Praise for *Fundamentals of LTE*

"*Fundamentals of LTE* is a clear yet detailed introduction to the 3GPP Long-Term Evolution. I would recommend it both to those wishing to get up to speed on the fundamentals of LTE and those who are already involved but in need of a reference for this critical technology."

—Dr. Alan Gatherer
   CTO of Baseband System-on-Chip
   Huawei

"Excellent .... A comprehensive and in-depth treatment of what is likely to become the dominant world broadband wireless standard."

—Dr. Reinaldo Valenzuela
   Director of Wireless Communications Research
   Bell Labs, Alcatel-Lucent

"*Fundamentals of LTE* is a well-written and self-contained book featuring a unique blend of leading industry and academic perspectives. Comprehensive and highly accessible."

—Dr. Angel Lozano
   Professor, Information & Communication Technologies
   University of Pompeu, Fabra

"This book offers a good entry point to the world of LTE for newcomers, since it contains useful background material for understanding the technology. It can serve as an instrumental reference for the general LTE community."

—Dr. Eko Onggosanusi
   Senior member of technical staff and 3GPP RAN1 lead delegate
   Texas Instruments

Fundamentals of LTE

Fundamentals of LTE

Arunabha Ghosh
Jun Zhang
Jeffrey G. Andrews
Rias Muhamed

PRENTICE
HALL

Upper Saddle River, NJ • Boston • Indianapolis • San Francisco
New York • Toronto • Montreal • London • Munich • Paris • Madrid
Capetown • Sydney • Tokyo • Singapore • Mexico City

Many of the designations used by manufacturers and sellers to distinguish their products are claimed as trademarks. Where those designations appear in this book, and the publisher was aware of a trademark claim, the designations have been printed with initial capital letters or in all capitals.

The authors and publisher have taken care in the preparation of this book, but make no expressed or implied warranty of any kind and assume no responsibility for errors or omissions. No liability is assumed for incidental or consequential damages in connection with or arising out of the use of the information or programs contained herein.

Credits and permissions appear on pages 417 and 418.

The publisher offers excellent discounts on this book when ordered in quantity for bulk purchases or special sales, which may include electronic versions and/or custom covers and content particular to your business, training goals, marketing focus, and branding interests. For more information, please contact:

U.S. Corporate and Government Sales
(800) 382-3419
corpsales@pearsontechgroup.com

For sales outside the United States please contact:

International Sales
international@pearson.com

Visit us on the Web: informit.com/ph

Library of Congress Cataloging-in-Publication Data

Fundamentals of LTE / Arunabha Ghosh ... [et al.].
      p. cm.
  Includes bibliographical references and index.
  ISBN-10: 0-13-703311-7 (hardcover : alk. paper)
  ISBN-13: 978-0-13-703311-9 (hardcover : alk. paper) 1. Long-Term Evolution (Telecommunications) I. Ghosh, Arunabha, 1969–
TK5103.48325.F86 2010
621.3845′6—dc22   2010021369

ISBN-13: 978-0-13-703311-9
ISBN-10:   0-13-703311-7

Text printed in the United States on recycled paper at Courier in Westford, Massachusetts.
First printing, August 2010

Dedicated to my wife Debolina

—Arunabha

To my parents Nanxian and Zhiying, and my sisters Ying and Li

—Jun

Dedicated to my daughter Jade

—Jeff

Dedicated to Shalin, Tanaz, and my parents

—Rias

Contents

Foreword

With the deployment of LTE, the wireless revolution will achieve an important milestone. For the first time, a wide-area wireless network will be universally deployed that has been primarily designed for IP-centric broadband data (rather than voice) from the very beginning. LTE also is rapidly becoming the dominant global standard for fourth generation cellular networks with nearly all the major cellular players behind it and working toward its success.

Having been personally involved in designing, developing, and promoting one of the first OFDM-based cellular systems since the late 1990s, back when such an approach was considered slightly eccentric, LTE's success is personally very satisfying for me to see. As with any standard, which by political necessity is "designed by committee," the LTE specification is not without flaws and there is room for progress and future evolution. The system architecture is not yet a fully flat IP platform, for example, and some interference issues are not fully addressed. But there can be no doubt that LTE is a giant step in the right direction and a necessary step to meet the anticipated growth in consumer and business mobile broadband applications and services. LTE provides a credible platform for wireless broadband access based on OFDMA, multiantenna technologies, and other cutting-edge techniques that provide improvements in spectral efficiency and significantly lower the cost of delivering mobile broadband. I expect the future evolution of LTE to continually improve the standard.

Fundamentals of LTE is an excellent introduction to the LTE standard and the various technologies that it incorporates, like OFDMA, SC-FDMA, and multiantenna transmission and reception. It is exceptionally well written, easy to understand, and concisely but completely covers the key aspects of the standard. Because of its diverse author team—including both LTE systems engineers as well as leading academic researchers who have worked extensively on the core underlying technologies—this book will be of use to a wide set of potential readers. I recommend it to folks in the industry who are involved with the development of LTE-based technology and products, as well as to students and faculty in academia who wish to understand the standard and participate in incorporating more advanced techniques into the future versions of the specification. The book also describes some of the "weak points" in the current specification of the standard. This helps ensure that these issues will be fixed as the specification evolves.

I hope you will enjoy reading the book and benefit from it, and am confident you will.

Rajiv Laroia
Senior vice president, Qualcomm Flarion Technologies

Preface

The Long-Term Evolution (LTE) is the next evolutionary step beyond 3G for mobile wireless communication. LTE brings together many technological innovations from different areas of research such as digital signal processing, Internet protocols, network architecture, and security, and is poised to dramatically change the way we use the worldwide mobile network in the future. Unlike 3G, LTE uses a clean-slate design approach for all the components of the network including the radio access network, the transport network, and the core network. This design approach, along with its built-in flexibility, allows LTE to be the first truly global wireless standard that can be deployed in a variety of spectrum and operating scenarios, and support a wide range of wireless applications. A large number of service providers around the world have already announced LTE as their preferred next generation technology.

Fundamentals of LTE is a comprehensive tutorial on the most innovative cellular standard since CDMA emerged in the early 1990s. The impending worldwide deployment of LTE (Long-Term Evolution, often called 4G cellular) will revolutionize the cellular networks by going to much larger bandwidths, data rates, and an all-IP framework. *Fundamentals of LTE* is the only book to provide an accessible but complete tutorial on the key enabling technologies behind LTE, such as OFDM, OFDMA, SC-FDMA, and MIMO, as well as provide a step-by-step breakdown of all the key aspects of the standard from the physical layer through the network stack. The book begins with a historical overview and the reasons for the radical departure from conventional voice-centric cellular systems that LTE represents. Following this, four tutorial chapters explain the essential underpinnings of LTE, which could also be used as the basis for an entry-level university course. Finally, five chapters on the LTE standard specifically attempt to illuminate its key aspects, explaining both how LTE works, and why certain choices were made by the LTE standards body. This collaboration between UT Austin and AT&T has resulted in a uniquely accessible and comprehensive book on LTE.

Chapter 1 provides an overview and history of the cellular wireless technologies, starting from first-generation systems such as AMPS to fourth-generation technologies such as LTE and WiMAX. This chapter provides a historical account of the mobile wireless networks and illustrates the key technological breakthroughs and market forces that drove the evolution of the mobile wireless network over the past two decades. This chapter also provides an executive summary of the LTE and some of its key technical enablers.

The balance of the book is organized into two parts, as noted. Part I consists of four tutorial chapters (Chapters 2–5) on the essential wireless networking and communications technologies underpinning LTE. Chapter 2 provides a tutorial introduction to broadband wireless channels and systems, and demonstrates the challenges inherent to the development of a broadband wireless system such as LTE. Chapter 3 provides a comprehensive tutorial on multicarrier modulation, detailing how it works in both theory and practice. This chapter emphasizes a practical understanding of OFDM system design, and discusses implementation issues, in particular the peak-to-average power ratio. An overview of single-carrier frequency domain equalization (SC-FDE), which overcomes the peak-to-average problem, is also provided. Chapter 4 extends Chapter 3 to provide an overview on the frequency domain multiple access techniques adopted in LTE: OFDMA in the downlink and SC-FDMA in the uplink. Resource allocation to the users, especially relevant opportunistic scheduling approaches, is discussed, along with important implementation issues pertinent to LTE. Chapter 5 provides a rigorous tutorial on multiple antenna techniques, covering techniques such as spatial diversity, interference cancellation, spatial multiplexing, and multiuser and networked MIMO. The inherent tradeoffs between different techniques and practical considerations for the deployment of MIMO in LTE are distinguishing features of this chapter.

Part II of the book, consisting of Chapters 6–10, provides a detailed description of the LTE standard with particular emphasis on the air-interface protocol. We begin this part in Chapter 6 with an introduction to the basic structure of the air-interface protocol and the channel structure utilized by LTE at different layers. This chapter also provides an overview of the physical layer and various OFDMA-related aspects of LTE. Chapters 7 and 8 provide a thorough description of the physical and MAC layer processing (at the transport channel level) for downlink (DL) and uplink (UL), respectively. Features such as channel encoding, modulation mapping, Hybrid-ARQ (H-ARQ), and multiantenna processing for the different DL and UL channels are discussed in detail. In Chapter 9 we discuss the various feedback mechanisms that are essential components of LTE and are needed to enable various features such as channel aware scheduling, closed-loop and open-loop multiantenna processing, adaptive modulation and coding, etc. These concepts are critical to a complete understanding of LTE and its operation. In this chapter we also discuss various MAC layer concepts related to scheduling, QoS, ARQ, etc. Finally, in Chapter 10 we discuss the higher layers of the LTE protocol stack, such as RLC, PDCP, and RRM, and the role of these in the overall operation of an LTE system. In this chapter we also provide an in-depth discussion on the mobility and handoff procedures in LTE from a radio access network point of view.

Acknowledgments

We sincerely thank our publisher Bernard Goodwin and the rest of the members of his team at Prentice Hall for providing us with this opportunity to write a book on LTE. Without their encouragement and constant support we would not have undertaken the challenging task of writing this book. We would also like to thank Angel Lozano, Mark Reed, and Steve Jones for reviewing our book. We realize that their unrivalled feedback and review is a critical component to the success of this book and we sincerely appreciate their efforts.

The authors also express their sincere gratitude to Rajiv Laroia for writing the foreword for this book. His work has truly been an inspiration to us and his confidence in this book is invaluable.

Arunabha Ghosh: I would like to thank my coauthors Jun Zhang, Jeffrey G. Andrews, and Rias Muhamed, without whose expertise, hard work, and valuable feedback it would have been impossible to bring this book to completion.

I am especially thankful to David R. Wolter of AT&T Labs for his support and encouragement in this venture. David has provided me with an environment at work that is unrivaled in my opinion and has provided me with umpteen opportunities for personal and professional growth. I would also like to thank my colleagues Milap Majmundar and Rich Kobylinski of AT&T Labs. Their hard work and thorough understanding of wireless systems in general and LTE in particular have been a critical component to my success in bringing this book to completion. I also thank them for providing me with key results and concepts that were necessary to ensure the quality and completeness of this book.

Most important of all, I would like to thank my beloved wife Debolina who has been an inspiration to me. Writing this book has been quite an undertaking for both of us as a family and it is her constant support and encouragement that gave me the courage and the motivation to accept the challenge of writing this book. I also want to thank my dearest friends Radhika and Rajesh for their support and encouragement, especially at moments when I needed them the most. On more than one occasion when I have faltered they have shown me the right path. I also want to thank my parents Amitabha and Meena, and my brother Siddhartha. No words can truly express my gratitude and feelings toward them and this book is a humble gesture on my part as a token of my appreciation and dedication to them.

Jun Zhang: First of all, I would like to thank my coauthors, without whose consistent encouragement and help it would be impossible for me, as a Ph.D. student, to coauthor a book on LTE. In particular, I would like to thank Professor Jeffrey Andrews for his invaluable guidance through my Ph.D. research and for his sincere invitation to join in writing this book. I would also like to thank Arunabha Ghosh and David Wolter for inviting me for summer internships at AT&T Labs during 2007–2008, during which period I started to build up my understanding of commercial wireless standards.

I would like to thank my colleagues at UT Austin for their helpful discussions and comments, and especially Rahul Mehta for his careful proofreading of our manuscript.

Most important of all, I would like to thank my parents Nanxian and Zhiying for their unconditional love and support throughout my life, and my sisters Ying and Li for their support and encouragement.

Jeffrey G. Andrews: I would, of course, like to thank my coauthors, who are a delight to work with. In particular, I would like to thank Arunabha for nurturing and valuing our long-running collaboration, which is sadly unusual in academia and industry these days. I would also like to thank Jun for having the courage and confidence to take on this challenge in the final year of his Ph.D.; this book would have been impossible without Jun's drive, initiative, and talent. And Rias, thanks for coming out of technical retirement in Dallas to work with us again! If there is an engineer around who is a better writer than you, I have not yet worked with that person.

I would like to acknowledge my student Tom Novlan and postdoc Illsoo Sohn for helping me on the new Fractional Frequency Reuse section, as well as my former students and postdocs who helped with earlier versions of some of this material, including Runhua Chen, Zukang Shen, Wan Choi, Aamir Hasan, Kaibing Huang, Jin Sam Kwak, Han Gyu Cho, Taeyoon Kim, Jaeweon Kim, and Kitaek Bae.

I would also like to thank Mark Reed and Steve Jones for reviewing this book in their valuable time, and especially Angel Lozano, who provided exceptionally detailed and sharp comments, which noticeably improved the book. I would also like to thank Bernard Goodwin for his encouragement to take on this project, and his and his staff's help in bringing this project to fast completion.

Finally, I would like to thank my wife Catherine and my daughter Jade whose love and support are fundamental to everything that I do.

Rias Muhamed: I sincerely thank my coauthors Arunabha Ghosh, Jeff Andrews, and Jun Zhang for inviting me to join them in writing this book. The extraordinary knowledge, expertise, and commitment that they brought to this effort made working with them a very rewarding and enjoyable experience. I have cherished every bit of it and have learned immensely from them. I take this opportunity to express my appreciation for all my colleagues at AT&T, past and present, from whom I have learned a lot.

Most of all, I thank my beloved wife Shalin and my precious daughter Tanaz for their love, support, and encouragement on this project and everything I do. I owe my gratitude to my parents for the continuous love and support they have offered for all my pursuits. My thanks are also due to my siblings and my in-laws for the support and encouragement I have received from them.

About the Authors

Arunabha Ghosh, Ph.D.

Arunabha Ghosh is a lead member of technical staff in the Wireless Communications Group in AT&T Laboratories. He received his B.S. with highest distinction from the Indian Institute of Technology at Kanpur in 1992 and his Ph.D. from the University of Illinois at Urbana Champaign in 1998. As a technical member at AT&T Labs, Dr. Ghosh's primary area of research is mobile wireless systems, with particular emphasis on MIMO-OFDM systems. Dr. Ghosh has worked extensively in the area of closed-loop single-user and multiuser MIMO solutions for technologies such as LTE and WiMAX and has been an active participant in many standards bodies such as 3GPP, IEEE, and WiMAX Forum.

Jun Zhang, Ph.D.

Jun Zhang is a visiting assistant professor in the Department of Electronic and Computer Engineering at the Hong Kong University of Science and Technology. He received his B.Eng. in electronic engineering from the University of Science and Technology of China (USTC) in 2004, his M.Phil. in information engineering from the Chinese University of Hong Kong (CUHK) in 2006, and his Ph.D. in electrical and computer engineering from the University of Texas at Austin in 2009. He was an intern at AT&T Labs in the summers of 2007 and 2008.

Jeffrey G. Andrews, Ph.D.

Jeffrey G. Andrews is an associate professor in the Department of Electrical and Computer Engineering at the University of Texas at Austin, where he is the director of the Wireless Networking and Communications Group. He received his B.S. in engineering with high distinction from Harvey Mudd College, and his M.S. and Ph.D. in electrical engineering from Stanford University. Dr. Andrews has industry experience at companies including Qualcomm, Intel, and Microsoft, and is the co-recipient of three IEEE best paper awards and the National Science Foundation CAREER Award.

Rias Muhamed

Rias Muhamed is a director of business development with the AT&T Corporate Strategy and Development Team. His area of focus is on developing and incubating new business applications and services for AT&T using emerging technologies. He was previously with

AT&T Labs, where he led technology assessment of a variety of wireless communication systems. He received his B.S. in electrical engineering from Pondicherry University, India in 1990; his M.S. in electrical engineering from Virginia Tech in 1996; and his M.B.A. from St. Edward University in Austin in 2000.

List of Acronyms

3GPP – 3rd Generation Partnership Project
3GPP2 – 3rd Generation Partnership Project 2
AAS – Advanced Antenna Systems
ADC – Analog to Digital Converter
AM – Amplitude Modulation
AMC – adaptive modulation and coding
AMPS – Analogue Mobile Phone System
AoA – Angle of Arrival
AoD – Angle of Departure
ARQ – automatic repeat request
AUC – Authentication Center
AWGN – Additive White Gaussian Noise
AWS – Advanced Wireless Services
BCCH – Broadcast Control Channel
BCH – Broadcast Channel
BER – Bit Error Rate
BF – Beamforming
BLAST – Bell labs LAyered Space-Time receiver
BLER – Block Error Rate
BP – Bandwidth Part
BPSK – Binary Phase Shift Keying
BS – Base station
BSC – Base Station Controller
BSR – Buffer Status Report
BTS – Base Transceiver Station
CAZAC – Constant-Amplitude Zero-Auto-Correlation
CCCH – Common Control Channel
CCDF – Complimentary Cumulative Distribution Function
CCI – co-channel interference
CDD – Cyclic Delay Diversity
CDF – Cumulative Distribution Function
CDMA – Code Division Multiple Access
CDPD – Cellular Digital Packet Data
CEPT – European Conference of Postal and Telecommunications Administrations

CFI – Control Format Indicator
CGF – Charging Gateway Function
CIR – Carrier to Interference Ratio
CL-MIMO – Closed-Loop MIMO
CLT – Central Limit Theorem
CN – core network
CoMP – Coordinated Multi-Point transmission/reception
CP – Cyclic Prefix
CQI – Channel Quality Indicator
CRC – Cyclic Redundancy Check
CRF – Charging Rules Function
C-RNTI – Cell Radio Network Temporary Identifier
CSI – channel state information
CSIT – Channel State Information at Transmitter
CSMA – Carrier Sense Multiple Access
DAC – Digital to Analog Converter
DAI – Downlink Assignment Index
D-BLAST – diagonal Bell labs LAyered Space-Time receiver
DCCH – Downlink Control Channel
DCI – downlink control information
DDFSE – Delayed-decision Feedback Sequence Estimation
DECT – Digital Enhanced Cordless Telephone
DFE – Decision Feedback Equalizer
DFT – Discrete Fourier Transform
DL – Downlink
DL-SCH – Downlink Shared Channel
DMT – Discrete Multitone
DMT – Diversity-Multiplexing Tradeoff
DPC – Dirty Paper Coding
DSL – Digital Subscriber Line
DSP – Digital Signal Processing
DS-SS – Direct Sequence Spread Spectrum
DSTTD – Double Space Time Transmit Diversity
DTCH – Dedicated Traffic Channel
DwPTS – Downlink Pilot Time Slot
ECC – Error Correction Code
E-DCH – Enhanced Dedicated Channel
EDGE – Enhanced Data rates for GSM Evolution
EGC – Equal Gain Combining
EPC – Evolved Packet Core
EPS – Evolved Packet System
ETACS – European Total Access Communication System
ETSI – European Telecommunications Standards Institute
ETWS – Earthquake and Tsunami Warning System
E-UTRAN – Evolved Universal Terrestrial Radio Access Network

EV-DO – Evolution Data Optimized
FCC – Federal Communications Commission
FDD – frequency division duplexing
FDMA – Frequency Division Multiple Access
FEC – forward error correction
FEQ – Frequency Domain Equalizer
FER – Frame Error Rate
FFR – Fractional Frequency Reuse
FFT – Fast Fourier Transform
FIR – Finite Impulse Response
FM – Frequency Modulation
FPC – Fractional Power Control
FSK – Frequency Shift Keying
FSTD – Frequency Shift Time Diversity
FSTD – Frequency Switched Transmit Diversity
GBR – Guaranteed Bit Rate
GERAN – GSM/EDGE Radio Access Network
GGSN – Gateway GPRS Support Node
GMSK – Gaussian Minimum Shift Keying
GP – Guard Period
GPRS – General Packet Radio Service
GPS – Global Positioning System
GSM – Global System for Mobile communications
GTP – GPRS Tunneling Protocol
H-ARQ – Hybrid Automatic Repeat Request
HF – High Frequency
HFN – Hyper Frame Number
HI – HARQ Indicator
HII – High Interference Indicator
HLR – Home Location Register
HSDPA – High Speed Downlink Packet Access
HS-DSC – High Speed Downlink Shared Channel
HS-DSCH – High Speed Downlink Shared Channel
HSPA – High Speed Packet Access
HSPA+ – High Speed Packet Access Evolved
HSS – Home Subscriber Server
HSUPA – High Speed Uplink Packet Access
ICI – Inter-carrier Interference
IDFT – Inverse Discrete Fourier Transform
IETF – Internet Engineering Task Force
IFFT – Inverse Fast Fourier Transform
IMS – IP Multimedia Services
IMT – International Mobile Telecommunications
IMTS – Improved Mobile Telephone System
IP – Internet Protocol

ISI – Inter-Symbol Interference
ITU – International Telecommunications Union
LAN – Local Area Network
LOS – Line of Sight
LTE – Long-Term Evolution
MAC – Media Access Control
MAC-I – Message Authentication Code for Integrity
MBMS – Multimedia Broadcast and Multicast Service
MB-SFN – Multicast/Broadcast Single Frequency Network
MC-CDMA – Multicarrier CDMA
MCCH – Multicast Control Channel
MCH – Multicast Channel
MF – Maximum Fairness algorithm
MIB – Master Information Block
MIMO – Multiple Input/Multiple Output
ML – Maximum Likelihood detection
MLSD – Maximum Likelihood Sequence Detection
MLSE – Maximum Likelihood Sequence Estimation
MME – Mobility Management Entity
MMS – Multimedia Messaging Service
MMSE – Minimum Mean Squared Error detection
MRC – Maximal Ratio Combining
MRT – Maximal Ratio Transmission
MS – Mobile Station
MSC – Mobile Switching Center
MSE – Minimum Squared Error
MSR – Maximum Sum Rate algorithm
MTCH – Multicast Traffic Channel
MTS – Mobile Telephone System
MUD – Multi-User Detection
MU-MIMO – Multi-user MIMO
NAS – Non-Access Stratum
NLOS – non-line of sight
NMT – Nordic Mobile Telephone
NSS – Network Switching Subsystem
NTACS – Narrowband Total Access Communication System
OC – Optimum Combiner
OCI – other cell interference
OFDM – Orthogonal Frequency Division Multiplexing
OFDMA – Orthogonal Frequency Division Multiple Access
OI – Overload Indicator
OSTBC – Orthogonal Space Time Block Code
PA – Power Amplifier
PAPR – Peak-to-Average Power Ratio
PAR – Peak-to-Average Ratio

PBCH – Physical Broadcast Channel
PCCC – Parallel Concatenated Convolutional Code
PCCH – Paging Control Channel
PCFICH – Physical Control Format Indicator Channel
PCH – Paging Channel
PCRF – Policy and Charging Rules Function
PCS – Personal Communication Services
PCU – Packet Control Unit
PDCCH – Physical Downlink Control Channel
PDCP – Packet Data Convergence Protocol
PDF – Policy Decision Function
PDF – probability density function
PDN – Packet Data Network
PDN-GW – Packet Data Network Gateway
PDSCH – Physical Downlink Shared Channel
PDU – protocol data unit
PER – Packet Error Rate
PF – Paging Frame
PF – Proportional Fairness algorithm
PGW – Packet Data Network Gateway
PHICH – Physical Hybrid ARQ Indicator Channel
PHS – Personal Handyphone System
PHY – Physical Layer
PMCH – Physical Multicast Channel
PMI – Precoding Matrix Index
PRACH – Physical Random Access Channel
PRB – physical resource block
PRC – Proportional Rate Constraints algorithm
P-RNTI – Paging-Radio Network Temporary Identifier
PSD – Power Spectral Density
PSTN – Public Switched Telephone Network
PUCCH – Physical Uplink Control Channel
PUSCH – Physical Uplink Shared Channel
QAM – Quadrature Amplitude Modulation
QCI – QoS Class Identifier
QoS – Quality of Service
QPP – Quadrature Permutation Polynomial
QPSK – Quadrature Phase Shift Keying
RACH – Random Access Channel
RAN – radio access network
RA-RNTI – Random Access Radio Network Temporary Identifier
RB – Resource Block
RBG – resource block group
RLC – Radio Link Control
RMS – Root Mean Square

RNC – Radio Network Controller
RNTI – radio network temporary identifier
RNTP – Relative Narrowband Transmit Power
ROHC – Robust Header Compression protocol
RRC – Radio Resource Control
RSCP – Reference Signal Code Power
RSRP – Reference Signal Received Power
RSSE – Reduced State Sequence Estimation
SAE – System Architecture Evolution
SAE-GW – System Architecture Evolution Gateway
SAP – Service Access Point
SC – Selection Combining
SC-FDE – Single-Carrier Frequency Domain Equalization
SC-FDMA – Single-Carrier Frequency Division Multiple Access
SDMA – Space Division Multiple Access
SDU – service data unit
SFBC – Space Frequency Block Code
SFN – Single-Frequency Network
SFR – Soft Frequency Reuse
SGSN – Serving GPRS Support Node
SGW – Serving Gateway
SIB – System Information Block
SINR – signal-to-interference-plus-noise ratio
SIR – signal-to-interference ratio
SISO – Single Input Single Output communication system
SMS – Short Messaging Service
SN – Sequence Number
SNDR – signal-to-noise-plus-distortion ratio
SNR – Signal-to-Noise Ratio
SR – Scheduling Request
SRB – Signaling Radio Bearer
SRNS – Serving Radio Network Subsystem
SRS – Sounding Reference Symbol
STBC – Space Time Block Code
SU-MIMO – Single User MIMO
SVD – Singular Value Decomposition
TACS – Total Access Communication System
TBS – Transport Block Size
TDD – Time Division Duplexing
TDM – Time Division Multiplexing
TDMA – Time Division Multiple Access
TD-SCDMA – Time Division Synchronous Code Division Multiple Access
TIA – Telecommunications Industry Association
TPC – Transmit Power Control
TPMI – Transmit Precoding Matrix Indication

TTI – Transmission Time Interval
UCI – Uplink Control Information
UE – User Equipment
UHF – Ultra High Frequency
UL – Uplink
ULA – Uniform Linear Array
UL-SCH – Uplink Shared Channel
UMTS – Universal Mobile Telecommunications System
UpPTS – Uplink Pilot Time Slot
UTRAN – UMTS Terrestrial Radio Access Network
V-BLAST – Vertical Bell labs Layered Space-Time receiver
VLR – Visitor Location Register
VoIP – Voice over Internet Protocol
VRB – virtual resource block
WAP – Wireless Access Protocol
WCDMA – Wideband Code Division Multiple Access
WiBro – Wireless Broadband
WiMAX – Worldwide Interoperability for Microwave Access
WMAN – Wireless Metropolitan Area Network
WSS – Wide Sense Stationary
WSSUS – Wide Sense Stationary Uncorrelated Scattering
ZF – Zero Forcing detection

Chapter 1

Evolution of Cellular Technologies

1.1   Introduction

All over the world, wireless communications services have enjoyed dramatic growth over the past 25 years. It was only in late 1983 that the first commercial cellular telephone system in the United States was deployed by Ameritech in the Chicago area. That was the analog service called Advanced Mobile Phone Service (AMPS). Today, digital cellular telephone services are available throughout the world, and have well surpassed fixed-line telephone services both in terms of availability and number of users. In fact, as of March 2010 we have over 4.8 billion mobile subscribers in the world, which is more than double the number of fixed line subscribers and amounts to a higher than 60% penetration. The relative adoption of wireless versus fixed line is even more dramatic in the developing world. For example, in India, wireless penetration is more than four times that of fixed line.

It took less then 20 years for mobile subscribers worldwide to grow from zero to over one billion users. This amazing growth demonstrates not only the strong desire of people around the world to connect with one another and have access to information while on the move, but also the tremendous strides that technology has made in fulfilling and further fueling this need. The developments in RF circuit fabrication, advanced digital signal processing, and several miniaturization technologies that made it possible to deploy and deliver wireless communication services at the scale and scope that we see today are indeed quite remarkable.

Today, we are at the threshold of another major revolution in wireless. While mobile voice telephony drove the past growth of wireless systems and still remains the primary application, it is abundantly clear that wireless data applications will drive its future growth. In the past two decades, the Internet transformed from being a curious academic tool to an indispensible global information network providing a vast array of services and applications—from e-mail to social networking and e-commerce to entertainment. As illustrated in Figure 1.1, the global growth in wireless over the past decade was accompanied by a parallel growth in Internet usage. Worldwide, over 1.5 billion people use the Internet today, and there are over 500 million subscribers to Internet access

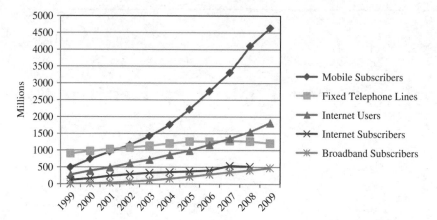

Figure 1.1 Global growth of mobile, Internet, broadband, and fixed telephone line subscribers from 1998–2009 [I].

services; of these over 400 million have broadband or high-speed connections to the Internet. In the United States, more than 60% of households have broadband access to the Internet.

Users worldwide are finding that having broadband access to the Internet dramatically changes how we share information, conduct business, and seek entertainment. Broadband access not only provides faster Web-surfing and quicker downloading but also enables several multimedia applications, such as real-time audio and video streaming, multimedia conferencing, and interactive gaming. Those who have experienced the richness and variety of applications accessible through broadband services in their home or office now clamor for a similar experience wherever they are and while on the move. Providing true broadband experience to mobile users is the next frontier for wireless, and Long-Term Evolution (LTE), the subject of this book, is a key enabling technology for delivering mobile broadband.

In this chapter we provide an overview of the evolution of mobile communication systems. We begin with a brief history of wireless communications and trace the evolution of cellular systems and standards from early developments to the current state of the art. We then cover the market drivers for LTE and the key technical requirements set forth for its development. In the subsequent section, we describe the key ingredient technologies that enable the superior performance of LTE. We then provide a brief overview of the LTE architecture and discuss the spectrum options and migration strategies for operators interested in deploying LTE. We close the chapter with a brief look into the future enhancements being envisioned for LTE.

1.2   Evolution of Mobile Broadband

Before we begin our discussion of modern mobile broadband systems, it is instructive to briefly review the history of mobile wireless communications to gain an appreciation of the remarkable achievements leading to the wireless services that we enjoy today.

The origin of radio communications is often traced back to Guglielmo Marconi, who is commonly credited with its invention and was awarded a patent for the development of a wireless telegraphy system in 1897. Around the same time, Nikola Tesla, Jagadish Bose, and Alexander Popov also demonstrated radio communications and controversy persists about who could claim to be the true inventor of radio. Several scientists and engineers did pioneering experiments with radio in the early years of the twentieth century and achieved remarkable success. The first verifiable transatlantic radio transmission was made in 1902 and voice signals were transmitted across the Atlantic for the first time in 1915. The following decades saw the development of shortwave radio, frequency modulation, and other key technologies that led to the development of the first mobile communication systems.

One of the early uses of mobile communications systems was in the area of public safety. Several U.S. municipalities deployed systems beginning in the 1930s. In 1946, AT&T introduced the first mobile telephone service in St. Louis, Missouri: a manual system with a capacity to support a maximum of three simultaneous calls. By 1948, AT&T expanded the service to 100 cities and had over 5,000 customers—mostly utilities, truck fleet operators, and reporters.

Early mobile telephone systems used base stations with large power amplifiers and tall towers to cover large geographic areas. Each base station was independent of the others, used all the available frequency channels, and was geographically separated from other base stations to avoid interference. Examples of early mobile telephone systems include Mobile Telephone System (MTS) which operated in the 40MHz band, and improved MTS (IMTS), which operated in the 150MHz and 450MHz bands. All these systems were extremely limited in their capacity. For example, in 1976, the IMTS system deployed in New York City had 12 channels and could only support 2,000 subscribers over a thousand square miles. Even those few customers often had to wait 30 minutes to place a call. There was growing demand for mobile services, and a way had to be found to support more users. Governments could not simply allocate spectrum in proportion to the growing demand for mobile service.

The breakthrough solution to the issue of limited capacity was the cellular concept—the idea of replacing a single high-powered transmitter with several lower-power transmitters, each providing coverage to a small portion of the service area and using a fraction of the total available spectrum. Frequencies could then be reused across the service area as long as base stations using the same frequency were sufficiently separated from one another. Although conceived by Bell Labs in 1947, the technology required to implement the cellular concept was not available until the 1970s. In 1971, AT&T submitted a proposal to the Federal Communications Commission (FCC) for a cellular mobile concept, and after more than a decade of deliberations, in 1983 the FCC allocated 40MHz of spectrum in the 800MHz band, which led to the deployment of the first generation of commercial cellular systems (see Table 1.1).

Table 1.1 Important Historical Milestones Toward the Development of Mobile Broadband

Year	Important Milestone
Before 1892	Nikola Tesla found theoretical basis for radio communication and demonstrated radio transmission.
1897	Guglielmo Marconi demonstrated radio communications; awarded patent for it.
1902	First verifiable transatlantic radio transmission (telegraphy) made from an Italian cruiser with Marconi aboard using 272kHz signals.
1906	Reginald Fessendon made first successful two-way transmission over North Atlantic and demonstrated voice transmission using amplitude modulation.
1915	First transatlantic radio transmission of voice from Arlington, Virginia to Paris, France.
1921	Short wave radio (HF radio: 2.3MHz to 25.82MHz) developed.
1934	AM radio systems used in 194 U.S. municipalities for public safety.
1935	Edwin Armstrong demonstrated FM.
1946	First mobile telephone service in St. Louis, Missouri introduced by AT&T.
1948	Claude Shannon published his seminal theory on channel capacity; $C=B\log_2(1+SNR)$.
1956	Ericsson developed first automatic mobile phone called Mobile Telephone A (weighed 40kg).
1960–1970	Bell Labs developed cellular concept.
1971	AT&T submits proposal for a cellular mobile system concept to FCC.
1979	First commercial cellular system deployed by NTT in Japan.
1983	FCC allocated 40MHz of spectrum in 800MHz for AMPS.
1983	Advanced Mobile Phone Service (AMPS) launched in Chicago.
1989	Qualcomm proposes CDMA as a more efficient, wireless voice technology.
1991	First commercial GSM deployment in Europe (Finland).
1995	First commercial launch of CDMA (IS-95) service by Hutchinson Telecom, Hong Kong.
1995	Personal Communication Services (PCS) license in the 1800/1900MHz band auctioned in the United States.
2001	NTT DoCoMo launched first commercial 3G service using UMTS WCDMA.
2002	South Korea Telecom launches first CDMA2000 EV-DO network.
2005	UMTS/HSDPA launched in 16 major markets by AT&T.
2005	IEEE 802.16e standard, the air-interface for Mobile WiMAX, completed and approved.
2006	WiBro (uses the IEEE 802.16e air-interface) commercial services launched in South Korea.
2007	Apple iPhone launched, driving dramatic growth in mobile data consumption.
2009	3GPP Release 8 LTE/SAE specifications completed.

1.2.1 First Generation Cellular Systems

The United States, Japan, and parts of Europe led the development of the first generation of cellular wireless systems. The first generation systems were characterized by their analog modulation schemes and were designed primarily for delivering voice services. They were different from their predecessor mobile communications systems in that they used the cellular concept and provided automatic switching and handover of on-going calls. Japan's Nippon Telephone and Telegraph Company (NTT) implemented the world's first commercial cellular system in 1979. Nordic Mobile Telephone (NMT-400) system, deployed in Europe in 1981, was the first system that supported automatic handover and international roaming. NMT-400 was deployed in Denmark, Finland, Sweden, Norway, Austria, and Spain. Most NMT-400 subscribers used car phones that transmitted up to 15 watts of power.

The more successful first generation systems were AMPS in the United States and its variant Total Access Communication Systems (ETACS and NTACS) in Europe and Japan. These systems were almost identical from a radio standpoint, with the major difference being the channel bandwidth. The AMPS system was built on a 30kHz channel size, whereas ETACS and NTACS used 25kHz and 12.5kHz, respectively. Table 1.2 provides a quick summary of first generation cellular systems.

1.2.1.1 Advanced Mobile Phone Service (AMPS)

AMPS was developed by AT&T Bell Labs in the late 1970s and was first deployed commercially in 1983 in Chicago and its nearby suburbs. The first system used large cell areas and omni-directional base station antennas. The system covered 2,100 square miles

Table 1.2 Major First Generation Cellular Systems

	AMPS	ETACS	NTACS	NMT-450/ NMT-900
Year of Introduction	1983	1985	1988	1981
Frequency Bands	D/L:869-894MHz U/L:824-849MHz	D/L:916-949MHz U/L:871-904MHz	D/L:860-870MHz U/L:915-925MHz	NMT-450:450-470MHz NMT-900:890-960MHz
Channel Bandwidth	30kHz	25kHz	12.5kHz	NMT-450:25kHz NMT-900:12.5kHz
Multiple Access	FDMA	FDMA	FDMA	FDMA
Duplexing	FDD	FDD	FDD	FDD
Voice Modulation	FM	FM	FM	FM
Number of Channels	832	1240	400	NMT-450:200 NMT-900:1999

with only ten base stations, each with antenna tower height between 150 ft. and 550 ft. Most of the early systems were designed for a carrier-to-interference ratio (CIR) of 18dB for satisfactory voice quality, and were deployed in a 7-cell frequency reuse pattern with 3 sectors per cell.

Besides the United States, AMPS was deployed in several countries in South America, Asia, and North America. In the United States, the FCC assigned spectrum to two operators per market—one an incumbent telecommunications carrier and the other a new non-incumbent operator. Each operator was assigned 20MHz of spectrum, supporting a total of 416 AMPS channels in each market. Of the 416 channels, 21 channels were designated for control information and the remaining 395 channels carried voice traffic. AMPS systems used Frequency Modulation (FM) for the transmission of analog voice and Frequency Shift Keying (FSK) for the control channel. Even after the deployment of second generation (2G) systems, AMPS continued to be used by operators in North America as a common fallback service available throughout the geography, as well as in the context of providing roaming between different operator networks that had deployed incompatible 2G systems.

1.2.2   2G Digital Cellular Systems

Improvements in processing abilities of hardware platforms over time enabled the development of 2G wireless systems. 2G systems were also aimed primarily toward the voice market but, unlike the first generation systems, used digital modulation. Shifting from analog to digital enabled several improvements in systems performance. System capacity was improved through (1) the use of spectrally efficient digital speech codecs, (2) multiplexing several users on the same frequency channel via time division or code division multiplexing techniques, and (3) tighter frequency re-use enabled by better error performance of digital modulation, coding, and equalization techniques, which reduced the required carrier-to-interference ratio from 18dB to just a few dB. Voice quality was also improved through the use of good speech codecs and robust link level signal processing. 2G systems also used simple encryption to provide a measure of security against eavesdropping and fraud, which were a source of major concern with first generation analog systems.

Examples of 2G digital cellular systems include the Global System for Mobile Communications (GSM), IS-95 CDMA, and IS-136 TDMA systems. GSM is by far the most widely deployed of these systems; IS-95 is deployed in North America and parts of Asia; IS-54 (later enhanced to IS-136) was initially deployed in North America but was later discontinued and replaced mostly by GSM. IS-136 was a TDMA-based system that was designed as a digital evolution of AMPS using 30kHz channels. The Personal Handyphone System (PHS) deployed in China, Japan, Taiwan, and some other Asian countries is also often considered a 2G system. PHS is a cordless telephone system like the Digital Enhanced Cordless Telephone (DECT) system but with capability to handover from one cell to another, and operated in the 1880–1930MHz frequency band. Table 1.3 provides a summary comparison of the various 2G digital cellular systems.

Besides providing improved voice quality, capacity, and security, 2G systems also enabled new applications. Prime among these was the Short Messaging Service (SMS). SMS was first deployed in Europe in 1991, and quickly became a popular conversational tool

Table 1.3 Major Second Generation Cellular Systems

	GSM	IS-95	IS-54/IS-136
Year of Introduction	1990	1993	1991
Frequency Bands	850/900MHz, 1.8/1.9GHz	850MHz/1.9GHz	850MHz/1.9GHz
Channel Bandwidth	200kHz	1.25MHz	30kHz
Multiple Access	TDMA/FDMA	CDMA	TDMA/FDMA
Duplexing	FDD	FDD	FDD
Voice Modulation	GMSK	DS-SS:BPSK, QPSK	$\pi/4$QPSK
Data Evolution	GPRS, EDGE	IS-95-B	CDPD
Peak Data Rate	GPRS:107kbps; EDGE:384kbps	IS-95-B:115kbps	$\sim$ 12kbps
Typical User Rate	GPRS:20-40kbps; EDGE:80-120kbps	IS-95B: <64kbps;	9.6kbps
User Plane Latency	600-700ms	> 600ms	> 600ms

among younger mobile subscribers. Today, over 2.5 billion SMS messages are sent each day in the United States alone, and the service has been used for delivering news updates, business process alerts, mobile payments, voting, and micro-blogging, among other things.

In addition to SMS, 2G systems also supported low data rate wireless data applications. Original 2G systems supported circuit switched data services (similar in concept to dial-up modems), and later evolved to support packet data services as well. Early wireless data services included information services such as the delivery of news, stock quotes, weather, and directions, etc. Limitations in data rate and available space for display in handheld devices meant that specialized technologies, such as the Wireless Access Protocol (WAP), had to be developed to tailor and deliver Internet content to handheld devices.

1.2.2.1 GSM and Its Evolution

In 1982, many European countries came together under the auspices of the Conference of European Posts and Telegraphs (CEPT) to develop and standardize a pan-European system for mobile services. The group was called the Groupe Spécial Mobile (GSM) and their main charter was to develop a system that could deliver inexpensive wireless voice services, and work seamlessly across all of Europe. Prior to GSM, the European cellular market was fragmented with a variety of mutually incompatible systems deployed in different countries: Scandinavian countries had NMT-400 and NMT-900, Germany had C-450, the United Kingdom had TACS, and France had Radiocom.

By 1989, the European Telecommunications Standards Institute (ETSI) took over the development of the GSM standard and the first version, called GSM Phase I, was released in 1990. Shortly thereafter, several operators in Europe deployed GSM. GSM quickly gained acceptance beyond Europe and the standard was appropriately renamed as the Global System for Mobile Communications. According to the Informa Telecoms and Media, an industry analyst, GSM and its successor technologies today boast over 4.2 billion subscribers spread across 220 countries, a 90% global market share. The broad worldwide adoption of GSM has made international roaming a seamless reality.

The GSM air-interface is based on a TDMA scheme where eight users are multiplexed on a single 200kHz wide frequency channel by assigning different time slots to each user. GSM employed a variant of FSK called Gaussian Minimum Shift Keying (GMSK) as its modulation technique. GMSK was chosen due to its constant envelope property providing good power and spectral efficiency characteristics.

Besides voice and SMS, the original GSM standard also supported circuit-switched data at 9.6kbps. By the mid-1990s, ETSI introduced the GSM Packet Radio Systems (GPRS) as an evolutionary step for GSM systems toward higher data rates. GPRS and GSM systems share the same frequency bands, time slots, and signaling links. GPRS defined four different channel coding schemes supporting 8kbps to 20kbps per slot. Under favorable channel conditions, the higher 20kbps rate can be used, and if all eight slots in the GSM TDM frame were used for data transmission, in theory, GPRS could provide a maximum data rate of 160kbps. Typical implementations of GPRS provided a user data rate of 20–40kbps.

Figure 1.2 provides a high-level architecture of a GSM/GPRS network. It is instructive to review this architecture as it formed the basis from which later 3G systems and LTE evolved. The original GSM architecture had two sub-components:

- **Base Station Subsystem**: This is comprised of the base-station transceiver (BTS) units that the mobile stations (MS) connect with over the air-interface and the base station controller (BSC), which manages and aggregates traffic from several BTSs for transport to the switching core, and manages mobility across BTSs connected

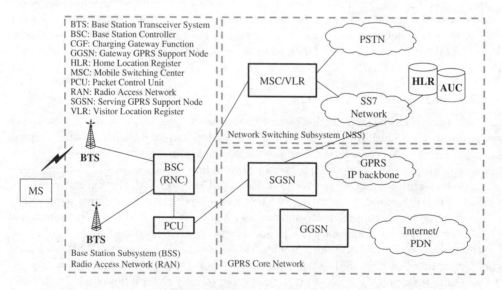

Figure 1.2 GSM network architecture.

directly to them. BSCs evolved to become Radio Network Controllers (RNC) in the 3G evolution of GSM.

- **Network Switching Sub-system**: This is comprised of the Mobile Switching Center (MSC) and subscriber data bases. The MSC provides the required switching to connect the calling party with the called party and is interconnected with the Public Switched Telephone Network (PSTN). The MSC uses the Home Location Register (HLR) and Visitor Location Register (VLR) to determine the location of mobile subscribers for call control purposes.

As shown in Figure 1.2, a GSM system may be upgraded to a GPRS system by introducing new elements, such as the Serving GPRS Support Node (SGSN) and Gateway GPRS Support Node (GGSN), and upgrading existing network elements such as the BTS with a packet control unit (PCU) for handling data. SGSN provides location and mobility management and may be thought of as the packet data equivalent of MSC. GGSN provides the IP access router functionality and connects the GPRS network to the Internet and other IP networks.

The GSM standard got a further boost in its data handling capabilities with the introduction of Enhanced Data Rate for GSM Evolution, or EDGE, in the early part of 1997. EDGE added support for 8PSK modulation to boost the data rate. This allowed for a maximum per slot data rate of 59.2kbps—a three-fold increase from GPRS speeds. Typical user rates for EDGE varied from 80 to 120kbps.

1.2.2.2 CDMA (IS-95) and Its Evolution

In 1989, Qualcomm, a then obscure start-up company in San Diego, California, proposed Code Division Multiple Access (CDMA) as a more efficient, higher quality wireless technology and demonstrated a system implementation of it. In a remarkable achievement, in 1993, Qualcomm was able to get the Telecommunications Industry Association (TIA) to adopt their proposal as an IS-95 standard providing an alternative to the IS-54 TDMA standard that was adopted earlier as the digital evolution of AMPS. Unlike in other digital wireless systems like GSM, in an IS-95 CDMA system multiple users share the same frequency channel at the same time. Instead of time-slicing multiple users in a given frequency channel, each user is assigned a different orthogonal spreading code that is used to separate their signals at the receiver. Codes are applied by multiplying user data symbols by a much higher rate code sequence, which leads to spreading the occupied bandwidth. IS-95 CDMA uses a 1.25MHz bandwidth to transmit a 9.2kbps or lower voice signal. Spreading signals over a larger bandwidth provides better immunity to multipath fading and interference.

IS-95 CDMA systems claimed a number of advantages over TDMA systems for voice. First, it enabled universal frequency reuse—that is, every cell can use the same frequency channel—which simplified frequency planning and provided increased capacity. Second, it used RAKE receivers that effectively combined multi-path signals to produce a stronger signal thereby reducing the required transmitter power. Third, it improved handoff performance by enabling soft-handoff, where a mobile can make a connection to a new base station before disconnecting from its current base station; this is possible since all base stations use the same frequency. Further, it implemented voice activity detection to turn off transmissions during silent periods, thereby reducing the overall interference level and increasing system capacity. All these features gave CDMA systems a higher voice capacity than GSM. It should be noted, though, that by implementing slow frequency hopping, GSM countered a lot of the frequency reuse advantages of CDMA. To keep the interference in check and improve system capacity, IS-95 implements fast (800Hz on uplink) and effective power control mechanisms, which were a huge challenge at that time.

In the early days of digital cellular, there was a rigorous debate between the proponents of TDMA and CDMA about which technology provided superior capacity and coverage. Practical deployments have tended to prove that IS-95 CDMA technology offered better coverage and capacity. This is further evidenced by the fact that even TDMA proponents adopted a CDMA-based technology as part of their evolution plan for 3G. IS-95 CDMA systems, however, did not succeed in gaining nearly as broad a global adoption as GSM. As of 2009, IS-95 and its evolutionary systems had about 480 million subscribers—most in North America, South Korea, Brazil, and India.

In addition to voice, the original (IS-95A) system supported a single dedicated data channel at 9.6kbps. A later evolution, called IS-95B, introduced a burst or packet mode transmission for improved efficiency. It also defined a new Supplemental Code Channel (SCH) that supported a data rate of 14.4kbps, and allowed for combining up to 7 SCH channels to provide a peak rate of 115.2kbps.

The CDMA community developed 3G evolution plans and aggressively deployed them well ahead of similar systems becoming available for GSM operators. They were able to get 3G rates without changing the 1.25MHz channel bandwidth or giving up on backward compatibility, which made the migration easier on operators. While GSM operators sought more gradual evolution to 3G through GPRS and EDGE, CDMA operators moved more rapidly to deploy their 3G networks: CDMA2000-1X and EV-DO.

1.2.3   3G Broadband Wireless Systems

Clearly, 2G digital cellular systems provided significant increase in voice capacity, improved voice quality, and began support for data applications such as Internet access. The circuit-switched paradigm based on which these systems were built made 2G systems very inefficient for data, and hence provided only low-data rate support—tens of kilobits per second, typically—and limited capacity.

Third generation (3G) systems were a significant leap over 2G, providing much higher data rates, significant increase in voice capacity, and supporting advanced services and applications, including multimedia. Work on 3G began in the early 1990s when the International Telecommunications Union (ITU) began invitation for proposals for 3G systems (known as IMT-2000) and started identifying spectrum for it. The ITU's objective was to create a globally harmonized specification for mobile communication that would facilitate global interoperability and provide the scale to lower cost. The ITU laid out the following data rate requirements as the criterion for IMT-2000:

- 2Mbps in fixed or in building environments

- 384kbps in pedestrian or urban environments

- 144kbps in wide area vehicular environments

Besides high data rate, 3G systems also envisioned providing better Quality of Service (QoS) control tailored for a variety of applications—from voice telephony and interactive games, to Web browsing, e-mail, and streaming multimedia applications.

A number of proposals were submitted to the ITU over the past 10–15 years, and six have been accepted so far. One of the more interesting aspects of the 3G proposals was the choice of CDMA as the preferred access technique for the majority of 3G systems. Not only did the IS-95 camp propose evolution toward a CDMA-based 3G technology called CDMA2000, but the GSM camp offered its own version of CDMA, called wideband CDMA (W-CDMA). So far, the ITU has accepted and approved the following terrestrial radio interfaces for IMT-2000:

- **IMT-2000 CDMA Direct Spread (IMT-DS)**: This standard is more commonly known as W-CDMA and was proposed as the air-interface for the Universal Mobile Telephone Service (UMTS) solution proposed by the Third Generation Partnership Project (3GPP) as the evolution of GSM systems.

- **IMT-2000 CDMA Multi-carrier (IMT-MC)**: This standard was proposed by the 3GPP2 organization and represents an evolution of the IS-95 systems. They are more commonly known as IX-EV-DO.

- **IMT-2000 CDMA TDD (IMT-TC)**: This standard is also proposed by 3GPP for operation in unpaired spectrum using Time Division Duplexing technology. It is also known as UMTS-TDD or TD-SCDMA (Time Division, Synchronous CDMA) and is mostly used in China.

- **IMT-2000 TDMA Single Carrier (IMT-SC)**: This standard was proposed by the Universal Wireless Consortium in the United States as a lower-cost evolution to 3G. Also called UWC-136, this is essentially the EDGE standard developed by 3GPP.

- **IMT-2000 FDMA/TDMA (IMT-FT)**: The Digital European Cordless Telephone (DECT) standard was also accepted as an IMT-2000 air-interface, primarily for indoor and pico-cell applications.

- **IMT-2000 IP-OFDMA**: This standard, more commonly known as WiMAX or IEEE 802.16e, was accepted by the ITU as a sixth air-interface in 2007.

Table 1.4 provides a quick summary of the major 3G system characteristics. A more detailed discussion of the four major 3G technologies is provided in the following subsections.

1.2.3.1 CDMA 2000 and EV-DO

The 3G evolution of IS-95 standards was called CDMA2000 by the CDMA community. Though most of the early work was done by Qualcomm and the CDMA development group, the official standardization process moved to a collaborative standards body called the Third Generation Partnership Project 2 (3GPP2) in 1999. CDMA2000-1X was the first evolution of IS-95 toward 3G accepted as an IMT-2000 interface. The 1X term implies

Table 1.4 Summary of Major 3G Standards

	W-CDMA	CDMA2000 1X	EV-DO	HSPA
Standard	3GPP Release 99	3GPP2	3GPP2	3GPP Release 5/6
Frequency Bands	850/900MHz, 1.8/1.9/2.1GHz	450/850MHz 1.7/1.9/2.1GHz	450/850MHz 1.7/1.9/2.1GHz	850/900MHz, 1.8/1.9/2.1GHz
Channel Band-width	5MHz	1.25MHz	1.25MHz	5MHz
Peak Data Rate	384–2048kbps	307kbps	DL:2.4–4.9Mbps UL:800–1800kbps	DL:3.6–14.4Mbps UL:2.3–5Mbps
Typical User Rate	150–300kbps	120–200kbps	400–600kbps	500–700kbps
User-Plane Latency	100–200ms	500–600ms	50–200ms	70–90ms
Multiple Access	CDMA	CDMA	CDMA/TDMA	CDMA/TDMA
Duplexing	FDD	FDD	FDD	FDD
Data Mod-ulation	DS-SS: QPSK	DS-SS: BPSK, QPSK	DS-SS: QPSK, 8PSK and 16QAM	DS-SS: QPSK, 16QAM and 64QAM

that it uses the same bandwidth (1.25MHz) as IS-95. The data capabilities were enhanced by adding separate logical channels termed *supplemental channels*. Each link can support a single fundamental channel (at 9.6kbps) and multiple supplemental channels (up to 307kbps). Strictly speaking, this is less than the 3G requirements, and for this reason, one may refer to CDMA2000-1X as a 2.5G system. The data rate can be increased up to 2Mbps through the use of multiple carriers as in CDMA2000-3X. CDMA2000-1X theoretically doubles the capacity of IS-95 by adding 64 more traffic channels to the forward link, orthogonal to the original set of 64. The uplink was improved through the use of coherent modulation; and the downlink through the addition of fast (800Hz) power control to match the uplink. Advanced antenna capabilities were also integrated into the new standard through options for transmit diversity as well as supplemental pilot options for beam-steering. A key to these upgrades is that they are backward compatible. CDMA2000 and IS-95A/B could be deployed on the same carrier, which allowed for a smooth migration.

In order to achieve higher data rates (up to 2Mbps) as well as improve overall system throughput for packet data scenarios, the CDMA2000-1X standard was also evolved to CDMA2000-1X-EVDO (*EV*olution, *D*ata *O*nly). As the name implies, the standard is applicable to data traffic only and there is no support for voice or other real time services.

Though it uses a 1.25MHz channel bandwidth and shares radio characteristics with IS-95, it cannot be deployed on the same carrier as CDMA2000-1X RTT or IS-95. This required service providers to dedicate a single carrier to data services in order to deploy data.

EV-DO originally was developed as a High-Data Rate (HDR) solution by Qualcomm for use in fixed and nomadic applications meeting the 2Mbps low mobility requirements of IMT-2000. It was, however, later upgraded to meet the full mobility requirements and was indeed the first system to provide real broadband-like speeds to mobile users. In fact, the first deployment of EV-DO occurred in 2002, a full three years ahead of a similar system—HSDPA—being deployed by GSM operators. According to the CDMA Development Group, as of July 2009, EV-DO had over 120 million subscribers.

EV-DO is designed to be an asymmetric system providing downlink rates up to 2.4Mbps and uplink rates up to 153kbps. The downlink is actually a TDMA link where multiple users are time multiplexed. The system supports QPSK and 16QAM modulation and coding rates from 1/5 to 1/3. Depending on the modulation and coding scheme chosen, user rates can vary from 38.4kbps to 2457.6kbps. EV-DO has the capability to adaptively change the modulation and coding based on link conditions.

Enhancements to EV-DO were made in EV-DO Rev. A, which improved the peak user data rates to 3.07Mbps and 1.8Mbps in the downlink and uplink, respectively, while providing a more symmetric link. In commercial deployments, Rev A achieves average throughput of 450–800kbps in the forward link and 300–400kbps in the reverse link.

1.2.3.2 UMTS WCDMA

Universal Mobile Telephone Service (UMTS) was originally developed by ETSI as the 3G system for IMT-2000 based on the evolution of GSM. As GSM went global, in 1998, the 3GPP was formed as a collaboration of six regional telecommunications standards bodies from around the world to continue the development of UMTS and other standards of GSM heritage. 3GPP completed and published the first 3G UMTS standard in 1999, and that standard is often called UMTS Release 99. UMTS Release 99 is widely deployed around the world and enjoys broad success. According to the trade groups 3G Americas and the UMTS Forum, as of May 2010, UMTS networks have been deployed by 346 operators in over 148 countries [2] and has over 450 million users [3].

UMTS includes (1) a core network (CN) that provides switching, routing, and subscriber management; (2) the UMTS Terrestrial Radio Access Network (UTRAN); and (3) the User Equipment (UE). The basic architecture is based on and backward compatible with the GSM/GPRS architecture described in Figure 1.2, with each element enhanced for 3G capabilities. The BTS becomes Node-B, BSC becomes the Radio Network Controller (RNC), the NSS becomes CN, and the MS is called the UE.

While UMTS retains the basic architecture of GSM/GPRS networks, the 3G air-interface called Wide-band CDMA (W-CDMA) is a radical departure from the 2G air-interface. The W-CDMA design was inspired by the success of IS-95 and builds on its basic features. It is a Direct Sequence Spread Spectrum CDMA system where user data is multiplied with pseudo-random codes that provide channelization, synchronization, and scrambling. W-CDMA is specified for both FDD and TDD operations, although FDD is by far the most widely deployed. The system operates on a larger 5MHz bandwidth, capable of supporting over 100 simultaneous voice calls, and providing peak data rates from 384 to 2048kbps. Besides the channel bandwidth, other notable distinguishing features of W-CDMA when compared to CDMA2000 include: (1) support for multi-code use by a single user to increase data rate, (2) wider choice of spreading factors and data rates, and (3) use of Alamouti space-time coding for transmit diversity.

1.2.3.3 HSPA

High-Speed Packet Access, or HSPA, is the term used to refer to the combination of two key enhancements by 3GPP to UMTS-WCDMA: (1) High-Speed Downlink Packet Access (HSDPA) introduced in Release 5 in 2002 and (2) High-Speed Uplink Packet Access (HSUPA) introduced in Release 6 in 2004. HSDPA was first deployed by AT&T in late 2005 and quickly became widely deployed around the world. As of February 2010, HSPA has been deployed by 303 operators in 130 countries, with many more being planned [2]. For the most part, HSPA was deployed as a software upgrade to existing UMTS systems.

Since Internet usage patterns in the late 1990s showed that most of the applications demanded higher throughput on the download, 3GPP UMTS evolution focused initially on improving the downlink. HSDPA defined a new downlink transport channel capable of providing up to 14.4Mbps peak theoretical throughput. This downlink transport channel called the High-Speed Downlink Shared Channel (HS-DSCH), unlike previous W-CDMA channels, uses time division multiplexing as the primary multi-access technique with limited code division multiplexing. HSDPA has 16 Walsh codes, 15 of which are used for user traffic. A single user could use 5, 10, or 15 codes to get higher throughputs, though this is often limited to 5 or 10 by UE implementations. To achieve higher speed, this channel uses a 2ms frame length, compared to frame lengths of 10, 20, 40, or 80ms used by W-CDMA channels. Practical deployments of HSDPA provided typical user throughputs in the 500kbps to 2Mbps range.

HSPA introduced a number of new advanced techniques to realize the high throughput and capacity [4,5]. These include

- **Adaptive Modulation and Coding (AMC)**: HSPDA supports QPSK and 16QAM modulation and rate 1/4 through rate 1 coding. AMC or link adaptation involves varying the modulation and coding scheme on a per user and per frame basis depending on instantaneous downlink channel quality. The idea is to maximize the throughput and system capacity by assigning each user link the highest modulation and coding technique that it can reliably support under the given signal to interference condition. HSDPA mobiles report a Channel Quality Indicator (CQI) measure to the base stations to enable the selection of the best possible modulation and coding scheme.

- **Fast Dynamic Scheduling**: Instead of scheduling users at fixed periods in time, HSDPA systems use a dynamic scheduler that attempts to exploit the diversity of channel conditions experienced by different users at different times. By scheduling delivery of packets to coincide with the fading peaks of each user and avoiding scheduling during their troughs, a dynamic scheduler can ensure that the system is always operating at the highest possible rate. A dynamic scheduler could, if so desired, allocate all the cell capacity to a single user for a very short time when conditions are favorable. This strategy leads to better utilization of available resources and hence increases the overall system capacity, although it may not be wise from a fairness or customer satisfaction point of view. In HSDPA, to enable faster scheduling, the scheduler is located at the Node-B as opposed to the RNC as in W-CDMA.

- **Hybrid Automatic Repeat Request (H-ARQ)**: Delays and inaccuracies in channel quality feedback could lead to incorrect link adaption causing errors. Link layer errors can be corrected using automatic repeat request (ARQ), where erroneous frames are retransmitted upon request, but multiple retransmissions can lead to intolerable delays. Hybrid-ARQ is an improved retransmission technique, where multiple erroneous retransmissions can be soft-combined to effectively recover from errors more quickly. This is referred to as *chase combining*. HSDPA also supports *incremental redundancy* where each subsequent retransmission provides additional error-correction coding in order to improve the chances of error-free reception. It should also be noted that in HSDPA, link layer retransmissions occur between the Node-B and UE as opposed to the RNC and UE as in Release 99 W-CDMA.

HSUPA, also known as Enhanced Uplink, introduced a new uplink channel called the Enhanced Dedicated Channel (E-DCH) to UMTS-WCDMA. HSUPA introduced to the uplink the same advanced technical features such as multi-code transmission, H-ARQ, short transmission time interval, and fast scheduling that HSDPA brought to the downlink. HSUPA is capable of supporting up to 5.8Mbps peak uplink throughput, with practical deployments offering typical user throughput in the 500kbps–1Mbps range. These higher uplink rates and low latency enable applications such as VoIP, uploading pictures and videos, and sending large e-mails.

1.2.4 Beyond 3G: HSPA+, WiMAX, and LTE

As of 2009, mobile operators around the world are planning their next step in the evolution of their networks. The choice they make will depend largely on their current network deployment status, the competitive pressures, and appetite for large capital investment [6,7]. It is reasonable to assume that most operators would choose from one of the following three options.

1. Deploy HSPA and its evolutionary technologies and delay migration to LTE as long as possible. Operators who have recently deployed UMTS/HSPA and wish to recoup their investment will find this option attractive.

2. Deploy WiMAX for broadband data. This option is most attractive to (a) greenfield operators who don't have legacy mobile networks and wish to quickly deploy a competitive broadband offering, (b) CDMA operators who wish to offer real broadband services quickly and do not see a viable CDMA evolutionary technology that is competitive, and (c) operators with unpaired spectrum who wish to deploy a TDD system quickly.

3. Deploy LTE as soon as possible. Many CDMA operators who find their 1X-EVDO network to be at a competitive disadvantage to the HSPA networks, and do not believe in WiMAX as a viable option, will likely wish to migrate to LTE as quickly as feasible, perhaps as early as 2010. Many operators who have not deployed 3G networks, for example, in the developing world, will likely find the option to leapfrog directly to LTE attractive.

In the following subsection we provide an overview of HSPA+ and WiMAX and compare it to LTE. Many in the industry refer to WiMAX and LTE as 4G systems, although technically they do not meet the requirements for 4G as laid out by the ITU (see Section 1.7). The 4G title is, however, somewhat justified from an engineering standpoint, as both WiMAX and LTE represent a clear break from other 3G systems in both the air-interface technology and network architecture. Each of these systems is capable of providing multi-megabits per second throughput, and achieves these high rates through the use of advanced signal processing techniques. It should also be noted that the 3GPP2 community had developed an evolution of IS-95 called IS-95 Rev. C, aka Ultra Mobile Broadband (UMB), which shares a number of technical characteristics with WiMAX and LTE. It does not, however, appear that many operators are considering deploying UMB, and therefore we have omitted it from our discussions.

1.2.4.1   HSPA+

3GPP Release 7 published in June 2007 had substantial enhancements included as a further evolution of HSPA. Release 7 HSPA, sometimes referred to as HSPA+, contains a number of additional features that improve the system capacity (including voice capacity), end-user throughput, and latency [8]. The key technical enhancements included in HSPA+ are

- **Higher-order modulation and MIMO to achieve higher peak rates**: HSPA+ introduces 64QAM as an additional downlink modulation scheme to the QPSK and 16QAM already supported in Release 6 HSPA. On the uplink, support for 16QAM is included in addition to the dual BPSK scheme supported in Release 6. Higher order modulation schemes require high signal-to-noise ratio and can only be practically used in a minority of situations and hence typically only increase the peak rate. Use of 64QAM and 16QAM pushes the peak downlink and uplink rates to 21.1Mbps and 11.5Mbps, respectively. HSPA+ also defines the use for up to two transmit antennas in the base station and two receive antennas in the mobile terminal for MIMO (multiple input multiple output) transmission supporting performance enhancing techniques such as open-loop and closed-loop transmit diversity, beamforming, and spatial multiplexing. The use of 2×2 MIMO spatial multiplexing increases the peak downlink theoretical rate to 28Mbps. While Release 7 HSPA+ does not allow the simultaneous use of 64QAM and MIMO, Release 8 does, and that takes the peak data rate to 42Mbps. It should be noted that the peak rates are seldom achieved in practical deployments. LTE further enhances the support for higher order modulation and MIMO.

- **Dual-carrier downlink operation**: In Release 8, dual-carrier operation in the downlink on adjacent carriers was also defined for HSPA+. This dual-carrier operation offers a very attractive means to achieving higher data rates when there are multiple carriers available and deployed in a single cell. Using this approach doubles the peak data rate from 21Mbps to 42Mbps as well as doubles the average data rate and substantially increases the overall cell capacity. This is unlike the case of using MIMO, which only provides peak data rate enhancements and also incurs the implementation challenges of running RF cables to multiple antennas at the base station. Given these advantages, service providers who do have multiple carriers available will likely prefer this approach. The standard allows scheduling for using dual carriers to be done on either carrier and supports load balancing between carriers in one sector.

- **Continuous packet connectivity for improved battery life**: 3GPP Release 6 HSPA requires that mobile terminals transmit the physical control channel even in the absence of any data channel transmission, which causes unnecessary battery drain. Release 7 HSPA+ allows the uplink transmission to be discontinuous such that the mobile transmitter can be completely turned off when there is no data transmission. On the downlink, similarly, discontinuous reception is supported where the mobile terminal is allowed to wake up for only parts of the frame and can go to sleep mode when there is no data to be received. Discontinuous transmission and reception are very useful power-saving techniques for bursty data applications such as Web browsing (typically, up to 50%). Discontinuous uplink transmissions also reduce interference and hence increase capacity. When applied to VoIP calls, this could provide up to 50% increase in VoIP capacity compared to Release 6.

- **Advanced mobile receivers for data rate and capacity enhancement**: Two-antenna chip equalizer is also defined as part of HSPA+ in addition to the one-antenna chip equalizer and two-antenna RAKE receivers defined in Release 6 HSPA. The antenna diversity improves signal-to-noise ratio and the chip equalizer removes intra-cell interference; together the advanced receiver allows for higher throughput transmissions in the downlink and hence improves capacity. It should be noted this comes at the cost of receiver complexity and is a key disadvantage when compared to the OFDM approach used in LTE.

- **Flexible RLC and MAC segmentation**: W-CDMA and HSPA specified a low, fixed-size Radio Link Control (RLC) layer packet structure (40 bytes, optional 80 bytes in HSPA). This was done largely to avoid having to retransmit large payloads in case of errors. With more robust link layer retransmission schemes in place for HSPA, Release 7 HSPA+ now allows the RLC block size to be flexible and can be as large as 1,500 bytes (typical IP Packet size) without requiring any segmentation at the RLC. Segmentation can be done by the MAC layer based on physical layer requirements. This flexible RLC reduces the RLC layer overhead (RLC header of 2 bytes is just 0.2% of a 1,000-byte packet versus 5% of a 40-byte packet), avoids the need for unnecessary padding to fit in a fixed size, and reduces the number of packets to process at the RLC. All of these lead to improved data throughput and peak rates.

- **Single frequency network for improved multi-cast and broadcast**: HSPA+ allows network synchronization across base stations and the use of same scrambling codes for multi-cast broadcast (MBMS) transmissions from multiple base stations. This realizes a single frequency network (SFN) for multi-cast broadcast services. Operating in SFN mode allows users at the cell-edge to combine the signals from multiple cells coherently and using an equalizer, eliminate any time-dispersion impacts. Release 6 of 3GPP allowed only for soft combining and not for a single frequency operation. Improving cell-edge performance of MBMS implies that higher-data broadcast services can be supported.

According to 3G Americas, 56 operators in 34 countries have already begun deploying HSPA+ as of May 2010 [2].

1.2.4.2   Mobile WiMAX

In 1998, the Institute of Electrical and Electronics Engineers (IEEE) formed a group called 802.16 to develop a standard for what was called a *wireless metropolitan area network* (WMAN). The group first produced a standard for fixed wireless applications in 2001 and later enhanced it to support mobility. The revised standard, called IEEE 802.16e, was completed in 2005 and is often referred to as Mobile WiMAX. The industry consortium called Worldwide Interoperability for Microwave Access (WiMAX) Forum was formed in 2001 to promote, develop, perform interoperability and conformance testing, and certify end-to-end wireless systems based on the IEEE 802.16 air-interface standards. In 2007, WiMAX was approved by ITU as an IMT-2000 terrestrial radio interface option called IP-OFDMA. The WiMAX network is designed using IP protocols, and does not offer circuit-switched voice telephony; voice services, however, can be provided using the VoIP (voice over IP). According to the WiMAX Forum, as of February 2010, there are 504 WiMAX networks deployed in 147 countries. WiMAX is generally seen as the only credible alternative to LTE for operators looking to deploy mobile broadband, though most analysts expect WiMAX to take a much smaller share of the worldwide mobile broadband market compared to LTE. It should also be noted that a number of aspects in the LTE design—especially the use of OFDM and OFDMA technology—was directly inspired by their implementation in WiMAX.

Some of the salient features of WiMAX that deserve highlighting are [10]:

- **Very High Peak Data Rates**: WiMAX peak physical layer data rate can be as high as 74Mbps when operating using a 20MHz wide spectrum. Using 5MHz spectrum, the peak physical layer (PHY) data rate is 18Mbps. These peak PHY data rates are achieved when using 64QAM modulation with rate $3/4$ error correction coding.

- **OFDM/OFDMA Based Physical Layer**: The WiMAX PHY is based on Orthogonal Frequency Division Multiplexing (OFDM), a scheme that offers good resistance to multipath, and allows WiMAX to operate in non-line-of-sight (NLOS) conditions even with large bandwidths. OFDM is now widely recognized as the method of choice for mitigating multipath for broadband wireless, and in fact has been chosen by LTE as well. WiMAX also uses OFDMA as the multiple access technique, which allows users to be multiplexed in both time and frequency in a dynamic manner. OFDM and OFDMA are subjects of Chapter 3 and 4, respectively.

- **Scalable Bandwidth and Data Rate Support**: WiMAX has a very scalable physical layer architecture that allows for the data rate to scale easily with available channel bandwidth. This scalability is supported by OFDMA, where the FFT size may be scaled based on the available channel bandwidth. For example, a WiMAX system may use 128-, 512-, or 1048-bit FFTs based on whether the channel bandwidth is 1.25MHz, 5MHz, or 10MHz, respectively. This scaling may be done dynamically, and supports user roaming across different networks that may have varying bandwidth allocations.

- **Support for TDD and FDD**: IEEE 802.16e-2005 supports both Time 1 Division Duplexing (TDD) and Frequency Division Duplexing (FDD), but WiMAX implementations thus far have been TDD. TDD has been attractive to WiMAX operators since it offers flexibility in choosing uplink-to-downlink data rate ratios, the ability to exploit channel reciprocity, and perhaps more importantly because it allows implementation in non-paired spectrum.

- **Flexible and Dynamic Per User Resource Allocation**: Both uplink and downlink resource allocation is controlled by a scheduler in the base station. Capacity is shared among multiple users on a demand basis employing a burst TDM multiplexing scheme. Multiplexing is additionally done in the frequency dimension, by allocating different subsets of OFDM subcarriers to different users. Resources may be allocated in the spatial domain as well when using optional advanced antenna systems (AAS). The standard allows for bandwidth resources to be allocated in time, frequency, and space, and has a flexible mechanism to convey the resource allocation information on a frame-by-frame basis.

- **Robust Link Layer**: WiMAX supports a number of modulation and forward error correction (FEC) schemes, and supports adaptive modulation and coding (AMC) to maximize the data rate on each link. For connections that require enhanced reliability, WiMAX supports automatic retransmissions (ARQ) at the link layer and optionally supports Hybrid-ARQ as well.

- **Support for Advanced Antenna Techniques**: The WiMAX solution has a number of features built into the physical layer design that allows for the use of multiple antenna techniques such as beamforming, space-time coding, and spatial multiplexing. These schemes can be used to improve the overall system capacity and spectral efficiency by deploying multiple antennas at the transmitter and/or the receiver.

- **IP-Based Architecture**: The WiMAX Forum has defined a reference network architecture that is based on an all-IP platform. All end-to-end services are delivered over an IP architecture relying on IP protocols for end-to-end transport, QoS, session management, security, and mobility. Reliance on IP allows WiMAX to ride the declining cost curves of IP processing, facilitate easy convergence with other networks, and exploit the rich application development ecosystem that exists for IP.

1.2.4.3   Comparison of HSPA+ and WiMAX to LTE

While we provide a more detailed introduction to LTE in Section 1.3, here we offer a quick comparison of LTE with HSPA+ and WiMAX. Since LTE is the latest of the three standards, it was obviously designed to perform better than HSPA+ and WiMAX. The three, however, have a lot in common as several of the ideas in LTE are derived directly from the design experience of HSPA and WiMAX. Table 1.5 provides a summary comparing the key characteristics of HSPA+, WiMAX, and LTE.

A few key observations to make are

- While HSPA+ and LTE are both developed by 3GPP as an evolution to the currently deployed GSM/UMTS networks, WiMAX was developed independently by the IEEE and WiMAX Forum as an alternative wireless broadband technology without any backward compatibility constraints.

- Though all three systems are designed to offer great flexibility in frequency selection, early deployments of WiMAX are likely to be in the 2.3GHz, 2.6GHz, and 3.5GHz frequency bands, while most HSPA+ and LTE deployments are likely to be in bands below 2.1GHz. All else being equal, lower frequencies will provide better coverage and building penetration. LTE supports both FDD and TDD and hence affords flexibility in operating in both paired and unpaired spectrum. WiMAX is mostly deployed in TDD mode and HSPA+ only supports FDD.

- Both LTE and WiMAX use OFDM/OFDMA as the underlying modulation and multi-access technology while HSPA+ uses CDMA/TDMA. LTE uses a variation of OFDMA called Single Carrier Frequency Division Multiple Access (SC-FDMA) on the uplink that offers better power efficiency. WiMAX uses OFDMA in both uplink and downlink.

- While HSPA uses a fixed 5MHz bandwidth, both WiMAX and LTE offer a flexible bandwidth architecture supporting up to a maximum of 20MHz. This makes it possible, given sufficient spectrum, to provide much higher peak rates in LTE and WiMAX when compared to HSPA+.

- All three standards support a variety of signal processing techniques to improve performance and spectral efficiency. Hybrid-ARQ retransmission schemes, dynamic channel dependent scheduling, and multiantenna schemes such as transmit diversity, beamforming, and spatial multiplexing are supported by HSPA+, LTE, and WiMAX.

Table 1.5 Summary Comparison of HSPA+, WiMAX, and LTE

	HSPA+	Mobile WiMAX	LTE
Standard	3GPP Release 7&8	IEEE 802.16e-2005	3GPP Release 8
Frequency Bands (Early Deployments)	850/900MHz, 1.8/1.9GHz,	2.3GHz, 2.6GHz, and 3.5GHz	700MHz, 1.7/2.1GHz, 2.6GHz, 1.5GHz
Channel Bandwidth	5MHz	5, 7, 8.75, and 10MHz	1.4, 3, 5, 10, 15, and 20MHz
Peak Downlink Data Rate	28–42Mbps	46Mbps (10MHz, 2 × 2 MIMO, 3:1 DL to UL ratio TDD); 32Mbps with 1:1	150Mbps (2 × 2 MIMO, 20MHz)
Peak Uplink Data Rate	11.5Mbps	7Mbps (10MHz, 3:1 DL to UL ratio TDD); 4Mbps with 1:1	75Mbps (10MHz)
User-Plane Latency	10–40ms	15–40ms	5–15ms
Frame Size	2ms frames	5ms frames	1ms sub-frames
Downlink Multiple Access	CDMA/TDMA	OFDMA	OFDMA
Uplink Multiple Access	CDMA/TDMA	OFDMA	SC-FDMA
Duplexing	FDD	TDD; FDD option planned	FDD and TDD
Data Modulation	DS-SS: QPSK, 16QAM, and 64QAM	OFDM: QPSK, 16QAM, and 64QAM	OFDM: QPSK, 16QAM, and 64QAM
Channel Coding	Turbo codes; rate 3/4, 1/2, 1/4	Convolutional, turbo RS codes, rate 1/2, 2/3, 3/4, 5/6	Convolutional and Turbo coding: rate 78/1024 to 948/1024
Hybrid-ARQ	Yes; incremental redundancy and chase combining	Yes; chase combining	Yes, various
MIMO	Tx diversity, spatial multiplexing, beamforming	Beamforming, open-loop Tx diversity, spatial multiplexing	Transmit Diversity, Spatial Multiplexing; 4 × 4 MIMO Uplink: Multi-user collaborative MIMO
Persistent Scheduling	No	No	Yes

- LTE supports higher peak data rates than HSPA+ and WiMAX. In the best case, assuming 20MHz spectrum and using 4 × 4 MIMO, LTE can support up to 326Mbps on the downlink and 86Mbps on the uplink. Spectral efficiency differences between these systems, although significant, are, however, less dramatic.

- LTE supports 10ms frames and 1ms sub-frames, which is much shorter than the frame sizes supported by HSPA+ and WiMAX. Shorter frame sizes allow for faster feedback for retransmission and provide better efficiency at high-speed.

- Among the three, LTE offers the best support for VoIP. It has the lowest (5–15ms) user plane latency and lowest (50ms) call setup time. LTE also supports persistent scheduling, which significantly reduces the control channel overhead for low bit rate voice transmission and thus improves VoIP capacity. Both HSPA+ and LTE use dedicated control channels, which are more efficient for VoIP than using mapping symbols to assign resources, as is done in WiMAX.

1.2.5 Summary of Evolution of 3GPP Standards

We have thus far covered a number of cellular wireless standards and systems, tracing the evolution from first generation analog voice systems to the development of LTE. Let us now summarize the major enhancements and performance improvements that have been achieved at each step of this evolution. Since LTE was developed by the 3GPP standards body, we will focus here only on 3GPP standards evolution.

The first version of a 3G standard by 3GPP was targeted for completion in 1999, and is often referred to as 3GPP Release 99, although the actual release occurred in 2000. Several UMTS networks around the world are based on this standard. Subsequent releases are identified by a release number as opposed to year of release. Each release provided enhancements in one or more of several aspects including (1) radio performance improvements such as higher data rates, lower latency, and increased voice capacity, (2) core network changes aimed at reducing its complexity and improving transport efficiency, and (3) support for new applications such as push-to-talk, multimedia broadcast, and multicast services and IP Multimedia Services. Table 1.6 summarizes the various 3GPP releases and the enhancements that each brought.

Table 1.7 summarizes the evolution of peak data rates and latency of wireless systems that evolved from GSM via 3GPP standards. Clearly, tremendous strides have been made over the past decade in both data rate and latency. Peak data rates in early GPRS systems were as low as 40kbps, while, in theory, LTE can provide up to 326Mbps; that is almost a ten thousand–fold increase. Typical end-user speeds grew from 10–20kbps with GPRS to 0.5–2Mbps with HSPA/HSPA+, and expect to get to 2–3Mbps or more with LTE. Advances in technology have pushed us very close to realizing the Shannon limit for channel capacity, which makes achieving further gains in spectral efficiency quite challenging. Changes in protocols, frame sizes, and network architecture over the years have also resulted in dramatic reduction in latency. While GPRS and EDGE systems had user plane latencies around 350–700ms, HSPA systems got it down to less than 100ms, and LTE systems will get it below 30ms. Lower latency improves the quality of experience of real-time applications such as VoIP, gaming, and other interactive applications.

Table 1.6 3GPP Standards Evolution

3GPP Standards Release	Year Completed	Major Enhancements
Release 99	2000	Specified the original UMTS 3G network using W-CDMA air-interface. Also included Enhancements to GSM data (EDGE).
Release 4	2001	Added multimedia messaging support and took steps toward using IP transport in core network.
Release 5	2002	Specified HSDPA with up to 1.8Mbps peak downlink data rate. Introduced IP Multimedia Services (IMS) architecture.
Release 6	2004	Specified HSUPA with up to 2Mbps uplink speed. Multimedia Broadcast/Multicast Services (MBMS). Added advanced receiver specifications, push-to-talk over cellular (PoC) and other IMS enhancements, WLAN interworking option, limited VoIP capability.
Release 7	2007	Specified HSPA+ with higher order modulation (64QAM downlink and 16QAM uplink) and downlink MIMO support offering up to 28Mbps downlink and 11.5Mbps uplink peak data rates. Reduced latency and improved QoS for VoIP.
Release 8	2009	Further evolution of HSPA+: combined use of 64QAM and MIMO; dual-carrier with 64QAM. Specifies new OFDMA-based LTE radio interface and a new all IP flat architecture with Evolved Packet Core (EPC).
Release 9	2010	Expected to include HSPA and LTE enhancements.
Release 10	2012?	Expected to specify LTE-Advanced that meets the ITU IMT-Advanced Project requirements for 4G.

1.3 The Case for LTE/SAE

As fixed-line broadband adoption began growing rapidly around the world, the mobile community recognized the need to develop a mobile broadband system that is commensurate with DSL and capable of supporting the rapid growth in IP traffic. Around 2005, two groups within 3GPP started work on developing a standard to support the expected heavy growth in IP data traffic. The Radio Access Network (RAN) group initiated work

Table 1.7 Performance Evolution of 3GPP Standards

Standard	3GPP Release	Peak Down-link Speed	Peak Uplink Speed	Latency
GPRS	Release 97/99	40–80kbps	40–80kbps	600–700ms
EDGE	Release 4	237–474kbps	237kbps	350–450ms
UMTS (WCDMA)	Release 4	384kbps	384kbps	<200ms
HSDPA/UMTS	Release 5	1800kbps	384kbps	<120ms
HSPA	Release 6	3600–7200kbps	2000kbps	<100ms
HSPA+	Release 7 and 8	28–42Mbps	11.5Mbps	<80ms
LTE	Release 8	173–326Mbps	86Mbps	<30ms

on the Long Term Evolution (LTE) project and the Systems Aspects group initiated work on the Systems Architecture Evolution (SAE) project. These two groups completed their initial study by mid-2006 and transitioned it into standards development. The LTE group developed a new radio access network called Enhanced UTRAN (E-UTRAN) as an evolution to the UMTS RAN. The SAE group developed a new all IP packet core network architecture called the Evolved Packet Core (EPC). Together, EUTRAN and EPC are formally called the Evolved Packet System (EPS).

In this section we discuss the market demand drivers for the development and deployment of LTE and enumerate the key requirements that LTE design had to meet.

1.3.1 Demand Drivers for LTE

The dramatic growth of the Internet over the past decade is clearly the underlying driver for mobile broadband. The Internet today is the platform for delivering a vast variety of applications and has become the media of choice for all our information, communication, and entertainment needs. The availability of broadband access services has made it possible for users to experience the Internet in its full multimedia richness, and users now expect to have the same on-demand access to multimedia content from anywhere and while on the move. This is evidenced by the dramatic growth in wireless data subscription over the past few years. Informa Telecoms & Media, a consultancy, reports that at the end of March 2009, worldwide mobile broadband subscribers reached 225 million, representing a 93% year-on-year growth. The same consultancy predicts that there will be over 2 billion subscribers on 3G and beyond systems by 2013, 80% of whom would be on 3GPP networks [11].

We identify three broad trends that together drive demand for mobile broadband and make a compelling case for the development and deployment of LTE. These are

- **Growth in high-bandwidth applications**: Mobile applications are rapidly moving from SMS, Web and WAP access, multimedia messaging (MMS), and low MB content (e.g., ringtones) downloading to high bandwidth applications such as music downloads, video sharing, mobile video, and IPTV. The proliferation of Web sites with embedded video content and the popularity of video sharing sites such as YouTube are driving more and more users to access, view, and share video using their mobile devices. Video now accounts for a large fraction of all mobile data traffic and it is growing rapidly. Analysts predict that by 2014, more than 65% of mobile data traffic will be video [12].

- **Proliferation of smart mobile devices**: The past few years has witnessed a tremendous growth in the variety and availability of smartphones, that is, mobile phone devices with full keyboard and integrated data capabilities. Remarkable improvements in the user interface, the availability of full browsing, e-mail, and music and video playing capabilities in mobile devices are turning cell phone subscribers into prodigious consumers of wireless data services. The packaging of cameras, camcorders, GPS navigation systems, and other technologies into mobile phones has enabled a variety of exciting mobile applications and use cases, further driving the demand for these devices. According to analysts at Informa Telecoms and Media, in 2008, there were almost 162 million smartphones sold, surpassing laptop sales for the first time. They expect that by 2013 almost 25% of all phones sold will be smartphones. In fact, by mid-2009, in the United States, smartphones account for more than 30% of all mobile phone sales. Besides smartphones, a variety of other mobile devices are also emerging. These include laptops with integrated 3G interface, consumer devices with large screens, netbook computers, tablet computers, gaming devices, electronic readers, portable media players, cameras, camcorders and projectors with built-in wireless interfaces, health monitoring, asset tracking, and other machine-to-machine communication devices. Global adoption of LTE as a single standard will almost certainly lead to further proliferation of devices.

- **Intense competition leading to flat revenues**: In most of the world, the wireless market is an intensely competitive one. It can be argued that competition among service providers and device manufacturers was a key driver for the innovation and rapid growth we have seen thus far. As wireless penetration has deepened—in many countries it is higher than 100% as on average each person has more than one cell phone—mobile operators have had to poach customers from one another for growth leading to lower pricing and hence lower margins. The adoption of flat-rate pricing is leading to a widening gap between revenue and consumption. Usage and consumption is growing at a significantly higher pace, straining network resources and forcing operators to invest in upgrades. HSPA operators are reporting huge increases in mobile data consumption, and most analysts expect aggregate mobile data consumption to grow 50–100 times or more in the next five years. For example, according to Cisco Visual Networking Index, global mobile data traffic will grow from 90 petabytes (10^{15}) per month in 2009 to 3.6 exabytes (10^{18}) per month in 2014 [12]. While data revenues will also grow, the expectation is that they will grow only around two times over the same period. Clearly, operators have a strong need to reduce the cost per megabyte and find a network infrastructure and operating model that helps them achieve that. Lowering the cost per megabyte will be another key driver for LTE deployment.

1.3.2   Key Requirements of LTE Design

LTE was designed with the following objectives in mind to effectively meet the growing demand [13].

- **Performance on Par with Wired Broadband**: One of the goals of LTE was to make mobile Internet experience as good as or better than that achieved by residential wired broadband access systems deployed today. The two key network performance parameters that drive user experience are high throughput and low latency.

  To push toward high throughputs, 3GPP set the peak data rate targets to be at 100Mbps and 50Mbps for the downlink and uplink, respectively. This is an order of magnitude better than what is achieved by 3G systems today. In addition to peak data rates, which may be experienced only by a fraction of users who happen to be in close radio proximity to the base stations, an average user data rate target was also set. The LTE design goal was to achieve an average downlink throughput that is 3–4 times better than that of the original HSPA and an average uplink throughput that is 2–3 times better. It was also stipulated that these higher data rates be achieved by making a 2–4 times improvement in spectral efficiency. LTE requirements also call for increased cell edge bit rate while maintaining the same site locations as deployed today.

  To enable support for delay sensitive applications like voice and interactive gaming, it is required that the network latency is kept very low. The target round-trip latency for LTE radio network is set to be less than 10ms. This is better than the 20–40ms delay observed in many DSL systems. In addition, LTE aims to reduce latency associated with control plane functions such as session setup. Enhancing QoS capabilities to support a variety of applications is another LTE goal.

  While LTE aims for performance parity with wired broadband systems, it does so while simultaneously elevating the requirements on mobility. The system is required to support optimized high quality handoff and connections up to speeds of 15kmph with only minor degradations allowed for connections up to speeds of 120kmph. A lower quality support is envisioned for up to 350kmph.

- **Flexible Spectrum Usage**: The frequency band and amount of spectrum owned by different mobile operators around the world vary significantly. Since many LTE deployments are likely to be in refarmed spectrum that is currently used for 3G or 2G services, the amount of spectrum that could be made available for LTE will also depend on how aggressively individual operators wish to migrate to LTE. In order to be a truly global standard and to make it attractive for deployment by a wide variety of operators, 3GPP mandated a high degree of spectrum flexibility.

  Operators can deploy LTE in 900MHz, 1800MHz, 700MHz, and 2.6GHz bands. LTE supports a variety of channel bandwidths: 1.4, 3, 5, 10, 15, and 20MHz. It is also mandated that end user devices are able to operate at all the channel bandwidths lower than their maximum capability; for example, a 10MHz mobile device will support all bandwidths up to 10MHz. The smaller 1.4MHz and 5MHz channels are optimized for GSM and CDMA refarming to support deployments where operators are unable to free larger amounts of spectrum. LTE also supports both frequency division duplexing (FDD) and time division duplexing (TDD) to accommodate paired as well as unpaired spectrum allocations. However, most deployments are likely to be FDD, and for the most part, the coverage in this book will be limited to FDD.

- **Co-existence and Interworking with 3G Systems as well as Non-3GPP Systems**: Given the large base of existing mobile subscribers, it is a critical requirement that LTE networks interwork seamlessly with existing 2G and 3G systems. Most existing cellular operators are likely to phase in LTE over a period of time with initial deployments being made in areas of high demand such as urban cores. Service continuity and mobility—handoff and roaming—between LTE and existing 2G/3G systems are critical to obtain a seamless user experience. As LTE aims to be a truly global standard attractive to a variety of operators, interworking requirements have been extended to non-3GPP systems such as the 3GPP2 CDMA and WiMAX networks. Further, to facilitate fixed-mobile convergence, interworking requirements apply to all IP networks including wired IP networks

- **Reducing Cost per Megabyte**: As discussed in the previous section, there is a growing gap between wireless data consumption and revenue. To bridge this gap, it is essential that substantial reductions be achieved in the total network cost to deliver data to end users. 3GPP recognizes this issue and has made reducing the cost per megabyte of data a key design criterion for LTE. A number of design criteria are tied directly to cost efficiency. These include:

  - High-capacity, high-spectral efficiency air-interface
  - Ability to deploy in existing spectrum and reuse cell sites and transmission equipment
  - Interworking with legacy systems to allow for cost-effective migration
  - Interworking with non-3GPP systems to drive toward one global standard to achieve higher economies of scale
  - A flat architecture with fewer network components and protocols
  - A single IP packet core for voice and data
  - IP architecture to leverage larger development community and gain economies of scale through convergence with wired communication systems
  - Support for lower-cost Ethernet-based backhaul networks
  - Base stations with lower power and space requirements; could in many cases be put inside existing base station cabinets or mounted beside them
  - Support for self-configuring and self-optimizing network and technologies to reduce installation and management cost

1.4   Key Enabling Technologies and Features of LTE

To meet its service and performance requirements, LTE design incorporates several important enabling radio and core network technologies [14–16]. Here, we provide a brief introduction to some of the key enabling technologies used in the LTE design. Subsequent chapters in this book elaborate on each of these in much greater detail.

1.4.1   Orthogonal Frequency Division Multiplexing (OFDM)

One of the key differences between existing 3G systems and LTE is the use of Orthogonal Frequency Division Multiplexing (OFDM) as the underlying modulation technology. Widely deployed 3G systems such as UMTS and CDMA2000 are based on Code Division Multiple Access (CDMA) technology. CDMA works by spreading a narrow band signal over a wider bandwidth to achieve interference resistance, and performs remarkably well for low data rate communications such as voice, where a large number of users can be multiplexed to achieve high system capacity. However, for high-speed applications, CDMA becomes untenable due to the large bandwidth needed to achieve useful amounts of spreading.

OFDM has emerged as a technology of choice for achieving high data rates. It is the core technology used by a variety of systems including Wi-Fi and WiMAX. The following advantages of OFDM led to its selection for LTE:

- **Elegant solution to multipath interference**: The critical challenge to high bit-rate transmissions in a wireless channel is intersymbol interference caused by multipath. In a multipath environment, when the time delay between the various signal paths is a significant fraction of the transmitted signal's symbol period, a transmitted symbol may arrive at the receiver during the next symbol and cause intersymbol interference (ISI). At high data rates, the symbol time is shorter; hence, it only takes a small delay to cause ISI, making it a bigger challenge for broadband wireless. OFDM is a multicarrier modulation technique that overcomes this challenge in an elegant manner. The basic idea behind multicarrier modulation is to divide a given high-bit-rate data stream into several parallel lower bit-rate streams and modulate each stream on separate carriers—often called subcarriers, or tones. Splitting the data stream into many parallel streams increases the symbol duration of each stream such that the multipath delay spread is only a small fraction of the symbol duration. OFDM is a spectrally efficient version of multicarrier modulation, where the subcarriers are selected such that they are all orthogonal to one another over the symbol duration, thereby avoiding the need to have non-overlapping subcarrier channels to eliminate inter-carrier interference. In OFDM, any residual intersymbol interference can also be eliminated by using guard intervals between OFDM symbols that are larger than the expected multipath delay. By making the guard interval larger than the expected multipath delay spread, ISI can be completely eliminated. Adding a guard interval, however, implies power wastage and a decrease in bandwidth efficiency.

- **Reduced computational complexity**: OFDM can be easily implemented using Fast Fourier Transforms (FFT/IFFT), and the computational requirements grow only slightly faster than linearly with data rate or bandwidth. The computational complexity of OFDM can be shown to be $O(BlogBT_m)$ where B is the bandwidth and T_m is the delay spread. This complexity is much lower than that of a time-domain equalizer-based system—the traditional means for combating multipath interference—which has a complexity of $O(B^2T_m)$. Reduced complexity is particularly attractive in the downlink as it simplifies receiver processing and thus reduces mobile device cost and power consumption. This is especially important given the wide transmission bandwidths of LTE coupled with multistream transmissions.

- **Graceful degradation of performance under excess delay**: The performance of an OFDM system degrades gracefully as the delay spread exceeds the value designed for. Greater coding and low constellation sizes can be used to provide fallback rates that are significantly more robust against delay spread. In other words, OFDM is well suited for adaptive modulation and coding, which allows the system to make the best of the available channel conditions. This contrasts with the abrupt degradation owing to error propagation that single-carrier systems experience as the delay spread exceeds the value for which the equalizer is designed.

- **Exploitation of frequency diversity**: OFDM facilitates coding and interleaving across subcarriers in the frequency domain, which can provide robustness against burst errors caused by portions of the transmitted spectrum undergoing deep fades. OFDM also allows for the channel bandwidth to be scalable without impacting the hardware design of the base station and the mobile station. This allows LTE to be deployed in a variety of spectrum allocations and different channel bandwidths.

- **Enables efficient multi-access scheme**: OFDM can be used as a multi-access scheme by partitioning different subcarriers among multiple users. This scheme is referred to as OFDMA and is exploited in LTE. OFDMA offers the ability to provide fine granularity in channel allocation, which can be exploited to achieve significant capacity improvements, particularly in slow time-varying channels.

- **Robust against narrowband interference**: OFDM is relatively robust against narrowband interference, since such interference affects only a fraction of the subcarriers.

- **Suitable for coherent demodulation**: It is relatively easy to do pilot-based channel estimation in OFDM systems, which renders them suitable for coherent demodulation schemes that are more power efficient.

- **Facilitates use of MIMO**: MIMO stands for multiple input multiple output and refers to a collection of signal processing techniques that use multiple antennas at both the transmitter and receiver to improve system performance. For MIMO techniques to be effective, it is required that the channel conditions are such that the multipath delays do not cause intersymbol interference—in other words, the channel has to be a flat fading channel and not a frequency selective one. At very high data rates, this is not the case and therefore MIMO techniques do not work well in traditional broadband channels. OFDM, however, converts a frequency selective broad band channel into several narrowband flat fading channels where the MIMO models and techniques work well. The ability to effectively use MIMO techniques to improve system capacity gives OFDM a significant advantage over other techniques and is one of the key reasons for its choice. MIMO and OFDM have already been combined effectively in Wi-Fi and WiMAX systems.

- **Efficient support of broadcast services**: By synchronizing base stations to timing errors well within the OFDM guard interval, it is possible to operate an OFDM network as a single frequency network (SFN). This allows broadcast signals from different cells to combine over the air to significantly enhance the received signal power, thereby enabling higher data rate broadcast transmissions for a given transmit power. LTE design leverages this OFDM capability to improve efficient broadcast services.

While all these advantages drove 3GPP to adopt OFDM as their modulation choice, it should be noted that OFDM also suffers from a few disadvantages. Chief among these is the problem associated with OFDM signals having high peak-to-average ratio (PAR), which causes non-linearities and clipping distortion when passed through an RF amplifier. Mitigating this problem requires the use of expensive and inefficient power amplifiers with high requirements on linearity, which increases the cost of the transmitter and is wasteful of power.

While the increased amplifier costs and power inefficiency of OFDM is tolerated in the downlink as part of the design, for the uplink LTE selected a variation of OFDM that has a lower peak-to-average ratio. The modulation of choice for the uplink is called Single Carrier Frequency Division Multiple Access (SC-FDMA).

1.4.2   SC-FDE and SC-FDMA

To keep the cost down and the battery life up, LTE incorporated a power efficient transmission scheme for the uplink. Single Carrier Frequency Domain Equalization (SC-FDE) is conceptually similar to OFDM but instead of transmitting the Inverse Fast Fourier Transform (IFFT) of the actual data symbols, the data symbols are sent as a sequence of QAM symbols with a cyclic prefix added; the IFFT is added at the end of the receiver. SC-FDE retains all the advantages of OFDM such as multipath resistance and low complexity, while having a low peak-to-average ratio of 4-5dB. The uplink of LTE implements a multi-user version of SC-FDE, called SC-FDMA, which allows multiple users to use parts of the frequency spectrum. SC-FDMA closely resembles OFDMA and can in fact be thought of as "DFT precoded OFDMA." SC-FDMA also preserves the PAR properties of SC-FDE but increases the complexity of the transmitter and the receiver.

1.4.3   Channel Dependent Multi-user Resource Scheduling

The OFDMA scheme used in LTE provides enormous flexibility in how channel resources are allocated. OFDMA allows for allocation in both time and frequency and it is possible to design algorithms to allocate resources in a flexible and dynamic manner to meet arbitrary throughput, delay, and other requirements. The standard supports dynamic, channel-dependent scheduling to enhance overall system capacity.

Given that each user will be experiencing uncorrelated fading channels, it is possible to allocate subcarriers among users in such a way that the overall capacity is increased. This technique, called frequency selective multiuser scheduling, calls for focusing transmission power in each user's best channel portion, thereby increasing the overall capacity. Frequency selective scheduling requires good channel tracking and is generally only viable in slow varying channels. For fast varying channels, the overhead involved in doing this negates the potential capacity gains. In OFDMA, frequency selective scheduling can be combined with multi-user time domain scheduling, which calls for scheduling users during the crests of their individual fading channels. Capacity gains are also obtained by adapting the modulation and coding to the instantaneous signal-to-noise ratio conditions for each user subcarrier.

For high-mobility users, OFDMA can be used to achieve frequency diversity. By coding and interleaving across subcarriers in the frequency domain using a uniform random distribution of subcarriers over the whole spectrum, the signal can be made more robust against frequency selective fading or burst errors. Frequency diverse scheduling is best suited for control signaling and delay sensitive services.

1.4.4   Multiantenna Techniques

The LTE standard provides extensive support for implementing advanced multiantenna solutions to improve link robustness, system capacity, and spectral efficiency. Depending on the deployment scenario, one or more of the techniques can be used. Multiantenna techniques supported in LTE include:

- **Transmit diversity**: This is a technique to combat multipath fading in the wireless channel. The idea here is to send copies of the same signal, coded differently, over multiple transmit antennas. LTE transmit diversity is based on space-frequency block coding (SFBC) techniques complemented with frequency shift time diversity (FSTD) when four transmit antenna are used. Transmit diversity is primarily intended for common downlink channels that cannot make use of channel-dependent scheduling. It can also be applied to user transmissions such as low data rate VoIP, where the additional overhead of channel-dependent scheduling may not be justified. Transmit diversity increases system capacity and cell range.

- **Beamforming**: Multiple antennas in LTE may also be used to transmit the same signal appropriately weighted for each antenna element such that the effect is to focus the transmitted beam in the direction of the receiver and away from interference, thereby improving the received signal-to-interference ratio. Beamforming can provide significant improvements in coverage range, capacity, reliability, and battery life. It can also be useful in providing angular information for user tracking. LTE supports beamforming in the downlink.

- **Spatial multiplexing**: The idea behind spatial multiplexing is that multiple independent streams can be transmitted in parallel over multiple antennas and can be separated at the receiver using multiple receive chains through appropriate signal processing. This can be done as long as the multipath channels as seen by the different antennas are sufficiently decorrelated as would be the case in a scattering

rich environment. In theory, spatial multiplexing provides data rate and capacity gains proportional to the number of antennas used. It works well under good
SNR and light load conditions, and hence tends to have a more pronounced effect
on peak rates rather than overall system capacity. LTE standard supports spatial
multiplexing with up to four transmit antennas and four receiver antennas.

- **Multi-user MIMO**: Since spatial multiplexing requires multiple transmit chains,
  it is currently not supported in the uplink due to complexity and cost considerations. However, multi-user MIMO (MU-MIMO), which allows multiple users in
  the uplink, each with a single antenna, to transmit using the same frequency and
  time resource, is supported. The signals from the different MU-MIMO users are
  separated at the base station receiver using accurate channel state information of
  each user obtained through uplink reference signals that are orthogonal between
  users.

1.4.5   IP-Based Flat Network Architecture

Besides the air-interface, the other radical aspect of LTE is the flat radio and core network
architecture [15]. "Flat" here implies fewer nodes and a less hierarchical structure for
the network. The lower cost and lower latency requirements drove the design toward
a flat architecture since fewer nodes obviously implies a lower infrastructure cost. It
also means fewer interfaces and protocol-related processing, and reduced interoperability
testing, which lowers the development and deployment cost. Fewer nodes also allow better
optimization of radio interface, merging of some control plane protocols, and short session
start-up time.

Figure 1.3 shows how the 3GPP network architecture evolved over a few releases.
3GPP Release 6 architecture, which is conceptually very similar to its predecessors,
has four network elements in the data path: the base station or Node-B, radio network
controller (RNC), serving GPRS service node (SGSN), and gateway GRPS service node
(GGSN). Release 7 introduced a direct tunnel option from the RNC to GGSN, which
eliminated SGSN from the data path. LTE on the other hand, will have only two network
elements in the data path: the enhanced Node-B or eNode-B, and a System Architecture
Evolution Gateway (SAE-GW). Unlike all previous cellular systems, LTE merges the
base station and radio network controller functionality into a single unit. The control
path includes a functional entity called the Mobility Management Entity (MME), which
provides control plane functions related to subscriber, mobility, and session management.
The MME and SAE-GW could be collocated in a single entity called the access gateway
(a-GW). More details about the network architecture are provided in the next section.

A key aspect of the LTE flat architecture is that all services, including voice, are
supported on the IP packet network using IP protocols. Unlike previous systems, which
had a separate circuit-switched subnetwork for supporting voice with their own Mobile
Switching Centers (MSC) and transport networks, LTE envisions only a single evolved
packet-switched core, the EPC, over which all services are supported, which could provide huge operational and infrastructure cost savings. It should be noted, however, that
although LTE has been designed for IP services with a flat architecture, due to backwards
compatibility reasons certain legacy, non-IP aspects of the 3GPP architecture such as

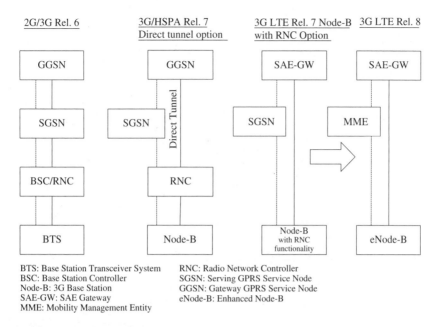

Figure 1.3 3GPP evolution toward a flat LTE SAE architecture.

the GPRS tunneling protocol and PDCP (packet data convergence protocol) still exists within the LTE network architecture.

1.5   LTE Network Architecture

While the focus of this book is on the radio network aspects of LTE, a basic understanding of the overall end-to-end architecture is useful to gain an appreciation of how services are delivered over an LTE network. To that end, we provide a brief overview of the LTE network architecture in this section.

As already mentioned, the core network design presented in 3GPP Release 8 to support LTE is called the Evolved Packet Core (EPC). EPC is designed to provide a high-capacity, all IP, reduced latency, flat architecture that dramatically reduces cost and supports advanced real-time and media-rich services with enhanced quality of experience. It is designed not only to support new radio access networks such as LTE, but also provide interworking with legacy 2G GERAN and 3G UTRAN networks connected via SGSN. Functions provided by the EPC include access control, packet routing and transfer, mobility management, security, radio resource management, and network management.

The EPC includes four new elements: (1) Serving Gateway (SGW), which terminates the interface toward the 3GPP radio access networks; (2) Packet Data Network Gateway (PGW), which controls IP data services, does routing, allocates IP addresses, enforces policy, and provides access for non-3GPP access networks; (3) Mobility Management Entity (MME), which supports user equipment context and identity as well as authenticates and authorizes users; and (4) Policy and Charging Rules Function (PCRF), which

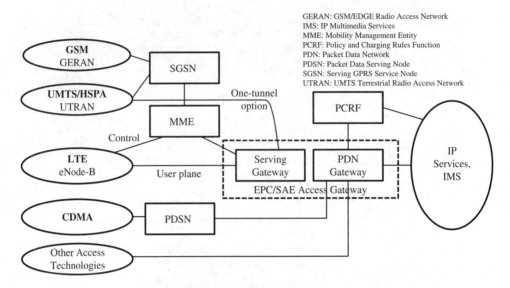

Figure 1.4 Evolved Packet Core architecture.

manages QoS aspects. Figure 1.4 shows the end-to-end architecture including how the EPC supports LTE as well as current and legacy radio access networks.

A brief description of each of the four new elements is provided here:

- **Serving Gateway (SGW)**: The SGW acts as a demarcation point between the RAN and core network, and manages user plane mobility. It serves as the mobility anchor when terminals move across areas served by different eNode-B elements in E-UTRAN, as well as across other 3GPP radio networks such as GERAN and UTRAN. SGW does downlink packet buffering and initiation of network-triggered service request procedures. Other functions include lawful interception, packet routing and forwarding, transport level packet marking in the uplink and the downlink, accounting support for per user, and inter-operator charging.

- **Packet Data Network Gateway (PGW)**: The PGW acts as the termination point of the EPC toward other Packet Data Networks (PDN) such as the Internet, private IP network, or the IMS network providing end-user services. It serves as an anchor point for sessions toward external PDN and provides functions such as user IP address allocation, policy enforcement, packet filtering, and charging support. Policy enforcement includes operator-defined rules for resource allocation to control data rate, QoS, and usage. Packet filtering functions include deep packet inspection for application detection.

- **Mobility Management Entity (MME)**: The MME performs the signaling and control functions to manage the user terminal access to network connections, assignment of network resources, and mobility management function such as idle mode location tracking, paging, roaming, and handovers. MME controls all control plane functions related to subscriber and session management. The MME provides security functions such as providing temporary identities for user terminals, interacting with Home Subscriber Server (HSS) for authentication, and negotiation of ciphering and integrity protection algorithms. It is also responsible for selecting the appropriate serving and PDN gateways, and selecting legacy gateways for handovers to other GERAN or UTRAN networks. Further, MME is the point at which lawful interception of signaling is made. It should be noted that an MME manages thousands of eNode-B elements, which is one of the key differences from 2G or 3G platforms using RNC and SGSN platforms.

- **Policy and Charging Rules Function (PCRF)**: The Policy and Charging Rules Function (PCRF) is a concatenation of Policy Decision Function (PDF) and Charging Rules Function (CRF). The PCRF interfaces with the PDN gateway and supports service data flow detection, policy enforcement, and flow-based charging. The PCRF was actually defined in Release 7 of 3GPP ahead of LTE. Although not much deployed with pre-LTE systems, it is mandatory for LTE. Release 8 further enhanced PCRF functionality to include support for non-3GPP access (e.g., Wi-Fi or fixed line access) to the network.

1.6   Spectrum Options and Migration Plans for LTE

3GPP specifications allow for the deployment of LTE in a wide variety of spectrum bands globally. It is deployable in any of the existing 2G and 3G spectrum bands as well as several new frequency bands. 3GPP and other standards bodies along with several industry consortiums continue to negotiate with authorities around the world for global harmonization of spectrum to enable larger economies of scale and faster development.

Tables 1.8 and 1.9 list a number of the more common paired and unpaired frequency bands in which LTE could be deployed in FDD or TDD mode, respectively [17, 18]. Bands 1 through 10 in FDD and bands 33 through 38 in TDD are spectrum that currently has 3GPP systems deployed. In most cases, deployment of LTE in these bands will require spectrum to be refarmed; that is, existing 2G or 3G systems will have to be vacated from those bands and replaced with LTE systems. Bands 11 through 17 in FDD mode and bands 39 and 40 in TDD mode are new spectrum that is mostly unencumbered by the presence of existing 2G/3G networks, and hence can more readily be used for LTE. Operators who have access to new spectrum will most likely begin deployment of LTE as an overlay solution to existing networks using the new spectrum. Table 1.10 summarizes the various bands by region that are likely to see LTE deployments.

Figure 1.5 shows the various spectrum options available in the United States. The 850MHz cellular band and the 1900MHz PCS band have various 3GPP and 3GPP2 systems deployed today. The advanced wireless services (AWS) spectrum and the recently auctioned 700MHz UHF spectrum are likely to be prime candidates for initial LTE deployment in the United States.

In Europe, many operators may look to refarm the 900MHz GSM band for LTE deployment. As many operators continue migration of their customers to 3G systems in the UMTS bands (1920–1980MHz/2110–2179MHz), the load on 900MHz is reducing. While some operators may deploy 3G UMTS/HSPA systems in 900MHz, others may wait for LTE to replace GSM there. HSPA requires carving out 5MHz at a time, while

Table 1.8 3GPP Designated FDD Frequency Bands for LTE

3GPP Band #	Band (Common) Name	Amount of Spectrum	Uplink (MHz)	Downlink (MHz)	Available Regions
1	2.1GHz (IMT)	2 × 60MHz	1920–1980	2110–2170	Europe, Asia, Japan, Oceania
2	1900MHz (PCS)	2 × 60MHz	1850–1910	1930–1990	North America
3	1800MHz (DCS)	2 × 75MHz	1710–1985	1805–1880	Europe, Asia
4	1.7/2.1GHz (AWS)	2 × 45MHz	1710–1755	2110–2155	United States, Canada (Future)
5	850MHz (CLR)	2 × 25MHz	824–849	869–894	North America, Oceania
6	800MHz (IMT-E)	2 × 10MHz	830–840	875–885	Japan
7	2.6GHz	2 × 70MHz	2500–2570	2620–2690	Europe (Future)
8	900MHz (GSM)	2 × 35MHz	880–915	925–960	Europe, Asia, Oceania
9	1700MHz	2 × 35MHz	1749.9–1784.9	1844.9–1879.9	Japan
10	Ext.1.7/ 2.1MHz	2 × 60MHz	1710–1770	2110–2170	North America excluding United States
11	1500MHz	2 × 25MHz	1427.9–1452.9	1475.9–1500.9	Japan
12	Lower 700MHz (UHF)	2 × 18MHz	698–716	728–746	United States
13	Lower 700MHz (UHF)	2 × 10MHz	777–787	746–756	United States
14	Upper 700MHz (UHF) public safety/private	2 × 10MHz	788–798	758–768	United States
17	Lower 700MHz (UHF)	2 × 12MHz	704–716	734–746	United States

Table 1.9 Designated TDD Frequencies for LTE

3GPP Band #	Band (Common) Name	Amount of Spectrum	Frequency	Available Regions
33	TDD 2000	20MHz	1900–1920MHz	Europe
34	TDD 2000	15MHz	2010–2025MHz	Europe and China
35	TDD 1900	60MHz	1850–1910MHz	United States/ Canada
36	TDD 1900	60MHz	1850–1910MHz	United States/ Canada
37	PCS Center Gap	20MHz	1910–1930MHz	United States/ Canada
38	IMT Extension Center Gap	50MHz	2570–2620MHz	Europe
39	China TDD	40MHz	1880–1920MHz	China
40	2.3GHz TDD	100MHz	2300–2400MHz	China

LTE allows operating with as low as 1.4MHz, which makes it attractive to spectrum-constrained operators. We are also likely to see LTE deployments in the UMTS bands as several operators have not yet fully used up all the bandwidth in those bands. Additional candidate frequencies for LTE deployment in Europe are the IMT Extension Band frequencies in the 2.6GHz range.

Next, we discuss in more detail the newer and more likely spectrum options for early LTE deployments.

- **AWS Band**: In 2006, the FCC auctioned 90MHz (2 × 45MHz) of unpaired spectrum for advanced wireless services (AWS). A total of 1,087 licenses were awarded to 104 bidders netting $13.9 billion dollars for the U.S. treasury at $0.53 permegahertz per population. This spectrum, called AWS-I, spans 1710–1755MHz for mobile

Table 1.10 Spectrum Options for LTE in Various Global Regions

	Candidate Spectrum For	
	Initial LTE Deployment	**Potential Future LTE Deployment**
North America	AWS: 2100MHz UHF: 700MHz	850MHz (refarm) 1.9GHz (refarm)
Asia Pacific	1.5GHz (Japan) 2.6GHz (Japan)	2.1GHz (Japan) 2.3–2.4GHz (China) 470–854MHz 1.8GHz (refarm)
Europe, Middle East, Africa	2.1GHz 2.6GHz	900MHz (refarm) 1.8GHz (refarm) 450MHz (refarm) 470–854MHz

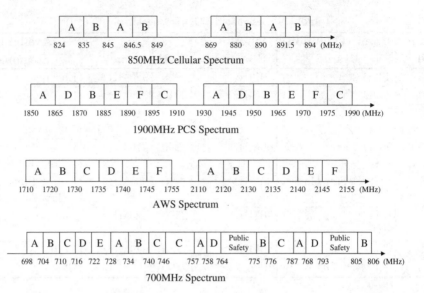

Figure 1.5 Available wireless spectrum in the United States for potential LTE deployment.

transmissions and 2100–2155MHz for base station transmissions. The upper band overlaps the IMT-2000 downlink, which spans 2110–2170MHz. The AWS spectrum was split into six pairs—three 2 × 10MHz pairs and three 2 × 5MHz pairs—for the auction. The band is used by Broadband Radio Services (BRS) and Fixed Microwave Services (FMS) operators who need to be vacated prior to deploying mobile services. Several operators in the United States have started 3G deployments in AWS, while others may wait for LTE before deploying in this spectrum. Canada auctioned AWS in 2008, and Latin American countries are expected to make it available shortly. Currently, FCC is formulating rules for auctioning additional 20MHz of paired frequencies designated AWS-II targeting 1915–1920MHz/1995–2000MHz and 2020–2025MHz/2175–2180MHz and 20MHz unpaired frequencies designated AWSIII at 2155–2175MHz. The FCC is proposing to allow TDD operation in AWS-III, but many in the industry have concerns about TDD operation right next to the AWS-I FDD spectrum.

- **700MHz UHF Band**: In 2008, the FCC auctioned 52MHz of spectrum in the 700MHz UHF band. Much of this spectrum was previously allocated to TV broadcast, and reclaimed by FCC as part of the transition to digital TV. The FCC divided the spectrum into a lower 700MHz band spanning 698–746MHz and an upper 700MHz band spanning 746–806MHz. The lower 700MHz band has several paired and unpaired spectrum blocks, each 6MHz wide and corresponding to 6MHz TV channels. The upper 700MHz band had a 2 × 5MHz paired block that was auctioned on a nationwide license basis. It also had another two 2 × 1MHz paired bands as well as a large 2 × 11MHz pair band called the "C Band." The C Band came with FCC regulations for "open access."

A total of 101 bidders won 1,090 licenses netting about $19 billion, which was more than any other auction in the last 15 years had fetched. AT&T and Verizon, the two largest mobile operators in the United States, won the lion's share of licenses. The 700MHz spectrum was so coveted by operators due to the attractive propagation characteristics of this lower frequency band, which provides better coverage range and building penetration. This is particularly attractive for new deployments in rural and suburban areas, since it will take fewer LTE base stations to cover at 700MHz than at higher frequencies. The 700MHz auction was viewed as the last opportunity to obtain UHF spectrum, and participants paid on average $1.28 permegahertz per population for licenses, double the rate paid for AWS. Parts of the 700MHz spectrum have been licensed in large enough chunks to allow LTE operation using 10MHz and 20MHz bandwidths, allowing for the possibility of very high peak data rates.

While the United States has led the auction of 700MHz UHF spectrum, the transition to digital television is happening all over the world, and that transition will certainly yield spectrum dividends. It is very likely that parts of the 470–862MHz band spectrum traditionally occupied by analog TV will be auctioned off for new services including mobile broadband in the rest of the world as well.

- **IMT Extension Band**: In the 2000 World Radio Congress, the 2500–2690MHz band was identified as an additional IMT2000 band. European nations have begun allocating as much as 140MHz of IMT2000 expansion spectrum for FDD operation using 2500–2570MHz for uplink and 2630–2690MHz for downlink. Additional unpaired TDD allocation of up to 50MHz will also be made shortly in the 2570–2620MHz band. Like the 700MHz UHF band, this band offers the potential for LTE deployments using 20MHz channel bandwidths.

Each operator's spectrum situation along with their competitive position and capacity for capital investment will dictate their timing and approach to deploying LTE and migrating customers to it. Operators will also have to manage the technology risk, maintain service and network quality during transition, control operational cost including transport costs, and develop a device eco-system that can support and fuel the migration of customers to LTE.

Those operators who have obtained new spectrum for LTE will most likely deploy LTE as an overlay solution in the new spectrum beginning with dense urban areas and then building out slowly. As more and more customers migrate to LTE, these operators may begin freeing up their existing 3G spectrum and refarming them for LTE deployment. It is likely that many operators will continue to use 2G/3G circuit-switched voice network even after transitioning their data to LTE. Full voice transition to LTE may not happen until operators are convinced about the quality and capacity, have fully deployed IP Multimedia Subsystem (IMS) to support real-time services over packet bearers, and have a solid mechanism for voice handoffs across LTE and legacy domains.

1.7 Future of Mobile Broadband—Beyond LTE

Work is already under way to develop systems beyond LTE. Though many in the industry refer to LTE as a 4G system, strictly speaking it does not meet the requirements set out by the ITU for the fourth generation (4G) wireless standard. The ITU definition of a

4G system, called IMT-Advanced, requires a target peak data rate of 100Mbps for high mobility and 1Gbps for low mobility applications [19]. Besides peak data rates, IMT-Advanced also sets out requirements for spectral efficiency including peak, average, and cell-edge spectral efficiency. It envisions a peak downlink spectral efficiency of 15bps/Hz, an average downlink spectral efficiency of 2.6bps/Hz per cell, and a cell edge efficiency of 0.075bps/Hz per user. While the techniques for increasing peak efficiency are clear—higher order MIMO and higher order modulation—it is unclear yet how the cell-edge and average spectral efficiency required by IMT-Advanced can be met. Researchers and developers of wireless systems have a formidable challenge ahead.

Finding the necessary spectrum to achieve the 100Mbps and 1Gbps requirements is another challenge. The World Radio congress of 2007 identified a few new IMT spectrum, but very few places have continuous blocks of 100MHz—for example, 2.6GHz and 3.5GHz. This implies that network and spectrum sharing across operators and aggregation of non-contiguous channels from different bands may be required.

3GPP is investigating a number of technologies to realize the requirements for IMT-Advanced. The standards body has formed a study group for developing LTE-Advanced, which will then be proposed as an IMT-Advanced standard to ITU. 3GPP has developed preliminary requirements for LTE-Advanced [20] and they are shown in Table 1.11. Some of the technologies being considered for LTE-Advanced include:

- Higher order MIMO and beamforming (up to 8×8)

- Several new MIMO techniques: improved multi-user MIMO, collaborative and network MIMO, single-user uplink MIMO, etc.

Table 1.11 Summary of LTE-Advanced Target Requirements

	LTE-Advanced Target Requirement
Peak Data Rate	1Gbps downlink and 500Mbps uplink; assumes low mobility and 100MHz channel
Peak Spectral Efficiency	Downlink: 30bps/Hz assuming no more than 8×8 MIMO Uplink: 15bps/Hz assuming no more than 4×4 MIMO
Average Downlink Cell Spectral Efficiency	3.7bps/Hz/cell assuming 4×4 MIMO; 2.4bps/Hz/cell assuming 2×2 MIMO; IMT-Advanced requires 2.6bps/Hz/cell
Downlink Cell-Edge Spectral Efficiency	0.12bps/Hz/user assuming 4×4 MIMO; 0.07bps/Hz/user assuming 2×2 MIMO; IMT-Advanced requires 0.075bps/Hz/user
Latency	<10ms from dormant to active; <50ms from camped to active
Mobility	Performance equal to LTE; speeds up to 500kmph considered
Spectrum Flexibility	FDD and TDD; focus on wider channels up to 100MHz, including using aggregation
Backward Compatibility	LTE devices should work on LTE-Advanced; reuse LTE architecture; co-exist with other 3GPP systems

- Inter-cell interference co-ordination and cancellation

- Use of multi-hop relay nodes to improve and extend high data rate coverage

- Carrier aggregation to support larger bandwidths while simultaneously being backward compatible with lower bandwidth LTE

- Femto-cell/Home Node-B using self-configuring and self-optimizing networks

In the final analysis, wireless system capacity is driven by three factors: amount of spectrum, spectral efficiency, and the number of cells. Given the scarcity of useful spectrum, we are unlikely to see huge increases there in the near future. Spectral efficiency gains will also be limited since we have already developed and deployed technologies that get us close to the theoretical Shannon limit for capacity. This leaves us largely with the need to increase the number of cells—to move from microcells to pico-cells and femto-cells to achieve significant capacity gains. As we look toward achieving the IMT-Advanced requirements and beyond, much effort will be focused on evolving the topology of the cellular network and intelligently managing interference and dynamically assigning resources across a more complex topology to maximize system capacity.

1.8   Summary and Conclusions

In this chapter we provided an overview of the evolution of mobile wireless broadband systems and made the case for LTE. The key points made are

- Wireless services have grown at a remarkable rate over the past 25 years with over 4 billion users around the world today.

- Voice telephony has been the traditional killer application for wireless systems, but data consumption is growing rapidly and will dominate future growth.

- Wireless systems evolved from early single cell systems to first generation analog voice cellular systems to second generation digital voice (mostly) systems to third generation packet data systems and toward mobile broadband wireless systems.

- We provided an overview of various wireless standards: AMPS, GSM, CDMA, IX-EVDO, UMTS, HSPA, WiMAX, and LTE.

- We discussed the market drivers, salient features, and key technologies included in the LTE standard.

- We briefly described the end-to-end network architecture of LTE supporting all services over a flat IP network.

- We discussed the spectrum options for LTE deployments emphasizing the newer spectrum options that have become available.

- Provided a peek into future evolution of LTE toward a true 4G system capable of up to 1Gbps peak data rates.

Bibliography

[1] ITU Telecommunications indicators update—2009. www.itu.int/ITU-D/ict/statistics/

[2] 3G Americas. List of 3G deployments worldwide. www.3gamericas.org

[3] UMTS Forum. www.umts-forum.org

[4] Holma, H. et al. "High-Speed Packet Access Evolution in 3GPP Release 7." *IEEE Communications Magazine*, 45(12):29–35, December 2007.

[5] Holma, H. and A. Toskala. "High-Speed Downlink Packet Access." Chapter 11. *WCDMA for UMTS*. New York: John Wiley & Sons, Inc., 2002.

[6] Wiggins, R. "North American Operator Perspectives of 4G Migration Paths." *Yankee Group Survey Analysis*, August 13, 2008.

[7] Marshall, P. "HSPA+ Challenges Both WiMAX and LTE on the Road to 4G." *Yankee Group Trend Analysis*, September 29, 2008.

[8] 3G Americas White Paper. The mobile broadband revolution: 3GPP Release 8 and beyond, HSPA+, SAE/LTE and LTE-Advanced. February 2009.

[9] Bakshi, S.K. and R.T. Llamas. Worldwide Converged Mobile Device 2008–2012 Forecast Update: September 2008. *IDC*. Report 214293. September 2008.

[10] Andrews, J., A. Ghosh, and R. Muhamed. *Fundamentals of WiMAX*. Upper Saddle River, NJ: Prentice Hall, 2007.

[11] World Cellular Information Service. Iforma Telecoms and Media. May 2009.

[12] Cisco Visual Networking Index: Global Mobile Data Traffic Forecast Update, 2009–2014. www.cisco.com/en/US/solutions/collateral/ns341/ns525/ns537/ns705/ns827/white_paper_c11-520862.html

[13] 3GPP TR 25.913., "Requirements for Evolved UTRA (E-UTRA) and Evolved UTRAN (E-UTRAN)," v8.0.0, December 2008.

[14] *IEEE Communications Magazine*, Special issue on LTE—LTE Part II: Radio Access, April 2009.

[15] *IEEE Communications Magazine*, Special issue on LTE—LTE Part I: Core Network, February 2009.

[16] *EURASIP Journal on Wireless Communications and Networking*, Special issue on 3GPP LTE and LTE Advanced, August 2009.

[17] 3GPP TS 36.104: "Evolved Universal Terrestrial Radio Access (E-UTRA); Base Station (BS) radio transmission and reception (Release 8)."

[18] 3G Americas White Paper. 3GPP technology approaches for maximizing fragmented spectrum allocations. July 2009.

[19] *ITU-R Report M.2134*, "Requirements Related to Technical Performance for IMT-Advanced Radio Interface(s)," November 2008.

[20] 3GPP TR 36.913, "Requirements for Further Advancements for E-UTRA," v8.0.1, March 2009.

Part I

LTE Tutorials

Chapter 2

Wireless Fundamentals

Wireless data rates have typically lagged wired data rates by a factor of between 10 and 100, or equivalently, by about 10–15 years for the same data rate. For example, wireless LANs were 1 Mbps (and largely unavailable) when Ethernet was 10 Mbps, advanced to 10+ Mbps when Ethernet was at 100 Mbps, and so on. Similarly, cellular communication systems have trailed residential wired broadband services by roughly the same factor. At the time of writing, 3G cellular data services such as HSDPA have finally become widespread and advertise *peak* data rates in the 10 Mbps and above range, but despite such claims empirically offer typical throughput only approaching 1 Mbps, which has been available in DSL or cable modem for over a decade. Why is this?

Large-scale wireless networks such as LTE and its ancestors are inherently power-inefficient and interference-limited. It is very difficult to support mobility while simultaneously achieving a high degree of power efficiency, for example, through directional antennas. To be cost-efficient, base stations must be deployed sparingly but support large user populations, resulting in a large amount of self-interference. For these reasons, it is very difficult—if not impossible—to simultaneously achieve high coverage, capacity, and reliability at low cost and consumed power.

This chapter provides a tutorial introduction to wireless channels and systems and identifies their key properties and parameters. It will help the reader appreciate why universal wireless broadband has been so difficult to achieve, and why the design of LTE has been taken in a very different direction from its predecessors.

2.1 Communication System Building Blocks

All wireless digital communication systems must possess a few key building blocks, as shown in Figure 2.1. Even an LTE system can be conceptually broken down into a collection of *links*, with each link consisting of a transmitter, channel, and receiver.

The transmitter receives packets of bits from a higher protocol layer, and its duty is to send those bits as electromagnetic waves toward the receiver. The key steps in the digital domain are encoding and modulation. The encoder generally adds redundancy that will allow error correction at the receiver. The modulator prepares the digital signal for the wireless channel, and may comprise a number of different operations. The modulated

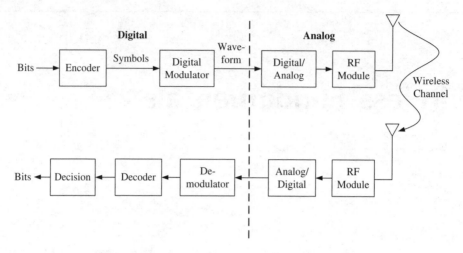

Figure 2.1 Wireless digital communication system.

digital signal is converted into a representative analog waveform by a digital-to-analog (D/A) convertor, and then upconverted to one of the desired LTE radio frequency (RF) bands. This RF signal is then radiated as electromagnetic waves by a suitable antenna.

The receiver performs essentially the reverse of these operations. After downconverting the received RF signal and filtering out signals at other frequencies, the resulting baseband signal is converted to a digital signal by an analog-to-digital (A/D) convertor. This digital signal can then be demodulated and decoded with energy and space-efficient integrated circuits to (hopefully) reproduce the original bit stream.

There are, however, a nearly endless number of choices presented to the designer of a digital communication system. The LTE standard is primarily relevant to the *digital* aspects of wireless communication, in particular at the transmitter side. The receiver implementation is unspecified: each equipment manufacturer is welcome to develop efficient proprietary receiver algorithms. Aside from agreeing on a carrier frequency and transmit spectrum mask, there are few requirements placed on the RF units. The main reason that the standard is primarily interested in the digital transmitter is that the receiver must understand what the transmitter did in order to make sense of the received signal—but not vice versa.

Next, we describe the large-scale characteristics of broadband wireless channels, and see why they present such a large design challenge.

2.2   The Broadband Wireless Channel: Path Loss and Shadowing

The main goal of this chapter is to explain the fundamental factors affecting the received signal in a wireless system, and how they can be modelled using a handful of parameters. The relative values of these parameters, which are summarized in Table 2.1 and described throughout this section, make all the difference when designing a wireless communication system. In this section we will introduce the overall channel model, and discuss the *large-scale* trends that affect this model.

Table 2.1 Key Wireless Channel Parameters

Symbol	Parameter
α	Path loss exponent
v	Number of ISI taps in channel ($v + 1$ is total number of taps)
σ_s	Log normal shadowing standard deviation
f_D	Doppler spread (maximum Doppler frequency), $f_D = \frac{\nu f_c}{c}$
c	Speed of light
ν	Relative speed between transmitter and receiver
f_c	Carrier frequency
λ	Carrier wavelength, $f_c \lambda = c$
T_c	Channel coherence time, $T_c \approx f_D^{-1}$
$\tau_{\max}$	Channel delay spread (maximum)
τ_{rms}	Channel delay spread (Root Mean Square)
B_c	Channel coherence bandwidth, $B_c \approx \tau^{-1}$
θ_{rms}	Angular spread (Root Mean Square)

The overall model we will use for describing the channel in discrete time is a simple tap-delay line (TDL):

$$h[k, t] = h_0 \delta[k, t] + h_1 \delta[k - 1, t] + \ldots + h_v \delta[k - v, t]. \tag{2.1}$$

Here, the discrete-time channel is time-varying (so changes with respect to t), and has non-negligible values over a span of $v + 1$ channel taps. Generally, we will assume that the channel is sampled at a frequency $f_s = 1/T$, where T is the symbol period,[1] and hence the duration of the channel in this case is about vT. The $v + 1$ sampled values are, in general, complex numbers.

Assuming that the channel is static over a period of $(v + 1)T$ seconds, the output of the channel can then be described as

$$y[k, t] = \sum_{j=-\infty}^{\infty} h[j, t] x[k - j] \tag{2.2}$$

$$\triangleq h[k, t] * x[k], \tag{2.3}$$

where $x[k]$ is an input sequence of data symbols with rate $1/T$, and $*$ denotes convolution. In simpler notation, the channel can be represented as a time-varying $(v + 1) \times 1$ column vector:[2]

$$\mathbf{h}(t) = [h_0(t) \ h_1(t) \ldots h_v(t)]^T. \tag{2.4}$$

---

1 The symbol period T is the amount of time over which a single data symbol is transmitted. Hence, the data rate in a digital transmission system is directly proportional to $\frac{1}{T}$.

2 $(\cdot)^T$ denotes the standard transpose operation.

Although this tapped-delay line model is general and accurate, it is difficult to design a communication system for the channel without knowing some of the key attributes about $\mathbf{h}(t)$. Some likely questions one might have are

- What is the value for the total received power? In other words, what are the relative values of the h_i terms?

   Answer: As we will see, a number of different effects cause the received power to vary over long (path loss), medium (shadowing), and short (fading) distances.

- How quickly does the channel change with the parameter t?

   Answer: The *channel coherence time* specifies the period of time over which the channel's value is correlated. The coherence time depends on how fast the transmitter and receiver are moving relative to each other.

- What is the approximate value of the channel duration v?

   Answer: This value is known as the *delay spread*, and is measured or approximated based on the propagation distance and environment.

The rest of the chapter explores these questions more deeply in an effort to characterize and explain these key wireless channel parameters, which are given in Table 2.1.

2.2.1 Path Loss

The first obvious difference between wired and wireless channels is the amount of transmitted power that actually reaches the receiver. Assuming an isotropic antenna is used, as shown in Figure 2.2, the propagated signal energy expands over a spherical wavefront, so the energy received at an antenna a distance d away is inversely proportional to the sphere surface area, $4\pi d^2$. The *free-space path loss formula*, or Friis formula, is given

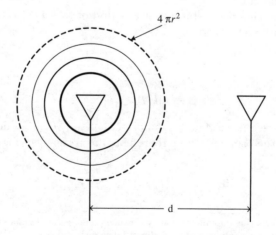

Figure 2.2 Free space propagation.

more precisely as

$$P_r = P_t \frac{\lambda^2 G_t G_r}{(4\pi d)^2},$$ (2.5)

where P_r and P_t are the received and transmitted powers and λ is the wavelength. In the context of the TDL model of (2.1), P_r/P_t is the average value of the channel gain; that is, $P_r/P_t = E||\mathbf{h}||^2$, where $E[\cdot]$ denotes the expected value, or mathematical mean. If directional antennas are used at the transmitter or receiver, a gain of G_t and/or G_r is achieved, and the received power is simply increased by the gain of these antennas.[3] An important observation from (2.5) is that since $c = f_c\lambda \Rightarrow \lambda = c/f_c$, the received power fall offs quadratically with the carrier frequency. In other words, for a given transmit power, the range is decreased when higher frequency waves are used. This has important implications for high-data rate systems, since most large bandwidths are available at higher frequencies.

Range vs. Bandwidth

As observed in (2.5), $P_r \propto \lambda^2$, which means that $P_r \propto \frac{1}{f_c^2}$. Clearly, higher frequencies suffer greater power loss than lower frequencies. As a result, lower carrier frequencies are generally more desirable, and hence very crowded. For example, compare an LTE system at 2100MHz (the new PCS frequencies) with one deployed in the newly available 700MHz spectrum. All else being equal, the 700MHz system will have nine times the received power. In fact, measurement campaigns have consistently shown that the effective path loss exponent α also increases at higher frequencies, due to increased absorption and attenuation of high frequency signals [27,32,33,55], so the difference can be greater still. From a coverage point of view, this creates a distinct advantage for 700MHz systems.

On the other hand, bandwidth at higher carrier frequencies is more plentiful, more consistently available on a global basis, and almost always less expensive. Hence, a high-rate, low-cost system would generally prefer to operate at higher frequencies, if the customer base is dense enough to overcome the coverage problems at those frequencies. Perhaps an ideal scenario from an operator standpoint would be to initially roll out LTE at low frequencies (like 700MHz) in order to serve many customers with few base stations. Then, as the subscriber base grows to a critical mass, shift to a shorter-range network operating at higher frequencies to support higher density at lower cost.

The terrestrial propagation environment is not free space. Intuitively, it seems that reflections from the Earth or other objects would actually increase the received power since

---

3 For an ideal isotropic radiator, $G_t = G_r = 1$.

more energy would reach the receiver. However, because a reflected wave often experiences a 180-degree phase shift, at relatively large distances (usually over a kilometer) the reflection serves to create destructive interference, and the common *2-ray approximation* for path loss is:

$$P_r = P_t \frac{G_t G_r h_t^2 h_r^2}{d^4}, \tag{2.6}$$

which is significantly different from free-space path loss in several respects. First, the antenna heights now assume a very important role in the propagation, as is anecdotally familiar: radio transmitters are usually placed on the highest available object. Second, the wavelength and hence carrier frequency dependence has disappeared from the formula, which is not typically observed in practice, however. Third, and crucially, the distance dependence has changed to d^{-4}, implying that energy loss is more severe with distance in a terrestrial system than in free space.

In order to more accurately describe different propagation environments, empirical models are often developed using experimental data. One of the simplest and most common is the *empirical path loss formula*:

$$P_r = P_t P_o \left(\frac{d_o}{d}\right)^{\alpha}, \tag{2.7}$$

which groups all the various effects into two parameters, the path loss exponent α and the measured path loss P_o at a reference distance of d_o, which is often chosen as 1 meter. Although P_o should be determined from measurements, it is often well approximated (within several dB) as simply $(\lambda/4\pi)^2$ when $d_o = 1$. This simple empirical path loss formula is capable of reasonably representing most of the important path loss trends with just these two parameters, at least over some range of interest.

Example 2.1. Consider a user in the downlink of a cellular system, where the desired base station is at a distance of 500 meters (.5 km), and there are numerous nearby interfering base stations transmitting at the same power level. If there are three interfering base stations at a distance of 1 km, three at a distance of 2 km, and ten at a distance of 4 km, use the empirical path loss formula to find the signal-to-interference ratio (SIR, i.e., the noise is neglected) when $\alpha = 3$, and then when $\alpha = 5$.

For $\alpha = 3$ and d_0 in units of kilometers, the desired received power is

$$P_{r,d} = P_t P_o d_o^3 (0.5)^{-3}, \tag{2.8}$$

and the interference power is

$$P_{r,I} = P_t P_o d_o^3 \left[3(1)^{-3} + 3(2)^{-3} + 10(4)^{-3} \right]. \tag{2.9}$$

The SIR expressions compute to

$$\text{SIR}(\alpha = 3) = \frac{P_{r,d}}{P_{r,I}} = 2.27 \quad (3.55 \text{ dB}),$$

$$\text{SIR}(\alpha = 5) = 10.32 \quad (10.32 \text{ dB}),$$

demonstrating that the overall system performance can be substantially improved when the path loss is in fact large. These calculations can be viewed as an upper bound, where the signal-to-interference plus noise ratio (SINR) is less than the SIR, due to the addition of noise. This means that as the path loss worsens, microcells grow increasingly attractive since the required signal power can be decreased down to the noise floor, and the overall performance will actually be better than in a system with lower path loss at the same transmit power level.

2.2.2 Shadowing

As we have seen in the last section, path loss models attempt to account for the distance-dependent relationship between transmitted and received power. However, many factors other than distance can have a large effect on the total received power. For example, as shown in Figure 2.3, obstacles such as trees and buildings may be located between the transmitter and receiver, and cause temporary degradation in received signal strength, while on the other hand a temporary line-of-sight transmission path would result in abnormally high received power. Since modelling the locations of all objects in every possible communication environment is generally impossible, the standard method of accounting for these variations in signal strength is to introduce a random effect called *shadowing*. With shadowing, the empirical path loss formula becomes

$$P_r = P_t P_o \chi \left(\frac{d_o}{d}\right)^\alpha, \tag{2.10}$$

where χ is a sample of the *shadowing* random process. Hence, the received power is now also modelled as a random process. In effect, the distance-trend in the path loss can be

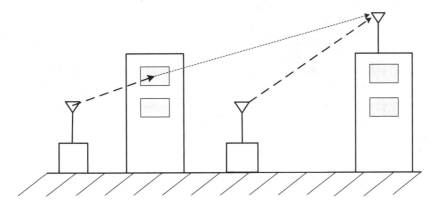

Figure 2.3 Shadowing can cause large deviations from path loss predictions.

thought of as the mean (or expected) received power, while the χ shadowing value causes a perturbation from that expected value. It should be emphasized that since shadowing is caused by macroscopic objects, typically it has a correlation distance on the order of meters or tens of meters. Hence, shadowing is often alternatively called "large-scale fading."

The shadowing value χ is typically modelled as a lognormal random variable, that is

$$\chi = 10^{x/10}, \quad \text{where } x \sim N(0, \sigma_s^2), \tag{2.11}$$

where $N(0, \sigma_s^2)$ is a Gaussian (normal) distribution with mean 0 and variance σ_s^2. With this formulation, the standard deviation σ_s is expressed in dB. Typical values for σ_s are in the 6–12 dB range. Figure 2.4 shows the very important effect of shadowing, where $\sigma = 11.8$ dB and $\sigma = 8.9$ dB, respectively.

Shadowing is an important effect in wireless networks because it causes the received SINR to vary dramatically over long time scales. In some locations in a given cell, reliable high-rate communication may be nearly impossible. The system design and base station deployment must account for lognormal shadowing either through macrodiversity, variable transmit power, and/or by simply accepting that some users will experience poor performance at a certain percentage of locations. While on occasion shadowing can be beneficial—for example, if there is an object blocking interference—it is generally detrimental to system performance because it requires a several-dB margin to be built into the system. Let's do a realistic numerical example to see how shadowing affects wireless system design.

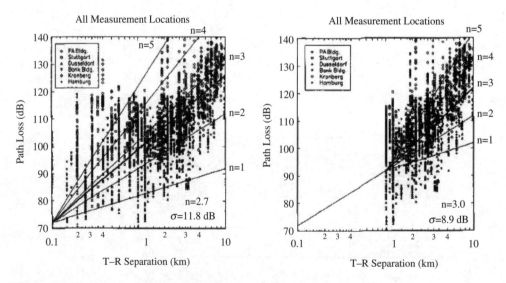

Figure 2.4 Shadowing causes large random fluctuations about the path loss model. Figure from [42], courtesy of IEEE.

Example 2.2. The Effect of Shadowing Consider an LTE base station (BS) communicating to a subscriber, with the channel parameters $\alpha = 3$, $P_o = -40$ dB, $d_0 = 1$ m, $\sigma_s = 6$ dB. We assume a transmit power of $P_t = 1$ Watt (30 dBm),[4] a bandwidth of $B = 10$MHz and due to error correction coding, a received SNR of 14.7 dB is required for 16QAM, while just 3 dB is required for BPSK. Finally, we consider only ambient noise with a typical power spectral density of $N_o = -173$ dBm/Hz, with an additional receiver noise figure of $N_f = 5$ dB.[5]

The question is this: At a distance of 500 meters from the base station, what is the likelihood that the BS can reliably send BPSK or 16QAM?

To solve this problem, we must find an expression for received SNR, and then compute the probability that it is above the BPSK and 16QAM thresholds.

First, let's compute the received power, P_r in dB based on (2.10)

$$P_r(\text{dB}) = 10\log_{10} P_t + 10\log_{10} P_o - 10\log_{10} d^\alpha + 10\log_{10} \chi \qquad (2.12)$$

$$= 30 \text{ dBm} - 40 \text{ dB} - 81 \text{ dB} + \chi(\text{dB}) = -91 \text{ dBm} + \chi(\text{dB}) \qquad (2.13)$$

Next, we can compute the total noise/interference power I_{tot} in dB similarly:

$$I_{tot}(\text{dB}) = N_o + N_f + 10\log_{10} B \qquad (2.14)$$

$$= -173 \text{ dBm} + 5 \text{ dB} + 70 \text{ dB} = -98 \text{ dBm} \qquad (2.15)$$

The resulting SNR $\gamma = P_r/I_{tot}$ can be readily computed in dB as

$$\gamma = -91 \text{ dBm} + \chi(\text{dB}) + 98 \text{ dBm} = 7 \text{ dB} + \chi(\text{dB}). \qquad (2.16)$$

In this scenario, the average received SNR is 7 dB, good enough for BPSK but not good enough for 16QAM. Since we can see from Equation (2.11) that $\chi(\text{dB}) = x$ has a zero mean Gaussian distribution with standard deviation 6, the probability that we are able to achieve BPSK can be derived in terms of the complimentary cumulative distribution function (CCDF) of a normalized Gaussian random variable, which is known as the Q function:[6]

$$P[\gamma \geq 3 \text{ dB}] = P\left[\frac{\chi + 7}{\sigma} \geq \frac{3}{\sigma}\right] \qquad (2.17)$$

$$= P\left[\frac{\chi}{6} \geq -\frac{4}{6}\right] \qquad (2.18)$$

$$= Q\left(-\frac{4}{6}\right) = 0.75 \qquad (2.19)$$

---

4 A positive real number x representing a *ratio* of powers can be expressed in dB as $X = 10\log_{10} x$ dB, and is unitless. If a number y is a power in units of Watts (W) or z in milliwatts (mW), it could also be expressed as $Y = 10\log_{10} x$ dBW or $Z = 10\log_{10} x$ dBm, respectively, where 1 W = 1000 mW so 0 dBW = 30 dBm. Note also that in this lexicon $x \cdot y$ gives units of Watts, so this corresponds to $X + Y$ dBW.

5 5 dB can be considered the total additional noise from all sources.

6 The Q function is the tail of a zero mean, unit variance Gaussian distribution, i.e., $Q(x) = \mathbb{P}[X > x] = \frac{1}{\sqrt{2\pi}} \int_x^\infty e^{y^2/2} \text{d}y$. It is related to the so-called erf function as $Q(x) = \frac{1}{2} - \frac{1}{2}\text{erf}\left(\frac{x}{\sqrt{2}}\right)$.

And similarly for 16QAM:

$$P[\gamma \geq 14.7 \text{ dB}] = P\left[\frac{\chi + 7}{\sigma} \geq \frac{14.7}{\sigma}\right] \tag{2.20}$$

$$= Q\left(\frac{7.7}{6}\right) = .007 \tag{2.21}$$

To summarize the example, while 75% of users can use BPSK modulation and hence get a raw data rate of 10MHz · 1 bit/symbol ·1/2 = 5 Mbps, less than 1% of users can reliably use 16QAM (4 bits/symbol) for a more desirable data rate of 20 Mbps. Additionally, whereas without shadowing *all* the users could at least get low-rate BPSK through, with shadowing 25% of the users appear unable to communicate at all. Interestingly though, without shadowing 16QAM could never be sent, whereas with shadowing it can be sent a small fraction of the time. In fact, such fluctuations can be exploited using *adaptive modulation and coding*, which we will describe generally in Section 2.6.5 and specifically for LTE in Sections 9.2 and 9.6.

Why is the Shadowing Lognormal?

While the primary rationale for the lognormal distribution for the shadowing value χ is accumulated evidence from channel measurement campaigns, one plausible explanation is as follows. Neglecting the path loss for a moment, if a transmission experiences N random attenuations β_i, $i = 1, 2, \ldots, N$ between the transmitter and receiver, the received power can be modelled as

$$P_r = P_t \prod_{i=1}^{N} \beta_i, \tag{2.22}$$

which can be expressed in dB as

$$P_r(\text{dB}) = P_t(\text{dB}) + 10 \sum_{i=1}^{N} \log_{10} \beta_i. \tag{2.23}$$

Then, using the Central Limit Theorem (CLT), it can be argued that the sum term will become Gaussian as N becomes large (and often the CLT is accurate for fairly small N), and since the expression is in dB, the shadowing is hence lognormal.

2.3   Cellular Systems

As explained in the previous section, due to path loss and to a lesser extent shadowing, given a maximum allowable transmit power, it is only possible to reliably communicate over some limited distance. However, path loss allows for spatial isolation of different transmitters operating on the same frequency at the same time. As a result, path loss and short-range transmissions in fact *increase* the overall capacity of the system by allowing more simultaneous transmissions to occur. This straightforward observation is the theoretical basis for the ubiquity of modern cellular communication systems.

In this section, we briefly explore the key aspects of cellular systems, and the closely related topics of sectoring and frequency reuse. Since LTE systems are expected to be deployed primarily in a cellular architecture, the concepts presented in this section will be fundamental to understanding LTE system design and performance.

2.3.1 The Cellular Concept

In cellular systems, the service area is subdivided into smaller geographic areas called *cells* that are each served by their own base station. In order to minimize interference between cells, the transmit power level of each base station is regulated to be just enough to provide the required signal strength at the cell boundaries. Then, as we have seen, propagation path loss allows for spatial isolation of different cells operating on the same frequency channels at the same time. Therefore, the same frequency channels can be reassigned to different cells, as long as those cells are spatially isolated.

Although perfect spatial isolation of different cells cannot be achieved, from a practical point of view, the rate at which frequencies can be reused should be determined such that the interference between base stations is kept to an acceptable level. In this context, *frequency planning* is required to determine a proper frequency reuse factor and a geographic reuse pattern. The frequency reuse factor f is defined as $f \leq 1$, where $f = 1$ means that all cells reuse all the frequencies. Accordingly, $f = 1/3$ implies that a given frequency band is used by only 1 out of every 3 cells.

The reuse of the same frequency channels should be intelligently planned in order to maximize the geographic distance between the co-channel base stations. Figure 2.5 shows an example of hexagonal cellular system model with frequency reuse factor $f = 1/7$, where cells labelled with the same letter use the same frequency channels. In this model, a cluster is outlined in bold and consists of seven cells with different frequency channels. Even though the hexagonal cell shape is conceptual, it has been widely used in the analysis of a cellular system owing to its simplicity and analytical convenience.

Cellular systems allow the overall system capacity to increase by simply making the cells smaller and turning down the power. In this manner, cellular systems have a very desirable scaling property—more capacity can be supplied by installing more base stations. As the cell size decreases, the transmit power of each base station also decreases correspondingly. For example, if the radius of a cell is reduced by half when the propagation path loss exponent is 4, the transmit power level of a base station is reduced by 12 dB ($=10 \log 16$ dB).

Since cellular systems support user mobility, seamless call transfer from one cell to another should be provided. The handoff process provides a means of the seamless transfer of a connection from one base station to another. Achieving smooth handoffs is a challenging aspect of cellular system design.

Although small cells give a large capacity advantage and reduce power consumption, their primary drawbacks are the need for more base stations (and their associated hardware costs), and the need for frequent handoffs. The offered traffic in each cell also

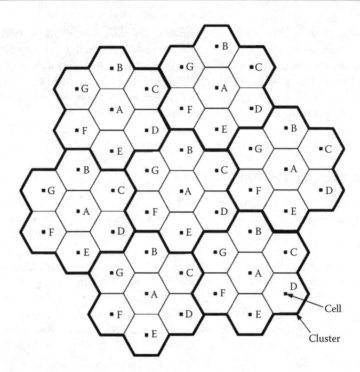

Figure 2.5 Standard figure of a hexagonal cellular system with $f = 1/7$.

becomes more variable as the cell shrinks, resulting in inefficiency. As in most aspects of wireless systems, an appropriate tradeoff between these competing factors needs to be determined depending on the system requirements.

2.3.2 Analysis of Cellular Systems

The performance of wireless cellular systems is significantly limited by co-channel interference (CCI), which comes from other users in the same cell or from other cells. In cellular systems, other cell interference (OCI) is a decreasing function of the radius of the cell (R) and the distance to the center of the neighboring co-channel cell and an increasing function of transmit power. However, what determines performance (capacity, reliability) is the SIR, i.e., the amount of desired power to the amount of transmitted power. Therefore, if all users (or base stations) increased or decreased their power at once, the SIR and hence the performance is typically unchanged—which is known as an interference-limited system. The spatial isolation between co-channel cells can be measured by defining the parameter Z, called *co-channel reuse ratio*, as the ratio of the distance to the center of the nearest co-channel cell (D) to the radius of the cell. In a hexagonal cell structure, the co-channel reuse ratio is given by

$$Z = \frac{D}{R} = \sqrt{3/f} \tag{2.24}$$

where $1/f$ is the size of a cluster and the inverse of the frequency reuse factor. Obviously, a lower value of f reduces co-channel interference so that it improves the quality of the communication link and capacity. However, the overall spectral efficiency decreases with the size of a cluster, so f should be chosen just small enough to keep the received signal-to-interference-plus-noise ratio (SINR) above acceptable levels.

Since the background noise power is negligible compared to the interference power in an interference-limited environment, the received signal-to-interference ratio (SIR) can be used instead of SINR. If the number of interfering cells is N_I, the SIR for a mobile station can be given by

$$\frac{S}{I} = \frac{S}{\sum_{i=1}^{N_I} I_i} \tag{2.25}$$

where S is the received power of the desired signal and I_i is the interference power from the ith co-channel base station. The received SIR depends on the location of each mobile station, and it should be kept above an appropriate threshold for reliable communication. The received SIR at the cell boundaries is of great interest since this corresponds to the worst interference scenario. For example, if the empirical path loss formula given in (2.10) and universal frequency reuse are considered, the received SIR for the worst case given in Figure 2.6 is expressed as

$$\frac{S}{I} = \frac{\chi_0}{\chi_0 + \sum_{i=1}^{2} \chi_i + 2^{-\alpha} \sum_{i=3}^{5} \chi_i + (2.633)^{-\alpha} \sum_{i=6}^{11} \chi_i} \tag{2.26}$$

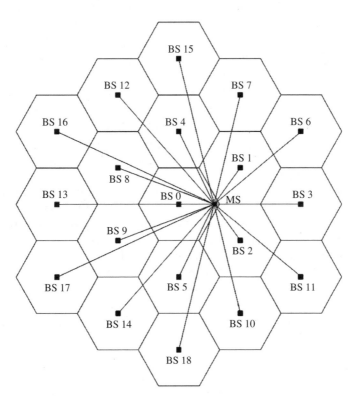

Figure 2.6 Forward link interference in a hexagonal cellular system (worst case).

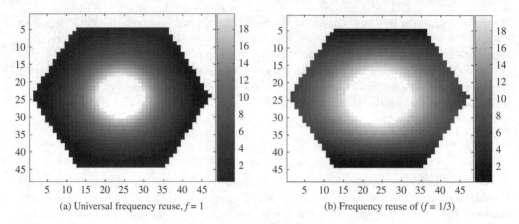

(a) Universal frequency reuse, $f = 1$ (b) Frequency reuse of ($f = 1/3$)

Figure 2.7 The received SIR in a cell with path-loss exponent $\alpha = 3.5$. The scale on the right indicates the SIR bins, i.e., darker indicates lower SIR.

where χ_i denotes the shadowing from the ith base station. Since the sum of lognormal random variables are well approximated by a lognormal random variable [15, 41], the denominator can be approximated as a lognormal random variable and then the received SIR follows a lognormal distribution [9]. Therefore, the outage probability that the received SIR falls below a threshold can be derived from the distribution. If the mean and standard deviation of the lognormal distribution are μ and σ in dB, the outage probability is derived in the form of Q function

$$P_{\text{out}} = \mathbb{P}[\text{SIR} < \gamma] = Q\left(\frac{\gamma - \mu}{\sigma}\right) \tag{2.27}$$

where γ is the threshold SIR level in dB. Usually, the SINR at the cell boundaries is too low to achieve the outage probability design target if universal frequency reuse is adopted. Therefore, a lower frequency reuse factor is typically adopted in the system design to satisfy the target outage probability at the sacrifice of spectral efficiency.

Figure 2.7 highlights the OCI problem in a cellular system if universal frequency reuse is adopted. It shows the regions of a cell in various SIR bins of the systems with universal frequency reuse and $f = 1/3$ frequency reuse. The figure is based on a two-tier cellular structure and the simple empirical path loss model given in (2.7) with $\alpha = 3.5$. The SIR in most parts of the cell is very low if universal frequency reuse is adopted. The OCI problem can be mitigated if higher frequency reuse is adopted as shown in Figure 2.7b. However, as previously emphasized, this improvement in the quality of communication is achieved at the sacrifice of spectral efficiency, in this case the available bandwidth is cut by a factor of 3. Frequency planning is a delicate balancing act of using the highest reuse factor possible, while still having most of the cell have at least some minimum SIR.

2.3.3 Sectoring

Since the SIR is so bad in most of the cell, it is desirable to find techniques to improve it without sacrificing so much bandwidth, as frequency reuse does. A popular technique

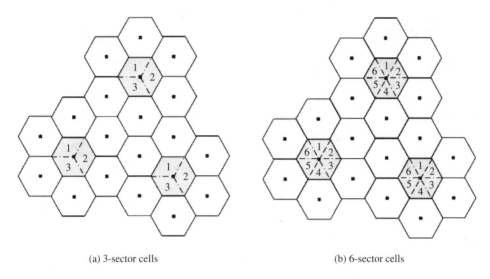

(a) 3-sector cells   (b) 6-sector cells

Figure 2.8 3-sector (120-degree) and 6-sector (60-degree) cells.

is to sectorize the cells, which is effective if frequencies are reused in each cell. By using directional antennas instead of an omni-directional antenna at the base station, the co-channel interference can be significantly reduced. An illustration of sectoring is shown in Figure 2.8. Although the absolute amount of bandwidth used is 3X before (assuming 3-sector cells), the capacity increase is in fact more than 3X. No capacity is lost from sectoring because each sector can reuse time and code slots, so each sector has the same nominal capacity as an entire cell. Furthermore, the capacity in each sector is actually higher than that in a non-sectored cellular system because the interference is reduced by sectoring, since users only experience interference from the sectors at their frequency. Referring again to Figure 2.8a, if each sector 1 points the same direction in each cell, then the interference caused by neighboring cells will be dramatically reduced. An alternative way to use sectors that is not shown in Figure 2.8 is to reuse frequencies in each sector. In this case, all of the time/code/frequency slots can be reused in each sector, but there is no reduction in the experienced interference.

Figure 2.9 shows the regions of a 3-sector cell in various SIR bins of the systems with universal frequency reuse and 1/3 frequency reuse. All the configurations are the same as those of Figure 2.7 except sectoring is added. Compared to Figure 2.7, sectoring improves SIR especially at the cell boundaries even when universal frequency reuse is adopted. If sectoring is adopted with frequency reuse, the received SIR can be significantly improved as shown in Figure 2.9b where both $f = 1/3$ frequency reuse and 120-degree sectoring are used.

Although sectoring is an effective and practical approach to the OCI problem, it is not without cost. Sectoring increases the number of antennas at each base station and reduces trunking efficiency due to channel sectoring at the base station. Even though intersector handoff is simpler compared to intercell handoff, sectoring also increases the overhead due to the increased number of intersector handoffs. Finally, in channels with

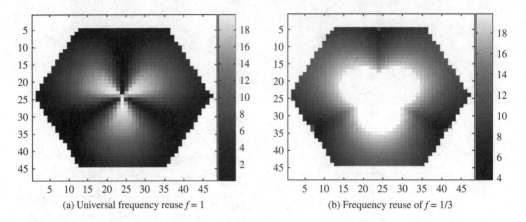

(a) Universal frequency reuse $f = 1$ (b) Frequency reuse of $f = 1/3$

Figure 2.9 The received SIR in a sectorized cell (three sectors). The path-loss exponent $= \alpha = 3.5$.

heavy scattering, desired power can be lost into other sectors, which can cause intersector interference as well as power loss.

New Approaches to Other Cell Interference. While the problem of co-channel interference has existed in cellular systems for many years, its effect on LTE is more important since LTE's requirements for high data rate and spectral efficiency—and hence high SINR—go beyond 3G systems, and LTE does not have built-in features to reduce the effects of this interference, unlike, for example, CDMA. The deployment of multiple antennas does not help, and in fact is likely to make the system even more sensitive to other cell interference [2, 5, 11]. A straightforward approach to this problem is advanced signal processing techniques at the receiver [1, 11] and/or transmitter [25, 43, 57] as a means of reducing or cancelling the perceived interference. Although those techniques have important merits and are being actively researched and considered, they have some important shortcomings when viewed in a practical context of near-future cellular systems such as LTE. As an alternative, network-level approaches such as cooperative scheduling or encoding across base stations [8, 28, 31, 35, 48, 59], multicell power control [6, 18, 23, 38, 53, 56], and distributed antennas [7, 22, 24, 37, 58] can be considered. These network-level approaches require relatively little channel knowledge (with the exception of cooperative encoding) and effectively reduce other cell interference through macro-diversity and efficient sharing of the spectrum. The simpler of these techniques are being actively considered for LTE and beyond.

2.4 The Broadband Wireless Channel: Fading

One of the more intriguing aspects of wireless channels is the fading phenomenon. Unlike path loss or shadowing, which are large-scale attenuation effects due to distance or obstacles, fading is caused by the reception of multiple versions of the same signal. The multiple received versions are caused by reflections that are referred to as *multipath*, as introduced briefly in Chapter 1. The reflections may arrive at very close to the same time—for example, if there is local scattering around the receiver—or the reflections may

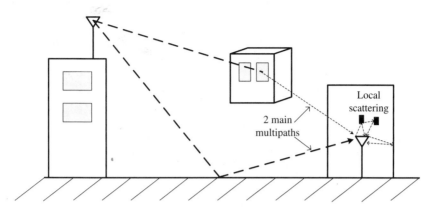

Figure 2.10 The channel may have a few major paths with quite different lengths, and then the receiver may see a number of locally scattered versions of those paths.

arrive at relatively longer intervals—for example, due to multiple different paths between the transmitter and receiver. A visualization of this is shown in Figure 2.10.

When some of the reflections arrive at nearly the same time, the combined effect of those reflections can be seen in Figure 2.11. Depending on the phase difference between the arriving signals, the interference can be either constructive or destructive, which causes a very large observed difference in the amplitude of the received signal even over very short distances. In other words, moving the transmitter or receiver even a very short distance can have a dramatic effect on the received amplitude, even though the path loss and shadowing effects may not have changed at all.

To formalize this discussion, we will now return to the time-varying tapped-delay line channel model of (2.1). As either the transmitter or receiver move relative to each other, the channel response $\mathbf{h}(t)$ will change.[7] This channel response can be thought of as having two dimensions: a delay dimension τ and a time-dimension t, as shown in Figure 2.12. Since the channel changes over distance (and hence time), the values of $h_0, h_1, \ldots, h_v$ may be totally different at time t vs. time $t + \Delta t$. Because the channel is highly variant in both the τ and t dimensions, in order to be able to discuss what the channel response is, we must use statistical methods.

The most important and fundamental function used to statistically describe broadband fading channels is the two-dimensional autocorrelation function, $A(\Delta\tau, \Delta t)$. Although this autocorrelation function is over two dimensions (and hence requires a three-dimensional plot), it can usefully be thought of as two simpler functions, $A_t(\Delta t)$ and $A_\tau(\Delta\tau)$, where $\Delta\tau$ and Δt have been set to zero, respectively. The autocorrelation function is defined as

$$
\begin{aligned}
A(\Delta\tau, \Delta t) &= E\big[h(\tau_1, t_1)h^*(\tau_2, t_2)\big] \\
&= E\big[h(\tau_1, t)h^*(\tau_2, t + \Delta t)\big] \\
&= E\big[h(\tau, t)h^*(\tau + \Delta\tau, t + \Delta t)\big]
\end{aligned}
\tag{2.28}
$$

---

7 Movement in the propagation environment will also cause the channel response to change over time.

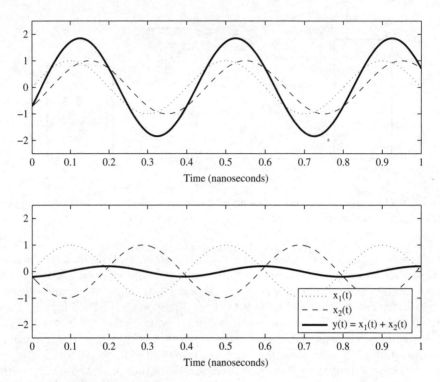

Figure 2.11 The difference between constructive interference (top) and destructive interference (bottom) at $f_c = 2.5\text{GHz}$ is less than 0.1 nanoseconds in phase, which corresponds to about 3 cm.

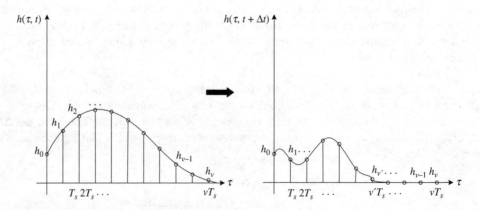

Figure 2.12 The delay τ corresponds to how *long* the channel impulse response lasts. The channel is time varying, so the channel impulse response is also a function of time, i.e., $h(\tau, t)$, and can be quite different at time $t + \Delta t$ than it was at time t.

where in the first step we have assumed that the channel response is Wide Sense Stationary (WSS) (and hence the autocorrelation function only depends on $\Delta t = t_2 - t_1$), and in the second step we have assumed that the channel response of paths arriving at different times τ_1 and τ_2 are uncorrelated. This allows the dependence on specific times τ_1 and τ_2 to be replaced simply by $\tau = \tau_1 - \tau_2$. Channels that can be described by the autocorrelation in (2.28) are thus referred to as Wide Sense Stationary Uncorrelated Scattering (WSSUS), which is the most popular model for wideband fading channels, and relatively accurate in many practical scenarios, largely because the scale of interest for τ (usually μsecs) and t (usually msec) generally differ by a few orders of magnitude.

The next three sections will explain how many of the key wireless channel parameters can be estimated from the autocorrelation function $A(\Delta\tau, \Delta t)$, and how they are related (see Table 2.2).

Table 2.2 Summary of Broadband Fading Parameters, with Rules of Thumb

Quantity	If "Large"?	If "Small"?	LTE Design Impact
Delay Spread, τ	If $\tau \gg T$, then frequency selective	If $\tau \ll T$, then frequency flat	The larger the delay spread relative to the symbol time, the more severe the ISI.
Coherence Bandwidth, B_c	If $\frac{1}{B_c} \ll T$, then frequency flat	If $\frac{1}{B_c} \gg T$, then frequency selective	Provides a guideline to subcarrier width $B_{\mathrm{sc}} \approx B_c/10$, and hence number of subcarriers needed in OFDM: $L \geq 10B/B_c$.
Doppler Spread, $f_D = \frac{f_c \nu}{c}$	If $f_c \nu \gg c$, then fast fading	If $f_c \nu \leq c$, then slow fading	As f_D/B_{sc} becomes non-negligible, subcarrier orthogonality is compromised.
Coherence Time, T_c	If $T_c \gg T$, then slow fading	If $T_c \leq T$, then fast fading	T_c small necessitates frequent channel estimation and limits the OFDM symbol duration, but provides greater time diversity.
Angular Spread, θ_{rms}	Non-LOS channel, lots of diversity	Effectively LOS channel, not much diversity	Multiantenna array design, beamforming vs. diversity.
Coherence Distance, D_c	Effectively LOS channel, not much diversity	Non-LOS channel, lots of diversity	Determines antenna spacing.

2.4.1   Delay Spread and Coherence Bandwidth

The delay spread is a very important property of a wireless channel, since it specifies the duration of the channel impulse response $h(\tau, t)$. Intuitively, the delay spread is the amount of time that elapses between the first arriving path and the last arriving (non-negligible) path. The delay spread can be found by inspecting $A(\Delta\tau, 0) \triangleq A_\tau(\Delta\tau)$; that is, by setting $\Delta t = 0$ in the channel autocorrelation function. $A_\tau(\Delta\tau)$ is often referred to as the *Multipath Intensity Profile*, or *power delay profile*. If $A_\tau(\Delta\tau)$ has non-negligible values from $(0, \tau_{\max})$, the maximum delay spread is $\tau_{\max}$. Intuitively, this is an important definition because it specifies how many taps v will be needed in the discrete representation of the channel impulse response, since

$$v \approx \frac{\tau_{\max}}{T_s}, \tag{2.29}$$

where T_s is the sampling time. But, this definition is not rigorous since it is not clear what "non-negligible" means mathematically. In order to speak more quantitatively, the average and rms delay spread are often used instead of $\tau_{\max}$, and are defined as follows:

$$\mu_\tau = \frac{\int_0^\infty \Delta\tau A_\tau(\Delta\tau) d(\Delta\tau)}{\int_0^\infty A_\tau(\Delta\tau) d(\Delta\tau)} \tag{2.30}$$

$$\tau_{\mathrm{rms}} = \sqrt{\frac{\int_0^\infty (\Delta\tau - \mu_\tau)^2 A_\tau(\Delta\tau) d(\Delta\tau)}{\int_0^\infty A_\tau(\Delta\tau) d(\Delta\tau)}} \tag{2.31}$$

Intuitively, τ_{rms} gives a measure of the "width" or "spread" of the channel response in time. A large τ_{rms} implies a highly dispersive channel in time and a long channel impulse response (i.e., large v), whereas a small τ_{rms} indicates that the channel is not very dispersive, and hence might require just a few taps to accurately characterize. A general rule of thumb is that $\tau_{\max} \approx 5\tau_{\mathrm{rms}}$.

The channel coherence bandwidth B_c is the frequency domain dual of the channel delay spread. The coherence bandwidth gives a rough measure for the maximum separation between a frequency f_1 and a frequency f_2 where the channel frequency response is correlated. That is:

$$|f_1 - f_2| \le B_c \implies H(f_1) \approx H(f_2)$$
$$|f_1 - f_2| > B_c \implies H(f_1) \text{ and } H(f_2) \text{ are uncorrelated}$$

Just as $\tau_{\max}$ is a "ballpark" value describing the channel duration, B_c is a ballpark value describing the range of frequencies over which the channel stays constant. Given the channel delay spread, it can be shown that

$$B_c \approx \frac{1}{5\tau_{\mathrm{rms}}} \approx \frac{1}{\tau_{\max}}. \tag{2.32}$$

"Exact" relations can be found between B_c and τ_{rms} by arbitrarily defining notions of coherence, but the important and prevailing feature is that B_c and τ are inversely related.

2.4.2   Doppler Spread and Coherence Time

Whereas the power delay profile gave the statistical power distribution of the channel over time for a signal transmitted for just an instant, the *Doppler power spectrum* gives the statistical power distribution of the channel versus frequency for a signal transmitted at just one exact frequency (generally normalized as $f = 0$ for convenience). Whereas the power delay profile was caused by multipath between the transmitter and receiver, the Doppler power spectrum is caused by *motion* between the transmitter and receiver. The Doppler power spectrum is the Fourier transform of $A_t(\Delta t)$, that is:

$$\rho_t(\Delta f) = \int_{-\infty}^{\infty} A_t(\Delta t) e^{-\Delta f \cdot \Delta t}(d\Delta t) \tag{2.33}$$

Unlike the power delay profile, the Doppler power spectrum is non-zero strictly for $\Delta f \in (-f_D, f_D)$, where f_D is called the maximum Doppler, or Doppler spread. That is, $\rho_t(\Delta f)$ is strictly "band-limited." The Doppler spread is

$$f_D = \frac{\nu f_c}{c}, \tag{2.34}$$

where ν is the maximum speed between the transmitter and receiver, f_c is the carrier frequency, and c is the speed of light. As can be seen, over a large bandwidth the Doppler will change since the frequency over the entire bandwidth is *not* f_c. However, as long as the communication bandwidth $B << f_c$, the Doppler power spectrum can be treated as approximately constant. This generally is true for all but ultrawideband systems.

Due to the time-frequency uncertainty principle,[8] since $\rho_t(\Delta f)$ is strictly band-limited, its time-frequency dual $A_t(\Delta t)$ cannot be strictly time-limited. Since $A_t(\Delta t)$ gives the correlation of the channel over time, what this means is that strictly speaking, the channel exhibits non-zero correlation between any two time instants. However, in practice it is possible to define a channel coherence time T_c, which, similarly to coherence bandwidth, gives the period of time over which the channel is significantly correlated. Mathematically:

$$|t_1 - t_2| \leq T_c \;\; \Rightarrow \;\; \mathbf{h}(t_1) \approx \mathbf{h}(t_2)$$
$$|t_1 - t_2| > t_c \;\; \Rightarrow \;\; \mathbf{h}(t_1) \text{ and } \mathbf{h}(t_2) \text{ are uncorrelated}$$

The coherence time and Doppler spread are also inversely related,

$$T_c \approx \frac{1}{f_D}. \tag{2.35}$$

This makes intuitive sense: if the transmitter and receiver are moving fast relative to each other and hence the Doppler is large, the channel will change much more quickly than if the transmitter and receiver are stationary.

Values for the Doppler spread and the associated channel coherence time are given in Table 2.3 for two plausible LTE frequency bands. This table demonstrates one of the reasons that mobility places severe constraints on the system design. At high frequency

---

8 The time-frequency uncertainty principle mandates that no waveform can be perfectly isolated in both time and frequency.

Table 2.3 Doppler Spreads and Approximate Coherence Times for LTE at Pedestrian, Vehicular, and Maximum Speeds

f_c	Speed (km/hr)	Speed (mph)	Max. Doppler, f_D (Hz)	Coherence Time, $T_c \approx \frac{1}{f_D}$ (msec)
700MHz	2	1.2	1.3	775
700MHz	45	27	29.1	34
700MHz	350	210	226.5	4.4
2.5GHz	2	1.2	4.6	200
2.5GHz	45	27	104.2	10
2.5GHz	350	210	810	1.2

and mobility, the channel may change up to 1000 times per second, placing a large burden on overhead channels, channel estimation algorithms, and making the assumption of accurate transmitter channel knowledge questionable. Additionally, the large Doppler at high mobility and frequency can also degrade the OFDM subcarrier orthogonality, as discussed in Chapter 3.

2.4.3   Angular Spread and Coherence Distance

In this chapter we have focused on how the channel response varies over time, and how to quantify its delay and correlation properties. However, channels also vary over space. We will not attempt to rigorously treat all the aspects of spatial-temporal channels, but we will summarize a few important points.

The rms angular spread of a channel can be denoted as θ_{rms}, and refers to the statistical distribution of the angle of the arriving energy. A large θ_{rms} implies that channel energy is coming in from many directions, whereas a small θ_{rms} implies that the received channel energy is more focused. A large angular spread generally occurs when there is a lot of local scattering, and this results in more statistical diversity in the channel, whereas more focused energy results in less statistical diversity.

The dual of angular spread is coherence distance, D_c. As the angular spread increases, the coherence distance decreases, and vice versa. A coherence distance of d means that any physical positions separated by d have an essentially uncorrelated received signal amplitude and phase. An approximate rule of thumb is [13]

$$D_c \approx \frac{.2\lambda}{\theta_{\mathrm{rms}}}. \tag{2.36}$$

For the case of Rayleigh fading, which assumes a uniform angular spread, the well-known relation is

$$D_c \approx \frac{9\lambda}{16\pi}. \tag{2.37}$$

An important trend to note from the above relations is that the coherence distance increases with the carrier wavelength λ, so higher-frequency systems have shorter coherence distances.

Angular spread and coherence distance are particularly important in multiple antenna systems. The coherence distance gives a rule of thumb for how far antennas should be spaced apart, in order to be statistically independent. If the coherence distance is very small, antenna arrays can be effectively employed to provide rich diversity. The importance of diversity will be introduced later in Section 2.6. On the other hand, if the coherence distance is large, it may not be possible due to space constraints to take advantage of spatial diversity. In this case, it would be preferable to have the antenna array cooperate and use beamforming. The tradeoffs between beamforming and linear array processing will be discussed in Chapter 4.

2.5 Modelling Broadband Fading Channels

In order to design and benchmark wireless communication systems, it is important to develop channel models that incorporate their variations in time, frequency, and space. The two major classes of models are *statistical* and *empirical*. Statistical models are simpler, and are useful for analysis and simulations. The empirical models are more complicated but usually represent a specific type of channel more accurately.

A Pedagogy for Developing Statistical Models

The methods we will describe for modelling wireless channels are broken into three steps:

1. Section 2.5.1: First consider just a single channel sample corresponding to a single principle path between the transmitter and receiver, that is:

$$h(\tau, t) \rightarrow h_0 \delta(\tau, t)$$

   Attempt to quantify: How is the value of $|h_0|$ statistically distributed?

2. Section 2.5.2: Next consider how this channel sample h_0 evolves over time, that is:

$$h(\tau, t) \rightarrow h_0(t) \delta(\tau)$$

   Attempt to quantify: How does the value $|h_0(t)|$ change over time? That is, how is $h_0(t)$ correlated with some $h_0(t + \Delta t)$?

3. Sections 2.5.2 and 2.5.3: Finally, $h(\tau, t)$ is represented as a general time varying function. One simple approach would be to model $h(\tau, t)$ as a general multipath channel with $v + 1$ tap values. The channel sample value for each of these taps is distributed as determined in step 1 above, and evolves over time as specified by step 2.

2.5.1 Statistical Channel Models

As we have noted, the received signal in a wireless system is the superposition of numerous reflections, or multipath components. The reflections may arrive very closely spaced in time—for example, if there is local scattering around the receiver—or the reflections may arrive at relatively longer intervals. As we saw in Figure 2.11, when the reflections arrive at nearly the same time, constructive and destructive interference between the different reflection causes the envelope of the aggregate received signal $r(t)$ to vary substantially.

In this section, we will overview statistical methods that can be used to characterize the amplitude and power of $r(t)$ when all the reflections arrive at about the same time. In terms of the previous section, we will first consider the special case of the Multipath Intensity Profile where $A_\tau(\Delta\tau) \approx 0$ for $\Delta\tau \neq 0$. That is, we only concern ourselves with the scenario where all the received energy arrives at the receiver at the same instant—this is step 1. In practice, this is only true when the symbol time is much greater than the delay spread, i.e., $T \gg \tau_{\max}$, so these models are often said to be valid for "narrowband fading channels." In addition to assuming a negligible multipath delay spread, we will first consider just a "snapshot" value of $r(t)$, and we will provide statistical models for its amplitude and power under various assumptions. In the following section, we will consider how these statistical values are correlated in time, frequency, and space—this is step 2. Then finally, we will relax all the assumptions and consider how wideband fading channels evolve in time, frequency, and space—this is step 3.

Rayleigh Fading

If the number of scatterers is large and the angles of arrival between them are uncorrelated, from the Central Limit Theorem it can be shown that the in-phase (cosine) and quadrature (sine) components of $r(t)$, denoted as $r_I(t)$ and $r_Q(t)$, follow two independent time-correlated Gaussian random processes.

Consider a snapshot value of $r(t)$ at time $t = 0$, and note that $r(0) = r_I(0) + r_Q(0)$. Since the values $r_I(0)$ and $r_Q(0)$ are Gaussian random variables, it can be shown that the distribution of the envelope amplitude $|r| = \sqrt{r_I^2 + r_Q^2}$ is Rayleigh, and the received power $|r|^2 = r_I^2 + r_Q^2$ is exponentially distributed. Formally,

$$f_{|r|}(x) = \frac{2x}{P_r} e^{-x^2/P_r}, \quad x \geq 0, \tag{2.38}$$

and

$$f_{|r|^2}(x) = \frac{1}{P_r} e^{-x/P_r}, \quad x \geq 0, \tag{2.39}$$

where P_r is the average received power due to shadowing and path loss, as described for example in Equation (2.10). The path loss and shadowing determine the mean received power (assuming they are fixed over some period of time), and the total received power fluctuates around this mean due to the fading. This is demonstrated in Figure 2.13. It

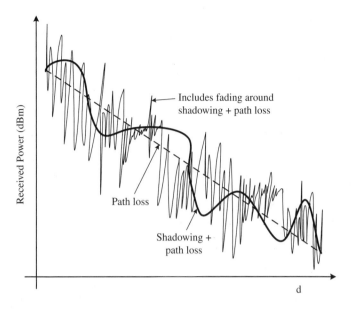

Figure 2.13 The three major channel attenuation factors are shown in terms of their relative spatial (and hence temporal) scales.

can also be noted that in this setup, the Gaussian random variables r_I and r_Q each have zero mean and variance $\sigma^2 = P_r/2$. The phase of $r(t)$ is defined as

$$\theta_r = \tan^{-1}\left(\frac{r_Q}{r_I}\right), \tag{2.40}$$

which is uniformly distributed from 0 to 2π, or equivalently from $[-\pi, \pi]$ any other contiguous full period of the carrier signal.[9]

Line-of-Sight Channels—The Ricean Distribution

An important assumption in the Rayleigh fading model is that all the arriving reflections have a mean of zero. This will not be the case if there is a dominant path, for example, a line-of-sight (LOS) path, between the transmitter and receiver. For a LOS signal, the received envelope distribution is more accurately modelled by a Ricean [36] distribution, which is given by

$$f_{|r|}(x) = \frac{x}{\sigma^2} e^{-(x^2+\mu^2)/2\sigma^2} I_0\left(\frac{x\mu}{\sigma^2}\right), \quad x \geq 0, \tag{2.41}$$

where μ^2 is the power of the LOS component and I_0 is the 0th order, modified Bessel function of the first kind. Although this expression is more complicated than a Rayleigh distribution, it is really a generalization of the Rayleigh distribution. This can be confirmed by observing that $\mu = 0 \Rightarrow I_0(\frac{x\mu}{\sigma^2}) = 1$, so the Ricean distribution reduces to

---

9 Strictly, (2.40) will only give values from $[0, \pi]$ but it is conventional that the sign of r_I and r_Q determine the actual quadrant of the phase. For example, if r_I and r_Q are negative, then $\theta_r \in [\pi, 3\pi/2]$.

the Rayleigh distribution in the absence of a LOS component. Except in this special case, the Ricean phase distribution θ_r is not uniform in $[0, 2\pi]$ and is not described by a straightforward expression.

Since the Ricean distribution depends on the LOS component's power μ^2, a common way to characterize the channel is by the relative strengths of the LOS and scattered paths. This factor K is quantified as

$$K = \frac{\mu^2}{2\sigma_2} \tag{2.42}$$

and is a natural description of how strong the LOS component is relative to the non-LOS (NLOS) components. For $K = 0$, again the Ricean distribution reduces to Rayleigh, and as $K \to \infty$, the physical meaning is that there is only a single LOS path and no other scattering. Mathematically, as K grows large, the Ricean distribution is quite Gaussian about its mean μ with decreasing variance, physically meaning that the received power becomes increasingly deterministic.

The average received power under Ricean fading is just the combination of the scattering power and the LOS power, i.e., $P_r = 2\sigma^2 + \mu^2$. Although it is not straightforward to directly find the Ricean power distribution $f_{|r|^2}(x)$, the Ricean envelope distribution in terms of K can be found by subbing $\mu^2 = KP_r/(K + 1)$ and $2\sigma^2 = P/(K + 1)$ into (2.41).

Although its simplicity makes the Rayleigh distribution more amenable to analysis than the Ricean distribution, the Ricean distribution is usually a more accurate depiction of wireless broadband systems, which typically have one or more dominant components. This is especially true of fixed wireless systems, which do not experience fast fading and often are deployed to maximize LOS propagation (see Figure 2.14 for a comparison of the most popular fading distributions).

A More General Model: Nakagami-m Fading

The last statistical fading model that we will discuss is the Nakagami-m fading distribution [30]. The probability density function (PDF) of Nakagami fading is parameterized by m and given as

$$f_{|r|}(x) = \frac{2m^m x^{2m-1}}{\Gamma(m)P_r^m} e^{-mx^2/P_r}, \quad m \geq 0.5. \tag{2.43}$$

Although this expression appears to be just as ungainly as (or even more so than) the Ricean distribution, the dependence on x is simpler and hence the Nakagami distribution can in many cases be used in tractable analysis of fading channel performance [45]. Additionally, it is more general as $m = (K + 1)^2/(2K + 1)$ gives an approximate Ricean distribution, and $m = 1$ gives a Rayleigh. As $m \to \infty$, the receive power tends to be a constant, P_r. The power distribution for Nakagami fading is

$$f_{|r|^2}(x) = \left(\frac{m}{P_r}\right)^m \frac{x^{m-1}}{\Gamma(m)} e^{-mx/P_r}, \quad m \geq 0.5. \tag{2.44}$$

Similarly, the power distribution is also amenable to integration.

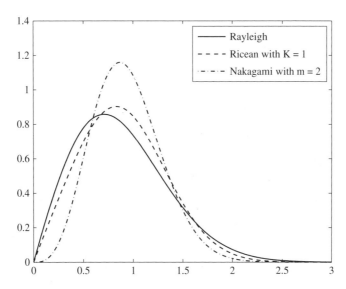

Figure 2.14 Probability distributions $f_{|r|}(x)$ for Rayleigh, Ricean w/$K = 1$, and Nakagami with $m = 2$. All have average received power $P_r = 1$.

2.5.2 Statistical Correlation of the Received Signal

The statistical methods in the last section discussed how *samples* of the received signal were statistically distributed. We considered three specific statistical models—Rayleigh, Ricean, and Nakagami-m—and provided the probability density functions (PDFs) that gave the likelihoods of the received signal envelope and power at a given time instant. What is of more interest, though, is how to link those statistical models with the channel autocorrelation function, $A_c(\Delta\tau, \Delta t)$, in order to understand how the envelope signal $r(t)$ evolves over time, or changes from one frequency or location to another.

For simplicity and consistency, we will use Rayleigh fading as an example distribution during this section, but the concepts apply equally for any PDF. We will first discuss correlation in different domains separately, but will conclude with a brief discussion of how the correlations in different domains interact.

Time Correlation

In the time domain, the channel $h(\tau = 0, t)$ can intuitively be thought of as consisting of approximately one new sample from a Rayleigh distribution every T_c seconds, with the values in between interpolated. But, it will be useful to be more rigorous and accurate in our description of the fading envelope. As discussed in Section 2.4, the autocorrelation function $A_t(\Delta t)$ describes how the channel is correlated in time (see Figure 2.15). Similarly, its frequency domain Doppler power spectrum $\rho_t(\Delta f)$ provides a band-limited description of the same correlation since it is simply the Fourier transform of $A_t(\Delta t)$. In other words, the power spectral density of the channel $h(\tau = 0, t)$ should be $\rho_t(\Delta f)$. Since uncorrelated random variables have a flat power spectrum, this means that a sequence of independent complex Gaussian random numbers can be multiplied by the

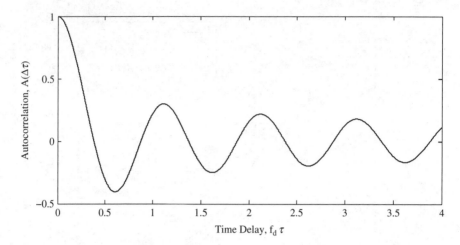

Figure 2.15 Autocorrelation of the signal envelope in time, $A_c(\Delta t)$, which here is normalized by the Doppler f_D. For example, from this figure it can be seen that for $\Delta t \approx 0.4/f_D$, which means that after $0.4/f_D$ seconds, the fading value is uncorrelated with the value at time 0.

desired Doppler power spectrum $\rho_t(\Delta f)$, and then by taking the Inverse Fast Fourier Transform (IFFT), a correlated narrowband sample signal $h(\tau = 0, t)$ can be generated. The signal will have a time correlation that is defined by $\rho_t(\Delta f)$, and be Rayleigh due to the Gaussian random samples in frequency.

For the specific case of uniform scattering [26], it can been shown that the Doppler power spectrum becomes

$$
\rho_t(\Delta f) = \begin{cases} \dfrac{P_r}{4\pi} \dfrac{1}{f_D \sqrt{1 - \left(\frac{\Delta f}{f_D}\right)^2}}, & |\Delta f| \leq f_D \\ 0, & \Delta_f > f_D \end{cases}
\tag{2.45}
$$

A plot of this realization of $\rho_t(\Delta f)$ is shown in Figure 2.16. It is well known that the Inverse Fast Fourier Transform of this function is the 0th order Bessel function of the 1st kind, which is often used to model the time autocorrelation function $A_c(\delta t)$, and hence predict the time correlation properties of narrowband fading signals.

Frequency Correlation

Similar to time correlation, a simple intuitive notion of fading in frequency is that the channel in the frequency domain, $H(f, t = 0)$, can be thought of as consisting of approximately one new random sample every B_c Hz, with the values in between interpolated. The Rayleigh fading model assumes that the received quadrature signals in time are complex Gaussian. Similar to the development in the last section where complex Gaussian values in the frequency domain can be converted to a correlated Rayleigh envelope in the time domain, complex Gaussian values in the time domain can likewise be converted to a correlated Rayleigh frequency envelope $|H(f)|$. (See Figure 2.17).

The correlation function that maps from uncorrelated time domain (τ domain) random variables to a correlated frequency response is the Multipath Intensity Profile,

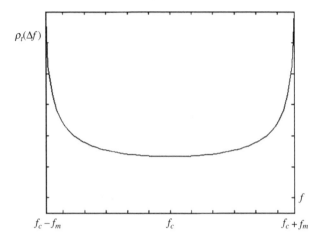

Figure 2.16 The spectral correlation due to Doppler, $\rho_t(\Delta f)$ for uniform scattering, i.e., Equation (2.45).

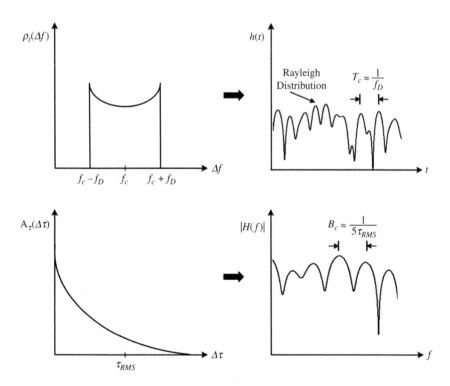

Figure 2.17 The shape of the Doppler power spectrum $\rho_t(\Delta f)$ determines the correlation envelope of the channel in time (top). Similarly, the shape of the Multipath Intensity Profile $A_\tau(\Delta \tau)$ determines the correlation pattern of the channel frequency response (bottom).

$A_\tau(\Delta\tau)$. This makes sense: just as $\rho_t(\Delta f)$ describes the channel time correlation in the frequency domain, $A_\tau(\Delta\tau)$ describes the channel frequency correlation in the time domain. Note that one familiar special case is the case where there is only one arriving path, in which case $A_\tau(\Delta\tau) = \delta(\Delta\tau)$. Hence, the values of $|H(f)|$ are correlated over all frequencies since the Fourier transform of $\delta(\Delta\tau)$ is a constant over all frequency. We refer to this scenario as "flat fading," and in practice whenever $A_\tau(\Delta\tau)$ is narrow (i.e., $\tau_{\max} \ll T$), the fading is approximately flat.

If the arriving quadrature components are approximately complex Gaussian, then a correlated Rayleigh distribution might be a reasonable model for the gain $|H(f)|$ on each subcarrier of a typical OFDM system. These gain values could also be generated by a suitably modified version of the provided simulation, where in particular the correlation function used changes from that in (2.45) to something like an exponential or uniform distribution, or any function that reasonably reflects the Multipath Intensity Profile $A_\tau(\Delta\tau)$,

The Dispersion-Selectivity Duality

As we have seen, there are two quite different effects from fading that we can refer to as *selectivity* and *dispersion*. By *selectivity*, we mean that the signal's received value is changed by the channel over time or frequency. By *dispersion*, we mean that the channel is dispersed, or spread out, over time or frequency. Selectivity and dispersion are time-frequency duals of each other: selectivity in time causes dispersion in frequency, and selectivity in frequency causes dispersion in time—or vice versa. This is illustrated in Figure 2.18.

For example, we have seen that the Doppler effect causes dispersion in frequency, as described by the Doppler power spectrum $\rho_t(\Delta f)$. This means that frequency components of the signal received at a specific frequency f_0 will be dispersed about f_0 in the frequency domain with a probability distribution function described by $\rho_t(\Delta f)$. As we have seen, this dispersion can be interpreted as a time varying amplitude, or selectivity, in time.

Similarly, a dispersive multipath channel that causes the paths to be received over a period of time $\tau_{\max}$ causes selectivity in the frequency domain, known as frequency-selective fading. Because symbols are traditionally sent one after another in the time domain, time dispersion usually causes much more damaging interference than frequency dispersion, since adjacent symbols are smeared together.

Multidimensional Correlation

In order to present the concepts as clearly as possible, we have thus far treated time, frequency, and spatial correlations separately. In reality, signals are correlated in all three domains.

A broadband wireless data system with mobility and multiple antennas is an example of a system where all three types of fading will play a significant role. The concept of doubly selective (in time and frequency) fading channels [39] has received recent attention for OFDM. The reason that the combination of these two types of correlation is important is that in the context of OFDM, they appear to compete with each other. On

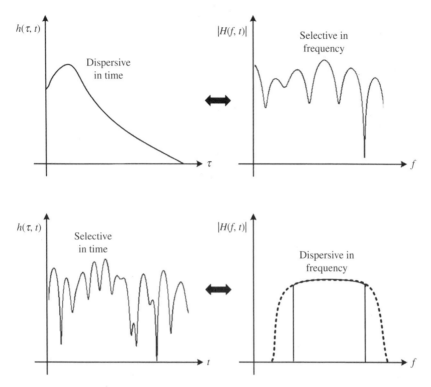

Figure 2.18 The dispersion-selectivity duality: Dispersion in time causes frequency selectivity, while dispersion in frequency causes time selectivity.

one hand, a highly frequency-selective channel—resulting from a long multipath channel as in a wide area wireless broadband network—requires a large number of potentially closely spaced subcarriers to effectively combat the intersymbol interference and small coherence bandwidth. On the other hand, a highly mobile channel with a large Doppler causes the channel to fluctuate over the resulting long symbol period, which degrades the subcarrier orthogonality. In the frequency domain, the Doppler frequency shift can cause significant inter-carrier interference as the carriers become more closely spaced. Although the mobility and multipath delay spread must reach fairly severe levels before this doubly selective effect becomes significant, this is a problem facing mobile LTE systems that does not have a comparable precedent. The scalable nature of the LTE physical layer—notably variable numbers of subcarriers and guard intervals—will allow custom optimization of the system for different environments and applications.

2.5.3 Empirical Channel Models

The parametric statistical channel models discussed thus far in the chapter do not take into account specific wireless propagation environments. While exactly modelling a wireless channel requires complete knowledge of the surrounding scatterers (e.g., buildings, plants, etc.), the time and computational demands of such a methodology is unrealistic due to the near infinite number of possible transmit-receive locations, and the fact that objects are subject to movement. Therefore, empirical and semi-empirical wireless channel models have been developed to accurately estimate the path loss, shadowing, and small-scale fast fading. Although these models are generally not analytically tractable, they are very useful for simulations and to fairly compare competing designs. Empirical models are based on extensive measurement of various propagation environments, and they specify the parameters and methods for modeling the typical propagation scenarios in different wireless systems. Compared to parametric channel models, the empirical channel models take into account realistic factors such as angle of arrival (AoA), angle of departure (AoD), antenna array fashion, angle spread (AS), and antenna array gain pattern.

Different empirical channel models exist for different wireless scenarios, such as suburban macro, urban macro, urban micro cells, and so on. For channels experienced in different wireless standards, the empirical channel models are also different. In the following sections, we briefly introduce the common physical parameters and methodologies used in several major empirical channel models. These models are also applicable to the multiple antenna systems described in Chapter 4.

LTE Channel Models for Path Loss

In this section we briefly introduce the empirical LTE channel models, which are widely used in modelling the outdoor macro- and micro-cell wireless environments. These are also referred to as "3GPP" channel models as they derive from the earlier channel models from the same standards body.

First, we need to specify the environment where an empirical channel model is used, e.g., suburban macro, urban macro, or urban micro environment. The BS to BS distance is typically larger than 3 km for a macro-cell environment and less than 1 km for an urban micro-cell environment.

The path loss can then be specified by empirical models for these different scenarios. For the 3GPP macro-cell environment, the path loss is given by the so-called COST Hata model, which is given by the following easily computable, if not immediately intuitive, formula:

$$PL_c[\text{dB}] = (44.9 - 6.55\log_{10}(h_b))\log_{10}(d) + 46.3 + 33.9\log_{10}(f_c) - 13.82\log_{10}(h_b)$$

$$- a(h_m) + C_o, \tag{2.46}$$

where h_b is the BS antenna height in meters, f_c is the carrier frequency in MHz, d is the distance between the BS and MS in kilometers, $a(h_m)$ is a relatively negligible correction function for the mobile height defined as $a(h_m) = (1.1\log_{10}(f_c) - 0.7)h_m - 1.56\log_{10}(f_c) - 0.8$ where h_m is the mobile antenna height in meters. The COST Hata model is generally considered to be accurate when d is between 100 meters and 20 km and $f_c \in (1500, 2000)\text{MHz}$.

Since LTE systems are also envisioned to operate below 1500MHz, for example at 700MHz, the empirical channel model used in such scenarios is the Hata model, which is closely related to the COST Hata model, but with slightly different parameters. Several slightly different Hata models exist, depending on whether the environment is urban, suburban, or for open areas. The Hata Model for Urban Areas is:

$$PL_u[\text{dB}] = (44.9 - 6.55\log_{10}(h_b))\log_{10}(d) + 69.55 + 26.16\log_{10}(f_c) - 13.82\log_{10}(h_b) + C_1,$$
$$(2.47)$$

where C_1 is a corrective factor that further varies depending on the size of the city, but for a medium or small city is

$$C_1 = 0.8 + (1.1\log_{10}(f_c) - 0.7)h_m - 1.56\log_{10}(f_c)$$

The Hata Model for both Suburban and Open Areas derives from the Urban model. The Suburban path loss is given as

$$PL_s[\text{dB}] = PL_u - 2\left(\log_{10}\left(\frac{f_c}{28}\right)\right)^2 - 5.4$$

while the Open Area Hata Model is

$$PL_o[\text{dB}] = PL_u - 4.78(\log_{10}f_c)^2 + 18.33\log_{10}(f_c) - 40.94$$

We do not suggest that readers spend too long searching for deep meaning in these equations—they can be viewed essentially as statistical curvefits based on experimentation.

LTE Channel Models for Multipath

The 3GPP channel models also include considerations for multipath modelling and scattering. The received signal at the mobile receiver consists of N time-delayed versions of the transmitted signal. The N paths are characterized by powers and delays that are chosen according to prescribed channel generation procedures, as follows. The number of paths N ranges from 1 to 20 and is dependent on the specific channel models. For example, the 3GPP channel model has $N = 6$ multipath components. The power distribution normally follows the exponential profile, but other power profiles are also supported. In the next subsection, specific semi-empirical models are given for the power profiles.

Each multipath component further corresponds to a cluster of M subpaths, where each subpath characterizes the incoming signal from a scatterer. The M subpaths define a cluster of adjacent scatterers, and therefore have the same multipath delay. The M subpaths have random phases and subpath gains, specified by the given procedure in different stands. For 3GPP, the phases are random variables uniformly distributed from 0 to 360 degrees, and the subpath gains are given by the following equation.

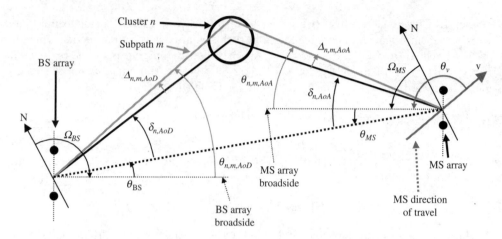

Figure 2.19 3GPP channel model for MIMO simulations.

The Angle of Departure (AoD) is usually within a narrow range in outdoor applications due to the lack of scatterers around the BS transmitter, and is often assumed to be uniformly distributed in indoor applications. The Angle of Arrival (AoA) is typically assumed to be uniformly distributed due to the abundance of local scattering around the mobile receiver. The final channel is created by summing up the M subpath components. In the 3GPP channel model, the nth multipath component from the uth transmit antenna to the sth receive antenna, is given as

$$h_{u,s,n}(t) = \sqrt{\frac{P_n \sigma_{SF}}{M}} \sum_{m=1}^{M} \left(\begin{array}{l} \sqrt{G_{BS}(\theta_{n,m,AoD})}\exp\left(j\left[kd_s\sin\left(\theta_{n,m,AoD}+\Phi_{n,m}\right)\right]\right) \\ \times \sqrt{G_{BS}(\theta_{n,m,AoA})}\exp\left(jkd_u\sin\left(\theta_{n,m,AoA}\right)\right) \\ \times \exp\left(jk\|\mathbf{v}\|\cos\left(\theta_{n,m,AoA}-\theta_v\right)t\right) \end{array} \right)$$

$$(2.48)$$

where the following are the key parameters, shown visually in Figure 2.19:

- P_n is the power of the nth path, following exponential distribution.

- σ_{SF} is the lognormal shadow fading, applied as a bulk parameter to the n paths. The shadow fading is determined by the delay spread (DS), angle spread (AS), and shadow fading (SF) parameters, which are correlated random variables generated with specific procedures.

- M is the number of subpaths per path.

- $\theta_{n,m,AoD}$ is the AoD for the mth subpath of the nth path.

- $\theta_{n,m,AoA}$ is the AoA for the mth subpath of the nth path.

- $G_{BS}(\theta_{n,m,AoD})$ is the BS antenna gain of each array element.

- $G_{BS}(\theta_{n,m,AoA})$ is the MS antenna gain of each array element.

- k is the wave number $\frac{2\pi}{\lambda}$ where λ is the carrier wavelength in meters.

- d_s is the distance in meters from BS antenna element s from the reference ($s = 1$) antenna.

- d_u is the distance in meters from MS antenna element u from the reference ($u = 1$) antenna.

- $\Phi_{n,m}$ is the phase of the mth subpath of the nth path, uniformly distributed between 0 and 360 degrees.

- $\|\mathbf{v}\|$ is the magnitude of the MS velocity vector, which consists of the velocity of the MS array elements.

- θ_v is the angle of the MS velocity vector.

LTE Semi-Empirical Channel Models

The above empirical multipath model provides a very thorough description of a number of propagation environments. However, due to the sheer number of parameters involved, constructing a fully empirical channel model is relatively time-consuming and computationally intensive. Semi-empirical channel models are therefore alternatives, which provide the accurate inclusion of the practical parameters in a real wireless system, while maintaining the simplicity of statistical channel models.

Well-known examples of the simpler multipath channel models include the 3GPP2 Pedestrian A, Pedestrian B, Vehicular A, and Vehicular B models, suited for low-mobility pedestrian mobile users and higher mobility vehicular mobile users. The power delay profile of the channel is determined by the number of multipath taps and the power and delay of each multipath component. Each multipath component is modelled as independent Rayleigh fading with a different power level, and the correlation in the time domain is created according to a Doppler spectrum corresponding to the specified speed. The Pedestrian A is a flat fading model corresponding to a single Rayleigh fading component with a speed of 3 km/hr, while the Pedestrian B model corresponds to a power delay profile with four paths of delays [0 .11 .19 .41] microseconds, and the power profile given as [1 0.1071 0.0120 0.0052], also at 3 km/hr. For the vehicular A model, the mobile speed is specified at 30 km/hr. Four multipath components exist, each with delay profile [0 0.11 0.19 0.41] microseconds and power profile [1 0.1071 0.0120 0.0052]. For the vehicular B model, the mobile speed is 30 km/h, with six multipath components, delay profile [0 0.2 0.8 1.2 2.3 3.7] microseconds and power profile [1 0.813 0.324 0.158 0.166 0.004]. These models are often referred to as Ped A/B and Veh A/B. It is easy to see how these four models can be used to coarsely model the scenarios of low (Ped) and high (Veh) mobility, and small (A) and large (B) delay spreads.

The LTE standard has additionally defined *Extended* delay profiles with increased multipath resolution known as Extended Pedestrian A, Extended Vehicular A, and Extended Typical Urban. These profiles are given in Tables 2.4, 2.5, and 2.6.

Table 2.4 Extended Pedestrian A Model

Delay [nsec]	0	30	70	90	110	190	410
Relative Power [dB]	0	−1.0	−2.0	−3.0	−8.0	−17.2	−20.8

Table 2.5 Extended Vehicular A Model

Delay [nsec]	0	30	150	310	370	710	1090	1730	2510
Relative Power [dB]	0	−1.5	−1.4	−3.6	−0.6	−9.1	−7.0	−12.0	−16.9

Table 2.6 Extended Typical Urban Model

Delay [nsec]	0	50	120	200	230	500	1600	2300	5000
Relative Power [dB]	−1.0	−1.0	−1.0	0.0	0.0	0.0	−3.0	−5.0	−7.0

These empirical channel models follow the fundamental principles of the statistical parametric models discussed previously in this chapter, while considering empirical measurement results. As such, semi-empirical channel models are suitable for link-level simulations and performance evaluation in real broadband wireless environments.

2.6 Mitigation of Narrowband Fading

There are many different techniques used to overcome narrowband fading in modern communication systems, but most can be collectively referred to as *diversity*. Because the received signal power is random, if several (mostly) uncorrelated versions of the signal can be received, chances are good that at least one of the versions has adequate power. Without diversity, high data rate wireless communication is virtually impossible. We now briefly quantify the potential cost of narrowband fading, before describing the principal techniques used in LTE to overcome these deleterious effects.

2.6.1 The Effects of Unmitigated Fading

The probability of bit error (BER) is the principle metric of interest for the physical layer (PHY) of a communication system. For a QAM-based modulation system, the BER in an additive white Gaussian noise (AWGN, no fading) can accurately be approximated by the following bound [16]:

$$P_b \leq 0.2e^{-1.5\text{SNR}/(M-1)} \tag{2.49}$$

where $M \geq 4$ is the MQAM alphabet size.[10] Note that the probability of error decreases very rapidly (exponentially) with the SNR, so decreasing the SNR linearly causes the

---

10 For example, $M = 2$ is BPSK, $M = 4$ is QPSK, $M = 16$ is 16 QAM, and so on.

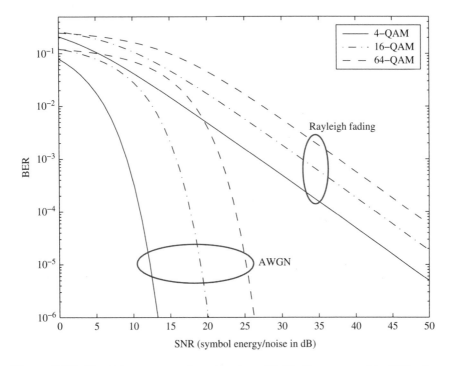

Figure 2.20 Flat fading causes a loss of at least 20–30 dB at reasonable BER values.

BER to increase exponentially. Since the channel is constant, the BER is constant over time.

However, in a fading channel, the BER become a random variable that depends on the instantaneous channel strength, and the occasional instances when the channel is in a deep fade therefore dominate the average BER. When the required average BER is very low (say 10^{-6}), virtually all errors are made while in deep fades. The average BER varies depending on the precise constellation used, but roughly follows the relationship

$$\bar{P}_b \propto \frac{M}{SNR} \tag{2.50}$$

The key point being that now BER goes down very slowly with SNR, only inversely. This trend is captured plainly in Figure 2.20, where we see that at reasonable system BERs like $10^{-5} - 10^{-6}$, the required SNR is over 30 dB higher in fading! Clearly, it is not desirable, or even possible, to increase the power by over a factor of 1000 to overcome occasional deep fades. Furthermore, in an interference-limited system, increasing the power will not significantly raise the effective SINR.

Although BER is a more analytically convenient measure since it is directly related to the SINR, for example via (2.49), a more common and relevant measure in LTE is the Packet Error Rate (PER), or equivalently Block Error Rate (BLER) or Frame Error Rate (FER). All these measures refer to the probability that at least one bit is in error in a block of L bits. This is the more relevant measure since the detection of a single bit error in a packet by the Cyclic Redundancy Check (CRC) requires the packet to either be discarded by the receiver or retransmitted. An expression for PER is

$$PER \leq 1 - (1 - P_b)^L \tag{2.51}$$

where P_b is the BER and L is the packet length. This expression is true with equality when all bits are equally likely to be in error. If the bit errors are correlated, then the PER actually improves. It is clear that PER and BER are directly related, so reducing PER and BER are roughly equivalent objectives.

Diversity is the key to overcoming the potentially devastating performance loss from fading channels, and to improving PER and BER. We now discuss the three most important types of diversity deployed in LTE systems.

2.6.2 Spatial Diversity

Spatial diversity is a powerful form of diversity, and particularly desirable since it does not necessitate redundancy in time or frequency. It usually is achieved by having two or more antennas at the receiver and/or the transmitter. The simplest form of space diversity consists of two receive antennas, where the stronger of the two signals is selected. As long as the antennas are spaced sufficiently, the two received signals will undergo approximately uncorrelated fading. This type of diversity is sensibly called *selection diversity*, and is illustrated in Figure 2.21. Even though this simple technique completely discards "half" of the received signal, most of the deep fades can be avoided and the average SNR is also increased. More sophisticated forms of spatial diversity include receive antenna arrays (two or more antennas) with maximal ratio combining, transmit diversity using

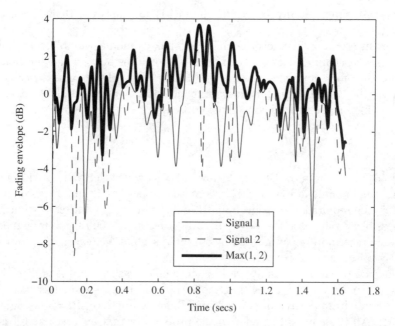

Figure 2.21 Simple two-branch selection diversity eliminates most deep fades.

space-time codes, transmit precoding, and other combinations of transmit and receive diversity. Spatial signaling techniques are so important, the ultimate success of LTE, that Chapter 4 is dedicated to this topic.

2.6.3 Coding and Interleaving

A ubiquitous form of diversity in nearly all contemporary digital communication systems is the natural pair of coding and interleaving. Traditionally thought of as a form of time diversity, in a multicarrier system they also can capture frequency diversity.

By coding, we mean the use of error correction codes (ECCs), which is also sometimes known as forward error correction. ECCs efficiently introduce redundancy at the transmitter to allow the receiver to recover the input signal even if the received signal is significantly degraded by attenuation, interference, and noise. Coding techniques can be categorized by their *coding rate* $r \leq 1$, which is the inverse of the redundancy added. For example, the output of a rate $\frac{1}{3}$ code has three times the original rate, or in other words has introduced two redundant bits for every original information bit. Equivalently, if the transmission rate is held constant, a rate $\frac{1}{3}$ code lowers the transmitted bit rate by a factor of 3, which is to say the data rate is multiplied by $\frac{1}{3}$. Somewhat counter-intuitively, though, well-designed error correction codes actually *increase* the achieved data rate even for $r < 1$ because the reliability increase they provide is so great that the number of bits per symbol that can be successfully transmitted increases by a factor greater than $1/r$, producing a net gain.

In Figure 2.22 we reproduce a figure of the convolutional encoder defined by LTE for use in the Broadcast Channel (BCH). This is clearly a rate $\frac{1}{3}$ code since there is one input bit (c_k) and 3 outputs $d_k^{(i)}$. The constraint length of this code is 7; equivalently, there are 6 delay elements or 64 possible states. The generator polynomial **G**, which consists of the generators G_i for each of the three outputs, are by a somewhat archaic convention denoted in octal notation. For example, $G_0 = 133$ in binary form is 1 0 1 1 0 1 1, where a 0 means the output does not include this tap and a 1 means it does. Therefore, d_k^0 includes modulo-2 summed contributions from the input and after delay elements 2, 3, 5, and 6. Notably, all optimal convolutional codes will include in each output the first and last taps, for maximum memory. The job of the decoder is to take degraded output symbols $\hat{d}_k$ after demodulation, and produce an estimate $\hat{c}_k$ of the original information signal c_k. If for a given packet $\hat{c}_k = c_k$, then the packet was successfully received; otherwise, it must be retransmitted. The most common decoding technique for convolutional codes

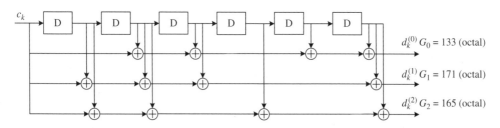

Figure 2.22 The rate $\frac{1}{3}$ convolutional encoder defined by LTE for use in the Broadcast Channel (BCH).

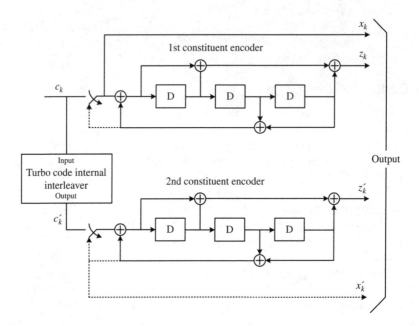

Figure 2.23 The rate $\frac{1}{3}$ parallel concatenated turbo encoder defined by LTE for use in the uplink and downlink shared channels, among others.

is the reduced-state sliding-window maximum likelihood sequence estimator, popularly known as the Viterbi decoder [50]. A detailed discussion of how convolutional coding and decoding works is outside the scope of this book, and the interested reader is referred to the vast literature on this topic, for example [29, 52].

Turbo codes [4] build upon convolutional codes to provide increased resilience to errors through iterative decoding [3, 21]. A rate $\frac{1}{3}$ turbo code is also deployed by LTE as shown in Figure 2.23, including for the uplink and downlink shared channels. In particular, the encoder is a parallel concatenated convolutional code that comprises an 8-state rate $\frac{1}{2}$ *systematic* encoder and an 8-state rate 1 systematic encoder that operates on an interleaved input sequence, for a net coding rate of $\frac{1}{3}$. By *systematic*, we mean that one output is generated by a linear modulo-2 sum of the current encoder state that is a function of both the input bit(s) and the previous states (i.e., there is feedback in the state machine), while the other outputs are simply passed through to the output, like x_k in Figure 2.23. Note that the convolutional encoder in Figure 2.22 was not systematic: there is no feedback in that state machine, and all outputs are linear combinations of the current state in addition to the current input.

Although not shown in either figure, codes in LTE can also be *punctured*, which means that some of the output coded bits are simply dropped, in order to lower the transmission rate. For example, if the output of a rate $\frac{1}{2}$ convolutional code had a puncturing factor of $\frac{1}{4}$, this means that out of every four output bits, one is dropped. Hence, the effective code rate would become $\frac{2}{3}$, since only three coded bits are transmitted for every two information bits. At the decoder, a random or fixed coded bit is inserted in the decoding process, which of course has a 50% chance of being incorrect. The decoded sequence is therefore less reliable than in the case of a lower-rate, unpunctured code, but if the received SINR was relatively good, the transmitted bit sequence can usually still be decoded correctly with the intended benefit of having a higher overall data rate in the same bandwidth, due to using a lower rate code. In general, a punctured code has worse performance than an unpunctured code of the same rate. For example, a rate $\frac{1}{2}$ code with every fourth bit punctured to achieve a rate $\frac{2}{3}$ code will usually have worse performance than a well-designed rate $\frac{2}{3}$ code that actually produced three bits as a linear combination of every two input bits using two-state machines. The reason puncturing is used is one of simplicity and complexity: since encoders and decoders must have a different structure depending on the coding polynomial, switching between many different encoder structures places a large complexity burden particularly on the decoder. Simply puncturing the same code to achieve different coding rates allows the decoder structure to remain the same regardless of the code rate.

Interleaving is typically used in both convolutional coding and turbo coding. For use with a conventional convolutional code, the interleaver shuffles coded bits to provide robustness to burst errors that can be caused by either bursty noise and interference, or a sustained fade in time or frequency. In such noise or fading, many adjacent bits in the transmitted signal will be degraded, which without interleaving makes it very difficult for the error correcting decoder to reconstruct the intended bits, even accounting for considerable redundancy. Interleaving seeks to spread out coded bits so that the effects of a burst error, after deinterleaving, are spread roughly evenly over a frame, or block.

For turbo coding, the intuition is a bit different: here an interleaver is used between the concatenated codes in order to provide statistical independence between the two encoder outputs. At the receiver, the decoders for each encoder pass their soft outputs (conditional probabilities) back and forth via a deinterleaver that decorrelates these values. The decoder proceeds to iterate back and forth between each decoder until the symbol estimates converge, i.e., the interleaver is no longer able to decorrelate the soft outputs.

For both conventional convolutional codes and turbo codes, the interleaver block size would, from a data reliability standpoint, ideally be quite large: several coherence times or coherent bandwidths for convolutional codes in order to maximize the attained diversity, and the larger the better for turbo codes and other iterative decoders as well. However, large interleaving blocks cause long interleaving and deinterleaving delays since typically the entire block must be populated with coded bits (a serial operation) before the interleaving is performed and the output generated. For this reason, the interleaver block size is usually constrained to be at most over a single packet, and often much less than that. Deinterleaving delays have been one of the primary impediments to turbocoding since they cause considerable latency. Nevertheless, interleaving has proven very effective in allowing ECCs designed for constant, time-invariant additive noise channels to also work well on fading, time-variant noisy channels.

Specifically to LTE, interleaving is used in several capacities. It is used in the turbo code as seen in Figure 2.23, in the rate matching functions, and finally there is an additional channel interleaver used to send control information over the uplink shared channel in order to spread it out over a wide range of subcarriers.

2.6.4   Automatic Repeat Request (ARQ)

Another technique that is often used in modern wireless communication systems including LTE is ARQ (automatic repeat request) and Hybrid-ARQ. ARQ simply is a MAC layer retransmission protocol that allows erroneous packets to be quickly retransmitted. Such a protocol works in conjunction with PHY layer ECCs and parity checks to ensure reliable links even in hostile channels. Since a single bit error causes a packet error, with ARQ the entire packet must be retransmitted even when nearly all of the bits already received were correct, which is clearly inefficient. Imagine the situation where the same packet is "dropped" twice in a row, despite the fact that 99% of its bits were received correctly. In such cases, it is likely that every bit was received correctly in one of the two packets.

Hybrid-ARQ combines the two concepts of ARQ and FEC to avoid such waste, by combining received packets. Hybrid-ARQ, therefore, is able to extract additional time diversity in a fading channel as well. In H-ARQ a channel encoder such as a convolution encoder or turbo encoder is used to generate additional redundancy to the information bits. However, instead of transmitting all the encoded bits (systematic bits + redundancy bits), only a fraction of the encoded bits are transmitted. This is achieved by puncturing some of the encoded bits to create an effective code rate greater than the native code rate of the encoder. After transmitting the encoded and punctured bits, the transmitter waits for an acknowledgment from the receiver telling it whether the receiver was able to successfully decode the information bits from the transmission. If the receiver was able to decode the information bits, then nothing else needs to be done. If, on the other hand, the receiver was unable to decode the information bits, then the transmitter can resend another copy of the encoded bits.

In type I H-ARQ—commonly referred to as *chase combining*—during a retransmission the transmitter sends a copy of the encoded bits that is identical to the first transmission and the receiver soft combines the received bits with the previous transmission. Since the encoded bits are the same in all the transmissions and the noise/interference is uncorrelated, the receiver can combine all the transmissions to increase the effective SINR. Thus, with every subsequent transmission the error probability is reduced and this process continues until the receiver is able to decode the information without error. In type II H-ARQ—commonly referred to as *incremental redundancy*—the transmitter changes the bits that are punctured during a retransmission. This way with every retransmission the effective code rate at the receiver decreases, which reduces the error probability.

2.6.5   Adaptive Modulation and Coding (AMC)

LTE systems employ adaptive modulation and coding (AMC) in order to take advantage of fluctuations in the channel over time and frequency. The basic idea is quite simple: transmit as high a data rate as possible when and where the channel is good, and transmit at a lower rate when and where the channel is poor in order to avoid excessive dropped packets. Lower data rates are achieved by using a small constellation—such as QPSK—and low rate error correcting codes such as rate $\frac{1}{3}$ turbo codes. The higher data rates are achieved with large constellations—such as 64QAM—and less robust error correcting codes, for example, either higher rate (like $\frac{3}{4}$) codes, or in LTE's case, *punctured* turbo codes for the reduced-complexity reasons discussed in the previous section.

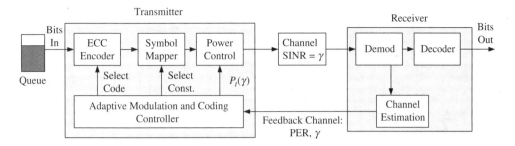

Figure 2.24 Adaptive modulation and coding block diagram.

To perform AMC, the transmitter must have some knowledge of the instantaneous channel gain. Once it does, it can choose the modulation technique that will achieve the highest possible data rate while still meeting a BER or packet error rate (PER) requirement. An alternative objective is to pick the modulation and/or coding combination that simply maximizes the successful throughput, i.e., $\max br(1 - \text{PER})$ where $b = \log_2 M$ is the number of bits per symbol (modulation type) and $r \leq 1$ is the coding rate. For example, in (2.49) it can be seen that as the constellation alphabet size M increases, the BER also increases. Since the data rate is proportional to $\log_2 M$, we would like to choose the largest alphabet size M such that either the required BER/PER is met or the throughput is maximized.

A block diagram of an AMC system is given in Figure 2.24. For simplicity, we will first consider just a single user system attempting to transmit as quickly as possible through a channel with a variable SINR, for example, due to fading. The goal of the transmitter is to transmit data from its queue as rapidly as possible, subject to the data being demodulated and decoded reliably at the receiver. Feedback is critical for adaptive modulation and coding: the transmitter needs to know the "channel SINR" γ—which is defined as the received SINR γ_r divided by the transmit power P_t (which itself is usually a function of γ). The received SINR is thus $\gamma_r = P_t \gamma$.

A Practical Example of AMC Figure 2.25 shows a possible realization of AMC, using three different code rates $(\frac{1}{2}, \frac{2}{3}, \frac{3}{4})$, and three different modulation types (QPSK, 16QAM, 64QAM). We note that these are not the precise configurations used in LTE, but are used here as a demonstrative example. Using just six of the possible nine combinations, a "gap" to Shannon capacity[11] of approximately 2–4 dB can be maintained over a wide range of SINR. This allows the throughput to increase as the SINR increases. In this example, the lowest offered data rate is QPSK and rate $\frac{1}{2}$ turbo codes, while the highest data rate burst profile is with 64QAM and rate $\frac{3}{4}$ turbo codes. The achieved throughput normalized by the bandwidth is defined as

$$T = (1 - \text{PER}) r \log_2(M) \text{ bps/Hz} \tag{2.52}$$

where PER is the packet error rate, $r \leq 1$ is the coding rate, and M is the number of points in the constellation. For example, 64QAM with rate $\frac{3}{4}$ codes achieves a max-

---

11 Shannon capacity is the theoretical maximum throughput as a function of SINR that no (single-input) communication system can possibly exceed in Gaussian noise, given by the equation $C = \log_2(1 + \text{SINR})$ [44].

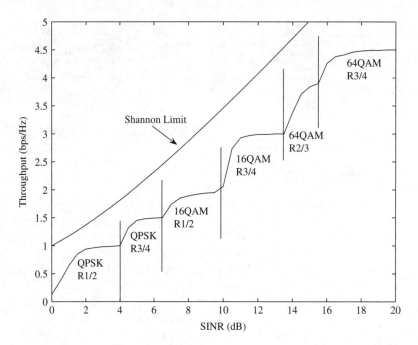

Figure 2.25 Throughput vs. SINR, assuming the best available constellation and coding configuration is chosen for each SINR. Only 6 configurations are used in this figure, and the turbo decoder is a max log MAP decoder with 8 iterations of message passing.

imum throughput of 4.5 bps/Hz (when PER → 0), while QPSK with rate $\frac{1}{2}$ codes achieves a best case throughput of 1 bps/Hz. Some combinations are never used: for example, 64QAM with rate $\frac{1}{2}$ coding has the same data rate as 16QAM with rate $\frac{3}{4}$ coding (3 bits/symbol) but worse performance over all SINR values, while the slight gain from using a rate $\frac{2}{3}$ code with QPSK or 16QAM does not justify its inclusion.

The results shown here are for the idealized case of perfect channel knowledge and do not consider retransmissions, for example, with ARQ. In practice, the feedback will incur some delay, and perhaps also be degraded due to imperfect channel estimation or errors in the feedback channel. LTE systems heavily protect the feedback channel with error correction, so usually the main source of degradation is due to mobility, which causes channel estimates to rapidly become obsolete. Empirically, with speeds greater than about 30 km/hr (on a 2GHz carrier) even the faster feedback configurations do not allow timely and accurate channel state information to be available at the transmitter.

Tuning the Adaptive Modulation and Coding Controller A key challenge in AMC is to efficiently control three different quantities at once: transmit power, transmit rate (constellation), and the coding rate. This corresponds to developing an appropriate policy for the AMC controller shown in Figure 2.24. Although reasonable guidelines can be developed from a theoretical study of adaptive modulation, in practice the system engineer needs to develop and fine-tune the algorithm based on extensive simulations since the performance depends on many factors. We list a few considerations here, which are by no means exhaustive.

- **PER and Received SINR** In adaptive modulation theory, the transmitter needs only to know the statistics and instantaneous channel SINR. From the channel SINR, it can determine the optimum coding/modulation strategy and transmit power [10]. In practice, however, the PER should be carefully monitored as the final word on whether the data rate should be increased (if the PER is low) or decreased to a more robust setting.

- **Automatic Repeat Request (ARQ)** ARQ allows rapid retransmissions, and Hybrid-ARQ generally increases the ideal PER operating point by about a factor of 10, e.g., from 1% to 10%. For delay-tolerant applications, it may be possible to accept a PER approaching even 70%, if chase combining is used in conjunction with H-ARQ to make use of unsuccessful packets.

- **Power Control: A balancing act** Power control is a subtle system level issue, because competing objectives must be balanced. For example, in theory the best power control policy for the capacity of parallel channels (over time or frequency) is the so-called waterfilling strategy, in which more power is allocated to strong channels, and less power allocated to weak channels [19, 20]. In practice though, the opposite approach—sometimes referred to as channel inversion—is often taken, because a sensible goal is to use as little power as possible to achieve a given target rate and reliability. Excess power over this amount causes interference to the network. For example, referring to Figure 2.25, there is almost nothing gained with a 13 dB SINR vs. an 11 dB SINR: in both cases the throughput is 3 bps/Hz. Therefore, as the SINR improved from 11 dB to 13 dB, the transmitter would be well advised to lower the transmit power, in order to save power and generate less interference to neighboring cells. Power control mechanisms in LTE are discussed in Section 9.10, and additional discussion can be found in [47, 54].

- **Adaptive Modulation in OFDMA** In an OFDMA system, each user will be allocated a block of subcarriers, each of which will have a different set of SINRs. Therefore, care needs to be paid to which constellation/coding set is chosen based on the varying SINRs across the subcarriers.

2.6.6 Combining Narrowband Diversity Techniques—The Whole Is Less Than the Sum of the Parts

It should be noted that the use of diversity in one domain can decrease the gain of diversity in another domain. For example, if selection diversity is deployed on the received signals in Figure 2.21, the resulting "combines" signal will become increasingly flat in time, since at each instant, the best signal is selected. Therefore, the *gain* (in say, dB) from adaptive modulation and coding would be less than if there was no selection combining, since there would be less variation to exploit. Although the overall robustness is maximized by using all available forms of diversity, more diversity causes the effective channel to get closer to an AWGN channel (constant SNR), so additional sources of diversity achieve diminishing returns. In short, the aggregate diversity gain from multiple techniques is less than the sum of the individual diversity gains. Failure to recognize this will result in optimistic projections of system performance.

2.7   Mitigation of Broadband Fading

In Section 2.4.1 we discussed how frequency-selective fading causes dispersion in time, which causes adjacent symbols to interfere with each other unless $T \gg \tau_{\max}$. Since the data rate R is proportional to $1/T$, high data rate systems almost invariably have a substantial multipath delay spread, i.e., $T \ll \tau_{\max}$, and experience very serious *intersymbol interference* (ISI) as a result. Choosing a technique to effectively combat ISI is a central design decision for any high data rate system. Increasingly, OFDM is the most popular choice for combatting ISI in a range of high rate systems, including 802.11/WiFi, 802.16/WiMAX, and of course LTE. OFDM is the focus of the next chapter, so now let us briefly consider the other main techniques for ISI mitigation.

2.7.1   Spread Spectrum and RAKE Receivers

Somewhat counter-intuitively, actually speeding up the *transmission* rate can help combat multipath fading, assuming the *data* rate is kept the same. Since speeding up the transmission rate for a narrowband data signal results in a wideband transmission, this technique is called *spread spectrum*. Spread spectrum techniques are generally broken into two quite different categories: direct sequence and frequency hopping. Direct sequence spread spectrum, also known as Code Division Multiple Access (CDMA), is used widely in cellular voice networks and is effective at multiplexing a large number of variable rate users in a cellular environment. Frequency hopping is used in some low-rate wireless LANs like Bluetooth, and also for its interference averaging properties in GSM cellular networks.

Some of LTE's natural competitors for wireless broadband data services have grown out of the CDMA cellular voice networks—notably 1xEVDO (from cdma2000) and HSDPA/HSUPA (from W-CDMA)—as discussed in Chapter 1. However, CDMA is not an appropriate technology for high data rates, and 1xEVDO and HSDPA are CDMA in name only.[12] For both types of spread spectrum, a large bandwidth is used to send a relatively small data rate. This is a reasonable approach for low data rate communications, like voice, where a large number of users can be statistically multiplexed to yield a high overall system capacity. For high rate data systems, it requires each user to employ several codes simultaneously, which generally results in self-interference. Although this self-interference can be corrected with an equalizer (see next section), this largely defeats the purpose of using spread spectrum to help with intersymbol interference.

In short, spread spectrum is not a natural choice for wireless broadband networks, since by definition, the data rate of a spread spectrum system is less than its bandwidth. The same trend has been observed in wireless LANs: early wireless LANs (802.11 and 802.11b) were spread spectrum[13] and had relatively low spectral efficiency; later wireless LANs (802.11a and 802.11g) used OFDM for multipath suppression and achieved much higher data rates in the same bandwidth.

---

12 In higher-rate versions of 1xEVDO and HSDPA, users are multiplexed primarily in the time rather than the code domain, and the spreading factor is very small.

13 Note that the definition of spread spectrum is somewhat loose. The FCC has labeled even the 11 Mbps in 20MHz 802.11b system as "spread spectrum," but this is generally inconsistent with its historical definition that the bandwidth be much larger than the data rate; see, for example, [40, 46, 51] and the references therein.

2.7.2 Equalization

Equalizers are perhaps the most logical alternative for ISI-suppression to OFDM, since they don't require additional antennas or bandwidth, and have moderate complexity. Equalizers are implemented at the receiver, and attempt to reverse the distortion introduced by the channel. Generally, equalizers are broken into two classes: linear and decision-directed (nonlinear).

Linear Equalizers A linear equalizer simply runs the received signal through a filter that roughly models the inverse of the channel. The problem with this approach is that it inverts not only the channel, but also the received noise. This noise enhancement can severely degrade the receiver performance, especially in a wireless channel with deep frequency fades. Linear receivers are relatively simple to implement, but achieve poor performance in a time-varying and severe-ISI channel.

Nonlinear Equalizers A nonlinear equalizer uses previous symbol decisions made by the receiver to cancel out their subsequent interference, and so is often called a decision feedback equalizers (DFE). Recall that the problem with multipath is that many separate paths are received at different time offsets, so that prior symbols cause interference with later symbols. If the receiver knows the prior symbols, it can subtract their interference out. One problem with this approach is that it is common to make mistakes about what the prior symbols were (especially at low SNR), which causes "error propagation." Also, nonlinear equalizers pay for their improved performance relative to linear receivers with sophisticated training and increased computational complexity.

Maximum Likelihood Sequence Detection Maximum Likelihood Sequence Detection (MLSD) is the optimum method of suppressing ISI, but has complexity that scales like $O(M^v)$, where as before M is the constellation size and v is the channel delay. Therefore, MLSD is generally impractical on channels with a relatively long delay spread or high data rate, but it is often used in some low–data rate outdoor systems like GSM. For a high–data rate broadband wireless channel, MLSD is not expected to be practical in the foreseeable future, although suboptimal approximations like delayed-decision feedback sequence estimation (DDFSE)—which is a hybrid of MLSE and decision feedback equalization [12] and reduced-state sequence estimation (RSSE) [14]—are reasonable suboptimal approximations for MLSE in practical scenarios [17].

2.7.3 Multicarrier Modulation: OFDM

The philosophy of multicarrier modulation is that rather than fighting the time-dispersive ISI channel, why not utilize its diversity? For this, a large number of subcarriers (L) are used in parallel, so that the symbol time for each goes from $T \rightarrow LT$. In other words, rather than sending a single signal with data rate R and bandwidth B, why not send L signals at the same time, each having bandwidth B/L and data rate R/L? In this way, if $B/L \ll B_c$, each of the signals will undergo approximately flat fading and the time dispersion for each signal will be negligible. As long as the number of subcarriers L is large enough, the condition $B/L \ll B_c$ can be met. This elegant idea is the basic principle of Orthogonal Frequency Division Multiplexing, or OFDM. In the next chapter, we will take a close look at this increasingly popular modulation technique, discussing its theoretical basis and implementation challenges.

2.7.4   Single-Carrier Modulation with Frequency Domain Equalization

A primary drawback of the OFDM approach to ISI-suppression is that the transmit signal
has a high peak-to-average ratio (PAR) relative to a single carrier signal. Put simply,
the dynamic range of the transmit power is too large, which results in either significant
clipping and distortion, or in a requirement for highly linear power amps (which are
expensive and inefficient). Needless to say, both of these outcomes are bad.

Is there a way to effectively do OFDM without generating a high PAR? The answer
is yes: one can transmit a single carrier signal with a cyclic prefix, which has a low
PAR, and then do all the processing at the receiver. Said processing consists of a Fast
Fourier Transform (FFT) to move the signal into the frequency domain, a 1-tap frequency
equalizer (just like in OFDM), and then an Inverse FFT to convert back to the time
domain for decoding and detection. In addition to eliminating OFDM's PAR problem,
an additional advantage of this approach for the uplink is the potential to move the
FFT and IFFT operations to the base station. In LTE, however, because multiple uplink
users share the frequency channel at the same time, the mobile station still must perform
FFT and IFFT operations. The resulting approach, known in LTE as Single-Carrier
Frequency Division Multiple Access (SC-FDMA), will be described in more detail in
Chapter 3.

2.8   Chapter Summary

In this chapter, we attempted to understand and characterize the challenging and
multifaceted broadband wireless channel, and how it drives design decisions made in
the LTE standard. Specifically:

- We observed how the average value of the channel power could be modelled based
  simply on the distance between the transmitter and receiver, the carrier frequency,
  and the path loss exponent.

- We characterized the large-scale perturbations from this average channel as *lognormal shadowing*.

- We took a brief break from modelling the channel to show how cellular systems must
  contend with severe interference from neighboring cells, and how this interference
  can be reduced through sectoring and frequency reuse patterns.

- We characterized the small-scale channel effects, known collectively as *fading*. We
  showed how broadband wireless channels have autocorrelation functions that tell
  us a lot about their behavior (see Table 2.2).

- We overviewed popular statistical channel models such as Rayleigh, Ricean, and
  Nakagami, and developed realistic models for time, frequency, and spatial
  correlation.

- We overviewed diversity-achieving techniques for narrowband fading, namely error
  correcting codes and adaptive modulation (with spatial diversity left to Chapter 4).

- We considered broadband fading countermeasures not adopted in LTE, comprising spread spectrum (which is not appropriate for wireless broadband), equalization, and sequence detection, before introducing OFDM and the related Frequency Domain Equalization techniques that will be studied in detail in the coming chapters.

Bibliography

[1] Andrews, J. G. Interference cancellation for cellular systems: A contemporary overview. *IEEE Wireless Communications Magazine*, 12(2):19–29, Apr. 2005.

[2] Andrews, J. G., W. Choi, and R. W. Heath. Overcoming interference in spatial multiplexing MIMO cellular networks. *IEEE Wireless Communications Magazine*, 14(6):95–104, Dec. 2007.

[3] Benedetto, S., G. Montorsi, and D. Divsalar. Concatenated convolutional codes with interleavers. *IEEE Communications Magazine*, 41(8):102–109, Aug. 2003.

[4] Berrou, C., A. Glavieux, and P. Thitmajshima. Near shannon limit error-correcting coding and decoding: turbo-codes. In *Proc., IEEE Intl. Conf. on Communications*, pages 1064–1070, Geneva, Switzerland, May 1993.

[5] Catreux, S., P. Driessen, and L. Greenstein. Attainable throughput of an interference-limited multiple-input multiple-output (MIMO) cellular system. *IEEE Trans. on Communications*, 49(8):1307–1311, Aug. 2001.

[6] Chen, R., J. G. Andrews, R. W. Heath, and A. Ghosh. Uplink power control in multi-cell spatial multiplexing wireless systems. *IEEE Trans. on Wireless Communications*, 4(7):2700–2711, July 2007.

[7] Choi, W. and J. G. Andrews. Downlink performance and capacity of distributed antenna systems in a multicell environment. *IEEE Trans. on Wireless Communications*, pages 69–73, Jan. 2007.

[8] Choi, W. and J. G. Andrews. The capacity gain from base station cooperation in multi-antenna systems. *IEEE Trans. on Wireless Communications*, pages 714–725, Feb. 2008.

[9] Choi, W. and J. Y. Kim. Forward-link capacity of a DS/CDMA system with mixed multirate sources. *IEEE Trans. on Veh. Technology*, 50(3):737–749, May 2001.

[10] Chua, S. G. and A. Goldsmith. Adaptive coded modulation for fading channels. *IEEE Trans. on Communications*, pages 595–602, May 1998.

[11] Dai, H., A. Molisch, and H. V. Poor. Downlink capacity of interference-limited MIMO systems with joint detection. *IEEE Trans. on Wireless Communications*, 3(2):442–453, Mar. 2004.

[12] Duel-Hallen, A. and C. Heegard. Delayed decision-feedback sequence estimation. *IEEE Trans. on Communications*, 37:428–436, May 1989.

[13] Durgin, G. *Space-Time Wireless Channels*. Upper Saddle River, NJ: Prentice Hall, 2003.

[14] Eyuboglu, M. V. and S. U. Qureshi. Reduced-state sequence estimation with set partitioning and decision feedback. *IEEE Trans. on Communications*, 36:13–20, Jan. 1988.

[15] Fenton, L. F. The sum of log-normal probability distributions in scatter transmission systems. *IRE Trans. Commun.*, 8:57–67, Mar. 1960.

[16] Foschini, G. and J. Salz. Digital communications over fading radio channels. *Bell Systems Technical Journal*, 429–456, Feb. 1983.

[17] Gerstacker, W. H. and R. Schober. Equalization concepts for EDGE. *IEEE Trans. on Wireless Communications*, 1(1):190–199, Jan. 2002.

[18] Gesbert, D. and M. Kountouris. Joint power control and user scheduling in multicell wireless networks: Capacity scaling laws. *IEEE Trans. on Info. Theory*, Submitted.

[19] Goldsmith, A. and P. Varaiya. Capacity of fading channels with channel side information. *IEEE Trans. on Info. Theory*, 1986–1992, Nov. 1997.

[20] Goldsmith, A. J. *Wireless Communications*. Cambridge University Press, 2005.

[21] Hagenauer, J., E. Offer, and L. Papke. Iterative decoding of binary block and convolutional codes. *IEEE Trans. on Info. Theory*, 42(2):429–445, Mar. 1996.

[22] Hasegawa, R., M. Shirakabe, R. Esmailzadeh, and M. Nakagawa. Downlink performance of a CDMA system with distributed base station. In *Proc., IEEE Veh. Technology Conf.*, 882–886, Oct. 2003.

[23] Herdtner, J. and E. Chong. Analysis of a class of distributed asynchronous power control algorithms for cellular wireless systems. *IEEE Journal on Sel. Areas in Communications*, 18(3), Mar. 2000.

[24] Hu, H., Y. Zhang, and J. L. (Editors). *Distributed Antenna Systems: Open Architecture for Future Wireless Communications*. Boca Raton, FL: CRC Press, 2007.

[25] Jafar, S., G. Foschini, and A. Goldsmith. PhantomNet: Exploring optimal multicellular multiple antenna systems. In *Proc., IEEE Veh. Technology Conf.*, 24–28, Sept. 2002.

[26] Jakes, W. C. *Microwave Mobile Communications*. Wiley-Interscience, 1974.

[27] Janssen, G. J. M., P. A. Stigter, and R. Prasad. Wideband indoor channel measurements and BER analysis of frequency selective multipath channels at 2.4, 4.75, and 11.5GHz. *IEEE Trans. on Communications*, 44(10):1272–1288, Oct. 1996.

[28] Karakayali, K., G. J. Foschini, and R. A. Valenzuela. Network coordination for spectrally efficient communications in cellular systems. *IEEE Wireless Communications Magazine*, 13(4):56–61, Aug. 2006.

[29] Lin, S. and D. Costello. *Error Control Coding*. 2nd edition, Upper Saddle River, NJ: Prentice Hall, 2004.

[30] Nakagami, M. *Statistical Methods in Radio Wave Propagation*. Oxford, England: Pergamon, 1960.

[31] Ng, B. L., J. S. Evans, S. V. Hanly, and D. Aktas. Transmit beamforming with cooperative base stations. In *Proc., IEEE Intl. Symposium on Information Theory*, Sept. 2005.

[32] Papazian, P. Basic transmission loss and delay spread measurements for frequencies between 430 and 5750MHz. *IEEE Trans. on Antennas and Propagation*, 53(2):694–701, Feb. 2005.

[33] Parsons, D. *The Mobile Radio Propagation Channel*. New York: John Wiley & Sons, 1992.

[34] Rappaport, T. S. *Wireless Communications: Principles and Practice*. 2nd edition. Upper Saddle River, NJ: Prentice Hall, 2002.

[35] Rashid-Farrokhi, F., K. R. Liu, and L. Tassiulas. Transmit beamforming and power control for cellular wireless systems. *IEEE Journal on Sel. Areas in Communications*, 16(8):1437–1450, Oct. 1998.

[36] Rice, S. O. Statistical properties of a sine wave plus random noise. *Bell Systems Technical Journal*, 27:109–157, Jan. 1948.

[37] Saleh, A., A. J. Rustako, and R. S. Roman. Distributed antennas for indoor radio communications. *IEEE Trans. on Communications*, 35:1245–1251, Dec. 1987.

[38] Saraydar, C. U., N. B. Mandayam, and D. J. Goodman. Pricing and power control in a multicell wireless data network. *IEEE Journal on Sel. Areas in Communications*, 1883–1892, Oct. 2001.

[39] Schniter, P. Low-complexity equalization of OFDM in doubly-selective channels. *IEEE Trans. on Signal Processing*, 52(4):1002–1011, Apr. 2004.

[40] Scholtz, R. The origins of spread-spectrum communications. *IEEE Trans. on Communications*, 30(5):822–854, May 1982.

[41] Schwartz, S. and Y. S. Yeh. On the distribution function and moments of power sums with log-normal components. *Bell System Tech. Journal*, 61:1441–1462, Sept. 1982.

[42] Seidel, S. Y., T. Rappaport, S. Jain, M. Lord, and R. Singh. Path loss, scattering and multipath delay statistics in four European cities for digital cellular and microcellular radiotelephone. *IEEE Trans. on Veh. Technology*, 40(4):721–730, Nov. 1990.

[43] Shamai, S. and B. Zaidel. Enhancing the cellular downlink capacity via co-processing at the transmitting end. In *Proc., IEEE Veh. Technology Conf.*, 1745–1749, May 2001.

[44] Shannon, C. E. A mathematical theory of communication (part 1). *Bell System Tech. Journal*, 27:379–423, 1948.

[45] Simon, M. K. and M. S. Alouini. *Digital Communication over Generalized Fading Channels: A Unified Approach to the Performance Analysis*. New York: John Wiley & Sons, 2000.

[46] Simon, M. K., J. K. Omura, R. A. Scholtz, and B. K. Levitt. *Spread Spectrum Communications Handbook*. Rev. ed. New York: McGraw Hill, 1994.

[47] Simonsson, S. and A. Furuskar. Uplink power control in LTE—overview and performance. In *Proc., IEEE Veh. Technology Conf.*, 1–5, Sept. 2008.

[48] Somekh, O., B. M. Zaidel, and S. S. (Shitz). Sum rate characterization of joint multiple cell-site processing. *IEEE Trans. on Info. Theory*, 4473–4497, Dec. 2007.

[49] Stuber, G. L. *Principles of Mobile Communication*. 2nd edition, Kluwer, 2001.

[50] Viterbi, A. J. Error bounds for convolutional codes and an asymptotically optimum decoding algorithm. *IEEE Trans. on Info. Theory*, 13(2):260–269, Apr. 1967.

[51] Viterbi, A. J. *CDMA—Principles of Spread Spectrum Communication*. 1st edition. Reading, MA: Addison-Wesley, 1995.

[52] Wicker, S. B. *Error Control Systems for Digital Communication and Storage*. Englewood Cliffs, NJ: Prentice Hall, 1994.

[53] Xiao, M., N. B. Shroff, and E. K. P. Chong. A utility-based power control scheme in wireless cellular systems. *IEEE/ACM Trans. Networking*, 210–221, Apr. 2003.

[54] Xiao, W., R. Ratasuk, A. Ghosh, R. Love, Y. Sun, and R. Nory. Uplink power control, interference coordination and resource allocation for 3GPP E-UTRA. In *Proc., IEEE Veh. Technology Conf.*, 1–5, Sept. 2006.

[55] Yacoub, M. D. *Foundations of Mobile Radio Engineering*. Boca Raton, FL: CRC Press, 1993.

[56] Yates, R. D. A framework for uplink power control in cellular radio systems. *IEEE Journal on Sel. Areas in Communications*, 13(7):1341–1347, Sept. 1995.

[57] Zhang, H. and H. Dai. Co-channel interference mitigation and cooperative processing in downlink multicell multiuser MIMO networks. *European Journal on Wireless Communications and Networking*, 4th Quarter 2004.

[58] Zhang, J. and J. G. Andrews. Distributed antenna systems with randomness. *IEEE Transactions on Wireless Communications*, 7(9):3636–3646, Sept. 2008.

[59] Zhang, J., R. Chen, J. G. Andrews, A. Ghosh, and R. W. Heath. Networked MIMO with clustered linear precoding. *IEEE Transactions on Wireless Communications*, To appear.

Multicarrier Modulation

M ulticarrier modulation underlies many of the most successful modern wireless data systems, including Digital Subscriber Lines (DSL), Wireless LANs (802.11a/g/n), Digital Video Broadcasting, and most recently, beyond 3G cellular technologies such as WiMAX and LTE. The unifying common feature of multicarrier modulation techniques is the use of multiple parallel subcarriers, invariably generated by the (inverse) discrete Fourier transform. By far the most common type of multicarrier modulation is Orthogonal Frequency Division Multiplexing (OFDM), along with its close cousins Discrete Multitone (DMT) in DSL[1] and the somewhat oddly named Single-Carrier Frequency Division Multiple Access (SC-FDMA) in the LTE uplink.

The main reason for OFDM's popularity for high data rate applications stems primarily from its efficient and flexible management of intersymbol interference (ISI) in highly dispersive channels. As emphasized in Chapter 2, as the channel delay spread τ becomes an increasingly large multiple of the symbol time T_s—for example, due to significant multipath—the ISI becomes very severe. By definition, a high data rate system like LTE will generally have $\tau \gg T_s$ since the number of symbols sent per second is high. In a non-line of sight (NLOS) system like LTE that must transmit over moderate to long distances, the delay spread will also frequently be large. This makes the use of a robust ISI-suppression technique mandatory.

As discussed at the end of the last chapter, there are essentially three possible directions for ISI suppression. The method of choice in 3G technology is spread spectrum, which becomes increasingly unviable as the data rate increases since it requires a bandwidth much larger than the data rate. Therefore, in higher data rate 3G systems like HSPA, an equalizer must be used in addition. Although time-domain equalization still has its advocates, the overhead and especially the complexity inherent to accurate equalization is significantly higher than that of OFDM in highly dispersive channels (relative to the symbol rate), as we show in Section 3.7.

---

1 DMT is an OFDM system that supports adaptive modulation and power control per subcarrier.

This chapter has the following main goals:

1. Demonstrate the elegance of multicarrier modulation, and how it works in both theory and practice.

2. Emphasize a practical understanding of OFDM system design, covering key concepts such as the cyclic prefix, frequency equalization, and synchronization.[2]

3. Discuss implementation issues for OFDM systems, in particular the peak-to-average ratio.

4. Overview Single-Carrier Frequency Domain Equalization (SC-FDE), an alternative block modulation approach that utilizes the cyclic-prefix and FFT and is very similar to OFDM, but avoids its peak-to-average ratio problem.

3.1 The Multicarrier Concept

The basic idea of multicarrier modulation is quite simple, and follows naturally from the competing desires for high data rates and intersymbol interference (ISI) free channels. In order to have a channel that does not have ISI, the symbol time T_s has to be larger—often significantly larger—than the channel delay spread τ. Digital communication systems simply cannot function if ISI is present—an error floor quickly develops and as T_s approaches or falls below τ, the bit error rate becomes intolerable. As we have noted previously, for wideband channels that provide the high data rates needed by today's applications, the desired symbol time is usually much smaller than the delay spread, so intersymbol interference is severe.

In order to overcome this, multicarrier modulation divides the high-rate transmit bitstream into L lower-rate substreams, where L is chosen so that *each* of the subcarriers has effective symbol time $T_s L >> \tau$, and is hence effectively ISI-free. These individual substreams can then be sent over L parallel subcarriers, maintaining the total desired data rate. Typically, the subcarriers are orthogonal under ideal propagation conditions, in which case multicarrier modulation is often referred to as Orthogonal Frequency Division Multiplexing (OFDM). The data rate on each of the subcarriers is much less than the total data rate, and so the corresponding subcarrier bandwidth is much less than the total system bandwidth. The number of substreams is chosen to ensure that each subcarrier has a bandwidth less than the coherence bandwidth of the channel, so the subcarriers experience relatively flat fading. Thus, the ISI on each subcarrier is small. Moreover, in the digital implementation of OFDM, the ISI can be completely eliminated through the use of a cyclic prefix.

---

2 Channel estimation for OFDM is covered in Chapter 5 in the context of MIMO-OFDM.

Example 3.1. A certain wideband wireless channel has a delay spread of 1 μsec. In order to overcome ISI, assume a requirement that $T_s \geq 10\tau$.

1. What is the maximum bandwidth allowable in this system if the ISI constraint is to be met without using multicarrier modulation?

2. If multicarrier modulation is used, and we desire a 10MHz bandwidth, what is the required number of subcarriers?

For part (1), if it is assumed that $T_s = 10\tau$ in order to satisfy the ISI-free condition, the maximum bandwidth would be $1/T_s = .1/\tau = 100$KHz, two orders of magnitude below the intended bandwidths for LTE systems.

In part (2), if multicarrier modulation is employed, the symbol time goes to $T = LT_s$. The delay spread criterion mandates that the new symbol time is still bounded to 10% of the delay spread, that is, $(LT_s)^{-1} = 100$KHz. But the 10MHz bandwidth requirement gives $(T_s)^{-1} = 10$MHz. Hence, $L \geq 100$, so a suitable[3] choice of L might be 128 subcarriers to allow the full 10MHz bandwidth to be used with negligible ISI.

3.1.1 An Elegant Approach to Intersymbol Interference

Multicarrier modulation in its simplest form divides the wideband incoming data stream into L narrowband substreams, each of which is then transmitted over a different orthogonal frequency subcarrier. As in Example 3.1, the number of substreams L is chosen to make the symbol time on each substream much greater than the delay spread of the channel or, equivalently, to make the substream bandwidth less than the channel coherence bandwidth. This ensures that the substreams will not experience significant ISI.

A simple illustration of a multicarrier transmitter and receiver is given in Figures 3.1 and 3.2. Essentially, a high-rate data signal of rate R bps and with a passband bandwidth B is broken into L parallel substreams each with rate R/L and passband bandwidth B/L. After passing through the channel $H(f)$, the received signal would appear as shown in Figure 3.3, where we have assumed for simplicity that the pulse-shaping allows a perfect spectral shaping so that there is no subcarrier overlap.[4] As long as the number of subcarriers is sufficiently large to allow for the subcarrier bandwidth to be much less than the coherence bandwidth, that is, $B/L \ll B_c$, then it can be ensured that each subcarrier experiences approximately flat fading. The mutually orthogonal signals can then be individually detected, as shown in Figure 3.2.

---

3 The number of subcarriers is always an exponential factor of 2, that is, $L = 2^k = 2, 4, 8, 16, 32, 64,$ $128, \ldots$, because the FFT is most efficient and natural for such numbers.

4 In practice, there would be some rolloff factor of β, so the actual consumed bandwidth of such a system would be $(1 + \beta)B$. However, OFDM, as we will see, avoids this inefficiency by using an IFFT to do the modulation.

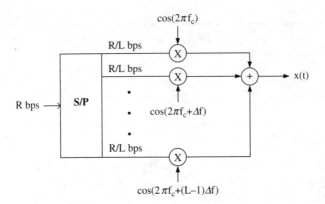

Figure 3.1 A basic multicarrier transmitter: a high-rate stream of R bps is broken into L parallel streams each with rate R/L and then multiplied by a different carrier frequency.

Hence, the multicarrier technique has an interesting interpretation in both the time and the frequency domains. In the time domain, the symbol duration on each subcarrier has increased to $T = LT_s$, so by letting L grow larger, it can be assured that the symbol duration exceeds the channel delay spread, that is, $T \gg \tau$, which is a requirement for ISI-free communication. In the frequency domain, the subcarriers have bandwidth $B/L \ll B_c$, which assures "flat fading," the frequency domain equivalent to ISI-free communication.

Although this simple type of multicarrier modulation is easy to understand, it has several crucial shortcomings. First, as noted above, in a realistic implementation, a large bandwidth penalty will be inflicted since the subcarriers can't have perfectly rectangular pulse shapes and still be time-limited. Additionally, very high-quality (and hence, expensive), low-pass filters will be required to maintain the orthogonality of the subcarriers at the receiver. Most importantly, this scheme requires L independent RF units and demodulation paths. In Section 3.2, we show how OFDM overcomes these shortcomings.

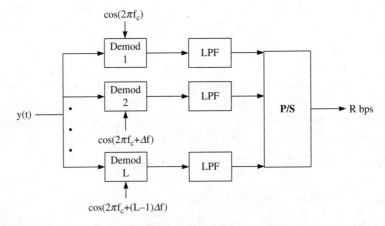

Figure 3.2 A basic multicarrier receiver: each subcarrier is decoded separately, requiring L independent receivers.

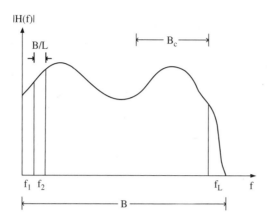

Figure 3.3 The transmitted multicarrier signal experiences approximately flat fading on each sub-carrier since $B/L \ll B_c$, even though the overall channel experiences frequency selective fading, that is, $B > B_c$.

3.2 OFDM Basics

In order to overcome the daunting requirement for L RF radios in both the transmitter and receiver, OFDM employs an efficient computational technique known as the Discrete Fourier Transform (DFT), which lends itself to a highly efficient implementation commonly known as the Fast Fourier Transform (FFT). In this section, we will learn how the FFT (and its inverse, the IFFT) are able to create a multitude of orthogonal subcarriers using just a single radio.

3.2.1 Block Transmission with Guard Intervals

We begin by grouping L data symbols into a block known as an *OFDM symbol*. An OFDM symbol lasts for a duration of T seconds, where $T = LT_s$. In order to keep each OFDM symbol independent of the others after going through a wireless channel, it is necessary to introduce a guard time in between each OFDM symbol, as shown here:

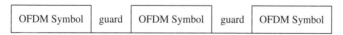

This way, after receiving a series of OFDM symbols, as long as the guard time T_g is larger than the delay spread of the channel τ, each OFDM symbol will only interfere with itself.

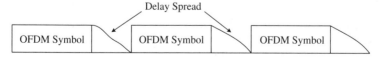

Put simply, OFDM transmissions allow ISI *within* an OFDM symbol, but by including a sufficiently large guard band, it is possible to guarantee that there is no interference *between* subsequent OFDM symbols.

3.2.2 Circular Convolution and the DFT

Now that subsequent OFDM symbols have been rendered orthogonal with a guard interval, the next task is to attempt to remove the ISI *within* each OFDM symbol. As described in Chapter 2, when an input data stream $x[n]$ is sent through a linear time-invariant FIR channel $h[n]$, the output is the linear convolution of the input and the channel, that is, $y[n] = x[n] * h[n]$. However, let's imagine for a moment that it was possible to compute $y[n]$ in terms of a *circular* convolution, that is

$$y[n] = x[n] \circledast h[n] = h[n] \circledast x[n], \tag{3.1}$$

where

$$x[n] \circledast h[n] = h[n] \circledast x[n] \triangleq \sum_{k=0}^{L-1} h[k]x[n-k]_L \tag{3.2}$$

and the circular function $x[n]_L = x[n \bmod L]$ is a *periodic* version of $x[n]$ with period L. In other words, each value of $y[n] = h[n] \circledast x[n]$ is the sum of the product of L terms.[5]

In this case of circular convolution, it would then be possible to take the DFT of the channel output $y[n]$ to get:

$$\text{DFT}\{y[n]\} = \text{DFT}\{h[n] \circledast x[n]\} \tag{3.3}$$

which yields in the frequency domain

$$Y[m] = H[m]X[m]. \tag{3.4}$$

Note that the duality between circular convolution in the time domain and simple multiplication in the frequency domain is a property unique to the DFT. The L point DFT is defined as

$$\text{DFT}\{x[n]\} = X[m] \triangleq \frac{1}{\sqrt{L}} \sum_{n=0}^{L-1} x[n]e^{-j\frac{2\pi nm}{L}}, \tag{3.5}$$

while its inverse, the IDFT is defined as

$$\text{IDFT}\{X[m]\} = x[n] \triangleq \frac{1}{\sqrt{L}} \sum_{m=0}^{L-1} X[m]e^{j\frac{2\pi nm}{L}}. \tag{3.6}$$

Referring to (3.4), this innocent formula actually describes an ISI-free channel in the frequency domain, where each input symbol $X[m]$ is simply scaled by a complex-value $H[m]$. So, given knowledge of the channel frequency response $H[m]$ at the receiver, it is trivial to recover the input symbol by simply computing

$$\hat{X}[m] = \frac{Y[m]}{H[m]}, \tag{3.7}$$

---

5 For a more thorough tutorial on circular convolution, the reader is referred to [31] or the "Connexions" Web resource http://cnx.rice.edu/.

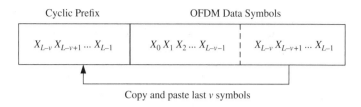

Figure 3.4 The OFDM cyclic prefix.

where the estimate $\hat{X}[m]$ will generally be imperfect due to additive noise, co-channel interference, imperfect channel estimation, and other imperfections that will be discussed later. Nevertheless, in principle, the ISI—which is the most serious form of interference in a wideband channel—has been mitigated.

But, where does this circular convolution come from? After all, nature provides a linear convolution when a signal is transmitted through a linear channel. The answer is that this circular convolution can be "faked" by adding a specific type of redundancy called the *cyclic prefix* onto the transmitted vector.

3.2.3   The Cyclic Prefix

The key to making OFDM realizable in practice is the utilization of the FFT algorithm for computing the DFT and the IFFT algorithm for computing the IDFT, which reduces the number of required multiplications and additions from $O(L^2)$ to $O(L \log L)$, which is very significant. The IFFT operation at the transmitter allows all the subcarriers to be created in the digital domain, and thus requires only a single radio to be used, rather than L radios as in Figure 3.1. In order for the IFFT/FFT to create an ISI-free channel, the channel must appear to provide a circular convolution, as seen in (3.4). If a cyclic prefix is added to the transmitted signal, as shown in Figure 3.4, then this creates a signal that appears to be $x[n]_L$, and so $y[n] = x[n] \circledast h[n]$.

Let's see how this works. If the maximum channel delay spread has a duration of $v+1$ samples, then by adding a guard band of at least v samples between OFDM symbols, each OFDM symbol is made independent of those coming before and after it, and so just a single OFDM symbol can be considered. Representing such an OFDM symbol in the time domain as a length L vector gives

$$\mathbf{x} = [x_1 \ x_2 \ldots x_L]. \tag{3.8}$$

After applying a cyclic prefix of length v, the actual transmitted signal is

$$\mathbf{x}_{cp} = [\underbrace{x_{L-v} \ x_{L-v+1} \ \cdots \ x_{L-1}}_{\text{Cyclic prefix}} \underbrace{x_0 \ x_1 \ \cdots \ x_{L-1}}_{\text{Original data}}]. \tag{3.9}$$

The output of the channel is by definition $\mathbf{y}_{cp} = \mathbf{h} * \mathbf{x}_{cp}$, where $\mathbf{h}$ is a length $v+1$ vector describing the impulse response of the channel during the OFDM symbol.[6] The output

---

6 It can generally be reasonably assumed that the channel remains constant over an OFDM symbol, since the OFDM symbol time T is usually much less than the channel coherence time, T_c.

$\mathbf{y}_{cp}$ has $(L + v) + (v + 1) - 1 = L + 2v$ samples. The first v samples of $\mathbf{y}_{cp}$ contain interference from the preceding OFDM symbol, and so are discarded. The last v samples disperse into the subsequent OFDM symbol, and so also are discarded. This leaves exactly L samples for the desired output $\mathbf{y}$, which is precisely what is required to recover the L data symbols embedded in $\mathbf{x}$.

Our claim is that these L samples of $\mathbf{y}$ will be equivalent to $\mathbf{y} = \mathbf{h} \circledast \mathbf{x}$. Various proofs are possible, the most intuitive being a simple inductive argument, shown also in Figure 3.5. Consider for the moment just y_0, that is, the first element in $\mathbf{y}$. As shown in Figure 3.5, due to the cyclic prefix, y_0 depends on x_0 and the circularly wrapped values $x_{L-v} \ldots x_{L-1}$. That is:

$$y_0 = h_0 x_0 + h_1 x_{L-1} + \cdots + h_v x_{L-v}$$
$$y_1 = h_0 x_1 + h_1 x_0 + \cdots + h_v x_{L-v+1}$$
$$\vdots$$
$$y_{L-1} = h_0 x_{L-1} + h_1 x_{L-2} + \cdots + h_v x_{L-v-1} \tag{3.10}$$

From inspecting (3.2), it can be seen that this is exactly the value of $y_0, y_1, \ldots, y_{L-1}$ resulting from $\mathbf{y} = \mathbf{x} \circledast \mathbf{h}$. Thus, by mimicking a circular convolution, a cyclic prefix that is at least as long as the channel duration allows the channel output $\mathbf{y}$ to be decomposed into a simple multiplication of the channel frequency response $\mathbf{H} = \mathrm{DFT}\{\mathbf{h}\}$ and the channel frequency domain input, $\mathbf{X} = \mathrm{DFT}\{\mathbf{x}\}$.

The cyclic prefix, although elegant and simple, is not entirely free. It comes with both a bandwidth and power penalty. Since v redundant symbols are sent, the required

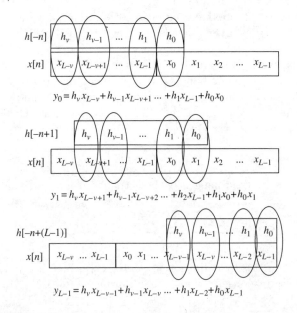

Figure 3.5 The OFDM cyclic prefix creates a circular convolution at the receiver (signal y) even though the actual channel causes a linear convolution.

bandwith for OFDM increases from B to $\frac{L+v}{L}B$. Similarly, an additional v symbols must be counted against the transmit power budget. Hence, the cyclic prefix carries a power penalty of $10\log_{10}\frac{L+v}{L}$ dB in addition to the bandwidth penalty. In summary, the use of cyclic prefix entails data rate and power losses that are both

$$\text{Rate Loss} = \text{Power Loss} = \frac{L}{L+v}.$$

The "wasted" power has increased importance in an interference-limited wireless system, since it causes interference to neighboring users.

It can be noted that for $L \gg v$, the inefficiency due to the cyclic prefix can be made arbitrarily small by increasing the number of subcarriers. However, as the latter parts of this chapter will explain, there are numerous other important sacrifices that must be made as L grows large. As with most system design problems, desirable properties such as efficiency must be traded off against cost and required tolerances.

Example 3.2. In this example, we will find the minimum and maximum data rate loss due to using the cyclic prefix in LTE. We will consider a channel where the maximum delay spread has been determined to be $\tau = 2\mu\text{sec}$. What is the minimum and maximum data rate loss due to the cyclic prefix? What is the minimum theoretical loss if a shorter cyclic prefix could be used?

In LTE, there are two possible cyclic prefix (CP) lengths, per Section 6.3.1. The "normal" CP length is $T_g = 144T_s \approx 4.7\mu\text{sec}$,[7] which is clearly longer than $2\mu\text{sec}$ and so sufficient for this channel. Since the CP length is fixed, it would appear that the least overhead (rate loss) will be incurred for the longest block size, which is $L = 2048$ subcarriers, while the most overhead would be incurred for the shortest block, $L = 128$. However, LTE indexes the block (FFT) size to the transmission bandwidth so the subcarrier width is fixed at 15KHz. So, at $L = 128$ the CP length is $T_g = 144T_s = 144 \cdot \frac{128}{2048} = 9$ data symbols, whereas at $L = 2048$ the CP length is 144 data symbols. Hence, the rate loss factor is in fact the same: $L/(L+v) = 0.934$ for both cases, that is, there is a rate loss of less than 7%.

If the cylic prefix was even shorter, the rate loss would be less. Since $\tau = 2\mu\text{sec}$, the cyclic prefix could shrink by over 50% to about 4 symbols for the $L = 128$ case and to 62 symbols for the $L = 2048$ case. This would decrease the overhead to about 3%.

3.2.4 Frequency Equalization

In order for the received symbols to be estimated, the complex channel gains for each subcarrier must be known, which corresponds to knowing the amplitude and phase of the subcarrier. For simple modulation techniques like QPSK that do not use the amplitude to transmit information, just the phase information is sufficient.

---

7 We will neglect the first symbol in the slot, which has a slightly longer CP length of $T_g = 160T_s$.

After the FFT is performed, the data symbols are estimated using a one-tap frequency domain equalizer, or FEQ, as

$$\hat{X}_l = \frac{Y_l}{H_l} \quad . \tag{3.11}$$

where H_l is the *complex* response of the channel at the frequency $f_c + (l-1)\Delta f$, and therefore it both corrects the phase and equalizes the amplitude before the decision device. Note that although the FEQ inverts the channel, there is no problematic noise enhancement or coloring since both the signal and the noise will have their powers directly scaled by $|\frac{1}{H_l}|^2$.

3.2.5   An OFDM Block Diagram

Let us now briefly review the key steps in an OFDM communication system, each of which can be observed in Figure 3.6.

1. The first step in OFDM is to break a wideband signal of bandwidth B into L narrowband signals (subcarriers) each of bandwidth B/L. This way, the aggregate symbol rate is maintained, but each subcarrier experiences flat fading, or ISI-free communication, as long as a cyclic prefix that exceeds the delay spread is used. The L subcarriers for a given OFDM symbol are represented by a vector $\mathbf{X}$, which contains the L current symbols.

2. In order to use a single wideband radio instead of L independent narrow band radios, the subcarriers are created digitally using an IFFT operation.

3. In order for the IFFT/FFT to decompose the ISI channel into orthogonal subcarriers, a cyclic prefix of length v must be appended after the IFFT operation. The resulting $L + v$ symbols are then sent in serial through the wideband channel.

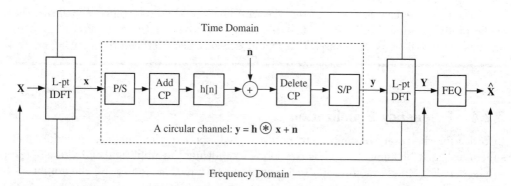

Figure 3.6 An OFDM system in vector notation. In OFDM, the encoding and decoding is done in the frequency domain, where **X**, **Y**, and $\hat{\mathbf{X}}$ contain the L transmitted, received, and estimated data symbols.

4. At the receiver, the cyclic prefix is discarded, and the L received symbols are demodulated using an FFT operation, which results in L data symbols, each of the form $Y_l = H_l X_l + N_l$ for subcarrier l.

5. Each subcarrier can then be equalized via an FEQ by simply dividing by the complex channel gain $H[i]$ for that subcarrier. This results in $\hat{\mathbf{X}}_l = X_l + N_l/H_l$.

We have neglected a number of important practical issues thus far. For example, we have assumed that the transmitter and receiver are perfectly synchronized, and that the receiver perfectly knows the channel (in order to perform the FEQ). In the next section, we overview the key implementation issues for OFDM in LTE.

3.3 OFDM in LTE

To gain an appreciation for the time and frequency domain interpretations of OFDM, LTE systems can be used as an example. Although simple in concept, the subtleties of OFDM can be confusing if each signal processing step is not understood. To ground the discussion, we will consider a passband OFDM system, and then give specific values for the important system parameters.

Figure 3.7 shows an up close view of a passband OFDM modulation engine. The inputs to this figure are L independent QAM symbols (the vector $\mathbf{X}$), and these L symbols are treated as separate subcarriers. These L data-bearing symbols can be created from a bit stream by a symbol mapper and serial-to-parallel convertor (S/P). The L-point IFFT then creates a time domain L-vector $\mathbf{x}$ that is cyclic extended to have length $L(1 + G)$, where G is the fractional overhead. As just seen in Example 3.2 and with further description in Section 6.3.1, in LTE $G \approx 0.07$ for the normal cyclic prefix and grows to $G = 0.25$ for the extended cyclic prefix. This longer vector is then parallel-to-serial (P/S) converted into a wideband digital signal that can be amplitude modulated with a single radio at a carrier frequency of $f_c = \omega_c/2\pi$.

This procedure appears to be relatively straightforward, but in order to be a bit less abstract, we will now use some plausible values for the different parameters. The key

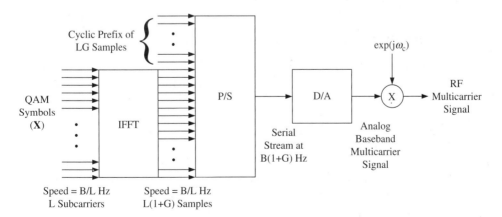

Figure 3.7 A close-up of the OFDM baseband to passband transmitter.

Table 3.1 Summary of Key OFDM Parameters in LTE and Example Values for 10MHz

Symbol	Description	Relation	Example LTE value
B	Nominal bandwidth	$B = 1/2f_s$	7.68MHz
B_{chan}	Transmission bandwidth	Channel spacing	10MHz
L	No. of subcarriers	Size of IFFT/FFT	1024
G	Guard fraction	% of L for CP	0.07
L_d	Data subcarriers	$L-$ pilot/null subcarriers	600
Δf	Subcarrier spacing	Independent of L	15KHz
T_s	Sample time	$T_s = 1/\max(B) = 1/\Delta f \cdot 2048$	$1/15\text{KHz} \cdot 2048$ $= 32.55$ nsec
N_g	Guard symbols	$N_g = GL$	72
T_g	Guard time	$T_g = 144T_s$ or $160T_s$	4.7 or 5.2 μsec
T	OFDM symbol time	$T = (L + N_g)/B$	142.7 μsec

OFDM parameters are summarized in Table 3.1, along with some potential numerical values for these parameters. As an example, if 16QAM modulation was used ($M = 16$) with the normal cyclic prefix, the raw (neglecting coding) data rate of this LTE system would be:

$$R = \frac{B}{L} \frac{L_d \log_2(M)}{1 + G} \tag{3.12}$$

$$= \frac{10^7 \text{MHz}}{1024} \frac{600 \log_2(16)}{1.07} = 21.9 \, \text{Mbps}. \tag{3.13}$$

In other words, there are $L_d = 600$ data-carrying subcarriers of bandwidth B/L, each carrying $\log_2(M)$ bits of data. An additional overhead penalty of $(1+G)$ must be paid for the cyclic prefix, since it consists of redundant information and sacrifices the transmission of actual data symbols.

3.4   Timing and Frequency Synchronization

In order to demodulate an OFDM signal, there are two important synchronization tasks that need to be performed by the receiver. First, the timing offset of the symbol and the optimal timing instants need to be determined. This is referred to as *timing synchronization*. Second, the receiver must align its carrier frequency as closely as possible with the transmitted carrier frequency. This is referred to as *frequency synchronization*. Compared to single-carrier systems, the timing synchronization requirements for OFDM are in fact somewhat relaxed, since the OFDM symbol structure naturally accommodates a reasonable degree of synchronization error. On the other hand, frequency synchronization requirements are significantly more stringent, since the orthogonality of the data symbols is reliant on their being individually discernible in the frequency domain.

Figure 3.8 shows a representation of an OFDM symbol in time (top) and frequency (bottom). In the time domain, the IFFT effectively modulates each data symbol onto a unique carrier frequency. In Figure 3.8 only two of the carriers are shown—the actual transmitted signal is the superposition of all the individual carriers. Since the time window is $T = 1\,\mu\text{sec}$ and a rectangular window is used, the frequency response of each subcarrier becomes a "sinc" function with zero crossings every $1/T = 1\text{MHz}$. This can be confirmed using the Fourier Transform $\mathcal{F}\{\cdot\}$ since

$$\mathcal{F}\{\cos(2\pi f_c t) \cdot \text{rect}(t/T)\} = \mathcal{F}\{\cos(2\pi f_c t)\} * \mathcal{F}\{\text{rect}(2t/T)\} \qquad (3.14)$$

$$= \text{sinc}\left(T(f - f_c)\right), \qquad (3.15)$$

where $\text{rect}(x) = 1$, $x \in (-0.5, 0.5)$, and zero elsewhere. This frequency response is shown for $L = 8$ subcarriers in the bottom part of Figure 3.8.

The challenge of timing and frequency synchronization can be appreciated by inspecting these two figures. If the timing window is slid to the left or right, a unique phase change will be introduced to each of the subcarriers. In the frequency domain, if the carrier frequency synchronization is perfect, the receiver samples at the peak of each subcarrier, where the desired subcarrier amplitude is maximized and the inter-carrier interference (ICI) is zero. However, if the carrier frequency is misaligned by some amount δ, then some of the desired energy is lost, and more significantly, inter-carrier interference is introduced.

The following two subsections will more carefully examine timing and frequency synchronization. Although the development of good timing and frequency synchronization algorithms for LTE systems is the responsibility of each equipment manufacturer, we will give some general guidelines on what is required of a synchronization algorithm, and discuss the penalty for imperfect synchronization. It should be noted that synchronization is one of the most challenging problems in OFDM implementation, and the development of efficient and accurate synchronization algorithms presents an opportunity for technical differentiation and intellectual property.

3.4.1   Timing Synchronization

The effect of timing errors in symbol synchronization is somewhat relaxed in OFDM due to the presence of a cyclic prefix. In Section 3.2.3, we assumed that only the L time domain samples after the cyclic prefix were utilized by the receiver. Indeed, this corresponds to "perfect" timing synchronization, and in this case even if the cyclic prefix length N_g is equivalent to the length of the channel impulse response v, successive OFDM symbols can be decoded ISI free.

In the case that perfect synchronization is not maintained, it is still possible to tolerate a timing offset of τ seconds without any degradation in performance as long as $0 \leq \tau \leq T_g - T_m$, where as usual T_g is the guard time (cyclic prefix duration) and T_m is the maximum channel delay spread. Here, $\tau < 0$ corresponds to sampling earlier than at the ideal instant, whereas $\tau > 0$ is later than the ideal instant. As long as $0 \leq \tau \leq T_g - T_m$, the timing offset simply results in a phase shift per subcarrier of $\exp(-j\Delta f\tau)$, which is fixed for all subcarriers. As long as τ remains constant, the channel estimator simply includes it as part of a fixed phase offset and it can be corrected by the FEQ without

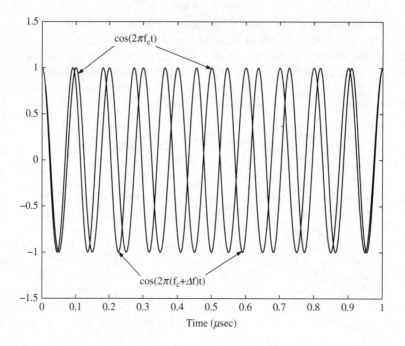

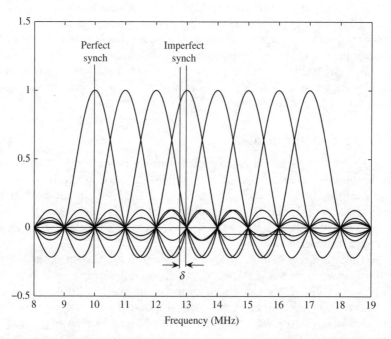

Figure 3.8 OFDM synchronization in time (top) and frequency (bottom). Here, two subcarriers in the time domain and eight subcarriers in the frequency domain are shown, where $f_c = 10\text{MHz}$ and the subcarrier spacing $\Delta f = 1\text{Hz}$.

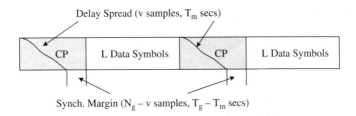

Figure 3.9 Timing synchronization margin. OFDM is actually less sensitive to timing synchronization errors than single-carrier modulation, assuming a bit of margin is allowed in the cyclic prefix length.

any loss in performance. This acceptable range of τ is referred to as the *timing synchronization margin*, and is shown in Figure 3.9.

On the other hand, if the timing offset τ is not within this window $0 \leq \tau \leq T_m - T_g$, inter-symbol interference (ISI) occurs regardless of whether the phase shift is appropriately accounted for. This can be confirmed intuitively for the scenario that $\tau > 0$ and for $\tau < T_m - T_g$. For the case $\tau > 0$, the receiver loses some of the desired energy (since only delayed versions of the early samples $x_0, x_1, \ldots$ are received), and also incorporates undesired energy from the subsequent symbol. Similarly for $\tau < T_m - T_g$, desired energy is lost while interference from the preceding symbol is included in the receive window. For both of these scenarios, the SNR loss can be approximated by

$$\Delta SNR(\tau) \approx -2 \left(\frac{\tau}{LT_s} \right)^2, \tag{3.16}$$

which makes intuitive sense given the above arguments, and has been shown more rigorously in the literature on synchronization for OFDM [37]. Important observations from this expression are that:

- SNR decreases quadratically with the timing offset.

- Longer OFDM symbols are increasingly immune from timing offset, that is, more subcarriers helps.

- Since in general $\tau \ll LT_s$, timing synchronization errors are not that critical as long as the induced phase change is corrected.

In summary, to minimize SNR loss due to imperfect timing synchronization, the timing errors should be kept small compared to the guard interval, and a small margin in the cyclic prefix length is helpful.

For LTE, the primary and secondary synchronization channels (PHY layer channels) are used for time and frequency synchronization. The primary and secondary sync signals occupy the 31 tones on either side of the DC subcarrier in the 5th and 6th OFDM symbols, respectively, of the 0th and 10th slots in every subframe. The five adjacent tones on "top" and "bottom" of the sync signals are not used, so 62 tones in all are used for this purpose, or a total of $62 \cdot 15\text{kHz} = 930\text{kHz}$. Current state-of-the-art phase lock loops can achieve a timing synchronization that is roughly $0.1B_s^{-1}$, where B_s is the amount of bandwidth used for synchronization, that is, $930\text{kHz} \approx 1\text{MHz}$. Thus, a timing synchronization offset of about $\tau \approx 0.1\,\mu\text{sec}$ can be considered typical, which is clearly far less than the cyclic prefix length of about $5\,\mu\text{sec}$.

3.4.2 Frequency Synchronization

OFDM achieves a high degree of bandwidth efficiency compared to other wideband systems. The subcarrier packing is extremely tight compared to conventional modulation techniques, which require a guard band on the order of 50% or more, in addition to special transmitter architectures such as the Weaver architecture or single-sideband modulation that suppress the redundant negative-frequency portion of the passband signal. The price to be paid for this bandwidth efficiency is that the multicarrier signal shown in Figure 3.8 is very sensitive to frequency offsets due to the fact that the subcarriers overlap, rather than having each subcarrier truly spectrally isolated.

Since the zero crossings of the frequency domain sinc pulses all line up as seen in Figure 3.8, as long as the frequency offset $\delta = 0$, there is no interference between the subcarriers. One intuitive interpretation for this is that since the FFT is essentially a frequency sampling operation, if the frequency offset is negligible the receiver simply samples **y** at the peak points of the sinc functions, where the ICI is zero from all the neighboring subcarriers.

In practice, of course, the frequency offset is not always zero. The major causes for this are mismatched oscillators at the transmitter and receiver and Doppler frequency shifts due to mobility. Since precise crystal oscillators are expensive, tolerating some degree of frequency offset is essential in a consumer OFDM system like LTE. For example, if an oscillator is accurate to 0.1 parts per million (ppm), $f_{\text{offset}} \approx (f_c)(0.1\text{ ppm})$. If $f_c = 3\text{GHz}$ and the Doppler is 100Hz, then $f_{\text{offset}} = 300+100\text{Hz}$, which will degrade the orthogonality of the received signal, since now the received samples of the FFT will contain interference from the adjacent subcarriers. We'll now analyze this inter-carrier interference (ICI) in order to better understand its effect on OFDM performance.

The matched filter receiver corresponding to subcarrier l can be simply expressed for the case of rectangular windows (neglecting the carrier frequency) as

$$x_l(t) = X_l e^{j\frac{2\pi l t}{LT_s}}, \tag{3.17}$$

where $1/LT_s = \Delta f$, and again LT_s is the duration of the data portion of the OFDM symbol, that is, $T = T_g + LT_s$. An interfering subcarrier m can be written as

$$x_{l+m}(t) = X_m e^{j\frac{2\pi(l+m)t}{LT_s}}. \tag{3.18}$$

If the signal is demodulated with a fractional frequency offset of δ, $|\delta| \leq \frac{1}{2}$

$$\hat{x}_{l+m}(t) = X_m e^{j\frac{2\pi(l+m+\delta)t}{LT_s}}. \tag{3.19}$$

The ICI between subcarriers l and $l+m$ using a matched filter (i.e., the FFT) is simply the inner product between them:

$$I_m = \int\limits_0^{LT_s} x_l(t)\hat{x}_{l+m}(t)dt = \frac{LT_sX_m\left(1 - e^{-j2\pi(\delta+m)}\right)}{j2\pi(m+\delta)}. \tag{3.20}$$

It can be seen that in the above expression, $\delta = 0 \Rightarrow I_m = 0$, and $m = 0 \Rightarrow I_m = 0$, as expected. The total average ICI energy per symbol on subcarrier l is then

$$ICI_l = E\left[\sum_{m\neq l}|I_m|^2\right] \approx C_0(LT_s\delta)^2\mathcal{E}_x, \tag{3.21}$$

where C_0 is a constant that depends on various assumptions and $\mathcal{E}_x$ is the average symbol energy [23,33]. The approximation sign is due to the fact that this expression assumes that there are an infinite number of interfering subcarriers. Since the interference falls off quickly with m, this assumption is very accurate for subcarriers near the middle of the band, and is pessimistic by a factor of 2 at either end of the band.

The SNR loss induced by frequency offset is given by

$$\Delta SNR = \frac{\mathcal{E}_x/N_o}{\mathcal{E}_x/\left(N_o + C_0(LT_s\delta)^2\mathcal{E}_x\right)} \tag{3.22}$$

$$= 1 + C_0(LT_s\delta)^2 SNR \tag{3.23}$$

Important observations from the ICI expression (3.23) and Figure 3.10 are that:

- SNR decreases quadratically with the frequency offset.

- SNR decreases quadratically with the number of subcarriers.

- The loss in SNR is also proportional to the SNR itself.

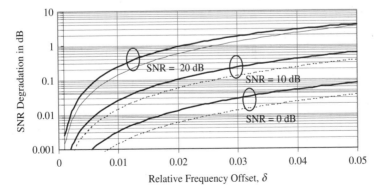

Figure 3.10 SNR loss as a function of the frequency offset δ, relative to the subcarrier spacing. The solid lines are for a fading channel and the dotted lines are for an AWGN channel.

- In order to keep the loss negligible, say less than 0.1 dB, the relative frequency offset needs to be about 1–2% of the subcarrier spacing, or even lower to preserve high SNRs.

- Therefore, this is a case where reducing the CP overhead by increasing the number of subcarriers causes an offsetting penalty, introducing a tradeoff.

In order to further reduce the ICI for a given choice of L, non-rectangular windows can also be used [27, 34].

3.5   The Peak-to-Average Ratio

OFDM signals have a higher peak-to-average ratio (PAR)—often called a peak-to-average power ratio (PAPR)—than do single-carrier signals. The reason for this is that in the time domain, a multicarrier signal is the sum of many narrowband signals. At some times, this sum is large; at other times it is small, which means that the peak value of the signal is substantially larger than the average value. This high PAR is one of the most important implementation challenges that face OFDM because it reduces the efficiency and hence increases the cost of the RF power amplifier, which is one of the most expensive components in the radio. Alternatively, the same power amplifier can be used but the input power to the PA must be reduced: this is known as input backoff (IBO) and results in a lower average SNR at the receiver, and hence a reduced transmit range. In this section, we will quantify the PAR problem, explain its severity in LTE, and briefly overview some strategies for reducing the PAR.

3.5.1   The PAR Problem

When a high-peak signal is transmitted through a nonlinear device such as a high-power amplifier (HPA) or digital-to-analog converter (DAC), it generates out-of-band energy (spectral regrowth) and in-band distortion (constellation tilting and scattering). These degradations may affect the system performance severely. The nonlinear behavior of HPA can be characterized by amplitude modulation/amplitude modulation (AM/AM) and amplitude modulation/phase modulation (AM/PM) responses. Figure 3.11 shows a typical AM/AM response for an HPA, with the associated input and output backoff regions: IBO and OBO, respectively.

To avoid the undesirable nonlinear effects just mentioned, a waveform with high-peak power must be transmitted in the linear region of the HPA by decreasing the average power of the input signal. This is called input *backoff* (IBO) and results in a proportional output backoff (OBO). High backoff reduces the power efficiency of the HPA, and may limit the battery life for mobile applications. In addition to inefficiency in terms of power, the coverage range is reduced and the cost of the HPA is higher than would be mandated by the average power requirements.

The input backoff is defined as

$$IBO = 10 \log_{10} \frac{P_{inSat}}{\bar{P}_{in}}, \tag{3.24}$$

where P_{inSat} is the saturation power (above which is the nonlinear region) and $\bar{P}_{in}$ is the average input power. The amount of backoff is usually greater than or equal to the PAR of the signal.

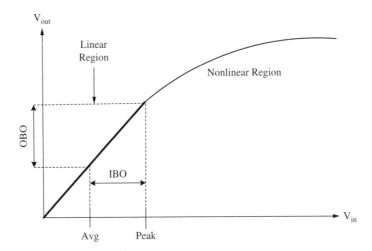

Figure 3.11 A typical power amplifier response. Operation in the linear region is required in order to avoid distortion, so the peak value must be constrained to be in this region, which means that on average, the power amplifier is underutilized by a "backoff" amount.

The power efficiency of an HPA can be increased by reducing the PAR of the transmitted signal. For example, the efficiency of a class A amplifier is halved when the input PAR is doubled or the operating point (average power) is halved [4, 11]. The theoretical efficiency limits for two classes of HPAs are shown in Figure 3.12. Clearly, it would be desirable to have the average and peak values be as close together as possible in order to maximize the efficiency of the power amplifier.

In addition to the large burden placed on the HPA, a high PAR requires high resolution for both the transmitter's digital-to-analog convertor (DAC) and the receiver's

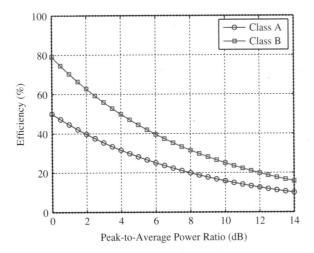

Figure 3.12 Theoretical efficiency limits of linear amplifiers [22]. A typical OFDM PAR is in the 10 dB range, so the PA efficiency is 50–75% lower than in a single-carrier system.

analog-to-digital convertor (ADC), since the dynamic range of the signal is proportional to the PAR. High-resolution D/A and A/D conversion places an additional complexity, cost, and power burden on the system.

3.5.2 Quantifying the PAR

Since multicarrier systems transmit data over a number of parallel frequency channels, the resulting waveform is the superposition of L narrowband signals. In particular, each of the L output samples from an L-point IFFT operation involves the sum of L complex numbers, as can be seen from (3.6). Due to the Central Limit Theorem, the resulting output values $\{x_1, x_2, \ldots, x_L\}$ can be accurately modelled (particularly for large L) as complex Gaussian random variables with zero mean and variance $\sigma^2 = \mathcal{E}_x/2$, that is, the real and imaginary parts both have zero mean and variance $\sigma^2 = \mathcal{E}_x/2$. The amplitude of the output signal is

$$|x[n]| = \sqrt{(\Re\{x[n]\})^2 + (\Im\{x[n]\})^2},$$ (3.25)

where $\Re$ and $\Im$ give the real and imaginary parts. Since $x[n]$ is complex Gaussian, just as for narrowband fading in Chapter 2, the envelope $|x[n]|$ is Rayleigh distributed with parameter σ^2. The output power is therefore

$$|x[n]|^2 = (\Re\{x[n]\})^2 + (\Im\{x[n]\})^2,$$ (3.26)

which is exponentially distributed with mean $2\sigma^2$. The important thing to note is that the output amplitude and hence power are *random*, so the PAR is not a deterministic quantity either.

The PAR of the transmitted analog signal can be defined as

$$PAR \triangleq \frac{\max_t |x(t)|^2}{E[|x(t)|^2]},$$ (3.27)

where naturally the range of time to be considered has to be bounded over some interval. Generally, the PAR is considered for a single OFDM symbol, which consists of $L + N_g$ samples, or a time duration of T, as this chapter has explained. Similarly, the discrete-time PAR can be defined for the IFFT output as

$$PAR \triangleq \frac{\max_{l \in (0, L+N_g)} |x_l|^2}{E[|x_l|^2]} = \frac{\mathcal{E}_{\max}}{\mathcal{E}_x}.$$ (3.28)

Although the average energy of IFFT outputs $x[n]$ is the same as the average energy of the inputs $X[m]$ and equal to $\mathcal{E}_x$, the analog PAR is not exactly the same as the PAR of the IFFT samples, due to the interpolation performed by the D/A convertor. Usually, the analog PAR is higher than the digital (Nyquist sampled) PAR. Since the PA is by definition analog, the analog PAR is what determines the PA performance. Similarly, DSP techniques developed to reduce the digital PAR may not always have the anticipated effect on the analog PAR, which is what matters. In order to bring the analog PAR expression in (3.27) and the digital PAR expression in (3.28) closer together, oversampling can be considered for the digital signal. That is, an oversampling factor of M can be used to interpolate the digital signal in order to better approximate its analog PAR, that is, a given OFDM symbol is sampled LM times rather than simply L.

The maximum possible value of the PAR is L or $10\log_{10} L$ dB, which would occur if all the subcarriers add up constructively at a single point. However, although it is theoretically possible to find an input sequence that results in this maximum PAR, such an upper bound for the PAR is misleading. For independent binary inputs, for example, the probability of this maximum peak value occurring is on the order of 2^{-L}.

Since the theoretical maximum PAR value seldom (in practice, never) occurs and the PAR is a random variable, statistical descriptions are used. The complementary cumulative distribution function (CCDF = 1 − CDF) of the PAR is the most commonly used measure. The CCDF is an intuitive measure as it gives the probability that the PAR is larger than a target value. For example, in Figure 3.13 for $L = 64$ subcarriers, the probability that the PAR is greater than 10 dB is about 0.005.

The distribution of the OFDM PAR has been studied by many researchers [2, 28, 29, 39]. Among these, van Nee and de Wild introduced a simple and accurate approximation of the CCDF for large $L(\geq 64)$:

$$\text{CCDF}(L, \mathcal{E}_{\max}) = 1 - F(L, \mathcal{E}_{\max})^{\beta L} = 1 - \left(1 - \exp\left(-\frac{\mathcal{E}_{\max}}{2\sigma^2}\right)\right)^{\beta L}, \qquad (3.29)$$

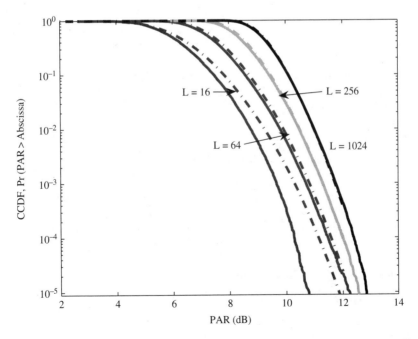

Figure 3.13 CCDF of PAR for QPSK OFDM system: $L = 16, 64, 256, 1024$. Solid line: simulation results, dotted line: approximation using $\beta = 2.8$.

where $\mathcal{E}_{\max}$ is the peak power level and β is a pseudo-approximation of the oversampling factor, which is given empirically as $\beta = 2.8$ [39]. Note that the PAR is $\mathcal{E}_{\max}/2\sigma^2$ and $F(L, \mathcal{E}_{\max})$ is the CDF of a single Rayleigh distributed subcarrier with parameter σ^2. The basic idea behind this approximation is that unlike a Nyquist[8] sampled signal, the samples of an oversampled OFDM signal are correlated, making it hard to derive an exact peak distribution. The CDF of the Nyquist sampled signal power can be obtained by

$$G(L, \mathcal{E}_{\max}) = P(\max \|\mathbf{x}(t)\| \leq \mathcal{E}_{\max}) = F(L, \mathcal{E}_{\max})^L, \qquad (3.30)$$

Using this result as a baseline, the oversampled case can be approximated heuristically by regarding the oversampled signal as generated by βL Nyquist sampled subcarriers. Note however that β is not equal to the oversampling factor M. This simple expression is quite effective for generating accurate PAR statistics for various scenarios, and sample results are displayed in Figure 3.13. As expected, the approximation is accurate for large L and the PAR of OFDM systems increases with L but not nearly linearly.

The Cubic Metric

Although the PAR gives a reasonable estimate of the amount of PA backoff required, it is not precise. That is, backing off on the output power by 3 dB may not reduce the effects of nonlinear distortion by 3 dB. Similarly, the penalty associated with the PAR does not necessarily follow a dB-for-dB relationship. A typical PA gain can be reasonably modelled as

$$v_{out}(t) = c_1 v_{in}(t) + c_2 (v_{in}(t))^3, \qquad (3.31)$$

where c_1 and c_2 are amplifier-dependent constants. The cubic term in the above equation causes several types of distortion, including both in and out of band distortion. Therefore, in [25] Motorola proposed a "Cubic Metric" for estimating the amount of amplifier backoff that is actually needed in order to reduce the distortion affects by a prescribed amount. The cubic metric (CM) is defined as

$$CM = \frac{20 \log_{10} [\bar{v}^3]_{\mathrm{rms}} - 20 \log_{10} [\bar{v}^3_{\mathrm{ref}}]_{\mathrm{rms}}}{c_3} \qquad (3.32)$$

where $\bar{v}$ is the signal of interest normalized to have an RMS value of 1, and $\bar{v}_{\mathrm{ref}}$ is a low-PAR reference signal (usually a simple BPSK voice signal), also normalized to have an RMS value of 1. The constant c_3 is found empirically through curve fitting; it was found that $c_3 \approx 1.85$ in [25].

The advantage of the cubic metric is that initial studies show that it very accurately predicts—usually within 0.1 dB—the amount of backoff required by the PA in order to meet distortion constraints.

---

8 Nyquist sampling means the minimum allowable sampling frequency without irreversible information loss, that is, no oversampling is performed.

3.5.3 Clipping and Other PAR Reduction Techniques

In order to avoid operating the PA in the nonlinear region, the input power can be reduced up to an amount about equal to the PAR. This, of course, is very inefficient and will reduce the range and/or SINR of the system by the same amount. However, two important facts related to this IBO amount can be observed from Figure 3.13. First, since the highest PAR values are uncommon, it might be possible to simply "clip" off the highest peaks, at the cost of some hopefully minimal distortion of the signal. Second and conversely, it can be seen that even for a conservative choice of IBO, say 10 dB, there is still a distinct possibility that a given OFDM symbol will have a PAR that exceeds the IBO and causes clipping.

Clipping, sometimes called "soft limiting," truncates the amplitude of signals that exceed the clipping level as

$$\tilde{x}[n] = \begin{cases} Ae^{j\angle x[n]}, & \text{if } |x[n]| > A \\ x[n], & \text{if } |x[n]| \le A, \end{cases} \tag{3.33}$$

where $x[n]$ is the original signal, $\tilde{x}[n]$ is the output after clipping, and A is the *clipping level*, that is, the maximum output envelope value. The clipping ratio can be used as a metric and is defined as

$$\gamma \triangleq \frac{A}{\sqrt{E\{|x[n]|^2\}}} = \frac{A}{\sqrt{\mathcal{E}_x}} \tag{3.34}$$

Obviously, clipping reduces the PAR at the expense of distorting the desired signal. The two primary drawbacks from clipping are (1) spectral regrowth (frequency domain leakage), which causes unacceptable interference to users in neighboring RF channels, and (2) distortion of the desired signal.

Spectral Regrowth The clipping noise can be expressed in the frequency domain through the use of the DFT. The resulting clipped frequency domain signal $\tilde{X}$ is

$$\tilde{X}_k = X_k + C_k, \quad k = 0, \dots, L-1, \tag{3.35}$$

where C_k represents the clipped off signal in the frequency domain. In Figure 3.14, the power spectral density of the original (X), clipped $(\tilde{X})$, and clipped-off (C) signals are plotted for different clipping ratios γ of 3, 5, and 7 dB. The following deleterious effects are observed. First, the clipped-off signal C_k is strikingly increased as the clipping ratio is lowered from 7 dB to 3 dB. This increase shows the correlation between X_k and C_k inside the desired band at low clipping ratios, and causes the in-band signal to be attenuated as the clipping ratio is lowered. Second, it can be seen that the out-of-band interference caused by the clipped signal $\tilde{X}$ is determined by the shape of clipped-off signal C_k. For example, even the seemingly conservative clipping ratio of 7 dB still violates the specification of a typical transmit spectral mask (specifically, of IEEE 802.16e-2005), albeit not by much.

In-band Distortion Although the desired signal and the clipping signal are clearly correlated, it is possible based on the Bussgang Theorem to model the in-band distortion due to the clipping process as the combination of uncorrelated additive noise and an

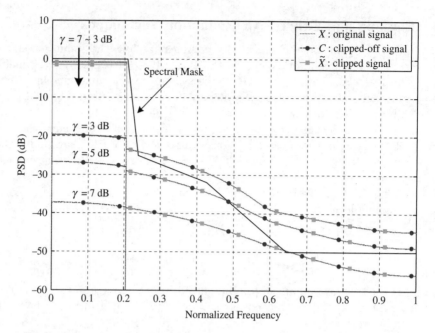

Figure 3.14 Power spectral density (PSD) of the unclipped (original) and clipped (nonlinearly distorted) OFDM signals with 2048 block size and 64 QAM when clipping ratio (γ) is 3, 5, and 7 dB in soft limiter.

attenuation of the desired signal [12, 14, 30]:

$$\tilde{x}[n] = \alpha x[n] + d[n], \quad \text{for } n = 0, 1, \ldots, L - 1. \tag{3.36}$$

Now, $d[n]$ is uncorrelated with the signal $x[n]$ and the attenuation factor α is obtained by

$$\alpha = 1 - e^{-\gamma^2} + \frac{\sqrt{\pi}\gamma}{2}\text{erfc}(\gamma). \tag{3.37}$$

The attenuation factor α is plotted in Figure 3.15 as a function of the clipping ratio γ. The attenuation factor α is negligible when the clipping ratio γ is greater than 8 dB, so for high clipping ratios, the correlated time-domain clipped-off signal $c[n]$ can be approximated by uncorrelated noise $d[n]$. That is, $c[n] \approx d[n]$ as $\gamma \uparrow$. The variance of the uncorrelated clipping noise can be expressed assuming a stationary Gaussian input $x[n]$ as

$$\sigma_d^2 = \mathcal{E}_x(1 - \exp(-\gamma^2) - \alpha^2). \tag{3.38}$$

It is possible to define the signal-to-noise-plus-distortion ratio (SNDR) of one OFDM symbol in order to estimate the impact of clipped OFDM signals over an AWGN channel under the assumption that the distortion $d[n]$ is Gaussian and uncorrelated with the

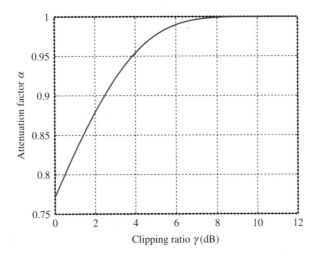

Figure 3.15 Attenuation factor α as a function of the clipping ratio γ.

input and channel noise (that has variance $N_0/2$):

$$\text{SNDR} = \frac{\alpha^2 \mathcal{E}_x}{\sigma_d^2 + N_0/2}. \tag{3.39}$$

The bit-error probability (BEP) can be evaluated for different modulation types using the SNDR [12]. In the case of M-QAM and average power $\mathcal{E}_x$, the BEP can then be approximated as

$$P_b \approx \frac{4}{\log_2 M} \left(1 - \frac{1}{\sqrt{M}} \right) Q \left(\sqrt{ \frac{3 \mathcal{E}_x \alpha^2}{(\sigma_d^2 + N_0/2)(M - 1)} } \right). \tag{3.40}$$

Figure 3.16 shows the BER for an OFDM system with L = 2048 subcarriers and 64-QAM modulation. As the SNR increases, the clipping error dominates the additive noise and an error floor is observed. The error floor can be inferred from (3.40) by letting the noise variance $N_0/2 \to 0$.

A number of additional studies of clipping in OFDM systems have been completed in recent years, for example, [2,3,12,28,35]. In some cases clipping may be acceptable, but in LTE systems the margin for error is quite tight, as much of this book has emphasized. Other techniques for reducing the PAR (or cubic metric) are peak cancellation or signal mapping [20,26,32], iterative clipping and filtering [1,6], tone reservation [16,38], and active constellation extension (ACE) [21]. A useful overview of many of these techniques can be found in [18].

3.5.4   LTE's Approach to PAR in the Uplink

LTE has taken a pioneering new approach to PAR. In the downlink, PAR is less important because the base stations are fewer in number and generally higher in cost, and so are

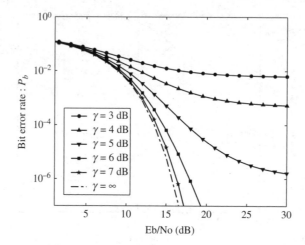

Figure 3.16 Bit error rate probability for a clipped OFDM signal in AWGN with different clipping ratios.

not especially sensitive to the exact PAR. If the PAR is still considered to be too high, a number of techniques can be utilized to bring it down, all with some complexity and performance tradeoffs [18, 38]. Typically, the high PAR is basically tolerated and sufficient input power backoff is undertaken in order to keep the in-band distortion and spectral regrowth at an acceptable level.

For the uplink, the mobiles are many in number and are very sensitive to cost. So, a technique known as single-carrier frequency division multiple access (SC-FDMA) is used. SC-FDMA will be discussed in Chapter 4, and it is a multiple access adaption of single-carrier frequency domain equalization (SC-FDE), which is discussed in the next section.

3.6   Single-Carrier Frequency Domain Equalization (SC-FDE)

An alternative approach to OFDM is the less popular but conceptually similar single-carrier frequency domain equalization (SC-FDE) approach to ISI suppression [13, 36]. SC-FDE maintains OFDM's three most important benefits: (1) low complexity even for severe multipath channels (see Section 3.7); (2) excellent BER performance, close to theoretical bounds; and (3) a decoupling of ISI from other types of interference, notably spatial interference, which is very useful when using multiple antenna transmission. By utilizing single-carrier transmission, the peak-to-average ratio is also reduced significantly (by several dB) relative to multicarrier modulation.

3.6.1   SC-FDE System Description

Frequency domain equalization is used in both OFDM and SC-FDE systems primarily in order to reduce the complexity inherent to time-domain equalization, as discussed in Section 3.7. The block diagrams for OFDM and SC-FDE are compared in Figure 3.17, in which we can see that the only apparent difference between the two systems is that the

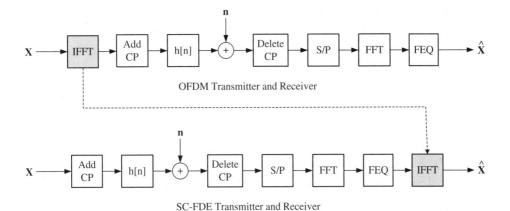

Figure 3.17 Comparison between an OFDM system and an SC-FDE system. The principle difference is that the IFFT formerly in the transmitter is in the SC-FDE receiver.

IFFT is moved to the end of the receive chain rather than operating at the transmitter, to create a multicarrier waveform as in OFDM.

An SC-FDE system still utilizes a cyclic prefix at least as long as the channel delay spread, but now the transmitted signal is simply a sequence of QAM symbols, which have low PAR, on the order of 4–5 dB depending on the constellation size. Considering that an unmodulated sine wave has a PAR of 3 dB, it is clear that the PAR cannot be lowered much below that of an SC-FDE system.

The action, in an SC-FDE system, is at the receiver. As in an OFDM system, an FFT is applied, but in an SC-FDE system this operation moves the received signal into the frequency domain. Because of the application of the cyclic prefix, the received signal appears to be circularly convolved, that is, $y[n] = x[n] \circledast h[n] + w[n]$, where $w[n]$ is noise. Therefore,

$$\text{FFT}\{y[n]\} \triangleq Y[m] = H[m]X[m] + W[m]$$

just as in OFDM, with the important distinction being that now the frequency domain version $X[m]$ is not precisely the data symbols, but rather the FFT of the data symbols $x[n]$. Analogously, recall that in an OFDM system the transmitted time-domain signal $x[n]$ was not the actual data symbols, but rather the IFFT of the actual data symbols.

After the FFT, a simple 1-tap FEQ can be applied that inverts each virtual subcarrier, so that

$$\hat{X}[m] = \frac{Y[m]}{H[m]}.$$

The resulting signal can then be converted back into the time domain using an IFFT operation to give $\hat{x}[n]$, which are estimates of the desired data symbols. Naturally, in practice $H[m]$ must be estimated at the receiver using pilot signals or other standard methods.

3.6.2   SC-FDE Performance vs. OFDM

The primary difference in terms of performance between SC-FDE and OFDM comes from the way they treat noise. In both OFDM and SC-FDE receivers, the FEQ typically inverts each frequency bin, that is, the FEQ consists of L complex taps each of value $1/H_l$. As noted earlier for OFDM in Section 3.2.4, this does *not* result in damaging noise enhancement since the SNR of each data symbol is unchanged by multiplying by a constant factor. High SNR symbols remain at high SNR, and low SNR symbols remain at low SNR. The discrepancies between the SNR on each carrier can be handled by either per-subcarrier adaptive modulation or coding and interleaving. In LTE, short-scale variations in SNR would generally be addressed by coding and interleaving, which would allow a considerable number of degraded (low-SNR) symbols to be corrected.

In SC-FDE, however, the FEQ does not operate on data symbols themselves but rather on the frequency domain dual of the data symbols. Therefore, just as in OFDM's FEQ, low SNR parts of the spectrum have their power increased by a factor of $|1/H_l|^2$ while the noise power is increased by a factor of $|1/H_l^2|$. Unlike in OFDM, however, in SC-FDE when the ensuing IFFT is applied to move the signal back into the time domain for detection, the amplified noise is spread by the IFFT operation over all the data symbols. Therefore, although the total noise amplification is the same in OFDM and SC-FDE, the noise amplification is not isolated to a single symbol in SC-FDE, but instead affects all the symbols prior to decoding and detection.

Although this sounds daunting for SC-FDE, in fact the performance difference is often insignificant between SC-FDE and OFDM. In some cases OFDM slightly outperforms SC-FDE, while in others SC-FDE does a little better [13]. The primary determinants of this are the strength of the coding and the size of the constellation. OFDM does a bit better when the coding is strong and/or the constellation is large, while the opposite is true for SC-FDE. This makes intuitive sense: Higher-order constellations are more sensitive to even modest amounts of noise, which hurts SC-FDE since it subjects all its symbols to amplified noise. And strong coding helps OFDM because a few very low SNR symbols can usually be more readily corrected through a Trellis-style decoder (such as that used for Viterbi decoding) than a larger number of fairly low SNR symbols.

In most cases, the BER vs. SNR performance differences are negligible, and other factors like the reduced PA backoff of SC-FDE or the symmetric complexity of OFDM are likely to be more important factors in selecting which approach to use.

3.6.3   Design Considerations for SC-FDE and OFDM

Since the performance difference between SC-FDE and OFDM is not that significant, other considerations are more important in determining which is the appropriate method to use for a given application. An obvious difference is that SC-FDE has a lower-complexity transmitter but a higher-complexity receiver, compared to OFDM. Since the receiver was already considerably more complex than the transmitter in a typical OFDM system due to channel estimation, synchronization, and the error correction decoder, this further skews the asymmetry.

In a cellular system like LTE, this asymmetry can in fact be a favorable feature, since the uplink could utilize SC-FDE and the downlink could utilize OFDM. In such a situation, the base station would therefore perform 3 IFFT/FFT operations and the mobile, which is more power- and cost-sensitive, would perform only a single FFT operation (to receive its OFDM waveform from the base station). Adding in SC-FDE's benefits of reduced PAR and the commensurate cost and power savings, it appears that the case for using SC-FDE in the uplink of a wideband data system is favorable indeed.

Channel estimation and synchronization are a bit different in practice for an SC-FDE system vs. an OFDM system. In a typical wireless OFDM system—including LTE, WiMAX, and 802.11a/g/n—channel estimation and synchronization are accomplished via a preamble of known data symbols, and then pilot tones, which are inserted at known positions in all subsequent OFDM symbols. Although SC-FDE systems would typically also include a preamble, this preamble is in the time domain so it is not as straightforward to estimate the frequency domain values H_l. Similarly, it is not possible to insert pilot tones on a per-frame basis. As we will see, however, in Chapter 4, SC-FDMA overcomes these potential problems for LTE by using both a DFT and an IFFT at the transmitter.

Another commonly cited disadvantage of SC-FDE is that it has a nominally more dispersive spectrum compared to OFDM. OFDM's sharper spectrum results in less co-channel interference and/or less restrictive RF roll-off requirements. On the other hand, because OFDM has a higher PAR, it is more subject to clipping that can cause spectral dispersion as discussed in Section 3.5.3. Finally, the combination of SC-FDE with MIMO is not as natural because detection cannot be done in the frequency domain. Hence, it is not possible to use maximum likelihood detection for MIMO with SC-FDE; suboptimal linear detectors (such as MMSE) or interference cancellation approaches must instead be adopted.

On the whole, OFDM continues to be much more popular than SC-FDE, but the fundamental technical arguments for this imbalance are not very clear. Instead, it is reasonable to posit that the longevity and familiarity with OFDM are bigger factors. In that sense, LTE has broken the mold slightly by using an uplink transmission technique inspired by SC-FDE, as will be seen in the next chapter.

3.7 The Computational Complexity Advantage of OFDM and SC-FDE

One of the principal advantages of frequency domain equalization relative to time domain equalization is that FDE—whether in OFDM or SC-FDE systems—requires much lower computational complexity, especially for high data rates. In this section, we compare the computational complexity of an equalizer with that of a standard IFFT/FFT implementation of OFDM.

A time-domain equalizer consists of a series of multiplications with several delayed versions of the signal. The number of delay taps in an equalizer depends on the symbol rate of the system and the delay spread in the channel. To be more precise, the number of equalizer taps is proportional to the bandwidth-delay spread product $T_m/T_s \approx BT_m$. We have been calling this quantity v, or the number of ISI channel taps. An equalizer with

v taps performs v complex multiply and accumulate (CMAC) operations per received symbol. Therefore, the complexity of an equalizer is of the order

$$O(v \cdot B) = O(B^2 T_m). \tag{3.41}$$

In an OFDM or SC-FDE system, the IFFT and FFT are the principal computational operations. It is well known that the IFFT and FFT each have a complexity of $O(L \log_2 L)$, where L is the FFT block size. In the case of OFDM, L is the number of subcarriers. As this chapter has shown, for a fixed cyclic prefix overhead, the number of subcarriers L must grow linearly with the bandwidth-delay spread product $v = BT_m$. Therefore, the computational complexity for each OFDM symbol (or SC-FDE block) is of the order $O(BT_m \log_2 BT_m)$. There are B/L OFDM symbols sent each second. Since $L \propto BT_m$, this means there are order $O(1/T_m)$ OFDM symbols per second, so the computational complexity in terms of CMACs for OFDM is

$$O(BT_m \log_2 BT_m)O(1/T_m) = O(B \log_2 BT_m). \tag{3.42}$$

The complexity of a time-domain equalizer grows as the square of the data rate since both the symbol rate and the number of taps increases linearly with the data rate. For an OFDM or SC-FDE system, the increase in complexity grows with the data rate only slightly faster than linearly. This difference is dramatic for very large data rates, as shown in Figure 3.18. It should be noted, however, that LTE uses SC-FDMA, which is not precisely the same as SC-FDE. The complexity of SC-FDMA still scales as $O(B \log_2 BT_m)$, but there are twice as many FFT/IFFT operations as there are in SC-FDE.

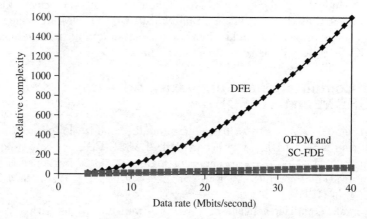

Figure 3.18 OFDM and SC-FDE have an enormous complexity advantage over equalization for broadband data rates. The delay spread is $T_m = 2\mu$sec, the OFDM symbol period is $T = 20\mu$sec, 16 QAM (4 bps/Hz) is used, and the considered time-domain equalizer is a DFE.

A Brief History of OFDM

Although OFDM has become widely used only recently, the concept dates back some 40 years. In order to provide context for the reader, we give a brief history of some landmark dates in OFDM.

1958: The "Kineplex" system was developed, which was a multicarrier modem for the HF bands (3 to 30MHz) [24]. This is widely considered the first ever multicarrier system—it actually used multiple HF radios as the FFT was not re-discovered[9] until 1954 [10].

1966: Chang shows in the Bell Labs technical journal that multicarrier modulation can solve the multipath problem without reducing data rate [5]. This is generally considered the first theoretical publication on multicarrier modulation, although there were naturally precursory studies, including Holsinger's 1964 MIT dissertation [19] and some of Gallager's early work on waterfilling [15].

1971: Weinstein and Ebert show that multicarrier modulation can be accomplished using a "Discrete Fourier Transform" (DFT) [40].

1985: Cimini at Bell Labs identifies many of the key issues in OFDM transmission and does a proof of concept design [7].

1993: DSL adopts OFDM, also called "Discrete Multitone," following successful field trials/competitions at Bellcore vs. equalizer-based systems.

1999: IEEE 802.11 committee on wireless LANs releases 802.11a standard for OFDM operation in 5GHz UNI band.

2002: IEEE 802.16 committee releases OFDM-based standard for wireless broadband access for metropolitan area networks under revision 802.16a.

2003: IEEE 802.11 committee releases 802.11g standard for operation in the 2.4GHz band.

2003: The "multiband OFDM" standard for ultrawideband is developed, showing OFDM's usefulness in low-SNR systems.

2005: 802.16e standard is ratified, supporting mobile OFDMA for WiMAX.

2006: First commercial LTE demonstrations by Siemens (now Nokia Siemens Networks).

2008: Qualcomm, the primary backer of Ultramobile Broadband (UMB), the main future competition to LTE and WiMAX and also OFDM/OFDMA-based, announces it will end UMB development and transition to LTE, solidifying LTE as the leading beyond 3G cellular standard.

2009: 3GPP Release 8 LTE/SAE specifications completed and released.

2009: 802.11n standard is ratified, which performs MIMO-OFDM for wireless LANs for peak data rates of 600 Mbps.

---

9 It turns out that the legendary mathematician C. F. Gauss knew of the FFT as early as 1805—but didn't publish it.

3.8   Chapter Summary

This chapter has covered the theory of multicarrier modulation, as well as the important design- and implementation-related issues. The following were the key points:

- OFDM overcomes even severe inter-symbol interference through the use of the IFFT and a cyclic prefix.

- OFDM is the core modulation strategy used in the LTE downlink. Its multiple-access version OFDMA is the subject of Chapter 4.

- Single-carrier frequency domain equalization, which is closely related to OFDM, is the core modulation strategy used in the LTE uplink. Its multiple access version SC-FDMA is described in Chapter 4.

- Key details on OFDM implementation, such as synchronization and managing the peak-to-average ratio, were covered in depth.

Bibliography

[1] Armstrong, J. Peak-to-average power reduction for OFDM by repeated clipping and frequency domain filtering. *Electronics Letters*, 38(8):246–247, Feb. 2002.

[2] Bahai, A., M. Singh, A. Goldsmith, and B. Saltzberg. A new approach for evaluating clipping distortion in multicarrier systems. *IEEE Journal on Selected Areas in Communications*, 20(5):1037–1046, 2002.

[3] Banelli, P., and S. Cacopardi. Theoretical analysis and performance of OFDM signals in nonlinear AWGN channels. *IEEE Trans. on Communications*, 48(3):430–441, Mar. 2000.

[4] Baxley, R., and G. Zhou. Power savings analysis of peak-to-average power ratio in OFDM. *IEEE Transactions on Consumer Electronics*, 50(3):792–798, 2004.

[5] Chang, R. W. Synthesis of band-limited orthogonal signals for multichannel data transmission. *Bell Systems Technical Journal*, 45:1775–1796, Dec. 1966.

[6] Chen, H. and A. Haimovich. Iterative estimation and cancellation of clipping noise for OFDM signals. *IEEE Communications Letters*, 7(7):305–307, July 2003.

[7] Cimini, L. J. Analysis and simulation of a digital mobile channel using orthogonal frequency division multiplexing. *IEEE Trans. on Communications*, 33(7):665–675, July 1985.

[8] Cioffi, J. M. *Digital Communications, Chapter 4: Multichannel Modulation*. Unpublished course notes, available at www.stanford.edu/class/ee379c/.

[9] Cioffi, J. M. A multicarrier primer. Stanford University/Amati T1E1 contribution, I1E1.4/91-157, Nov. 1991.

[10] Cooley, J. W. and J. W. Tukey. An algorithm for the machine calculation of complex Fourier series. *Mathematics of Computation*, pages 297–301, Apr. 1965.

[11] Cripps, S. C. *RF Power Amplifiers for Wireless Communications*. Norwood, MA: Artech House, 1999.

[12] Dardari, D., V. Tralli, and A. Vaccari. A theoretical characterization of nonlinear distortion effects in OFDM systems. *IEEE Trans. on Communications*, 48(10):1755–1764, Oct. 2000.

[13] Falconer, D., S. L. Ariyavisitakul, A. Benyamin-Seeyar, and B. Eidson. Frequency domain equalization for single-carrier broadband wireless systems. *IEEE Communications Magazine*, pages 58–66, Apr. 2002.

[14] Friese, M. On the degradation of OFDM-signals due to peak-clipping in optimally predistorted power amplifiers. In *Proc., IEEE Globecom*, pages 939–944, Nov. 1998.

[15] Gallager, R. G. *Information Theory and Reliable Communications*. Wiley, 1968.

[16] Gatherer, A. and M. Polley. Controlling clipping probability in DMT transmission. In *Proceedings of the Asilomar Conference on Signals, Systems and Computers*, pages 578–584, Nov. 1997.

[17] Goldsmith, A. J. *Wireless Communications*. Cambridge University Press, 2005.

[18] Han, S. H. and J. H. Lee. An overview of peak-to-average power ratio reduction techniques for multicarrier transmission. *IEEE Wireless Communications*, 12(2):56–65, 2005.

[19] Holsinger, J. L. *Digital communication over fixed time-continuous channels with memory, with special application to telephone channels*. PhD thesis, Massachusetts Institute of Technology, 1964.

[20] Jones, A. E., T. A. Wilkinson, and S. K. Barton. Block coding scheme for reduction of peak to mean envelope power ratio of multicarrier transmission schemes. *Electronics Letters*, 30(25):2098–2099, Dec. 1994.

[21] Krongold, B. and D. Jones. PAR reduction in OFDM via active constellation extension. *IEEE Transactions on Broadcasting*, 49(3):258–268, 2003.

[22] Miller, S. and R. O'Dea. Peak power and bandwidth efficient linear modulation. *IEEE Trans. on Communications*, 46(12):1639–1648, Dec. 1998.

[23] Moose, P. A technique for orthogonal frequency division multiplexing frequency offset correction. *IEEE Trans. on Communications*, 42(10):2908–2914, Oct. 1994.

[24] Mosier, R. R. and R. G. Clabaugh. Kineplex, a bandwidth efficient binary transmission system. *AIEE Trans.*, 76:723–728, Jan. 1958.

[25] Motorola. Comparison of PAR and cubic metric for power de-rating. TSG-RAN WG1#37 Meeting, Montreal, Canada, Doc # R1-040522, May 2004.

[26] Müller, S. and J. Huber. A comparison of peak power reduction schemes for OFDM. In *Proc., IEEE Globecom*, pages 1–5, Nov. 1997.

[27] Muschallik, C. Improving an OFDM reception using an adaptive nyquist windowing. *IEEE Trans. Consumer Electron.*, 42(3):259–269, Aug. 1996.

[28] Nikopour, H. and S. Jamali. On the performance of OFDM systems over a Cartesian clipping channel: a theoretical approach. *IEEE Transactions on Wireless Communications*, 3(6):2083–2096, 2004.

[29] Ochiai, H. and H. Imai. On the distribution of the peak-to-average power ratio in OFDM signals. *IEEE Transactions on Communications*, 49(2):282–289, 2001.

[30] Ochiai, H. and H. Imai. Performance analysis of deliberately clipped OFDM signals. *IEEE Trans. on Communications*, 50(1):89–101, Jan. 2002.

[31] Oppenheim, A. V. and R. W. Schafer. *Discrete-Time Signal Processing*. Englewood Cliffs, NJ: Prentice-Hall, 1989.

[32] Paterson, K. G. and V. Tarokh. On the existence and construction of good codes with low peak-to-average power ratios. *IEEE Trans. on Info. Theory*, 46(6):1974–1987, Sept. 2000.

[33] Pollet, T., M. V. Bladel, and M. Moeneclaey. BER sensitivity of OFDM systems to carrier frequency offset and Wiener phase noise. *IEEE Trans. on Communications*, 43(234):191–193, Feb/Mar/Apr 1995.

[34] Redfern, A. Receiver window design for multicarrier communication systems. *IEEE Journal on Sel. Areas in Communications*, 20(5):1029–1036, June 2002.

[35] Santella, G. and F. Mazzenga. A hybrid analytical-simulation procedure for performance evaluation in M-QAM-OFDM schemes in presence of nonlinear distortions. *IEEE Trans. on Veh. Technology*, 47(1):142–151, Feb. 1998.

[36] Sari, H., G. Karam, and I. Jeanclaude. Frequency domain equalization of mobile radio and terrestrial broadcast channels. In *Proc., IEEE Globecom*, pages 1–5, San Francisco, CA, Dec. 1994.

[37] Schmidl, T. M. and D. C. Cox. Robust frequency and timing synchronization for OFDM. *IEEE Trans. on Communications*, 45(12):1613–1621, Dec. 1997.

[38] Tellado, J. *Multicarrier Modulation with Low PAR: Applications to DSL and Wireless*. Boston: Kluwer Academic Publishers, 2000.

[39] Van Nee, R. and A. de Wild. Reducing the peak-to-average power ratio of OFDM. In *Vehicular Technology Conference, 1998. VTC 98. 48th IEEE*, 3:2072–2076, 1998.

[40] Weinstein, S. and P. Ebert. Data transmission by frequency-division multiplexing using the Discrete Fourier Transform. *IEEE Trans. on Communications*, 19(5):628–634, Oct. 1971.

Chapter 4

Frequency Domain Multiple Access: OFDMA and SC-FDMA

T he multiple access strategy is perhaps the defining choice of a cellular communication system. Previous generations of cellular systems have been popularly referred to simply as "FDMA"—First Generation (1G), notably AMPS—followed by "TDMA"—2G GSM or IS-54—and then "CDMA" for 2G IS-95 (Qualcomm) and 3G WCDMA.[1] LTE evolved from the 3G W-CDMA standards body but does not use CDMA. Rather, LTE employs two different multiple access approaches, both of which are effectively hybrids of TDMA and FDMA adapted to multicarrier modulation. In the downlink LTE utilizes Orthogonal Frequency Division Multiple Access (OFDMA), while in the uplink Single-Carrier Frequency Division Multiple Access (SC-FDMA) is preferred. Conceptually and practically, these approaches are very similar, and both allocate each subscriber some portion of the subcarriers (or frequency channel) for some duration of time.

Because LTE traffic is expected to be very diverse—including VoIP, video streaming, and broadband data sessions—the multiple access scheme needs to be highly flexible and efficient. It must be flexible enough to support many low-rate continuous voice streams, while also providing very high data rates over very short time periods to broadband data users. Simultaneously handling these two very different types of traffic efficiently poses major challenges for the design of the protocol, since sessions must be set up and taken down quickly for bursty data, while maintaining reliable ongoing service for voice users.

This chapter explains OFDMA and SC-FDMA in the following steps:

1. Multiple access techniques are overviewed with special attention to their interaction with OFDM modulation.

2. OFDMA and SC-FDMA are described, and their particular features and tradeoffs are discussed.

---

1 It should be noted that nearly all commercial wireless systems inherently use FDMA since they use only a portion of the frequency spectrum. Therefore, TDMA, CDMA, and OFDMA all include a higher-level FDMA as well to separate out the band of interest.

3. A key potential source of performance gain for OFDMA and SC-FDMA is multiuser diversity harnessed through adaptive scheduling of users (and adaptive modulation per user). We describe several possible approaches to resource allocation, and weigh their tradeoffs.

4. OFDMA and SC-FDMA's implementation in LTE is briefly overviewed, along with challenges and opportunities to make them perform better.

4.1 Multiple Access for OFDM Systems

OFDM is not a multiple-access strategy, but rather a technique for mitigating frequency selectivity (inter-symbol interference). OFDM does, however, create many parallel streams of data that can in principle be used by different users. Most previous OFDM systems such as DSL, 802.11a/g, and earlier 802.16/WiMAX systems (prior to the 802.16e standard) have used what can be called "single-user OFDM" or often simply "OFDM"— all the subcarriers are used by a single user at a time. For example, in 802.11a/g WiFi sytems, nearby users share the 20MHz bandwidth by transmitting at different times after contending for the channel. Naturally, in these "single-user OFDM" systems multiple users can be (and often are) accommodated by simply time-sharing the channel. As we will see over the next few pages, such an approach would not be effective for LTE, and a more sophisticated multiple-access scheme is required.

Note that although we will focus the discussion on OFDM and OFDMA, nearly all the concepts are equivalent for SC-FDMA, which we describe in detail in Section 4.3. When necessary, we will point out when statements apply only to OFDMA or SC-FDMA but not both.

4.1.1 Multiple Access Overview

Multiple-access strategies typically attempt to provide *orthogonal*, that is, non-interfering, communication channels for each active base station–subscriber link. The most common ways to divide the available dimensions among the multiple users is through the use of frequency, time, or code division multiplexing. In Frequency Division Multiple Access (FDMA), each user receives a unique carrier frequency and bandwidth. In Time Division Multiple Access (TDMA), each user is given a unique time slot, either on demand or in a fixed rotation. Wireless TDMA systems almost invariably also use FDMA in some form, since using the entire electromagnetic spectrum is not allowable. Orthogonal Code Division Multiple Access (CDMA) systems allow each user to share the bandwidth and time slots with many other users, and rely on orthogonal or nearly orthogonal binary codes to separate out the users. More generally, in all CDMA systems (including the popular non-orthogonal ones) many users share the available time and frequency dimensions.

It can be easily proven that TDMA, FDMA, and orthogonal CDMA all have the same theoretical capacity in an additive noise channel [16, 26], since they all can be designed to have the same number of orthogonal dimensions in a given bandwidth and amount of time.[2] For example, assume it takes one unit of bandwidth to send a user's signal,

---

2 It may be complicated to find orthogonal codes for divisions that are not factors of two. Nevertheless, they are provably the same in their efficiency.

and eight units of bandwidth are available. Eight users can be accommodated with each technique. In FDMA, eight orthogonal frequency slots would be created, one for each user. In TDMA, each user would use all eight frequency slots, but only transmit one-eighth of the time. In CDMA, each user would transmit all of the time over all of the frequencies, but would use one of eight available orthogonal codes to ensure that there was no interference with the other seven users.

So why all the debate over multiple access? One reason is that orthogonality is not possible in dense wireless systems. The above techniques only guarantee orthogonality between users in the *same* cell, whereas users in *different*, potentially neighboring cells will likely be given the same time or frequency slot. Secondly, different multiple access techniques have different delay characteristics and so may be appropriate for different types of data. In the FDMA-TDMA example above with eight slots, it can be seen that TDMA data would arrive in periodic short bursts with high rate, whereas FDMA traffic would arrive continuously at a slower, smooth rate. Perhaps most importantly, each technique has a number of positives and negatives, and different systems will have different sensitivities to the various pros and cons. One of the principle merits of OFDMA is that by adjusting how subcarriers are allocated in time and frequency, many of the desirable features of both FDMA and TDMA can be achieved, while the negatives can be mitigated.

4.1.2 Random Access vs. Multiple Access

Before describing in more detail how TDMA, FDMA, and CDMA can be applied to OFDM, it is useful to consider an alternate *random access* technique known as Carrier Sense Multiple Access (CSMA). CSMA is commonly used in packet-based communication systems, notably Ethernet and wireless LANs such as 802.11. In random access, users *contend* for the channel, rather than being allocated a reserved time, frequency, or code resource. Well-known random access techniques include ALOHA and slotted ALOHA, as well as CSMA. In ALOHA, users simply transmit packets at will without regard to other users. If the packet is not acknowledged by the receiver after some period, it is assumed lost and is retransmitted. Naturally, this scheme becomes increasingly inefficient and delay prone as the intensity of the traffic increases, as many transmissions result in collisions and hence retransmissions. Slotted ALOHA improves on this by about a factor of two since users transmit on specified time boundaries, and hence collisions are about half as likely.

CSMA improves upon ALOHA and slotted ALOHA through carrier sensing, in which users "listen" to the channel before transmitting in order to avoid collisions whenever possible. Numerous contention algorithms have been developed for CSMA systems; the most well known includes the Distributed Coordination Function (DCF) of 802.11 in which users wait for a random amount of time after the channel is clear before transmitting in order to reduce the probability of two stations transmitting immediately after the channel becomes available. Although the theoretical efficiency of CSMA is often around 60–70%, in wireless LANs the efficiency is often empirically observed to be less than 50%, even when there is only a single user [43].

Although random access is almost always pursued in the time dimension, there is no reason that frequency and code slots could not be contended for in an identical fashion. However, because random access tends to be inefficient, systems sophisticated enough to have frequency and especially code slots generally opt for coordinated multiple access, rather than random access. Most CSMA systems can reasonably be classified as a type of TDMA, where some inefficiency due to contention and collisions is tolerated in order to have a very simple distributed channel acquisition procedure in which users only acquire resources when they actually have packets to send. It should be noted that although FDMA and TDMA are certainly more efficient than CSMA when all users have packets to send, wasted (unused) frequency and time slots in FDMA and TDMA can also bring down the efficiency considerably. In fact, around half the bandwidth is typically wasted in TDMA and FDMA voice systems, which is one major reason that CDMA has proven so successful for voice [15]. Assuming full queues, the efficiency of a connection-oriented MAC can approach 90%, compared to at best 50% or less in most CSMA wireless systems such as 802.11. The need for extremely high spectral efficiency and low delay in LTE precludes the use of CSMA, and the burden of resource assignment is placed on the base stations.

4.1.3 Frequency Division Multiple Access (OFDM-FDMA)

Frequency Division Multiple Access (FDMA) can be readily implemented in OFDM systems by assigning different users their own sets of subcarriers. There are a number of ways this allocation can be performed. The simplest method is a static allocation of subcarriers to each user, as shown on the left of Figure 4.1. For example, in a 64-subcarrier OFDM system, user 1 could take subcarriers 1–16, with users 2, 3, and 4 using subcarriers 17–32, 33–48, and 49–64, respectively. The allocations are enforced with a multiplexer for the various users before the IFFT operation. Naturally, there could also be uneven allocations with high data rate users being allocated more subcarriers than lower rate users. In fact, such a system as this could reasonably be referred to as OFDMA since it allows multiple users to share the OFDM subcarriers. In fact, before the term "OFDMA" was coined and became popular, OFDM-FDMA was sometimes used to describe what would now be called an OFDMA system [42, 53]. OFDMA in LTE, however, has explicit time-sharing and procedures to allow for the dynamic allocation of subcarriers.

An improvement upon static allocation made possible in LTE is dynamic subcarrier allocation based upon channel state conditions. For example, due to frequency selective

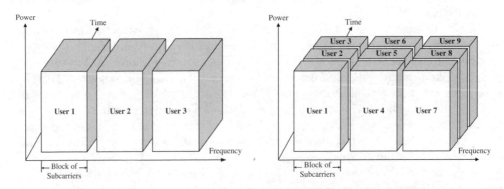

Figure 4.1 FDMA (left) and a combination of FDMA with TDMA (right).

fading, user 1 may have relatively good channels on subcarriers 33–48, while user 3 might have good channels on subcarriers 1–16. Obviously, it would be mutually beneficial for these users to swap the static allocations given above. There are well-developed theories for how the dynamic allocation of subcarriers should be performed, and we discuss these in detail in the next section.

4.1.4 Time Division Multiple Access (OFDM-TDMA)

In addition to or instead of FDMA, multiple users can also be accommodated with TDMA. In reality, all wireless TDMA systems employ both FDMA and TDMA at some level since the electromagnetic spectrum must be shared with many other users and systems. In an OFDM cellular system, some degree of TDMA is essential since there will generally be more users in the system than can be simultaneously carried on a single OFDM symbol. Furthermore, users often will not have data to send, so it is also important that subcarriers be dynamically allocated in order to avoid waste.

Static TDMA is shown on the right of Figure 4.1. Such a static TDMA methodology is appropriate for constant data-rate (i.e., circuit-switched) applications like voice and streaming video, but in general, a packet-based system like LTE can employ more sophisticated scheduling algorithms based on queue-lengths, channel conditions, and delay constraints to achieve much better performance than static TDMA. In the context of a packet-based system, static TDMA is often called *round robin* scheduling: each user simply waits for their pre-determined turn and then transmits.

4.1.5 Code Division Multiple Access (OFDM-CDMA or MC-CDMA)

CDMA is the dominant multiple access technique for 3G cellular systems, at least as of 2009, but is not particularly appropriate for high-speed data since the entire premise of CDMA is that a bandwidth much larger than the data rate is used to suppress the interference (Figure 4.2). In wireless broadband networks the data rates already are very large, so spreading the spectrum further is not viable. Even the nominally CDMA broadband standards such as HSDPA and 1xEVDO[3] have very small spreading factors and/or allow each user to employ multiple codes at the same time. They are therefore TDMA as well as CDMA (or multicode CDMA) systems, since users must take turns transmitting based on scheduling objectives such as channel conditions and latency.

OFDM and CDMA are not fundamentally incompatible; they can be combined to create a Multicarrier CDMA (MC-CDMA) waveform [19,56]. It is possible to use spread spectrum signalling and to separate users by codes in OFDM by spreading in either the time or frequency domain. Time domain spreading entails each subcarrier transmitting the same data symbol on several consecutive OFDM symbols, that is, the data symbol is multiplied by a length N code sequence and then sent on a specific subcarrier for the next N OFDM symbols. Frequency domain spreading, which generally has slightly better performance than time domain spreading [17], entails each data symbol being sent

---

3 HSDPA is a UMTS/3GPP standard and closely related to WCDMA. It is LTE's predeceessor in that standards body as discussed in Chapter 1. EVDO is a 3GPP2 standard and closely related to cdma2000, both of which are often associated with Qualcomm. Both of these standards are similar in that for higher data rates they become increasingly like TDMA systems.

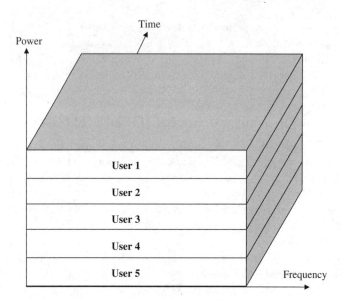

Figure 4.2 CDMA's users share time and frequency slots but employ codes that allow the users to be separated by the receiver.

simultaneously on N different subcarriers. MC-CDMA is not part of the LTE standard, at least at present.

4.2   Orthogonal Frequency Division Multiple Access (OFDMA)

OFDMA systems allocate subscribers time-frequency slices (in LTE, "resource grids") consisting of M subcarriers over some number of consecutive OFDM symbols in time (in LTE, most commonly seven). The M subcarriers can either be (1) spread out over the band, often called a "distributed," "comb," or "diversity" allocation or (2) bunched together in M contiguous subcarriers, which is often called a "band AMC," "localized," or "grouped" cluster. The distributed allocation achieves frequency diversity over the entire band, and would typically rely on interleaving and coding to correct errors caused by poor subcarriers. The band AMC mode, as the name suggests, instead attempts to use subcarriers where the SINR is roughly equal (and, presumably, higher than other possible clusters) and to choose the best coding and modulation scheme for that SINR.

Broadly speaking, if accurate SINR information can be obtained at the receiver about each band's SINR, then band AMC outperforms distributed subcarrier allocation. If this is not possible, for example, in a highly mobile system, then a distributed allocation would typically be preferred in order to maximize diversity. More details of how both types of subcarrier allocations are made in LTE are provided in Section 6.3.3, Resource Allocation. Table 4.1 summarizes the notation that will be used throughout this section.

Table 4.1 OFDMA Notation

K	Number of active users
L	Total number of subcarriers
M_k, M	Number of subcarriers per active user k
$h_{k,l}$	Envelope of channel gain for user k in subcarrier l
$P_{k,l}$	Transmit power allocated for user k in subcarrier l
σ^2	AWGN power spectrum density
P_{tot}	Total transmit power available at the base station
B	Total transmission bandwidth

4.2.1 OFDMA: How It Works

The block diagram for a downlink OFDMA system is shown in Figures 4.3 and 4.4. The basic flow is very similar to an OFDM system except for now K users share the L subcarriers, with each user being allocated M_k subcarriers. The method or rules for how users are mapped to subcarriers is not specified by the LTE standard but some general principles on how this should be performed are discussed in Section 4.4. Although in theory it is possible to have users share subcarriers, this never occurs in practice, so $\sum_k M_k = L$ and each subcarrier only has one user assigned to it.

At each receiver, the user cares only about its own M_k subcarriers, but still has to apply an L point FFT to the received digital waveform in order to extract the desired subset of subcarriers. Of course, the receiver has to know which time-frequency resources it has been allocated in order to extract the correct subcarriers—the control signalling that achieves this is discussed in Chapter 9. Thus, an OFDMA downlink receiver must mostly demodulate the entire waveform, which wastes power, but digital separation of users is simple to enforce at the receiver and the amount of residual interuser interference is very low compared to either CDMA or conventional FDMA where analog filters must be used to separate the users.

Although OFDMA is not used in the LTE uplink, we show OFDMA uplink block diagrams in Figures 4.5 and 4.6 to clearly illuminate the differences and numerous similarities

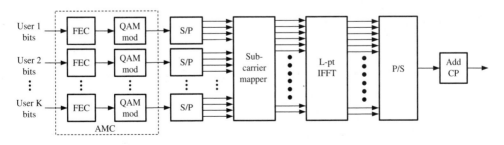

Figure 4.3 OFDMA downlink transmitter.

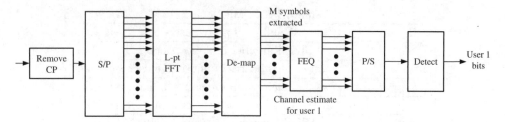

Figure 4.4 OFDMA downlink receiver for user 1. Each of the K active users—who by design have orthogonal subcarrier assignments—have a different receiver that only detects the M_k subcarriers intended for it.

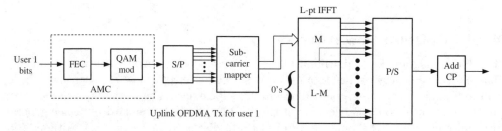

Figure 4.5 OFDMA uplink transmitter for user 1, where user 1 is allocated subcarriers $1, 2, \ldots,$ M of L total subcarriers.

between OFDMA and SC-FDMA. The transmitter modulates user k's bits over just the M_k subcarriers of interest: in this case, we have chosen $M_k = M$ for all users, and shown user 1 occupying subcarriers $1, 2, \cdots, M$ of the L total subcarriers. All the users' signals collide at the receiver's antenna, and are collectively demodulated using the receiver's FFT. Assuming each subcarrier has only a single user on it, the demodulated subcarriers can be de-mapped to the detectors for each of the K served users.

It should be noted that uplink OFDMA is considerably more challenging than downlink OFDMA since the uplink is naturally asynchronous, that is the users' signals arrive

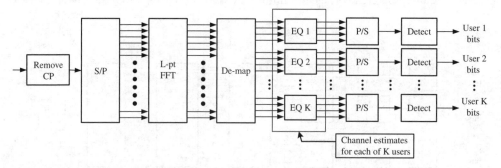

Figure 4.6 OFDMA uplink receiver. All K active users—who by design have orthogonal subcarrier assignments—are aggregated at the receiver and demultiplexed after the FFT.

at the receiver offset slightly in time (and frequency) from each other. This is not the case in the downlink since the transmitter is common for all users. These time and frequency offsets can result in considerable self-interference if they become large. Particularly in the distributed subcarrier mode, sufficiently large frequency offsets can severely degrade the orthogonality across all subcarriers. The timing offsets also must typically be small, within a fraction of a cyclic prefix, analogous to Figure 3.9. In LTE the uplink multiaccess scheme uses only the localized subcarrier mode due to the SC-FDMA nature of the uplink. In this case, the lack of perfect frequency and time synchronization between the multiple users leads to some inter-carrier interference but this is limited only to the subcarriers at the edge of the transmission band of each user. Frequency and timing synchronization for the uplink is achieved relative to the downlink synchronization, which is done using the synchronization channels as discussed in the previous chapter.

A higher level view of OFDMA can be seen in Figure 4.7. Here, a base station is transmitting a band AMC-type OFDMA waveform to four different devices simultaneously. The three arrows for each user indicate the signalling that must happen in order for band AMC-type OFDMA to work. First, the mobiles measure and feed back the quality of their channel, or channel state information (CSI) to the base station. Usually, the CSI feed back would be a measurement corresponding to SINR. The base station would then allocate subcarriers to the four users and send that subcarrier allocation information to the four users in an overhead message. Finally, the actual data is transmitted over the subcarriers assigned to each user. Here, it can be seen that the base station was successful in assigning each user a portion of the spectrum where it had a relatively strong signal.

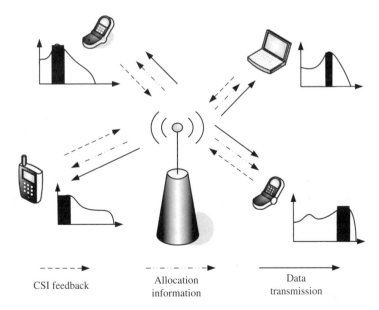

CSI feedback   Allocation information   Data transmission

Figure 4.7 In OFDMA, the base station allocates each user a fraction of the subcarriers, preferably, in a range where they have a strong channel.

4.2.2 OFDMA Advantages and Disadvantages

The advantages of OFDMA start with the advantages of single-user OFDM in terms of robust multipath suppression, relatively low complexity, and the creation of frequency diversity. In addition, OFDMA is a flexible multiple access technique that can accommodate many users with widely varying applications, data rates, and QoS requirements. Because the multiple access is performed in the digital domain (before the IFFT operation), dynamic, flexible, and efficient bandwidth allocation is possible. This allows sophisticated time and frequency domain scheduling algorithms to be integrated in order to best serve the user population. Some of these algorithms will be discussed in the next section.

Lower data rates (such as voice) and bursty data are handled much more efficiently in OFDMA than in single-user OFDM (i.e., OFDM-TDMA) or with CSMA. Take the first case, voice, as an example. If OFDMA was not used, each downlink user would receive a very high rate signal for a very short period of time—especially in channels with a large bandwidth such as 10 or 20MHz—and then be dormant for a relatively long time. This would require the receiver to quickly process a large amount of data, and could have bad latency and jitter properties as voice decompressor (vocoder) would frequently have to wait for a while before new decoded bits were available. Furthermore, since the switching between users would have to be very rapid, more frequency overhead signalling would be required, reducing the overall system throughput. In the uplink, OFDM-TDMA would be even more toxic as in addition to these concerns, the subscriber would have to transmit a wideband signal at very high total power for a very short time, and then again be dormant. This would put a large strain on the power amplifier.

OFDMA does not suffer from these problems because the allocation of time-frequency resources to users is extremely flexible and can be adapted dynamically to meet arbitrary throughput, delay, and possibly other QoS constraints.

4.3 Single-Carrier Frequency Division Multiple Access (SC-FDMA)

Single-carrier FDMA, or SC-FDMA, is employed in the LTE uplink. Conceptually, this system evolves naturally from the single-carrier frequency domain equalization (SC-FDE) modulation approach discussed in Section 3.6. However, as a practical matter, SC-FDMA more closely resembles OFDMA because it still requires an IFFT operation at the transmitter in order to separate the users. Because SC-FDE is truly a single-carrier modulation technique, it is not possible for an uplink user to use only part of the spectrum, or part of an SC-FDE block. Therefore, the goal of SC-FDMA is to take the low peak-to-average ratio (PAR) properties of SC-FDE and achieve them in an OFDMA-type system that allows partial usage of the frequency band. In fact, SC-FDMA can reasonably be called "FFT (or DFT) precoded OFDMA" [37].

4.3.1 SC-FDMA: How It Works

An SC-FDMA uplink transmitter is shown in Figure 4.8. Clearly, this is very similar to the OFDMA uplink transmitter in Figure 4.5, the only difference being that the user's

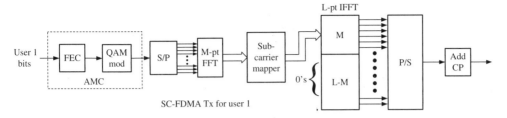

Figure 4.8 SC-FDMA uplink transmitter for user 1, where user 1 is allocated subcarriers 1, 2, ..., M of L total subcarriers.

M_k complex symbols are pre-processed with an FFT of size M_k. Let us refer to these time-domain complex symbols as $x[n]$. In LTE, M_k is related to the number of resource blocks allocated to the user k for its uplink transmission. The FFT operation creates a frequency domain version of the signal $X[m] = \text{FFT}(x[n])$, so that when the L point IFFT is applied later, the time-domain outputs of the IFFT correspond to an over-sampled and phase-shifted version of the original time-domain signal $x[n]$. Specifically, $x[n]$ is oversampled by a factor of L/M and experiences a phase shift that depends on which inputs to the IFFT are used. Although L/M is not required to be an integer, it usually is.

The SC-FDMA uplink receiver is shown in Figure 4.9. Clearly, this is also very similar to the OFDMA uplink receiver of Figure 4.6, the difference now being that for each user's M_k "subcarriers," an additional small IFFT must be applied prior to detection to bring the received data back into the time domain. Just like in OFDMA, frequency domain equalization is applied to each user's signal independently after the FFT, and users' signals are de-mapped based on the current subcarrier allocation.

4.3.2 SC-FDMA Advantages and Disadvantages

Since SC-FDMA is so similar to OFDMA, the natural question that arises is "what's the point of all this? Why not just use OFDMA?" The rationale for SC-FDMA is twofold. First, the key advantage of OFDMA is preserved: only part of the frequency spectrum

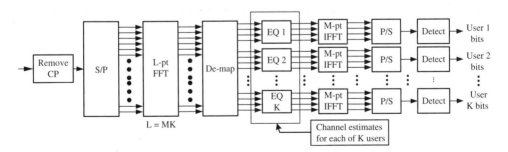

Figure 4.9 SC-FDMA uplink receiver. Much like the OFDMA receiver, here we explicitly assume that each user occupies a fraction M/L of the spectrum.

is used by any one user at a time. This allows the band used to be chosen adaptively for higher throughput, and perhaps more crucially allows for much lower total transmit power than if the entire spectrum had to be used, as in SC-FDE or OFDM-TDMA. In other words, the first rationale is that it basically *is* OFDMA.

The second rationale is that the PAR of SC-FDMA is significantly lower than OFDMA, and this is the real justification. Because the transmitted SC-FDMA signal for each user is simply an oversampled single-carrier signal, the PAR is about the same as for the corresponding single-carrier signal. This follows directly from the discussion in Section 3.6 on SC-FDE improving the PAR relative to OFDM. Reducing the PAR—and hence the power amplifier cost—is particularly important in the uplink due to the cost and power constraints experienced by mobile handsets.

The tradeoffs between SC-FDMA and OFDMA are also closely related to the tradeoffs SC-FDE faces versus OFDM. In particular, SC-FDMA can experience more spectral leakage than OFDMA, and achieve frequency diversity differently, leading to slight differences in performance. On the complexity side, unlike SC-FDE, which had very favorable complexity for the uplink due to its simple transmitter, SC-FDMA has a complexity disadvantage versus OFDMA in both the transmitter and receiver as an additional FFT of size M_k has to be performed for each user at the transmitter and receiver.

4.4   Multiuser Diversity and Opportunistic Scheduling

In OFDMA and SC-FDMA, users are allocated a portion of the spectrum. It only stands to reason that they should, if at all possible, be allocated a portion of the spectrum where they have the best SINR. For a frequency selective fading channel as discussed in Chapter 2, this corresponds to picking a part of the channel where constructive rather than destructive interference exists. Additionally, since SINR is used for a metric rather than SNR, a portion of the channel that has lower interference—due to the particular subcarrier allocations in neighboring cells and their fading values—can also be selected.

In this section, we first provide some necessary background discussion on the principle behind this exploitation of frequency diversity, known specifically as multiuser diversity and generally first attributed to an observation made by Knopp and Humblet [30]. Multiuser diversity describes the gains available by selecting a user from a subset of users that have "good" conditions. Adaptive modulation, as discussed in Section 2.6.5, is the means by which "good" channels can be exploited to achieve the higher data rates their high SINRs make viable.

4.4.1   Multiuser Diversity

The main motivation for adaptive subcarrier allocation in OFDMA systems is to exploit multiuser diversity. Although OFDMA systems have a number of subcarriers, we will focus temporarily on the allocation for a single subcarrier among multiple users for illustrative purposes.

Consider a K-user system, where the subcarrier of interest experiences independent and identically distributed (i.i.d.) Rayleigh fading, that is, each user's channel gain is independent of the others, and is denoted by h_k. The probability density function (PDF)

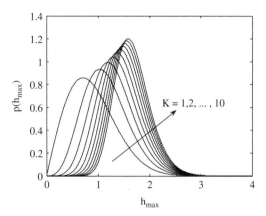

Figure 4.10 Probability density function of h_{max}, the maximum of the K users' channel gains.

of user k's channel gain $p(h_k)$ is given by

$$p(h_k) = \begin{cases} 2h_k e^{-h_k^2} & \text{if } h_k \geq 0 \\ 0 & \text{if } h_k < 0. \end{cases} \quad (4.1)$$

Now suppose the base station only transmits to the user with the highest channel gain, denoted as $h_{max} = \max\{h_1, h_2, \ldots, h_K\}$. It is easy to verify that the PDF of h_{max} is

$$p(h_{max}) = 2K h_{max} \left(1 - e^{-h_{max}^2}\right)^{K-1} e^{-h_{max}^2}. \quad (4.2)$$

Figure 4.10 shows the PDF of h_{max} for different values of K. As the number of users increases, the PDF of h_{max} shifts to the right, which means the probability of getting a large channel gain improves. Figure 4.11 shows how this increased channel gain improves the capacity and bit error rate (BER) for uncoded QPSK. Both plots show that the multiuser diversity gain improves as the number of users in the system increases, but

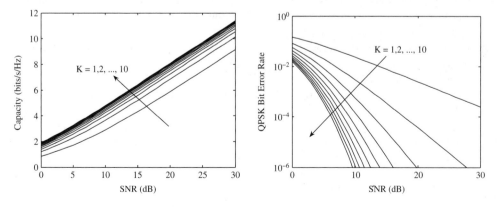

Figure 4.11 Average capacity (left) and QPSK bit error rate (right) for different numbers of users K.

the majority of the gain is achieved from just the first few users. Specifically, it has been proven using extreme value theory that in a K-user system the average capacity scales as $\log \log K$ [44], assuming just Rayleigh fading. If i.i.d. lognormal shadowing is also present for each of the users, which is a reasonable assumption in cellular systems, the scaling improves to $\sqrt{\log K}$ [7].

In an LTE system, the multiuser diversity gain can be reduced by averaging effects such as spatial diversity and the need to assign users contiguous blocks of subcarriers. This conflict is discussed in more detail in Section 4.6.3. Nevertheless, the gains from multiuser diversity can be considerable in practical systems, around a factor of two is an empirical rule of thumb. Although we will focus on the gains in terms of throughput (capacity) in this chapter, it should be noted that in some cases the largest impact from multiuser diversity is on the link reliability and overall coverage area.

4.4.2   Opportunistic Scheduling Approaches for OFDMA

There are a number of different ways to take advantage of multiuser diversity and adaptive modulation in OFDMA systems. Algorithms that take advantage of these gains are not specified by the LTE standard, and each LTE developer has the freedom to develop their own innovative procedures. The idea is to develop algorithms for determining which users to schedule, how to allocate subcarriers to them, and how to determine the appropriate power levels for each user on each subcarrier. In this section, we will overview some of the different possible approaches to resource allocation. We focus on the class of techniques that attempt to balance the desire for high throughput with fairness among the users in the system. We generally assume that the outgoing queues for each user are full, but in practice the algorithms discussed here can be modified to adjust for queue length or delay constraints, which in many applications may be as important (or more) than raw throughput.[4]

Referring to the downlink OFDMA system shown in Figure 4.7, users estimate and feed back the channel state information (CSI) to a centralized base station, where subcarrier and power allocation is determined according to users' CSI and the resource allocation procedure. Once the subcarriers for each user have been determined, the base station must inform each user which subcarriers have been allocated to it. This subcarrier mapping must be broadcast to all users whenever the resource allocation changes: the format of these messages is discussed in Chapter 7. Typically, the resource allocation must be performed on the order of the channel coherence time, although it may be performed more frequently than that if there are a lot of users competing for resources.

The resource allocation is usually formulated as a constrained optimization problem, to either (1) minimize the total transmit power with a constraint on the user data rate [29, 53] or to (2) maximize the total data rate with a constraint on total transmit power [24, 33, 35, 59]. The first objective is appropriate for fixed-rate applications (e.g., voice), while the second is more appropriate for bursty applications like data and other IP applications. Therefore, in this section we will focus on the rate adaptive algorithms (category 2), which are more relevant to LTE systems. We also note that considerable related work on resource allocation has been done for multicarrier DSL systems, for

---

4 Queueing theory and delay-constrained scheduling is a rich topic in its own right and doing it justice here is outside the scope of this chapter.

example, [5, 8, 9, 57]; the coverage and references in this section are by no means comprehensive. Unless otherwise stated, we assume in this section that the base station has obtained perfect instantaneous channel station information for all users.

4.4.3 Maximum Sum Rate Algorithm

The objective of the maximum sum rate (MSR) algorithm, as the name indicates, is to maximize the sum rate of all users, given a total transmit power constraint [59]. This algorithm is optimal if the goal is to get as much data as possible through the system. The drawback of the MSR algorithm is that it is likely that a few users that are close to the base station (and hence have excellent channels) will be allocated all the system resources. We will now briefly characterize the SINR, data rate, and power and subcarrier allocation that is achieved by the MSR algorithm.

Let $P_{k,l}$ denote user k's transmit power in subcarrier l. The signal-to-interference-plus-noise ratio for user k in subcarrier l, denoted as $\text{SINR}_{k,l}$, can be expressed as

$$\text{SINR}_{k,l} = \frac{P_{k,l}h_{k,l}^2}{\sum_{j=1, j\neq k}^{K} P_{j,l}h_{k,l}^2 + \sigma^2 \frac{B}{L}}. \tag{4.3}$$

Using the Shannon capacity formula as the throughput measure,[5] the MSR algorithm maximizes the following quantity:

$$\max_{P_{k,l}} \sum_{k=1}^{K} \sum_{l=1}^{L} \frac{B}{L} \log\left(1 + \text{SINR}_{k,l}\right) \tag{4.4}$$

with the total power constraint

$$\sum_{k=1}^{K} \sum_{l=1}^{L} P_{k,l} \leq P_{tot}.$$

The sum capacity is maximized if the total throughput in each subcarrier is maximized. Hence, the max sum capacity optimization problem can be decoupled into L simpler problems, one for each subcarrier. Further, the sum capacity in subcarrier l, denoted as C_l, can be written as

$$C_l = \sum_{k=1}^{K} \log\left(1 + \frac{P_{k,l}}{P_{tot,l} - P_{k,l} + \frac{\sigma^2}{h_{k,l}^2}\frac{B}{L}}\right), \tag{4.5}$$

where $P_{tot,l} - P_{k,l}$ denotes other users' interference to user k in subcarrier l. It is easy to show that C_l is maximized when all available power $P_{tot,l}$ is assigned to just the single user with the largest channel gain in subcarrier l. This result agrees with intuition: give

---

5 Throughout this section, we will use the Shannon capacity formula as the throughput measure. In practice, there is a gap between the achieved data rate and the maximum (Shannon) rate, which can be simply characterized with an SINR gap of a few dB. Therefore, this approach to resource allocation is valid, but the exact numbers given here are optimistic.

each channel to the user with the best gain in that channel. This is sometimes referred to as a "greedy" optimization. The optimal power allocation proceeds according to a rich-get-richer "waterfilling" solution [14, 16] or more realistically for the multiuser scenario with QAM, "mercury waterfilling" [34]. The total sum capacity is readily determined by adding up the rate on each of the subcarriers.

4.4.4 Maximum Fairness Algorithm

Although the total throughput is maximized by the MSR algorithm, in a cellular system like LTE where the path loss attenuation will vary by several orders of magnitude between users, some users will be extremely underserved by an MSR-based scheduling procedure. At the alternate extreme, the maximum fairness algorithm [41] aims to allocate the subcarriers and power such that the *minimum* user's data rate is maximized. This essentially corresponds to equalizing the data rates of all users, hence the name "Maximum Fairness."

The maximum fairness algorithm can be referred to as a *Max-Min* problem, since the goal is to maximize the minimum data rate. The optimum subcarrier and power allocation is considerably more difficult to determine than in the MSR case because the objective function is not concave. It is particularly difficult (NP-hard) to simultaneously find the optimum subcarrier and power allocation. Therefore, low-complexity suboptimal algorithms are necessary, in which the subcarrier and power allocation are done separately.

A common approach is to assume initially that equal power is allocated to each subcarrier, and then to iteratively assign each available subcarrier to a low-rate user with the best channel on it [41, 54]. Once this generally suboptimal subcarrier allocation is completed, an optimum (waterfilling) power allocation can be performed. It is typical for this suboptimal approximation to be very close to the performance obtained with an exhaustive search for the best joint subcarrier-power allocation, both in terms of the fairness achieved and the total throughput.

4.4.5 Proportional Rate Constraints Algorithm

A weakness of the Maximum Fairness algorithm is that the rate distribution among users is not flexible. Further, the total throughput is largely limited by the user with the worst SINR, as most of the resources are allocated to that user, which is clearly suboptimal. In a wireless broadband network, it is likely that different users require application-specific data rates that vary substantially. A generalization of the Maximum Fairness algorithm is the Proportional Rate Constraints (PRC) algorithm, whose objective is to maximize the sum throughput, with the additional constraint that each user's data rate is proportional to a set of pre-determined system parameters $\{\beta_k\}_{k=1}^K$. Mathematically, the proportional data rate's constraint can be expressed as

$$\frac{R_1}{\beta_1} = \frac{R_2}{\beta_2} = \cdots = \frac{R_K}{\beta_K} \tag{4.6}$$

where each user's achieved data rate R_k is

$$R_k = \sum_{l=1}^{L} \frac{\rho_{k,l} B}{L} \log_2 \left(1 + \frac{P_{k,l} h_{k,l}^2}{\sigma^2 \frac{B}{L}} \right), \tag{4.7}$$

and $\rho_{k,l}$ can only be the value of either 1 or 0, indicating whether subcarrier l is used by user k or not. Clearly, this is the same setup as the Maximum Fairness algorithm if $\beta_k = 1$ for each user. The advantage is that any arbitrary data rates can be achieved by varying the β_k values.

The PRC optimization problem is also generally very difficult to solve directly, since it involves both continuous variables $P_{k,l}$ and binary variables $\rho_{k,l}$ and the feasible set is not convex. As for the Maximum Fairness case, the prudent approach is to separate the subcarrier and power allocation, and to settle for a near-optimal subcarrier and power allocation that can be achieved with manageable complexity. The near optimal approach is derived and outlined in [45,46] and a low-complexity implementation developed in [54].

4.4.6 Proportional Fairness Scheduling

The three algorithms we have discussed thus far attempt to *instantaneously* achieve an objective such as the total sum throughput (MSR algorithm), maximum fairness (equal data rates among all users), or pre-set proportional rates for each user. Alternatively, one could attempt to achieve such objectives over time, which provides significant additional flexibility to the scheduling algorithms. In this case, in addition to throughput and fairness, a third element enters the tradeoff, which is *latency*. In an extreme case of latency tolerance, the scheduler could simply just wait for the user to get close to the base station before transmitting. In fact, the MSR algorithm achieves both fairness *and* maximum throughput if the users are assumed to have the same average channels in the long term (on the order of minutes, hours, or more), and there is no constraint with regard to latency. Since latencies even on the order of seconds are generally unacceptable, scheduling algorithms that balance latency and throughput and achieve some degree of fairness are needed. The most popular framework for this type of scheduling is Proportional Fairness (PF) scheduling [49,50,52].

The PF scheduler is designed to take advantage of multiuser diversity, while maintaining comparable long-term throughput for all users. Let $R_k(t)$ denote the instantaneous data rate that user k can achieve at time t, and $T_k(t)$ be the average throughput for user k up to time slot t. The Proportional Fairness scheduler selects the user, denoted as k^*, with the highest $R_k(t)/T_k(t)$ for transmission. In the long-term, this is equivalent to selecting the user with the highest instantaneous rate relative to its mean rate. The average throughput $T_k(t)$ for all users is then updated according to

$$T_k(t+1) = \begin{cases} \left(1 - \frac{1}{t_c}\right) T_k(t) + \frac{1}{t_c} R_k(t) & k = k^* \\ \left(1 - \frac{1}{t_c}\right) T_k(t) & k \neq k^*. \end{cases} \tag{4.8}$$

Since the Proportional Fairness scheduler selects the user with the largest instantaneous data rate relative to its average throughput, "bad" channels for each user are unlikely to be selected. On the other hand, users that have been consistently underserved receive scheduling priority, which promotes fairness. The parameter t_c controls the latency of the system. If t_c is large, then the latency increases, with the benefit of higher sum throughput. If t_c is small, the latency decreases since the average throughput values change more quickly, at the expense of some throughput. The Proportional

Fairness scheduler has been widely adopted in packet data systems such as HSDPA and 1xEV-DO, where t_c is commonly set between 10 and 20. One interesting property of PF scheduling is that as $t_c \to \infty$, the sum of the logs of the user data rates is maximized. That is, PF scheduling maximizes $\sum_{k=1}^{K} \log T_k$ or equivalently $\prod_{k=1}^{K} T_k$.

Although the Proportional Fairness scheduler was originally designed for a single-channel, time-slotted system, it can be adapted to an OFDMA system. In an OFDMA system, due to the multiple parallel subcarriers in the frequency domain, multiple users can transmit on different subcarriers simultaneously. The original PF algorithm can be extended to OFDMA by treating each subcarrier independently. Let $R_k(t, n)$ be the supportable data rate for user k in subcarrier n at time slot t. Then for each subcarrier, the user with the largest $R_k(t, n)/T_k(t)$ is selected for transmission. Let $\Omega_k(t)$ denote the set of subcarriers in which user k is scheduled for transmission at time slot t, then the average user throughput is updated as

$$T_k(t+1) = \left(1 - \frac{1}{t_c}\right) T_k(t) + \frac{1}{t_c} \sum_{n \in \Omega_k(t)} R_k(t, n) \tag{4.9}$$

for $k = 1, 2, \ldots, K$. Other weighted adaptations and evolutions of PF scheduling of OFDMA are certainly possible.

4.4.7 Performance Comparison

In this section, we briefly compare the performance of the various scheduling algorithms for OFDMA that we have discussed, in order to gain intuition on their relative performance and merits. In these results, an exponentially decaying multipath profile with six multipath components was used to generate the frequency diversity. All users have the same average SNR. The absolute capacity numbers are not especially important; what is important are the trends between the different curves.

Throughput First, we consider the multiuser diversity gains of the different types of algorithms. Figure 4.12 shows the capacity (normalized by the total bandwidth) for static TDMA (round robin), Proportional Fairness, and the maximum sum rate (MSR) algorithm. As expected, the MSR algorithm achieves the best total throughput, and the gain increases as the number of users increases, on the order of $\log \log K$. Static TDMA achieves no multiuser gain, since the users transmit independent of their channel realizations. It can be seen that the proportional fairness algorithm approaches the throughput of the MSR algorithm, with an expected penalty due to its support for under-served users.

Fairness Now, let us consider how the worst user in the system does: this is shown in the left of Figure 4.13. As expected, the Maximum Fairness algorithm achieves the best performance for the most under-served user, with a slight gain for optimal power allocation over its allocated subcarriers (waterfilling) relative to an equal power allocation. Also as expected, the MSR algorithm results in a starved worst-case user—in fact, it is typical for several users to receive no resources at all for substantial periods of time. Static TDMA performs in-between the two, with the percentage loss relative to the Maximum Fairness algorithm increasing as the number of users increases, since TDMA does not take advantage of multiuser diversity.

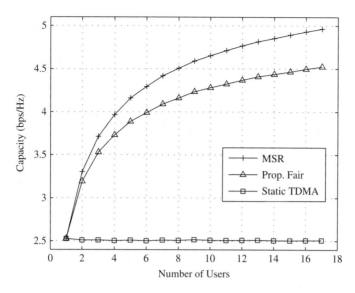

Figure 4.12 Sum capacity vs. number of users for a single-carrier system (scheduling is in the time-domain only).

Next we consider a heterogeneous environment with eight users. The first user has an average SINR of 20 dB, the second user has an average SINR of 10 dB, and users 3–8 have average SINRs of 0 dB. This is a reasonable scenario in which user 1 is close to the base station, users 3–8 are near the cell edge, and user 2 is in-between. Clearly, the bulk of the resources will be allocated to users 1 and 2 by the MSR algorithm, and this can be readily observed in the right of Figure 4.13. The downside of this approach, of course, is that users 3–8 have a throughput of approximately zero. A more balanced approach would be to use the Proportional Rate Constraints algorithm (PRC) and adopt proportional rate

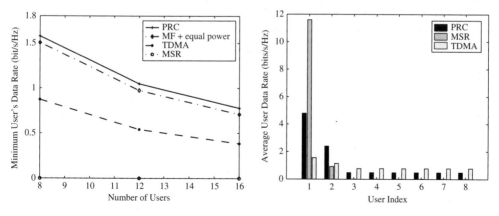

Figure 4.13 (Left) Minimum user's capacity in multiuser OFDM vs. the number of users; (right) normalized average throughput per user in a heterogeneous environment.

Table 4.2 Comparison of Different OFDMA Rate-Adaptive Resource Allocation Schemes

Algorithm	Sum Capacity	Fairness	Complexity	Simple Algorithm?
Maximum Sum Rate (MSR)	Best	Poor and inflexible	Low	Very simple [24]
Maximum Fairness (MF)	Poor	Best but inflexible	Medium	Available [41]
Proportional Constraints (PRC)	Good	Most flexible	High	Available [46]
Proportional Fairness (PF)	Good	Flexible	Low	Available [52]

constraints equal to the relative SINRs, that is, $\beta_1 = 100, \beta_2 = 10, \beta_3 = 1, \ldots \beta_8 = 1$. This allows the under-served users to get at least some throughput, while preserving the bulk of the multiuser diversity gains. Naturally, a more equal assignment of the β_k's will increase the fairness, with the extreme case $\beta_k = 1$ for all users k equalizing the data rates for all users.

Summary of Comparison Table 4.2 compares the four resource allocation algorithms that this chapter introduced for OFDMA systems. In summary, the Maximum Sum Rate allocation is the best in terms of total throughput, achieves a low computational complexity, but has a terribly unfair distribution of data rates. Hence, the MSR algorithm is viable only when all users have nearly identical channel conditions and a relatively large degree of latency is tolerable. The Maximum Fairness algorithm achieves complete fairness while sacrificing significant throughput, and so is appropriate only for fixed, equal rate applications. The Proportional Rate Constraints (PRC) algorithm allows a flexible tradeoff between these two extremes, but it may not always be possible to aptly set the desired rate constraints in real time. We also described the popular Proportional Fairness algorithm, which is fairly simple to implement and also achieves a practical balance between throughput and fairness.

4.5   OFDMA and SC-FDMA in LTE

LTE, like any OFDMA-based standard, must specify several things in order for the system to work. First, it must specify the "quanta," or units, of time-frequency resources that can be assigned. Second, it must specify messaging protocols that allow the mobile units to request resources when necessary, and to know what resources they have been assigned, both for transmission and reception. Third, ranging procedures must be specified so that simultaneous uplink transmissions from several different mobile units can be reliably decoded at the base station.

Although we leave details of these procedures to later chapters, we now overview how LTE accomplishes these three tasks. Note that although scheduling algorithms such as those discussed in the previous section can be very important in determining system throughput, delay, and fairness, they are not specified by LTE. Rather, LTE simply specifies how resources may be assigned, and how to notify the mobile units of the assignment.

4.5.1   The LTE Time-Frequency Grid

In LTE, mobile units are allocated groups of subcarriers over time and frequency known as a *resource block*. The size of the resource block is chosen to balance a tradeoff between granularity and overhead. On the one hand, it would be nice to be able to assign any subcarrier to any user in any time slot; but then it would take a very large amount of overhead to specify the current allocation to all the mobile units. On the other hand, the much lower overhead would be achieved by an OFDM-TDMA type system where one user has access to all the subcarriers and uses the same AMC level on all of them—but as discussed this is not efficient in many respects including total throughput, delay, and the required peak power. The downlink resource block of LTE is shown in Figure 6.10: a typical resource block consists of 12 subcarriers over 7 OFDM symbols, also referred to as a timeslot. A timeslot in LTE spans 0.5 msec and two consecutive timeslots create a subframe. Resources are allocated to users in units of resource blocks over a subframe, that is, 12 subcarriers over $2 \times 7 = 14$ OFDM symbols for a total of 168 "resource elements," which in practice are QAM symbols. Not all the 168 resource elements can be used for data since some are used for various layer 1 and layer 2 control messages.

The subcarriers of a resource block can be allocated in one of two ways. The first way, known as *distributed subcarrier allocation*, takes advantage of frequency diversity by spreading the resource block hop across the entire channel bandwidth. This can be accomplished by using a "comb" pattern at any given point of time for a given user, so that its subcarriers occur at even intervals across the entire frequency bandwidth. This approach is typically used in the downlink (OFDMA) when distributed subcarrier allocation is used. Alternatively, frequency diversity can be achieved by hopping a contiguous block of subcarriers in time, for example, the 12 subcarriers in a resource block could hop to a different part of the spectrum over each of the 14 OFDM symbols utilized. Since the channel is generally relatively constant over 14 OFDM symbols, frequency diversity is achieved as long as sufficient interleaving is employed: this is certainly the case in LTE systems, which are heavy on interleaving. This approach is used in the uplink, since SC-FDMA transmitters in general operate on contiguous sets of subcarriers as seen in Figure 4.8. Even more fundamentally, because the distributed uplink transmitters are difficult to precisely align in time and frequency, and can have radically different path loss values to the base station receiver, even if OFDMA was used in the uplink, a comb-style subcarrier allocation may prove troublesome.

The second way to allocate subcarriers is *adjacent subcarrier allocation*. This approach relies on a channel-aware allocation of resources, so that each user can be allocated a resource block where they have a strong channel. Since a block of 12 subcarriers is typically smaller than the coherence bandwidth of the channel, frequency diversity is not achieved, which is helpful as long as the scheduler is able to assign "good" blocks to each user. More details on distributed and adjacent allocations are given in Section 6.3.3.

4.5.2   Allocation Notification and Uplink Feedback

In order for each MS to know which subcarriers to use in downlink reception and uplink transmission, the BS must broadcast this information to the pool of active users in its cell. Similar to previous UMTS standards such as wideband CDMA, overhead signalling is done on a logical control channel, in this case, the PDCCH (physical downlink control channel). The PDCCH specifies the following:

- Downlink resource block allocation

- Uplink resource block allocation

- QAM constellation to use per resource block

- Type and rate of coding to use per resource block

Once a user is able to decode the PDCCH, it knows precisely where to receive (downlink) or to transmit (uplink), and how. The PDCCH is sent over the first 2–3 OFDM symbols of each subframe across all the subcarriers. Recall that each allocation, which consists of a resource block subframe, consisted of 168 subcarriers over 14 OFDM sybmols. Since the first 2–3 symbols in each subframe are used by the PDCCH, about 14–21% of the total downlink capacity is used by the PDCCH. Additional downlink capacity is also used by other control channels and the pilot symbols. More details on PDCCH and the downlink signal structure is provided in Section 7.3. To aid the base station in uplink scheduling, LTE units utilize buffer status reporting (BSR), wherein each user can notify the BS about its queue length, and channel quality information (CQI) feedback. Once the BS is well informed about the channels to/from the users and their respective queue lengths, it can more appropriately determine the optimum allocation among the various users. In the downlink, the BS has inherent knowledge of the amount of buffered data for each user, while in the uplink it can estimate the channel from each user. Hence, BSR feedback is only used for uplink scheduling while CQI feedback is only used for downlink scheduling and AMC-mode selection. The CQI reporting can be either periodic or aperiodic, wideband or subband, and multiple CQI feedback modes are defined for different scenarios. The feedback for CQI in LTE is discussed in detail in Section 9.2.

4.5.3   Power Control

Although OFDMA (and SC-FDMA) systems are designed to have orthogonality within a cell (unlike many CDMA systems, for example), they still suffer from two forms of self-interference. The first is intercell interference, whereby neighboring cells allocate the same time-frequency resource blocks and hence cause interference. This intercell interference can occur in either the uplink or the downlink, but is typically the most problematic for cell-edge users in the downlink since they are approximately equidistant between two base stations and hence doubly suffer from lower desired power and higher interference power. Interference-aware allocation approaches that can mitigate this are discussed shortly in Section 4.6.1. Power control is one part of the solution as well, since it can try to equalize SINR values over the cell.

The second form of self-interference was discussed briefly in Section 4.5.1, and is related to imperfect time-frequency-power synchronization between the different uplink users. This is not a problem in the downlink since each mobile station receives a single waveform from the base station. On the other hand, in the uplink, the received waveform is aggregated "in the air" as the summation of the different transmit waveforms for each user. Because these distributed transmitters are bound to be at least slightly unsynchronized in time and frequency, the orthogonality of the subcarriers will be degraded at the receiver, as discussed in some detail in Section 3.4 for OFDM. Furthermore, if power control is not used, the different signals may be received with very different powers, which causes a dynamic range problem when the signal is A/D converted—that is, the strong users will dominate the A/D dynamic range and the weak users will experience severe quantization noise, making digital reconstruction of those signals difficult or impossible. In short, some uplink power control is needed in OFDMA (or SC-FDMA) systems.

In LTE, closed-loop power control is possible in the uplink where the BS can explicitly indicate the maximum transmit power density (power per resource block) that can be used by each user. This information is carried on the PDCCH when the uplink allocation for each user is specified. The uplink loop power control algorithm in LTE is flexible in terms of the amount of channel inversion it performs. On one extreme, channel inversion can be used, which results in the same received power for all users regardless of their channel conditions. This maximizes fairness. On the other hand, no power control can be used—all users transmit at full power—which results in high average spectral efficiency but low battery efficiency and poor fairness, as cell edge users are disadvantaged. These two extremes can be balanced by *fractional power control* [25, 55], whereby the channel is partially inverted, that is, the transmit power is proportional to h^{-s} where s is a fractional value between 0 and 1. Note that fixed transmit power corresponds to $s = 0$ and full channel inversion to $s = 1$. Fractional power control is the open-loop power control scheme in LTE.

In the downlink, no closed-loop power control is specified in the standard; however, LTE systems can specify a relative power offset between different users. This is done using a higher layer message and thus can only be performed at much longer timescales compared to uplink power control. By allocating different power offsets among the different users according to their location, the system can try to improve the fairness in terms of the data rate of a user who is at the cell edge relative to that of a user closer to the BS. More details on both uplink and downlink power control in LTE can be found in Section 9.10.

4.6 OFDMA System Design Considerations

We conclude the chapter by considering two important considerations for the implementation of an OFDMA-based cellular system. The first concerns the allocation of resources in a cellular network, where the actions of one base station affect its neighbors. The second is a cautionary tail regarding the diversity gain from opportunistic scheduling in a system like LTE that attempts to milk every last bit of diversity out of the channel using coding, ARQ, adaptive modulation, OFDM, and multiple antenna techniques.

4.6.1   Resource Allocation in Cellular Systems

Readers may have noticed that since the scheduling algorithms discussed thus far in this chapter are all very dependent on the perceived SINR for each user, the scheduling choices of each base station affect the users in the adjacent cells. For example, if a certain MS near the cell edge (presumably with a low SINR) is selected to transmit in the uplink at high power, this will lower the effective SINRs of all the users in the cell next to it, hence perhaps changing the ideal subcarrier allocation and burst profile for that cell. Therefore, a cellular OFDMA system greatly benefits from methods for suppressing or avoiding the interference from adjacent cells.

A simple approach is to use a unique frequency hopping pattern for each base station to randomize to the other cell interference [38], an approach popularized by the Flarion (now part of Qualcomm) scheme called FLASH-OFDM. Although this scheme reduces the probability of a worst-case interference scenario, under a high-system load the interference levels can still rapidly approach untenable levels and the probability of collision can grow large [48, 51]. A more sophisticated approach is to develop advanced receivers that are capable of cancelling the interference from a few dominant interference sources. This is a challenging proposition even in a single-carrier system [1], and its viability in a cellular OFDMA system is open to debate.

An appealing approach is to revisit the resource allocation algorithms discussed in Section 4.4.2 in the context of a multi-cell system. If each base station is unaware of the exact conditions in the other cells, and no cooperation among neighboring base stations is allowed, the subcarrier and power allocation follows the theory of non-cooperative games [6, 10, 18, 57] and typically results in a Nash equilibrium, where no user can benefit by unilaterally deviating from their current allocation. Simply put, this scenario is the equivalent of gridlock: for example, the users reach a point where neither increasing nor decreasing their power improves their capacity. The convergence time of such approaches is generally not fast enough to be of much use in an LTE system, anyway.

Better performance can be obtained if there is some cooperation between the base stations. For example, there could be a master scheduler for all the base stations that knew the channels in each and every base station and made multi-cell resource allocation schedules accordingly. This would be prohibitively complex, though, due to (1) transferring large amounts of real-time information to and from this centralized scheduler, and (2) the computational difficulties involved in processing this quantity of information to determine a globally optimal or near-optimal resource allocation. Simpler approaches are possible: for example, just neighboring base stations could share simple information to make sure they do not assign the same subcarriers to vulnerable users, for example. Research on cellular cooperation and encoding continues to be active, including fundamental work from an information theory perspective [7, 13, 21, 23, 36, 47, 58], as well as more heuristic techniques specifically for cellular OFDMA [11, 27, 32, 39, 40]. Although in many cases the standard will leave such details unspecified, LTE systems are very likely to adopt some of these techniques to improve their coverage and spectral efficiency, particularly for cell-edge users.

4.6.2 Fractional Frequency Reuse in Cellular Systems

Compared to CDMA-based cellular systems, OFDMA-based systems are more vulnerable to inter-cell interference, which especially degrades the performance of users at the cell edge. Frequency planning techniques have been proposed for LTE systems to mitigate inter-cell interference instead of standard universal frequency reuse [22]. Fractional frequency reuse (FFR) is one such strategy that partitions a cell into several regions and applies different frequency reuse factors in each region. The inter-cell interference can be significantly reduced since FFR increases the spatial distance between neighboring interferers.

Figure 4.14 shows examples of the two main types of FFR deployments: Strict FFR and Soft Frequency Reuse (SFR). In a Strict FFR system, users in the interior of the cells universally share a common sub-band of frequencies, while the cell edge users' bandwidth is partitioned based on a reuse factor of N, requiring a total of $N + 1$ sub-bands. It is termed "strict" because interior users do not share any spectrum with edge users, which reduces interference for both interior users and edge cell users.

Soft Frequency Reuse employs a similar partitioning strategy as Strict FFR, with the exception that interior users can share the same bandwidth as edge users in adjacent cells. As a result, cell interior users typically transmit at lower power levels than the cell-edge users in order to reduce interference to neighboring cells. While SFR is more bandwidth efficient than Strict FFR, it allows more interference to both cell interior and edge users.

Since the cell partitions are based on the geometry of the network, the locations of the users are important in order to determine the frequency partitions. However, one practical method to determine user classifications is for each cell to use the average received SINR of its users, which is usually a good indicator of the distance of the user from its base station. The base station then classifies users with average SINR less than a pre-determined threshold as edge users, while users with average SINR greater than the threshold are classified as interior users.

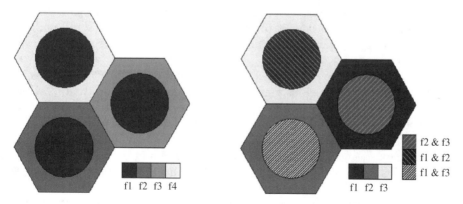

Figure 4.14 Strict Fractional Frequency Reuse (left) and Soft Frequency Reuse (right) geometry with $N = 3$ cell-edge reuse factors.

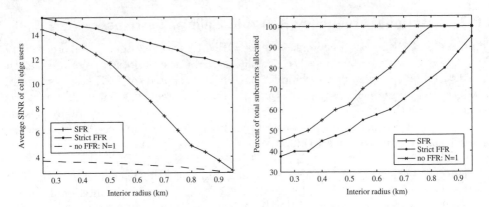

Figure 4.15 Edge user performance (left); spectral efficiency of the reuse schemes (right).

Figure 4.15 shows the results of a simulation comparing the two main FFR schemes with standard $N = 1$ frequency reuse. A total of 48 resource blocks (RBs) are available, users are uniformly distributed over the 12-cell network, and a high traffic load is assumed. The cell coverage radius is 1 km and the interior radius, which determines the number of interior and edge users served, is varied from .25 to .95 km.

The plot on the left of Figure 4.15 shows the significant benefit the Strict FFR scheme provides for edge users over SFR and universal frequency reuse. However, the plot on the right shows that if the network has a moderate or high traffic load, this benefit comes at a cost of not being able to fairly serve all users. For example, an interior radius two-thirds of the total cell radius results in allocating 20% fewer RBs per cell under Strict FFR as could be allocated under SFR and 40% fewer RBs than under universal frequency reuse, resulting in fewer users being able to be served by the cell. Another way to view this result is to note that the peak throughput of the cell is reduced under both FFR schemes since some of the available RBs are "wasted" by not being allocated in order to reduce interference to users in neighboring cells who were allocated those RBs. So we see that there is a tradeoff between interference reduction and total spectral efficiency under both FFR schemes. However, one benefit of SFR is the ability to balance the performance gains experienced under Static FFR while more efficiently utilizing all of the available RBs in every cell.

Recent research on FFR has focused on the optimal design of FFR systems by utilizing advanced techniques such as game theory and convex optimization [2]. However, since in practice it is computationally prohibitive to derive an optimal solution, various suboptimal solutions have been developed based on some simple assumptions of FFR system models. These assumptions typically include static traffic loads, equal transmit power per subcarrier, and global channel state information at every base station [3,12]. Variations and hybrids of strict FFR and SFR systems have also been investigated, which further partition the cell and refine the frequency reuse pattern [20,28].

Base station cooperation is an expected enhancement of future multicell network standards. This allows FFR to be implemented dynamically alongside resource allocation strategies to adapt to different channel conditions and user traffic loads in each cell [4]. For example, based on user channel conditions or data rate requirements, base stations would be able to send or receive requests from neighboring base stations using the X2 signaling interface requesting a transition to or from different FFR modes for a pre-determined time window. See Section 10.5 for a discussion of inter-base-station coordination support in the LTE standard.

4.6.3 Multiuser Diversity vs. Frequency and Spatial Diversity

Diversity is a key source of performance gain in OFDMA systems. In particular, OFDMA exploits multiuser diversity among the different MSs, frequency diversity across the subcarriers, and time diversity by allowing latency. Spatial diversity is also a key aspect of LTE systems, as discussed in the next chapter. One important observation is that these sources of diversity will generally compete with each other. For example, imagine that the receiver has two sufficiently spaced antennas. If two-branch selection diversity is used for each subcarrier, then the amount of variation between each subcarrier will decrease significantly, since most of the deep fades will be eliminated by the selection process. Now, if ten different users were to execute an OFDMA scheduling algorithm, although the overall performance would increase further, the multiuser diversity gain would be less than that without the selection diversity, since each user has already eliminated their worst channels with the selection combining. The intuition of this simple example can be extended to other diversity-exploiting techniques, like coding and interleaving, space-time and space-frequency codes, and so on. In short, *the total diversity gain will be less than the sum of the diversity gains from the individual techniques.*

Figure 4.16 shows the combined effect of multiuser and spatial diversity for five different configurations of 2×1 MIMO systems: single antenna (SISO), opportunistic beamforming [52], Alamouti STBCs, and transmit beamforming with limited feedback (1-bit

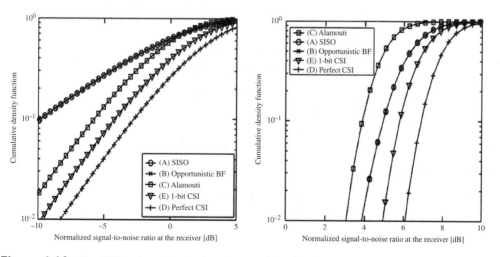

Figure 4.16 The SINR of multiuser diversity combined with antenna diversity techniques. The number of users is $K = 1$ (left), $K = 50$ (right). Figure from [31], courtesy of IEEE.

CSI) and perfect CSI. For a single user, the SISO and opportunistic BF are the least effective, since opportunistic BF requires multiuser diversity to get a performance gain over SISO. Alamouti codes increase performance, in particular reducing the probability of a very low SINR from occurring. The CSI-endowed techniques do the best; notably the perfect CSI case is always 3 dB better than Alamouti codes regardless of the number of users. When the system does have 50 users, however, some of the conclusions change considerably. Now, Alamouti codes actually perform worse than single-antenna transmission! This is because Alamouti codes harden the received SINR toward the average and so the SINR difference between the users is attenuated—but this is exactly what is exploited by a multiuser scheduler that picks the best out of the 50 users. The advantage of perfect CSI is also narrowed relative to SISO and opportunistic beamforming. The key point here is that the diversity gains from different techniques may interfere with each other, and only a complete system characterization can reliably predict the overall system performance.

4.7   Chapter Summary

This chapter has overviewed the key aspects of multiple access in OFDM systems.

- Traditional multiple access techniques (FDMA, TDMA, CDMA, CSMA) can all be applied to OFDM but suffer from important inefficiencies if applied in a naive manner.

- The preferred approach—adopted in LTE—is conceptually an FDMA-TDMA hybrid called "OFDMA" in the downlink and "SC-FDMA" in the uplink.

- OFDMA and SC-FDMA achieve both high performance and flexibility through *multiuser and/or frequency diversity, opportunistic scheduling*, and low-overhead protocols that support efficient real-time assignment of subcarriers.

- A number of resource allocation procedures are possible for OFDMA. We introduced and compared four such algorithms that achieve various tradeoffs in terms of sum throughput, fairness to under-served users, and complexity.

- To practically implement OFDMA or SC-FDMA, some overhead messaging is required. We overviewed how this is done in LTE, with more details to come in Chapter 9.

Bibliography

[1] Andrews, J. G. Interference cancellation for cellular systems: A contemporary overview. *IEEE Wireless Communications Magazine*, 12(2):19–29, Apr. 2005.

[2] Assad, M. Optimal fractional frequency reuse (FFR) in multicellular OFDMA system. In *IEEE Vechicular Technology Conference*, pages 1–5, September 2008.

[3] Assad, M. and N. Hassan. Optimal fractional frequency reuse (FFR) and resource allocation in multiuser OFDMA system. In *International Conference on Information and Communication Technologies*, pages 88–92, Aug. 2009.

[4] Boudreau, G., J. Panicker, N. Guo, R. Chang, N. Wang, and S. Vrzic. Interference coordination and cancellation for 4G networks. *IEEE Communications Magazine*, 47(4):74–81, Apr. 2009.

[5] Cendrillon, R., M. Moonen, J. Verliden, T. Bostoen, and W. Yu. Optimal multiuser spectrum management for digital subscriber lines. In *Proc. IEEE International Conference on Communications*, 1:1–5, Jun. 2004.

[6] Chen, Y., K. H. Teo, S. Kishore, and J. Zhang. Inter-cell interference management in WiMAX downlinks by a Stackelberg game between BSs. In *Proc., IEEE Intl. Conf. on Communications*, pages 3442–46, Beijing, China, May 2008.

[7] Choi, W. and J. G. Andrews. The capacity gain from base station cooperation in multi-antenna systems. *IEEE Trans. on Wireless Communications*, 714–725, Feb. 2008.

[8] Chow, J., J. Tu, and J. Cioffi. A discrete multitone transceiver system for HDSL applications. *IEEE Journal on Sel. Areas in Communications*, 9(6):895–908, Aug. 1991.

[9] Chow, P., J. Cioffi, and J. Bingham. A practical discrete multitone transceiver loading algorithm for data transmission over spectrally shaped channels. *IEEE Trans. on Communications*, 43(2/3/4):773–775, Feb.–Apr. 1995.

[10] Chung, S. T., S. J. Kim, J. Lee, and J. M. Cioffi. A game-theoretic approach to power allocation in frequency-selective Gaussian interference channels. In *Proc., IEEE Intl. Symposium on Information Theory*, page 316, July 2003.

[11] Ergen, M., S. Coleri, and P. Varaiya. QoS aware adaptive resource allocation techniques for fair scheduling in OFDMA based broadband wireless access systems. *IEEE Transactions on Broadcasting*, 49(4):362–370, Dec. 2003.

[12] Fang, L. and X. Zhang. Optimal fractional frequency reuse in OFDMA based wireless networks. In *Proc. 4th International Conference on Wireless Communications, Networking and Mobile Computing*, pages 1–4, Oct. 12–14, 2008.

[13] Foschini, G. J., H. Huang, K. Karakayali, R. A. Valenzuela, and S. Venkatesan. The value of coherent base station coordination. In *Proc., Conference on Information Sciences and Systems (CISS)*, Johns Hopkins University, Mar. 2005.

[14] Gallager, R. G. *Information Theory and Reliable Communications*. Wiley, 1968.

[15] Gilhousen, K. S. et. al. On the capacity of a cellular CDMA system. *IEEE Trans. on Veh. Technology*, 40(2):303–312, May 1991.

[16] Goldsmith, A. J. *Wireless Communications*. Cambridge University Press, 2005.

[17] Gui, X. and T. S. Ng. Performance of asynchronous orthogonal multicarrier system in a frequency selective fading channel. *IEEE Trans. on Communications*, 47(7): 1084–1091, July 1999.

[18] Han, Z., Z. Ji, and K. R. Liu. Power minimization for multi-cell OFDM networks using distributed non-cooperative game approach. In *Proc., IEEE Globecom*, pages 3742–3747, Dec. 2004.

[19] Hara, S. and R. Prasad. Overview of multicarrier CDMA. *IEEE Communications Magazine*, 35(12):126–133, Dec. 1997.

[20] Hernandez, A., I. Guio, and A. Valdovinos. Interference management through resource allocation in multi-cell OFDMA networks. In *Proc. IEEE Vehicular Technology Conference*, pages 1–5, Apr. 26–29, 2009.

[21] Huang, H. and S. Venkatesan. Asymptotic downlink capacity of coordinated cellular network. In *Proc., IEEE Asilomar*, Mar. 2004.

[22] Huawei. R1-050507: Soft frequency reuse scheme for UTRAN LTE. *3GPP TSG RAN WG1 Meeting #41*, May 2005.

[23] Jafar, S. A., G. Foschini, and A. J. Goldsmith. Phantomnet: Exploring optimal multicellular multiple antenna systems. *EURASIP Journal on Appl. Signal Processing, Special issue on MIMO Comm. and Signal Processing*, 591–605, May 2004.

[24] Jang, J. and K. Lee. Transmit power adaptation for multiuser OFDM systems. *IEEE Journal on Sel. Areas in Communications*, 21(2):171–178, Feb. 2003.

[25] Jindal, N., S. Weber, and J. G. Andrews. Fractional power control for decentralized wireless networks. *IEEE Trans. on Wireless Communications*, 7(12):5482–5492, Dec. 2008.

[26] Jung, P., P. Baier, and A. Steil. Advantages of CDMA and spread spectrum techniques over FDMA and TDMA in cellular mobile radio applications. *IEEE Trans. on Veh. Technology*, 357–64, Aug. 1993.

[27] Kim, H., Y. Han, and J. Koo. Optimal subchannel allocation scheme in multicell OFDMA systems. In *Proc., IEEE Veh. Technology Conf.*, pages 1821–1825, May 2004.

[28] Kim, S. G., K. Cho, D. Yoon, Y.-J. Ko, and J. K. Kwon. Performance analysis of downlink inter cell interference coordination in the LTE-Advanced system. In *Proc. Fourth International Conference on Digital Telecommunications*, pages 30–33, July 20–25, 2009.

[29] Kivanc, D., G. Li, and H. Liu. Computationally efficient bandwidth allocation and power control for OFDMA. *IEEE Transactions on Wireless Communications*, 2(6):1150–1158, Nov. 2003.

[30] Knopp, R. and P. Humblet. Information capacity and power control in single-cell multiuser communications. In *Proc., IEEE Intl. Conf. on Communications*, pages 331–335, June 1995.

[31] Larsson, E. G. On the combination of spatial diversity and multiuser diversity. *IEEE Communications Letters*, 8(8):517–519, Aug. 2004.

[32] Li, G. and H. Liu. Downlink dynamic resource allocation for multi-cell OFDMA system. In *Proc., IEEE Veh. Technology Conf.*, pages 1698–1702, Oct. 2003.

[33] Li. G. and H. Liu. On the optimality of the OFDMA network. *IEEE Communications Letters*, 9(5):438–440, May 2005.

[34] Lozano, A., A. Tulino, and S. Verdu. Optimum power allocation for multiuser OFDM with arbitrary signal constellations. *IEEE Trans. on Communications*, 56(5): 828–837, May 2008.

[35] Mohanram, C. and S. Bhashyam. A sub-optimal joint subcarrier and power allocation algorithm for multiuser OFDM. *IEEE Communications Letters*, 9(8):685–687, Aug. 2005.

[36] Ng, T. C. and W. Yu. Joint optimization of relay strategies and power allocation in a cooperative cellular network. *IEEE J. Select. Areas Commun.*, pages 328–339, Feb. 2007.

[37] Noune, M. and A. Nix. Frequency-domain precoding for single carrier frequency-division multiple access. *IEEE Communications Magazine*, 68–74, June 2009.

[38] Olofsson, H., J. Naslund, and J. Skold. Interference diversity gain in frequency hopping GSM. In *Proc., IEEE Veh. Technology Conf.*, 1:102–106, Aug. 1995.

[39] Pietrzyk, S. and G. J. Janssen. Subcarrier allocation and power control for QoS provision in the presence of CCI for the downlink of cellular OFDMA systems. In *Proc., IEEE Veh. Technology Conf.*, pages 2221–2225, Apr. 2003.

[40] Pischella, M. and J.-C. Belfiore. Power control in distributed cooperative OFDMA cellular networks. *IEEE Trans. on Wireless Communications*, 7(5):2008, May 2008.

[41] Rhee, W. and J. M. Cioffi. Increase in capacity of multiuser OFDM system using dynamic subchannel allocation. In *Proc., IEEE Veh. Technology Conf.*, pages 1085–1089, Tokyo, May 2000.

[42] Rohling, H. and R. Grunheid. Performance comparison of different multiple access schemes for the downlink of an OFDM communication system. In *Proc., IEEE Veh. Technology Conf.*, pages 1365–1369, Phoenix, AZ, May 1997.

[43] Shakkottai, S., T. S. Rappaport, and P. Karlson. Cross-layer design for wireless networks. *IEEE Communications Magazine*, 74–80, Oct. 2003.

[44] Sharif, M. and B. Hassibi. Scaling laws of sum rate using time-sharing, DPC, and beamforming for MIMO broadcast channels. In *Proc., IEEE Intl. Symposium on Information Theory*, page 175, July 2004.

[45] Shen, Z., J. G. Andrews, and B. Evans. Optimal power allocation for multiuser OFDM. In *Proc., IEEE Globecom*, pages 337–341, San Francisco, Dec. 2003.

[46] Shen, Z., J. G. Andrews, and B. L. Evans. Adaptive resource allocation for multiuser OFDM with constrained fairness. *IEEE Trans. on Wireless Communications*, 4(6):2726–2737, Nov. 2005.

[47] Shitz, S. S., O. Somekh, and B. M. Zaidel. Multi-cell communications: An information theoretic perspective. In *Joint Workshop on Communications and Coding (JWCC)*, Florence, Italy, Oct. 2004.

[48] Stamatiou, K. and J. Proakis. A performance analysis of coded frequency-hopped OFDMA [cellular system]. In *Proc., IEEE Wireless Communications and Networking Conf.*, 2:1132–1137, Mar. 2005.

[49] Svedman, P., S. K. Wilson, L. J. Cimini, and B. Ottersten. Opportunistic beamforming and scheduling for OFDMA systems. *IEEE Trans. on Communications*, 55(5):941–952, May 2007.

[50] Tse, D. Multiuser diversity in wireless networks. In *Stanford Wireless Communications Seminar*, available at: http://www.stanford.edu/group/wcs/, Apr. 2001.

[51] Tsumura, S., R. Mino, S. Hara, and Y. Hara. Performance comparison of OFDM-FH and MC-CDMA in single- and multi-cell environments. In *Proc., IEEE Veh. Technology Conf.*, 3:1730–1734, May 2005.

[52] Viswanath, P., D. Tse, and R. Laroia. Opportunistic beamforming using dumb antennas. *IEEE Trans. on Info. Theory*, 48(6):1277–1294, June 2002.

[53] Wong, C., R. Cheng, K. Letaief, and R. Murch. Multiuser OFDM with adaptive subcarrier, bit, and power allocation. *IEEE Journal on Sel. Areas in Communications*, 17(10):1747–1758, Oct. 1999.

[54] Wong, I., Z. Shen, B. Evans, and J. Andrews. A low complexity algorithm for proportional resource allocation in OFDMA systems. In *Proc., IEEE Signal Processing Workshop*, pages 1–6, Austin, TX, Oct. 2004.

[55] Xiao, W., R. Ratasuk, A. Ghosh, R. Love, Y. Sun, and R. Nory. Uplink power control, interference coordination and resource allocation for 3GPP E-UTRA. In *Proc., IEEE Veh. Technology Conf.*, pages 1–5, Sept. 2006.

[56] Yee, N., J. Linnartz, and G. Fettweis. Multicarrier cdma in indoor wireless radio networks. In *Proc., IEEE PIMRC*, pages 109–113, Yokohama, Japan, Sept. 1993.

[57] Yu, W., G. Ginis, and J. Cioffi. Distributed multiuser power control for digital subscriber lines. *IEEE Journal on Sel. Areas in Communications*, 20(5):1105–1115, June 2002.

[58] Zhang, H., H. Dai, and Q. Zhou. Base station cooperation for multiuser MIMO: Joint transmission and BS selection. In *Proc., Conference on Information Sciences and Systems (CISS)*, Mar. 2004.

[59] Zhang, Y. J. and K. B. Letaief. Multiuser adaptive subcarrier-and-bit allocation with adaptive cell selection for OFDM systems. *IEEE Transactions on Wireless Communications*, 3(4):1566–1575, Sep. 2004.

Chapter 5

Multiple Antenna Transmission and Reception

T he expanded and more advanced use of multiple antennas at both the transmitter and receiver promises to be among LTE's largest advantages over incumbent technologies. Multicarrier modulation enables richer, more efficient use of multiple antennas and receivers in wideband channels. Multiple antenna techniques can be grouped into roughly three different categories: diversity, interference suppression, and spatial multiplexing. Spatial diversity allows a number of different versions of the signal to be transmitted and/or received, and provides considerable resilience against fading. Interference suppression uses the spatial dimensions to reject interference from other users, either through the physical antenna gain pattern or through other forms of array processing such as linear precoding, postcoding, or interference cancellation. Spatial multiplexing allows two or more independent streams of data to be sent simultaneously in the same bandwidth, and hence is useful primarily for increasing the data rate. And, of course, combinations of techniques from these broad categories can be used simultaneously, to achieve some of the benefits of each. LTE's current options include techniques from each of the three categories.

All three of these different approaches are often collectively referred to as multiple input-multiple output (MIMO) communication, although this is inaccurate unless there are at least two antennas at both the transmitter and the receiver.[1] This chapter will provide a tutorial on multiantenna technologies organized around the above three categories, and attempt to provide intuition on the strengths and weaknesses of each technique. We will particularly highlight the approaches that are specified or likely to be used in LTE, with precise implementation details left mostly to Chapter 7 (downlink) and Chapter 8 (uplink). As LTE matures in the future, more advanced techniques will be offered, but this chapter provides a technical foundation broad enough to cover nearly any possible

---

1 Another common, and stricter, convention is for MIMO to specifically refer to only the third type, spatial multiplexing, since only this technique actually transmits multiple independent data streams and hence has multiple inputs and outputs.

multiantenna technique. For example, many possible multiuser MIMO techniques[2] can be viewed as a hybrid of all three categories.

5.1 Spatial Diversity Overview

As we have seen in Chapters 2–4, diversity is indispensable for reliability in wireless systems. The primary advantage of spatial diversity relative to most forms of time and frequency diversity is that no additional bandwidth or power is needed in order to take advantage of spatial diversity. Instead, spatial diversity is exploited through two or more antennas, which are separated by enough distance so that the fading is approximately decorrelated between them. The cost of and space consumed by each additional antenna, its RF transmit and/or receive chain, and the associated signal processing required to modulate or demodulate multiple spatial streams may not be negligible. However, for a small number of antennas, the gains are significant enough to warrant the space and expense in most modern wireless systems.

5.1.1 Array Gain

When multiple antennas are used, there are two forms of gain available, which we will refer to as *diversity gain* and *array gain*. Diversity gain, which will be treated shortly, results from the creation of multiple independent channels between the transmitter and receiver, and is a product of the statistical richness of those channels. Array gain, on the other hand, does not rely on statistical diversity between the different channels. Instead it achieves its performance enhancement by coherently combining the energy of each of the antennas to gain an advantage versus the noise signal on each antenna, which is uncorrelated and so does not add coherently. Due to array gain, even if the channels are completely correlated (as might happen in a line-of-sight system with closely spaced antennas) the received SNR increases linearly with the number of receive antennas, N_r.

For a $N_t \times N_r$ system, the array gain is N_r, which can be seen for a $1 \times N_r$ as follows. In correlated flat fading, each antenna $i \in (1, N_r)$ receives a signal that can be characterized as:

$$y_i = h_i x + n_i = hx + n_i, \tag{5.1}$$

where $h_i = h$ for all the antennas since they are perfectly correlated. Hence, the SNR on a single antenna is

$$\gamma_i = \frac{|h|^2}{\sigma^2}, \tag{5.2}$$

where the noise power is σ^2 and we assume unit signal energy ($\mathcal{E}_x = E|x|^2 = 1$). If all the receive antenna paths are added, the resulting signal is

$$y = \sum_{i=1}^{N_r} y_i = N_r hx + \sum_{i=1}^{N_r} n_i, \tag{5.3}$$

---

2 Also known as space division multiple access, as introduced in Chapter 4 and discussed in more detail here in Section 5.9.1.

and the combined SNR, assuming that just the noise on each branch is uncorrelated, is

$$\gamma_\Sigma = \frac{|N_r h|^2}{N_r \sigma^2} = \frac{N_r |h|^2}{\sigma^2}. \tag{5.4}$$

Hence, the received SNR also increases linearly with the number of receive antennas even if those antennas are correlated. However, because the channels are all correlated in this case (in fact, identical), there is no diversity gain.

5.1.2   Diversity Gain

Traditionally, the main objective of spatial diversity has been to improve the communication reliability by decreasing the sensitivity to fading. The physical layer reliability is typically measured by the outage probability or average bit error rate. In additive noise, the bit error probability (BEP) can be written for virtually any modulation scheme as:

$$P_b \approx c_1 e^{-c_2 \gamma}, \tag{5.5}$$

where c_1 and c_2 are constants that depend on the modulation type and γ is the received SNR. Because the error probability is *exponentially* decreasing with SNR, the few instances in a fading channel when the received SNR is low dominate the BEP, since even modestly higher SNR values have dramatically reduced BEP.

In contrast, with fading the SNR becomes a random variable and so the BEP is also a random variable. Without diversity, the average BEP decreases very slowly in a fading channel, and can be written as:

$$\bar{P}_b \approx c_3 \gamma^{-1}. \tag{5.6}$$

This simple inverse relationship between SNR and BEP is *much, much* weaker than a decaying exponential, which, as discussed in Section 2.6, results in terrible reliability for unmitigated fading channels.

If N_t transmit antennas and N_r receive antennas that are sufficiently spaced[3] are added to the system, it is said that the *diversity order* is $N_d = N_r N_t$, since that is the number of uncorrelated channel paths between the transmitter and receiver. Since the probability of all the N_d uncorrelated channels having low SNR is very small, the diversity order has a dramatic effect on the system reliability. With diversity, the average BEP improves to:

$$\bar{P}_b \approx c_4 \gamma^{-N_d}, \tag{5.7}$$

which is an enormous improvement. For example, if the BEP without any diversity was about 1 in 10—which is awful—the BEP with two antennas at both the transmitter and receiver would be closer to 1 in 10,000. Diversity gain is very powerful!

On the other hand, if only an array gain was possible (for example, if the antennas are not sufficiently spaced or the channel is LOS), the average BEP would only decrease from (5.6) to:

$$\bar{P}_b \approx c_5 (N_d \gamma)^{-1}, \tag{5.8}$$

---

3   Recall from Section 2.4.3 that generally about a half or even a quarter wavelength allows the antenna elements to be somewhat uncorrelated.

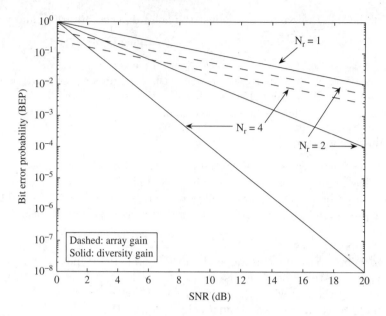

Figure 5.1 Relative bit error probability (BEP) curves for $N_t = 1$, $N_r = (1, 2, 4)$. The BEP (0 dB) is normalized to 1 for each technique. Statistical diversity has a very large impact on BEP, whereas the array gain only results in a fixed shift of the curve.

since the array gain only provides a linear increase in SNR. The difference between (5.7) and (5.8) is quite dramatic as γ and N_d increase, and is shown in Figure 5.1, where it is assumed that the constants $c_i = 1$ (which is equivalent to just normalizing the BEP to 1 for $\gamma = 1$). The trend is clear: sufficient spacing for the antennas is critical for increasing the system reliability.

5.1.3 Increasing the Data Rate with Spatial Diversity

As just discussed, diversity techniques are very effective at averaging out fades in the channel and thus increasing the system reliability. Receive diversity techniques also increase the average received SNR at best linearly due to the array gain. The Shannon capacity formula gives the maximum achievable data rate of a single communication link in additive white Gaussian noise (AWGN) as:

$$C = B \log_2(1 + \gamma), \tag{5.9}$$

where C is the "capacity," or maximum error-free data rate, B is the bandwidth of the channel, and γ is again the SNR (or SINR). Due to advances in coding, and with sufficient diversity, it may be possible to approach the Shannon limit in some wireless channels.

Since antenna diversity increases the SNR linearly, diversity techniques increase the capacity only *logarithmically* with respect to the number of antennas. In other words, the data rate benefit rapidly diminishes as antennas are added. However, it can be noted that when the SNR is low, the capacity increase is close to linear with SNR, since $\log(1+x) \approx x$

for small x. Hence, in low SNR channels, diversity techniques increase the capacity about linearly, but the overall throughput is generally still poor due to the low SNR.

In order to get a more substantial data rate increase at higher SNRs, the multiantenna channel can instead be used to send multiple independent streams. As we will also see in Section 5.5, spatial multiplexing has the ability to achieve a *linear* increase in the data rate with the number of antennas at moderate to high SINRs through the use of sophisticated signal processing algorithms. Specifically, the capacity can be increased as a multiple of $\min(N_t, N_r)$, that is, capacity is limited by the minimum of the number of antennas at either the transmitter or receiver.

5.1.4   Increased Coverage or Reduced Transmit Power

The benefits of diversity can also be harnessed to increase the coverage area and to reduce the required transmit power, although these gains directly compete with each other, as well as with the achievable reliability and data rate.

We first consider the increase in coverage area due to spatial diversity. For simplicity, assume that there are N_r receive antennas and just one transmit antenna. Due to just the array gain, the average SNR is approximately $N_r\gamma$, where γ is the average SNR per branch. From the simplified path loss model of Chapter 2, $P_r = P_t P_o d^{-\alpha}$, it can be found that the increase in coverage range is $N_r^{\frac{1}{\alpha}}$, and so the coverage area improvement is $N_r^{\frac{2}{\alpha}}$, without even considering the diversity gain. Hence, the system reliability could still be greatly enhanced even with this range extension. Similar reasoning can be used to show that the required transmit power can be reduced by $10\log_{10} N_r$ dB while maintaining a diversity gain of $N_t \times N_r$.

5.2   Receive Diversity

The most prevalent form of spatial diversity is receive diversity, often with just two antennas. This type of diversity is nearly ubiquitous—$N_r = 2$ being by far the most common—on cellular base stations and wireless LAN access points, and will be mandatory for LTE base stations and handsets. Receive diversity on its own places no particular requirements on the transmitter, but requires a receiver that processes the N_r received streams and combines them in some fashion. Because receive diversity places no requirements on the transmitter, these techniques are not specified in the LTE standard. Nevertheless, they most certainly will be used in nearly all LTE handsets and base stations.

In this section, we will overview two of the widely used combining algorithms, selection combining (SC) and maximal ratio combining (MRC) which are shown in Figure 5.2. Although receive diversity is highly effective in both flat fading and frequency selective fading channels, we will focus on the flat (narrowband) fading scenario where the signal received by each of the N_r antennas is uncorrelated and has the same average power.

5.2.1   Selection Combining

Selection combining is the simplest type of "combiner," in that it simply estimates the instantaneous strengths of each of the N_r streams, and selects the highest one. Since SC ignores the useful energy on the other streams, it is clearly suboptimal, but its simplicity and reduced hardware and power requirements make it attractive for narrowband

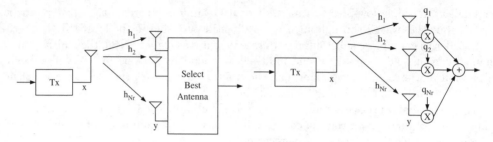

Figure 5.2 Receive diversity: selection combining (left) and maximal ratio combining (right).

channels. In a wideband channel, different coherence bands will have different SNRs, and so although selection diversity can be used on each band, that would likely require all antennas to be active for at least one band, which nullifies one of the main arguments in favor of selection diversity. If all the antennas and RF chains have to be active, it is usually better to use MRC, described next.

The diversity gain from employing selection combining can be confirmed quite quickly by considering the outage probability, defined as the probability that the received SNR drops below some required threshold, $P_{out} = P[\gamma < \gamma_o] = p$. Assuming N_r uncorrelated receptions of the signal,

$$
\begin{aligned}
P_{out} &= P[\gamma_1 < \gamma_o, \ \gamma_2 < \gamma_o, \ \ldots, \ \gamma_M < \gamma_o], \\
&= P[\gamma_1 < \gamma_o]P[\gamma_2 < \gamma_o]\ldots P[\gamma_M < \gamma_o], \\
&= p^{N_r}.
\end{aligned}
\tag{5.10}
$$

For a Rayleigh fading channel:

$$
p = 1 - e^{-\gamma_o/\bar{\gamma}},
\tag{5.11}
$$

where $\bar{\gamma}$ is the average received SNR at that location (for example, due to path loss). Thus, selection combining decreases the outage probability to:

$$
P_{out} = (1 - e^{-\gamma_o/\bar{\gamma}})^{N_r}.
\tag{5.12}
$$

The average received SNR for N_r-branch SC can be derived in Rayleigh fading to be:

$$
\begin{aligned}
\gamma_{sc} &= \bar{\gamma} \sum_{i=1}^{N_r} \frac{1}{i}, \\
&= \bar{\gamma}(1 + \frac{1}{2} + \frac{1}{3} + \ \ldots \ + \frac{1}{N_r}).
\end{aligned}
\tag{5.13}
$$

Hence, although each added (uncorrelated) antenna does increase the average SNR,[4] it does so with rapidly diminishing returns. The average BEP can be derived by averaging (integrating) the appropriate BEP expression in AWGN against the exponential

---

4 It can be noted that (5.13) does not in fact converge, i.e., $N_r \to \infty \Rightarrow \gamma_{sc} \to \infty$. This is due to the tail of the exponential function allowing arbitrarily high SNR. In practice, this is impossible since the number of co-located uncorrelated antennas could rarely exceed single digits, and because the SNR of a single branch never does approach infinity.

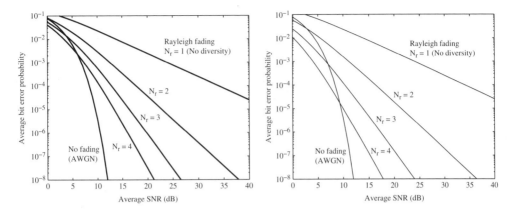

Figure 5.3 Average bit error probability for selection combining (left) and maximal ratio combining (right) using coherent BPSK. MRC typically achieves a few dB better SNR than SC due to its array gain.

distribution. Plots of the BEP with different amounts of selection diversity are shown in Figure 5.3, and although the performance improvement with increasing N_r diminishes, the improvement from the first few antennas is substantial. For example, at a target BEP of 10^{-4} about 15 dB of improvement is achieved by adding a single receive antenna, and the improvement increases to 20 dB with an additional antenna.

5.2.2 Maximal Ratio Combining

Maximal ratio combining (MRC) combines the information from all the received branches in order to maximize the ratio of signal-to-noise power, which gives it its name. MRC works by weighting each branch with a complex factor $q_i = |q_i|e^{j\phi_i}$ and then adding up the N_r branches, as shown in Figure 5.2. The received signal on each branch can be written as $x(t)h_i$, assuming the fading is flat with a complex value of $h_i = |h_i|e^{j\theta_i}$ on the ith branch.

The combined signal can then be written as:

$$y(t) = x(t) \sum_{i=1}^{N_r} |q_i||h_i| \exp\{j(\phi_i + \theta_i)\}. \tag{5.14}$$

If we let the phase of the combining coefficient $\phi_i = -\theta_i$ for all the branches, then the signal-to-noise ratio of $y(t)$ can be written as:

$$\gamma_{\text{mrc}} = \frac{\mathcal{E}_x(\sum_{i=1}^{N_r} |q_i||h_i|)^2}{\sigma^2 \sum_{i=1}^{N_r} |q_i|^2}, \tag{5.15}$$

where $\mathcal{E}_x$ is the transmit signal energy. Maximizing this expression by taking the derivative with respect to $|q_i|$ gives the maximizing combining values as $|q_i^*|^2 = |h_i|^2/\sigma^2$, i.e., each branch is multiplied by its SNR. In other words, branches with better signal energy should be enhanced, whereas branches with lower SNRs should be given relatively less weight. The resulting signal-to-noise ratio can be found to be:

$$\gamma_{\mathrm{mrc}} = \frac{\mathcal{E}_x \sum_{i=1}^{N_r} |h_i|^2}{\sigma^2} = \sum_{i=1}^{N_r} \gamma_i. \tag{5.16}$$

MRC is intuitively appealing: the total SNR is achieved by simply adding up the branch SNRs when the appropriate weighting coefficients are used.

It should be noted that although MRC does in fact maximize SNR and generally performs well, it may not be optimal in many cases since it ignores interference power (the statistics of which may differ from branch to branch). Equal gain combining (EGC), which only corrects the phase and hence as the name of the technique suggests uses $|q_i| = 1$ and $\phi_i = -\theta_i$ for all the combiner branches, achieves a post-combining SNR of:

$$\gamma_{\mathrm{EGC}} = \mathcal{E}_x \frac{\sum_{i=1}^{N_r} |h_i|^2}{N_r \sigma^2} = \frac{1}{N_r} \sum_{i=1}^{N_r} \gamma_i. \tag{5.17}$$

The most notable difference between (5.17) and (5.16) is that EGC incurs a noise penalty of N_r in trade for not requiring channel gain estimation. EGC is hence very suboptimal to MRC assuming that the MRC combiner has accurate knowledge of $|h_i|$, particularly when the noise variance is high and there are several receive branches. For an interference-limited cellular system like LTE, MRC would be strongly preferred to either EGC or SC, despite the fact that the latter techniques are somewhat simpler. The BEP performance of MRC is shown in Figure 5.3. Although the BEP slopes are similar to selection combining since the techniques have the same diversity order, the SNR gain is several dB due to its array gain, which may be especially significant at the SINR operating points expected in LTE (frequently less than 10 dB). An additional very important advantage of MRC in frequency selective fading channels is that all the frequency diversity can be utilized, whereas an RF antenna selection algorithm would simply select the best *average* antenna and then must live with the potentially deep fades at certain frequencies.

5.3 Transmit Diversity

Spatial transmit diversity is a more recent development than spatial receive diversity, and has become widely understood and implemented only in the early 2000s. Because the signals sent from different transmit antennas interfere with one another at the receiver, additional signal processing is required at both the transmitter and receiver in order to achieve diversity while removing or at least attenuating the spatial interference. Transmit diversity is particularly useful in the downlink since the base station can usually accommodate more antennas than the mobile station. Additionally, if multiple antennas are already present at the base station for uplink receive diversity, the incremental cost of using them for transmit diversity is small.

Multiple antenna transmit schemes (both transmit diversity and MIMO) are often categorized into two classes: *open-loop* and *closed-loop*. Open-loop refers to systems that do *not* require knowledge of the channel at the transmitter as shown in Figure 5.4. On

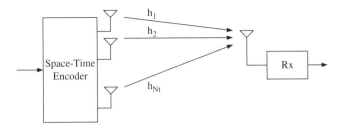

Figure 5.4 Open-loop transmit diversity (no feedback).

the contrary, closed-loop systems require channel knowledge at the transmitter, thus necessitating either channel reciprocity (same uplink and downlink channel, possible in TDD) or more commonly a feedback channel from the receiver to the transmitter.

5.3.1 Open-Loop Transmit Diversity: 2×1 Space-Frequency Block Coding

The most popular open-loop transmit diversity scheme is space-time (in LTE, space-frequency) coding, where a particular code known to the receiver is applied at the transmitter. Although the receiver must know the channel to decode a space-time code, this is not a large burden since the channel must be known for other decoding operations anyway. Space-time coding was first suggested in the early 1990s [72, 98] before generating intense interest in the late 1990s. Although there are many types of space-time codes, in this section we specifically focus on space-frequency block codes (SFBCs), which lend themselves to easy implementation and are supported in LTE.

A key breakthrough in the late 1990s was a space-time block code (STBC) referred to as either the Alamouti code (after its inventor [2]) or the orthogonal space-time block code (OSTBC). This simple code has become the most popular means of achieving transmit diversity due to its ease of implementation (linear at both the transmitter and receiver), and its optimality with regards to diversity order. Conceived for a narrowband fading channel, STBCs can easily be adapted to a wideband fading channel using OFDM by utilizing adjacent subcarriers rather than consecutive symbols. Mathematically and conceptually, there is no difference between SFBCs and the more common STBCs: instead of adjacent subcarriers as denoted below, STBCs use consecutive symbols in time [7]. SFBCs are preferred to STBCs because they experience less delay and are less likely to suffer from channel variations. STBCs would require two OFDM symbols to be encoded (and decoded) over, which significantly increases delay while also increasing the likelihood of channel variation over the code block, which as we will see is contrary to the standard decoding model.[5]

The simplest SFBC corresponds to two transmit antennas and a single receive antenna. If two symbols to be transmitted are s_1 and s_2, the Alamouti code sends the

---

5 There is a body of work on STBCs that are capable of handling channel variations over the block, e.g., [53, 71], but it is preferable to be able to simply assume that the channel is constant over the code block.

following over two subcarriers f_1 and f_2:

	Antenna	1	2
Subcarrier	f_1	s_1	s_2
	f_2	$-s_2^*$	s_1^*

The 2×1 Alamouti SFBC is referred to as a rate 1 code, since the data rate is neither increased nor decreased; two symbols are sent over two adjacent subcarriers. Rather than directly increasing the data rate, the goal of space-frequency block coding is to harness the spatial diversity of the channel.

Assuming a flat fading channel on each subcarrier, then $h_1(f_1)$ is the complex channel gain from transmit antenna 1 to the receive antenna and $h_2(f_2)$ is from transmit antenna 2. An additional assumption is that the channel is constant over the two adjacent subcarriers, that is $h_1(f_1) = h_1(f_2) = h_1$. This is a reasonable assumption if $B_c \gg B/L$, which by choosing a large enough number of subcarriers L can be forced to be true. From Chapter 3, we can recall that forcing flat fading per subcarrier is one of the main purposes of multicarrier systems, and a prerequisite for efficiently suppressing ISI.

The received signal $r(f)$ can be written as:

$$\begin{aligned} r(f_1) &= h_1 s_1 + h_2 s_2 + n(f_1), \\ r(f_2) &= -h_1 s_2^* + h_2 s_1^* + n(f_2), \end{aligned} \tag{5.18}$$

where $n(\cdot)$ is a sample of white Gaussian noise. The following diversity combining scheme can then be used, assuming the channel is known at the receiver:

$$\begin{aligned} y_1 &= h_1^* r(f_1) + h_2 r^*(f_2), \\ y_2 &= h_2^* r(f_1) - h_1 r^*(f_2). \end{aligned} \tag{5.19}$$

Hence, for example, it can be seen that:

$$\begin{aligned} y_1 &= h_1^*(h_1 s_1 + h_2 s_2 + n(f_1)) + h_2(-h_1^* s_2 + h_2^* s_1 + n^*(f_2)), \\ &= (|h_1|^2 + |h_2|^2) s_1 + h_1^* n(f_1) + h_2 n^*(f_2), \end{aligned} \tag{5.20}$$

and proceeding similarly that:

$$y_2 = (|h_1|^2 + |h_2|^2) s_2 + h_2^* n(f_1) - h_1 n^*(f_2). \tag{5.21}$$

Hence, this very simple decoder that just linearly combines the two received samples $r(f_1)$ and $r^*(f_2)$ is able to eliminate all the spatial interference. The resulting SNR can be computed as:

$$\begin{aligned} \gamma_\Sigma &= \frac{(|h_1|^2 + |h_2|^2)^2}{|h_1|^2 \sigma^2 + |h_2|^2 \sigma^2} \frac{\mathcal{E}_x}{2}, \\ &= \frac{(|h_1|^2 + |h_2|^2)}{\sigma^2} \frac{\mathcal{E}_x}{2}, \\ &= \frac{\sum_{i=1}^{2} |h_i|^2}{\sigma^2} \frac{\mathcal{E}_x}{2}. \end{aligned} \tag{5.22}$$

Referring to (5.16), it can be seen that this is similar to the gain from MRC. However, in order to keep the transmit power the same as in the MRC case, each transmit antenna must halve its transmit power so that the total transmit energy per actual data symbol is $\mathcal{E}_x$ for both cases. That is for SFBC, $E|s_1|^2 = E|s_2|^2 = \mathcal{E}_x/2$ since each are sent twice.

In summary, the 2×1 Alamouti code achieves the same diversity order and data rate as a 1×2 receive diversity system with MRC, but with a 3-dB penalty due to the redundant transmission that is required to remove the spatial interference at the receiver. An equivalent statement is that the Alamouti code sacrifices the array gain of MRC, while achieving the same diversity gain. The linear decoder used earlier is the maximum likelihood decoder (in zero mean noise), so is optimum as well as simple.

Space-time trellis codes [88,89] could also be converted to frequency domain versions. These codes introduce memory and achieve better performance than orthogonal STBCs (about 2 dB in many cases), but have decoding complexity that scales as $O(M^{\min\{N_t,N_r\}})$, where M is again the constellation order. Orthogonal STBCs (or SFBCs) on the other hand have complexity that scales only as $O(\min\{N_t, N_r\})$, so the complexity reduction is quite considerable for high-spectral efficiency systems with many antennas at both the transmitter and receiver.

5.3.2 Open-Loop Transmit Diversity with More Antennas

It would be desirable to achieve the gains of both MRC and the SFBC simultaneously, and that is indeed possible in several cases. In general, however, orthogonal SFBCs like the 2×1 Alamouti code do not exist for most combinations of transmit and receive antennas. As a result, a substantial amount of research has proposed different techniques for achieving transmit diversity for more general scenarios, and overviewing all this work is outside the scope of this chapter. Instead, we refer readers interested in space-time coding to the following overviews [23, 30, 64]. Here, we will overview two other popular open-loop transmit diversity approaches before concluding this section by comparing transmit and receive diversity.

2×2 SFBC

The 2×2 SFBC uses the same transmit encoding scheme as for 2×1 transmit diversity. Now, the channel description (still flat fading and constant over two symbols) can be represented as a 2×2 matrix rather than a 2×1 vector.

$$\mathbf{H} = \begin{bmatrix} h_{11} & h_{12} \\ h_{21} & h_{22} \end{bmatrix}.$$

The resulting signals at subcarriers f_1 and f_2 on antennas 1 and 2 can be represented as:

$$\begin{aligned}
r_1(f_1) &= h_{11}s_1 + h_{21}s_2 + n_1(f_1), \\
r_1(f_2) &= -h_{11}s_2^* + h_{21}s_1^* + n_1(f_2), \\
r_2(f_1) &= h_{12}s_1 + h_{22}s_2 + n_2(f_1), \\
r_2(f_2) &= -h_{12}s_2^* + h_{22}s_1^* + n_2(f_2).
\end{aligned} \qquad (5.23)$$

Using the following combining scheme:

$$y_1 = h_{11}^* r_1(f_1) + h_{21} r_1^*(f_2) + h_{12}^* r_2(f_1) + h_{22} r_2^*(f_2),$$
$$y_2 = h_{21}^* r_1(f_1) - h_{11} r_1^*(f_2) + h_{22}^* r_2(f_1) - h_{21} r_2^*(f_2),$$

yields the following decision statistics:

$$y_1 = (|h_{11}|^2 + |h_{12}|^2 + |h_{21}|^2 + |h_{22}|^2)s_1 + 4 \text{ noise terms},$$
$$y_2 = (|h_{11}|^2 + |h_{12}|^2 + |h_{21}|^2 + |h_{22}|^2)s_2 + 4 \text{ noise terms},$$

and results in the following SNR:

$$\gamma_\Sigma = \frac{\left(\sum_j \sum_i |h_{ij}|^2\right)^2}{\sigma^2 \sum_j \sum_i |h_{ij}|^2} \frac{\mathcal{E}_x}{2} = \frac{\sum_{j=1}^{2} \sum_{i=1}^{2} |h_{ij}|^2}{\sigma^2} \frac{\mathcal{E}_x}{2}. \tag{5.24}$$

This is like MRC with four receive antennas, where again there is a 3-dB penalty due to transmitting each symbol twice. An orthogonal, full-rate, full-diversity SFBC over an $N_t \times N_r$ channel will provide a diversity gain equivalent to that of an MRC system with $N_t N_r$ antennas, with a $10 \log_{10} N_t$ dB transmit power penalty due to the N_t transmit antennas. In other words, in theory it is generally beneficial to have somewhat evenly balanced antenna arrays, as this will maximize the diversity order for a fixed number of antenna elements. In practice, full-diversity, orthogonal SFBCs only exist for $N_t = 2$ and for certain values of N_r, although coding theorists have developed several near-orthogonal full-rate space-time block coding approaches [44, 73, 86].

4 × 2 Stacked STBCs

As presented in the previous section, the 2×2 Alamouti code achieves full diversity gain. In LTE, it will be common to have four transmit antennas at the base station. In this case, two data streams can be sent using a double space-time transmit diversity (DSTTD) scheme that essentially consists of operating two 2×1 Alamouti code systems in parallel [62, 91]. DSTTD, also called "stacked STBCs," combines transmit diversity and maximum ratio combining techniques along with a form of spatial multiplexing as shown in Figure 5.5. As in other space-time diversity techniques, the time dimension can be used interchangeably with frequency to create stacked SFBCs.

The received signals at subcarriers f_1 and f_2 on antennas 1 and 2 can be represented with the equivalent channel model as:

$$\begin{bmatrix} r_1(f_1) \\ r_1^*(f_2) \\ \hline r_2(f_1) \\ r_2^*(f_2) \end{bmatrix} = \begin{bmatrix} h_{11} & h_{12} & h_{13} & h_{14} \\ h_{12}^* & -h_{11}^* & h_{14}^* & -h_{13}^* \\ \hline h_{21} & h_{22} & h_{23} & h_{24} \\ h_{22}^* & -h_{21}^* & h_{24}^* & -h_{23}^* \end{bmatrix} \begin{bmatrix} s_1 \\ s_2 \\ \hline s_3 \\ s_4 \end{bmatrix} + \begin{bmatrix} n_1(f_1) \\ n_1^*(f_2) \\ \hline n_2(f_1) \\ n_2^*(f_2) \end{bmatrix}. \tag{5.25}$$

Then, the equivalent matrix channel model of DSTTD can be represented as:

$$\begin{bmatrix} \mathbf{r}_1 \\ \mathbf{r}_2 \end{bmatrix} = \begin{bmatrix} \mathbf{H}_{11} & \mathbf{H}_{12} \\ \mathbf{H}_{21} & \mathbf{H}_{22} \end{bmatrix} \begin{bmatrix} \mathbf{s}_1 \\ \mathbf{s}_2 \end{bmatrix} + \begin{bmatrix} \mathbf{n}_1 \\ \mathbf{n}_2 \end{bmatrix}. \tag{5.26}$$

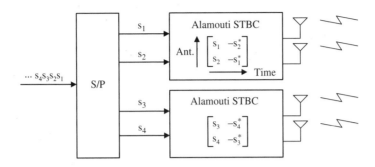

Figure 5.5 4 × 2 stacked STBC transmitter.

As shown in (5.26), each $\mathbf{H}_{ij}$ channel matrix is the equivalent channel of the Alamouti code. Thus, DSTTD can achieve a diversity order of $N_d = 2N_r$ (ML detection) or $N_d = 2$ (ZF detection) due to the 2×1 Alamouti code while also transmitting two data streams (spatial multiplexing order of 2).

If the same linear combining scheme is used as in the 2×2 STBC case, then the following decision statistics can be obtained:

$$
\begin{aligned}
y_1 &= (|h_{11}|^2 + |h_{12}|^2 + |h_{21}|^2 + |h_{22}|^2)s_1 + I_3 + I_4 + 4 \text{ noise terms,} \\
y_2 &= (|h_{11}|^2 + |h_{12}|^2 + |h_{21}|^2 + |h_{22}|^2)s_2 + I_3 + I_4 + 4 \text{ noise terms,} \\
y_3 &= (|h_{13}|^2 + |h_{14}|^2 + |h_{23}|^2 + |h_{24}|^2)s_3 + I_1 + I_2 + 4 \text{ noise terms,} \\
y_4 &= (|h_{13}|^2 + |h_{14}|^2 + |h_{23}|^2 + |h_{24}|^2)s_4 + I_1 + I_2 + 4 \text{ noise terms,} \qquad (5.27)
\end{aligned}
$$

where I_i is the interference from the ith transmit antenna due to transmitting two simultaneous data streams. The detection process of DSTTD should attempt to suppress the interference between the two STBC encoders, and for this purpose can turn to any of the spatial multiplexing receivers discussed in Section 5.5, such as ZF, MMSE, and BLAST. In contrast to OSTBCs (Alamouti codes), the ML receiver for stacked STBCs is *not* linear.

4 × 2 in LTE

In LTE, the rate 2 stacked SFBC approach just discussed is not supported. Instead, when four transmit antennas are available, a combination of SFBC and frequency switched transmit diversity (FSTD) is used. This combination of SFBC and FSTD is a rate 1 diversity scheme, i.e., four modulation symbols are sent over four OFDM symbols using the following space-frequency encoder, where the columns correspond to the subcarrier index and the rows to the transmit antenna:

$$
\frac{1}{\sqrt{2}} \begin{bmatrix} s_1 & s_2 & 0 & 0 \\ 0 & 0 & s_3 & s_4 \\ -s_2^* & s_1^* & 0 & 0 \\ 0 & 0 & -s_4^* & s_3^* \end{bmatrix} \qquad (5.28)
$$

The first and second symbols s_1 and s_2 are sent over antenna ports 0 and 2 on the first two OFDM subcarriers in the block. On the other two subcarriers, the third and fourth symbols are sent using antenna port 1 and 3. Just like 2×2 SFBCs, this encoder is rate 1 and can be detected using a simple linear ML receiver. To send two streams using four antennas, LTE uses an open-loop 4×2 spatial multiplexing approach as indicated in Section 7.2.2.

5.3.3 Transmit Diversity vs. Receive Diversity

The three example space-time block codes showed that transmit and receive diversity are capable of providing an enhanced diversity that increases the robustness of communication over wireless fading channels. The manner in which this improvement is achieved is quite different, however.

Receive Diversity For maximal ratio combining with N_r antennas and only one transmit antenna, the received SNR continuously grows as antennas are added, and the growth is linear, that is:

$$\gamma_{\mathrm{mrc}} = \frac{\mathcal{E}_x}{\sigma^2} \sum_{i=1}^{N_r} |h_i|^2 = \sum_{i=1}^{N_r} \gamma_i. \tag{5.29}$$

The expected value or average combined SNR can thus be found as:

$$\bar{\gamma}_{\mathrm{mrc}} = N_r \bar{\gamma}, \tag{5.30}$$

where $\bar{\gamma}$ is the average SNR on each branch. In other words, the SNR growth is *linear* with the number of receive antennas. Thus, from Shannon's capacity formula, it can be observed that since $C = B \log(1 + SNR)$, the throughput growth due to receive diversity is *logarithmic* with the number of receive antennas, since receive diversity serves to increase the SNR.

Transmit Diversity Due to the transmit power penalty inherent to transmit diversity techniques, the received SNR does not always grow as transmit antennas are added. Instead, if there is a single receive antenna, the received combined SNR in an orthogonal STBC scheme is generally of the form:

$$\gamma_\Sigma = \frac{\mathcal{E}_x}{N_t \sigma^2} \sum_{i=1}^{N_t} |h_i|^2. \tag{5.31}$$

As the number of transmit antennas grows large, this expression becomes

$$\gamma_\Sigma = \frac{\mathcal{E}_x}{\sigma^2} \frac{|h_1|^2 + |h_2|^2 + \ldots + |h_{N_t}|^2}{N_t} \rightarrow \frac{\mathcal{E}_x}{\sigma^2} E\big[|h_1|^2\big], \tag{5.32}$$

by the law of large numbers. Thus, open-loop transmit diversity causes the received SNR to "harden" to the average SNR. In other words, it eliminates the effects of fading but does not actually increase the average amount of useful received signal-to-noise ratio.

Example 5.1. Consider two possible antenna configurations that use a total of $N_a = 6$ antennas. In one system, we place two antennas at the transmitter and four at the receiver and implement the Alamouti SFBC scheme. In the other, we place just one antenna at the transmitter and five at the receiver and perform MRC. Which configuration will achieve a lower BEP in a fading channel?

An exact calculation is not very simple, and requires the BEP in AWGN to be integrated against a complex SNR expression. However, to get a feel for it two things should be considered: the average output SNR (array gain) and the diversity order. The diversity order of the 2×4 SFBC approach is 8, while it is just 5 for the 1×5 MRC system. However, the average post-combining SNR is higher for the 1×5 MRC system due to array gain, since

$$\bar{\gamma}_{1 \times 5}^{\mathrm{mrc}} = 5\bar{\gamma} \tag{5.33}$$

while

$$\bar{\gamma}_{2 \times 4}^{\mathrm{STBC}} = \frac{1}{2} 8\bar{\gamma} = 4\bar{\gamma} \tag{5.34}$$

due to the transmit power penalty. Since the array gains of SFBC and MRC over a single-input single-output (SISO) system are both equal to the number of receive antennas N_r, when the total number of transmit and receive antennas is fixed at $N_a = 6$, at high SNR the diversity order causes the occasional fades to be averaged out, and 2×4 SFBC is therefore preferable to 1×5 MRC. On the other hand, at low SNR a fixed array gain is a more significant contribution than the SNR averaging provided by the diversity gain, and so pure MRC is generally preferable at low SNR.

Figure 5.6 compares the BEP performance of Alamouti STBC (= SFBC) with MRC using coherent BPSK with various N_a in a Rayleigh fading channel and confirms this intuition. As expected, for a fixed $N_a > 3$, the Alamouti code outperforms MRC at high SNR due to the diversity order, whereas MRC has better BEP performance at low SNR due to the array gain. In the case of $N_a = 6$, we observe that the BEP crossing point between 2×4 STBC and 1×5 MRC is at 2.03 dB average SNR on each branch.

5.3.4 Closed-Loop Transmit Diversity

If feedback is added to the system, then the transmitter may be able to have knowledge of the channel between it and the receiver. Because the channel changes quickly in a highly mobile scenario, closed-loop transmission schemes tend to be feasible primarily in fixed or low-mobility scenarios. As we shall see, however, there is a substantial gain in many cases from possessing channel state information (CSI) at the transmitter, particularly in the spatial multiplexing setup discussed later in the chapter. This has motivated intensive research on techniques for achieving low-rate prompt feedback, often specifically for the multiantenna channel [55].

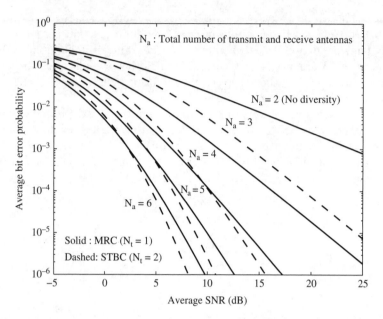

Figure 5.6 Comparison of the Alamouti STBC (SFBC) with MRC for coherent BPSK in a Rayleigh fading channel.

The basic configuration for closed-loop transmit diversity is shown in Figure 5.7, where in general the receiver could also have multiple antennas, but we neglect that here for simplicity. An encoding algorithm is responsible for using the channel state information to effectively use its N_t available channels. We will assume throughout this section that the transmitter has fully accurate CSI available to it due to the feedback channel. We will now overview two important types of closed-loop transmit diversity, focusing on how they affect the encoder design, and on their achieved performance.

Transmit Selection Diversity

Transmit selection diversity (TSD) is the simplest form of transmit diversity. In transmit selection diversity, first suggested by Winters [97], only a subset $N^* < N_t$ of the available

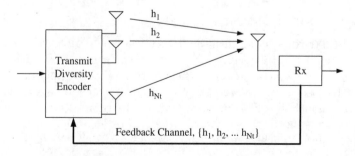

Figure 5.7 Closed-loop transmit diversity.

N_t antennas is used at a given time. The selected subset typically corresponds to the best channels between the transmitter and receiver. Some advantages of transmit antenna selection are (1) hardware cost and complexity are reduced, (2) spatial interference is reduced since fewer transmit signals are sent, and (3) somewhat surprisingly, the diversity order is still $N_t N_r$ even though only N^* of the N_t antennas are used. Despite its optimal diversity *order*, transmit selection diversity is not optimal in terms of diversity *gain*. Transmit selection can also be used in conjunction with spatial multiplexing, for example, to create two spatial streams in a 4×2 MIMO configuration [38]. The main drawback of antenna selection is that—just as with selection combining as discussed in Section 5.2.1— wideband channels have multiple coherence bands so the gain from selecting the best antenna averaged over all the coherence bands is likely to be small.

In the simplest case, a single transmit antenna is selected, where the chosen antenna results in the highest gain between the transmitter and the receive antenna. Mathematically, this is statistically identical to choosing the highest gain receive antenna in a receive diversity system, since they both result in an optimum antenna choice i^*:

$$i^* = \arg\max_{i \in (1, N_t)} |h_i|^2. \tag{5.35}$$

Hence, transmit selection diversity does not incur the power penalty relative to receive selection diversity that we observed in the case of SFBCs vs. MRC, while achieving the same diversity order. The average SNR with single transmit antenna selection in a $N_t \times 1$ system with i.i.d. Rayleigh fading is thus:

$$\gamma_{\text{tsd}} = \bar{\gamma} \sum_{i=1}^{N_t} \frac{1}{i}, \tag{5.36}$$

which is identical to (5.13) for receiver selection combining. This is, however, a lower average SNR than can be achieved with beamforming techniques that use all the transmit antennas. In other words, transmit selection diversity captures the full diversity order— and so is robust against fading—but sacrifices some overall SNR performance relative to techniques that use or capture all the available energy at the transmitter and receiver.

The feedback required for antenna transmit selection diversity is also quite low, since all that is needed is the index of the required antenna, rather than the full CSI. In the case of single transmit antenna selection, only $\log_2 N_t$ bits of feedback are needed for each channel realization. For example, if there were $N_t = 4$ transmit antennas and the channel coherence time was $T_c = 10$ msec (corresponding to a Doppler of about 100Hz), only about 1 Kbps of channel feedback would be needed, assuming the feedback rate was five times faster than the rate of channel decorrelation.

In the case of N^* active transmit antennas, choosing the best N^* out of the available N_t elements requires a potentially large search over

$$\binom{N_t}{N^*} \tag{5.37}$$

different possibilities, although for many practical configurations, the search is simple. For example, choosing the best two antennas out of four requires only six possible combinations to be checked. Even for very large antenna configurations, near-optimal results can be attained with much simpler searches. The required feedback for transmit antenna selection is about $N^* \log_2 N_t$ bits per channel coherence time. Because of its excellent performance vs. complexity tradeoffs, transmit selection diversity appears to be attractive as a technique for achieving spatial diversity. It has also been extended to other transmit diversity schemes like space-time block codes [15, 34], spatial multiplexing [38], and multiuser MIMO systems [14]. A detailed overview of transmit antenna selection can be found in [60].

A Brief Primer on Matrix Theory

As this chapter indicates, linear algebra and matrix analysis are inseparable parts of MIMO theory. Matrix theory is also useful in understanding OFDM. In this book, we have tried to keep all the matrix notation as standard as possible, so that any appropriate reference will be capable of clarifying any of the presented equations.

In this sidebar, we simply define some of the more important notation for clarity. First, in this chapter, two types of transpose operations are used. The first is the conventional transpose $\mathbf{A}^T$ which is defined as:

$$\mathbf{A}^T_{ij} = \mathbf{A}_{ji},$$

that is, just the rows and columns are reversed. The second type of transpose is the conjugate transpose, which is defined as:

$$\mathbf{A}^*_{ij} = (\mathbf{A}_{ji})^*.$$

That is, in addition to exchanging rows with columns, each term in the matrix is replaced with its complex conjugate. If all the terms in $\mathbf{A}$ are real, then clearly $\mathbf{A}^T = \mathbf{A}^*$. Sometimes the conjugate transpose is called the Hermitian transpose and denoted as $\mathbf{A}^H$. They are equivalent.

Another recurring theme is matrix decomposition, specifically the eigendecomposition and the singular value decomposition, which are related to each other. If a matrix is square and diagonalizable ($M \times M$), then it has the eigendecomposition

$$\mathbf{A} = \mathbf{T}\mathbf{\Lambda}\mathbf{T}^{-1}$$

where $\mathbf{T}$ contains the (right) eigenvectors of $\mathbf{A}$ and $\mathbf{\Lambda} = \mathrm{diag}[\lambda_1 \; \lambda_2 \ldots \lambda_M]$ is a diagonal matrix containing the eigenvalues of $\mathbf{A}$. $\mathbf{T}$ is invertible as long as $\mathbf{A}$ is symmetric or has full rank (M non-zero eigenvalues).

When the eigendecomposition does not exist, either because $\mathbf{A}$ is not square or for the above reasons, a generalization of matrix diagonalization is the singular value decomposition, which is defined as:

$$\mathbf{A} = \mathbf{U}\mathbf{\Sigma}\mathbf{V}^*,$$

where $\mathbf{U}$ is $M \times r$, $\mathbf{V}$ is $N \times r$, and $\mathbf{\Sigma}$ is $r \times r$, and the rank of $\mathbf{A}$, i.e., the number of non-zero singular values, is r. Although $\mathbf{U}$ and $\mathbf{V}$ are no longer inverses of each other as in eigendecomposition, they are both unitary, i.e., $\mathbf{U}^*\mathbf{U} = \mathbf{V}^*\mathbf{V} = \mathbf{I}_r$, $\mathbf{U}\mathbf{U}^* = \mathbf{I}_M$, and $\mathbf{V}\mathbf{V}^* = \mathbf{I}_N$, which means they have orthonormal columns and rows. The singular values of $\mathbf{A}$ can be related to eigenvalues of $\mathbf{A}^*\mathbf{A}$ by:

$$\sigma_i(\mathbf{A}) = \sqrt{\lambda_i(\mathbf{A}^*\mathbf{A})}.$$

Because $\mathbf{T}^{-1}$ is not unitary, it is not possible to find a more exact relation between the singular values and eigenvalues of a matrix, but these values generally are of the same order since the eigenvalues of $\mathbf{A}^*\mathbf{A}$ are on the order of the square of those of $\mathbf{A}$.

Linear Diversity Precoding

Linear precoding is a general technique for improving the data rate or the link reliability by exploiting the CSI at the transmitter. In this section we consider *diversity* precoding, a special case of linear precoding where the data rate is unchanged, and the linear precoder at the transmitter and a linear postcoder at the receiver are applied only to improve the link reliability. This will allow comparison with open-loop techniques (namely SFBCs), and the advantage of transmit CSI will become apparent.

With linear precoding in the general case, the received data vector $\mathbf{z}$ can be written as:

$$\mathbf{z} = \mathbf{G}\mathbf{y} = \mathbf{G}(\mathbf{H}\mathbf{F}\mathbf{x} + \mathbf{n}), \tag{5.38}$$

where the size of the transmitted vector ($\mathbf{x}$) is $M \times \mathbf{1}$ and the received vector $\mathbf{y}$ is $N_r \times \mathbf{1}$. The postcoder matrix $\mathbf{G}$ is $M \times N_r$ to give $\mathbf{z}$ dimensions of $M \times \mathbf{1}$, while the channel matrix $\mathbf{H}$ is $N_r \times N_t$, the precoder matrix $\mathbf{F}$ is $N_t \times M$, the noise vector $\mathbf{n}$ is $N_r \times \mathbf{1}$, and M is the number of spatial data "streams" sent in the general case. For the case of pure diversity precoding (comparable to a rate $\mathbf{1}$ STBC), only one data symbol is sent at a time, so $M = \mathbf{1}$ and the SNR maximizing precoder $\mathbf{F}$ and postcoder $\mathbf{G}$ are the right and left singular vectors of $\mathbf{H}$ corresponding to its largest singular value, $\sigma_{\max}$. Therefore, the equivalent channel model after precoding and postcoding for a transmitted data symbol x becomes

$$\mathbf{y} = \mathbf{h}x + \mathbf{n}, \tag{5.39}$$

which is $N_r \times \mathbf{1}$ and when left multiplying by a $\mathbf{1} \times N_r$ postcoding vector $\mathbf{g}$ gives simply:

$$z = \sigma_{\max} \cdot x + n_z, \tag{5.40}$$

Therefore, the received SNR is

$$\gamma = \frac{\mathcal{E}_x}{\sigma^2}\sigma^2_{\text{max}}, \tag{5.41}$$

where σ^2 is the noise variance of n_z. Since the value or expected value of σ^2_{max} is not deterministic, the SNR can only be bounded as [64]:

$$\frac{\|\mathbf{H}\|^2_{\mathbf{F}}}{N_t} \cdot \frac{\mathcal{E}_x}{\sigma^2} \le \gamma \le \|\mathbf{H}\|^2_{\mathbf{F}} \cdot \frac{\mathcal{E}_{\mathbf{x}}}{\sigma^2}, \tag{5.42}$$

where $\| \cdot \|_{\mathbf{F}}$ denotes the Frobenius norm, which is just the total sum of all the powers of each spatial channel, defined as:

$$\|\mathbf{H}\|_{\mathbf{F}} = \sqrt{\sum_{i=1}^{N_t}\sum_{j=1}^{N_r} h_{ij}^2}. \tag{5.43}$$

For the sake of comparison, by generalizing the SNR expression for 2×2 STBCs (5.24), the SNR for the case of STBC is given as:

$$\gamma_{\text{STBC}} = \frac{\|\mathbf{H}\|^2_{\mathbf{F}}\mathcal{E}_{\mathbf{x}}}{N_t\sigma^2}. \tag{5.44}$$

By comparing (5.42) and (5.44), it is clear that linear precoding achieves a higher SNR than the open-loop STBCs, by up to a factor of N_t. When $N_r = 1$, the full SNR gain of $10\log_{10}N_t$ dB is achieved, i.e., the upper bound on SNR in (5.42) becomes an equality. This special case of $M = \mathbf{1}$ is known by other names including maximal ratio transmission (MRT) [54] and eigen-beamforming. Spatial multiplexing occurs whenever $M \ge 2$, so we will revisit this approach in Section 5.5 when we discuss spatial multiplexing.

To employ linear diversity precoding in practice, CSI is required at the transmitter. This could be acquired (or at least accurately approximated) in a TDD system by channel reciprocity, since the uplink and downlink channels are in theory equivalent. In an FDD system, feedback from the receiver to the transmitter is required. For a multiantenna channel, accurate feedback of the entire channel matrix $\mathbf{H}$ would require a very large amount of overhead, particularly in mobile channels. Therefore, sophisticated quantization and compression techniques have been developed, and play a role in LTE. This is the subject of Section 5.7.2.

5.4 Interference Cancellation Suppression and Signal Enhancement

The available antenna elements at either the transmitter or receiver can be used to suppress undesired signals and/or enhance the power of the desired signal. In a multiantenna system, the channel is multidimensional and so the dimensions of the channel can be applied to null interference in a certain direction, while amplifying signals in another direction. Put another way, rather than increasing the statistical diversity of the total signal as in the preceding section, the energy can instead be steered. Perhaps most intuitively, the energy can be steered physically, resulting in actual electromagnetic wave patterns with certain properties. We discuss this approach first. Alternatively, the dimensions can be used to create linear transmitters and receivers that project desired signals into strong dimensions while attenuating the dimensions that interferers appear in. We consider two such approaches in Sections 5.4.2 and 5.4.3, depending on the amount of information available about the interfering channels.

5.4.1   DOA-Based Beamsteering

Electromagnetic waves can be physically steered to create beam patterns at either the transmitter or the receiver. At the transmitter, this causes energy to be sent predominantly in a desired direction, while only a small amount of residual energy is leaked in other directions. The more antennas are used, the more control over the beam pattern. The most common and simple form of this is static pattern-gain beamsteering, which is known as "sectoring" and was discussed in Section 2.3.3 in the context of cellular systems. In sectoring, static patterns are created. For example, in a three-sector cell, a strong beam is projected over approximately 120 degrees, while very little energy is projected over the remaining 240 degrees. At a sectored receiver, the idea is similar: energy is accepted from the desired direction while suppressed from other directions.

In this section we consider more sophisticated and general beamsteering approaches, where the beam patterns can be finely and, in theory, dynamically adjusted to attenuate undesired signals while amplifying desired signals. The incoming signals to a receiver typically consist of desired energy and interference energy (for example, from other users or from multipath reflections). The various signals can be characterized in terms of the direction of arrival (DOA) or angle of arrival (AOA) of each received signal.

Each DOA can be estimated using signal processing techniques such as the MUSIC, ESPRIT, and MLE algorithms (see [31, 51] and the references therein). From these acquired DOAs, a beamformer extracts a weighting vector for the antenna elements and uses it to transmit or receive the desired signal of a specific user while suppressing the undesired interference signals.

When the plane wave arrives at the d-spaced uniform linear array (ULA) with AOA θ, the wave at the first antenna element travels an additional distance of $d \sin \theta$ to arrive at the second element. This difference in propagation distance between the adjacent antenna elements can be formulated as an arrival time delay, $\tau = d/c \sin \theta$. As a result, the signal arriving at the second antenna can be expressed in terms of the signal at the first antenna element as:

$$
\begin{aligned}
y_2(t) &= y_1(t) \exp(-j 2\pi f_c \tau), \\
&= y_1(t) \exp(-j 2\pi \frac{d \sin \theta}{\lambda}).
\end{aligned}
\tag{5.45}
$$

For an antenna array with N_r elements all spaced by d, the resulting received signal vector can therefore be expressed as:

$$
\begin{aligned}
\mathbf{y}(t) &= [y_1(t)\ y_2(t)\ \cdots\ y_{N_r}(t)]^T \\
&= y_1(t)\underbrace{[1\ \ \exp(-j2\pi\frac{d\sin\theta}{\lambda})\ \ \cdots\ \ \exp(-j2\pi(N_r-1)\frac{d\sin\theta}{\lambda})]^T}_{\mathbf{a}(\theta)}, \quad (5.46)
\end{aligned}
$$

where $\mathbf{a}(\theta)$ is the *array response vector*.

In the following, we show an example to demonstrate the principle of DOA-based beamforming. Consider a three-element ULA with $d = \lambda/2$ spacing between the antenna elements. Assume that the desired user's signal is received with an AOA of $\theta_1 = 0$ (i.e., the signal is coming from the broadside of the ULA), and two interfering signals are received with AOAs of $\theta_2 = \pi/3$ and $\theta_3 = -\pi/6$, respectively. The array response vectors are then given by:

$$
\mathbf{a}(\theta_1) = [1\ 1\ 1]^T, \quad \mathbf{a}(\theta_2) = \left[1\ e^{-j\frac{\sqrt{3}}{2}\pi}\ e^{-j\sqrt{3}\pi}\right]^T, \quad \text{and} \quad \mathbf{a}(\theta_3) = \left[1\ e^{j\frac{\pi}{2}}\ e^{j\pi}\right]^T.
\tag{5.47}
$$

The beamforming weight vector $\mathbf{w} = [w_1\ w_2\ w_3]^T$ should increase the antenna gain in the direction of the desired user while simultaneously minimizing the gain in the directions of interferers. Thus, the weight vector $\mathbf{w}$ should satisfy the following criterion

$$
\mathbf{w}^*[\mathbf{a}(\theta_1)\ \ \mathbf{a}(\theta_2)\ \ \mathbf{a}(\theta_3)] = [1\ 0\ 0]^T,
\tag{5.48}
$$

and a unique solution for the weight vector is readily obtained as:

$$
\mathbf{w} = [0.3034 + j0.1966\ \ 0.3932\ \ 0.3034 - j0.1966]^T.
\tag{5.49}
$$

Figure 5.8 shows the beam pattern using this weight vector. As expected, the beamformer has unity gain for the desired user and two nulls at the directions of two interferers. Since the beamformer can place nulls in the directions of interferers, the DOA-based beamformer in this example is often called the *null-steering beamformer* [31]. The null-steering beamformer can be designed to completely null out interfering signals only if the number of such signals is strictly less than the number of antenna elements. That is, if the number of receive antennas is N_r, then $N_r - 1$ independent interferers can be cancelled.[6] The disadvantage of this approach is that a null is placed in the direction of the interferers and so the antenna gain is not maximized at the direction of the desired user. Typically, there exists a tradeoff between interference nulled and desired gain lost. A more detailed description on the DOA-beamformer with refined criterion can be found in [31, 51].

We have thus far assumed that the array response vectors of different users with corresponding AOAs are known. In practice, each resolvable multipath is likely to be

---

6 In some special cases it may be possible to null more than $N_r - 1$ interferers. For example, the special case where a third interferer was at an angle of $2\pi/3$ or $7\pi/6$ in Figure 5.8.

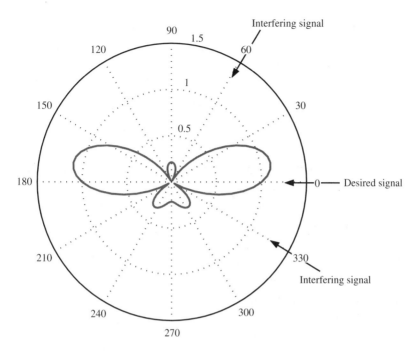

Figure 5.8 Null-steering beam pattern for the DOA-based beamforming using three-element ULA with $\lambda/2$ spacing at transmit antennas. The AOAs of the desired user and two interferers are 0, $\pi/3$, and $-\pi/6$, respectively.

comprised of several unresolved components coming from significantly different angles. In this case, it is not possible to associate a discrete AOA with a signal impinging the antenna array. Therefore, the DOA-based beamformer is really only viable in LOS environments or in environments with limited local scattering around the transmitter.

5.4.2 Linear Interference Suppression: Complete Knowledge of Interference Channels

We now change gears to a more general form of interference suppression. Unlike the preceding DOA-based approach, this technique is more easily expressed mathematically although its physical interpretation is not as straightforward. Consider a single transmitter with N_t antennas trying to communicate to a receiver with $N_r > N_t$ antennas, in the presence of one or more, say L_I, interfering transmitters, each with $N_{t,i}$ antennas. Thus, there are a total number

$$L = \sum_{i=1}^{L_I} N_{t,i} \tag{5.50}$$

interfering sources. To keep matters simple for now—we will generalize it in the next section—let us assume $L = 1$ and $N_t = 1$ for both the desired transmitter and the

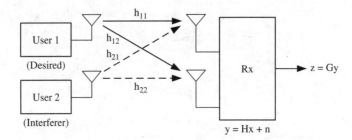

Figure 5.9 Simple two-user interference cancellation example for Sections 5.4.2 and 5.4.3.

interferer, and that $N_r = 2$. This means we have a total of two transmitted streams, to a two-antenna receiver, as shown in Figure 5.9. The received signal model is therefore:

$$\mathbf{y} = \mathbf{Hx} + \mathbf{n}$$

where $\mathbf{H}$ is a 2×2 matrix of both the desired and interfering channels. If we assume the receiver knows not only its own channel vector but the interfering channel as well, then detection of its desired signal x_1 is straightforward. For example, a zero-forcing receiver $\mathbf{G} = \mathbf{H}^{-1}$ would do the trick and produce

$$\mathbf{z} = \mathbf{x} + \mathbf{H}^{-1}\mathbf{n}.$$

As long as $\mathbf{H}$ is well-conditioned (no eigenvalues approximately equal to zero), this receiver would probably perform acceptably. Naturally, other (better) receivers could be used instead of a simple inverse, several of which are discussed in Section 5.5 in the context of spatial multiplexing for a more general setup of arbitrary N_t and N_r. Indeed, the above case is an example of spatial multiplexing where the transmitters are independent rather than co-located, which would also be known as uplink multiuser MIMO or uplink SDMA since two users are supported simultaneously. For a single-user system, though, the receiver is presumed to not be interested in decoding the interfering signal(s), x_2 in this example. Therefore, this system is "over-designed," and furthermore it may not be possible for the receiver to learn $\mathbf{h}_2$, the interfering user's channel to it. Next we consider the case where only a single desired stream is detected, and the other channels are suppressed with only statistical knowledge of the interference level rather than the instantaneous channel matrix.

5.4.3   Linear Interference Suppression: Statistical Knowledge of Interference Channels

We now consider the case where we again wish to suppress multiple interferers, but have only statistical knowledge of the interference. We consider a general setup where again the desired transmitter has N_t antennas for transmission and the desired receiver N_r antennas for reception in a flat fading channel. There are again L_I distinct cochannel interferers each equipped with $N_{t,i}$ antenna elements, giving $L = \sum_{i=1}^{L_I} N_{t,i}$ total interference sources. Now, we allow the transmitter to precode its signal with a $N_t \times 1$

beamforming vector $\mathbf{w}_t$, and so the N_r-dimensional received signal vector at the receiver is given by:

$$\mathbf{y} = \mathbf{H}\mathbf{w}_t x + \mathbf{H}_I \mathbf{x}_I + \mathbf{n} \qquad (5.51)$$

where x is the desired symbol with energy $\mathcal{E}_x$, $\mathbf{x}_I = [x_1\ x_2\ \cdots\ x_L]^T$ is the interference vector, and $\mathbf{n}$ is the noise vector with covariance matrix $\sigma^2 \mathbf{I}$, $\mathbf{H}$ is the $N_r \times N_t$ channel gain matrix for the desired user, and $\mathbf{H}_I$ is the $N_r \times L$ channel gain matrix for the interferers. In order to maximize the output SINR at the receiver, joint optimal weighting vectors at both the transmitter and the receiver can be obtained as [99]:

$$\mathbf{w}_t = \text{Eigenvector corresponding to the largest eigenvalue } \lambda_{\max}\left(\mathbf{H}^*\mathbf{R}^{-1}\mathbf{H}\right), \qquad (5.52)$$

and

$$\mathbf{w}_r = \alpha \mathbf{R}^{-1}\mathbf{H}\mathbf{w}_t, \qquad (5.53)$$

where α is an arbitrary constant that does not affect the SNR, $\mathbf{R} = \sigma^2 \mathbf{I} + \mathbb{E}[\mathbf{H}_I \mathbf{x}_I \mathbf{x}_I^* \mathbf{H}_I^*]$ is the interference-plus-noise covariance matrix, and $\lambda_{\max}(\mathbf{A})$ is the largest eigenvalue of $\mathbf{A}$. We then have the maximum output SINR:

$$\gamma = \mathcal{E}_x \lambda_{\max}\left(\mathbf{H}^*\mathbf{R}^{-1}\mathbf{H}\right). \qquad (5.54)$$

This shows that the transmit power is focused on the largest eigenchannel among $\min(N_t, N_r)$ eigenchannels in order to maximize post-beamforming SINR. This beamforming approach can be termed the *optimum eigen-beamformer, interference-aware beamforming*, and/or *optimum combiner* (OC).

It can be seen that this interference-aware beamformer is conceptually similar to the linear diversity precoding approach of Section 5.3.4, the only difference being that the eigen-beamformer takes interfering signals into account. If the interference terms are ignored, $\mathbf{R} \rightarrow \sigma^2 \mathbf{I}$ and $\mathbf{w}_r \rightarrow \mathbf{G}$ and $\mathbf{w}_t \rightarrow \mathbf{F}$. This special case just collapses back to maximal ratio transmission (MRT) [54] at the transmitter and MRC at the receiver when interference is ignored at either the transmitter or receiver. For example, the transmitter may not be able to learn its own channel or even the statistical description of the interference.

Figure 5.10 shows a performance comparison between the eigen-beamformer and other transmit/receive diversity schemes. We observe that the optimum beamformer nulls a strong interferer by sacrificing a degree of freedom at the receiver, i.e., the 2×2 optimum beamformer with one strong interferer is equivalent to the 2×1 MRT with no interference, which also has the same performance as 1×2 MRC. We also confirm that exploiting channel knowledge at the transmitter provides significant array gain and, especially in the case of a single receive antenna, the transmit diversity using MRT has the same array gain and diversity order of receive diversity MRC.

To summarize mathematically, in the absence of interference, the output SNR of optimum beamformer (i.e., MRT, since there is no interference) with $N_t > 1$ can be upper- and lower-bounded as follows:

$$\gamma_{N_t \times N_r}^{STBC} = \frac{\mathcal{E}_x}{N_t \sigma^2}||\mathbf{H}||_{\mathbf{F}}^2 < \gamma_{N_t \times N_r}^{MRT} = \frac{\mathcal{E}_x}{\sigma^2}\lambda_{\max}\left(\mathbf{H}^H\mathbf{H}\right) \leq \frac{\mathcal{E}_x}{\sigma^2}||\mathbf{H}||_{\mathbf{F}}^2 = \gamma_{1 \times N_t N_r}^{MRC} \qquad (5.55)$$

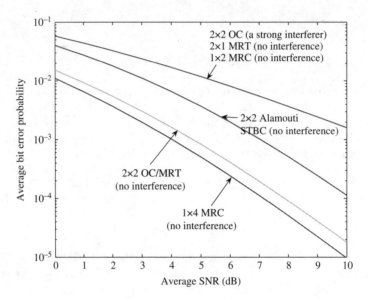

Figure 5.10 Performance comparison between optimal combining/beamforming and diversity approaches. MRT and MRC have the same performance for the same number of antennas.

where the equality between MRT and MRC holds if and only if $N_r = 1$. The above inequality is a generalization of (5.42). When L cochannel interferers exist, the average output SINR of the optimum combining/beamforming techniques will naturally exceed those of MRT and MRC systems that simply ignore the interference in their beamforming design.

The techniques of this subsection have been designed for transmitting a single data stream using perfect channel state information at both the transmitter and receiver. In order to further increase the system capacity using the acquired transmit CSI, up to $\mathrm{rank}(\mathbf{H}) = \min(N_t, N_r)$ eigenchannels can be used for transmitting multiple data steams. Because multiple streams are transmitted, this becomes spatial multiplexing and is discussed in the next section. In particular, Section 5.5.3 will generalize these results (in the absence of interference) to M data-bearing subchannels, where $1 \leq M \leq \min(N_r, N_t)$.

5.5   Spatial Multiplexing

Spatial multiplexing refers to breaking the incoming high rate data stream into M parallel data streams, as shown in Figure 5.11 for $M = N_t$ and $N_t \leq N_r$. Assuming that the streams can be successfully decoded, the spectral efficiency is increased by a factor of M. This is certainly exciting: it implies that adding antenna elements can greatly increase the data rate without any increase in bandwidth. Spatial multiplexing has proven challenging in practice, largely because this data rate increase comes at the expense of the diversity and/or interference suppression capabilities discussed in the last two sections. We will provide an overview of spatial multiplexing, but adopt a critical view to

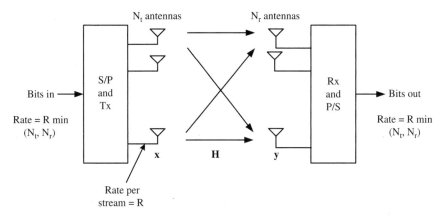

Figure 5.11 A spatial multiplexing MIMO system transmits multiple substreams to increase the data rate.

separate viable design principles from purely theoretical results that dominate much of the literature on the topic.

5.5.1 An Introduction to Spatial Multiplexing

First, we overview the classic theoretical results and model for spatial multiplexing that are widely used. The standard mathematical model for spatial multiplexing is very similar to what was used for linear precoding and interference suppression, i.e.:

$$\mathbf{y} = \mathbf{Hx} + \mathbf{n} \tag{5.56}$$

where the size of the received vector $\mathbf{y}$ is $N_r \times 1$, the channel matrix $\mathbf{H}$ is $N_r \times N_t$, the transmit vector $\mathbf{x}$ is $N_t \times 1$, and the noise $\mathbf{n}$ is $N_r \times 1$. Typically, the transmit vector is normalized by N_t so that each symbol in $\mathbf{x}$ has average energy $\mathcal{E}_x/N_t$. This keeps the total transmit energy constant with the SISO case for comparison. The channel matrix in particular is of the form:

$$\mathbf{H} = \begin{bmatrix} h_{11} & h_{12} & \dots & h_{1N_t} \\ h_{21} & h_{22} & \dots & h_{2N_t} \\ \vdots & \vdots & \ddots & \vdots \\ h_{N_r1} & h_{N_r2} & \dots & h_{N_rN_t} \end{bmatrix}, \tag{5.57}$$

and it is usually assumed that the entries in the channel matrix and the noise vector are complex Gaussian and i.i.d. with zero mean and diagonal covariance matrices. In other words, the spatial channels all experience uncorrelated Rayleigh fading and Gaussian noise, which is reasonable if there is significant scattering, sufficient antenna spacing, and no dominant interferers: all assumptions that deserve scrutiny in an LTE system. Under this model, using basic linear algebra arguments it is straightforward to confirm that decoding N_t streams is theoretically possible when there exist at least N_t non-zero eigenvalues in the channel matrix, i.e., rank($\mathbf{H}$) $\geq N_t$. This result has been generalized and made rigorous with information theory [26, 90].

This model enables a rich framework for mathematical analysis for MIMO systems based on random matrix theory [25, 94], information theory, and linear algebra. Using these tools, numerous insights on MIMO systems have been obtained, and we refer the interested reader to [23, 33, 64, 92] for detailed summaries. The key points we would like to summarize regarding this single-user MIMO system model are

- The capacity, or maximum data rate, grows as $\min(N_t, N_r)\log(1 + SNR)$ when the SNR is large [90]. When the SNR is high, spatial multiplexing is optimal.

- When the SNR is low, the capacity-maximizing strategy is to send a single stream of data using diversity precoding. Although the capacity is much smaller than at high SNR, it still grows approximately linearly with $\min(N_t, N_r)$ since capacity is linear with SNR in the low-SNR regime.

- Both of these cases are superior in terms of capacity to space-time coding, where the data rate grows at best logarithmically with N_r.

- The average SNR of all N_t streams can be maintained without increasing the total transmit power relative to a SISO system, since each transmitted stream is received at $N_r \geq N_t$ antennas and hence recovers the transmit power penalty of N_t due to the array gain. However, even a single low eigenvalue in the channel matrix can dominate the error performance.

5.5.2 Open-Loop MIMO: Spatial Multiplexing Without Channel Feedback

As with multiantenna diversity techniques, spatial multiplexing can be performed with or without channel knowledge at the transmitter. We will first consider the principal open-loop techniques; we will always assume that the channel is known at the receiver, ostensibly through pilot symbols or other channel estimation techniques. The open-loop techniques for spatial multiplexing attempt to suppress the interference that results from all N_t streams being received by each of the N_r antennas. The techniques discussed in this section are largely analogous to the interference-suppression techniques developed for equalization [65] and multiuser detection [96], as seen in Figure 5.12.

Optimum Decoding: Maximum Likelihood Detection

If the channel is unknown at the transmitter, the optimum decoder is the maximum-likelihood decoder, which finds the most likely input vector $\hat{\mathbf{x}}$ via a minimum distance criterion:

$$\hat{\mathbf{x}} = \arg\min ||\mathbf{y} - \mathbf{H}\hat{\mathbf{x}}||^2. \tag{5.58}$$

Unfortunately, there is no simple way to compute this, and an exhaustive search must be done over all M^{N_t} possible input vectors, where M is the order of the modulation (e.g., $M = 4$ for QPSK). The computational complexity is prohibitive for even a small

	Optimum	Interference Cancellation	Linear
Equalization (ISI)	Maximum Likelihood Sequence Detection (MLSD)	Decision feedback equalization	Zero-forcing, MMSE
Multiuser Detection	Optimum MUD	Successive/parallel interference cancellation, iterative MUD	Decorrelating, MMSE
Spatial Multiplexing Receivers	ML detector sphere decoder (near-optimum)	BLAST	Zero-forcing, MMSE

Figure 5.12 The similarity of interference suppression techniques for different applications. Complexity is decreasing from left to right.

number of antennas. Lower complexity approximations of the ML detector, notably the sphere decoder, can be used to nearly achieve the performance of the ML detector in many cases [39], and these have some potential for high-performance, open-loop MIMO systems. When optimum (or near-optimum) detection is achievable, the gain from transmitter channel knowledge is fairly small and is mainly limited to waterfilling over the channel eigenmodes, which only provides significant gain at low SNR.

Linear Detectors

As in other situations where the optimum decoder is an intolerably complex maximum likelihood detector, a sensible next step is to consider linear detectors that are capable of recovering the transmitted vector $\mathbf{x}$. A block diagram is shown in Figure 5.13. The most obvious such detector is the *zero-forcing detector* that sets the receiver equal to the inverse of the channel $\mathbf{G}_{zf} = \mathbf{H}^{-1}$ when $N_t = N_r$, or more generally to the pseudoinverse:

$$\mathbf{G}_{zf} = (\mathbf{H}^*\mathbf{H})^{-1}\mathbf{H}^*. \tag{5.59}$$

As the name implies, the zero-forcing detector completely removes the spatial interference from the transmitted signal, giving an estimated received vector:

$$\hat{\mathbf{x}} = \mathbf{G}_{zf}\mathbf{y} = \mathbf{G}_{zf}\mathbf{H}\mathbf{x} + \mathbf{G}_{zf}\mathbf{n} = \mathbf{x} + (\mathbf{H}^*\mathbf{H})^{-1}\mathbf{H}^*\mathbf{n}. \tag{5.60}$$

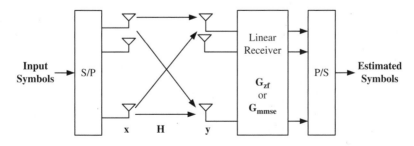

Figure 5.13 Spatial multiplexing with a linear receiver.

Because $\mathbf{G}_{zf}$ inverts the eigenvalues of $\mathbf{H}$, the bad spatial subchannels can severely amplify the noise in $\mathbf{n}$. This is particularly problematic in interference-limited MIMO systems, and will result in extremely poor performance. The zero-forcing detector is therefore not practical for LTE.

A logical alternative to the zero-forcing receiver is the MMSE receiver, which attempts to strike a balance between spatial interference suppression and noise enhancement by simply minimizing the distortion. Therefore:

$$\mathbf{G}_{mmse} = \arg \min_{\mathbf{G}} \mathrm{E} \|\mathbf{G}\mathbf{y} - \mathbf{x}\|^2, \tag{5.61}$$

which can be derived using the well-known orthogonality principle as:

$$\mathbf{G}_{mmse} = \left(\mathbf{H}^*\mathbf{H} + \frac{\sigma_z^2}{P_t}\mathbf{I}\right)^{-1} \mathbf{H}^*, \tag{5.62}$$

where P_t is the transmitted power. In other words, as the SNR grows large, the MMSE detector converges to the ZF detector, but at low SNR it prevents the worst eigenvalues from being inverted.

BLAST

The earliest known spatial multiplexing receiver was invented and prototyped in Bell Labs and is called *Bell labs LAyered Space-Time* (BLAST) [27]. Like other spatial multiplexing MIMO systems, BLAST consists of parallel "layers" supporting multiple simultaneous data streams. The layers (substreams) in BLAST are separated by interference cancellation techniques that decouple the overlapping data streams. The two most important techniques are the original *diagonal BLAST* (D-BLAST) [27] and its subsequent version, *vertical BLAST* (V-BLAST) [32].

D-BLAST groups the transmitted symbols into "layers," which are then coded in time independently of the other layers. These layers are then cycled to the different transmit antennas in a cyclical manner, resulting in each layer being transmitted in a *diagonal* of space and time. In this way, each symbol stream achieves diversity in time via coding, and in space since it rotates among all the different antennas. Therefore, the N_t transmitted streams will equally share the good and bad spatial channels, as well as their priority in the decoding process now described.

The key to the BLAST techniques lies in the detection of the overlapping and mutually interfering spatial streams. The diagonal layered structure of D-BLAST can be detected by decoding one layer at a time. The decoding process for the second of four layers is shown in the left side of Figure 5.14. Each layer is detected by *nulling* the layers that have not yet been detected, and *cancelling* the layers that have already been detected. In Figure 5.14, the layer to the left of the layer-2 block has already been detected and hence subtracted (cancelled) from the received signal while those to the right remain as interference but can be nulled using knowledge of the channel. The time-domain coding helps compensate for errors or imperfections in the cancellation and nulling process. Two drawbacks of D-BLAST are that the decoding process is iterative and somewhat complex, and the diagonal layering structure wastes space-time slots at the beginning and end of a D-BLAST block.

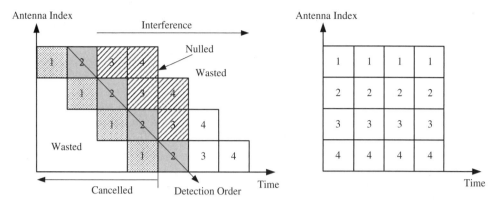

Figure 5.14 (Left) D-BLAST detection of layer 2 of 4. (Right) V-BLAST encoding. Detection is done dynamically; the layer (symbol stream) with the highest SNR is detected first and then cancelled.

V-BLAST was subsequently addressed in order to reduce the inefficiency and complexity of D-BLAST. V-BLAST is actually conceptually somewhat simpler than D-BLAST. In V-BLAST, each antenna simply transmits an independent symbol stream (for example, QAM symbols). A variety of techniques can be used at the receiver to separate the various symbol streams from each other, including several of the techniques discussed elsewhere in this chapter. These include linear receivers such as the ZF and MMSE, which take the form at each receive antenna of a length N_r vector that can be used to null out the contributions from the $N_t - 1$ interfering data streams. In this case, the post-detection SNR for the ith stream is

$$\gamma_i = \frac{\mathcal{E}_x}{\sigma^2 ||\mathbf{w}_{r,i}||^2} \quad i = 1, \cdots, N_t, \tag{5.63}$$

where $\mathbf{w}_{r,i}$ is the ith row of the zero-forcing or MMSE receiver $\mathbf{G}$ of (5.59) and (5.62), respectively.

Since this SNR is held hostage by the lower channel eigenvalues, the essence of V-BLAST is to combine a linear receiver with ordered successive interference cancellation. Instead of detecting all N_t streams in parallel, they are detected iteratively. First, the strongest symbol stream is detected (using a ZF or MMSE receiver, as before). After these symbols are detected, they can be subtracted out from the composite received signal. Then, the second strongest signal is detected, which now sees effectively $N_t - 2$ interfering streams. In general, the ith detected stream experiences interference from only $N_t - i$ of the transmit antennas, so that by the time the weakest symbol stream is detected, the vast majority of spatial interference has been removed. Employing the ordered successive interference cancellation lowers the block error rate by about a factor of 10 relative to a purely linear receiver, or equivalently, decreases the required SNR by about 4 dB [32]. Despite its apparent simplicity, V-BLAST prototypes have shown spectral efficiencies above 20 bps/Hz.

Despite demonstrating satisfactory performance in controlled laboratory environments, the BLAST techniques have not proven themselves to be useful in cellular systems at present. One challenge they face is their dependence on high SNR for the joint decoding of the different streams, which is difficult to achieve in a multicell environment. In both BLAST schemes, these imperfections can quickly lead to catastrophic error propagation when the layers are detected incorrectly.

5.5.3   Closed-Loop MIMO

The potential gain from transmitter channel knowledge is quite significant in spatial multiplexing systems. First we will consider a simple theoretical example using *singular value decomposition* (SVD) that shows the potential gain of closed-loop spatial multiplexing methods. Then we will turn our attention to more general linear precoding techniques of which the SVD approach is a special case, as is the linear diversity precoding in Section 5.3.4.

SVD Precoding and Postcoding

A relatively straightforward way to see the gain of transmitter channel knowledge is by considering the singular value decomposition (SVD, or generalized eigenvalue decomposition) of the channel matrix $\mathbf{H}$, which as noted previously can be written as:

$$\mathbf{H} = \mathbf{U}\Sigma\mathbf{V}^*, \tag{5.64}$$

where $\mathbf{U}$ and $\mathbf{V}$ are *unitary* and Σ is a diagonal matrix of singular values. As shown in Figure 5.15, with linear operations at the transmitter and receiver, i.e., multiplying by $\mathbf{V}$ and $\mathbf{U}^*$, respectively, the channel can be diagonalized. Mathematically, this can be confirmed by considering a decision vector $\mathbf{d}$ that should be close to the input symbol vector $\mathbf{b}$. The decision vector can be written systematically as

$$
\begin{aligned}
\mathbf{d} &= \mathbf{U}^*\mathbf{y}, \\
&= \mathbf{U}^*(\mathbf{H}\mathbf{x} + \mathbf{n}), \\
&= \mathbf{U}^*(\mathbf{U}\Sigma\mathbf{V}^*\mathbf{V}\mathbf{b} + \mathbf{n}), \\
&= \mathbf{U}^*\mathbf{U}\Sigma\mathbf{V}^*\mathbf{V}\mathbf{b} + \mathbf{U}^*\mathbf{n}, \\
&= \Sigma\,\mathbf{b} + \mathbf{U}^*\mathbf{n}, \tag{5.65}
\end{aligned}
$$

which has diagonalized the channel and removed all the spatial interference without any matrix inversions or non-linear processing. Because $\mathbf{U}$ is unitary, $\mathbf{U}^*\mathbf{n}$ still has the same variance as $\mathbf{n}$. Thus, the singular value approach does not result in noise enhancement, as did the open-loop linear techniques. SVD-MIMO is not particularly practical since the complexity of finding the SVD of an $N_t \times N_r$ matrix is on the order of $O(N_r N_t^2)$ if $N_r \geq N_t$ and requires a substantial amount of feedback. Nevertheless, it shows the promise of closed-loop MIMO in achieving high performance at much lower complexity than the ML detector in open-loop MIMO.

Linear Precoding and Postcoding

The SVD was an illustrative example of how linear precoding and postcoding can diagonalize the MIMO channel matrix to provide up to $\min(N_r, N_t)$ dimensions to communicate

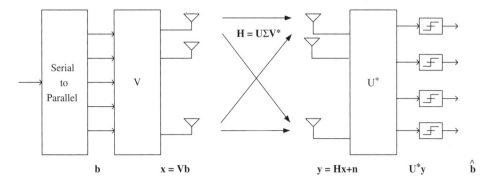

Figure 5.15 A MIMO system that has been diagonalized through SVD precoding.

data symbols through. More generally, the precoder and postcoder can be jointly designed based on a criteria such as the information capacity [68], the error probability [24], the detection MSE [70], or the received SNR [69]. From Section 5.3.4, we recall that the general precoding formulation is

$$\mathbf{y} = \mathbf{G}(\mathbf{HFx} + \mathbf{n}), \tag{5.66}$$

where $\mathbf{x}$ and $\mathbf{y}$ are $M \times 1$, the postcoder matrix $\mathbf{G}$ is $M \times N_r$, the channel matrix $\mathbf{H}$ is $N_r \times N_t$, the precoder matrix $\mathbf{F}$ is $N_t \times M$, and $\mathbf{n}$ is $N_r \times 1$. For the SVD example $M = \min(N_r, N_t)$, $\mathbf{G} = \mathbf{U}^*$, and $\mathbf{F} = \mathbf{V}$.

Regardless of the specific design criteria, the linear precoder and postcoder decompose the MIMO channel into a set of parallel subchannels as illustrated in Figure 5.16. Therefore, the received symbol for the ith subchannel can be expressed as:

$$y_i = \alpha_i \sigma_i \beta_i x_i + \beta_i n_i, \quad i = 1, \ldots, M, \tag{5.67}$$

where x_i and y_i are the transmitted and received symbols, respectively, with $E|x_i|^2 = \mathcal{E}_x$ as usual, σ_i are the singular values of $\mathbf{H}$, α_i and β_i are the precoder and the postcoder

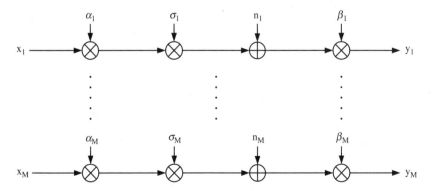

Figure 5.16 Spatial subchannels resulting from linear precoding and postcoding.

weights, and n_i is the noise per subchannel, which in addition to the usual noise also includes any residual spatial interference from the imperfect separation of the streams. The number of subchannels is bounded by:

$$1 \leq M \leq \min(N_t, N_r), \tag{5.68}$$

where $M = 1$ corresponds to the maximum diversity order (which we called *diversity precoding* in Section 5.3.4) and $M = \min(N_t, N_r)$ achieves the maximum number of parallel spatial streams. Intermediate values of M can be chosen to tradeoff between raw throughput and link reliability, as discussed in Section 5.6.

5.6   How to Choose Between Diversity, Interference Suppression, and Spatial Multiplexing

We have now discussed three quite different ways in which to use the antennas the system is endowed with: diversity, interference suppression, and spatial multiplexing. A natural question is, "how should I use them?" There is a basic tradeoff between them, since they all require the finite degrees of freedom in the system to be used. As we've seen, diversity provides robustness to fades and interference suppression provides robustness to interference. Neither increase the number of streams that can be sent, but they do increase the possible throughput on the stream that is sent by increasing the SINR $= S/(I+N)$. In particular, diversity increases and steadies S, while interference suppression (or nulling) reduces I. On the other hand, spatial multiplexing creates more parallel streams but does not necessarily increase the per-stream SINR.

Interference suppression and nulling is often considered impractical in a cellular system, and of questionable utility. The main reasons for this are (1) the interfering transmitters are numerous and fairly far away from the receiver, so the gain from cancelling just the few strongest ones is not always large; and (2) acquiring the needed channel state information from the interferers can be quite difficult, so accurate suppression is not usually possible. Therefore, most research has focused on diversity and multiplexing. When the transmitter has full CSI, the optimal precoder with link adaptation (i.e., per-stream waterfilling) will naturally select the optimum number of streams and the power sent on each. So with accurate CSIT, there is an inherently optimal tradeoff point between diversity and multiplexing. When the transmitter does not have exact CSIT, but instead partial CSIT, for example, knowledge of the average link SINR, the tradeoff is more subtle. Essentially, the choice comes down to the following question: would you rather have a thin, but very reliable pipe or a wide, but not very reliable pipe? Naturally, a compromise on each would often seem to be the preference.

The notion of switching or balancing between diversity and multiplexing based on a proxy for SINR was to our knowledge first introduced by Heath [37]. It was then developed into an elegant theory [109] known as the Diversity-Multiplexing Tradeoff (DMT), which has gained many adherents and spawned significant follow-up research. The DMT stipulates that both diversity gain and multiplexing gain can be achieved in a multiple antenna channel but that there is a fundamental tradeoff between how much of each gain can be achieved. Hence, *diversity gain*—the reliability exponent N_d in (5.7)—and *multiplexing gain*—in essence, the number of streams sent—are obtained at the expense of each other. The DMT captures the tension between the error probability and the rate of a system. Unfortunately, the model used in the formal DMT is largely irrelevant for modern wireless systems since it is typically narrowband and ignores other forms of (non-spatial) diversity like coding, ARQ, and frequency-selectivity, and is predicated on asymptotically high SNR and asymptotically small error rate.

In the context of LTE, a more relevant perspective on the DMT was recently developed by Lozano and Jindal [57], which results in several conclusions at odds with those of the traditional model. Lozano and Jindal use a model that includes frequency-selective fading, ARQ, and coding, and focuses on achieved rate at fixed error probability (instead of vanishing error probability)—all of which are appropriate adjustments for LTE. The principle—and somewhat surprising—conclusion is that all the spatial degrees of freedom should be used for multiplexing and none for spatial diversity. In short, there is no tradeoff! This is well-captured in Figure 5.17. On the left, with settings corresponding to the simplistic DMT model (and $N_t = N_r = 4$), we see that for all but the highest SNR values, transmit diversity indeed outperforms spatial multiplexing. In fact, spatial multiplexing even does worse than no transmit diversity, because so many errors are made on the weakest streams. However, with the wideband channel model on the right of Figure 5.17, specifically, the UMTS Typical Urban (TU) channel with $\tau_{\mathrm{max}} = 1\mu\mathrm{sec}$, and hybrid ARQ, the relation between them flips, and now transmit diversity is only very marginally better than the single-transmit antenna case while spatial multiplexing is much better, even at low to moderate SNR. What are the reasons for this major change?

First, modern wireless systems (like LTE) have many forms of diversity, most notably time and frequency diversity, which are exploited using coding, interleaving, retransmissions (ARQ), OFDMA, and adaptive modulation. There is very little diversity left in the channel to exploit with spatial diversity when these are considered. Second, link adaptation (adaptive modulation, ARQ, power control) is used to maintain a target block error probability, and there is very little benefit (but considerable cost in power and possibly

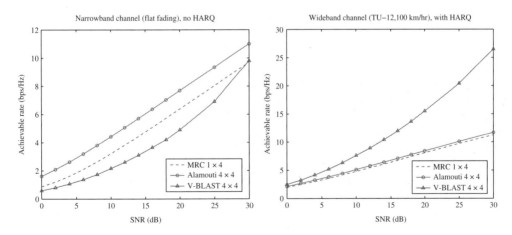

Figure 5.17 The Diversity-Multiplexing Tradeoff, for a narrowband system with no other forms of diversity (left) and for a wideband system with ARQ (right). Data provided by the authors of [57].

other resources) to beating this target. In short, transmit diversity and the gains in reliability it brings are redundant to other features of LTE. This points to aggressively using spatial multiplexing in LTE, something many companies and engineers have been reluctant to do previously because it was viewed as too "risky" as opposed to diversity.

5.7 Channel Estimation and Feedback for MIMO and MIMO-OFDM

When OFDM is used in conjunction with a MIMO transceiver, channel information is essential at the receiver in order to coherently detect the received signal, and for diversity combining or spatial interference suppression [85, 102]. Accurate channel information is also required at the transmitter for closed-loop MIMO. In this section, we first study channel estimation. Because channel estimation is performed at the receiver, how to perform it is not specified by the LTE standard, although pilot sequence patterns are specified by LTE (see Section 7.6 for downlink reference signals, Section 8.4 for uplink reference signals, and Section 9.4 for uplink channel sounding). We then discuss how channel estimates can be obtained at the transmitter in order to perform closed-loop MIMO techniques such as beamforming and linear precoding.

5.7.1 Channel Estimation

Channel estimation can be performed in two different ways: training-based and blind. In training-based channel estimation, known symbols are transmitted specifically to aid the receiver's channel estimation algorithms. In a blind channel estimation method, the receiver must determine the channel without the aid of known symbols. Although higher bandwidth efficiency can be obtained in blind techniques due to the lack of training overhead, the convergence speed and estimation accuracy is significantly compromised. For this reason, training-based channel estimation techniques are supported by the LTE standard and are the techniques considered in this section. Conventional OFDM channel estimation is just the special case in the below equations where $N_r = N_t = 1$.

Preamble and Pilot

There are two different ways to transmit training symbols: preamble or pilot tones. Preambles entail sending a certain number of training symbols prior to the user data symbols. In the case of OFDM, one or two preamble OFDM symbols are typical. Pilot tones involve inserting a few known pilot symbols among the subcarriers. Channel estimation in MIMO-OFDM systems can be performed in a variety of ways, but it is typical to use the preamble for synchronization[7] and initial channel estimation, and the pilot tones for tracking the time-varying channel in order to maintain accurate channel estimates.

In MIMO-OFDM, the received signal at each antenna is a superposition of the signals transmitted from the N_t transmit antennas. Thus, the training signals for each transmit antenna need to be transmitted without interfering with each other in order to accurately estimate the channel. Figure 5.18 shows three different patterns for MIMO-OFDM that avoid interfering with each other: independent, scattered, and orthogonal patterns [50].

---

7 Synchronization for OFDM is discussed in detail in Chapter 4.

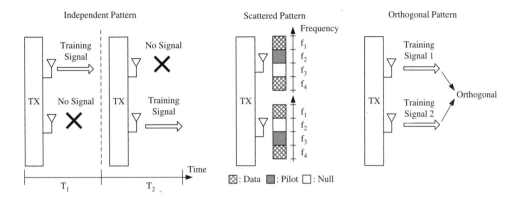

Figure 5.18 Three different patterns for transmitting training signals in MIMO-OFDM.

The independent pattern transmits training signals from one antenna at a time while the other antennas are silent, thus guaranteeing orthogonality between each training signal in the time domain. Clearly, an $N_t \times N_r$ channel can be estimated over N_t training signal times. The scattered pilot pattern prevents overlap of training signals in the frequency domain by transmitting each antenna's pilot symbols on different subcarriers, while other antennas are silent on that subcarrier. Finally, the orthogonal pattern transmits training signals that are mathematically orthogonal, similar to CDMA. The independent pattern is often the most appropriate for MIMO-OFDM, since the preamble is usually generated in the time domain. For transmitting the pilot tones, any of these methods or some combination of them can be used.

In MIMO-OFDM, frequency-domain channel information is required in order to detect the data symbols on each subcarrier (recall the FEQ of Chapter 3). Since the preamble consists of pilot symbols on many of the subcarriers,[8] the channel frequency response of each subcarrier can be reliably estimated from the preamble with simple interpolation techniques. In normal data OFDM symbols, there are typically a very small number of pilot tones, so interpolation between these estimated subchannels is required [20, 40]. The training symbol structure for the preamble and pilot tones are shown in Figure 5.19, with interpolation for pilot symbols. One-dimensional interpolation over either the time or frequency domain or two-dimensional interpolation over both the time and frequency domains can be performed with an assortment of well-known interpolation algorithms (linear, FFT, etc.). In the next section, we will focus on channel estimation in the time and frequency domain using the preamble and pilot symbols, and assume that interpolation can be performed by the receiver as necessary.

Time-Domain Channel Estimation

MIMO-OFDM channels can be estimated in either the time or frequency domain. The received time-domain signal can be directly used to estimate the channel impulse response,

---

8 Each preamble uses only 1/3 or 1/6 of all the subcarriers in order to allow different sectors in the cell to be distinguished.

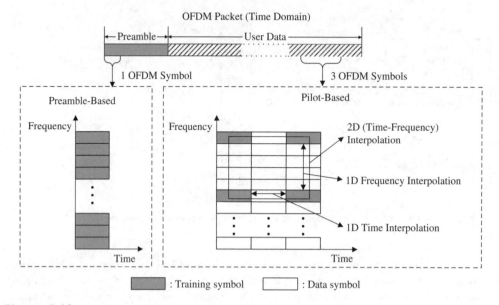

Figure 5.19 Training symbol structure of preamble-based and pilot-based channel estimation methods.

while frequency-domain channel estimation is performed using the received signal after processing it with the FFT. Here, we will overview both time- and frequency-domain channel estimation methods, assuming that each channel is clear of interference from the other transmit antennas, which can be ensured by using the pilot-designs described previously. Thus, the antenna indices i and j are neglected in this section and these techniques are directly applicable to single-antenna OFDM systems as well.

Channel estimation methods based on the preamble and pilot tones are different due to the difference in the number of known symbols. For preamble-based channel estimation in the time domain with a cyclic prefix, the received OFDM symbol for a training signal can be expressed with a circulant matrix as:

$$
\mathbf{y} =
\begin{bmatrix}
h(0) & \cdots & h(v) & 0 & \cdots & 0 \\
0 & h(0) & \cdots & h(v) & \cdots & 0 \\
\vdots & \vdots & \vdots & \vdots & \vdots & \vdots \\
h(1) & \cdots & h(v) & 0 & \cdots & h(0)
\end{bmatrix}
\begin{bmatrix}
x(L-1) \\
\vdots \\
x(0)
\end{bmatrix} + \mathbf{n}
$$

$$
=
\begin{bmatrix}
x(0) & x(L) & x(L-1) & \cdots & x(L-v+1) \\
x(1) & x(0) & x(L) & \cdots & x(L-v+2) \\
\vdots & \vdots & \vdots & \vdots & \vdots \\
x(L) & x(L-1) & \cdots & \cdots & x(L-v)
\end{bmatrix}
\begin{bmatrix}
h(0) \\
\vdots \\
h(v)
\end{bmatrix} + \mathbf{n}
$$

$$
= \mathbf{Xh} + \mathbf{n} \tag{5.69}
$$

where $\mathbf{y}$ and $\mathbf{n}$ are the L samples of the received OFDM symbol and AWGN noise, $x(l)$ is the lth time sample of the transmitted OFDM symbol, and $h(i)$ is the ith time sample of the channel impulse response. Using this matrix description, the estimated channel $\hat{\mathbf{h}}$ can be readily obtained using the least-squares (LS) or MMSE method. For example, the LS (i.e., zero forcing) estimate of the channel can be computed as:

$$\hat{\mathbf{h}} = (\mathbf{X}^*\mathbf{X})^{-1}\mathbf{X}^*\mathbf{y}, \tag{5.70}$$

since $\mathbf{X}$ is deterministic and hence known *a priori* by the receiver. When pilot tones are used for time-domain channel estimation, the received signal can be expressed as:

$$\mathbf{y} = \bar{\mathbf{F}}^*\mathbf{X}_P\bar{\mathbf{F}}\mathbf{h} + \mathbf{n}, \tag{5.71}$$

where $\mathbf{X}_P$ is a diagonal matrix whose diagonal elements are the pilot symbols in the frequency domain, $\bar{\mathbf{F}}$ is a $(P \times v)$ DFT matrix generated by selecting rows from $(L \times v)$ DFT matrix $\mathbf{F}$ according to the pilot subcarrier indices, and $[\mathbf{F}]_{i,j} = \frac{1}{\sqrt{L}}\exp(-j2\pi(i-1)(j-1)/L)$. Then, the LS pilot-based time-domain estimated channel is

$$\hat{\mathbf{h}} = (\bar{\mathbf{F}}^*\mathbf{X}_P^*\mathbf{X}_P\bar{\mathbf{F}})^{-1}\bar{\mathbf{F}}^*\mathbf{X}_P^*\bar{\mathbf{F}}\mathbf{y}. \tag{5.72}$$

Frequency-Domain Channel Estimation

Channel estimation is simpler in the frequency domain than in the time domain. For preamble-based frequency-domain channel estimation, the received symbol of the lth subcarrier in the frequency domain is

$$Y(l) = H(l)X(l) + N(l). \tag{5.73}$$

Since $X(l)$ is known *a priori* by the receiver, the channel frequency response of each subcarrier can easily be estimated. For example, the lth frequency-domain estimated channel using LS is

$$\hat{H}(l) = X(l)^{-1}Y(l). \tag{5.74}$$

Similarly, for pilot-based channel estimation, the received symbols for the pilot tones are the same as (5.73). To determine the complex channel gains for the data-bearing subcarriers, interpolation is required.

Least-squares channel estimation is often not very robust in high-interference or noisy environments since these effects are ignored. This can be improved by averaging the LS estimates over numerous symbols, or by utilizing MMSE estimation. MMSE estimation is usually more reliable, since it forms a more conservative channel estimate based on the strength of the noise and statistics on the channel covariance matrix. The MMSE channel estimate in the frequency domain is

$$\hat{\mathbf{H}} = \mathbf{A}\mathbf{Y}, \tag{5.75}$$

where $\mathbf{H}$ and $\mathbf{Y}$ here are the L point DFT of $\mathbf{H}$ and the received signal on each output subcarrier, and the estimation matrix $\mathbf{A}$ is computed as:

$$\mathbf{A} = \mathbf{R}_H(\mathbf{R}_H + \sigma^2(\mathbf{X}^*\mathbf{X})^{-1})^{-1}\mathbf{X}^{-1}, \tag{5.76}$$

and $\mathbf{R}_H = E[\mathbf{H}\mathbf{H}^*]$ is the channel covariance matrix and it is assumed that the noise/interference on each subcarrier is uncorrelated and has variance σ^2. It can be seen by setting $\sigma^2 = 0$ that if noise is neglected, the MMSE and LS estimators are the same.

One of the drawbacks of conventional LMMSE frequency-domain channel estimation is that it requires knowledge of the channel covariance matrix in both the frequency and time domains. Since the receiver usually does not possess this information *a priori*, it also needs to be estimated, which can be performed based on past channel estimates. However, in mobile applications the channel characteristics change rapidly, making it difficult to estimate and track the channel covariance matrix. In such cases, partial information about the channel covariance matrix may be the only possibility. For example, if only the maximum delay and the Doppler spread of the channel are known, then bounds on the actual channel covariance matrix can be derived. Surprisingly, the LMMSE estimator with only partial information often results in performance that is comparable to the conventional LMMSE estimator with full channel covariance information.

5.7.2   Channel Feedback

Closed-loop MIMO techniques naturally perform better than open-loop MIMO techniques, with the important caveat that the channel state information available at the transmitter is in fact accurate. This chapter has so far assumed for the closed-loop techniques that the transmitter has perfect knowledge of the current channel state, which is, of course, impossible. Two methods are possible for obtaining CSI at the transmitter (CSIT). First, the CSI may be fed back by the receiver to the transmitter over an overhead channel. Second, in time division duplex (TDD) systems, CSIT can be acquired by exploiting *channel reciprocity*, which means the downlink channel is assumed to be the same as the uplink channel and can be directly measured. However, in TDD systems some feedback may be needed in order to understand the interference conditions at the receiver, or SINR, which cannot be extracted by reciprocity. Assuming there is feedback, what form should it take? Even for a simple SISO channel, it is not possible to feedback the exact SINR: some quantization is needed. For a MIMO channel, especially one with significant frequency selectivity, the amount of feedback required to accurately know the full $N_t \times N_r$ channel over each active band of subcarriers will be enormous unless sophisticated quantization and compression techniques are utilized. This has led to a large amount of research on limited feedback techniques for MIMO systems in recent years, the body of which is well summarized by a recent tutorial article [56].

LTE systems have adopted some of the ideas developed in this line of research. In Figure 5.20, a quantized precoding system is illustrated. Specifically, the precoder is restricted to be one of P distinct matrices, the set of which is called a *precoding codebook*. Therefore, only $\log_2 P$ bits of feedback are required to indicate the index of the appropriate precoder matrix. If the set of precoding matrices is designed intelligently, even a very small number of feedback bits is sufficient to keep the distortion small (typically 3–8 bits).

In LTE, two distinct modes are defined by which the MS can provide feedback to the network needed for closed-loop operations. The first is the periodic mode where the MS sends the feedback on a periodic basis autonomously. The periodicity of the feedback can be determined by the network based on various factors such as speed, system load, etc.

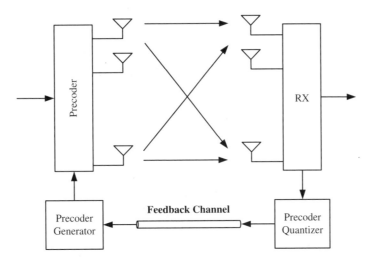

Figure 5.20 Linear precoding with quantized feedback.

The other is the aperiodic mode where the MS sends the feedback only when requested by the network. Due to the aperiodic nature of this mode, it is possible to send more detailed feedback compared to the periodic mode.

In both periodic and aperiodic modes the feedback specifies to the rank of the transmission, the Channel Quality Indicator (CQI) and the Precoding Matrix Index (PMI). The PMI is chosen from a predefined codebook and the codebook sizes are 4 and 16 for 2- and 4-antenna transmissions, respectively. The 2-antenna codebook with 4 entries is based on the HSDPA MIMO codebook, whereas the 4-antenna codebook with 16 entries is based on Householder generating functions. Further details on the codebook for CL-MIMO can be found in Section 7.2.2. The CQI indicates the modulation and code rate that should be used and is usually calculated to indicate the higher modulation and code rate that can be supported with a block error rate (BLER) of 10%.

Although both modes allow for CQI, PMI, and rank feedback, the MS can only send wideband feedback using the periodic mode, whereas more detailed narrowband (subband) feedback can be sent using the aperiodic mode. Due to the finer granularity of the feedback in the frequency domain, we expect the aperiodic mode to have superior performance. The superior performance of the aperiodic feedback mode comes with the cost of the more uplink bandwidth being required to send the feedback. In a real deployment we expect both feedback modes to be used. The periodic feedback mode is appropriate for applications such as VoIP where we expect the system to have a large number of users. A VoIP user generates traffic at a constant rate and since the VoIP packets are delay sensitive there is not much flexibility in the system as to how many VoIP packets can be transmitted at the same time. Typically, one or two VoIP packets of fixed size are sent on a periodic basis and the transmitter does not have much flexibility in adjusting the transport format, i.e., modulation, code rate, MIMO mode, etc. based on the channel condition. Therefore, a periodic feedback with a wideband CQI and PMI feedback is sufficient for such services. On the other hand, for data service such as best effort data where packet latency is less important than spectral efficiency, the aperiodic feedback mode is more appropriate.

5.8 Practical Issues That Limit MIMO Gains

In order to realistically consider the gains that might be achieved by MIMO in LTE systems, we emphasize that most of the well-known results for spatial multiplexing are based on the model in (5.56) of the previous section, which makes the following critical assumptions:

1. Because the entries of **H** are scalar random values, the multipath is assumed negligible, i.e., the fading is frequency flat.

2. Because the entries are i.i.d., this means that the antennas are all uncorrelated.

3. Usually, interference is ignored and the background noise is assumed to be small.

Clearly, all of these assumptions will be at least somewhat compromised in a cellular MIMO deployment. In many cases, they will be completely wrong. We now discuss how to address these important issues in a real system.

5.8.1 Multipath

Because LTE systems will have moderate to high bandwidths over non-negligible transmission distances, the multipath in LTE is expected to be substantial. Therefore, the flat-fading assumption appears to be unreasonable. However, OFDM can be introduced to convert a frequency-selective fading channel to L parallel flat-fading channels, as discussed in Chapter 3. If OFDM with sufficient subcarriers is combined with MIMO, the result is L parallel MIMO systems, and hence the model of (5.56) is again reasonable. For this reason, OFDM and MIMO are a natural pair, and the first commercial MIMO system employed OFDM in order to combat inter-symbol interference [66]. MIMO-OFDM has been widely researched [6, 85]. Since LTE is based on OFDM, using the flat-fading model for MIMO is reasonable, with the caveat that channel estimation and feedback must be done on a per-subcarrier basis. Of course, neighboring subcarriers will have nearly identical channels so interpolation or averaging can be used over blocks of subcarriers.

5.8.2 Uncorrelated Antennas

It is much more difficult to analyze MIMO systems with correlated antennas, so it is typically assumed that the spatial modes are uncorrelated. Uncorrelated antennas are generally assumed to be best case, and indeed this is true at the receiver. At the transmitter, if the correlation is known and exploited it can actually be beneficial at low SNR or at high SNR to focus transmit energy when $N_t > N_r$ [93]. For a single user, real-world channels will be at least partially correlated, particularly in the space-constrained mobile. Insufficient scattering—for example, in rural or line-of-sight channels—can also induce significant correlation. Fortunately, MIMO results based on uncorrelated antennas are often reasonably accurate even with a modest degree of spatial correlation [16, 19, 52, 80].

Nevertheless, as the number of antennas increases, particularly in the mobile, it should be recognized that the realized gains per antenna are likely to decrease due to antenna correlation.

5.8.3   Interference-Limited MIMO Systems

The third assumption, that the background noise is Gaussian and uncorrelated with the transmissions, is especially suspect in a cellular MIMO system. All well-designed cellular systems are by nature interference-limited: if they were not, it would be possible to increase the spectral efficiency by lowering the frequency reuse or increasing the average loading per cell. In the downlink of a cellular system, where MIMO is expected to be the most profitable and viable, there will be an effective number of $N_I \cdot N_t$ interfering signals, whereas in Chapter 2 the number of non-negligible interfering neighboring base stations is N_I. It is extremely difficult for a MIMO receiver at the MS to cope simultaneously with both the spatial interference (due to the N_t transmit antennas) and a high level of other cell interference. While most researchers have neglected this problem due to its lack of tractability, it has been shown using both information and communication theory that the capacity of a MIMO cellular system can actually *decrease* as the number of transmit antennas increases if the spatial interference is not suitably addressed [3–5, 10]. While most theoretical MIMO results are for high-SNR environments with idealized (ML) decoding, in practice MIMO must function in low-SINR environments with low-complexity receivers.

The other cell interference problem is a pressing problem confronting the use of spatial multiplexing in LTE systems. Various solutions for dealing with the other cell interference have been suggested, including interference-aware receivers [22], multicell power control [13], distributed antennas [17], and multicell coordination [18, 43, 104, 106]. None of these techniques is explicitly supported by the LTE standard as of press time of this book, although the deployment of interference-aware receivers is certainly not precluded by the standard. However, they are being actively considered. We discuss networked MIMO further in the next section.

5.9   Multiuser and Networked MIMO Systems

Thus far, we have considered "single-user" MIMO systems, although this is a slight misnomer for an OFDMA system since multiple users are supported in the frequency domain. "Single user" in the context of MIMO refers to sending data to only a single user in the spatial domain. Pure diversity approaches like the Alamouti code are inherently single user since only a single data stream is sent. For MIMO techniques that support two or more transmitted streams, e.g., linear precoding, it is possible to send the streams to different users. Similarly, in a multicell system, it is possible for the base stations to collaborate to form a larger virtual MIMO array that could serve multiple users. For example, two base stations with a single antenna each could in principle share data and channel information offline (through a wired backhaul connecting them) and form an effective $N_t = 2$ MIMO system. Although both of these techniques must overcome significant practical constraints and will likely not be supported in initial LTE deployments, the potential gains are large and so they are being seriously considered for later deployments, such as LTE-Advanced. We now briefly overview the key ideas and issues behind multiuser and networked MIMO systems.

5.9.1 Multiuser MIMO

The MIMO techniques developed so far in this chapter have implicitly assumed that only a single user is active on all the antennas at each instant in time and on each frequency channel. In fact, multiple users can utilize the spatial channels simultaneously, which can be advantageous, versus each user having to take turns sharing the channel. A simple example is a downlink channel with $N_t = 3$ transmit antennas at the base station and $N_r = 1$ antennas at each of three MSs, as shown in Figure 5.21. Using the techniques thus far presented in this chapter, only a single stream could be sent to a single user, for example, using 3×1 beamforming (MRT). In fact, it is possible to send a separate stream to each user, as long as the transmitter knows the total channel matrix $\mathbf{H}$ and precancels the interference caused by users 2 and 3 to user 1, and so on. This technique is also known as *Space Division Multiple Access* (SDMA).

SDMA has unique advantages compared to single-user MIMO (SU-MIMO) [29]. Due to space and cost/complexity constraints, current MSs can only support a small number of antennas, normally $N_r = 1$ or 2. Even if there are multiple receive antennas, each MS may have a single RF chain. In any case, it is obvious that a base station can support more antennas than a small, cost-sensitive handheld device. As we have noted, the capacity gain of SU-MIMO is linear with $\min\{N_t, N_r\}$, which in practice will be limited by N_r in the downlink or N_t in the uplink. SDMA provides the opportunity to overcome such a limitation by communicating with multiple MSs simultaneously by effectively increasing the dimension of the equivalent spatial channel. Put simply, MU-MIMO pools the antennas of K users until N_t and $K \cdot N_r$ are roughly equal: the resulting multiplexing gain becomes $\min\{N_t, KN_r\}$ and so is no longer constrained by the handheld antenna placement issues. In addition, unlike SU-MIMO where antennas at both the transmitter and receiver are co-located, the K users are presumably quite distant from each other, which decreases the antenna correlation. This provides SDMA higher immunity

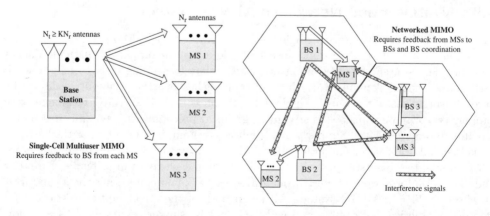

Figure 5.21 A 3×1 SDMA system (left) and a three-cell networked MIMO system (right).

to propagation limitations faced by SU-MIMO, namely channel rank loss due to antenna correlation.

Uplink SDMA is a straightforward extension of uplink SU-MIMO where the base station is able to jointly decode data for multiple users. For downlink SDMA, the capacity achieving approach involves a complex transmission procedure known as dirty paper coding (DPC) [9, 21, 47], which requires exact channel knowledge and involves iterative pre-cancellation and is therefore not considered practical. The capacity assuming DPC at high SNR is $C = N_t \log_2(1 + \text{SNR})$ where the number of possible users $K \geq N_t$. Compare this to a single-user system, which has $C = \log_2(1 + N_t \text{SNR})$ for beamforming to a single receive antenna. For even moderate N_t, the potential gain of SDMA is significant, and it is of practical interest since in the downlink it is assumed that generally $N_t \geq N_r$ due to cost and space restrictions at the mobile. SDMA also provides an enhanced multiuser diversity with opportunistic scheduling.[9] With N_t antennas at the base station and N_r antennas at each user, the multiuser diversity gain of SDMA with DPC is $N_t \log \log(N_r K)$ when the number of users K is large, compared to $\min(N_t, N_r) \log \log(K)$ achieved by single-user TDMA transmission [77]. Because DPC is not practical, linear techniques such as zero forcing and MMSE precoding are considered instead, where a simple matrix is applied at the transmitter to separate the spatial streams [14, 84, 100]. Although suboptimal compared to DPC, the loss is not very significant in many cases, and full spatial multiplexing gain and full multiuser diversity are sustained [46, 77, 78]. To further improve the performance, other precoding techniques can be employed, such as coordinated beamforming that jointly applies precoding and decoding matrices [11, 12].

One major requirement of downlink SDMA is obtaining accurate CSIT at the base station for each of the MSs. Without CSIT, the users cannot be separated by the base station, and the achievable spatial multiplexing gain reduces back to $\min(N_t, N_r)$, which is the same as SU-MIMO [36]. Limited feedback techniques as discussed in Section 5.7.2 are necessary to provide partial CSIT at reasonable feedback cost. Recently, limited feedback for SDMA has been studied rigorously in [42, 45]. Surprisingly, employing limited feedback and linear precoding, it was demonstrated in [45] that the full spatial multiplexing gain of SDMA can be obtained with carefully designed feedback strategies and a feedback rate that grows linearly with SNR (in dB) and the number of transmit antennas. In parallel, it was shown in [103] that zero forcing with limited feedback achieves full multiuser diversity. There is another low-complexity linear precoding SDMA transmission technique supported by limited feedback, called *random orthogonal beamforming* [76]. It employs N_t random orthogonal beamforming vectors and each user feeds back the preferred beam index and the associated SINR to the base station, from which the base station selects the N_t users with the highest SINR on each beam. Despite its low complexity, random beamforming provides full multiuser diversity with only $\lceil \log_2(N_t) \rceil$ bits feedback from each user. Per Unitary basis stream User and Rate Control (PU2RC) is an enhanced version of random beamforming, which employs multiple sets of orthogonal beamforming vectors [41]. The above discussion demonstrates that linear precoding combined with some form of limited feedback is a practically appealing option for harvesting the potential gains of SDMA.

---

9 Refer to Section 4.4 for a discussion on multiuser diversity and opportunistic scheduling.

Compared to SU-MIMO, the performance of SDMA tends to be much more sensitive to inaccurate CSI. In LTE—especially in mobile scenarios—there will inevitably be CSI inaccuracy due to feedback delay, mobility, and channel quantization error. These factors conspire to cause residual inter-user interference due to imperfect spatial pre-cancellation, and the effects accumulate quite quickly as the CSI accuracy degrades. In moderate to high mobility scenarios, SDMA is likely to be outperformed by SU-MIMO. In fact, Reference [108] indicates that SDMA is only likely to be viable at moderate SNR, and at low mobility-delay products, which seems to suggest that SDMA-enabled systems will also need to be able to revert to single-user MIMO when the mobility or cell position (and hence SNR) calls for it [107]. A final issue unique to MU-MIMO implementation is that since the channels for each user have to be fed back over a shared feedback channel, the amount of total feedback nominally increases with the number of total users. Opportunistic feedback and other compressive techniques will need to be used to overcome this [42, 87, 103]. Overall, due to the sensitivity of SDMA to mobility and imperfect feedback, we expect LTE to be quite conservative in adopting these techniques. As will be shown in Sections 7.2.2 and 8.2.3, SDMA is supported in both the downlink and uplink in LTE, but in a simple and optional form. LTE-Advanced is likely to carefully consider a more prominent role for SDMA.

5.9.2   Networked MIMO

Cellular networks are inherently interference-limited, so approaches that overcome this interference are highly desirable, and this is especially for MIMO systems as discussed in Section 5.8.3. An important extension of MIMO techniques for cellular networks is *networked MIMO*, also called *base station coordination* or *multicell processing*. In networked MIMO, multiple base stations collaborate with each other to communicate with multiple users. In this way, these base stations can be collectively regarded as a single "super base station," and the whole system is equivalent to a virtual MIMO system. A networked MIMO system with three base stations each with several antennas is shown in Figure 5.21. Note that sometimes networked MIMO refers to single-antenna base stations forming a virtual MIMO array instead. In theory, with enough cooperation between the base stations, networked MIMO can eliminate other cell interference completely and therefore change the cellular network from an interference-limited system to a noise-limited system, which is revolutionary.

The idea of coordinating multiple base stations to suppress other cell interference is not especially new, and it was originally proposed for the uplink [35, 75, 81, 101]. With the maturity of traditional MIMO techniques and promising theoretical gains [43, 79, 83], networked MIMO has received considerable recent attention. In the uplink, the super base station can separate signals for different users with multiuser detection, which is similar to the open-loop spatial multiplexing system discussed in Section 5.5.2. For the downlink, assuming the availability of channel state information and traffic data of all users, multiple base stations can jointly design downlink precoders to pre-cancel inter-user interference for different users. In addition to the significant amount of off-line cooperation required of the various base stations, another fundamental difference from single-cell MIMO transmission is the per-base-station transmit power constraint, which effectively becomes a per-antenna transmit power constraint. Both the optimal DPC and suboptimal linear precoding techniques introduced in Section 5.9.1 can be applied by the virtual MIMO super base station in any case [28, 48, 49, 74, 82, 104, 106]. Coordination among multiple base stations not only mitigates other cell interference but also increases the effective number of spatial degrees of freedom, so the spectral efficiency is significantly improved.

As in multiuser MIMO systems, there are practical constraints for the most powerful forms of networked MIMO, which in practice can prove even more difficult to overcome. One of the major difficulties is the requirement of timely channel state information at multiple base stations, the amount of which is proportional to both the number of base station antennas and the number of base stations. This poses challenges for channel estimation, feedback, and inter-cell communication (backhaul), which generally has its limitations both in terms of rate and delay [58, 59, 67]. In addition, the complexity of optimal processing is quite high, and grows rapidly with the network size. To reduce the complexity and the requirement of channel state information, cluster-based coordination is a feasible approach [8, 63, 95, 106], while another is to design distributed algorithms for computing the optimal transmitters and receivers [1, 61]. Accurate synchronization between base stations is also an important issue [105]. Although the best-performing theoretical approaches for networked MIMO face serious practical challenges, intermediate techniques such as cooperative scheduling (including transmit selection diversity) among base stations may provide a significant portion of the gains [18, 28], while being more robust and less complex and demanding on the network. The inter-cell interference mitigation techniques adopted in LTE will be discussed in Section 10.5. Although networked MIMO is not included in LTE, it is considered a key enabling technique for 3GPP LTE-Advanced. This is an area to watch closely in the next few years.

5.10 An Overview of MIMO in LTE

Unlike the previous generation of technologies such as HSDPA and UMTS, LTE has been designed to support a diverse set of multiantenna techniques from the very beginning. Along with scalable channel bandwidth, one of the key advantages of OFDMA is a relatively simpler implementation of multiantenna techniques, compared to single-carrier systems.

5.10.1 An Overview of MIMO in the LTE Downlink

The multiantenna techniques presently supported in the LTE downlink are the following.

Transmit Diversity The multiple antennas at the base station are used to transmit a single layer of data to the user. When two antennas are implemented at the base station, then 2×2 Alamouti block codes are used to perform the space-frequency coding at the transmitter. When four antennas are used, the base station uses the same 2×2 Alamouti block code by selecting two out of the four antennas at a time. During the first OFDM symbol antennas 1 and 3 are selected while during the second OFDM symbol antennas 2 and 4 are used in a similar fashion. Thus, the system alternates between antennas $\{1,3\}$ and antennas $\{2,4\}$, which provides some additional diversity over the second order diversity provided by the 2×2 Alamouti block codes when used in conjunction with error correction codes.

Open-Loop Spatial Multiplexing In spatial multiplexing, two or four transmit antennas at the base station are used to send more than one layer (stream) of data to the user. Each MIMO layer is mapped to one antenna. A cyclic delay diversity (CDD) precoder rotates each stream across the transmit antennas in order to equalize the channel SINRs across each layer. Since this is an open-loop technique, the total power to each antenna and therefore to each layer is simply kept constant.

Closed-Loop Spatial Multiplexing In this case a precoding matrix is used to map the MIMO layers to the antennas. Unlike the open-loop MIMO, in this case the number of layers can be equal to or less than the number of antennas. The precoding matrix is selected from a predefined codebook and the index of the optimum precoder is provided by the user using the feedback channels. Currently, the standard specifies a 2-bit codebook (four precoding matrices) when two antennas are used at the base station and a 4-bit codebook (16 precoding matrics) when four antennas are used at the base station. Along with the index of the optimum precoder, the user also indicates the effective rank of the MIMO channel, which is used by the base station to determine the number of MIMO layers that should be transmitted for each user.

Multiuser MIMO This is a special case of closed-loop spatial multiplexing where as just discussed in Section 5.9.1 the MIMO layers are intended for different users. For example, two users with a channel rank of one could be sent in a 2×2 system by each using only one stream. The precoding matrix for the different MIMO layers is based on the same codebook as used for the single-user closed-loop MIMO.

Beamforming Unlike the other multiantenna techniques just described, in the case of beamforming the mobile station does not have to be aware of the total number of physical antennas at the base station. The multiple physical antennas are combined using beamforming weights into a single transmission, and so the MS does not need to be aware of the number of physical antennas or how the weights are calculated. Therefore, the algorithm that determines the beamforming weights is not specified in the standard, and is left open to implementation.

5.10.2   An Overview of MIMO in the LTE Uplink

Compared to the downlink, the support for multiantenna techniques in the uplink is rather limited. The standard allows up to a maximum of two transmit antennas at the mobile station and the following multiantenna techniques are allowed.

Closed-Loop Switched Antenna Diversity This mode is applicable only for MSs that are equipped with two transmit antennas. During UL sounding, the base station instructs the MS to transmit two sounding signals, one from each antenna. These sounding signals can be orthogonal in frequency or time, which allows the base station to determine which of the two antennas is preferable. The base station indicates its choice using the

DL control channel, at which time the MS commences using the desired antenna until it is instructed to switch to the other antenna. Since the MS can transmit on only one antenna at a time, spatial multiplexing is not possible, but some gain can be realized through the selection diversity, although the gains are likely to be quite limited since the same antenna is used over the entire wideband channel, which already has significant diversity.

Multiuser Virtual MIMO In UL multiuser MIMO, two single transmit antenna mobile stations are multiplexed onto the same physical resource to form a virtual two-antenna transmitter. Naturally, if each MS has two antennas, it simply selects one of the two to transmit on and the other one is unused. Each MS uses a different pilot pattern—specified explicitly by the BS—which allows the BS to spatially separate the two MSs. In order to minimize the interference between the users, the system should select two users whose channels are nearly orthogonal to each other.

All of these multiantenna procedures are specified and discussed in much greater detail in Chapters 7 (downlink) and 8 (uplink).

5.11 Chapter Summary

This chapter has presented the wide variety of techniques that can be used when multiple antennas are deployed at the receiver and/or transmitter. In particular:

- We showed that spatial diversity offers very desirable improvements in reliability, comparable to increasing the transmit power by a factor of 10–100.

- We learned how these diversity gains could be attained with either multiple receive antennas, multiple transmit antennas, or a combination of both.

- Alternatively, we showed how the antennas can directly increase the desired signal energy while suppressing or cancelling interfering signals (Section 5.4).

- We overviewed spatial multiplexing, which allows multiple data streams to be simultaneously transmitted and received using sophisticated signal processing, to in theory increase the data rate by a linear factor $\min(N_t, N_r)$.

- Since multiple antenna techniques require channel knowledge, we showed how the MIMO-OFDM channel can be estimated, and also overviewed how this channel knowledge can be fed back to the transmitter to support closed-loop MIMO.

- Throughout the chapter, we adopted a critical view of MIMO systems and explained the practical issues and shortcomings of the various techniques in the context of a cellular broadband system like LTE, and we overviewed state-of-the-art research on these problems.

- We provided a brief summary of MIMO techniques in LTE, with details deferred to Chapters 7 and 8. See Table of MIMO techniques.

Table of MIMO Techniques

Technique	(N_r/N_t)	Feedback?	Rate r^*	Comments
Reliability Enhancement Techniques ($r \leq 1$)				
Selection combining (SC)	$N_r \geq 1$ $N_t = 1$	Open-loop	$r = 1$	Increases average SNR by $(1 + 1/2 + 1/3 + \ldots 1/N_r)$.
Maximal ratio combining (MRC)	$N_r \geq 1$ $N_t = 1$	Open-loop	$r = 1$	Increases SNR to $\gamma_\Sigma = \gamma_1 + \gamma_2 + \cdots + \gamma_{N_r}$.
Space time block codes (STBC)	$N_r \geq 1$ $N_t > 1$	Open-loop	$r \leq 1$	Increases SNR to $\gamma_\Sigma = \gamma\|\mathbf{H}\|_\mathbf{F}/N_t$.
Transmit selection diversity (TSD)	$N_r \geq 1$ $N_t > 1$	Closed-loop: feedback desired antenna index	$r = 1$ usually ($r < N_t$)	Same SNR as selection combining.
DOA beamforming	$N_r \geq 1$ $N_t \geq 1$ $N_r + N_t > 2$	Open-loop if $N_t = 1$ closed-loop if $N_t > 1$ or used for interference suppression	$r = 1$	Can suppress up to $(N_r - 1) + (N_t - 1)$ interference signals, and also increase gain in desired direction. Ineffective in multipath channels.
Precoding Techniques				
Linear diversity precoding	$N_r \geq 1$ $N_t > 1$	Closed-loop: feedback channel matrix	$r = 1$	Special case of linear beamforming where only one data stream is sent. Increases SNR to $\gamma_\Sigma = \gamma\|\mathbf{H}\|_\mathbf{F}$.
Eigenbeamforming	$N_r \geq 1$ $N_t > 1$	Closed-loop: feedback channel matrix and/or interfering signals	$1 \leq r \leq \min$ $(N_r - L, N_t - L)$	Can be used to both increase desired signal gain and suppress L interfering users.
General linear precoding	$N_r > 1$ $N_t > 1$	Closed-loop: feedback channel matrix	$1 \leq r \leq \min$ (N_r, N_t)	Similar to eigenbeamforming but interfering signals are generally not suppressed. Goal is to send multiple streams of data.
Spatial Multiplexing				
Open-loop spatial multiplexing	$N_r > 1$ $N_t > 1$	Open-loop	$r = \min (N_r, N_t)$	Can be received in a variety of ways: linear receiver (MMSE), ML receiver, sphere decoder. If $N_t > N_r$, can just select best N_r antennas to send streams on.
BLAST	$N_r > 1$ $N_t > 1$	Open-loop	$r = \min(N_r, N_t)$	Successively decode transmitted streams.
General linear precoding	$N_r > 1$ $N_t > 1$	Closed-loop: feedback channel matrix	$1 \leq r \leq \min(N_r, N_t)$	Same as above. Both a precoding technique and a spatial multiplexing technique.

* r is similar to the number of streams M but slightly more general since $r < 1$ is possible for some of the transmit diversity techniques.

Bibliography

[1] Aktas E., J. Evans, and S. Hanly. Distributed decoding in a cellular multiple access channel. *IEEE Trans. on Wireless Communications*, 7(1):241–250, Jan. 2008.

[2] Alamouti, S. M. A simple transmit diversity technique for wireless communications. *IEEE Journal on Sel. Areas in Communications*, 16(8):1451–1458, Oct. 1998.

[3] Andrews, J. G., W. Choi, and R. W. Heath. Overcoming interference in spatial multiplexing MIMO cellular networks. *IEEE Wireless Communications Magazine*, 14(6):95–104, Dec. 2007.

[4] Blum, R. MIMO capacity with interference. *IEEE Journal on Sel. Areas in Communications*, 21(5):793–801, June 2003.

[5] Blum, R., J. Winters, and N. Sollenberger. On the capacity of cellular systems with MIMO. *IEEE Communications Letters*, 6:242–244, June 2002.

[6] Bolcskei, H., R. W. Heath, and A. J. Paulraj. Blind channel identification and equalization in OFDM-based multiantenna systems. *IEEE Trans. on Signal Processing*, 50(1):96–109, Jan. 2002.

[7] Bolcskei, H. and A. J. Paulraj. Space-frequency coded broadband OFDM systems. In *Proc., IEEE Wireless Networking and Comm. Conf.*, 1–6, Chicago, IL, Sept. 2000.

[8] Caire, G., S. A. Ramprashad, H. C. Papadopoulos, C. Pepin, and C.-E. W. Sundberg. Multiuser MIMO downlink with limited inter-cell cooperation: Approximate interference alignment in time, frequency, and space. In *Allerton Conf. on Comm. Control and Comp.*, 730–737, Monticello, IL, Sept. 2008.

[9] Caire, G., and S. Shamai. On the achievable throughput of a multi-antenna Gaussian broadcast channel. *IEEE Trans. on Info. Theory*, 49(7):1691–1706, July 2003.

[10] Catreux, S., P. Driessen, and L. Greenstein. Attainable throughput of an interference-limited multiple-input multiple-output (MIMO) cellular system. *IEEE Trans. on Communications*, 49(8):1307–1311, Aug. 2001.

[11] Chae, C. B., D. Mazzarese, T. Inoue, and R. W. Heath Jr. Coordinated beamforming for the multiuser MIMO broadcast channel with limited feedforward. *IEEE Trans. on Signal Processing*, 56(12):6044–6056, Dec. 2008.

[12] Chae, C. B., D. Mazzarese, N. Jindal, and R. W. Heath Jr. Coordinated beamforming with limited feedback in the MIMO broadcast channel. *IEEE Journal on Sel. Areas in Communications*, 26(8):1505–1515, Oct. 2008.

[13] Chen, R., J. G. Andrews, R. W. Heath, and A. Ghosh. Uplink power control in multi-cell spatial multiplexing wireless systems. *IEEE Trans. on Wireless Communications*, 4(7):2700–2711, July 2007.

[14] Chen, R., R. W. Heath, and J. G. Andrews. Transmit selection diversity for multiuser spatial division multiplexing wireless systems. *IEEE Trans. on Signal Processing*, Mar. 2007.

[15] Chen, Z., J. Yuan, B. Vucetic, and Z. Zhou. Performance of Alamouti scheme with transmit antenna selection. *Electronics Letters*, 1666–1667, Nov. 2003.

[16] Chiani, M., M. Z. Win, and A. Zanella. On the capacity of spatially correlated MIMO Rayleigh-fading channels. *IEEE Trans. on Info. Theory*, 49(10):2363–2371, Oct. 2003.

[17] Choi, W. and J. G. Andrews. Downlink performance and capacity of distributed antenna systems in a multicell environment. *IEEE Trans. on Wireless Communications*, 69–73, Jan. 2007.

[18] Choi, W. and J. G. Andrews. The capacity gain from base station cooperation in multi-antenna systems. *IEEE Trans. on Wireless Communications*, 714–725, Feb. 2008.

[19] Chuah, C.-N., D. N. C. Tse, J. M. Kahn, and R. A. Valenzuela. Capacity scaling in MIMO wireless systems under correlated fading. *IEEE Trans. on Info. Theory*, 48:637–651, Mar. 2002.

[20] Cimini, L. J. Analysis and simulation of a digital mobile channel using orthogonal frequency division multiplexing. *IEEE Trans. on Communications*, 33(7):665–675, July 1985.

[21] Costa, M. Writing on dirty paper. *IEEE Trans. on Info. Theory*, 439–441, May 1983.

[22] Dai, H., A. Molisch, and H. V. Poor. Downlink capacity of interference-limited MIMO systems with joint detection. *IEEE Trans. on Wireless Communications*, 3(2):442–453, Mar. 2004.

[23] Diggavi, S., N. Al-Dhahir, A. Stamoulis, and 'A. Calderbank. Great expectations: The value of spatial diversity in wireless networks. *Proceedings of the IEEE*, 219–270, Feb. 2004.

[24] Ding, Y., N. Davidson, Z. Q. Luo, and K. M. Wong. Minimum BER block precoders for zero-forcing equalization. *IEEE Trans. on Signal Processing*, 51:2410–2423, Sept. 2003.

[25] Edelman, A. *Eigenvalues and condition number of random matrices*. PhD thesis, Dept. of Mathematics, MIT, 1989.

[26] Foschini, G. and M. Gans. On limits of wireless communications in a fading environment when using multiple antennas. *Wireless Personal Communications*, 6:311–335, Mar. 1998.

[27] Foschini, G. J. Layered space-time architecture for wireless communication in a fading environment when using multiple antennas. *Bell Labs Technical Journal*, 1(2):41–59, 1996.

[28] Foschini, G. J., K. Karakayali, and R. A. Valenzuela. Coordinating multiple antenna cellular networks to achieve enormous spectral efficiency. *IEE Proceedings*, 153(4):548–555, Aug. 2006.

[29] Gesbert, D., M. Kountouris, R. W. Heath Jr., C. B. Chae, and T. Salzer. Shifting the MIMO paradigm: From single user to multiuser communications. *IEEE Signal Processing Magazine*, 24(5):36–46, Sept. 2007.

[30] Gesbert, D., M. Shafi, D. Shiu, P. J. Smith, and A. Naguib. From theory to practice: An overview of MIMO spacetime coded wireless systems. *IEEE Journal on Sel. Areas in Communications*, 21(3):281–302, Apr. 2003.

[31] Godara, L. C. Application of antenna arrays to mobile communications, part II: Beam-forming and direction-of-arrival considerations. *Proceedings of the IEEE*, 85(8):1195–1245, Aug. 1997.

[32] Golden, G. D., G. J. Foschini, R. A. Valenzuela, and P. W. Wolniansky. Detection algorithm and initial laboratory results using V-BLAST space-time communication architecture. *IEE Electronics Letters*, 35:14–16, Jan. 1999.

[33] Goldsmith, A. J. *Wireless communications*. Cambridge University Press, 2005.

[34] Gore, D. and A. Paulraj. Space-time block coding with optimal antenna selection. In *Proc., IEEE Intl. Conf. on Acoustics, Speech, and Sig. Proc. (ICASSP)*, 2441–2444, May 2001.

[35] Hanly, S. and P. Whiting. Information-theoretic capacity of multi-receiver networks. *Telecommun. Syst.*, 1:1–42, 1993.

[36] Hassibi, B. and M. Sharif. Fundamental limits in MIMO broadcast channels. *IEEE Journal on Sel. Areas in Communications*, 25(7):1333–1344, Sept. 2007.

[37] Heath, R. W. and A. J. Paulraj. Switching between multiplexing and diversity based on constellation distance. In *Proc., Allerton Conf. on Comm., Control, and Computing*, Sept. 2000.

[38] Heath, R. W., S. Sandhu, and A. Paulraj. Antenna selection for spatial multiplexing systems with linear receivers. *IEEE Communications Letters*, 5(4):142–144, Apr. 2001.

[39] Hochwald, B. M. and S. ten Brink. Achieving near-capacity on a multiple-antenna channel. *IEEE Trans. on Communications*, 51(3):389–399, Mar. 2003.

[40] Hsieh, M. and C. Wei. Channel estimation for OFDM systems based on comb-type pilot arrangement in frequency selective fading channels. *IEEE Trans. Consumer Electron.*, 44(1):217–225, Feb. 1998.

[41] Huang, K., J. G. Andrews, and R. W. Heath Jr. Performance of orthogonal beamforming for SDMA with limited feedback. *IEEE Trans. on Veh. Technology*, 58(1):152–164, Jan. 2009.

[42] Huang, K., R. Heath, and J. Andrews. Space division multiple access with a sum feedback rate constraint. *IEEE Transactions on Signal Processing*, 55(7):3879–3891, July 2007.

[43] Jafar, S. A., G. Foschini, and A. J. Goldsmith. Phantomnet: Exploring optimal multicellular multiple antenna systems. *EURASIP Journal on Appl. Signal Processing, Special Issue on MIMO Comm. and Signal Processing*, 591–605, May 2004.

[44] Jafarkhani, H. A quasi-orthogonal space-time block code. *IEEE Trans. on Communications*, 49(1):1–4, Jan. 2001.

[45] Jindal, N. MIMO broadcast channels with finite rate feedback. *IEEE Trans. on Info. Theory*, 52(11):5045–5060, Nov. 2006.

[46] Jindal, N. and A. Goldsmith. Dirty-paper coding versus TDMA for MIMO broadcast channels. *IEEE Trans. on Info. Theory*, 51(5):1783–1794, May 2005.

[47] Jindal, N., S. Vishwanath, and A. Goldsmith. On the duality of Gaussian multiple-access and broadcast channels. *IEEE Trans. on Info. Theory*, 50(5):768–783, May 2004.

[48] Jing, S., D. N. C. Tse, J. Hou, J. B. Soriaga, J. E. Smee, and R. Padovani. Multi-cell downlink capacity with coordinated processing. *EURASIP Journal on Wireless Communications and Networking*, 2008. Volume 2008, Article ID 586878.

[49] Karakayali, K., G. J. Foschini, and R. A. Valenzuela. Network coordination for spectrally efficient communications in cellular systems. *IEEE Wireless Communications Magazine*, 13(4):56–61, Aug. 2006.

[50] Kim, T. and J. G. Andrews. Optimal pilot-to-data power ratio for MIMO-OFDM. In *Proc., IEEE Globecom*, 3:1481–1485, St. Louis, MO, Dec. 2005.

[51] Liberti, J. C. and T. S. Rappaport. *Smart Antennas for Wireless Communications: IS-95 and Third Generation CDMA Applications*. Upper Saddle River, NJ: Prentice Hall, 1999.

[52] Liu, K., V. Raghavan, and A. M. Sayeed. Capacity scaling and spectral efficiency in wide-band correlated MIMO channels. *IEEE Trans. on Info. Theory*, 49(10):2504–2527, Oct. 2003.

[53] Liu, Z., G. Giannakis, and B. Hughes. Double differential space-time block coding for time-selective fading channels. *IEEE Trans. on Communications*, 49(9):1529–1539, Sept. 2001.

[54] Lo, T. Maximum ratio transmission. *IEEE Trans. on Communications*, 1458–1461, Oct. 1999.

[55] Love, D. J. and R. W. Heath. Limited feedback unitary precoding for orthogonal space-time block codes. *IEEE Trans. on Signal Processing*, 64–73, Jan. 2005.

[56] Love, D. J., R. W. Heath, V. Lau, D. Gesbert, B. D. Rao, and M. Andrews. An overview of limited feedback in wireless communication systems. *IEEE Journal on Sel. Areas in Communications*, 26(8):1341–1365, Oct. 2008.

[57] Lozano, A. and N. Jindal. Transmit Diversity v. Spatial Multiplexing in Modern MIMO Systems. Submitted to *IEEE Trans. on Wireless Communications*, Oct. 2008.

[58] Marsch, P. and G. Fettweis. A framework for optimizing the downlink performance of distributed antenna systems under a constrained backhaul. In *Proc. European Wireless Conf. (EW' 07)*, Paris, France, Apr. 2007.

[59] Marsch, P. and G. Fettweis. A framework for optimizing the uplink performance of distributed antenna systems under a constrained backhaul. In *Proc., IEEE Intl. Conf. on Communications*, 975–979, Glasgow, Scotland, Jun. 2007.

[60] Molisch, A. F. and M. Z. Win. MIMO systems with antenna selection. *IEEE Microwave Magazine*, 5(1):46–56, Mar. 2004.

[61] Ng, B., J. Evans, S. Hanly, and D. Aktas. Distributed downlink beamforming with co-operative base stations. *IEEE Trans. on Info. Theory*, 54(12):5491–5499, Dec. 2008.

[62] Onggosanusi, E. N., A. G. Dabak, and T. A. Schmidl. High rate space-time block coded scheme: Performance and improvement in correlated fading channels. In *Proc., IEEE Wireless Communications and Networking Conf.*, 1:194–199, Orlando, FL, Mar. 2002.

[63] Papadogiannis, A., D. Gesbert, and E. Hardouin. A dynamic clustering approach in wireless networks with multi-cell cooperative processing. In *Proc., IEEE Intl. Conf. on Communications*, 4033–4037, Beijing, China, May 2008.

[64] Paulraj, A., D. Gore, and R. Nabar. *Introduction to Space-time Wireless Communications*. Cambridge, 2003.

[65] Proakis, J. G., *Digital Communications*. 3rd ed. New York: McGraw-Hill, 1995.

[66] Sampath, H., S. Talwar, J. Tellado, V. Erceg, and A. Paulraj. A fourth-generation MIMO-OFDM broadband wireless system: Design, performance, and field trial results. *IEEE Communications Magazine*, 40(9):143–149, Sept. 2002.

[67] Sanderovich, A., O. Somekh, and S. Shamai (Shitz). Uplink macro diversity with limited backhaul capacity. In *Proc., IEEE Intl. Symposium on Information Theory*, 11–15, Nice, France, Jun. 2007.

[68] Scaglione, A., S. Barbarossa, and G. B. Giannakis. Filterbank transceivers optimizing information rate in block transmissions over dispersive channels. *IEEE Trans. on Info. Theory*, 45:1988–2006, Apr. 1999.

[69] Scaglione, A., G. B. Giannakis, and S. Barbarossa. Redundant filterbank precoders and equalizers, Part I and II. *IEEE Trans. on Signal Processing*, 47:1988–2022, July 1999.

[70] Scaglione, A., P. Stoica, S. Barbarossa, G. B. Giannakis, and H. Sampath. Optimal designs for space-time linear precoders and decoders. *IEEE Trans. on Signal Processing*, 50(5):1051–1064, May 2002.

[71] Schniter, P. Low-complexity equalization of OFDM in doubly-selective channels. *IEEE Trans. on Signal Processing*, 52(4):1002–1011, Apr. 2004.

[72] Seshadri, N. and J. H. Winters. Two schemes for improving the performance of frequency-duplex (FDD) transmission systems using transmitter antenna diversity. *Int. J. Wireless Information Networks*, 1:49–60, Jan. 1994.

[73] Sethuraman, B., B. S. Rajan, and V. Shashidhar. Full-diversity, high-rate space-time block codes from division algebras. *IEEE Trans. on Info. Theory*, 49(10):2596–2616, Oct. 2003.

[74] Shamai, S. and B. Zaidel. Enhancing the cellular downlink capacity via co-processing at the transmitting end. In *Proc., IEEE Veh. Technology Conf.*, 1745–1749, May 2001.

[75] Shamai (Shitz), S. and A. D. Wyner. Information-theoretic considerations for symmetric, cellular, multiple-access fading channels—parts I & II. *IEEE Trans. on Info. Theory*, 43(11):1877–1911, Nov. 1997.

[76] Sharif, M. and B. Hassibi. On the capacity of MIMO broadcast channels with partial side information. *IEEE Trans. on Info. Theory*, 51(2):506–522, Feb. 2005.

[77] Sharif, M. and B. Hassibi. A comparison of time-sharing, DPC, and beamforming for MIMO broadcast channels with many users. *IEEE Trans. on Communications*, 55(1):11–15, Jan. 2007.

[78] Shen, Z., R. Chen, J. G. Andrews, R. W. Heath, and B. L. Evans. Sum capacity of multiuser MIMO broadcast channels with block diagonalization. *IEEE Trans. on Wireless Communications*, 6(5), May 2007.

[79] (Shitz), S. S., O. Somekh, and B. M. Zaidel. Multi-cell communications: An information theoretic perspective. In *Joint Workshop on Communications and Coding (JWCC)*, Florence, Italy, Oct. 2004.

[80] Shiu, D., G. J. Foschini, M. J. Gans, and J. M. Kahn. Fading correlation and its effect on the capacity of multielement antenna systems. *IEEE Trans. on Communications*, 48:502–513, Mar. 2000.

[81] Somekh, O. and S. S. (Shitz). Shannon-theoretic approach to a Gaussian cellular multi-access channel with fading. *IEEE Trans. on Info. Theory*, 46:1401–1425, July 2000.

[82] Somekh, O., O. Simeone, Y. Bar-Ness, and A. M. Haimovich. Distributed multi-cell zero-forcing beamforming in cellular downlink channels. In *Proc., IEEE Globecom*, 1–6, San Francisco, Nov. 2006.

[83] Somekh, O., B. M. Zaidel, and S. S. (Shitz). Sum rate characterization of joint multiple cell-site processing. *IEEE Trans. on Info. Theory*, 4473–4497, Dec. 2007.

[84] Spencer, Q., A. Swindlehurst, and M. Haardt. Zero-forcing methods for downlink spatial multiplexing in multi-user MIMO channels. *IEEE Trans. on Signal Processing*, 52:461–471, Feb. 2004.

[85] Stuber, G. L., J. R. Barry, S. W. McLaughlin, Y. Li, M. Ingram, and T. G. Pratt. Broadband MIMO-OFDM wireless communications. *Proceedings of the IEEE*, 271–94, Feb. 2004.

[86] Su, W. and X.-G. Xia. Signal constellations for quasi-orthogonal space-time block codes with full diversity. *IEEE Trans. on Info. Theory*, 50(10):2331–2347, Oct. 2004.

[87] Tang, T. and J. R. W. Heath. Opportunistic feedback for downlink multiuser diversity. *IEEE Communications Letters*, 9(10):948–950, Oct. 2005.

[88] Tarokh, V., H. Jafarkhani, and A. R. Calderbank. Space-time block codes from orthogonal designs. *IEEE Trans. on Info. Theory*, 45(5):1456–1467, July 1999.

[89] Tarokh, V., N. Seshadri, and A. R. Calderbank. Space-time codes for high data rate wireless communication: Performance criterion and code construction. *IEEE Trans. on Info. Theory*, 44(2):744–765, Mar. 1998.

[90] Teletar, E. Capacity of multi-antenna Gaussian channels. *European Trans. Telecommun.*, 6:585–595, Nov.-Dec. 1999.

[91] Texas Instruments. Double-STTD scheme for HSDPA systems with four transmit antennas: Link level simulation results. TSG-R WG1 document, TSGR1#20(01)0458, May 2001.

[92] Tse, D. and P. Viswanath. *Fundamentals of Wireless Communication*. Cambridge: Cambridge University Press, 2005.

[93] Tulino, A., A. Lozano, and S. Verdu. Impact of antenna correlation on the capacity of multiantenna channels. *IEEE Trans. on Info. Theory*, 51(7):2491–2509, July 2005.

[94] Tulino, A. and S. Verdu. Random matrix theory and wireless communications. *Foundations and Trends in Communications and Information Theory*, 1(1):1–186, 2004.

[95] Venkatesan, S. Coordinating base stations for greater uplink spectral efficiency in a cellular network. In *Proc., IEEE PIMRC*, 1–5, Athens, Greece, Sept. 2007.

[96] Verdu, S. *Multiuser Detection*. Cambridge: Cambridge University Press, 1998.

[97] Winters, J. H. Switched diversity with feedback for DPSK mobile radio systems. *IEEE Trans. on Veh. Technology*, 32:134–150, Feb. 1983.

[98] Wittneben, A. A new bandwidth efficient transmit antenna modulation diversity schme for linear digital modulation. In *Proc., IEEE Intl. Conf. on Communications*, 1630–1634, Geneva, Switzerland, May 1993.

[99] Wong, K.-K., R. D. Murch, and K. B. Letaief. Optimizing time and space MIMO antenna system for frequency selective fading channels. *IEEE Journal on Sel. Areas in Communications*, 19(7):1395–1407, July 2001.

[100] Wong, K. K., R. D. Murch, and K. B. Letaief. A joint-channel diagonalization for multiuser MIMO antenna systems. *IEEE Trans. on Wireless Communications*, 2(4):773–786, July 2003.

[101] Wyner, A. D. Shannon-theoretic approach to a Gaussian cellular multiple-access channel. *IEEE Trans. on Info. Theory*, 40(11):1713–1727, Nov. 1994.

[102] Yang, H. A road to future broadband wireless access: MIMO-OFDM-based air interface. *IEEE Communications Magazine*, 43(1):53–60, Jan. 2005.

[103] Yoo, T., N. Jindal, and A. Goldsmith. Multi-antenna broadcast channels with limited feedback and user selection. *IEEE Journal on Sel. Areas in Communications*, 1478–1491, Sept. 2007.

[104] Zhang, H. and H. Dai. Co-channel interference mitigation and cooperative processing in downlink multicell multiuser MIMO networks. *European Journal on Wireless Communications and Networking*, 4th Quarter 2004.

[105] Zhang, H., N. B. Mehta, A. F. Molisch, J. Zhang, and H. Dai. Asynchronous interference mitigation in cooperative base station systems. *IEEE Trans. on Wireless Communications*, 7(1):155–165, Jan. 2008.

[106] Zhang, J., R. Chen, J. G. Andrews, A. Ghosh, and R. W. Heath. Networked MIMO with clustered linear precoding. *IEEE Transactions on Wireless Communications*, To appear.

[107] Zhang, J., M. Kountouris, J. G. Andrews, and R. W. Heath. Achievable throughput of multi-mode multiuser MIMO with imperfect CSI constraints. *IEEE International Symposium on Information Theory*, June 2009.

[108] Zhang, J., R. W. Heath Jr., M. Kountouris, and J. G. Andrews. Mode switching for the multi-antenna broadcast channel based on delay and channel quantization. *EURASIP Journal on Advances in Signal Processing*, 2009. Article ID 802548.

[109] Zheng, L., and D. Tse. Diversity and multiplexing: A fundamental tradeoff in multiple antenna channels. *IEEE Trans. on Info. Theory*, 49(5), May 2003.

Part II

The LTE Standard

Chapter 6

Overview and Channel Structure of LTE

In Part I, we discussed the inherent challenges and associated technical solutions in designing a broadband wireless network. From here onward, we describe the technical details of the LTE specifications. As a starting point, in this chapter we provide an overview of the LTE radio interface. The 3rd Generation Partnership Project (3GPP) defines a separable network structure, that is, it divides the whole network into a radio access network (RAN) and a core network (CN), which makes it feasible to evolve each part independently. The *Long-Term Evolution (LTE)* project in 3GPP focuses on enhancing the UMTS Terrestrial Radio Access (UTRA)—the 3G RAN developed within 3GPP, and on optimizing 3GPP's overall radio access architecture. Another parallel project in 3GPP is the *Evolved Packet Core (EPC)*, which focuses on the CN evolution with a flatter all-IP, packet-based architecture. The complete packet system consisting of LTE and EPC is called the *Evolved Packet System (EPS)*. This book focuses on LTE, while EPC is discussed only when necessary. LTE is also referred to as *Evolved UMTS Terrestrial Radio Access (E-UTRA)*, and the RAN of LTE is also referred to as *Evolved UMTS Terrestrial Radio Access Network (E-UTRAN)*.

The radio interface of a wireless network is the interface between the mobile terminal and the base station, and thus in the case of LTE it is located between the RAN–E-UTRAN and the user equipment (UE, the name for the mobile terminal in 3GPP). Compared to the UMTS Terrestrial Radio Access Network (UTRAN) for 3G systems, which has two logical entities—the Node-B (the radio base station) and the radio network controller (RNC)—the E-UTRAN network architecture is simpler and flatter. It is composed of only one logical node—the evolved Node-B (eNode-B). The RAN architectures of UTRAN and E-UTRAN are shown in Figure 6.1. Compared to the traditional Node-B, the eNode-B supports additional features, such as radio resource control, admission control, and mobility management, which were originally contained in the RNC. This simpler structure simplifies the network operation and allows for higher throughput and lower latency over the radio interface.

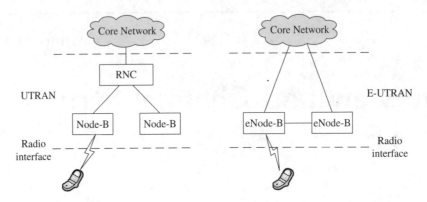

Figure 6.1 Radio interface architectures of UTRAN and E-UTRAN.

The LTE radio interface aims for a *long-term evolution,* so it is designed with a clean slate approach as opposed to High-Speed Packet Access (HSPA), which was designed as an add-on to UMTS in order to increase throughput of packet switched services. HSPA is a collection of *High-Speed Downlink Packet Access (HSDPA)* and *High-Speed Uplink Packet Access (HSUPA).* The clean slate approach allows for a completely different air interface, which means that advanced techniques, including *Orthogonal Frequency Division Multiplexing (OFDM)* and *multiantenna transmission and reception (MIMO),* could be included from the start of the standardization of LTE. For multiple access, it moves away from *Code Division Multiple Access (CDMA)* and instead uses *Orthogonal Frequency Division Multiple Access (OFDMA)* in the downlink and *Single-Carrier Frequency Division Multiple Access (SC-FDMA)* in the uplink. All these techniques were described in detail in Part I, so in Part II we assume a basic knowledge of a wireless system, antenna diversity, OFDMA, and other topics covered in Part I.

In this chapter, we provide an introduction to the LTE radio interface, and describe its hierarchical channel structure. First, an overview of the LTE standard is provided, including design principles, the network architecture, and radio interface protocols. We then describe the purpose of each channel type defined in LTE and the mapping between channels at various protocol layers. Next, the downlink OFDMA and uplink SC-FDMA aspects of the air interface are described, including frame structures, physical resource blocks, resource allocation, and the supported MIMO modes. This chapter serves as the foundation for understanding the physical layer procedures and higher layer protocols of LTE that are described in the chapters to follow.

6.1   Introduction to LTE

As mentioned previously, LTE is the next step in the evolution of mobile cellular systems and was standardized as part of the 3GPP Release 8 specifications. Unlike 2G and 3G cellular systems[1] that were designed mainly with voice services in mind, LTE was

---

1 Evolution of different 3GPP standards, including GPRS, UMTS, and HSPA, was discussed in Chapter 1.

designed primarily for high-speed data services, which is why LTE is a packet-switched network from end to end and has no support for circuit-switched services. However, the low latency of LTE and its sophisticated quality of service (QoS) architecture allow a network to emulate a circuit-switched connection on top of the packet-switched framework of LTE.

6.1.1 Design Principles

The LTE standard was designed as a completely new standard, with new numbering and new documentation, and it is not built on the previous versions of 3GPP standards. Earlier elements were brought in only if there was a compelling reason for them to exist in the new standard. The basic design principles that were agreed upon and followed in 3GPP while designing the LTE specifications include:[2]

- **Network Architecture**: Unlike 3G networks, LTE was designed to support packet-switched traffic with support for various QoS classes of services. Previous generations of networks such as UMTS/HSPA and 1xRTT/EvDO also support packet-switched traffic but this was achieved by subsequent add-ons to the initial version of the standards. For example, HSPA, which is a packet-switched protocol (packet-switched over the air), was built on top of the Release 99 UMTS network and as a result carried some of the unnecessary burdens of a circuit-switched network. LTE is different in the sense that it is a clean slate design and supports packet switching for high data rate services from the start. The LTE radio access network, E-UTRAN, was designed to have the minimum number of interfaces (i.e., the minimum number of network elements) while still being able to provide efficient packet-switched transport for traffic belonging to all the QoS classes such as conversational, streaming, real-time, non-real-time, and background classes.

- **Data Rate and Latency**: The design target for downlink and uplink peak data rates for LTE are 100 Mbps and 50 Mbps, respectively, when operating at the 20MHz frequency division duplex (FDD) channel size. The user-plane latency is defined in terms of the time it takes to transmit a small IP packet from the UE to the edge node of the radio access network or vice versa measured on the IP layer. The target for one-way latency in the user plane is 5 ms in an unloaded network, that is, if only a single UE is present in the cell. For the control-plane latency, the transition time from a camped state to an active state is less than 100 ms, while the transition time between a dormant state and an active state should be less than 50 ms.

- **Performance Requirements**: The target performance requirements for LTE are specified in terms of spectrum efficiency, mobility, and coverage, and they are in general expressed relative to the 3GPP Release 6 HSPA.

    - **Spectrum Efficiency** The average downlink user data rate and spectrum efficiency target is three to four times that of the baseline HSDPA network. Similarly, in the uplink the average user data rate and spectrum efficiency

---

2 See Section 1.2.4 for a comparison of different beyond-3G systems, including HSPA+, WiMAX, and LTE.

target is two to three times that of the baseline HSUPA network. The cell edge throughput, measured as the 5th percentile throughput, should be two to three times that of the baseline HSDPA and HSUPA.

- **Mobility** The mobility requirement for LTE is to be able to support hand-off/mobility at different terminal speeds. Maximum performance is expected for the lower terminal speeds of 0 to 15 km/hr, with minor degradation in performance at higher mobile speeds up to 120 km/hr. LTE is also expected to be able to sustain a connection for terminal speeds up to 350 km/hr but with significant degradation in the system performance.

- **Coverage** For the cell coverage, the above performance targets should be met up to 5 km. For cell ranges up to 30 km, a slight degradation of the user throughput is tolerated and a more significant degradation for spectrum efficiency is acceptable, but the mobility requirements should be met. Cell ranges up to 100 km should not be precluded by the specifications.

- **MBMS Service** LTE should also provide enhanced support for the Multimedia Broadcast and Multicast Service (MBMS) compared to UTRA operation.

- **Radio Resource Management**: The radio resource management requirements cover various aspects such as enhanced support for end-to-end QoS, efficient support for transmission of higher layers, and support for load sharing/balancing and policy management/enforcement across different radio access technologies.

- **Deployment Scenario and Co-existence with 3G**: At a high level, LTE shall support the following two deployment scenarios:

  - Standalone deployment scenario, where the operator deploys LTE either with no previous network deployed in the area or with no requirement for interworking with the existing UTRAN/GERAN (GSM EDGE radio access network) networks.

  - Integrating with existing UTRAN and/or GERAN deployment scenario, where the operator already has either a UTRAN and/or a GERAN network deployed with full or partial coverage in the same geographical area.

- **Flexibility of Spectrum and Deployment**: In order to become a truly global standard, LTE was designed to be operable under a wide variety of spectrum scenarios, including its ability to coexist and share spectrum with existing 3G technologies. Service providers in different geographical regions often have different spectrums in terms of the carrier frequency and total available bandwidth, which is why LTE was designed to have a scalable bandwidth from 1.4MHz to 20MHz. In order to accommodate flexible duplexing options, LTE was designed to operate in both frequency division duplex (FDD) and time division duplex (TDD) modes.

- **Interoperability with 3G and 2G Networks**: Multimode LTE terminals, which support UTRAN and/or GERAN operation, should be able to support measurement of, and handover from and to, both 3GPP UTRAN and 3GPP GERAN systems with acceptable terminal complexity and network performance.

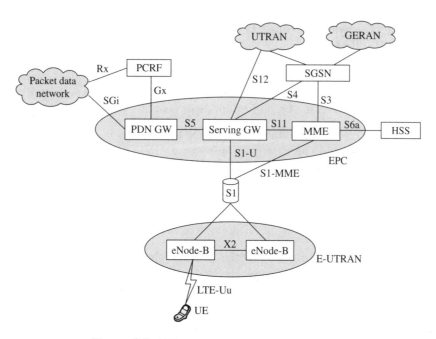

Figure 6.2 LTE end-to-end network architecture.

6.1.2 Network Architecture

Figure 6.2 shows the end-to-end network architecture of LTE and the various components of the network. The entire network is composed of the radio access network (E-UTRAN) and the core network (EPC), both of which have been defined as new components of the end-to-end network in Release 8 of the 3GPP specifications. In this sense, LTE is different from UMTS since UMTS defined a new radio access network but used the same core network as the previous-generation Enhanced GPRS (EDGE) network. This obviously has some implications for the service providers who are upgrading from a UMTS network to LTE. The main components of the E-UTRAN and EPC are

- **UE:** The mobile terminal.

- **eNode-B:** The eNode-B (also called the base station) terminates the air interface protocol and is the first point of contact for the UE. As already shown in Figure 6.1, the eNode-B is the only logical node in the E-UTRAN, so it includes some functions previously defined in the RNC of the UTRAN, such as radio bearer management, uplink and downlink dynamic radio resource management and data packet scheduling, and mobility management.

- **Mobility Management Entity (MME):** MME is similar in function to the control plane of legacy Serving GPRS Support Node (SGSN). It manages mobility aspects in 3GPP access such as gateway selection and tracking area list management.

- **Serving Gateway (Serving GW):** The Serving GW terminates the interface toward E-UTRAN, and routes data packets between E-UTRAN and EPC. In addition, it is the local mobility anchor point for inter-eNode-B handovers and also provides an anchor for inter-3GPP mobility. Other responsibilities include lawful intercept, charging, and some policy enforcement. The Serving GW and the MME may be implemented in one physical node or separate physical nodes.

- **Packet Data Network Gateway (PDN GW):** The PDN GW terminates the SGi interface toward the Packet Data Network (PDN). It routes data packets between the EPC and the external PDN, and is the key node for policy enforcement and charging data collection. It also provides the anchor point for mobility with non-3GPP accesses. The external PDN can be any kind of IP network as well as the IP Multimedia Subsystem (IMS) domain. The PDN GW and the Serving GW may be implemented in one physical node or separated physical nodes.

- **S1 Interface:** The S1 interface is the interface that separates the E-UTRAN and the EPC. It is split into two parts: the S1-U, which carries traffic data between the eNode-B and the Serving GW, and the S1-MME, which is a signaling-only interface between the eNode-B and the MME.

- **X2 Interface:** The X2 interface is the interface between eNode-Bs, consisting of two parts: the X2-C is the control plane interface between eNode-Bs, while the X2-U is the user plane interface between eNode-Bs. It is assumed that there always exists an X2 interface between eNode-Bs that need to communicate with each other, for example, for support of handover.

The specific functions supported by each component and the details about reference points (S1-MME, S1-U, S3, etc.) can be found in [1]. For other nodes in Figure 6.2, the Policy and Charging Rules Function (PCRF) is for policy and charging control, the Home Subscriber Server (HSS) is responsible for the service authorization and user authentication, and the Serving GPRS Support Node (SGSN) is for controlling packet sessions and managing the mobility of the UE for GPRS networks. The topics in this book mainly focus on the E-UTRAN and the LTE radio interface.

6.1.3   Radio Interface Protocols

As in other communication standards, the LTE radio interface is designed based on a layered protocol stack, which can be divided into control plane and user plane protocol stacks and is shown in Figure 6.3. The packet flow in the user plane is shown in Figure 6.4. The LTE radio interface protocol is composed of the following layers:

- **Radio Resource Control (RRC):** The RRC layer performs the control plane functions including paging, maintenance and release of an RRC connection-security handling-mobility management, and QoS management.

- **Packet Data Convergence Protocol (PDCP):** The main functions of the PDCP sublayer include IP packet header compression and decompression based

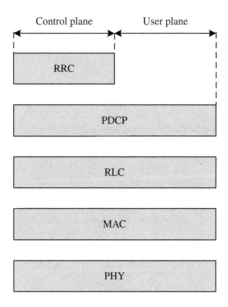

Figure 6.3 The LTE radio interface protocol stack.

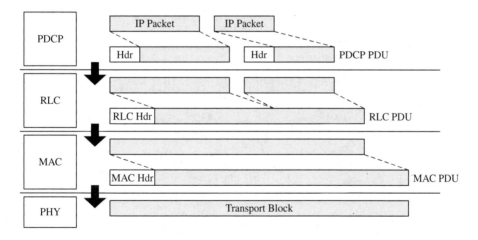

Figure 6.4 The packet flow in the user plane.

on the RObust Header Compression (ROHC) protocol, ciphering of data and signaling, and integrity protection for signaling. There is only one PDCP entity at the eNode-B and the UE per bearer.[3]

---

3 A bearer is an IP packet flow with a defined QoS between the PDN GW and the UE. It will be discussed in more detail in Chapter 10.

- **Radio Link Control (RLC):** The main functions of the RLC sublayer are segmentation and concatenation of data units, error correction through the Automatic Repeat reQuest (ARQ) protocol, and in-sequence delivery of packets to the higher layers. It operates in three modes:

  - **The Transparent Mode (TM):** The TM mode is the simplest one, without RLC header addition, data segmentation, or concatenation, and it is used for specific purposes such as random access.
  - **The Unacknowledged Mode (UM):** The UM mode allows the detection of packet loss and provides packet reordering and reassembly, but does not require retransmission of the missing protocol data units (PDUs).
  - **The Acknowledged Mode (AM):** The AM mode is the most complex one, and it is configured to request retransmission of the missing PDUs in addition to the features supported by the UM mode.

  There is only one RLC entity at the eNode-B and the UE per bearer.

- **Medium Access Control (MAC):** The main functions of the MAC sublayer include error correction through the Hybrid-ARQ (H-ARQ) mechanism, mapping between logical channels and transport channels, multiplexing/demultiplexing of RLC PDUs on to transport blocks, priority handling between logical channels of one UE, and priority handling between UEs by means of dynamic scheduling. The MAC sublayer is also responsible for transport format selection of scheduled UEs, which includes selection of modulation format, code rate, MIMO rank, and power level. There is only one MAC entity at the eNode-B and one MAC entity at the UE.

- **Physical Layer (PHY):** The main function of PHY is the actual transmission and reception of data in forms of transport blocks. The PHY is also responsible for various control mechanisms such as signaling of H-ARQ feedback, signaling of scheduled allocations, and channel measurements.

In Chapter 7 to Chapter 9, we focus on the PHY layer, also referred to as layer 1 of the Open Systems Interconnection (OSI) reference model. Higher layer processing is described in Chapter 10.

6.2   Hierarchical Channel Structure of LTE

To efficiently support various QoS classes of services, LTE adopts a hierarchical channel structure. There are three different channel types defined in LTE—logical channels, transport channels, and physical channels, each associated with a service access point (SAP) between different layers. These channels are used by the lower layers of the protocol stack to provide services to the higher layers. The radio interface protocol architecture and the SAPs between different layers are shown in Figure 6.5. Logical channels provide services at the SAP between MAC and RLC layers, while transport channels provide services at the SAP between MAC and PHY layers. Physical channels are the actual implementation of transport channels over the radio interface.

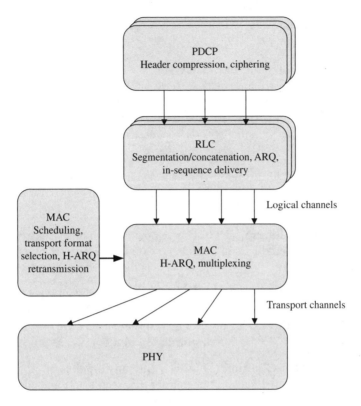

Figure 6.5 The radio interface protocol architecture and the SAPs between different layers.

The channels defined in LTE follow a similar hierarchical structure to UTRA/HSPA. However, in the case of LTE, the transport and logical channel structures are much more simplified and fewer in number compared to UTRA/HSPA. Unlike UTRA/HSPA, LTE is based entirely on shared and broadcast channels and contains no dedicated channels carrying data to specific UEs. This improves the efficiency of the radio interface and can support dynamic resource allocation between different UEs depending on their traffic/QoS requirements and their respective channel conditions. In this section, we describe in detail the various logical, transport, and physical channels that are defined in LTE. The description of different channel types and the channel mapping between different protocol layers provides an intuitive manner to understand the data flow of different services in LTE, which builds the foundation to understand the detail processing procedures in later chapters.

6.2.1 Logical Channels: What to Transmit

Logical channels are used by the MAC to provide services to the RLC. Each logical channel is defined based on the type of information it carries. In LTE, there are two categories of logical channels depending on the service they provide: *logical control channels* and *logical traffic channels*.

The logical control channels, which are used to transfer control plane information, include the following types:

- **Broadcast Control Channel (BCCH):** A downlink common channel used to broadcast system control information to the mobile terminals in the cell, including downlink system bandwidth, antenna configuration, and reference signal power. Due to the large amount of information carried on the BCCH, it is mapped to two different transport channels: the Broadcast Channel (BCH) and the Downlink Shared Channel (DL-SCH).

- **Multicast Control Channel (MCCH):** A point-to-multipoint downlink channel used for transmitting control information to UEs in the cell. It is only used by UEs that receive multicast/broadcast services.

- **Paging Control Channel (PCCH):** A downlink channel that transfers paging information to registered UEs in the cell, for example, in case of a mobile-terminated communication session. The paging process is discussed in Chapter 10.

- **Common Control Channel (CCCH):** A bi-directional channel for transmitting control information between the network and UEs when no RRC connection is available, implying the UE is not attached to the network such as in the idle state. Most commonly the CCCH is used during the random access procedure.

- **Dedicated Control Channel (DCCH):** A point-to-point, bi-directional channel that transmits dedicated control information between a UE and the network. This channel is used when the RRC connection is available, that is, the UE is attached to the network.

The logical traffic channels, which are to transfer user plane information, include:

- **Dedicated Traffic Channel (DTCH):** A point-to-point, bi-directional channel used between a given UE and the network. It can exist in both uplink and downlink.

- **Multicast Traffic Channel (MTCH):** A unidirectional, point-to-multipoint data channel that transmits traffic data from the network to UEs. It is associated with the multicast/broadcast service.

6.2.2 Transport Channels: How to Transmit

The transport channels are used by the PHY to offer services to the MAC. A transport channel is basically characterized by how and with what characteristics data is transferred over the radio interface, that is, the channel coding scheme, the modulation scheme, and antenna mapping. Compared to UTRA/HSPA, the number of transport channels in LTE is reduced since no dedicated channels are present.

LTE defines two MAC entities: one in the UE and one in the E-UTRAN, which handle the following downlink/uplink transport channels.

Downlink Transport Channels

- **Downlink Shared Channel (DL-SCH):** Used for transmitting the downlink data, including both control and traffic data, and thus it is associated with both logical control and logical traffic channels. It supports H-ARQ, dynamic link adaption, dynamic and semi-persistent resource allocation, UE discontinuous reception, and multicast/broadcast transmission. The concept of shared channel transmission originates from HSDPA, which uses the *High-Speed Downlink Shared Channel* (HS-DSCH) to multiplex traffic and control information among different UEs. By sharing the radio resource among different UEs the DL-SCH is able to maximize the throughput by allocating the resources to the optimum UEs. The processing of the DL-SCH is described in Section 7.2.

- **Broadcast Channel (BCH):** A downlink channel associated with the BCCH logical channel and is used to broadcast system information over the entire coverage area of the cell. It has a fixed transport format defined by the specifications. The processing of the BCH will be described in Section 7.4.

- **Multicast Channel (MCH):** Associated with MCCH and MTCH logical channels for the multicast/broadcast service. It supports *Multicast/Broadcast Single Frequency Network* (MBSFN) transmission, which transmits the same information on the same radio resource from multiple synchronized base stations to multiple UEs. The processing of the MCH is described in Section 7.5.

- **Paging Channel (PCH):** Associated with the PCCH logical channel. It is mapped to dynamically allocated physical resources, and is required for broadcast over the entire cell coverage area. It is transmitted on the Physical Downlink Shared Channel (PDSCH), and supports UE discontinuous reception.

Uplink Transport Channels

- **Uplink Shared Channel (UL-SCH):** The uplink counterpart of the DL-SCH. It can be associated to CCCH, DCCH, and DTCH logical channels. It supports H-ARQ, dynamic link adaption, and dynamic and semi-persistent resource allocation. The processing of the UL-SCH is described in Section 8.2.

- **Random Access Channel (RACH):** A specific transport channel that is not mapped to any logical channel. It transmits relatively small amounts of data for initial access or, in the case of RRC, state changes. The processing of the RACH is described in Section 8.5, while the random access procedure is described in Section 9.9.

The data on each transport channel is organized into *transport blocks*, and the transmission time of each transport block, also called Transmission Time Interval (TTI), is 1 ms in LTE. TTI is also the minimum interval for link adaptation and scheduling decision. Without spatial multiplexing, at most one transport block is transmitted to a UE in each TTI; with spatial multiplexing, up to two transport blocks can be transmitted in each TTI to a UE.

Besides transport channels, there are different types of control information defined in the MAC layer, which are important for various physical layer procedures. The defined control information includes

- **Downlink Control Information (DCI):** It carries information related to downlink/uplink scheduling assignment, modulation and coding scheme, and Transmit Power Control (TPC) command, and is sent over the Physical Downlink Control Channel (PDCCH). The DCI supports 10 different formats, listed in Table 6.1. Among them, Format 0 is for signaling uplink transmission allocation, Format 3 and 3A are for TPC, and the remaining formats are for signaling downlink transmission allocation. The detail content of each format can be found in [7], some of which is discussed in Section 7.3.

- **Control Format Indicator (CFI):** It indicates how many symbols the DCI spans in that subframe. It takes values CFI = 1, 2, or 3, and is sent over the Physical Control Format Indicator Channel (PCFICH).

- **H-ARQ Indicator (HI):** It carries H-ARQ acknowledgment in response to uplink transmissions, and is sent over the Physical Hybrid ARQ Indicator Channel (PHICH). HI = 1 for a positive acknowledgment (ACK) and HI = 0 for a negative acknowledgment (NAK).

Table 6.1 DCI Formats

Format	Carried Information
Format 0	Uplink scheduling assignment
Format 1	Downlink scheduling for one codeword
Format 1A	Compact downlink scheduling for one codeword and random access procedure
Format 1B	Compact downlink scheduling for one codeword with precoding information
Format 1C	Very compact downlink scheduling for one codeword
Format 1D	Compact downlink scheduling for one codeword with precoding and power offset information
Format 2	Downlink scheduling for UEs configured in closed-loop spatial multiplexing mode
Format 2A	Downlink scheduling for UEs configured in open-loop spatial multiplexing mode
Format 3	TPC commands for PUCCH and PUSCH with 2-bit power adjustments
Format 3A	TPC commands for PUCCH and PUSCH with 1-bit power adjustments

- **Uplink Control Information (UCI):** It is for measurement indication on the downlink transmission, scheduling request of uplink, and the H-ARQ acknowledgment of downlink transmissions. The UCI can be transmitted either on the Physical Uplink Control Channel (PUCCH) or the Physical Uplink Shared Channel (PUSCH). The detail transmission format is discussed in Section 8.3.

6.2.3 Physical Channels: Actual Transmission

Each physical channel corresponds to a set of resource elements in the time-frequency grid that carry information from higher layers. The basic entities that make a physical channel are resource elements and resource blocks. A resource element is a single sub-carrier over one OFDM symbol, and typically this could carry one (or two with spatial multiplexing) modulated symbol(s). A resource block is a collection of resource elements and in the frequency domain this represents the smallest quanta of resources that can be allocated. The details of the time-frequency resource structures for downlink and uplink are described in Section 6.3 and Section 6.4, respectively.

Downlink Physical Channels

- **Physical Downlink Control Channel (PDCCH):** It carries information about the transport format and resource allocation related to the DL-SCH and PCH transport channels, and the H-ARQ information related to the DL-SCH. It also informs the UE about the transport format, resource allocation, and H-ARQ information related to UL-SCH. It is mapped from the DCI transport channel.

- **Physical Downlink Shared Channel (PDSCH):** This channel carries user data and higher-layer signaling. It is associated to DL-SCH and PCH.

- **Physical Broadcast Channel (PBCH):** It corresponds to the BCH transport channel and carries system information.

- **Physical Multicast Channel (PMCH):** It carriers multicast/broadcast information for the MBMS service.

- **Physical Hybrid-ARQ Indicator Channel (PHICH):** This channel carries H-ARQ ACK/NAKs associated with uplink data transmissions. It is mapped from the HI transport channel.

- **Physical Control Format Indicator Channel (PCFICH):** It informs the UE about the number of OFDM symbols used for the PDCCH. It is mapped from the CFI transport channel.

Uplink Physical Channels

- **Physical Uplink Control Channel (PUCCH):** It carries uplink control information including Channel Quality Indicators (CQI), ACK/NAKs for H-ARQ in response to downlink transmission, and uplink scheduling requests.

- **Physical Uplink Shared Channel (PUSCH):** It carries user data and higher-layer signaling. It corresponds to the UL-SCH transport channel.

- **Physical Random Access Channel (PRACH):** This channel carries the random access preamble sent by UEs.

Besides physical channels, there are signals embedded in the downlink and uplink physical layer, which do not carry information from higher layers. The physical signals defined in the LTE specifications are

- **Reference signal:** It is defined in both downlink and uplink for channel estimation that enables coherent demodulation and for channel quality measurement to assist user scheduling. There are three different reference signals in the downlink:

    - Cell-specific reference signals, associated with non-MBSFN transmission
    - MBSFN reference signals, associated with MBSFN transmission
    - UE-specific reference signals

    There are two types of uplink reference signals:

    - Demodulation reference signal, associated with transmission of PUSCH or PUCCH
    - Sounding reference signal, to support uplink channel-dependent scheduling

    The processing of reference signals in the downlink and uplink are treated in Section 7.6.1 and Section 8.4, respectively.

- **Synchronization signal:** It is split into a primary and a secondary synchronization signal, and is only defined in the downlink to enable acquisition of symbol timing and the precise frequency of the downlink signal. It is discussed further in Section 7.6.2.

6.2.4 Channel Mapping

From the description of different channel types, we see that there exists a good correlation based on the purpose and the content between channels in different layers. This requires a mapping between the logical channels and transport channels at the MAC SAP and a mapping between transport channels and physical channels at the PHY SAP. Such channel mapping is not arbitrary, and the allowed mapping between different channel types is shown in Figure 6.6,[4] while the mapping between control information and physical channels is shown in Figure 6.7. It is possible for multiple channels mapped to a single channel, for example, different logical control channels and logical traffic channels are mapped to the DL-SCH transport channel. The channel mapping in Figures 6.6 and 6.7 will reappear in different sections in Chapters 7 and 8 when we discuss downlink and uplink transport channel processing.

---

4 The mapping of multicast-related channels, that is, MCCH, MTCH, MCH, and PMCH, is not specified in Release 8 but in Release 9.

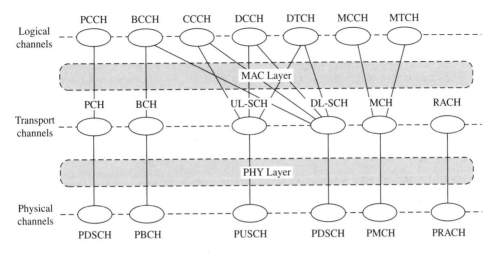

Figure 6.6 Mapping between different channel types.

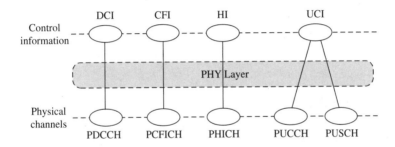

Figure 6.7 Mapping of control information to physical channels.

6.3 Downlink OFDMA Radio Resources

In LTE, the downlink and uplink use different transmission schemes due to different considerations. In this and the next section, we describe downlink and uplink radio transmission schemes, respectively. In the downlink, a scalable OFDM transmission/multiaccess technique is used that allows for high spectrum efficiency by utilizing multiuser diversity in a frequency selective channel. On the other hand, a scalable SC-FDMA transmission/ multiaccess technique is used in the uplink since this reduces the peak-to-average power ratio (PAPR) of the transmitted signal.

The downlink transmission is based on OFDM with a cyclic prefix (CP), which was described in Chapter 3 along with the associated multiple access scheme described in Chapter 4. We summarize some key advantages of OFDM that motivate using it in the LTE downlink:

- As shown in Chapter 3, OFDM is efficient in combating the frequency-selective fading channel with a simple frequency-domain equalizer, which makes it a suitable technique for wireless broadband systems such as LTE.

- As shown in Chapter 4, it is possible to exploit frequency-selective scheduling with OFDM-based multiple access (OFDMA), while HSPA only schedules in the time domain. This can make a big difference especially in slow time-varying channels.

- The transceiver structure of OFDM with FFT/IFFT enables scalable bandwidth operation with a low complexity, which is one of the major objectives of LTE.

- As each subcarrier becomes a flat fading channel, compared to single-carrier transmission OFDM makes it much easier to support multiantenna transmission, which is a key technique to enhance the spectrum efficiency.

- OFDM enables multicast/broadcast services on a synchronized single frequency network, that is, MBSFN, as it treats signals from different base stations as propagating through a multipath channel and can efficiently combine them.

The multiple access in the downlink is based on OFDMA. In each TTI, a scheduling decision is made where each scheduled UE is assigned a certain amount of radio resources in the time and frequency domain. The radio resources allocated to different UEs are orthogonal to each other, which means there is no intra-cell interference. In the remaining part of this section, we describe the frame structure and the radio resource block structure in the downlink, as well as the basic principles of resource allocation and the supported MIMO modes.

6.3.1 Frame Structure

Before going into details about the resource block structure for the downlink, we first describe the frame structure in the time domain, which is a common element shared by both downlink and uplink.

In LTE specifications, the size of elements in the time domain is expressed as a number of time units $T_s = 1/(15000 \times 2048)$ seconds. As the normal subcarrier spacing is defined to be $\Delta f = 15\text{kHz}$, T_s can be regarded as the sampling time of an FFT-based OFDM transmitter/receiver implementation with FFT size $N_{\text{FFT}} = 2048$. Note that this is just for notation purpose, as different FFT sizes are supported depending on the transmission bandwidths. A set of parameters for typical transmission bandwidths for LTE in the downlink is shown in Table 6.2, where the subcarrier spacing is $\Delta f = 15\text{kHz}$. The FFT size increases with the transmission bandwidth, ranging from 128 to 2048. With $\Delta f = 15\text{kHz}$, the sampling frequency, which equals $\Delta f \times N_{\text{FFT}}$, is a multiple or sub-multiple of the UTRA/HSPA chip rate of 3.84MHz. In this way, multimode UTRA/HSPA/LTE terminals can be implemented with a single clock circuitry. In addition to the 15kHz subcarrier spacing, a *reduced subcarrier spacing* of 7.5kHz is defined for MBSFN cells, which provides a larger OFDM symbol duration that is able to combat the large delay spread associated with the MBSFN transmission. Unless otherwise stated, we will assume $\Delta f = 15\text{kHz}$ in the following discussion.

In the time domain, the downlink and uplink multiple TTIs are organized into radio frames with duration $T_f = 307200 \cdot T_s = 10$ ms. For flexibility, LTE supports both FDD

Table 6.2 Typical Parameters for Downlink Transmission

Transmission bandwidth [MHz]	1.4	3	5	10	15	20
Occupied bandwidth [MHz]	1.08	2.7	4.5	9.0	13.5	18.0
Guardband [MHz]	0.32	0.3	0.5	1.0	1.5	2.0
Guardband, % of total	23	10	10	10	10	10
Sampling frequency [MHz]	1.92 $1/2 \times 3.84$	3.84	7.68 2×3.84	15.36 4×3.84	23.04 6×3.84	30.72 8×3.84
FFT size	128	256	512	1024	1536	2048
Number of occupied subcarriers	72	180	300	600	900	1200
Number of resource blocks	6	15	25	50	75	100
Number of CP samples (normal)	9×6 10×1	18×6 20×1	36×6 40×1	72×6 80×1	108×6 120×1	144×6 160×1
Number of CP samples (extended)	32	64	128	256	384	512

and TDD modes.[5] Most of the design parameters are common to FDD and TDD in order to reduce the terminal complexity and maximize reuse between the designs of FDD and TDD systems. Accordingly, LTE supports two kinds of frame structures: frame structure type 1 for the FDD mode and frame structure type 2 for the TDD mode.

Frame Structure Type 1

Frame structure type 1 is applicable to both full duplex and half duplex FDD. There are three different kinds of units specified for this frame structure, illustrated in Figure 6.8. The smallest one is called a *slot*, which is of length $T_{slot} = 15360 \cdot T_s = 0.5$ ms. Two consecutive slots are defined as a *subframe* of length 1 ms, and 20 slots, numbered from 0 to 19, constitute a *radio frame* of 10 ms. Channel-dependent scheduling and link adaptation operate on a subframe level. Therefore, the subframe duration corresponds to the minimum downlink TTI, which is of 1 ms duration, compared to a 2 ms TTI for the HSPA and a minimum 10 ms TTI for the UMTS. A shorter TTI is for fast link adaptation and is able to reduce delay and better exploit the time-varying channel through channel-dependent scheduling.

Each slot consists of a number of OFDM symbols including CPs. As shown in Chapter 3, CP is a kind of guard interval to combat inter-OFDM-symbol interference, which should be larger than the channel delay spread. Therefore, the length of CP depends on the environment where the network operates, and it should not be too large as it brings a bandwidth and power penalty. With a subcarrier spacing $\Delta f = 15$kHz, the OFDM symbol time is $1/\Delta f \approx 66.7 \mu s$. As shown in Figure 6.8, LTE defines two different

---

5 The LTE TDD mode, also referred to as TD-LTE, provides the long-term evolution path for TD-SCDMA-based networks.

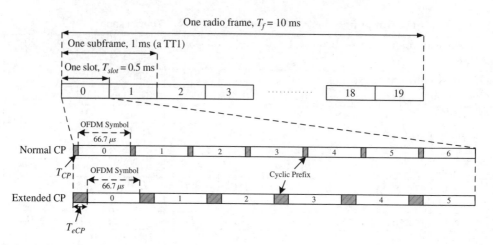

Figure 6.8 Frame structure type 1. For the normal CP, $T_{CP} = 160 \cdot T_s \approx 5.2\mu s$ for the first OFDM symbol, and $T_{CP} = 144 \cdot T_s \approx 4.7\mu s$ for the remaining OFDM symbols, which together fill the entire slot of 0.5 ms. For the extended CP, $T_{eCP} = 512 \cdot T_s \approx 16.7\mu s$.

CP lengths: a *normal CP* and an *extended CP*, corresponding to seven and six OFDM symbols per slot, respectively. The extended CP is for multicell multicast/broadcast and very-large-cell scenarios with large delay spread at a price of bandwidth efficiency, with length $T_{eCP} = 512 \cdot T_s \approx 16.7\mu s$. The normal CP is suitable for urban environment and high data rate applications. Note that the normal CP lengths are different for the first $(T_{CP} = 160 \cdot T_s \approx 5.2\mu s)$ and subsequent OFDM symbols $(T_{CP} = 144 \cdot T_s \approx 4.7\mu s)$, which is to fill the entire slot of 0.5 ms. The numbers of CP samples for different bandwidths are shown in Table 6.2. For example, with 10MHz bandwidth, the sampling time is $1/(15000 \times 1024)$ sec and the number of CP samples for the extended CP is 256, which provides the required CP length of $256/(15000 \times 1024) \approx 1.67\mu s$. In case of 7.5kHz subcarrier spacing, there is only a single CP length, corresponding to 3 OFDM symbols per slot.

For FDD, uplink and downlink transmissions are separated in the frequency domain, each with 10 subframes. In half-duplex FDD operation, the UE cannot transmit and receive at the same time while there are no such restrictions in full-duplex FDD. However, full-duplex FDD terminals need high quality and expensive RF duplex-filters to separate uplink and downlink channels, while half-duplex FDD allows hardware sharing between the uplink and downlink, which offers a cost saving at the expense of reducing data rates by half. Half-duplex FDD UEs are also considered a good solution if the duplex separation between the uplink and downlink transmissions is relatively small. In such cases, the half-duplex FDD is the preferable approach to mitigate the cross-interference between the transmit and receive chains.

Frame Structure Type 2

Frame structure type 2 is applicable to the TDD mode. It is designed for coexistence with legacy systems such as the 3GPP TD-SCDMA-based standard. As shown in Figure 6.9, each radio frame of frame structure type 2 is of length $T_f = 30720 \cdot T_s = 10$ ms, which

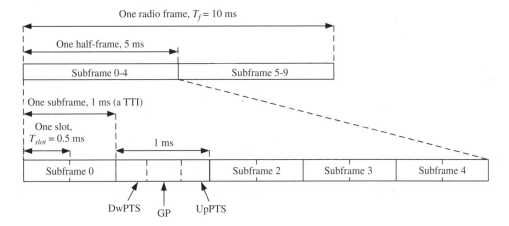

Figure 6.9 Frame structure type 2.

consists of two half-frames of length 5 ms each. Each half-frame is divided into five subframes with 1 ms duration. There are special subframes, which consist of three fields: Downlink Pilot TimeSlot (DwPTS), Guard Period (GP), and Uplink Pilot TimeSlot (UpPTS). These fields are already defined in TD-SCDMA and are maintained in the LTE TDD mode to provide sufficiently large guard periods for the equipment to switch between transmission and reception.

- **The DwPTS field:** This is the downlink part of the special subframe, and can be regarded as an ordinary but shorter downlink subframe for downlink data transmission. Its length can be varied from three up to twelve OFDM symbols.

- **The UpPTS field:** This is the uplink part of the special subframe, and has a short duration with one or two OFDM symbols. It can be used for transmission of uplink sounding reference signals and random access preambles.

- **The GP field:** The remaining symbols in the special subframe that have not been allocated to DwPTS or UpPTS are allocated to the GP field, which is used to provide the guard period for the downlink-to-uplink and the uplink-to-downlink switch.

The total length of these three special fields has a constraint of 1 ms. With the DwPTS and UpPTS durations mentioned above, LTE supports a guard period ranging from two to ten OFDM symbols, sufficient for cell size up to and beyond 100 km. All other subframes are defined as two slots, each with length $T_{slot} = 0.5$ ms.

Figure 6.9 only shows the detail structure of the first half-frame. The second half-frame has the similar structure, which depends on the uplink-downlink configuration. Seven uplink-downlink configurations with either 5 ms or 10 ms downlink-to-uplink switch-point periodicity are supported, as illustrated in Table 6.3, where "D" and "U" denote subframes reserved for downlink and uplink, respectively, and "S" denotes the special

Table 6.3 Uplink-Downlink Configurations for the LTE TDD Mode

Uplink-Downlink Configuration	Downlink-to-Uplink Switch-Point Periodicity	Subframe Number									
		0	1	2	3	4	5	6	7	8	9
0	5 ms	D	S	U	U	U	D	S	U	U	U
1	5 ms	D	S	U	U	D	D	S	U	U	D
2	5 ms	D	S	U	D	D	D	S	U	D	D
3	10 ms	D	S	U	U	U	D	D	D	D	D
4	10 ms	D	S	U	U	D	D	D	D	D	D
5	10 ms	D	S	U	D	D	D	D	D	D	D
6	5 ms	D	S	U	U	U	D	S	U	U	D

subframe. In the case of 5 ms switch-point periodicity, the special subframe exists in both half-frames, and the structure of the second half-frame is the same as the first one depicted in Figure 6.9. In the case of 10 ms switch-point periodicity, the special subframe exists in the first half-frame only. Subframes 0, 5, and the field DwPTS are always reserved for downlink transmission, while UpPTS and the subframe immediately following the special subframe are always reserved for uplink transmission.

6.3.2 Physical Resource Blocks for OFDMA

The physical resource in the downlink in each slot is described by a time-frequency grid, called a *resource grid*, as illustrated in Figure 6.10. Such a time-frequency plane representation is a common practice for OFDM systems, which makes it intuitive for radio resource allocation. Each column and each row of the resource grid correspond to one OFDM symbol and one OFDM subcarrier, respectively. The duration of the resource grid in the time domain corresponds to one slot in a radio frame. The smallest time-frequency unit in a resource grid is denoted as a *resource element*. Each resource grid consists of a number of *resource blocks*, which describe the mapping of certain physical channels to resource elements. The detail of these resource units is described as follows.

Resource Grid

The structure of each resource grid is characterized by the following three parameters:

- **The number of downlink resource blocks (N_{RB}^{DL}):** It depends on the transmission bandwidth and shall fulfill $N_{RB}^{min,DL} \leq N_{RB}^{DL} \leq N_{RB}^{max,DL}$, where $N_{RB}^{min,DL} = 6$ and $N_{RB}^{max,DL} = 110$ are for the smallest and largest downlink channel bandwidth, respectively. The values of N_{RB}^{DL} for several current specified bandwidths are listed in Table 6.2.

- **The number of subcarriers in each resource block (N_{sc}^{RB}):** It depends on the subcarrier spacing Δf, satisfying $N_{sc}^{RB}\Delta f = 180\text{kHz}$, that is, each resource block is

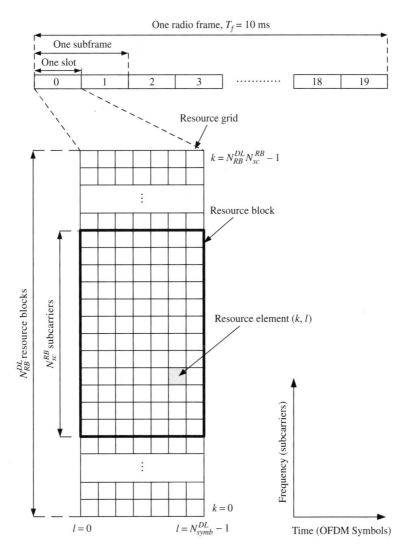

Figure 6.10 The structure of the downlink resource grid.

of 180kHz wide in the frequency domain. The values of N_{sc}^{RB} for different subcarrier spacings are shown in Table 6.4. There are a total of $N_{RB}^{DL} \times N_{sc}^{RB}$ subcarriers in each resource grid. For downlink transmission, the DC subcarrier is not used as it may be subject to a too high level of interference.

- **The number of OFDM symbols in each block (N_{symb}^{DL}):** It depends on both the CP length and the subcarrier spacing, specified in Table 6.4.

Therefore, each downlink resource grid has $N_{RB}^{DL} \times N_{RB}^{sc} \times N_{symb}^{DL}$ resource elements. For example, with 10MHz bandwidth, $\Delta f = 15$kHz, and normal CP, we get $N_{RB}^{DL} = 50$ from

Table 6.4 Physical Resource Block Parameters for the Downlink

Configuration		N_{sc}^{RB}	N_{symb}^{DL}
Normal CP	$\Delta f = 15\text{kHz}$	12	7
Extended CP	$\Delta f = 15\text{kHz}$	12	6
	$\Delta f = 7.5\text{kHz}$	24	3

Table 6.2, $N_{RB}^{sc} = 12$ and $N_{symb}^{DL} = 7$ from Table 6.4, so there are $50 \times 12 \times 7 = 4200$ resource elements in the downlink resource grid.

In case of multiantenna transmission, there is one resource grid defined per antenna port. An antenna port is defined by its associated reference signal, which may not correspond to a physical antenna. The set of antenna ports supported depends on the reference signal configuration in the cell. As discussed in Section 6.2.3, there are three different reference signals defined in the downlink, and the associated antenna ports are as follows:

- Cell-specific reference signals support a configuration of 1, 2, or 4 antenna ports and the antenna port number p shall fulfill $p = 0$, $p \in \{0, 1\}$, and $p \in \{0, 1, 2, 3\}$, respectively.

- MBSFN reference signals are transmitted on antenna port $p = 4$.

- UE-specific reference signals are transmitted on antenna port $p = 5$.

We will talk more about antenna ports when discussing MIMO transmission in the downlink in Section 7.2.2.

Resource Element

Each resource element in the resource grid is uniquely identified by the index pair (k, l) in a slot, where $k = 0, 1, \ldots, N_{RB}^{DL} N_{sc}^{RB} - 1$ and $l = 0, 1, \ldots, N_{symb}^{DL} - 1$ are indices in the frequency and time domains, respectively. The size of each resource element depends on the subcarrier spacing Δf and the CP length.

Resource Block

The resource block is the basic element for radio resource allocation. The minimum size of radio resource that can be allocated is the minimum TTI in the time domain, that is, one subframe of 1 ms, corresponding to two resource blocks. The size of each resource block is the same for all bandwidths, which is 180kHz in the frequency domain. There are two kinds of resource blocks defined for LTE: physical and virtual resource blocks, which are defined for different resource allocation schemes and are specified in the following section.

6.3.3 Resource Allocation

Resource allocation's role is to dynamically assign available time-frequency resource blocks to different UEs in an efficient way to provide good system performance. In LTE, channel-dependent scheduling is supported, and transmission is based on the shared channel structure where the radio resource is shared among different UEs. Therefore, with resource allocation techniques described in Chapter 4, *multiuser diversity* can be exploited by assigning resource blocks to the UEs with favorable channel qualities. Moreover, resource allocation in LTE is able to exploit the channel variations in both the time and frequency domain, which provides higher multiuser diversity gain than HSPA that can only exploit the time-domain variation. Given a wide bandwidth in LTE, this property is beneficial especially for slow-time varying channels, such as in the scenario with low mobility, where taking advantage of channel selectivity in the time domain is difficult.

With OFDMA, the downlink resource allocation is characterized by the fact that each scheduled UE occupies a number of resource blocks while each resource block is assigned exclusively to one UE at any time. Physical resource blocks (PRBs) and virtual resource blocks (VRBs) are defined to support different kinds of resource allocation types. The VRB is introduced to support both block-wise transmission (localized) and transmission on non-consecutive subcarriers (distributed) as a means to maximize frequency diversity. The LTE downlink supports three resource allocation types: type 0, 1, and 2 [8]. The downlink scheduling is performed at the eNode-B based on the channel quality information fed back from UEs, and then the downlink resource assignment information is sent to UEs on the PDCCH channel.

A PRB is defined as N_{symb}^{DL} consecutive OFDM symbols in the time domain and N_{sc}^{RB} consecutive subcarriers in the frequency domain, as demonstrated in Figure 6.10. Therefore, each PRB corresponds to one slot in the time domain (0.5 ms) and 180kHz in the frequency domain. PRBs are numbered from 0 to $N_{RB}^{DL} - 1$ in the frequency domain. The PRB number n_{PRB} of a resource element (k, l) in a slot is given by:

$$n_{PRB} = \left\lfloor \frac{k}{N_{sc}^{RB}} \right\rfloor.$$

The PRB is to support resource allocations of type 0 and type 1, which are defined for the DCI format 1, 2, and 2A.

- In **type 0 resource allocations**, several consecutive PRBs constitute a resource block group (RBG), and the resource allocation is done in units of RBGs. Therefore, a bitmap indicating the RBG is sufficient to carry the resource assignment. The allocated RBGs to a certain UE do not need to be adjacent to each other, which provides frequency diversity. The RBG size P, that is, the number of PRBs in each RBG, depends on the bandwidth and is specified in Table 6.5. An example of type 0

Table 6.5 Resource Allocation RBG Size vs. Downlink System Bandwidth

Downlink Resource Blocks $\left(N_{RB}^{DL} \right)$	RBG Size (P)
≤ 10	1
$11 - 26$	2
$27 - 63$	3
$64 - 110$	4

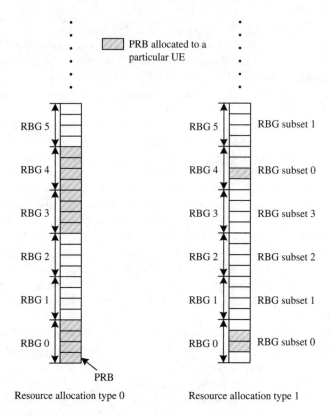

Figure 6.11 Examples of resource allocation type 0 and type 1, where the RBG size $P = 4$.

resource allocation is shown in Figure 6.11, where $P = 4$ and RBGs 0, 3, 4, ...,
are allocated to a particular UE.

- In **type 1 resource allocations**, all the RBGs are grouped into a number of RBG
subsets, and certain PRBs inside a selected RBG subset are allocated to the UE.
There are a total of P RBG subsets, where P is the RBG size. An RBG subset p,
where $0 \leq p < P$, consists of every P-th RBG starting from RBG p. Therefore,
the resource assignment information consists of three fields: the first field indicates
the selected RBG subset, the second field indicates whether an offset is applied,
and the third field contains the bitmap indicating PRBs inside the selected RBG
subset. This type of resource allocation is more flexible and is able to provide higher
frequency diversity, but it also requires a larger overhead. An example of type 1
resource allocation is shown in Figure 6.11, where $P = 4$ and the RBG subset 0 is
selected for the given UE.

In **type 2 resource allocations** that are defined for the DCI format 1A, 1B, 1C,
and 1D, PRBs are not directly allocated. Instead, VRBs are allocated, which are then
mapped onto PRBs. A VRB is of the same size as a PRB. There are two types of VRBs:
VRBs of the localized type and VRBs of the distributed type.

For each type of VRB, a pair of VRBs over two slots in a subframe are assigned together with a single VRB number, n_{VRB}. VRBs of the localized type are mapped directly to physical resource blocks such that the VRB number n_{VRB} corresponds to the PRB number $n_{PRB} = n_{VRB}$. For VRBs of the distributed type, the VRB numbers are mapped to PRB numbers according to the rule specified in [6].

For resource allocations of type 2, the resource assignment information indicates a set of contiguously allocated localized VRBs or distributed VRBs. A one-bit flag indicates whether localized VRBs or distributed VRBs are assigned.

Details about the downlink resource allocation can be found in [8]. The feedback for channel quality information and the related signaling is discussed in Chapter 9.

6.3.4 Supported MIMO Modes

Multiantenna transmission and reception (MIMO), as described in Chapter 5, is a physical layer technique that can improve both the reliability and throughput of the communications over wireless channels. It is considered a key component of the LTE physical layer from the start. The baseline antenna configuration in LTE is two transmit antennas at the cell site and two receive antennas at the UE. The higher-order downlink MIMO is also supported with up to four transmit and four receive antennas.

The downlink transmission supports both single-user MIMO (SU-MIMO) and multiuser MIMO (MU-MIMO). For SU-MIMO, one or multiple data streams are transmitted to a single UE through space-time processing; for MU-MIMO, modulation data streams are transmitted to different UEs using the same time-frequency resource. The supported SU-MIMO modes are listed as follows:

- Transmit diversity with space frequency block codes (SFBC)

- Open-loop spatial multiplexing supporting four data streams

- Closed-loop spatial multiplexing, with closed-loop precoding as a special case when channel rank = 1

- Conventional direction of arrival (DOA)-based beamforming

The supported MIMO mode is restricted by the UE capability. The PDSCH physical channel supports all the MIMO modes, while other physical channels support transmit diversity except PMCH, which only supports single-antenna–port transmission. The details about MIMO transmission on each downlink physical channel are provided in Chapter 7, while the feedback to assist MIMO transmission is discussed in Chapter 9.

6.4 Uplink SC-FDMA Radio Resources

For the LTE uplink transmission, SC-FDMA with a CP is adopted. As discussed in Chapter 4, SC-FDMA possesses most of the merits of OFDM while enjoying a lower PAPR. A lower PAPR is highly desirable in the uplink as less expensive power amplifiers are needed at UEs and the coverage is improved. In LTE, the SC-FDMA signal is generated by the DFT-spread-OFDM. Compared to conventional OFDM, the SC-FDMA receiver has higher complexity, which, however, is not considered to be an issue in the uplink given the powerful computational capability at the base station.

An SC-FDMA transceiver has a similar structure as OFDM, so the parametrization of radio resource in the uplink enjoys similarities to that in the downlink described in Section 6.3. Nevertheless, the uplink transmission has its own properties. Different from the downlink, only localized resource allocation on consecutive subcarriers is allowed in the uplink. In addition, only limited MIMO modes are supported in the uplink. In this section, we focus on the differences in the uplink radio resource from that in the downlink.

6.4.1   Frame Structure

The uplink frame structure is similar to that for the downlink. The difference is that now we talk about *SC-FDMA symbols* and *SC-FDMA subcarriers*. In frame structure type 1, an uplink radio frame consists of 20 slots of 0.5 ms each, and one subframe consists of two slots, as in Figure 6.8. Frame structure type 2 consists of ten subframes, with one or two special subframes including DwPTS, GP, and UpPTS fields, as shown in Figure 6.9. A CP is inserted prior to each SC-FDMA symbol. Each slot carries seven SC-FDMA symbols in the case of normal CP, and six SC-FDMA symbols in the case of extended CP.

6.4.2   Physical Resource Blocks for SC-FDMA

As SC-FDMA can be regarded as conventional OFDM with a DFT-based precoder, the *resource grid* for the uplink is similar to the one for the downlink, illustrated in Figure 6.12, that is, it comprises a number of resource blocks in the time-frequency plane. The number of resource blocks in each resource grid, N_{RB}^{UL}, depends on the uplink transmission bandwidth configured in the cell and should satisfy

$$N_{RB}^{min,UL} \leq N_{RB}^{UL} \leq N_{RB}^{max,UL},$$

where $N_{RB}^{min,UL} = 6$ and $N_{RB}^{max,UL} = 110$ correspond to the smallest and largest uplink bandwidth, respectively. There are $N_{sc}^{RB} \times N_{symb}^{RB}$ resource elements in each resource block. The values of N_{sc}^{RB} and N_{symb}^{UL} for normal and extended CP are given in Table 6.6. There is only one subcarrier spacing supported in the uplink, which is $\Delta f = 15\text{kHz}$. Different from the downlink, the DC subcarrier is used in the uplink, as the DC interference is spread over the modulation symbols due to the DFT-based precoding.

As for the downlink, each *resource element* in the resource grid is uniquely defined by the index pair (k, l) in a slot, where $k = 0, \ldots, N_{RB}^{UL} N_{sc}^{RB} - 1$ and $l = 0, \ldots, N_{symb}^{UL} - 1$ are the indices in the frequency and time domain, respectively. For the uplink, no antenna port is defined, as only single antenna transmission is supported in the current specifications.

A PRB in the uplink is defined as N_{symb}^{UL} consecutive SC-FDMA symbols in the time domain and N_{sc}^{RB} consecutive subcarriers in the frequency domain, corresponding to one slot in the time domain and 180kHz in the frequency domain. The relation between the

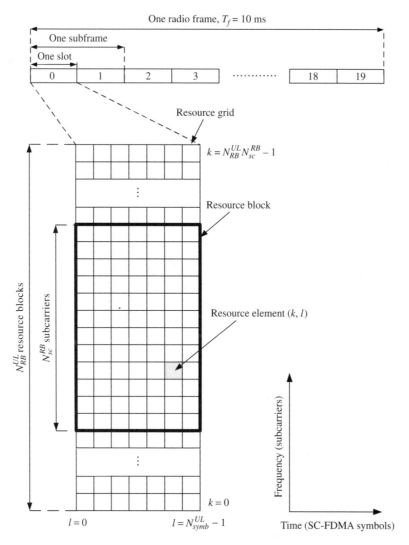

Figure 6.12 The structure of the uplink resource grid.

Table 6.6 Physical Resource Block Parameters for Uplink

Configuration	N_{sc}^{RB}	N_{symb}^{UL}
Normal CP	12	7
Extended CP	12	6

PRB number n_{PRB} in the frequency domain and resource elements (k, l) in a slot is given by:

$$n_{PRB} = \left\lfloor \frac{k}{N_{sc}^{RB}} \right\rfloor.$$

6.4.3 Resource Allocation

Similar to the downlink, shared-channel transmission and channel-dependent scheduling are supported in the uplink. Resource allocation in the uplink is also performed at the eNode-B. Based on the channel quality measured on the uplink sounding reference signals and the scheduling requests sent from UEs, the eNode-B assigns a unique time-frequency resource to a scheduled UE, which achieves orthogonal intra-cell transmission. Such intra-cell orthogonality in the uplink is preserved between UEs by using timing advance such that the transport blocks of different UEs are received synchronously at the eNode-B. This provides significant coverage and capacity gain in the uplink over UMTS, which employs non-orthogonal transmission in the uplink and the performance is limited by inter-channel interference. In general, SC-FDMA is able to support both localized and distributed resource allocation. In the current specification, only localized resource allocation is supported in the uplink, which preserves the single-carrier property and can better exploit the multiuser diversity gain in the frequency domain. Compared to distributed resource allocation, localized resource allocation is less sensitive to frequency offset and also requires fewer reference symbols.

The resource assignment information for the uplink transmission is carried on the PDCCH with DCI format 0, indicating a set of contiguously allocated resource blocks. However, not all integer multiples of one resource block are allowed to be assigned to a UE, which is to simplify the DFT design for the SC-FDMA transceiver. Only factors 2, 3, and 5 are allowed. The frequency hopping is supported to provide frequency diversity, with which the UEs can hop between frequencies within or between the allocated subframes. The resource mapping for different uplink channels is discussed in Chapter 8, and the uplink channel sounding and scheduling signaling is described in Chapter 9.

6.4.4 Supported MIMO Modes

For the MIMO modes supported in the uplink, the terminal complexity and cost are among the major concerns. MU-MIMO is supported, which allocates the same time and frequency resource to two UEs with each transmitting on a single antenna. This is also called Spatial Division Multiple Access (SDMA). The advantage is that only one transmit antenna per UE is required. To separate streams for different UEs, channel state information is required at the eNode-B, which is obtained through uplink reference signals that are orthogonal between UEs. Uplink MU-MIMO also requires power control, as the near-far problem arises when multiple UEs are multiplexed on the same radio resource.

For UEs with two or more transmit antennas, closed-loop adaptive antenna selection transmit diversity shall be supported. For this scenario, each UE only needs one transmit chain and amplifier. The antenna that provides the best channel to the eNode-B is selected based on the feedback from the eNode-B. The details of MIMO transmission in the uplink are described in Chapter 8.

6.5 Summary and Conclusions

This chapter provided an overview of the LTE radio interface, emphasizing the hierarchical channel structure and the radio resource in both downlink and uplink. The material covered should be adequate for the reader to get the unique characteristics of the LTE physical layer and understand the detailed physical layer procedures in the following chapters.

- LTE is the next step in the evolution of mobile cellular systems, and is a packet-switched network from end to end that is designed with a clean slate approach.

- LTE adopts the hierarchical channel structure from UTRA/HSPA. It simplifies the channel structure and is based totally on the shared channel transmission, which improves the efficiency of the air interface.

- LTE applies OFDMA in the downlink and SC-FDMA in the uplink, both of which have similar radio resource structures in the time-frequency plane. The capability of scheduling in both time and frequency domain provides a higher spectral efficiency in LTE than what is achieved in HSPA. Both localized and distributed resource allocations are supported in the downlink, while only localized resource allocation is supported in the uplink.

- MIMO transmission is a key component of LTE. In current specifications, downlink transmission supports a variety of MIMO modes, while uplink transmission has a limited MIMO support considering cost and complexity.

Bibliography

[1] 3GPP TS 23.401, "General Packet Radio Service (GPRS) enhancements for Evolved Universal Terrestrial Radio Access Network (E-UTRAN) access."

[2] 3GPP TR 25.814, "Physical layer aspects for evolved Universal Terrestrial Radio Access (UTRA)."

[3] 3GPP TR 25.912, "Feasibility study for evolved Universal Terrestrial Radio Access (UTRA) and Universal Terrestrial Radio Access Network (UTRAN)."

[4] 3GPP TR 25.913, "Requirements for Evolved UTRA (E-UTRA) and Evolved UTRAN (E-UTRAN)."

[5] 3GPP TS 36.201, "Evolved Universal Terrestrial Radio Access (E-UTRA); LTE Physical Layer—General Description."

[6] 3GPP TS 36.211, "Evolved Universal Terrestrial Radio Access (E-UTRA); Physical channels and modulation."

[7] 3GPP TS 36.212, "Evolved Universal Terrestrial Radio Access (E-UTRA); Multiplexing and channel coding."

[8] 3GPP TS 36.213, "Evolved Universal Terrestrial Radio Access (E-UTRA); Physical Layer Procedures."

[9] 3GPP TS 36.321, "Evolved Universal Terrestrial Radio Access (E-UTRA); Medium Access Control (MAC) protocol specification."

Chapter 7

Downlink Transport Channel Processing

In Chapters 7 to 9, we focus on the PHY layer of the LTE radio interface. As introduced in Chapter 6, the PHY layer provides services to the MAC layer through transport channels. In this and the next chapter, we provide a detailed description of physical layer processing on downlink and uplink transport channels, respectively. Data and control streams coming from the MAC layer are organized in the form of *transport blocks*. Each transport block is a group of resource blocks with a common modulation and coding scheme. The physical layer processing mainly consists of coding and modulation, which maps each transport block to specific physical time-frequency resources. A solid understanding of the transport channel processing is needed to continue on to the subsequent chapters on physical layer procedures and higher layer protocols.

This chapter starts with an overview of downlink transport channel processing, which contains common processes for different channel types. Then the detailed processing for different channels and control information is described. For data transmission on downlink shared channels, special attention is paid to MIMO transmission; for downlink multicast channels, Single-Frequency Network (SFN) operation is introduced; for downlink reference signals and synchronization signals that are important for physical layer procedures, detailed resource mapping is provided. The Hybrid-ARQ (H-ARQ) protocol in the downlink is also discussed.

7.1 Downlink Transport Channel Processing Overview

The downlink physical layer processing mainly consists of channel coding and modulation, as shown in Figure 7.1. Channel coding involves mapping the incoming transport blocks from the MAC layer into different codewords; modulation generates complex-valued OFDM baseband signals for each antenna port, which are then upconverted to the carrier frequency. In the remainder of this section, we describe the function of each processing block in Figure 7.1.

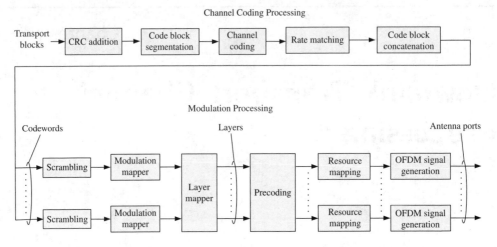

Figure 7.1 Overview of downlink transport channel processing.

7.1.1   Channel Coding Processing

This section describes generic channel coding procedures that are used for various data and control transport channels. These common aspects of channel coding are applicable to both downlink and uplink transmissions. Channel coding for the downlink is a combination of error detection, error correction, rate matching, interleaving, and transport channel/control information mapping onto physical channels. An example of the downlink channel coding processing is shown in Figure 7.2. Channel coding provides an error-control mechanism for data transmission using forward error correction (FEC) code and error detection based on cyclic redundancy check (CRC). For some transport

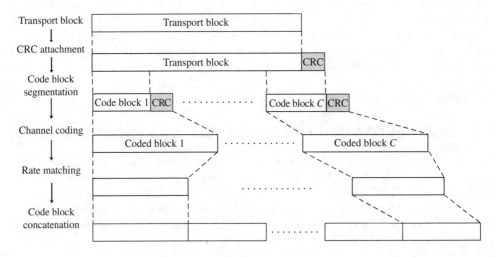

Figure 7.2 Channel coding processing.

channels such as the shared channel, the error-control mechanism is coupled with the re-transmission mechanism using what is called the Hybrid-ARQ (H-ARQ) protocol. This combined error-control and retransmission mechanism improves the link reliability significantly in fading channels, as opposed to performing these two steps separately. In LTE, the coding rate at the channel encoder is fixed, and different effective coding rates for the whole transport block are achieved by repetition/puncturing during the rate matching procedure.

CRC Addition

The CRC is used to provide error detection on the transport block [15]. It generates parity bits by cyclic generator polynomials that are specified in [4], which are then added at the end of the transport block. The number of parity bits can take the value of 8, 16, or 24. The 24-bit CRC is the baseline for the downlink shared channel.

Code Block Segmentation

Code block segmentation is performed when the number of bits in the sequence after CRC attachment, B, is larger than the maximum code block size for the turbo encoder, which is $Z = 6144$. It breaks the long sequence into C code blocks and adds an additional 24-bit CRC sequence to each block, where C is given by:

$$C = \begin{cases} 1 & \text{if} \quad B \leq Z \\ \lceil B/(Z-L) \rceil & \text{if} \quad B > Z, \end{cases} \tag{7.1}$$

and L is the number of CRC parity bits. Each of these C code blocks is then encoded independently. This is to prevent excessive complexity and memory requirement for decoding at the receiver. The number of bits in each code block after segmentation depends on B and is selected from the set of allowable code block sizes for the turbo encoder, specified in [4]. Filler bits are added to the beginning of the first block if needed. If $B < 40$, which is the minimum code block size for the turbo encoder, filler bits are added to the beginning of the incoming code block.

Channel Coding

In LTE, the channel encoders applied to transport channels include tail-biting convolutional coding and convolutional turbo coding. The usage of channel coding schemes and coding rates for different downlink transport channels is specified in Table 7.1. For control information, other channel coding schemes are supported, including block coding and repetition coding, specified in Table 7.2.

Table 7.1 Channel Coding Schemes and Coding Rates for Downlink Transport Channels

Transport Channel	Coding Scheme	Coding Rate
DL-SCH, PCH, MCH	Turbo coding	1/3
BCH	Tail-biting convolutional coding	1/3

Table 7.2 Channel Coding Schemes and Coding Rates for Downlink Control Information

Control Information	Coding Scheme	Coding Rate
DCI	Tail-biting convolutional coding	1/3
CFI	Block coding	1/16
HI	Repetition coding	1/3

Tail-Biting Convolutional Coding   The convolutional encoder used in LTE is a rate 1/3 encoder with a constraint length of 7 as shown in Figure 7.3. Since the transmitted code blocks are of finite length, trellis termination must be performed at the end of each code block in order to restore the state of the encoder to the initial state for the next code block. Also if the initial and the final states of the encoder are known, then a lower block error rate can be achieved at the decoder while using a Viterbi algorithm. Two of the most common approaches for trellis termination are padding and tail biting. In the case of padding, the end of the code block is padded with zeros. This forces the encoder to state '0' at the end of the code block, which is the starting state for the next code block. One of the main drawbacks of this method is that additional bandwidth is wasted due to the extra zeros that are added to the end of each code block. In this case, we would need to add six zeros in order to terminate the trellis. A more efficient method for trellis termination is tail biting, where the information bits from the end of each code block are appended to the beginning of the code block. Once these appended bits are passed through the encoder, it ensures that the start and end states of the encoder are the same. For example, if the input bit sequence is $c_0, c_1, \ldots, c_{K-1}$, the initial value of the shift register shall be set to $[s_0, s_1, s_2, s_3, s_4, s_5] = [c_{K-1}, c_{K-2}, c_{K-3}, c_{K-4}, c_{K-5}, c_{K-6}]$, and then the initial and final states of the shift register are the same. The parity bits generated from the appended bits in the beginning of the code block are discarded and not used for transmission. With tail biting, all the input bits are afforded the same amount of error protection, and there is no code-rate loss compared to zero padding, but the decoding algorithm becomes more complicated [10].

Convolution Turbo Coding   The turbo encoder in LTE is similar to the one used for HSPA [1]. It is a Parallel Concatenated Convolutional Code (PCCC) with two eight-state constituent encoders and one turbo code internal interleaver, with a coding rate of 1/3.

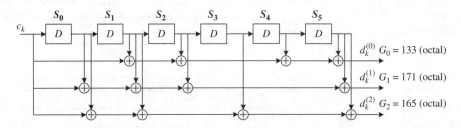

Figure 7.3   Rate 1/3 tail-biting convolutional encoder.

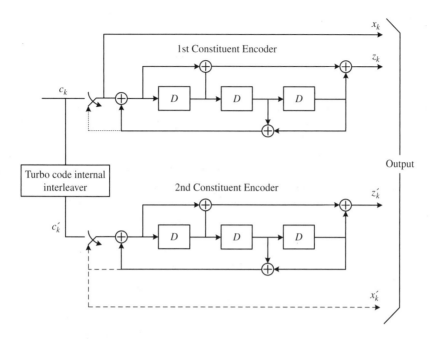

Figure 7.4 Structure of rate 1/3 turbo encoder (dotted lines apply for trellis termination only).

Unlike the convolutional codes, the encoder used for the turbo codes is systematic and therefore recursive in nature. Different from HSPA, LTE employs a new contention-free internal interleaver based on Quadrature Permutation Polynomial (QPP) [13]. The QPP interleaver requires a small parameter storage and allows highly flexible parallelization due to its maximum contention-free property [14], which substantially reduces the encoder-decoder complexity. The structure of the encoder is illustrated in Figure 7.4.

The transfer function of the eight-state constituent code for the PCCC is

$$G(D) = \left[1, \frac{g_1(D)}{g_0(D)} \right], \tag{7.2}$$

where

$$g_0(D) = 1 + D^2 + D^3,$$

$$g_1(D) = 1 + D + D^3.$$

The initial values of the shift registers shall be all zeros when starting to encode the input bits.

The input bits to the turbo code QPP-based internal interleaver, $c_0, c_1, \cdots, c_{K-1}$, are mapped to the output bits $c'_0, c'_1, \cdots, c'_{K-1}$, according to the following relationship:

$$c'_i = c_{\Pi(i)}, \quad i = 0, 1, \ldots, K-1, \tag{7.3}$$

where $\Pi(i)$ is a quadratic permutation polynomial given as $\Pi(i) = (f_1 \cdot i + f_2 \cdot i^2) \bmod K$. The parameter K is the number of input bits, which takes a specific value between 40 and 6,144 from a predefined set [4]. The values of parameters f_1 and f_2 depend on K, which is specified in [4].

Similar to the convolutional code, the turbo encoder needs to be terminated at the end of each code block. Unlike tail biting that is used for the convolution encoder, the trellis termination in this case is meant to re-initialize the state of the encoder to '0' state. Due to the recursive nature of the encoder, the termination is performed by taking the recursive bit and performing a modulo 2 addition with itself as shown in Figure 7.4.

For each K-bit input code block, the output of the turbo encoder consists of three K-bit data streams: one systematic bit stream and two parity bit streams. In addition, 12 tail bits due to trellis termination are added to the end of the output streams, so each bit stream has $K + 4$ bits. Therefore, the actual coding rate is slightly lower than $1/3$.

Rate Matching

The rate matching in LTE performs interleaving, as well as repetition or puncturing, in order to generate a transport block that fits the payload size determined by the modulation scheme and the number of resource blocks allocated for the transport block. Rate matching is defined per coded block and consists of the following stages: a) interleaving, b) bit collection, and c) bit selection, as illustrated in Figure 7.5. Interleaving is performed in order to spread out the occurrence of bursty errors across the code block, which improves the overall performance of the decoder. Since the interleaving is performed separately for the systematic and parity bits, a bit collection stage is required to place the systematic and parity bits in the right order as needed by the decoder. Finally, the bit selection stage is needed in order to repeat or puncture some of the parity bits to create the required payload.

Sub-block Interleaving   The interleaving is performed independently for each bit stream, done by a block interleaver with inter-column permutations. The inter-column permutation patterns are different for turbo coding and convolutional coding, specified in [4].

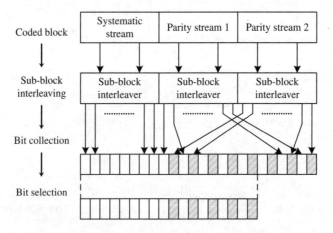

Figure 7.5 Rate matching for coded transport channels.

Bit Collection A virtual circular buffer is formed by collecting bits from the interleaved streams. The systematic bits are placed at the beginning, followed by bit-by-bit interlacing of the two interleaved parity streams, as shown in Figure 7.5. The interlacing guarantees that an equal number of parity 1 and parity 2 bits are transmitted.

Bit Selection To select the output bit sequence, the sequence length L should first be determined, which depends on the number of allocated resource blocks, the modulation scheme, and the MIMO mode. Then L bits are read from the virtual circular buffer. The starting point of the bit selection depends on the redundancy version of the current transmission, which is different for different retransmissions associated with the H-ARQ process. This means that from one H-ARQ transmission to the next even though the number of bits L is the same, the parity bits that are punctured or repeated can be different. This is indicated by the redundancy version of the H-ARQ transmission. During bit selection if the end of the buffer is reached, the reading continues by wrapping around to the beginning of the buffer. In this way, puncturing or repetition is achieved using a unified method. In the example in Figure 7.5, puncturing is achieved. With K input bits to the channel encoder, the effective coding rate is K/L, which can achieve any continuum of coding rates.

Code Block Concatenation

The code block concatenation consists of sequentially concatenating the rate matching outputs for different code blocks, forming the codeword input to the modulation processing. It is needed only for turbo coding when the number of code blocks is larger than one.

7.1.2 Modulation Processing

In this subsection, we describe the generic modulation procedures applicable to more than one physical channel type. Modulation takes in one or two codewords, depending on whether spatial multiplexing is used, and converts them to complex-valued OFDM baseband signals for each antenna port. As shown in Figure 7.1, the modulation processing consists of scrambling, modulation mapping, MIMO-related multiantenna processing, resource mapping, and OFDM signal generation.

Scrambling

Before modulation, the codeword generated through channel coding processing is first scrambled by a bit-level scrambling sequence. The block of bits for codeword q is denoted as $b^{(q)}(0), \ldots, b^{(q)}(M_b^{(q)} - 1)$, where $M_b^{(q)}$ is the number of bits transmitted in one subframe. The scrambling sequence $c^{(q)}$ is a pseudo-random sequence defined by a length-31 Gold sequence [3]. The scrambled bits are generated using a modulo 2 addition as:

$$\tilde{b}^{(q)}(i) = \left(b^{(q)}(i) + c^{(q)}(i) \right) \bmod 2, \quad i = 0, 1, \ldots, M_b^{(q)} - 1.$$

Up to two codewords can be transmitted in the same subframe, so $q = 0$ if spatial multiplexing is not used or $q \in \{0, 1\}$ if spatial multiplexing is used.

Except the multicast channel, for all other downlink transport channels and control information, the scrambling sequences are different for neighboring cells so that inter-cell interference is randomized, which is one of the approaches for interference mitigation. The same approach has already been taken in other systems such as UMTS. Details about inter-cell interference mitigation are discussed in Chapter 10. For the multicast channel, common scrambling is applied for all cells involved in a specific MBSFN transmission.

Modulation Mapping

For each codeword q, the block of scrambled bits $\tilde{b}^{(q)}(0), \ldots, \tilde{b}^{(q)}(M_b^{(q)}-1)$ are modulated into a block of complex-valued modulation symbols $d^{(q)}(0), \ldots, d^{(q)}(M_s^{(q)}-1)$, where $M_s^{(q)}$ is the number of the modulation symbols in each codeword and depends on the modulation scheme. The relation between $M_s^{(q)}$ and $M_b^{(q)}$ is as follows:

$$M_s^{(q)} = \frac{M_b^{(q)}}{Q_m},$$

where Q_m is the number of bits in the modulation constellation, with $Q_m = 2$ for QPSK, $Q_m = 4$ for 16QAM, and $Q_m = 6$ for 64QAM.

The supported data-modulation schemes in LTE include QPSK, 16QAM, and 64QAM, and BPSK is applied for the PHICH physical channel. Different physical channels employ different modulation schemes, listed in Table 7.3.

Layer Mapping and Precoding

Both layer mapping and precoding are associated with multiantenna transmission and reception (MIMO), the basis of which can be found in Chapter 5. The split between the two steps allows the inclusion of all the antenna processing schemes in a single framework. These two steps map the incoming codewords to up to four transmit antennas. As illustrated in Figure 7.6, the layer mapper maps N_c codewords to v spatial layers, while the precoder maps these v layers to P antenna ports. Some of the terminologies used in MIMO transmission are explained as follows.

Table 7.3 Modulation Schemes for Different Physical Channels

Physical Channel	Modulation Schemes
PDSCH	QPSK, 16QAM, 64QAM
PMCH	QPSK, 16QAM, 64QAM
PBCH	QPSK
PCFICH	QPSK
PDCCH	QPSK
PHICH	BPSK

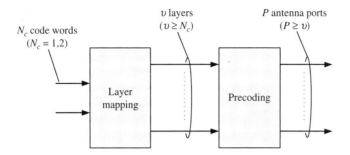

Figure 7.6 Layer mapping and precoding.

- **Codeword:** A codeword is defined as the output of each channel coding/rate matching stage associated with a single transport block coming from the MAC layer. For MIMO transmission with multiple codewords on different spatial channels, more efficient detectors with successive interference cancellation[1] can be used. In LTE, although up to four transmit/receive antennas are supported, the number of codewords is limited to two. This is to limit the uplink feedback overhead, as a separate H-ARQ process is operated for each codeword, which requires separate signaling in the uplink control channel.

- **Layer:** A layer corresponds to a data stream of the spatial multiplexing channel. Each codeword is mapped into one or multiple layers. Therefore, the number of layers, which is essentially the transmission rank, is at least as many as the number of codewords, that is, $v \geq N_c$.

- **Antenna port:** An antenna port is defined by its associated reference signal, which is a logical entity and may not correspond to an actual physical antenna. The number of transmit antenna ports at the eNode-B is sent to UEs through the PBCH channel, which can be 1, 2, or 4 in LTE. Antenna ports are divided into three groups:

  - Antenna ports 0-3 are cell specific, which are used for downlink MIMO transmission.
  - Antenna port 4 is MBSFN specific and is used for MBSFN transmission.
  - Antenna port 5 is UE specific, which is used for beamforming to a single UE using all physical antennas.

  Cell-specific ports and the UE-specific port cannot be simultaneously used. Different reference signals are defined for different types of antenna ports, as discussed in Section 7.6.1.

For a v-layer transmission, modulation symbols $d^{(q)}(0), \cdots, d^{(q)}(M_s^{(q)} - 1)$ for codeword q shall be mapped onto the layers $\mathbf{x}(i) = [x_0(i) \cdots x_{v-1}(i)]^T$, $i = 0, 1, \ldots,$

---

1 The BLAST system with successive interference cancellation was discussed in Section 5.5.2.

Table 7.4 Codeword-to-Layer Mapping for Spatial Multiplexing

Number of Layers	Codeword 0	Codeword 1
1	Layer 0	
2	Layer 0	Layer 1
2	Layer 0, 1	
3	Layer 0	Layer 1,2
4	Layer 0,1	Layer 2,3

$M_s^{\text{layer}} - 1$, where M_s^{layer} is the number of modulation symbols per layer. Layer mapping is different for different MIMO modes, described as follows.

- **Single antenna port:** One codeword is mapped to a single layer, which is straightforward.

- **Transmit diversity:** One codeword is mapped to two or four layers. It is an open-loop MIMO mode.

- **Spatial multiplexing:** N_c codewords are mapped to v layers, where $N_c = 1, 2$, $v = 1, 2, 3, 4$ and $v \geq N_c$. The detailed mapping is in Table 7.4. Note that the case of a single codeword mapped to two layers occurs only when the initial transmission contains two codewords and a codeword mapped onto two layers needs to be retransmitted. Both open-loop (OL) and closed-loop (CL) spatial multiplexing modes are supported in LTE, with rank-1 CL precoding as a special case.

The precoder takes a block of vectors $\mathbf{x}(i)$ as input, and generates a block of vectors $\mathbf{y}(i) = [y_0(i), \ldots, y_{P-1}(i)]^T$, $i = 0, 1, \ldots, M_s^{\text{ap}} - 1$ to be mapped onto resources on each of the antenna ports, where $y_p(i)$ is the signal for antenna port p and M_s^{ap} is the number of symbols on each antenna port. The precoder is either fixed or selected from a predefined codebook based on the feedback from UEs. The general form for precoding is

$$\mathbf{y}(i) = \mathbf{W}(i)\mathbf{x}(i),$$

where $\mathbf{W}(i)$ is the precoding matrix of size $P \times v$.

Different physical channels support different MIMO modes, specified in Table 7.5. The PDSCH channel supports all the specified MIMO modes, while the PMCH channel only supports single-antenna-port transmission (antenna port 4).

Shown in Figure 7.7 is the observed block error rate for some of the different modulation and coding rates in an additive white Gaussian noise (AWGN) channel.

Resource Mapping

For each of the antenna ports used for transmission of physical channels, the block of complex-valued symbols $y_p(0), \ldots, y_p(M_s^{\text{ap}} - 1)$ shall be mapped in sequence, starting

Table 7.5 Supported MIMO Modes for Different Physical Channels

Physical Channel	Single Antenna Port	OL Transmit Diversity	Spatial Multiplexing
PDSCH	✓	✓	✓
PDCCH	✓	✓	
PBCH	✓	✓	
PMCH	✓		
PHICH	✓	✓	
PCFICH	✓	✓	

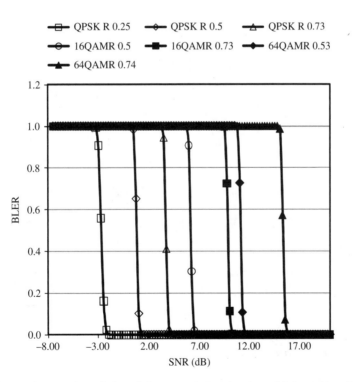

Figure 7.7 Simulation results of downlink transmission in the additive white Gaussian noise (AWGN) channel with different modulation and coding rates.

Table 7.6 Values of $N_{CP,l}$

Configuration		CP Length $N_{CP,l}$
Normal CP	$\Delta f = 15\text{kHz}$	160 for $l = 0$
		144 for $l = 1, 2, \ldots, 6$
Extended CP	$\Delta f = 15\text{kHz}$	512 for $l = 0, 1, \ldots, 5$
	$\Delta f = 7.5\text{kHz}$	1024 for $l = 0, 1, 2$

with $y_p(0)$, to resource blocks assigned for transmission. The mapping to resource element (k, l) on antenna port p not reserved for other purposes shall be in increasing order of first the index k and then the index l, starting with the first slot in a subframe.

OFDM Baseband Signal Generation

The continuous-time signal $s_l^{(p)}(t)$ on antenna port p in OFDM symbol l in a downlink slot is generated as:

$$s_l^{(p)}(t) = \sum_{k=-\lfloor N_{RB}^{DL} N_{sc}^{RB}/2 \rfloor}^{-1} a_{k^{(-)},l}^{(p)} \cdot e^{j2\pi k \Delta f(t - N_{CP,l}T_s)} + \sum_{k=1}^{\lceil N_{RB}^{DL} N_{sc}^{RB}/2 \rceil} a_{k^{(+)},l}^{(p)} \cdot e^{j2\pi k \Delta f(t - N_{CP,l}T_s)}$$

$$(7.4)$$

for $0 \leq t \leq (N_{CP,l} + N) \times T_s$, where $k^{(-)} = k + \lfloor N_{RB}^{DL} N_{sc}^{DL}/2 \rfloor$ and $k^{(+)} = k + \lfloor N_{RB}^{DL} N_{sc}^{DL}/2 \rfloor - 1$, and for 20MHz bandwidth the value of N is given by:

$$N = \begin{cases} 2048, & \text{if } \Delta f = 15\text{kHz} \\ 4096, & \text{if } \Delta f = 7.5\text{kHz}. \end{cases} \quad (7.5)$$

The cyclic prefix (CP) length $N_{CP,l}$ depends on the CP type and the subcarrier spacing, listed in Table 7.6.

In practice, the OFDM signal is generated using IFFT digital signal processing. At the receiver, FFT processing can be used to convert the time-domain signal back to the frequency domain. The implementation of the OFDM transceiver using IFFT and FFT is a major advantage of OFDM transmission due to its computational efficiency, as shown in Chapter 3. The OFDM signal generation with multiple users is illustrated in Figure 7.8.

7.2   Downlink Shared Channels

In this section, we describe the physical layer processing for specific transport channels including the downlink shared channel, the downlink control channel, the broadcast channel, and the multicast channel. Although most of the transport channels implement the various aspects of transport channel processing such as channel coding, rate matching,

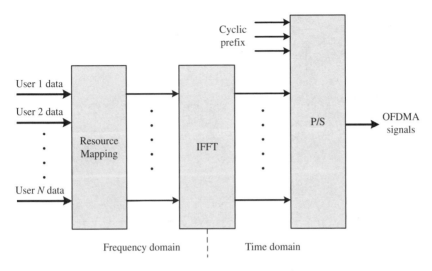

Figure 7.8 OFDMA signal generation with *N* users, where P/S denotes the parallel-to-serial converter.

symbol mapping, MIMO processing, and OFDM modulation, the specifics of each step vary from one transport channel to the other.

The DL-SCH is carried on the Physical Downlink Shared Channel (PDSCH). Data transmission in the PDSCH is based on the concept of shared-channel transmission, where the PHY layer resources, that is, resource blocks available for PDSCH, is treated as a common resource that can be dynamically shared among different UEs. The dynamic multiplexing of UEs on the PDSCH is done by the scheduler on a 1-msec interval. This way, a large portion of the radio resource can be allocated to a specific UE, which is suitable for packet-data applications. In addition, with shared-channel transmission and opportunistic scheduling, multiuser diversity can be obtained, as discussed in Chapter 4. The channel mapping around the DL-SCH is shown in Figure 7.9. We see that DL-SCHs carry both traffic and control data from logical channels, and the Paging Channel (PCH) is also carried on the PDSCH. In this section, we first briefly introduce channel coding and modulation of the DL-SCH, and then provide details about the supported MIMO transmission.

7.2.1 Channel Encoding and Modulation

The DL-SCH uses the rate 1/3 convolutional turbo code as described in Section 7.1.1. Rate matching is used in order to achieve an *effective channel coding rate* that matches the payload capacity determined by the number of resource blocks allocated to the transport block of the given UE and the modulation scheme. The redundancy version used for repetition or puncturing depends on the H-ARQ transmission number and is indicated explicitly by the eNode-B. The modulation scheme allowed for DL-SCH includes QPSK, 16QAM, and 64QAM and is chosen based on the Channel Quality Indicator (CQI) provided by the UE and various other parameters such as the size of the transport block. The transport block size, the redundancy version, and the modulation order are

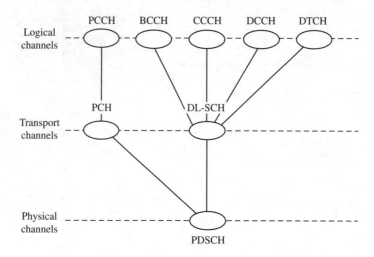

Figure 7.9 Channel mapping around the downlink shared channel.

indicated in the Downlink Control Information (DCI). For MIMO spatial multiplexing with two codewords, different modulation and coding can be used for each codeword, which requires individual signaling.

The resource mapping of the PDSCH physical channel depends on whether UE-specific reference signals are transmitted. In resource blocks without UE-specific reference signals, the PDSCH shall be transmitted on the same set of antenna ports as the PBCH, which is one of $\{0\}$, $\{0, 1\}$, or $\{0, 1, 2, 3\}$; if UE-specific reference signals are transmitted, the PDSCH shall be transmitted on antenna port $\{5\}$, that is, beamforming is applied. The complex-valued symbols are mapped to resource elements in the physical resource blocks corresponding to the virtual resource blocks assigned for transmission and not used for transmission of PCFICH, PHICH, PDCCH, PBCH, synchronization signals, or reference signals. Channel coding for the PCH transport channel is the same as that for the DL-SCH channel, both of which are mapped to the PDSCH physical channel.

7.2.2 Multiantenna Transmission

As the main channel for downlink traffic data transmission, the PDSCH supports all the MIMO modes specified in LTE, which makes this subsection an appropriate place to describe the transmission of the various MIMO modes. There are seven different transmission modes defined for data transmission on the PDSCH channel:

- **Single-antenna port (port 0):** One transport block is transmitted from a single physical antenna corresponding to antenna port 0.

- **Transmit diversity:** One transport block is transmitted from more than one physical antenna, that is, ports 0 and 1 if two physical antennas are used and ports 0, 1, 2, and 3 if four physical antennas are used.

- **Open-loop (OL) spatial multiplexing:** One or two transport blocks are transmitted from two or four physical antennas. In this case, predefined precoder matrices are used based on the Rank Indicator (RI) feedback. The precoding matrix is fixed and not adapted.

- **Closed-loop (CL) spatial multiplexing:** One or two transport blocks are transmitted from two or four physical antennas. The precoding in this case is adapted based on the Precoding Matrix Indicator (PMI) feedback from the UE.

- **Multiuser MIMO:** Two UEs are multiplexed onto two or four physical antennas with one transport block to each UE. The rank-1 PMI feedback from each UE is used to create the overall precoding matrix.

- **Closed-loop rank-1 precoding:** It is a special case of the CL spatial multiplexing with single-layer transmission, that is, a $P \times 1$ precoder is applied.

- **Single-antenna port (port 5):** A single transport block is transmitted from two or more physical antennas. The eNode-B performs beamforming to a single UE using all physical antennas. Unlike other modes, in this case the reference signal is also transmitted using the same beamforming vector that is used for the data symbols. Thus for this mode, the beamforming technique used at the eNode-B is transparent to the UE, and the UE is able to decode the transport block with the help of this UE-specific reference signal. Beamforming can be used to improve the received signal power and/or reduce the interference signal power, which is especially important for cell edge users.

Transmission mode 1 can be classified as a Single-Input-Single-Output (SISO) mode that does not require any layer mapping and precoding. On the other hand, transmission modes 2–6 can be classified as MIMO modes, which require explicit layer mapping and precoding. We categorize these MIMO modes into OL and CL modes, which will be described separately. Cell-specific reference signals are used to assist the MIMO transmission. Downlink MIMO transmission, especially CL MIMO modes, requires explicit feedback from UEs, including RI and PMI contained in Uplink Control Information (UCI). The feedback for MIMO transmission is treated in Chapter 9. Layer mapping has already been described in Section 7.1.2, and in this subsection we focus on MIMO precoding. For other technical details on MIMO transmission, please refer to Chapter 5.

OL MIMO Techniques

The OL MIMO technique requires no or little feedback from UEs, so it is suitable for scenarios where accurate feedback is difficult to obtain or the channel changes rapidly enough, making the feedbacks obsolete, such as the high mobility scenario. OL MIMO modes include OL transmit diversity and OL spatial multiplexing.

OL Transmit Diversity For the OL transmit diversity, the space-time block code discussed in Section 5.3 is applied, which is different for two- and four- antenna ports transmission.

For diversity transmission using two antenna ports, $p \in \{0,1\}$, the output $y(i) = [y_0(i) \ldots y_1(i)]^T$, $i = 0, 1, \ldots, M_s^{\mathrm{ap}} - 1$ of the precoding operation is determined as:

$$\begin{bmatrix} y_0(2i) & y_0(2i+1) \\ y_1(2i) & y_1(2i+1) \end{bmatrix} = \frac{1}{\sqrt{2}} \begin{bmatrix} x_0(i) & x_1(i) \\ -x_1^*(i) & x_0^*(i) \end{bmatrix} \tag{7.6}$$

for $i = 0, 1, \ldots, M_s^{\mathrm{layer}} - 1$ with $M_s^{\mathrm{ap}} = 2M_s^{\mathrm{layer}}$. It is similar to the Alamouti space-time block code [6], with the difference that the index i is in the frequency domain rather than the time domain. Thus, this transmit diversity technique is referred to as the space frequency block code (SFBC). As the Alamouti code, SFBC also achieves a diversity order of 2.

For transmission using four antenna ports, the output $\mathbf{y}(i) = [y_0(i), y_1(i), y_2(i), y_3(i)]^T$, $i = 0, 1, \ldots, M_s^{\mathrm{ap}} - 1$ of the precoding operation is defined by:

$$\begin{bmatrix} y_0(4i) & y_0(4i+1) & y_0(4i+2) & y_0(4i+3) \\ y_1(4i) & y_1(4i+1) & y_1(4i+2) & y_1(4i+3) \\ y_2(4i) & y_2(4i+1) & y_2(4i+2) & y_2(4i+3) \\ y_3(4i) & y_3(4i+1) & y_3(4i+2) & y_3(4i+3) \end{bmatrix} = \frac{1}{\sqrt{2}} \begin{bmatrix} x_0(i) & x_1(i) & 0 & 0 \\ 0 & 0 & x_2(i) & x_3(i) \\ -x_1^*(i) & x_0^*(i) & 0 & 0 \\ 0 & 0 & -x_3^*(i) & x_2^*(i) \end{bmatrix}$$
$$\tag{7.7}$$

for $i = 0, 1, \ldots, M_s^{\mathrm{layer}} - 1$ with $M_s^{\mathrm{ap}} = \begin{cases} 4M_s^{\mathrm{layer}} & \text{if } M_s^{(0)} \bmod 4 = 0 \\ 4M_s^{\mathrm{layer}} - 2 & \text{if } M_s^{(0)} \bmod 4 \neq 0 \end{cases}$. This is the

SFBC combined with Frequency Switched Transmit Diversity (FSTD), which achieves diversity order of 2. This rate 1 diversity scheme is used as no orthogonal rate 1 space-time block code exists. It is also able to provide robustness against the spatial channel correlation and simplify the UE receiver implementation. Note that mapping of symbols to antenna ports is in an interlaced fashion on every other antenna port instead of consecutive antenna ports. This is because the first two cell-specific antenna ports have a higher reference signal density than the last two, which is shown in Section 7.6.1, and hence provide better channel estimates. Interlacing ensures a more balanced decoding performance of the two SFBC codes. In addition, the switching between antenna ports can provide additional spatial diversity when used together with the outer bit-level channel coding.

OL Spatial Multiplexing   This mode can be applied only if the channel rank is greater than 1 (RI > 1). Codebook-based precoding is used. For OL spatial multiplexing, the precoding is defined by:

$$\begin{bmatrix} y_0(i) \\ \vdots \\ y_{P-1}(i) \end{bmatrix} = \mathbf{W}(i)\mathbf{D}(i)\mathbf{U} \begin{bmatrix} x_0(i) \\ \vdots \\ x_{v-1}(i) \end{bmatrix},$$

where i is the index of modulation symbols in each layer, $i = 0, 1, \ldots, M_s^{\mathrm{ap}} - 1$, and $M_s^{\mathrm{ap}} = M_s^{\mathrm{layer}}$, P and v are numbers of antenna ports and layers, respectively. Therefore, the precoder for OL spatial multiplexing consists of three different matrices, described as follows.

The $P \times v$ precoding matrix $\mathbf{W}(i)$ is selected from the same codebook defined for CL spatial multiplexing, which will be specified later and is shown in Table 7.9. For two antenna ports, it is always the same:

$$\mathbf{W}(i) = \frac{1}{\sqrt{2}} \begin{bmatrix} 1 & 0 \\ 0 & 1 \end{bmatrix}, \tag{7.8}$$

that is, the normalized identity matrix. For four antenna ports with v layers, v different precoding matrices are selected from the predefined codebooks. These v precoding matrices are cyclically applied in turn on every v vector. This is to provide additional decorrelation between the spatial streams. In particular, the precoder is selected according to $\mathbf{W}(i) = C_k$, where k is the precoder index given by:

$$k = \left(\left\lfloor \frac{i}{v} \right\rfloor \bmod 4 \right) + 1 \in \{1, 2, 3, 4\} \tag{7.9}$$

and C_1, C_2, C_3, C_4 denote precoder matrices corresponding to precoder indices 12, 13, 14, and 15, respectively, in Table 7.9.

The diagonal $v \times v$ matrix $\mathbf{D}(i)$ is to support large-delay cyclic delay diversity (CDD). CDD is originally used to provide single-rank transmit diversity for OFDM-based transmissions [7]. In LTE, large-delay CDD is used with spatial multiplexing to induce variations in the channel quality over different subcarriers. The benefit of CDD is reduced by antenna correlation, and the $v \times v$ matrix $\mathbf{U}$, which is a fixed unitary DFT-based precoding matrix, is applied to avoid this problem. Both $\mathbf{D}(i)$ and $\mathbf{U}$ are given in Table 7.7 for different values of v. When applied together, $\mathbf{D}(i)\mathbf{U}$ effectively makes sure that all layers undergo the same channel quality, which reduces signaling overhead as only a single CQI needs to be fed back and also provides increased robustness against imperfect link adaptation.

CL MIMO Techniques

CL MIMO transmission requires explicit feedback from UEs regarding the optimum precoding matrix (or vector). The UE determines this based on its current MIMO channel

Table 7.7 Large-Delay Cyclic Delay Diversity

v	U	$\mathbf{D}(i)$
2	$\frac{1}{\sqrt{2}} \begin{bmatrix} 1 & 1 \\ 1 & e^{-j2\pi/2} \end{bmatrix}$	$\begin{bmatrix} 1 & 0 \\ 0 & e^{-j2\pi i/2} \end{bmatrix}$
3	$\frac{1}{\sqrt{3}} \begin{bmatrix} 1 & 1 & 1 \\ 1 & e^{-j2\pi/3} & e^{-j4\pi/3} \\ 1 & e^{-j4\pi/3} & e^{-j8\pi/3} \end{bmatrix}$	$\begin{bmatrix} 1 & 0 & 0 \\ 0 & e^{-j2\pi i/3} & 0 \\ 0 & 0 & e^{-j4\pi i/3} \end{bmatrix}$
4	$\frac{1}{2} \begin{bmatrix} 1 & 1 & 1 & 1 \\ 1 & e^{-j2\pi/4} & e^{-j4\pi/4} & e^{-j6\pi/4} \\ 1 & e^{-j4\pi/4} & e^{-j8\pi/4} & e^{-j12\pi/4} \\ 1 & e^{-j6\pi/4} & e^{-j12\pi/4} & e^{-j18\pi/4} \end{bmatrix}$	$\begin{bmatrix} 1 & 0 & 0 & 0 \\ 0 & e^{-j2\pi i/4} & 0 & 0 \\ 0 & 0 & e^{-j4\pi/4} & 0 \\ 0 & 0 & 0 & e^{-j6\pi i/4} \end{bmatrix}$

and sends this information to the eNode-B using the uplink control channel. This is able to provide additional performance gain and simplify the receiver structure. The precoder of CL MIMO modes is based on the predefined codebook, which is selected at the eNode-B with the help of the feedback of RI and PMI from UEs. The codebook-based feedback ensures that the UE only needs to send the index of the precoder, also referred to as the Precoder Matrix Index (PMI), instead of sending the precoder itself. This reduces the feedback bandwidth significantly and has been shown to cause only minor degradation in performance due to the quantization of the precoder [8, 9, 11].

CL Spatial Multiplexing (RI > 1)   For CL spatial multiplexing, each UE feeds back the index of the precoder from a predefined codebook that achieves the best performance, and then the eNode-B can get the unitary precoding matrices from this codebook. The details about the precoder feedback are discussed in Chapter 9.

The precoding for CL spatial multiplexing is defined by:

$$
\begin{bmatrix} y_0(i) \\ \vdots \\ y_{P-1}(i) \end{bmatrix} = \mathbf{W}(i) \begin{bmatrix} x_0(i) \\ \vdots \\ x_{v-1}(i) \end{bmatrix},
$$

where the precoding matrix $\mathbf{W}(i)$ is of size $P \times v$, and $i = 0, 1, \dots, M_s^{\mathrm{ap}} - 1$, $M_s^{\mathrm{ap}} = M_s^{\mathrm{layer}}$.

For two antenna ports, the precoding matrix $\mathbf{W}(i)$ is selected from Table 7.8 or a subset thereof. For four antenna ports, the codebook uses a Householder generating function:

$$
\mathbf{W}_n = \mathbf{I} - 2\mathbf{u}_n \mathbf{u}_n^H / \mathbf{u}_n^H \mathbf{u}_n,
$$

where input vectors $\mathbf{u}_n$, $n = 0, 1, \dots, 15$, are given in Table 7.9. The precoding matrix $\mathbf{W}$ will be selected from Table 7.9 with a given number of layers, where the quantity $\mathbf{W}_n^{\{s\}}$ denotes the matrix defined by the columns given by the set $\{s\}$ from $\mathbf{W}_n$.

CL Rank-1 Precoding (RI = 1)   In LTE, rank-1 precoding is treated as a special case of CL spatial multiplexing. The precoder can be obtained in the same way as for CL spatial multiplexing by setting the number of layers to be $v = 1$. It is used to improve cell coverage and has lower overhead than spatial multiplexing.

Table 7.8 Codebook for Transmission on Antenna Ports {0,1}

Codebook Index	Number of Layers v	
	1	2
0	$\frac{1}{\sqrt{2}} \begin{bmatrix} 1 \\ 1 \end{bmatrix}$	$\frac{1}{\sqrt{2}} \begin{bmatrix} 1 & 0 \\ 0 & 1 \end{bmatrix}$
1	$\frac{1}{\sqrt{2}} \begin{bmatrix} 1 \\ -1 \end{bmatrix}$	$\frac{1}{\sqrt{2}} \begin{bmatrix} 1 & 1 \\ 1 & -1 \end{bmatrix}$
2	$\frac{1}{\sqrt{2}} \begin{bmatrix} 1 \\ j \end{bmatrix}$	$\frac{1}{\sqrt{2}} \begin{bmatrix} 1 & 1 \\ j & -j \end{bmatrix}$
3	$\frac{1}{\sqrt{2}} \begin{bmatrix} 1 \\ -j \end{bmatrix}$	N/A

Table 7.9 Codebook for Transmission on Antenna Ports $\{0,1,2,3\}$

Codebook Index	$\mathbf{u}_n$	Number of Layers v			
		1	2	3	4
0	$\mathbf{u}_0 = [1 \ -1 \ -1 \ -1]^T$	$\mathbf{W}_0^{\{1\}}$	$\mathbf{W}_0^{\{14\}}/\sqrt{2}$	$\mathbf{W}_0^{\{124\}}/\sqrt{3}$	$\mathbf{W}_0^{\{1234\}}/2$
1	$\mathbf{u}_1 = [1 \quad -j \quad 1 \quad j]^T$	$\mathbf{W}_1^{\{1\}}$	$\mathbf{W}_1^{\{12\}}/\sqrt{2}$	$\mathbf{W}_1^{\{123\}}/\sqrt{3}$	$\mathbf{W}_1^{\{1234\}}/2$
2	$\mathbf{u}_2 = [1 \quad 1 \quad -1 \quad 1]^T$	$\mathbf{W}_2^{\{1\}}$	$\mathbf{W}_2^{\{12\}}/\sqrt{2}$	$\mathbf{W}_2^{\{123\}}/\sqrt{3}$	$\mathbf{W}_2^{\{3214\}}/2$
3	$\mathbf{u}_3 = [1 \quad j \quad 1 \quad -j]^T$	$\mathbf{W}_3^{\{1\}}$	$\mathbf{W}_3^{\{12\}}/\sqrt{2}$	$\mathbf{W}_3^{\{123\}}/\sqrt{3}$	$\mathbf{W}_3^{\{3214\}}/2$
4	$\mathbf{u}_4 = [1 \quad \frac{-1-j}{\sqrt{2}} \quad -j \quad \frac{1-j}{\sqrt{2}}]^T$	$\mathbf{W}_4^{\{1\}}$	$\mathbf{W}_4^{\{14\}}/\sqrt{2}$	$\mathbf{W}_4^{\{124\}}/\sqrt{3}$	$\mathbf{W}_4^{\{1234\}}/2$
5	$\mathbf{u}_5 = [1 \quad \frac{1-j}{\sqrt{2}} \quad j \quad \frac{-1-j}{\sqrt{2}}]^T$	$\mathbf{W}_5^{\{1\}}$	$\mathbf{W}_5^{\{14\}}/\sqrt{2}$	$\mathbf{W}_5^{\{124\}}/\sqrt{3}$	$\mathbf{W}_5^{\{1234\}}/2$
6	$\mathbf{u}_6 = [1 \quad \frac{1+j}{\sqrt{2}} \quad -j \quad \frac{-1+j}{\sqrt{2}}]^T$	$\mathbf{W}_6^{\{1\}}$	$\mathbf{W}_6^{\{13\}}/\sqrt{2}$	$\mathbf{W}_6^{\{134\}}/\sqrt{3}$	$\mathbf{W}_6^{\{1324\}}/2$
7	$\mathbf{u}_7 = [1 \quad \frac{-1+j}{\sqrt{2}} \quad j \quad \frac{1+j}{\sqrt{2}}]^T$	$\mathbf{W}_7^{\{1\}}$	$\mathbf{W}_7^{\{13\}}/\sqrt{2}$	$\mathbf{W}_7^{\{134\}}/\sqrt{3}$	$\mathbf{W}_7^{\{1324\}}/2$
8	$\mathbf{u}_8 = [1 \quad -1 \quad 1 \quad 1]^T$	$\mathbf{W}_8^{\{1\}}$	$\mathbf{W}_8^{\{12\}}/\sqrt{2}$	$\mathbf{W}_8^{\{124\}}/\sqrt{3}$	$\mathbf{W}_8^{\{1234\}}/2$
9	$\mathbf{u}_9 = [1 \quad -j \quad -1 \quad -j]^T$	$\mathbf{W}_9^{\{1\}}$	$\mathbf{W}_9^{\{14\}}/\sqrt{2}$	$\mathbf{W}_9^{\{134\}}/\sqrt{3}$	$\mathbf{W}_9^{\{1234\}}/2$
10	$\mathbf{u}_{10} = [1 \quad 1 \quad 1 \quad -1]^T$	$\mathbf{W}_{10}^{\{1\}}$	$\mathbf{W}_{10}^{\{13\}}/\sqrt{2}$	$\mathbf{W}_{10}^{\{123\}}/\sqrt{3}$	$\mathbf{W}_{10}^{\{1324\}}/2$
11	$\mathbf{u}_{11} = [1 \quad j \quad -1 \quad j]^T$	$\mathbf{W}_{11}^{\{1\}}$	$\mathbf{W}_{11}^{\{13\}}/\sqrt{2}$	$\mathbf{W}_{11}^{\{134\}}/\sqrt{3}$	$\mathbf{W}_{11}^{\{1324\}}/2$
12	$\mathbf{u}_{12} = [1 \quad -1 \quad -1 \quad 1]^T$	$\mathbf{W}_{12}^{\{1\}}$	$\mathbf{W}_{12}^{\{12\}}/\sqrt{2}$	$\mathbf{W}_{12}^{\{123\}}/\sqrt{3}$	$\mathbf{W}_{12}^{\{1234\}}/2$
13	$\mathbf{u}_{13} = [1 \quad -1 \quad 1 \quad -1]^T$	$\mathbf{W}_{13}^{\{1\}}$	$\mathbf{W}_{13}^{\{13\}}/\sqrt{2}$	$\mathbf{W}_{13}^{\{123\}}/\sqrt{3}$	$\mathbf{W}_{13}^{\{1324\}}/2$
14	$\mathbf{u}_{14} = [1 \quad 1 \quad -1 \quad -1]^T$	$\mathbf{W}_{14}^{\{1\}}$	$\mathbf{W}_{14}^{\{13\}}/\sqrt{2}$	$\mathbf{W}_{14}^{\{123\}}/\sqrt{3}$	$\mathbf{W}_{14}^{\{3214\}}/2$
15	$\mathbf{u}_{15} = [1 \quad 1 \quad 1 \quad 1]^T$	$\mathbf{W}_{15}^{\{1\}}$	$\mathbf{W}_{15}^{\{12\}}/\sqrt{2}$	$\mathbf{W}_{15}^{\{123\}}/\sqrt{3}$	$\mathbf{W}_{15}^{\{1234\}}/2$

MU-MIMO in Downlink

In current specifications of 3GPP Release 8, there is a limited support for MU-MIMO in the downlink. The precoder for MU-MIMO is the same as that for the rank-1 precoding, that is, the eNode-B transmits to two UEs simultaneously with a rank-1 precoder for each UE, and no inter-user interference cancellation is applied during the precoding process. Mutual interference can be suppressed during the scheduling process by selecting UEs with near-orthogonal channel directions, or with advanced interference cancellation at the UE. The scheduling algorithm and receiver structure, however, are not specified in the standard. This kind of MU-MIMO mode is able to provide a throughput gain when there is transmit spatial correlation [12] or with a large number of UEs.

As discussed in Chapter 5, the main difficulty with MU-MIMO lies in channel state information (CSI) measurement and feedback. CSI requirements of MU-MIMO at the

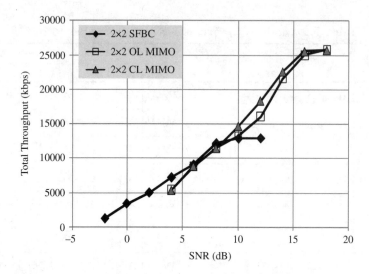

Figure 7.10 Simulation results of downlink transmission with different MIMO modes.

eNode-B are substantial: while imperfect CSI only causes a constant SNR loss for SU-MIMO, it affects the spatial multiplexing gain for MU-MIMO [17]. Therefore, more CSI feedback bits or advanced feedback schemes are required. With simultaneous transmission to multiple UEs, the CQI calculation for determining the modulation and coding scheme is also difficult, as the UE requires some knowledge about the precoder applied for the other UEs. In addition, the receiver structure has an impact on the CQI calculation. In Release 9 and beyond, the eNode-B will be able to utilize the UE specific reference signals for the newly defined antenna ports 7 and 8 to assist the MU-MIMO transmission. The reference signals on these two ports are precoded with the precoding vectors for the two scheduled UEs, respectively. Based on these reference signals each UE can explicitly measure the effective channel of the interfering stream and thus cancel it. This is also called *dual layer beamforming*.

The performance of various OL and CL MIMO techniques such as SFBC and spatial multiplexing are shown in Figure 7.10. The results shown here are based on a 2×2 10MHz FDD LTE system in an EVA (enhanced vehicular A) multipath fading channel for a UE speed of 3km/hr. The results are for MCS level of 16QAM R1/2 and take into account H-ARQ. For H-ARQ we assumed a total of eight processes per UE and with six maximum transmissions per H-ARQ process. An MMSE receiver structure was used for both OL and CL MIMO, and an optimum ML receiver architecture was used for SFBC. In the case of CL MIMO the PMI feedback interval was set to 10 msec. The throughput shown in this figure can be interpreted as the product of the peak throughput (for the given MCS level) and the successful transmission rate, that is, $1-$ block error rate.

7.3 Downlink Control Channels

Downlink control channels are carried over the Physical Downlink Control Channel (PDCCH) and they contain control information from the MAC layer, including downlink

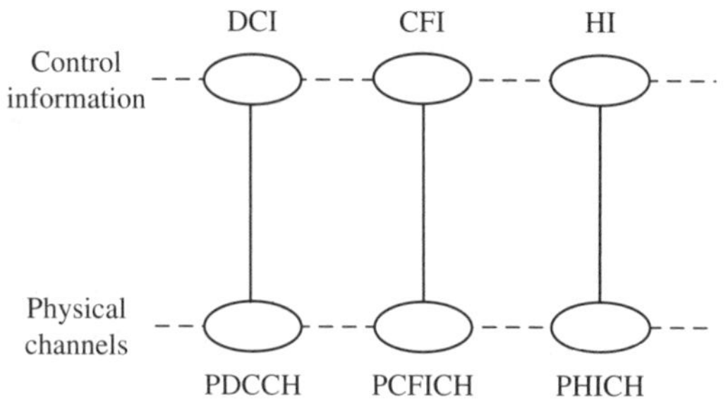

Figure 7.11 Channel mapping for control information in the downlink.

control information (DCI), Control Format Indicator (CFI), and H-ARQ Indicator (HI). Channel mapping between control information and physical channels in the downlink is shown in Figure 7.11. There is a specific physical channel for each type of control information. On the physical layer the PDCCH and the PDSCH are time multiplexed, such that the PDCCH is carried over the first few OFDM symbols of each subframe and the PDSCH is carried over the rest of the OFDM symbols. The number of OFDM symbols allocated for PDCCH can vary from one to four and is conveyed by the CFI. The CFI is carried on yet another control channel known as the Physical Control Format Indicator Channel (PCFICH), which is always carried in a predetermined format over the first OFDM symbol of each subframe. This predetermined format of PCFICH allows each UE to decode the CFI without ambiguity and thus determine the number of OFDM symbols in the beginning of each subframe that are used as the control region.

7.3.1 Downlink Control Information (DCI) Formats

Among the control information in the downlink, the DCI is the most important as it carries detailed control information for both downlink and uplink transmissions. Therefore, in this section, we first describe different DCI formats. Then, the coding and modulation processing for each control channel is discussed, followed by the supported MIMO transmission. The DCI carries the downlink scheduling assignments, uplink scheduling grants, power control commands, and other information necessary for the scheduled UEs to decode and demodulate data symbols in the downlink or encode and modulate data symbols in the uplink. As shown in Table 6.1 in Chapter 6, LTE defines ten different DCI formats for different transmission scenarios, summarized as follows:

- DCI format 0 carries uplink scheduling grants and necessary control information for uplink transmission.

- DCI format 1/1A/1B/1C/1D provides scheduling information for one codeword transmission without spatial multiplexing. This category has the largest number of types in order to save signaling resources on the PDCCH, as these formats are optimized for specific use cases and transmission modes.

- DCI formats 2 and 2A provide downlink scheduling information for CL and OL spatial multiplexing, respectively. In this case, DCI contains information about the

Table 7.10 Fields of DCI Format 0

Information Type	Number of Bits	Purpose
Flag for format 0/1A differentiation	1	Indicates format 0 or format 1A
Hopping flag	1	Indicates whether PUSCH frequency hopping is performed
Resource block assignment and hopping resource allocation	$\lceil \log_2(N_{RB}^{DL}(N_{RB}^{DL}+1)/2) \rceil$	Indicates assigned resource blocks
Modulation and coding scheme and redundancy version	5	For determining the modulation order, redundancy version and the transport block size
New data indicator	1	Indicates whether the packet is a new transmission or a retransmission
TPC command for scheduled PUSCH	2	Transport Power Control (TPC) command for adapting the transmit power on the PUSCH
Cyclic shift for demodulation reference signal	3	Indicates the cyclic shift for the demodulation reference signal for PUSCH
UL index	2	Indicates the scheduling grant and only applies to TDD operation with uplink-downlink configuration 0
Downlink Assignment Index (DAI)	2	For ACK/NAK reporting and only applies to TDD operating with uplink-downlink configurations 1-6
CQI request	1	Requests an aperiodic CQI from the UE

modulation and coding scheme and the redundancy version for each of the two codewords.

- DCI formats 3 and 3A carry Transmit Power Control (TPC) commands for the uplink.

DCI contains important information for different physical layer procedures that will be discussed in Chapter 9. Taking format 0 and format 1 as examples, the different fields are explained in Table 7.10 and Table 7.11, respectively. We see that there are common fields for both formats, including the resource assignment indication, the modulation and coding scheme, the new data indicator, and the downlink assignment index. The DCI format 0 is for scheduling of the PUSCH, so it has unique fields such as hopping flag and

Table 7.11 Fields of DCI Format 1

Information Type	Number of Bits	Purpose
Resource allocation header	1	Indicates whether it is of resource allocation type 0 or 1
Resource block assignment	Depends on resource allocation type	Indicates assigned resource blocks
Modulation and coding scheme	5	For determining the modulation order and the transport block size
H-ARQ process number	3 (TDD), 4 (FDD)	Indicates the H-ARQ process
New data indicator	1	Indicates whether the packet is a new transmission or a retransmission
Redundancy version	2	Identifies the redundancy version used for coding the packet
TPC command for PUCCH	2	TPC command for adapting the transmit power on the PUCCH
Downlink Assignment Index (DAI)	2	For ACK/NAK reporting and only applies to TDD operation

cyclic shift for demodulation reference signals. The DCI format 1 is for scheduling of one PDSCH codeword, and it provides other information such as the H-ARQ process number and the redundancy version of the current transmission. An exhaustive breakdown of the different DCI formats can be found in [4].

To receive the PDSCH, the UE shall monitor a set of PDCCH candidates for control information. Upon detecting a PDCCH with DCI format 1, 1A, 1B, 1C, 1D, 2, or 2A intended for itself, the UE then decodes the corresponding PDSCH in the same frame. To transmit the PUSCH, the UE shall first detect a PDCCH with format 0 intended for itself.

7.3.2 Channel Encoding and Modulation

Downlink Control Information (DCI)

The DCI is mapped to the PDCCH physical channel, and multiple PDCCHs can be transmitted in a subframe. A 16-bit CRC is attached to the control information symbols. The CRC parity bits are then scrambled according to the following rules:

- If UE transmit antenna selection is not configured or applicable, the CRC parity bits are scrambled with one radio network temporary identifier (RNTI), which is the UE identity. Then the UE is able to detect its own DCI.

Table 7.12 UE Transmit Antenna Selection Mask

UE Transmit Antenna Selection	Antenna Selection Mask
UE port 0	0, 0, 0, 0, 0, 0, 0, 0, 0, 0, 0, 0, 0, 0, 0, 0
UE port 1	0, 0, 0, 0, 0, 0, 0, 0, 0, 0, 0, 0, 0, 0, 0, 1

- If UE transmit antenna selection is configured and applicable, the CRC parity bits of PDCCH with DCI format 0 are scrambled with the corresponding RNTI and the antenna selection mask indicated in Table 7.12, which informs the UE about the selected antenna port.

The tail-biting convolutional code with rate 1/3 is used as the channel coding scheme, while QPSK is the modulation scheme. After channel coding, cell-specific scrambling is applied, and the PDCCH shall be transmitted on the same set of antenna ports as the PBCH.

The PDCCH is located in the first n OFDM symbols of each subframe, $1 \leq n \leq 4$. Such a special location can be used to support micro-sleep that saves UE battery life, and to reduce buffering and latency, that is, the UE can go to sleep if it sees no assignment. For frame structure type 2, PDCCH can also be mapped onto the first two OFDM symbols of the DwPTS field, while the third OFDM symbol is for the primary synchronization signal. The set of OFDM symbols possible to use for PDCCH in a subframe is given in Table 7.13. Before being mapped to resource elements, the PDCCH complex-valued symbols are first organized into quadruplets, which are then permuted according to the sub-block interleaver described in Section 7.1.1 for rate matching. Each PDCCH is transmitted using one or more so-called control channel elements (CCEs), where each CCE corresponds to nine sets of four physical resource elements known as resource element groups (REGs). Four QPSK symbols are mapped to each REG. The PDCCH can be transmitted using one or more CCEs, depending on the size of DCI and the channel condition. There are four different PDCCH formats defined in LTE with different numbers of CCEs, as listed in Table 7.14.

Control Format Indicator (CFI)

The CFI indicates how many OFDM symbols the DCI spans in the subframe. Such an indicator is needed because the load on PDCCH varies, depending on the number of resource blocks and the signaling format conveyed on PDCCH. For example, the PDCCH loads are different for DCI format 0 and format 1 as illustrated in Table 7.10 and Table 7.11. The CFI takes values CFI = 1, 2, or 3. As shown in Table 7.13, for system bandwidths $N_{RB}^{DL} > 10$, the DCI spans 1, 2, or 3 OFDM symbols, given by the value of the CFI; for system bandwidths $N_{RB}^{DL} \leq 10$, the DCI spans 2, 3, or 4 OFDM symbols, given by CFI+1.

The CFI uses a block code predefined based on $(3, 2)$ simplex coding with repetition of coding rate 1/16, the codewords of which are listed in Table 7.15. QPSK is the modulation scheme. In addition, cell-specific scrambling tied to the cell identity is used.

Table 7.13 Number of OFDM Symbols Used for PDCCH

Subframe	Number of OFDM Symbols for PDCCH When $N_{RB}^{DL} > 10$	Number of OFDM Symbols for PDCCH When $N_{RB}^{DL} \leq 10$
Subframe 1 and 6 for frame structure type 2	1,2	2
MBSFN subframes on a carrier supporting both PMCH and PDSCH for one or two cell-specific antenna ports	1,2	2
MBSFN subframes on a carrier supporting both PMCH and PDSCH for four cell-specific antenna ports	2	2
MBSFN subframes on a carrier not supporting PDSCH	0	0
All other cases	1,2,3	2,3,4

Table 7.14 PDCCH Formats

PDCCH Format	# CCEs (n)	# REGs	# PDCCH Bits
0	1	9	72
1	2	18	144
2	4	36	288
3	8	72	576

Table 7.15 CFI Codeword

CFI	CFI Codeword $b_0, b_1, \ldots, b_{31}$
1	0,1,1,0,1,1,0,1,1,0,1,1,0,1,1,0,1,1,0,1,1,0,1,1,0,1,1,0,1,1,0,1
2	1,0,1,1,0,1,1,0,1,1,0,1,1,0,1,1,0,1,1,0,1,1,0,1,1,0,1,1,0,1,1,0
3	1,1,0,1,1,0,1,1,0,1,1,0,1,1,0,1,1,0,1,1,0,1,1,0,1,1,0,1,1,0,1,1
4 (Reserved)	0,0,0,0,0,0,0,0,0,0,0,0,0,0,0,0,0,0,0,0,0,0,0,0,0,0,0,0,0,0,0,0

The CFI is mapped to the PCFICH physical channel carried on specific resource elements in the first OFDM symbol of the subframe. The PCFICH is transmitted when the number of OFDM symbols for PDCCH is greater than zero. In addition, the PCFICH shall be transmitted on the same set of antenna ports as the PBCH.

H-ARQ Indicator (HI)

The control information HI is for H-ARQ acknowledgement in response to uplink transmission. As spatial multiplexing is not supported in the uplink in current specifications, only one information bit is required for H-ARQ acknowledgment. It has two values: HI = 1 for a positive acknowledgment (ACK) and HI = 0 for a negative acknowledgment (NAK). A repetition code with rate $1/3$ is applied, which has two codewords: $\langle 0, 0, 0 \rangle$ and $\langle 1, 1, 1 \rangle$. Such a repetition is able to provide frequency diversity by mapping different code bits to different resource elements. BPSK modulation is applied.

HI is mapped onto the PHICH physical channel. Multiple PHICHs mapped to the same set of resource elements constitute a PHICH group, where PHICHs within the same group are separated through different orthogonal sequences with a spreading factor of four. A PHICH is identified by the index pair $(n_{\text{group}}, n_{\text{seq}})$, where n_{group} is the PHICH group number and n_{seq} is the orthogonal sequence index within the group. The numbers of PHICH groups are different for frame structure type 1 and type 2, specified in [3] along with the orthogonal sequence. In addition, cell-specific scrambling is applied.

7.3.3 Multiantenna Transmission

To improve the transmission reliability, OL transmit diversity is supported for downlink control information. For PDCCH and PCFICH, the precoding is the same as the OL transmit diversity for PDSCH presented in Section 7.2.2. For PHICH, the precoding for two-antenna-port transmission is the same as PDSCH. For transmission on four antenna ports, the precoding is different. As each PHICH symbol is spread with a spreading factor of four and carried on four subcarriers, and a repetition code with rate $1/3$ is applied, the same PHICH is repeated three times in the frequency domain with four subcarriers in each repetition. There are two alternative precoding types. Denoting $[x_0, x_1, x_2, x_3]^T$ as the vector after layer mapping, the transmission in three repetitions is either

$$\frac{1}{\sqrt{2}} \begin{bmatrix} x_0 & x_1 & x_2 & x_3 \\ 0 & 0 & 0 & 0 \\ -x_1^* & x_0^* & -x_3^* & x_2^* \\ 0 & 0 & 0 & 0 \end{bmatrix}, \frac{1}{\sqrt{2}} \begin{bmatrix} 0 & 0 & 0 & 0 \\ x_0 & x_1 & x_2 & x_3 \\ 0 & 0 & 0 & 0 \\ -x_1^* & x_0^* & -x_3^* & x_2^* \end{bmatrix}, \frac{1}{\sqrt{2}} \begin{bmatrix} x_0 & x_1 & x_2 & x_3 \\ 0 & 0 & 0 & 0 \\ -x_1^* & x_0^* & -x_3^* & x_2^* \\ 0 & 0 & 0 & 0 \end{bmatrix},$$

or

$$\frac{1}{\sqrt{2}} \begin{bmatrix} 0 & 0 & 0 & 0 \\ x_0 & x_1 & x_2 & x_3 \\ 0 & 0 & 0 & 0 \\ -x_1^* & x_0^* & -x_3^* & x_2^* \end{bmatrix}, \frac{1}{\sqrt{2}} \begin{bmatrix} x_0 & x_1 & x_2 & x_3 \\ 0 & 0 & 0 & 0 \\ -x_1^* & x_0^* & -x_3^* & x_2^* \\ 0 & 0 & 0 & 0 \end{bmatrix}, \frac{1}{\sqrt{2}} \begin{bmatrix} 0 & 0 & 0 & 0 \\ x_0 & x_1 & x_2 & x_3 \\ 0 & 0 & 0 & 0 \\ -x_1^* & x_0^* & -x_3^* & x_2^* \end{bmatrix}.$$

In fact, the vector $[x_0, x_1, x_2, x_3]^T$ is a combination of different orthogonal sequences, which is to separate different PHICHs. To maintain the orthogonality, this vector needs to be transmitted from the same antenna within each repetition, that is, antenna switching as in the precoding specified by (7.7) cannot be used. The precoding and repetition for PHICH achieves frequency and spatial diversity. In addition, using type 1 and type 2 precoding alternatively, it is able to keep uniform power distribution over eNode-B transmit antennas.

7.4 Broadcast Channels

Broadcast channels carry system information such as downlink system bandwidth, antenna configuration, and reference signal power. The UEs can get the necessary system information after the cell search (or synchronization) procedure. Due to the large size of the system information field, it is divided into two portions—Master Information Block (MIB) transmitted on the PBCH and System Information Blocks (SIB) transmitted on the PDSCH. The PBCH contains basic system parameters necessary to demodulate the PDSCH, which contains the remaining SIB. The transmission of the PBCH is characterized by a fixed pre-determined transport format and resource allocation, that is, there is no higher-layer control.

Error detection is provided through a 16-bit CRC, and then the CRC parity bits are scrambled according to the eNode-B transmit antenna configuration with the scrambling sequence specified in Table 7.16. This implicitly tells the UE about the eNode-B antenna configuration. The tail-biting convolutional coding with rate 1/3 is used, and the coded bits are rate matched to 1920 bits for the normal CP and to 1728 bits for the extended CP.

The modulation scheme is QPSK. No H-ARQ is supported. For MIMO modes, PBCH supports single-antenna transmission and OL transmit diversity. Dynamic adaptation modulation and coding is not possible, due to the lack of channel quality feedback. The complex-valued modulation symbols are mapped onto the 72 subcarriers centered around the DC subcarrier in slot 1 in subframe 0 during four consecutive radio frames, that is, the Transmission Time Interval (TTI) for the PBCH is 40 ms. The PBCH occupies the most narrow bandwidth supported by LTE (1.4MHz) and is located in the subframe guaranteed to be used in the downlink. Therefore, the resource mapping of the PBCH is independent of the system bandwidth and the duplex mode. This allows the UE to detect and decode the PBCH without any prior knowledge of the system bandwidth and the duplex mode. Once the PBCH is detected and the MIB is decoded, the UE can then extract the system bandwidth and the duplex mode.

Table 7.16 CRC Scrambling Sequences for PBCH

# Transmit Antenna Ports at eNode-B	Scrambling Sequence
1	$0,0,0,0,0,0,0,0,0,0,0,0,0,0,0,0$
2	$1,1,1,1,1,1,1,1,1,1,1,1,1,1,1,1$
4	$0,1,0,1,0,1,0,1,0,1,0,1,0,1,0,1$

7.5 Multicast Channels

Multimedia Broadcast and Multicast Services (MBMS), introduced in 3GPP Release 6 for the UTRA [2], supports multicast/broadcast services in a cellular system. It sends the same content information to all the UEs (broadcast) or to a given set of UEs (multicast), and is envisaged for delivering services such as mobile TV. In principle, the MBMS transmission can originate from a single base station or multiple base stations, but multicell transmission is preferred as large gains can be achieved through soft combining of transmissions from multiple base stations. For MBMS in the UTRA, to receive the same data information from multiple cells, the complexity at the receiver is high and there will be interference between signals from different base stations. One major design requirement for LTE is to provide enhanced support for the MBMS transmission, which is called *Enhanced MBMS (E-MBMS)* and is achieved through the so-called Single-Frequency Network (SFN) operation.

With the OFDM-based transmission in the downlink, over-the-air combining of multicast/broadcast transmissions from multiple base stations is possible in LTE with an extended CP. The extended CP is used as the propagation delay from multiple cells and will typically be larger than the delay spread in a single cell. A longer CP can ensure that signals from different base stations still fall within the CP at the receiver, which avoids inter-symbol interference at the cost of a slight reduction in peak data rate. Essentially, it makes synchronous multicell multicast/broadcast transmissions appear as a single transmission over a multipath channel, and since OFDM is efficient in combating multipath channels, there is no resulting interference. In such *Multicast/Broadcast Single Frequency Networks* (MBSFNs), the same information is broadcast on the same radio resources from multiple synchronized neighboring base stations to multiple UEs. The SFN operation has already been used in the terrestrial Digital Video Broadcasting system (DVB-T).

The E-MBMS transmission in LTE occurs on the MCH transport channel, along with the 7.5kHz subcarrier spacing and the extended CP. There are two types of E-MBMS transmissions:

- **Single-cell transmission (non-MBSFN operation):** The MBMS service (MTCH and MCCH) is transmitted on the MCH, and combining of MBMS transmission from multiple cells is not supported.

- **Multicell transmission (MBSFN operation):** The MBMS service (MTCH and MCCH) is transmitted synchronously on the MCH, and combining is supported with the SFN operation.

The BCCH indicates whether there is one (or none) MCCH per cell for cell specific transmission, or there is MCCH sent in MBSFN area for non-cell specific transmission.

The transport channel processing for the MCH is similar to that for the DL-SCH, with a few exceptions. As MBSFN transmission typically uses the point-to-multipoint mode, UE feedback such as ACK/NAK and CQI cannot be used. Therefore, the transport format and resource allocation cannot be dynamically selected, and H-ARQ is not applicable. In addition, only single-antenna port transmission is supported for the PMCH channel and the transmission shall use antenna port 4. Special reference signals are defined for MBSFN transmission, which is discussed in Section 7.6.1. The PMCH and DL-SCH can be multiplexed with the following rules:

- The MBSFN and DL-SCH transmission can be multiplexed in a time-division multiplexing (TDM) manner on a subcarrier basis, but cannot be transmitted within the same subframe.

- In the subframes where PMCH is transmitted on a carrier supporting a mix of PDSCH and PMCH transmissions, up to two of the first OFDM symbols of a subframe can be reserved for non-MBSFN transmission and shall not be used for PMCH transmission.

- In a cell with four cell-specific antenna ports, the first OFDM symbols of a subframe are reserved for non-MBSFN transmission in the subframes in which the PMCH is transmitted.

- The non-MBSFN symbols shall use the same CP as used for subframe 0.

- PMCH shall not be transmitted in subframes 0 and 5 on a carrier supporting a mix of PDSCH and PMCH transmissions.

7.6   Downlink Physical Signals

In this section, we describe the structure and processing of downlink physical signals, including downlink reference signals and synchronization signals. The emphasis is on the resource mapping of different signals.

7.6.1   Downlink Reference Signals

Downlink reference signals consist of known reference symbols that are intended for downlink channel estimation at the UE needed to perform coherent demodulation. To facilitate the channel estimation process, scattered reference signals are inserted in the resource grid at pre-determined intervals. The time and frequency intervals are mainly determined by the characteristics of the channels, and should make a tradeoff between the estimation accuracy and the overhead.

As introduced in Chapter 6, there are three different types of downlink reference signals: cell-specific reference signals, MBSFN reference signals, and UE-specific reference signals. The reference sequence is generated from a pseudo-random sequence, with different initializations for different types of reference signals. There is one reference signal transmitted per downlink antenna port. For MBSFN reference signals, identical sequence is transmitted from cells involved in the MBSFN transmission, while cell-specific sequences are used for other types of reference signals. In this subsection, we describe how the various reference signals are mapped on to the physical layer resource elements.

Cell-Specific Reference Signals

Cell-specific reference signals are transmitted in all downlink subframes in a cell supporting non-MBSFN transmission. In the subframe used for transmission with MBSFN,

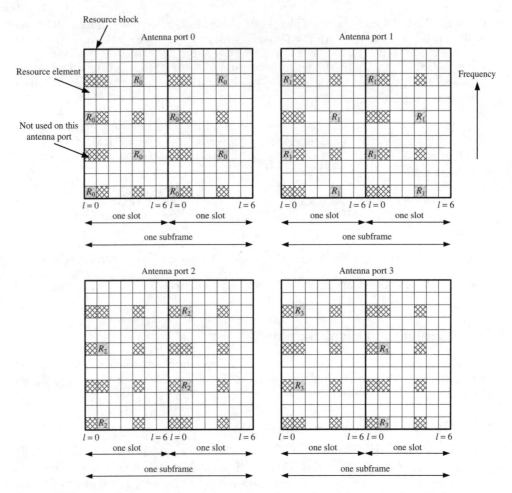

Figure 7.12 An example of mapping of downlink cell-specific reference signals, with four antenna ports and the normal CP. R_p denotes the resource element used for reference signal transmission on antenna port p.

only the first two OFDM symbols can be used for cell-specific reference symbols. Cell-specific reference signals are defined separately for antenna ports 0, 1, 2, and 3 as shown in Figure 7.12. Therefore, in LTE a maximum of four antennas can be used while transmitting the cell specific reference signal. The cell specific reference signals are defined only for the normal subcarrier spacing of $\Delta f = 15 \mathrm{kHz}$.

In the time domain, for the antenna port $p \in \{0, 1\}$, the reference symbols are inserted within the first and the third last OFDM symbols in each slot, which are the first and fifth OFDM symbols for the normal CP and the first and fourth OFDM symbols for the extended CP; for $p \in \{2, 3\}$, the reference symbols are only inserted in the second OFDM symbol. So antenna ports 0 and 1 have twice as many reference symbols as antenna ports 2 and 3. This is to reduce the reference signal overhead but also causes an imbalance in the quality of the respective channel estimates. This impacts the benefits of using four antennas relative to two and affects the MIMO transmission design, for example, the transmit diversity of the PHICH channel considers such imbalance as discussed in Section 7.3.3.

In the frequency domain, the spacing between neighboring reference symbols in the same OFDM symbol is five subcarriers, that is, the reference symbols are transmitted every six subcarriers. There is a staggering of three subcarriers between the first and second reference symbols.

The resource elements (k, l) occupied by reference symbols on any of the antenna ports in a slot shall not be used for any transmission on any other antenna port in the same slot and set to zero. With such resource mapping, the reference signals on different antennas are orthogonal to each other. In addition, there is a frequency shift determined by the slot number and the cell identity. So cell-specific reference signals from different eNode-Bs will have different frequency shifts, which allows the UE to detect the neighboring eNode-B and estimate the associated channel.

An example of resource mapping for cell-specific reference signals is shown in Figure 7.12, where R_p is used to denote a resource element used for reference signal transmission on antenna port p. Note that there are four reference symbols per resource block for $p \in \{0, 1\}$ and two reference symbols per resource block for $p \in \{2, 3\}$.

MBSFN Reference Signals

MBSFN reference signals are only transmitted in subframes allocated for MBSFN transmission, which is only defined for extended CP and transmitted on antenna port 4.

In the time domain, for even-numbered slots, the reference symbols are inserted in the third OFDM symbol for $\Delta f = 15$kHz and in the second OFDM symbol for $\Delta f = 7.5$kHz; for odd-numbered slots, the reference symbols are inserted in the first and fifth OFDM symbols for $\Delta f = 15$kHz and in the first and third OFDM symbols for $\Delta f = 7.5$kHz.

In the frequency domain, the reference symbols are transmitted every two subcarriers for $\Delta f = 15$kHz and every four subcarriers for $\Delta f = 7.5$kHz. In the 0-th OFDM symbols, the reference symbols are transmitted from the second and the third subcarrier for $\Delta f = 15$kHz and $\Delta f = 7.5$kHz, respectively; otherwise, they start from the first subcarrier.

Based on these rules, an example of the resource mapping of MBSFN reference signals is shown in Figure 7.13 with the extended CP, and $\Delta f = 15$kHz. Note that the density of the MBSFN reference signal in the frequency domain is three times higher than that of the cell-specific reference signal. This is because the SFN transmission includes a highly frequency selective channel, so it requires a high density of reference signals in the frequency domain.

UE-Specific Reference Signals

UE-specific reference signals support single-antenna-port transmission with beamforming for the PDSCH and are transmitted on antenna port 5. They are transmitted only on the resource blocks upon which the corresponding PDSCH is mapped. The UE-specific signal is not transmitted in resource elements in which one of the other physical signals or physical channels is transmitted.

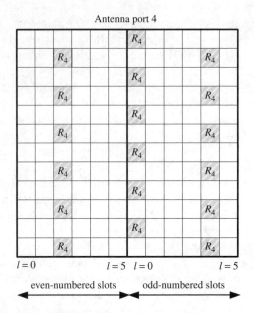

Figure 7.13 An example of mapping of MBSFN reference signals, with the extended CP and $\Delta f = 15\text{kHz}$.

An example of resource mapping of UE-specific reference signals is shown in Figure 7.14 with the normal CP. In the even-numbered slots, the reference symbols are inserted in the fourth and seventh OFDM symbols; in the odd-number slots, the reference symbols are inserted in the third and sixth OFDM symbols. There is a frequency shift of two subcarriers in neighboring reference symbols.

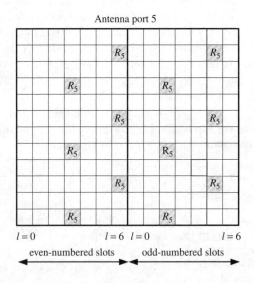

Figure 7.14 An example of mapping of UE-specific signals, with the normal CP.

7.6.2   Synchronization Signals

The downlink synchronization signals are sent to facilitate the cell search procedure, during which process the time and frequency synchronization between the UE and the eNode-B is achieved and the cell ID is obtained. There are a total of 504 unique physical-layer cell IDs, which are grouped into 168 physical-layer cell-ID groups. A physical-layer cell ID is uniquely defined as:

$$N_{ID}^{cell} = 3N_{ID}^{(1)} + N_{ID}^{(2)}, \tag{7.10}$$

where $N_{ID}^{(1)} = 0, 1, \dots, 167$ represents the physical-layer cell-ID group and $N_{ID}^{(2)} = 0, 1, 2$ represents the physical-layer ID within the cell-ID group. Each cell is assigned a unique physical-layer cell ID. The synchronization signals are classified as *primary synchronization signals* and *secondary synchronization signals*. Primary synchronization signals identify the symbol timing and the cell ID index $N_{ID}^{(2)}$, while secondary synchronization signals are used for detecting the cell-ID group index $N_{ID}^{(1)}$ and the frame timing.

The synchronization signals are designed in such a way to make the cell search procedure fast and of low complexity. The sequence used for the primary synchronization signal is generated from a frequency-domain Zadoff-Chu sequence. The Zadoff-Chu sequence possesses the Constant Amplitude Zero Auto-Correlation (CAZAC) property, which means low peak-to-average power ratio (PAPR). This property is desirable for synchronization signals as it improves coverage, which is an important design objective. There are three different root sequence indices, corresponding to cell indices $N_{ID}^{(2)} = 0, 1, 2$, which makes the primary synchronization signals for different cell IDs orthogonal to each other.

The sequence used for the secondary synchronization signal is an interleaved concatenation of two length 31 binary sequences. The two base sequences are cyclic shifts of the m-sequence, with shifts specified by the cell-ID group index $N_{ID}^{(1)}$, which are then scrambled with a scrambling sequence specified by the value of $N_{ID}^{(2)}$. Therefore, the secondary synchronization signal can only be detected after detecting the primary synchronization signal. The usage of two length 31 sequences makes it feasible to detect all 168 cell ID groups. The details of sequence generation can be found in [3].

Both primary and secondary synchronization signals are transmitted on the 62 subcarriers centered around the DC subcarrier, with five reserved subcarriers on either side in the frequency domain, so there are a total of 72 subcarriers occupied by synchronization signals, corresponding to the most narrow bandwidth supported by LTE (1.4MHz). In the time domain, both primary and secondary synchronization signals are transmitted twice per 10 ms in predefined slots.

The primary signal sequences transmitted in both slots are the same, so they can be used to detect the symbol timing but are unable to detect the frame timing. For the secondary synchronization signals, the combination of the two length-31 sequences differs between these two slots. If the sequence pair $(\mathbf{d}_1, \mathbf{d}_2)$ is defined, then $(\mathbf{d}_2, \mathbf{d}_1)$ is not allowed. With this property, the frame timing can be determined from the secondary synchronization signal.

For frame structure type 1, the primary and secondary synchronization signals are mapped to the last and the second to last OFDM symbols in slot 0 and 10. For frame

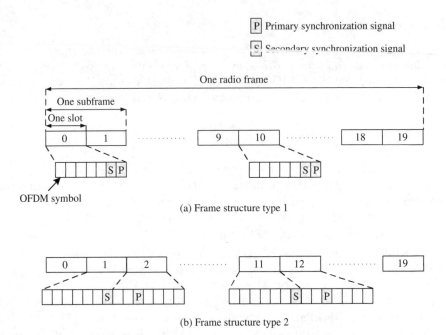

Figure 7.15 The mapping of primary and secondary synchronization signals to OFDM symbols for frame structure type 1 and type 2, with the normal CP. 'P' and 'S' denote primary and secondary synchronization signals, respectively.

structure type 2, the primary synchronization signal is mapped to the third OFDM symbol in slot 2 and 12 (or the third OFDM symbol of the DwPTS field), and the secondary synchronization signal is mapped to the last OFDM symbol in slot 1 and 11. The difference in the location of the synchronization signal enables the UE to detect the duplex mode of the cell. The resource mapping for synchronization signals is illustrated in Figure 7.15.

7.7 H-ARQ in the Downlink

In a wireless network, due to the effects of channel fading and interference from neighboring cells, it is nearly impossible to guarantee error-free transmission no matter how robust the channel coding is. Moreover, as the coding rate decreases, the transmission becomes more robust but at the same time power efficiency is lost, that is, a significant amount of power is used to transmit a few bits of information. An elegant approach to solve this problem is to use the H-ARQ protocol, which combines FEC and retransmission within a single framework, as described in Section 2.6.4. Similar to the HSPA system, in the case of LTE both Type I *Chase Combining* (CC) H-ARQ and Type II *Incremental Redundancy* (IR) H-ARQ schemes have been defined. The H-ARQ operation is part of the MAC layer, while the PHY layer handles soft combining. As shown in Section 7.1, the 1/3 turbo coding is used as the FEC code while a CRC is applied for error detection.

- **At the receiver** turbo decoding is first applied on the received code block. If this is a retransmission, which is indicated in the DCI, the code block will be combined with the previously received versions for decoding. If there is no error detected in the output of the decoder, an ACK signal is fed back to the transmitter through the PUCCH physical channel and the decoded block is passed to the upper layer; otherwise, an NAK signal is fed back and the received code block is stored in the buffer for subsequent combining. The coding and modulation for H-ARQ-ACK information carried in the uplink for the downlink H-ARQ process is discussed in Chapter 8, while the ACK/NAK feedback is treated in Chapter 9.

- **At the transmitter** for each (re)transmission, the same turbo-encoded data is transmitted with different puncturing, so each of these (re)transmissions has a different redundancy version and each is self-decodable. Puncturing is performed during the rate matching process as shown in Figure 7.5. The rate matcher can produce four different redundancy versions of the original coded block. H-ARQ transmissions are indexed with the redundancy version rv_{idx}, which indicates whether it is a new transmission ($rv_{idx} = 0$) or the rv_{idx}-th retransmission ($rv_{idx} = 1, 2,$ or 3).

As it takes a certain amount of time for the H-ARQ ACK/NAK to be received and for the system to be ready to retransmit, there is a time interval between two successive H-ARQ transmissions, which is typically 8 msec in LTE. During this 8 msec, the transport block can either be transmitted (if received with errors) or be discarded from the transmit buffer (if received without errors). This implies a certain amount of inefficiency in transmission since the transmitter has to wait for 8 msec before it can take any action. In order to mitigate this issue, an *N-channel Stop-and-Wait protocol* is used for downlink H-ARQ operation. An N-channel Stop-and-Wait protocol consists of N parallel H-ARQ processes. When one or more of the processes are busy waiting for the H-ARQ ACK/NAK, the processes that are free can be used to transmit other transport blocks.

There is one H-ARQ entity in the eNode-B for each UE that maintains a number of parallel H-ARQ processes. For the FDD mode, a maximum of eight H-ARQ processes is allowed in the downlink; for the TDD mode, the maximum number of H-ARQ processes in the downlink is determined by the UL/DL configuration, specified in Table 7.17, which

Table 7.17 Maximum Number of Downlink H-ARQ Processes for TDD

TDD UL/DL Configuration	Maximum Number of H-ARQ Processes
0	4
1	7
2	10
3	9
4	12
5	15
6	6

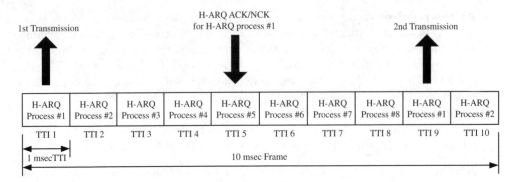

Figure 7.16 An example of a 10-msec frame with eight H-ARQ processes. The H-ARQ process 1 is transmitted in the first TTI, for which the H-ARQ ACK/NAK is received in the 5-th TTI, and then the H-ARQ process 1 is transmitted again in the 9-th TTI.

ranges from 4 to 15. Each H-ARQ process is associated with an H-ARQ process ID. When spatial multiplexing is used, both transport blocks are associated with the *same* H-ARQ process. Figure 7.16 shows a 10 msec frame with TTI index 1 transmitting the H-ARQ process 1, TTI index 2 transmitting the H-ARQ process 2, and so on. The H-ARQ ACK/NAK for the H-ARQ process 1 is received in TTI index 5.[2] Then in TTI index 9 the H-ARQ process 1 is transmitted again, either a new transmission if an ACK is received or a retransmission if an NAK is received.

LTE downlink applies the asynchronous H-ARQ protocol, where the H-ARQ processes can be transmitted in any order without fixed timing. Therefore, in the example in Figure 7.16, the retransmission of H-ARQ process 1 does not necessarily occur in the 9 th TTI. As we will see in Chapter 8, the uplink, on the other hand, uses the synchronous H-ARQ, where the H-ARQ process is assigned to a specific subframe. The asynchronous H-ARQ makes it possible to reflect channel quality measurements at the instance of re-transmission, which is able to provide a higher throughput with re-scheduling or changing the modulation and coding scheme, called *adaptive H-ARQ*. In addition, asynchronous operation makes it possible for the eNode-B to avoid potential collision of H-ARQ retrans-missions with other high priority scheduled transmissions such as persistent scheduling. Meanwhile, the asynchronous H-ARQ requires more overhead, as the receiver does not know ahead of time what is being transmitted and when the retransmission occurs. To support asynchronous H-ARQ in the downlink, PDCCH contains fields indicating the H-ARQ process number and the current redundancy version (see Table 7.11 for an ex-ample with DCI format 1).

The maximum number of H-ARQ retransmissions of each transport block is con-figured by the Radio Resource Control (RRC) layer. When this maximum number is reached without a successful transmission of the transport block or the transmission is in error due to the error in H-ARQ-ACK signaling, a Radio Link Control (RLC) layer ARQ protocol will be triggered to handle the error event. The interaction between the MAC layer H-ARQ protocol and the RLC layer ARQ protocol is discussed in Section 10.2.4.

---

2 As will be shown in Section 9.1.1, for the FDD mode, the UE shall feed back H-ARQ-ACK/NAK in subframe $n + 4$ for a PDSCH transmission in subframe n.

7.8   Summary and Conclusions

In this chapter, we described the physical layer processing for downlink transport channels and control information.

- The downlink data stream transmission is based on a shared-channel concept, which allows channel-dependent scheduling and adaptive modulation and coding. Convolutional turbo coding with a QPP contention-free internal interleaver is applied as the channel code. A variety of MIMO modes are supported in the downlink shared channel, but current specifications provide a limited support for the MU-MIMO mode.

- For each downlink subframe, the PDCCH carrying DCI is mapped to the first n OFDM symbols ($n \leq 4$), where the PCFICH located in the first OFDM symbol indicates the value of n. The PHICH carries H-ARQ ACK/NAK in response to the uplink H-ARQ transmission. Different DCI formats are defined, optimized for different scenarios.

- LTE supports E-MBMS services by the SFN operation, which transmits the same data symbols from multiple base stations and combines them efficiently using OFDM. It is supported by the 7.5kHz subcarrier spacing and the extended CP.

- Different types of reference signals are defined for different transmission modes, and they are inserted in the radio resource grid at pre-determined intervals. The density of reference symbols in the time-frequency plane is determined by making a tradeoff between the channel estimation accuracy and the overhead. For cell-specific reference signals, antenna ports 0 and 1 have twice as many reference symbols as antenna ports 2 and 3. The density of the MBSFN reference signal in the frequency domain is three times higher than that of the cell-specific reference signal.

- LTE downlink employs H-ARQ protocols with soft combining to improve the transmission reliability. The N-channel Stop-and-Wait protocol is used where each H-ARQ entity maintains a number of parallel H-ARQ processes. Asynchronous and adaptive H-ARQ protocol is used.

Bibliography

[1] 3GPP TS 25.212: "Multiplexing and channel coding (FDD)."

[2] 3GPP TS 25.346: "Introduction of the Multimedia Broadcast Multicast Service (MBMS) in the Radio Access Network (RAN)."

[3] 3GPP TS 36.211: "Evolved Universal Terrestrial Radio Access (E-UTRA); Physical channels and modulation."

[4] 3GPP TS 36.212: "Evolved Universal Terrestrial Radio Access (E-UTRA); Multiplexing and channel coding."

[5] 3GPP TS 36. 213: "Evolved Universal Terrestrial Radio Access (E-UTRA); Physical layer procedures."

[6] Alamouti, S. "A simple transmitter diversity technique for wireless communications," *IEEE J. Select. Areas. Commun.*, 16:1451–1458, October 1998.

[7] Dammann, A. and S. Kaiser. "Standard conformable antenna diversity techniques for OFDM and its application to the DVB-T system," in *Proc. IEEE Globecom*, San Antonio, TX, November 2001, pp. 3100–3105.

[8] Love, D. J., R. W. Heath, and T. Strohmer. "Grassmannian beamforming for multiple-input multiple-output wireless systems," *IEEE Trans. Inform. Theory*, 49(10):2735–2747, October 2003.

[9] Love, D. J. and R. W. Heath. "Limited feedback unitary precoding for spatial multiplexing," *IEEE Trans. on Inform. Theory*, 51(8):2967–2976, August 2005.

[10] Ma, H. H. and J. K. Wolf. "On tail-biting convolutional codes," *IEEE Trans. Commun.*, 34(2): 104–111, February 1986.

[11] Mukkavilli, K. K., A. Sabharwal, E. Erkip, and B. Aazhang. "On beamforming with finite rate feedback in multiple-antenna systems," *IEEE Trans. Inform. Theory*, 49(10): 2562–2579, October 2003.

[12] Ribeiro, C. B., K. Hugl, M. Lampinen, and M. Kuusela. "Performance of linear multi-user MIMO precoding in LTE system," *3rd International Symposium on Wireless Pervasive Computing*, May 2008, pp. 410–414.

[13] Sun, J. and O. Y. Takeshita. "Interleavers for turbo codes using permutation polynomials over integer rings," *IEEE Trans. Inform. Theory*, 51(1): 101–119, January 2005.

[14] Takeshita, O. Y. "On maximum contention-free interleavers and permutation polynomials over integer rings," *IEEE Trans. Inform. Theory*, 52(3): 1249–1253, March 2006.

[15] Wicker, S. B. *Error Control Systems for Digital Communication and Storage.* Englewood Cliffs, NJ: Prentice Hall, 1995.

[16] Wozencraft, J. M. and M. Horstein. "Digitalised communication over two-way channels," *Fourth London Symp. Information Theory*, London, U.K., September 1960.

[17] Zhang, J., R. W. Heath Jr., M. Kountouris, and J. G. Andrews. "Mode switching for the multi-antenna broadcast channel based on delay and channel quantization," *EURASIP Special Issue on Multiuser MIMO Transmission with Limited Feedback, Cooperation, and Coordination*, Volume 2009 (2009), Article ID 802548, 15 pages, 2009.

Chapter 8

Uplink Transport Channel Processing

As shown in Chapter 6, there are major differences between downlink and uplink in LTE, including different transmission and multiple access schemes, and different types of channel and control information, which result, in different physical layer processing. Low complexity and high power efficiency are among the major factors for the transmitter design in the uplink. As a result, the multiple access in the uplink is based on SC-FDMA due to its low peak-to-average power ratio (PAPR) compared to OFDMA, which subsequently has an impact on the resource allocation and baseband signal generation. Due to the SC-FDMA nature of the uplink, each UE can only be allocated contiguous resource blocks, unlike downlink where each UE can be allocated non-contiguous resource blocks in order to extract frequency diversity gain. In addition, the uplink only supports a limited number of MIMO modes compared to the downlink.

Nevertheless, there are similarities between the downlink and uplink transport channel processing. For example, the same channel coding processing is applied on both downlink and uplink shared channels and the time-frequency structure of the uplink resource blocks is similar to that of the downlink. There are also interactions between downlink and uplink transmissions. The downlink control information carries scheduling grants for the uplink transmission, while the uplink control information provides necessary information such as channel quality and channel rank for downlink scheduling and transport format selection.

In this chapter, we describe the physical layer processing of uplink transport channels and control information. First, an overview of the uplink transport channel processing is provided, highlighting the similarities and differences between the uplink and downlink processing. Then the channel processing of each individual uplink transport channel is described, including that of the control information and the reference signals. Finally, the H-ARQ protocol in the uplink is discussed.

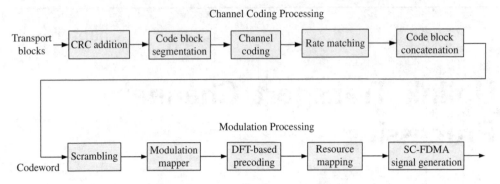

Figure 8.1 Overview of uplink transport channel processing.

8.1 Uplink Transport Channel Processing Overview

The transport channel processing in the uplink is very similar to that of the downlink, which can be divided into two distinct steps, that is, channel coding and modulation, as shown in Figure 8.1. Since spatial multiplexing is not supported in the uplink, data streams from the MAC layer are presented to the encoding unit only one transport block every subframe. The codeword after encoding is passed to the symbol mapping unit where the bits are mapped onto complex valued symbols. Subsequently, the modulated symbols are processed to generate SC-FDMA signals and mapped onto the assigned resource blocks. In this section, we describe the general framework of channel processing, which is common to all uplink transport channels/control information. We will focus mostly on the specific features in the uplink that are different from that of the downlink. The features that are common between uplink and downlink can be found in Chapter 7.

8.1.1 Channel Coding Processing

The channel coding processing in the uplink is similar to that in the downlink, that is, it includes CRC addition, code block segmentation, channel coding, rate matching, and code block concatenation. The general channel coding processing was illustrated in Figure 7.2 in Chapter 7. The usage of the channel coding scheme and coding rate for the uplink shared channel and control information is specified in Table 8.1 and Table 8.2, respectively. The same turbo encoder used for downlink shared channels is also used for uplink shared channels. For control information, the channel coding scheme depends on the type of control information and also on the type of the physical channel that carries the control information. Unlike the downlink, the control information in the uplink can be

Table 8.1 Usage of Channel Coding Scheme and Coding Rate for Uplink Transport Channels

Transport Channel	Coding Scheme	Coding Rate
UL-SCH	Turbo coding	1/3

Table 8.2 Usage of Channel Coding Scheme and Coding Rate for Uplink Control Information

Control Information	Coding Scheme	Coding Rate
UCI	Block coding	Variable
	Tail-biting convolutional coding	1/3

mapped either to the Physical Uplink Shared Channel (PUSCH) or the Physical Uplink Control Channel (PUCCH). Details about channel coding for control information in the uplink are discussed later in Section 8.3.1.

8.1.2 Modulation Processing

For the modulation in the uplink, the various steps such as scrambling and modulation mapping are done in the same way as in the downlink. Unlike downlink, in uplink a UE-specific scrambling is applied in order to randomize the interference. Also, since spatial multiplexing is not supported in the uplink there is no layer mapping or MIMO precoding. The main difference from the downlink comes from the nature of the SC-FDMA-based transmission, which is different from the OFDMA-based transmission that is used in the downlink.

The generation of the SC-FDMA baseband signal is illustrated in Figure 8.2.

1. First, the DFT-based precoding is applied to the block of complex-valued modulation symbols, which transforms the time-domain signal into the frequency domain. In LTE, the DFT size is constrained to be products of the integers two, three, and five, which is a tradeoff between the complexity of the implementation and the flexibility on the assigned bandwidth. The DFT size also depends on the number of resource blocks assigned to the UE.

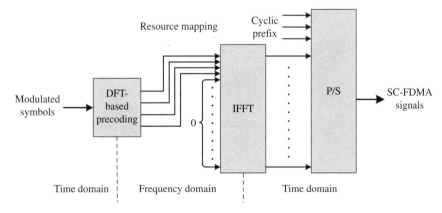

Figure 8.2 Generation of SC-FDMA baseband signals, where P/S denotes the parallel-to-serial converter.

2. Then the output of the DFT-based precoder is mapped to the resource blocks that have been allocated for the transmission of the transport block. In LTE, only localized resource allocation is supported in the uplink, that is, contiguous resource blocks are assigned to each UE.

3. The baseband signal $s_l(t)$ in SC-FDMA symbol l in an uplink slot is defined by:

$$s_l(t) = \sum_{k=-\lfloor N_{RB}^{UL} N_{sc}^{RB}/2 \rfloor}^{\lceil N_{RB}^{UL} N_{sc}^{RB}/2 \rceil - 1} a_{k^{(-)},l} \cdot e^{j2\pi(k+1/2)\Delta f(t - N_{CP,l} T_s)} \tag{8.1}$$

for $0 \leq t < (N_{CP,l} + N) \times T_s$, where $k^{(-)} = k + \lfloor N_{RB}^{UL} N_{sc}^{RB}/2 \rfloor$, N is the FFT size, $\Delta f = 15\text{kHz}$, and $a_{k,l}$ is the content of resource element (k, l). It is generated with an IFFT operation, after which the cyclic prefix (CP) is inserted. Different from the OFDM baseband signal in the downlink, the DC SC-FDMA subcarrier is used in the uplink. Direction conversion will introduce distortion in the DC subcarrier, and in LTE uplink all the subcarriers are shifted by half a subcarrier spacing to reduce this influence. The operation combining DFT-based precoding and IFFT applies to all uplink physical signals and physical channels except the physical random access channel.

Note that the generation of the SC-FDMA signal shares the similar structure as that for the OFDMA signal, with an additional DFT operation.

8.2 Uplink Shared Channels

In this section, we describe the transport channel processing for Uplink Shared Channels (UL-SCH). In the uplink, the UL-SCH is the only transport channel that carries traffic data. As mentioned previously it can also be used to transfer control signals for higher layers. The channel mapping around the UL-SCH is shown in Figure 8.3.

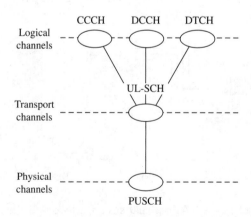

Figure 8.3 Channel mapping around the uplink shared channel.

8.2.1 Channel Encoding and Modulation

The channel coding scheme for data streams on the UL-SCH is the same as that for the DL-SCH. A rate 1/3 turbo encoder is used to encode the transport block. Effective code rates other than 1/3 are achieved by either puncturing or repetition of the encoded bits, depending on the transport block size, the modulation scheme, and the assigned radio resource. The encoded symbols are scrambled prior to modulation, which is done to randomize the interference. Instead of using a cell-specific scrambling as in the downlink, a UE-specific scrambling is applied in the uplink. The UL-SCH is mapped to the PUSCH, which supports QPSK, 16QAM, and 64QAM modulation schemes. The QPSK and 16QAM modulation schemes are mandatory and support for the 64QAM modulation is optional and depends on the UE capability. The modulation order and the redundancy version for the channel coding of the H-ARQ protocol are contained in the 5-bit "modulation and coding scheme and redundancy version" field (I_{MCS}) in the downlink control information (DCI) carried on the PDCCH with format 0.

8.2.2 Frequency Hopping

The resource mapper maps the complex-valued modulation symbols in sequence on to the physical resource blocks assigned for transmission of PUSCH. In LTE, only localized resource allocation is supported in the uplink due to its robustness to frequency offset compared to distributed resource allocation. Localized resource allocation also retains the single-carrier property in the uplink transmission. As a consequence, there is very little frequency diversity gain. On the contrary, in the downlink it is possible to allocate disjoint sets of resource blocks to a UE to extract some frequency diversity gain. To alleviate this issue, LTE supports frequency hopping on PUSCH, which provides additional frequency diversity gain in the uplink. Frequency hopping can also provide interference averaging when the system is not 100% loaded.

In LTE both *intra-subframe* and *inter-subframe* frequency hopping are supported, as illustrated in Figure 8.4. In intra-subframe hopping, the UE hops to another frequency allocation from one slot to another within the same subframe; in inter-subframe hopping, the frequency resource allocation changes from one subframe to another. Higher layers determine if the hopping is "inter-subframe" or "intra- and inter-subframe." In general, "intra-subframe" hopping provides higher frequency diversity gain since this gain can be extracted over a single H-ARQ transmission, which always spans only one subframe. In the case of "inter-subframe" hopping, multiple H-ARQ transmissions are needed in order to extract the frequency diversity gain.

If the single bit Frequency Hopping (FH) field in the corresponding PDCCH with DCI format 0 is set to 1, the UE shall perform PUSCH frequency hopping; otherwise, no PUSCH frequency hopping is performed.

- **No frequency hopping** If uplink frequency hopping is disabled (FH = 0), the set of physical resource blocks to be used for transmission is given by $n_{PRB} = n_{VRB}$, where n_{VRB} is the virtual resource block index obtained from the uplink scheduling grant.

- **Frequency hopping** If uplink frequency hopping is enabled (FH = 1), there are two frequency hopping types. *Type 1 hopping* uses an explicit offset in the second

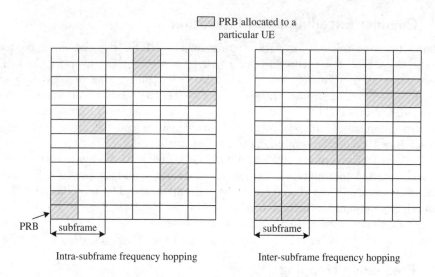

Figure 8.4 Illustrations of frequency hopping on PUSCH.

slot, determined by parameters in DCI format 0. In *Type 2 hopping*, the set of physical resource blocks to be used for transmission is given by the scheduling grant together with a predefined hopping pattern.

The UE first determines the allocated resource blocks after applying all the frequency hopping rules, and then the data is mapped onto these resources.

8.2.3   Multiantenna Transmission

As discussed in Chapter 6, considering cost and complexity of the UE, LTE only supports a limited number of multiantenna transmission schemes in the uplink: a) transmit antenna selection and b) multiuser MIMO (MU-MIMO).

Transmit Antenna Selection

With two or more transmit antennas at the UE, transmit antenna selection can be applied, which is able to provide spatial diversity gain. The multiantenna transmission at the UE depends on the signaling from higher layers.

- **No antenna selection** If transmit antenna selection is disabled or not supported by the UE, the UE shall transmit from antenna port 0.

- **Closed-loop (CL) antenna selection** If CL UE transmit antenna selection is enabled by higher layers, the UE shall perform transmit antenna selection in response to commands received via DCI format 0 from the eNode-B. The DCI format 0 is scrambled with the antenna selection mask as shown in Table 7.12 in Chapter 7, which enables the UE to determine which antenna port to select.

- **Open-loop (OL) antenna selection** If OL UE transmit antenna selection is enabled by higher layers, the transmit antenna to be selected by the UE is not specified. Although in this mode there is no closed-loop feedback from the eNode-B, the UE can determine the optimum antenna based on H-ARQ ACK/NAK feedbacks. The UE can transmit from antenna 0 for some time instance and then switch to antenna 1 for a next time instance. During both of these time instances, the UE also monitors the H-ARQ ACK/NAK ratio. If the ACK/NAK ratio in the time instance when antenna 0 was used is less than the ACK/NAK ratio for the time instance when antenna 1 was used, then clearly antenna 1 is a better choice and vice versa.

MU-MIMO in Uplink

MU-MIMO is supported in the uplink, which is also referred to as "virtual" MIMO transmission. Two UEs transmit simultaneously on the same radio resource, forming a virtual MIMO channel, and the eNode-B separates the data streams for each UE, for example, using multiuser detection. This transmission mode provides a spatial multiplexing gain to increase the uplink spectrum efficiency, even with single-antenna UEs.

The MU-MIMO mode mainly affects the operation at eNode-B, as the Channel Quality Indicator (CQI) calculation and the scheduling process will change due to the interaction between data streams for different UEs. As the eNode-B can estimate the channel information from the uplink reference signal, it is capable of performing CQI calculation and scheduling without further feedback from UEs, which makes it easier to implement MU-MIMO in the uplink than in the downlink. For the eNode-B to differentiate and demodulate signals from the two UEs, orthogonal reference signals are assigned for each of them, which is discussed in Section 8.4.

8.3   Uplink Control Information

The Uplink Control Information (UCI) is to assist physical layer procedures by providing the following types of physical layer control information:

- Downlink CQI, which is used to assist the adaptive modulation and coding and the channel-dependent scheduling of the downlink transmission. The CQI indicates the highest modulation and coding rate that can be supported in the downlink with a 10% block error rate on the first H-ARQ transmission.

- H-ARQ acknowledgment (H-ARQ-ACK) associated with the downlink H-ARQ process.

- Scheduling Request (SR) to request radio resources for the uplink transmission.

- Precoding Matrix Indicator (PMI) and Rank Indication (RI) for downlink MIMO transmission. RI indicates the maximum number of layers that can be used for spatial multiplexing in the downlink, while PMI indicates the preferred precoding matrix.

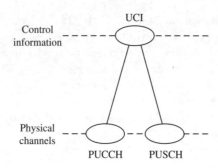

Figure 8.5 Channel mapping for control information in the uplink.

The channel mapping for control information in the uplink is shown in Figure 8.5. Unlike the downlink, which has three different physical control channels, there is only one physical control channel defined for the UCI—the PUCCH. The UCI can also be mapped onto PUSCH when the UE has been assigned uplink radio resources. When this happens, the UCI is frequency-multiplexed with the UL-SCH data on the PUSCH unless the PUSCH carries a random access response grant or a retransmission as part of the contention-based random access procedure. When the UE does not have uplink allocation on the PUSCH, the UCI is transmitted on the PUCCH in the specifically assigned radio resource. In this section, we first describe the channel coding processing for the UCI, which depends on whether it is transmitted on PUCCH or PUSCH, and then modulation and resource mapping for the UCI are discussed. The physical layer procedures related to the UCI transmission such as the CQI and PMI/RI feedback are discussed in Chapter 9.

8.3.1 Channel Coding for Uplink Control Information

As mentioned previously, the UCI can be transmitted on PUCCH, or on PUSCH if there is uplink assignment. The channel coding for UCI therefore depends on whether it is carried on the PUCCH or PUSCH. In addition, different types of control information are encoded differently, which allows individual adjustments of transmission energy using different coding rates.

UCI on PUCCH

When the UCI is transmitted on the PUCCH, three channel coding scenarios are considered: 1) the UCI contains CQI/PMI but not H-ARQ-ACK, 2) the UCI contains H-ARQ-ACK and/or SR but not CQI/PMI, and 3) the UCI contains both CQI/PMI and H-ARQ-ACK. The channel coding processing for each of these scenarios is described in the following:

- **Encoding CQI/PMI** The CQI/PMI is encoded using a $(20, N_{CQI})$ code, with codewords being a linear combination of the 13 basis sequences that are defined in Table 8.3, and N_{CQI} is the number of CQI and PMI bits, which is discussed in Section 9.2. Denote a_i, $i = 1, \ldots, N_{CQI}$ as the input channel quality bits, and the encoding is performed as:

$$b_i = \sum_{n=0}^{N_{CQI}} (a_n \cdot M_{i,n}) \bmod 2, \; i = 0, 1, \ldots, 19. \tag{8.2}$$

- **Encoding H-ARQ-ACK and SR** The H-ARQ-ACK bits and SR indication are received from higher layers. Each positive acknowledgement (ACK) is encoded as a binary '1' while each negative acknowledgment (NAK) is encoded as a binary '0'. There is one H-ARQ-ACK bit for single-codeword transmission and two H-ARQ-ACK bits for two-codeword transmission (spatial multiplexing).

- **Encoding CQI/PMI + H-ARQ-ACK** When CQI/PMI and H-ARQ-ACK are transmitted in the same subframe, the following coding scheme is used:

  - With the normal CP, the CQI/PMI is encoded using the $(20, N_{CQI})$ code as in (8.2), and then the H-ARQ-ACK bits are added at the end of the resulting codeword.

  - With the extended CP, the CQI/PMI and H-ARQ-ACK are jointly encoded using the same $(20, N)$ code as that for encoding CQI/PMI alone, with N as the sum of CQI/PMI bits and H-ARQ-ACK bits.

Table 8.3 Basis Sequences for (20, N) Code

i	$M_{i,0}$	$M_{i,1}$	$M_{i,2}$	$M_{i,3}$	$M_{i,4}$	$M_{i,5}$	$M_{i,6}$	$M_{i,7}$	$M_{i,8}$	$M_{i,9}$	$M_{i,10}$	$M_{i,11}$	$M_{i,12}$
0	1	1	0	0	0	0	0	0	0	0	1	1	0
1	1	1	1	0	0	0	0	0	0	1	1	1	0
2	1	0	0	1	0	0	1	0	1	1	1	1	1
3	1	0	1	1	0	0	0	0	1	0	1	1	1
4	1	1	1	1	0	0	0	1	0	0	1	1	1
5	1	1	0	0	1	0	1	1	1	0	1	1	1
6	1	0	1	0	1	0	1	0	1	1	1	1	1
7	1	0	0	1	1	0	0	1	1	0	1	1	1
8	1	1	0	1	1	0	0	1	0	1	1	1	1
9	1	0	1	1	1	0	1	0	0	1	1	1	1
10	1	0	1	0	0	1	1	1	0	1	1	1	1
11	1	1	1	0	0	1	1	0	1	0	1	1	1
12	1	0	0	1	0	1	0	1	1	1	1	1	1
13	1	1	0	1	0	1	0	1	0	1	1	1	1
14	1	0	0	0	1	1	0	1	0	0	1	0	1
15	1	1	0	0	1	1	1	1	0	1	1	0	1
16	1	1	1	0	1	1	1	0	0	1	0	1	1
17	1	0	0	1	1	1	0	0	1	0	0	1	1
18	1	1	0	1	1	1	1	1	0	0	0	0	0
19	1	0	0	0	0	1	1	0	0	0	0	0	0

Table 8.4 Supported PUCCH Formats

PUCCH Format	Contents	M_{bit}
1	Scheduling Request (SR)	N/A
1a	H-ARQ-ACK, H-ARQ-ACK+SR	1
1b	H-ARQ-ACK, H-ARQ-ACK+SR	2
2	CQI/PMI or RI, (CQI/PMI or RI)+H-ARQ-ACK (extended CP)	20
2a	(CQI/PMI or RI)+H-ARQ-ACK (normal CP)	21
2b	(CQI/PMI or RI)+H-ARQ-ACK (normal CP)	22

Based on different types of control information carried on the PUCCH, there are six different PUCCH formats defined in LTE, as shown in Table 8.4. The parameter M_{bit} is the number of encoded bits for each PUCCH format, which can be easily inferred from the channel coding scheme discussed above. For example, if the UCI carries CQI/PMI only, or carries CQI/PMI and H-ARQ-ACK with the extended CP, the $(20, N_{CQI})$ encoder is applied, so there are 20 coded bits, corresponding to PUCCH format 2. The SR is carried by the presence/absence of transmission of PUCCH from the UE, so there are no extra bits.

UCI on PUSCH with UL-SCH Data

If there is uplink radio resource assigned to the UE, the UCI can be multiplexed with the UL-SCH data on the PUSCH channel and there is no need to send SR. In this case, the channel coding for H-ARQ-ACK, RI, and CQI/PMI is done independently. Different coding rates can be achieved by allocating different numbers of coded symbols, depending on the amount of allocated radio resource.

Coding for H-ARQ-ACK For the FDD mode, there is one or two H-ARQ-ACK bits. For the TDD mode, two ACK/NAK feedback modes are supported,[1] with different information bits:

- ACK/NAK bundling, which consists of one or two bits of information

- ACK/NAK multiplexing, which consists of between one and four bits of information

Denote N_{HARQ} as the number of H-ARQ-ACK bits. For $N_{HARQ} = 1$ or 2, the H-ARQ-ACK bits are first encoded into a $N_{HARQ}Q_m$-bit codeword, with the encoding specified in [2], where Q_m is the modulation order and is equal to 2 for QPSK, 4 for 16QAM, and 6 for 64QAM.

- For both FDD and TDD ACK/NAK multiplexing with $N_{HARQ} \leq 2$, the output sequence from the channel encoder is obtained by concatenating multiple encoded H-ARQ-ACK blocks.

---

1 Different ACK/NAK feedback modes are discussed further in Section 9.1.1.

- For TDD with ACK/NAK bundling, the output sequence from the channel encoder is obtained by scrambling the concatenation of multiple encoded H-ARQ-ACK blocks with a specified scrambling sequence.

- For TDD with ACK/NAK multiplexing with $N_{HARQ} > 2$, the H-ARQ-ACK bits are encoded using a linear combination of a set of basis sequences.

Coding for RI The mapping between the RI bits and the channel rank is shown in Table 8.5. Denote N_{RI} as the number of RI bits. Similar to H-ARQ-ACK, the N_{RI}-bit RI is first encoded into an $N_{RI}Q_m$ codeword, and then multiple encoded RI blocks are concatenated to form a bit sequence.

Coding for CQI/PMI The coding scheme for CQI/PMI depends on the total number of CQI and PMI bits.

- If the payload size N_{CQI} is less than or equal to 11 bits, the CQI/PMI bits are first encoded using a $(32, N_{CQI})$ block code, with the codewords as a linear combination of 11 length-32 basis sequences given in [2]. The 11 basis sequences allow encoding a maximum of 11 CQI/PMI bits. The encoded CQI/PMI block is $b_0, b_1, \ldots, b_{31}$, and then the output bit sequence $q_0, q_1, \ldots, q_Q$ is obtained by circular repetition of the encoded block as $q_i = b_{(i \bmod 32)}$, where $i = 1, 2, \ldots, Q$. The length of the output sequence (Q) depends on the assigned radio resource for PUSCH.

- If $N_{CQI} > 11$, first a CRC is added, and then the tail-biting convolutional code with rate 1/3 described in Section 7.1.1 is used as the coding scheme.

After channel encoding, the CQI encoded sequence is multiplexed with the UL-SCH data, the output of which is interleaved with the RI and H-ARQ-ACK encoded sequence as depicted in Figure 8.6. The multiplexing ensures that control and data information bits are mapped to different modulation symbols. The channel interleaving, together with resource mapping, is to ensure that H-ARQ-ACK information is present on both slots in a subframe and is mapped to the radio resource around the uplink demodulation reference signals. It is done in this way since the H-ARQ ACK/NAK bits are not transmitted with much protection and placing them close to the reference signal ensures that they are decoded properly at the eNode-B.

Table 8.5 RI Mapping

RI Bits	Channel Rank
0	1
1	2
0, 0	1
0, 1	2
1, 0	3
1, 1	4

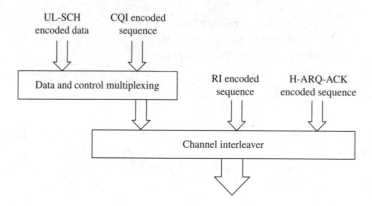

Figure 8.6 Multiplexing of data and control information on the PUSCH channel.

UCI on PUSCH Without UL-SCH Data

For this case, the channel coding for CQI, RI, and H-ARQ-ACK information is performed in the same manner as if the UCI is transmitted with UL-SCH data, and then the coded sequences are interleaved. The same interleaver as in Figure 8.6 is applied without the UL-SCH data.

8.3.2   Modulation of PUCCH

When the UCI is transmitted on the PUSCH, the modulation scheme is determined by the scheduler in the MAC layer. In this subsection, we focus on the scenario when the UCI is transmitted on the PUCCH, that is, no uplink resource is assigned to the UE. The modulation scheme and the number of bits per subframe for different PUCCH formats are specified in Table 8.6. All PUCCH formats use a cyclic shift of a based sequence to transmit in each SC-FDMA symbol, so UCI from multiple UEs can be transmitted on the same radio resource through code division multiplexing (CDM).

Table 8.6 Modulation for Different PUCCH Formats

PUCCH Format	Modulation Scheme	M_{bit}
1	N/A	N/A
1a	BPSK	1
1b	QPSK	2
2	QPSK	20
2a	QPSK+BPSK	21
2b	QPSK+QPSK	22

Table 8.7 Modulation Symbol $d(0)$ for PUCCH Formats 1a and 1b

PUCCH Format	$b(0), b(M_{bit}-1)$	$d(0)$
1a	0	1
	1	-1
1b	00	1
	01	$-j$
	10	j
	11	-1

PUCCH Formats 1, 1a, and 1b

The PUCCH formats 1a and 1b are used to transmit H-ARQ-ACK and/or SR, without CQI bits. When both ACK/NAK and SR are transmitted in the same subframe, a UE shall transmit the ACK/NAK on its assigned ACK/NAK PUCCH resource for a negative SR transmission and transmit the ACK/NAK on its assigned SR PUCCH resource for a positive SR transmission. As shown in Table 8.4, one or two explicit bits are transmitted, respectively, the modulation for which is described in Table 8.7, resulting in a complex-valued symbol $d(0)$. For PUCCH format 1, the SR information is carried by the presence/absence of transmission of the PUCCH from the UE, that is, the on-off keying is applied. When there is an SR, $d(0) = 1$.

Then $d(0)$ is multiplied with a cyclically shifted sequence with length 12, corresponding to 12 subcarriers in each uplink radio resource block. The Zadoff-Chu sequence[2] is used as the base sequence. This achieves frequency-domain CDM and the cyclic shift varies between symbols and slots within a subframe to randomize inter-cell interference. The resulting symbol block is scrambled and block-wise spread with an orthogonal sequence in the time domain, where the sequence length depends on the number of symbols available for transmission in each slot. In this way, multiple UEs' PUCCHs are multiplexed on the same time-frequency resource using frequency-domain and time-domain CDM.

PUCCH Formats 2, 2a, and 2b

As specified in Table 8.4, in each subframe the number of bits for format 2, 2a, or 2b is $M_{bit} \geq 20$. The block of the first 20 bits, $b(0), \ldots, b(19)$, shall be scrambled with a UE-specific scrambling sequence, producing a block of scrambled bits $\tilde{b}(0), \ldots, \tilde{b}(19)$. Then the scrambled bits will be QPSK modulated, resulting in a block of complex-valued

---

2 The Zadoff-Chu sequence [3] is a type of Constant-Amplitude Zero-Auto-Correlation (CAZAC) sequence. It has the constant amplitude property, which means low PAPR that is desirable for uplink transmission. In addition, cyclically shifted versions of the sequence do not cross-correlate with each other when the signal is recovered at the receiver. Due to these properties, the Zadoff-Chu sequence is used for uplink reference signals, random access preambles, and control channels.

Table 8.8 Modulation symbol $d(10)$ for PUCCH formats 2a and 2b

PUCCH Format	$b(20), b(M_{bit}-1)$	$d(10)$
2a	0	1
	1	-1
2b	00	1
	01	$-j$
	10	j
	11	-1

modulation symbols $d(0), \ldots, d(9)$. Similar to formats 1, 1a, and 1b, each of these complex-valued symbols is multiplied with a length-12 cyclically shifted version of a Zadoff-Chu sequence. This allows PUCCHs from multiple UEs to be transmitted on the same resource block with CDM.

For PUCCH formats 2a and 2b that apply only for normal CP, the extra bits $b(20)$, $b(M_{bit} - 1)$ represent ACK/NAK information. The modulation of these H-ARQ-ACK bits are described in Table 8.8. The resulting modulated symbol $d(10)$ will be used in the generation of the reference signal for PUCCH format 2a and 2b, from which the eNode-B can decode the ACK/NAK information.

8.3.3   Resource Mapping

The PUCCH is never transmitted simultaneously with the PUSCH from the same UE, that is, the PUCCH is time-division multiplexed with the PUSCH from the same UE. This is done in order to retain the single-carrier property of SC-FDMA. However, the PUCCH can be frequency-division multiplexed with the PUSCH from other UEs in the same subframe. For frame structure type 2 (the TDD mode), the PUCCH is not transmitted in the UpPTS field, which is only for the transmission of uplink sounding reference signals or random access. If the UE has not been assigned any uplink resource for the UL-SCH transmission, a certain set of uplink resources are assigned for the transmission of the PUCCH. The PUCCH uses one resource block in each of the two slots in a subframe.

The physical resource blocks to be used for PUCCH transmission in slot n_s are given by:

$$n_{PRB} = \begin{cases} \lfloor \frac{m}{2} \rfloor & \text{if } (m + n_s \bmod 2) \bmod 2 = 0 \\ N_{RB}^{UL} - 1 - \lfloor \frac{m}{2} \rfloor & \text{if } (m + n_s \bmod 2) \bmod 2 = 1 \end{cases} \qquad (8.3)$$

where the parameter m depends on the PUCCH format. According to this rule, the mapping of PUCCH to physical resource blocks in one subframe is shown in Figure 8.7 for different values of m. We see that the PUCCH is transmitted at the bandwidth edge, which is to provide the contiguous bandwidth in the middle for data transmission as only

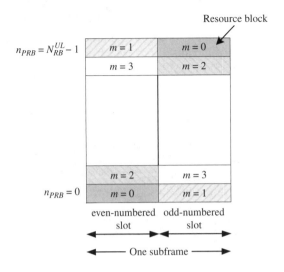

Figure 8.7 Mapping to physical resource blocks for PUCCH.

localized resource allocation is allowed in the uplink. In addition, the frequency hopping between different slots provides frequency diversity. The PUCCH symbols are mapped to resource elements not used for reference signal transmission. The resource mapping of PUCCH symbols within each slot, together with reference symbols, is discussed in Section 8.4.2.

8.4 Uplink Reference Signals

In LTE there are two types of reference signals defined in the uplink:

- **Demodulation reference signals,** which are transmitted on uplink resources assigned to the UE, are for coherent demodulation of data and control information at the eNode-B. As PUCCH cannot be transmitted simultaneously with PUSCH, there are demodulation reference signals defined for each of them, that is, there are demodulation reference signals for PUSCH and demodulation reference signals for PUCCH.

- **Sounding reference signals** are wideband reference signals for the eNode-B to measure uplink channel quality information for uplink resource allocation. They are not associated with the transmission of PUSCH or PUCCH.

The reason for having two types of reference signals in the uplink is because, unlike the downlink, the demodulation reference signals in uplink are only transmitted on subcarriers assigned to the UE and therefore cannot provide sufficient wideband channel quality information for resource allocation, particularly over the resource blocks that are not allocated to the UE. Unlike the downlink, the reference signal in the uplink cannot be transmitted at the same time as user data. Instead, the uplink reference signals are time-division multiplexed with the uplink data on the assigned subcarriers. In this way, the power level of the reference signal can be different from that of the data symbol as they are transmitted over different SC-FDMA symbols, so the PAPR is minimized over each SC-FDMA symbol.

8.4.1 Reference Signal Sequence

Both the demodulation reference signal and the sounding reference signal are defined by a cyclic shift of the same base sequence. The generation of the base sequence depends on the reference signal sequence length, which is $M_{sc}^{RS} = mN_{sc}^{RB}$ with $1 \leq m \leq N_{RB}^{max,UL}$, where m is the size of the resource blocks assigned to the UE.

- If $m \geq 3$ (the UE is assigned three resource blocks or more), the base sequence is based on prime-length Zadoff-Chu sequences that are cyclically extended to the desired length.

- For $m = 1$ or $m = 2$, the base sequence is of the form $e^{j\varphi(n)\pi/4}$, where $0 \leq n \leq M_{sc}^{RS} - 1$ and the value of $\varphi(n)$ is given in [1].

Multiple reference signals can then be created by different shifts of the same base sequence. As the Zadoff-Chu sequence has the property that cyclic shifted versions of the same sequence are orthogonal to each other, generating reference signals in such a manner can reduce inter-cell interference for the reference signal transmission. The orthogonality of reference signals within the same cell is obtained via frequency-domain multiplexing, as the reference signals for each UE are only carried in resource blocks assigned to that UE. The reference signal in the uplink is always UE-specific.

8.4.2 Resource Mapping of Demodulation Reference Signals

The resource mapping of the demodulation reference signal is different for PUSCH and PUCCH channels. In addition, different from the downlink, the reference signals are inserted in the time domain, which is to preserve the low PAPR property of SC-FDMA.

For PUSCH, the demodulation reference signal sequence is mapped to resource elements (k, l) with $l = 3$ for normal CP and $l = 2$ for extended CP, with increasing order first in k and then in the slot number. An example of demodulation reference signal mapping for PUSCH is shown in Figure 8.8, with the normal CP.

As shown in Section 8.3, PUCCH supports six different formats, and the resource mapping to SC-FDMA symbols for different formats is listed in Table 8.9. Note that the number of PUCCH demodulation reference symbols are different for different formats, which is related to the number of control symbols for each format. For example, as discussed in Section 8.3.2, there are 10 CQI/PMI modulated symbols for PUCCH format 2/2a/2b, and there are 2 reference symbols in each slot as shown in Table 8.9, so there are a total of 14 symbols that fill the whole subframe, which is of 14 SC-FDMA symbols. As PUCCH format 1/1a/1b has fewer information bits than PUCCH format 2/2a/2b, there are more reference symbols for format 1/1a/1b than there are for format 2/2a/2b, which can be used to improve the channel estimation performance. The resource mapping

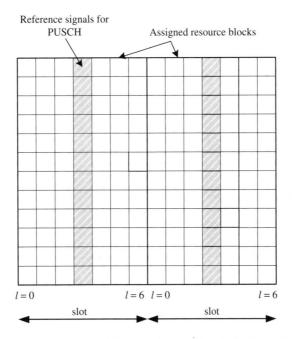

Reference signals for
PUSCH

Assigned resource blocks

$l=0$ $l=6$ $l=0$ $l=6$

slot   slot

Figure 8.8 Resource mapping of demodulation reference signals for PUSCH with the normal CP.

of PUCCH demodulation reference signals, together with PUCCH symbols, which are modulated as in Section 8.3.2, is shown in Figure 8.9 with the normal CP. Note that due to the resource mapping of PUCCH, the two consecutive slots shown in Figure 8.9(a) and 8.9(b) are at the two edges of the whole bandwidth, as in Figure 8.7.

8.4.3 Resource Mapping of Sounding Reference Signals

For the FDD mode, the sounding reference signal is transmitted in the last SC-FDMA symbol in the specified subframe. For the TDD mode, the sounding reference signal is transmitted only in configured uplink subframes or the UpPTS field in the special subframe. The subframes in which the sounding reference signals are transmitted are indicated by the broadcast signaling, and there are 15 different configurations. In the

Table 8.9 Demodulation Reference Signal Location for Different PUCCH Formats

PUCCH Format	Set of Values for l	
	Normal Cyclic Prefix	**Extended Cyclic Prefix**
1, 1a, 1b	2,3,4	2,3
2	1,5	3
2a, 2b	1,5	N/A

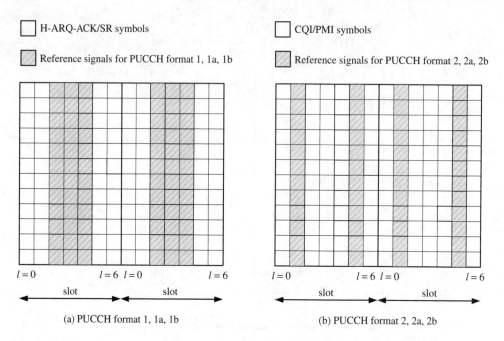

(a) PUCCH format 1, 1a, 1b   (b) PUCCH format 2, 2a, 2b

Figure 8.9 Resource mapping of demodulation reference signals for PUCCH with the normal CP.

frequency domain, the mapping starts from the position k_0, which is determined by system parameters, and fills every other subcarrier. The bandwidth of sounding reference signals is configured by higher layers and also depends on the system bandwidth. An example of resource mapping of sounding reference signals is shown in Figure 8.10.

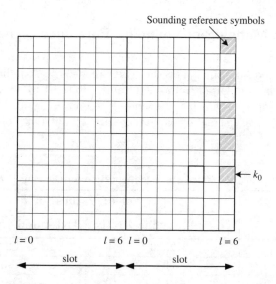

Figure 8.10 An example of resource mapping of sounding reference signals, with the normal CP.

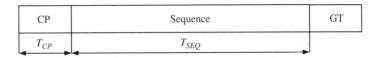

Figure 8.11 The random access preamble format.

The uplink channel sounding procedure is discussed in Section 9.4. By allocating every other subcarrier to a UE for the sounding reference signal, the system allows two UEs to use the same resource for sounding. The second UE uses the subcarriers not used by the first UE.

8.5 Random Access Channels

The uplink random access procedure is used during initial access or to re-establish uplink synchronization. Details about the random access procedure is provided in Chapter 9. In this section, we describe the random access channel that carries random access preambles.

As shown in Figure 8.11, the random access preamble consists of a CP of length T_{CP} and a sequence part of length T_{SEQ}. As uplink synchronization may not be established prior to the random access procedure, a Guard Time (GT) is also needed to account for the round trip propagation delay between the UE and the eNode-B. The values of T_{CP} and T_{SEQ} depend on the cell size and base station implementation. There are five different preamble formats defined in LTE, specified in Table 8.10, where $T_s = 1/(15000 \times 2048)$ sec. Format 0 is for normal cells; format 1, also known as the extended format, is used for large cells; format 2 and format 3 use repeated preamble sequences to compensate for increased path loss, and are used for small cells and large cells, respectively; format 4 is defined for frame structure type 2 only.

The random access preambles are generated from Zadoff-Chu sequences, which are similar to reference signals. The network configures the set of preamble sequences that the UE is allowed to use. In each cell, there are 64 available preambles, which are generated from one or several root Zadoff-Chu sequences. Due to the zero cross-correlation between different cyclic shifts of the same Zadoff-Chu sequence, there is no intra-cell interference from multiple random access attempts using different preambles in the same cell.

Table 8.10 Random Access Preamble Parameters

Preamble Format	T_{CP}	T_{SEQ}
0	$3168 \cdot T_s$	$24576 \cdot T_s$
1	$21024 \cdot T_s$	$24576 \cdot T_s$
2	$6240 \cdot T_s$	$2 \cdot 24576 \cdot T_s$
3	$21024 \cdot T_s$	$2 \cdot 24576 \cdot T_s$
4	$448 \cdot T_s$	$4096 \cdot T_s$

Table 8.11 Parameters for Random Access Preamble

Preamble Format	Δf_{RA}	N_{ZC}	φ
0–3	1.25 kHz	839	7
4	7.5 kHz	139	2

The transmission of a random access preamble is restricted to certain time and frequency resources. The Physical Random Access Channel (PRACH) resources within a radio frame are indicated by a PRACH configuration index, which is given by higher layers. For frame structure type 1 with preamble format 0–3, there is at most one random access resource per subframe; for frame structure type 2 with preamble format 0–4, there might be multiple random access resources in an uplink subframe depending on the uplink/downlink configuration.

In the frequency domain, the random access burst occupies a bandwidth corresponding to six consecutive resource blocks (72 subcarriers) in a subframe or a set of consecutive subframes. The PRACH uses a different subcarrier spacing (Δf_{RA}) than other physical channels, which is listed in Table 8.11 together with the preamble sequence length N_{ZC}. Note that the data symbol subcarrier spacing $\Delta f = 15$kHz is an integer multiple of the PRACH subcarrier spacing Δf_{RA}. This is to minimize the orthogonality loss in the frequency domain and can also reuse the IFFT/FFT component.

The baseband signal generation for the PRACH is different from other uplink physical channels, and no DFT-based precoding is applied, as the DFT of a Zadoff-Chu sequence is also a Zadoff-Chu sequence. The continuous-time random access signal is defined by:

$$s(t) = \beta \sum_{k=0}^{N_{ZC}-1} \sum_{n=0}^{N_{ZC}-1} x_{u,v}(n) \cdot e^{-j\frac{2\pi nk}{N_{ZC}}} \cdot e^{j2\pi(k+\varphi+K(k_0+1/2))\Delta f_{RA}(t-T_{CP})}, \qquad (8.4)$$

where $0 \leq t \leq (T_{SEQ} + T_{CP})$ and:

- β is an amplitude scaling factor for power control;

- $x_{u,v}(n)$ is the uth root Zadoff-Chu sequence with cyclic shift v;

- φ is a fixed offset determining the frequency-domain location of the random preamble within the physical resource blocks, given in Table 8.11;

- $K = \Delta f/\Delta f_{RA}$ accounts for the difference in subcarrier spacing between the random access preamble and uplink data transmission;

- $k_0 = n_{PRB}^{RA} N_{sc}^{RB} - N_{RB}^{UL} N_{sc}^{RB}/2$ controls the random access preamble location in the frequency domain, with $0 \leq n_{PRB}^{RA} \leq (N_{RB}^{UL} - 6)$ as the physical resource block number configured by higher layers.

8.6   H-ARQ in the Uplink

As in the downlink, the H-ARQ retransmission protocol is also used in the LTE uplink, so the eNode-B has the capability to request retransmissions of incorrectly received data packets. For the uplink H-ARQ process, the corresponding ACK/NAK information is carried on the PHICH, for which the coding and modulation processing was discussed in Chapter 7.

LTE uplink applies the synchronous H-ARQ protocol, that is, the retransmissions are scheduled on a periodic interval unlike downlink where the scheduler determines the timing of retransmissions. Synchronous retransmission is preferred in the uplink because it does not require to explicitly signal the H-ARQ process number so there is less protocol overhead. The number of H-ARQ processes and the time interval between the transmission and retransmission depend on the duplexing mode and the H-ARQ operation type, discussed later in this section.

There are two types of H-ARQ operation in the uplink: the non-subframe bundling operation (normal H-ARQ operation), and the subframe bundling operation (also called TTI[3] bundling), in which four redundancy versions are transmitted over four consecutive uplink subframes. This essentially is the same as sending four H-ARQ retransmissions back to back without waiting for the H-ARQ ACK/NAK feedback. When TTI bundling is used, the eNode-B waits for four TTIs to receive and decode the four redundancy versions jointly before sending an H-ARQ ACK/NAK over the PHICH in the downlink. Similar to the downlink, the N-channel Stop-and-Wait protocol is used in the uplink.

8.6.1   The FDD Mode

For the FDD mode, there are eight parallel H-ARQ processes in the uplink for the non-subframe bundling operation, and four H-ARQ processes for the subframe bundling operation. For the FDD mode with the normal H-ARQ operation, upon detection of an NAK in subframe n, the UE retransmits the corresponding PUSCH in subframe $n + 4$; for the FDD mode with the subframe bundling operation, upon detection of an NAK in subframe $n - 5$, the UE retransmits the corresponding first PUSCH transmission in the bundle in subframe $n + 4$.

8.6.2   The TDD Mode

For the TDD mode, the number of H-ARQ processes is determined by the DL/UL configuration, listed in Table 8.12.

- For TDD UL/DL configurations 1–6 and the normal H-ARQ operation, upon detection of an NAK in subframe n, the UE retransmits in subframe $n + k$, with k given in Table 8.13.

---

3 Transmission Time Interval, defined in Section 6.2.2.

Table 8.12 Number of Synchronous UL H-ARQ Processes for TDD

TDD UL/DL Configuration	Number of H-ARQ Processes for Normal H-ARQ Operation	Number of H-ARQ Processes for Subframe Bundling Operation
0	7	3
1	4	2
2	2	N/A
3	3	N/A
4	2	N/A
5	1	N/A
6	6	3

- For TDD UL/DL configuration 0 and the normal H-ARQ operation, upon detection of an NAK in subframe n, the UE will retransmit in subframe $n+7$ or $n+k$ with k given in Table 8.13, which depends on the UL index field in DCI and the value of n.

- For TDD UL/DL configurations 1 and 6 with subframe bundling, upon detection of an NAK in subframe $n-l$ with l given in Table 8.14, the UE retransmits the corresponding first PUSCH transmission in the bundle in subframe $n+k$, with k given in Table 8.13.

- For TDD UL/DL configuration 0 and the subframe bundling operation, upon detection of an NAK in subframe $n-l$ with l given in Table 8.14, the UE retransmits in subframe $n+7$ or $n+k$ with k given in Table 8.13, depending on the UL index field in DCI and the value of n.

Table 8.13 The Value of k for TDD Configurations 0–6

TDD UL/DL Configuration	DL Subframe Number n									
	0	1	2	3	4	5	6	7	8	9
0	4	6				4	6			
1		6			4		6			4
2				4					4	
3	4								4	4
4									4	4
5									4	
6	7	7				7	7			5

Table 8.14 The Value of *l* for TDD Configurations 0, 1, and 6

TDD UL/DL Configuration	DL Subframe Number n									
	0	**1**	**2**	**3**	**4**	**5**	**6**	**7**	**8**	**9**
0	9	6				9	6			
1		2		3		2				3
6	5	5				6	6			8

8.7 Summary and Conclusions

In this chapter we described the physical layer processing for uplink transport channels. The processing in the uplink shares similarities with the downlink but also has some differences, which we highlighted in this chapter.

- Downlink and uplink share similar coding and modulation procedures. Different from the downlink, the uplink transmission is based on SC-FDMA, so the baseband signal generation is different. Uplink shared channels only support localized resource allocation, and frequency hopping is introduced to increase frequency diversity. For MIMO transmission, transmit antenna selection and MU-MIMO (or virtual MIMO) are supported in the uplink.

- If uplink resource is assigned for the UE, the UCI is multiplexed with the uplink data stream on the PUSCH; otherwise, the UCI is carried on the PUCCH that is time-division multiplexed with the PUSCH from the same UE. Multiple UEs' PUCCHs are transmitted on the same resource blocks with CDM. Different contents in UCI have different coding and modulation schemes.

- There are two types of reference signals defined in the uplink: demodulation reference signals for coherent demodulation, and sounding reference signals to assist the uplink scheduling. The uplink reference signals are time-division multiplexed with the uplink data.

- LTE uplink supports the H-ARQ protocol with synchronous retransmission. The number of H-ARQ processes and the time interval between the transmission and retransmission depend on the duplexing mode and the H-ARQ operation type.

Bibliography

[1] 3GPP TS 36.211: "Evolved Universal Terrestrial Radio Access (E-UTRA); Physical channels and modulation."

[2] 3GPP TS 36.212: "Evolved Universal Terrestrial Radio Access (E-UTRA); Multiplexing and channel coding."

[3] Chu, D. C. "Polyphase codes with good periodic correlation properties," *IEEE Transaction on Information Theory*, 18(4): 531–532, July 1972.

Chapter 9

Physical Layer Procedures and Scheduling

In previous chapters, we have described the hierarchical channel structure, the physical radio resource structure, and transport channel processing of the LTE radio interface. In this chapter, we specify the physical layer procedures that provide crucial services to higher layers. Dynamic channel-dependent scheduling and MIMO transmission, including open-loop (OL) and closed-loop (CL) MIMO modes, are two key features of LTE that provide high-spectrum efficiency, both of which require specific feedback support and signaling. Channel Quality Indicator (CQI) feedback and channel sounding provide channel quality information (signal to noise ratio) for downlink and uplink, respectively. The Rank Indicator (RI) and Precoder Matrix Indicator (PMI) feedback are reported from UEs to support the different MIMO modes and enable dynamic switching between them. However, resources in the uplink are limited, so keeping the overhead low requires careful design of uplink reporting. In this chapter we also describe the various aspects of the different scheduling algorithms that are enabled in LTE. The type of scheduling used depends on the nature of the data traffic and its QoS requirements. In this chapter we also discuss the synchronization procedures used by the UE through cell search and random access procedures.

We first describe feedback procedures to enable dynamic scheduling, adaptive MIMO transmission, including H-ARQ ACK/NAK feedback, CQI reporting, and RI and PMI feedback. For uplink scheduling, channel sounding provides uplink channel quality information at the eNode-B and buffer status reporting from UEs are discussed. Then the signaling required for the dynamic scheduling of data traffic and semi-persistent scheduling of VoIP services are described. Finally, the network access procedure and uplink power control are discussed.

9.1 Hybrid-ARQ Feedback

In LTE, the H-ARQ protocol is applied to improve the transmission reliability over the wireless channel, as discussed in Section 7.7 and Section 8.6 for downlink and uplink, respectively, also tutored in Chapter 2 (Section 2.6.4). The LTE downlink employs the asynchronous adaptive H-ARQ protocol, for which the retransmissions are scheduled in a similar fashion to the first transmission, i.e., the TTI and resource allocation for the retransmission is dynamically determined by the scheduler. In the uplink, synchronous adaptive H-ARQ protocol is used, for which the retransmissions are automatically scheduled after a certain time window and the UE does not need to send the H-ARQ process number. This reduces the amount of signaling overhead in the uplink. With different frame structures, the H-ARQ feedback is different for FDD and TDD modes. In this section, we discuss the H-ARQ feedback for both downlink and uplink transmissions.

9.1.1 H-ARQ Feedback for Downlink (DL) Transmission

For H-ARQ transmissions in the downlink, UEs need to feed back the associated ACK/NAK information on PUCCH or PUSCH. One ACK/NAK bit is transmitted in case of single-codeword downlink transmission, while two ACK/NAK bits are transmitted in case of two-codeword downlink transmission. For two-codeword transmission, codeword swap is enabled by a 1-bit transport block to codeword swap flag, which allows both codewords to experience similar channel conditions after H-ARQ retransmission when the channel is static or experiences little or no variation between subsequent H-ARQ transmissions. The coding and modulation for ACK/NAK bits were discussed in Section 8.3.

For the FDD mode, the UE transmits H-ARQ-ACK in subframe n for a PDSCH transmission in subframe $n - 4$. When both H-ARQ-ACK and Scheduling Request (SR) are transmitted in the same subframe, i.e., with PUCCH format 1a or 1b, a UE shall transmit the H-ARQ-ACK on its associated H-ARQ-ACK PUCCH resource for a negative SR transmission and transmit the H-ARQ-ACK on its assigned SR PUCCH resource for a positive SR transmission.

For the TDD mode, in asymmetric uplink/downlink cases with more downlink subframes than uplink subframes, it may happen that more than one acknowledgment needs to be sent in a certain UL subframe. Therefore, H-ARQ reporting is different from the FDD mode. For TDD, two ACK/NAK feedback modes are supported by higher layer configuration:

- ACK/NAK bundling using PUCCH format 1a or 1b, which is the default mode and consists of one or two bits of information

- ACK/NAK multiplexing using PUCCH format 1b, which consists of between one and four bits of information

The feedback of H-ARQ-ACK in the UL subframe n corresponds to the detection of the PDSCH transmission within subframe(s) $n - k$, where the parameter k is different for different UL/DL configurations and different subframes, and $k \in K$ with K specified in Table 9.1. We see that for some UL/DL configurations and in some subframes multiple acknowledgments are needed, with a maximum number of 4, so the number of information bits for ACK/NAK multiplexing is between one and four. For ACK/NAK bundling, multiple acknowledgments are combined by a logical AND operation, and then the bundled 1 or 2 ACK/NAK bits are transmitted using PUCCH format 1a and PUCCH format 1b, respectively.

Table 9.1 Downlink Association Set Index $K : \{k_0, k_1, \ldots, k_{M-1}\}$ for TDD

TDD UL/DL	Subframe n									
Configuration	0	1	2	3	4	5	6	7	8	9
0			6		4			6		4
1			7,6	4			7,6	4		
2			8,7,4,6				8,7,4,6			
3			7,6,11	6,5	5,4					
4			12,8,7,11	6,5,4,7						
5			TBD							
6			7	7	5		7	7		

9.1.2   H-ARQ Indicator for Uplink (UL) Transmission

For the uplink H-ARQ process, as spatial multiplexing of transport blocks is not supported, only a single-bit H-ARQ Indicator (HI) needs to be sent to each scheduled UE, which is carried on the PHICH physical channel. The coding and modulation for HI were discussed in Section 7.3.2.

For the FDD mode, an ACK/NAK received on the PHICH assigned to a UE in subframe n is associated with the PUSCH transmission in subframe $n - 4$. For the TDD mode, different from the feedback for downlink transmission, there is no problem to transmit multiple acknowledgments on PHICH, as discussed in Section 7.3.2. For UL/DL configurations 1–6, an ACK/NAK received on the PHICH in subframe n is associated with the PUSCH transmission in the subframe $n - k$ as indicated in Table 9.2. For TDD with UL/DL configuration 0:

1. If there is PUSCH transmission in subframe 4 or 9, an ACK/NAK received on the PHICH in subframe n is associated with the PUSCH transmission in the subframe $n - 6$.

2. Otherwise, an ACK/NAK received on the PHICH in subframe n is associated with the PUSCH transmission in the subframe $n - k$ with k indicated in Table 9.2.

Table 9.2 The Value of k for TDD Configurations 0–6

TDD UL/DL	DL Subframe Number n									
Configuration	0	1	2	3	4	5	6	7	8	9
0	7	4				7	4			
1		4			6		4			6
2				6				6		
3	6								6	6
4									6	6
5									6	
6	6	4				7	4			6

9.2   Channel Quality Indicator (CQI) Feedback

The Channel Quality Indicator (CQI) contains information sent from a UE to the eNode-B to indicate a suitable downlink transmission data rate, i.e., a Modulation and Coding Scheme (MCS) value. CQI is a 4-bit integer and is based on the observed signal-to-interference-plus-noise ratio (SINR) at the UE. The CQI estimation process takes into account the UE capability such as the number of antennas and the type of receiver used for detection. This is important since for the same SINR value the MCS level that can be supported by a UE depends on these various UE capabilities, which needs to be taken into account in order for the eNode-B to select an optimum MCS level for the transmission. The CQI reported values are used by the eNode-B for downlink scheduling and link adaptation, which are important features of LTE.

LTE supports wideband and subband CQI reporting. A wideband CQI value is a single 4-bit integer that represents an *effective* SINR as observed by the UE over the entire channel bandwidth. With wideband CQI, the variation in the SINR across the channel due to frequency selective nature of the channel is masked out. Therefore, frequency selective scheduling where a UE is placed only in resource blocks with high SINR is not possible with wideband CQI reporting. To support frequency selective scheduling, each UE needs to report the CQI with a fine frequency granularity, which is possible with subband CQI reporting. A subband CQI report consists of a vector of CQI values where each CQI value is representative of the SINR observed by the UE over a subband. A subband is a collection of n adjacent Physical Resource Blocks (PRBs) where the value of n can be 2, 3, 4, 6, or 8 depending on the channel bandwidth and the CQI feedback mode. The various CQI feedback modes are discussed in further detail later in Section 9.2.2.

One of the critical aspects of designing the CQI feedback mechanism for LTE is the optimization between the downlink system performance and the uplink bandwidth consumed by the feedback mechanism. The wideband CQI is the most efficient in terms of uplink bandwidth consumption since it requires only a single 4-bit feedback. However, this is not the optimum feedback mechanism since frequency selective scheduling cannot be done using a wideband CQI feedback. On the other hand, subband CQI feedback requires more uplink bandwidth but is more efficient since it allows for a frequency selective scheduling, which maximizes the multiuser diversity gain of an OFDMA system. Wideband CQI is the preferred mode to use for high speeds where the channel changes rapidly since frequent subband reporting would exhaust a large portion of the uplink bandwidth. Wideband CQI is also the preferred mode for services such as VoIP where a large number of simultaneous UEs are supported and latency is more critical than the overall throughput since VoIP is typically a low data rate application with very strict latency requirement. The LTE standard does not specify how to select between wideband and subband CQI reporting depending on the UE speed or the QoS requirements of the application. It is left up to the equipment manufacturer to develop their proprietary algorithms in order to accomplish this.

In this section, we first describe the CQI estimation, and then move on to detailed discussion about different CQI reporting modes.

9.2.1 A Primer on CQI Estimation

Downlink cell-specific reference signals as discussed in Section 7.6.1 are used by each UE to estimate the MIMO channel from the eNode-B. The estimated MIMO channel along with the known reference signal is then used to calculate the other-cell interference level. The UE uses the estimated channel and interference plus noise variance to compute the SINR on the physical resource element (PRE) carrying the reference signal. The UE computes SINR samples over multiple OFDM symbols and subcarriers, which are then used to calculate an *effective SINR*. The effective SINR is given as:

$$
\text{SINR}_{\text{eff}} = \alpha_1 I^{-1} \left(\frac{1}{N} \sum_{k=1}^{N} I \left(\frac{\text{SINR}_k}{\alpha_2} \right) \right)
\tag{9.1}
$$

where N is the number of samples. The function $I(\cdot)$ maps the SINR to a performance metric that is averaged over all the samples, and $I^{-1}(\cdot)$ is its inverse. The parameters α_1 and α_2 adapt to different modulation and coding schemes. The most commonly used functions for I are

- Identity function: $I(\gamma) = \gamma$;

- Shannon capacity: $I(\gamma) = \log_2(1 + \gamma)$;

- Exponential Effective SINR Mapping (EESM): $I(\gamma) = e^{-\gamma}$;

- Mutual Information Equivalent SINR Mapping (MIESM) or modulation constrained capacity:

$$
I(\gamma) = \log_2(M) + \frac{1}{2\pi M} \sum_{m=1}^{M-1} \int e^{-\gamma(y-x_m)^2} \log_2 \left\{ \frac{e^{-\gamma(y-x_m)^2}}{\sum_{k=0}^{M-1} e^{-\gamma(y-x_k)^2}} \right\} dy, \tag{9.2}
$$

where M is the size of the modulation alphabet (4 for QPSK, 16 for 16QAM, and 64 for 64QAM), and x_m are the modulation symbols.

The EESM and the mutual information-based methods are preferred since they have been shown to give a more accurate estimate of the channel quality [6].

In the case of wideband CQI feedback, the UE measures the SINR from the reference signal over all the PRBs, and then computes its CQI based on the effective SINR across the entire channel bandwidth. On the other hand, for subband CQI the UE measures the SINR over the PRBs contained in the given subband, and then computes the CQI. A subband is a set of k contiguous PRBs where k is semi-statically configured by higher layers. The set of subbands ($\mathcal{S}$) a UE shall evaluate for CQI reporting spans the entire downlink system bandwidth. Note that the last subband in the set $\mathcal{S}$ may have fewer than k contiguous PRBs depending on N_{RB}^{DL}. The number of subbands for a system bandwidth given by N_{RB}^{DL} is determined by:

$$
N = \lceil N_{RB}^{DL}/k \rceil. \tag{9.3}
$$

If a UE reports a CQI value for a particular subband, it is called *subband feedback*; if a UE reports a single CQI value for the set $\mathcal{S}$, i.e., the whole system bandwidth, it is called *wideband feedback*.

Based on the estimated effective SINR, the UE picks the CQI index that indicates the highest MCS level (modulation and code rate) that can be supported with a 10% BLER on the first H-ARQ transmission. The CQI feedback is used by the eNode-B to select an optimum PDSCH transport block with a combination of modulation scheme and transport block size corresponding to the CQI index that could be received with target block error probability after the first H-ARQ transmission. While this target block error probability is left open as an implementation choice, typical values are in the range of 10–25%. It should be noted that the target BLER of the transmission is not the same as the BLER of 10% based on which the CQI is computed. Thus, the eNode-B needs to take this into account while selecting the optimum transport block size. If the achieved block error rate is not equal to the target value based on the H-ARQ ACK/NAK ratio, then a fudge factor can be added to the CQI to ensure that the selection of the block size based on the CQI leads to the desired target block error rate. A positive fudge factor implies a more aggressive transport block size selection, whereas a negative fudge factor implies a more conservative transport block size selection.

The supported CQI indices and their interpretations are given in Table 9.3. In total, there are 16 CQI values, which require a 4-bit CQI feedback. In Table 9.3, the efficiency for a given CQI index is calculated as:

$$\text{efficiency} = Q_m \times \text{code rate}, \tag{9.4}$$

Table 9.3 4-Bit CQI Table

CQI Index	Modulation	Code Rate × 1024	Efficiency
0	out of range		
1	QPSK	78	0.1523
2	QPSK	120	0.2344
3	QPSK	193	0.3770
4	QPSK	308	0.6016
5	QPSK	449	0.8770
6	QPSK	602	1.1758
7	16QAM	378	1.4766
8	16QAM	490	1.9141
9	16QAM	616	2.4063
10	64QAM	466	2.7305
11	64QAM	567	3.3223
12	64QAM	666	3.9023
13	64QAM	772	4.5234
14	64QAM	873	5.1152
15	64QAM	948	5.5547

where Q_m is the number of bits in the modulation constellation. Taking CQI index 4 as an example, as $Q_m = 2$ for QPSK, we have

$$\text{efficiency} = 2 \times \frac{308}{1024} \approx 0.6016 \text{ information bits/symbol.}$$

9.2.2 CQI Feedback Modes

CQI is reported with other uplink control information including Precoder Matrix Indicator (PMI) and Rank Indicator (RI) on PUSCH or PUCCH. The reporting of CQI, PMI, and RI in the time domain can be categorized into two classes:

- **Periodic reporting:** The UE reports CQI, PMI, and RI with reporting periods configured by the higher layer on the PUCCH. If the UE is scheduled in the uplink, the periodic reporting is carried on PUSCH.

- **Aperiodic reporting:** The UE reports CQI, PMI, and RI using the PUSCH upon receiving either a DCI format 0 or a random access response grant. Feedback via PUSCH can be used to provide large and more detailed reporting in a single reporting instance compared to the periodic feedback.

In cases where both periodic reporting on the PUCCH and the aperiodic reporting PUSCH happen to be on the same subframe, the UE will only transmit the aperiodic report over the PUSCH and ignore the periodic PUCCH report.

As we discussed previously, in the frequency domain the CQI reporting can be classified as subband CQI and wideband CQI. Both periodic and aperiodic reporting modes support wideband and subband CQI reporting. In the case of periodic CQI reporting mode when subband CQI is requested, the UE cycles through the different subbands from one reporting instance to the next. This allows for subband CQI reporting without requiring too much overhead in the uplink. The only problem with this is that it could take a while for the eNode-B to develop a complete picture in order to effectively utilize the CQI information for frequency selective scheduling. For aperiodic reporting, the UE can report the subband CQI across all the bands in one single report. This is possible since the available bandwidth on PUSCH is much larger than that of PUCCH. In LTE there are two distinct reporting mechanisms for subband CQI feedback when the aperiodic reporting mode is used:

- **Higher Layer Configured Subband Report:** In this case, the UE reports the subband CQI for each band in a single feedback report. The size of a band is specified by a higher layer message and is contingent on the system bandwidth.

- **UE Selected Subband Report:** In this case, the UE reports the subband CQI for the 'M' bands with the highest CQI values. The CQI for the rest of the bands is not reported. In this case, the value of M and the size of a band is given by a higher layer message and is also contingent on the system bandwidth.

Figure 9.1 shows the average per sector downlink throughput for the various wideband and subband CQI feedback modes. The results are typical of a 10MHz FDD system in a multicell deployment.

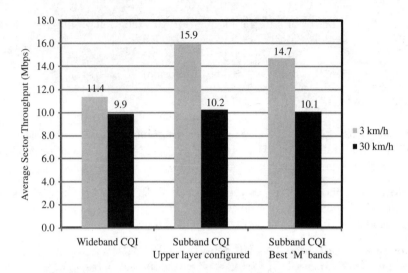

Figure 9.1 The average downlink throughput per sector for various CQI feedback modes.

Each reporting class supports a number of different *reporting modes*, where each reporting mode is characterized by a specific CQI feedback type and a PMI feedback type, which are listed in Table 9.4 and Table 9.5 for periodic reporting and aperiodic reporting, respectively. There are seven *transmission modes* in the downlink, as described in Section 7.2.2, and each of them supports a specific subset of the reporting modes, the details of which are shown in Table 9.6. In the remainder of this subsection, details about different CQI feedback modes are described.

Periodic CQI Reporting

First, we describe periodic CQI reporting, where a UE is semi-statically configured by higher layers to periodically feed back CQI on the PUCCH in one of the reporting modes given in Table 9.4. Note that mode 1-0 and 2-0 do not report PMI and they are used for OL MIMO modes and single-antenna port transmission. Mode 1-1 and mode 2-1

Table 9.4 CQI and PMI Feedback Types for Periodic PUCCH Reporting Modes

PUCCH CQI Feedback Type	PMI Feedback Type	
	No PMI	Single PMI
Wideband (Wideband CQI)	Mode 1-0	Mode 1-1
UE Selected (Subband CQI)	Mode 2-0	Mode 2-1

Table 9.5 CQI and PMI Feedback Types for Aperiodic PUSCH Reporting Modes

PUSCH CQI Feedback Type	PMI Feedback Type		
	No PMI	Single PMI	Multiple PMI
Wideband (Wideband CQI)			Mode 1-2
UE Selected (Subband CQI)	Mode 2-0		Mode 2-2
Higher Layer-Configured (Subband CQI)	Mode 3-0	Mode 3-1	

report a single PMI for CL MIMO modes, i.e., only the wideband PMI is reported. The periodic CQI feedback is useful for scheduling and adaptive modulation and coding, and can also be used to check or change semi-static parameters such as the MIMO mode or transmission mode.

Considering the reporting for CQI/PMI and RI, there are four different reporting types supported for each of these reporting modes as given in Table 9.7:

- Type 1 report supports CQI feedback for the UE selected subbands.

- Type 2 report supports wideband CQI and PMI feedback.

- Type 3 report supports RI feedback.

- Type 4 report supports wideband CQI.

Periodic reporting supports both UE-selected subband reporting and wideband reporting. In the following, we will first describe these two reporting types, and then describe the reporting period for each type.

Table 9.6 The Supporting CQI Reporting Modes for Different Transmission Modes

Transmission Mode	Periodic Reporting Mode	Aperiodic Reporting Mode
1. Single-antenna port, port 0	Modes 1-0, 2-0	Modes 2-0, 3-0
2. Transmit diversity	Modes 1-0, 2-0	Modes 2-0, 3-0
3. Open-loop spatial multiplexing	Modes 1-0, 2-0	Modes 2-0, 3-0
4. Closed-loop spatial multiplexing	Modes 1-1, 2-1	Modes 1-2, 2-2, 3-1
5. Multiuser MIMO	Modes 1-1, 2-1	Mode 3-1
6. Closed-loop Rank = 1 precoding	Modes 1-1, 2-1	Modes 1-2, 2-2, 3-1
7. Single-antenna port, port 5	Modes 1-0, 2-0	Modes 2-0, 3-0

Table 9.7 PUCCH Report Type Payload Size Per Reporting Mode

PUCCH Report Type	Mode State	PUCCH Reporting Modes			
		Mode 1-1 (bits/BP)	Mode 2-1 (bits/BP)	Mode 1-0 (bits/BP)	Mode 2-0 (bits/BP)
1. Subband CQI	RI= 1	NA	4+L	NA	4+L
	RI > 1	NA	7+L	NA	4+L
2. Wideband CQI/PMI	2 TX Antennas RI= 1	6	6	NA	NA
	4 TX Antennas RI= 1	8	8	NA	NA
	2 TX Antenna RI > 1	8	8	NA	NA
	4 TX Antennas RI > 1	11	11	NA	NA
3. RI	2-layer spatial multiplexing	1	1	1	1
	4-layer spatial multiplexing	2	2	2	2
4. Wideband CQI	RI= 1	NA	NA	4	4

UE-Selected Subband CQI   For the UE-selected subband CQI, a CQI report describes the channel quality in a particular part of the bandwidth. For this reporting type, two concepts are important to understand the feedback scheme:

- **Subband:** The system bandwidth, given by N_{RB}^{DL}, is divided into N subbands, where $\lfloor N_{RB}^{DL}/k \rfloor$ subbands are of size k and one is of size $N_{RB}^{DL} - k \cdot \lfloor N_{RB}^{DL}/k \rfloor$. The CQI report is for one of these subbands.

- **Bandwidth part:** A bandwidth part (BP) j consists of N_J consecutive subbands, and a total of J BPs span the system bandwidth N_{RB}^{DL}. If $J = 1$, then $N_J = \lceil N_{RB}^{DL}/k \rceil$. If $J > 1$, then $N_J = \lceil N_{RB}^{DL}/k/J \rceil$ or $N_J = \lceil N_{RB}^{DL}/k/J \rceil - 1$, depending on the values of N_{RB}^{DL}, k, and J.

The subband size k and the number of BPs J are given in Table 9.8 for different bandwidths. An example of $N_{RB}^{DL} = 24$ is shown in Figure 9.2, with $k = 4$ and $J = 2$. The UE selects the single subband with the best CQI out of N_J subbands of the j-th BP and feeds back the corresponding CQI together with an L-bit label where $L = \lceil \log_2 \lceil N_{RB}^{DL}/k/J \rceil \rceil$. From Table 9.8, we see that the value of L is 1 or 2. The value of j (the BP index) is determined by $j = \text{mod}(N_{SF}, J)$, where N_{SF} is a counter that a UE increments after each subband report transmission, so it does not need to be fed back to the eNode-B. Therefore, the UE-selected subband reporting only selects to report CQI for a subband from a certain BP but not from the whole bandwidth, which reduces the feedback overhead.

Table 9.8 Subband Size (k) and Bandwidth Parts (J) vs. Downlink System Bandwidth in Periodic Reporting

System Bandwidth N_{RB}^{DL}	Subband Size (k)	Bandwidth Parts (J)
6–7	NA	NA
8–10	4	1
11–26	4	2
27–63	6	3
64–110	8	4

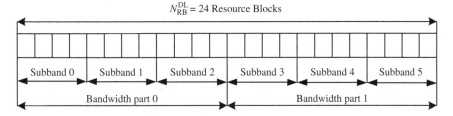

Figure 9.2 The structure of subbands and bandwidth parts.

The number of CQI feedback bits for type 1 subband CQI reporting is shown in Table 9.7. For mode 2-0, the feedback consists of a 4-bit CQI and an L-bit subband label. For OL spatial multiplexing, the preferred subband selection and CQI calculation are conditioned on the last reported RI; for other transmission modes, they are calculated conditioned on RI = 1. For mode 2-1, the feedback consists of an L-bit subband label and a 4-bit or 7-bit CQI, where the 4-bit CQI is for single-codeword CL spatial multiplexing and the 7-bit CQI is for two-codeword CL spatial multiplexing, with 4 bits for codeword 0 and 3 bits for the spatial differential value for codeword 1. The 3-bit spatial differential CQI value for codeword 1 is defined by:

$$\text{Codeword 1 offset level} = \text{CQI index for codeword 0} - \text{CQI index for codeword 1.} \tag{9.5}$$

The mapping from the 3-bit spatial differential value to the offset level is shown in Table 9.9. For CL spatial multiplexing, the subband selection and CQI values are calculated conditioned on the last reported wideband PMI and RI; for other transmission modes, they are calculated conditioned on the last reported PMI and RI = 1.

Wideband CQI For wideband CQI, a CQI report describes the channel quality over the set $\mathcal{S}$ of all the subbands. Different reporting modes with wideband CQI are described as follows:

- For single-antenna port and transmit diversity, as well as OL spatial multiplexing, i.e., for mode 1-0 and 2-0, a single 4-bit CQI is reported.

- The reporting is similar for mode 1-1 and 2-1. The feedback consists of a 4-bit (for single-codeword spatial multiplexing) or 7-bit CQI (for two-codeword spatial

Table 9.9 Mapping Spatial Differential CQI Value to Offset Level

Subband Differential CQI Value	Offset Level
0	0
1	1
2	2
3	≥ 3
4	≤ -4
5	-3
6	-2
7	-1

multiplexing) and a single PMI. The single PMI is selected assuming transmission on set S subbands and conditioned on the last reported periodic RI. The wideband CQI value is calculated assuming the use of the selected PMI in all subbands.

Based on these rules, together with the PMI feedback that will be discussed in Section 9.3, we are able to determine the payload size for each reporting mode in Table 9.7. For example, the payload size for reporting type 2 is 8 bits (RI = 1) or 11 bits (RI > 1) for mode 1-1 and 2-1, which consists of a 4-bit PMI and a 4-bit or 7-bit CQI.

Reporting Period   The reporting periods for the CQI feedback depend on the reporting type:

- The period N_p of the subband CQI reporting is selected from the set $\{2, 5, 10, 20, 40, 80, 160, \text{OFF}\}$ for the FDD mode and from the set $\{1, 5, 10, 20, 40, 80, 160, \text{OFF}\}$ for the TDD mode. The value of N_p is configured by higher-layer signaling.

- The wideband CQI/PMI reporting period is N_p if it is not configured with subband CQI reporting; otherwise, the wideband CQI/PMI reporting period is $H \cdot N_p$. The integer H is defined as $H = J \cdot K + 1$, where J is the number of bandwidth parts and K is selected from the set $\{1, 2, 3, 4\}$. In this case, between every two consecutive wideband CQI/PMI reports, the remaining $J \cdot K$ reporting instances are used for subband CQI reports on K full cycles of BPs.

- For the RI reporting, if RI and wideband CQI/PMI are configured, the reporting interval of the RI reporting is $N_p \cdot M_{RI}$, where M_{RI} is configured by higher-layer signaling and is selected from the set $\{1, 2, 4, 8, 16, 32, \text{OFF}\}$; if RI is configured with both wideband CQI/PMI and subband CQI reporting, the reporting interval of the RI reporting is $H \cdot N_p \cdot M_{RI}$. In case of a collision between RI and wideband CQI/PMI or subband CQI reporting, the wideband CQI/PMI or subband CQI is dropped.

Therefore, the report period is the longest for RI while shortest for subband CQI.

Aperiodic CQI Reporting

If a UE receives either a DCI format 0 or a random access response grant in subframe n, and if the respective CQI request field is set to 1 and is not reserved, the UE shall perform aperiodic CQI, PMI, and RI reporting using the PUSCH channel in subframe $n + k$. The value of k is specified as follows:

- For FDD, $k = 4$.

- For TDD UL/DL configuration 1–6, k is given in Table 9.10.

- For TDD UL/DL configuration 0:

  - If the Most Significant Bit (MSB) of the UL index is set to 1 and the Least Significant Bit (LSB) is set to 0 or 1, k is given in Table 9.10.

  - If the MSB of the UL index is set to 0 and the LSB is set to 1, k is equal to 7.

As shown in Table 9.5, there are three different aperiodic CQI feedback types: wideband feedback, higher layer-configured subband feedback, and UE-selected subband feedback, and five reporting modes. Modes 2-0 and 3-0 are for single-antenna-port transmission and OL MIMO modes, while Mode 3-1 with single PMI and Modes 1-2 and 2-2 with multiple PMI are for CL MIMO modes.

Wideband Feedback For wideband feedback, a UE selects a preferred precoding matrix for each subband, assuming transmission only in that subband. Then each UE reports one wideband CQI value for each codeword, assuming the use of the selected precoding matrix in each subband, and it also reports the selected PMI for each subband, i.e., multiple PMIs are reported.

Higher Layer-Configured Subband Feedback There are two different reporting modes with higher layer-configured subband feedback: Mode 3-0 (without PMI) and Mode 3-1 (with single PMI). The supported subband size k is the same as that for the periodic

Table 9.10 The Values of k for TDD Configuration 0–6

TDD UL/DL Configuration	DL Subframe Number n									
	0	1	2	3	4	5	6	7	8	9
0	4	6				4	6			
1		6			4		6			4
2				4					4	
3	4								4	4
4									4	4
5									4	
6	7	7				7	7			5

Table 9.11 Mapping Subband Differential CQI Value to Offset Level

Subband Differential CQI Value	Offset Level for Mode 3-0 and 3-1	Offset Level for Mode 2-0 and 2-2
0	0	≤ 1
1	1	2
2	≥ 2	3
3	≤ -2	≥ 4

reporting, as in Table 9.8. As a separate CQI is reported for each subband, this reporting type provides the finest frequency granularity but also has the highest overhead.

- For Mode 3-0, a UE reports one subband CQI for each subband, together with a wideband CQI. Both the wideband and subband CQI represent channel quality for the first codeword, even when RI > 1. No PMI is reported for this mode.

- For Mode 3-1, a single precoding matrix is selected, assuming transmission over the whole system bandwidth. A UE reports one subband CQI value per codeword for each subband, together with a wideband CQI value per codeword, assuming the use of the single precoding matrix in all subbands. A 4-bit wideband CQI is reported for each of codeword 0 and codeword 1. The selected precoding matrix is also reported.

The subband CQI values for each codeword are encoded differentially with respect to their respective wideband CQI using 2 bits defined by:

$$\text{subband differential CQI offset level} = \text{subband CQI index} - \text{wideband CQI index.}$$
$$(9.6)$$

The mapping from the 2-bit differential value to the offset level is show in Table 9.11.

UE-Selected Subband Feedback   For UE-selected subband feedback, there are two different reporting modes: Mode 2-0 (without PMI) and Mode 2-2 (with multiple PMI).

- For Mode 2-0, the UE selects a set of M preferred subbands of size k, where the values of M and k are given in Table 9.12 for different system bandwidths. The UE will report one CQI value reflecting transmission only over the M selected

Table 9.12 Subband Size (k) and Number of Subbands (M) vs. Downlink System Bandwidth in Aperiodic Reporting

System Bandwidth N_{RB}^{DL}	Subband Size (k)	M
6–7	NA	NA
8–10	2	1
11–26	2	3
27–63	3	5
64–110	4	6

subbands. This is called the *best-M method*. Additionally, the UE will also report a wideband CQI value.

- For Mode 2-2, the UE first jointly selects the set of M preferred subbands of size k and a preferred single precoding matrix. Then it will report one CQI value per codeword reflecting transmission only over the selected M preferred subbands, together with the selected single precoding matrix. The UE will also select a precoding matrix assuming transmission over the whole system bandwidth. Then it reports a wideband CQI per codeword together with the selected single PMI for the whole system bandwidth.

The CQI value for the M selected subbands for each codeword is encoded differentially using 2 bits relative to its respective wideband CQI, with the mapping from the 2-bit differential value to the offset level shown in Table 9.11. For all UE-selected feedback modes, the UE shall report the position of the M selected subbands using a combinatorial index r defined as:

$$r = \sum_{i=0}^{M-1} \left\langle \begin{array}{c} N - s_i \\ M - i \end{array} \right\rangle, \tag{9.7}$$

where the set $\{s_i\}_{i=0}^{M-1}$ $(1 \leq s_i \leq N, s_i < s_{i+1})$ contains the M sorted subband indices and

$$\left\langle \begin{array}{c} x \\ y \end{array} \right\rangle = \left\{ \begin{array}{cc} \binom{x}{k} & x \geq y \\ 0 & x < y \end{array} \right. \tag{9.8}$$

is the extended binomial coefficient, resulting in unique label $r \in \left\{ 0, \ldots, \binom{N}{M} - 1 \right\}$. So the number of bits to denote the positions of the M selected subbands is $L = \left\lceil \log_2 \binom{N}{M} \right\rceil$.

9.3 Precoder for Closed-Loop MIMO Operations

MIMO transmission is a key technique in LTE and can provide a significant throughput gain, especially with the spatial multiplexing mode. The amount of feedback required to provide the full CSI to the eNode-B is large, particularly in multicarrier systems. In order to mitigate the feedback issue, limited feedback mechanisms are used in LTE as indicated in Chapter 5. The UE chooses the optimum rank and precoder for downlink transmission based on a predefined set of precoders, also known as a codebook. In this case, instead of indicating the full precoding matrix, the UE only needs to indicate the index of the precoding matrix from the codebook. RI is reported by the UE to indicate the number of layers, i.e., the number of data streams used in spatial multiplexing. For CL MIMO modes, i.e., the transmission modes 4, 5, and 6, the preferred precoding matrix in the predefined codebook needs to be reported, which is provided by the PMI. In this section, we describe the feedback of PMI and RI.

9.3.1 Precoder Estimation for Multicarrier Systems

The precoder estimation at the UE can be done based on a few different metrics. The most common metric is the capacity-based one. The precoder is chosen to maximize the MIMO capacity of the effective channel, which includes the radio channel and the precoder. This metric is suitable for the receivers based on maximum likelihood detection. For a simpler receiver, such as the one based on Minimum Mean Square Error (MMSE), this approach is not optimal, as the rate achieved by MMSE receivers is not given by the MIMO capacity equation. For MMSE receivers, the optimal precoder is chosen such that the post-MMSE SINR across both streams is optimized in order to achieve maximum sum rate throughput across both streams.

In a CL MIMO system, the interference is dynamic in nature, as the precoders used at interfering cells change from one TTI to the next. Thus, choosing a precoder based on the instantaneous interference seen by a UE can lead to suboptimal performance, since the spatial characteristics of the interference can change from the time the precoder was chosen to the time the precoder was applied. It has been shown that in such cases it is better to choose the precoder based on long-term characteristics of the interference such as the interference variance at each receive antenna.

For the l-th subcarrier, the achievable rate for an MMSE receiver is

$$R_l = \sum_{k=1}^{M} \log_2(1 + \text{SINR}_k)$$
$$= -\sum_{k=1}^{M} \log_2\left(\left(\mathbf{I}_M + \frac{\rho}{M}\mathbf{F}^H\mathbf{H}^H\mathbf{H}\mathbf{F}\right)^{-1}_{k,k}\right), \qquad (9.9)$$

where $M = 1$ to 4, depending on the number of layers, and $\mathbf{H}$ and $\mathbf{F}$ are the channel matrix and precoding matrix, respectively. For a multicarrier system, the sum capacity over a subband with N subcarriers is

$$R_{\text{sum}} = \sum_{l=1}^{N} R_l. \qquad (9.10)$$

The precoder is chosen to maximize R_{sum} for a given subband (subband PMI) or the entire bandwidth (wideband PMI). For the MU-MIMO mode, the rank-1 precoder of the SU-MIMO mode is applied. The eNode-B schedules two UEs with orthogonal precoders and similar CQI level on the same radio resource. The two rank-1 precoders are used together to create a rank-2 precoding matrix for the two streams for two different UEs.

9.3.2   Precoding Matrix Index (PMI) and Rank Indication (RI) Feedback

The RI report is determined from the supported set of RI values for the corresponding eNode-B and the UE antenna configuration. The value of RI can be 1 or 2 for two-antenna ports and from 1 to 4 for four-antenna ports. The mapping between RI bits and the channel rank is shown in Table 9.13. UEs need to report RI for both CL and OL MIMO modes. For the CL spatial multiplexing, the RI report, together with the PMI, informs the eNode-B to select the suitable precoder; for OL MIMO, the RI report

Table 9.13 RI Mapping

RI Bits	Channel Rank
0	1
1	2
0, 0	1
0, 1	2
1, 0	3
1, 1	4

supports selection between transmit diversity (RI = 1) and OL spatial multiplexing (RI > 1). Only wideband RI reporting is supported, i.e., only a single RI is reported for the whole bandwidth, as subband RI reporting provides little performance gain. In addition, as the channel rank normally changes slowly, the reporting period for RI is longer than CQI in periodic reporting.

PMI reports the channel-dependent precoding matrix for CL MIMO modes. The codebooks for two-antenna and four-antenna ports are described in Table 7.8 and 7.9 in Section 7.2.2, respectively.

- **For two-antenna ports:** When RI = 1, a PMI value of $n \in \{0, 1, 2, 3\}$ corresponds to the codebook index n given in Table 7.8 with $v = 1$; when RI = 2, a PMI value of $n \in \{0, 1\}$ corresponds to the codebook index $n+1$ given in Table 7.8 with $v = 2$.

- **For four-antenna ports:** A PMI value of $n \in \{0, 1, \dots, 15\}$ corresponds to the codebook index n given in Table 7.9 with $v = $ RI.

Accordingly, the number of feedback bits for PMI reporting can be determined and is shown in Table 9.14.

Although the codebooks are given in Tables 7.8 and 7.9, each UE can be restricted to report PMI within a subset of the predefined precoder codebook when specified by higher layer signaling. A bitmap is used to specify all possible precoder codebook subsets from which the UE can assume the eNode-B may be using. The codebook subset restriction is supported for OL and CL spatial multiplexing, multiuser MIMO, and closed-loop rank = 1 precoding, with the number of bits given in Table 9.15 for different transmission modes. In the case of OL spatial multiplexing, these precoders are used for the four-antenna case, as discussed in Section 7.2.2. A bit value of zero in the bitmap indicates

Table 9.14 Number of Feedback Bits for PMI

Two-Antenna Ports	Four-Antenna Ports
2 (RI = 1)	4
1 (RI = 2)	

Table 9.15 Number of Bits in Codebook Subset Restriction Bitmap

Transmission Mode	Number of Bits A_c	
	Two-Antenna Ports	Four-Antenna Ports
Open-loop spatial multiplexing	2	4
Closed-loop spatial multiplexing	6	64
Multiuser MIMO	4	16
Closed-loop rank = 1 precoding	4	16

that the PMI reporting is not allowed to correspond to the precoder associated with the bit. The association of bits to precoders for different MIMO modes is given as follows:

- **Open-loop spatial multiplexing**

  - **Two-antenna ports:** There are 2 bits in the bitmap. The bit a_0 is associated with the precoder for the open-loop transmit diversity; the bit a_1 is associated with the precoder in Table 7.8 with index 0 and $v = 2$, i.e., the normalized identity matrix.

  - **Four-antenna ports:** There are 4 bits in the bitmap. The bit a_0 is associated with the open-loop transmit diversity precoder for four-antenna ports; bit a_{v-1}, $v = 2, 3, 4$ is associated with the precoders in Table 7.9 corresponding to v layers and codebook indices 12, 13, 14, and 15, and these precoders for each v will be applied cyclically to the v vectors on the PDSCH.

- **Closed-loop spatial multiplexing**

  - **Two-antenna ports:** There are 6 bits associated with the 6 precoders in Table 7.8 except the precoder with index 0 and $v = 2$.

  - **Four-antenna ports:** There are 64 bits associated with all the precoders in Table 7.9.

- **Multiuser MIMO and closed-loop Rank = 1 precoding**

  - **Two-antenna ports:** There are 4 bits associated with the precoders in Table 7.8 for $v = 1$.

  - **Four-antenna ports:** There are 16 bits associated with the precoders in Table 7.9 for $v = 1$.

Therefore, each reported PMI value corresponds to a codebook index given in Table 7.8 or Table 7.9 for two-antenna ports and four-antenna ports, respectively, with the subset restriction discussed above. In aperiodic reporting modes, PMI can be either wideband or subband, while only wideband PMI reporting is supported in periodic reporting modes.

The eNode-B can override the PMI reported by UEs. The actual precoding matrix used may be different from the PMI reported from the UE, and the eNode-B needs to send precoding information on PDCCH, which either indicates the actual PMI or informs the UE that the reported PMI is applied. This information field is called Transmit Precoding

Matrix Indication (TPMI), which is contained in DCI format 2 for CL spatial multiplexing with 3 bits for two transmit antennas and 6 bits for four transmit antennas. If the TPMI indicates a precoding matrix, this matrix is used on all frequency resources allocated. The eNode-B may also decide to perform transmit diversity and indicate this in the TPMI. For OL spatial multiplexing, there is also a TPMI field contained in DCI format 2A, which indicates whether the transmit diversity or OL spatial multiplexing is used.

9.4 Uplink Channel Sounding

Channel sounding is mainly used for uplink channel quality measurement at the eNode-B. The Sounding Reference Symbol (SRS) is transmitted by the UE in the uplink for the eNode-B to estimate the channel state information, which includes the MIMO channel of the desired signal, SINR, noise, interference level, etc. The SRS can also be used for uplink timing estimation and uplink power control. The signal sequence and resource mapping of the SRS were discussed in Section 8.4. The SRS transmission is always in the last SC-FDMA symbol in the configured subframe, on which PUSCH data transmission is not allowed. The eNode-B can either request an individual SRS transmission from a UE or configure a UE to periodically transmit SRS. The periodicity may take any value of 2, 5, 10, 20, 40, 80, 160, and 320 ms.

The UE-specific SRS parameters include the starting physical resource block assignment, duration of SRS transmission, SRS periodicity and SRS subframe offset, SRS bandwidth, frequency hopping bandwidth, and cyclic shift. These parameters are semi-statically configured by higher layers. A UE shall not transmit SRS in the following scenarios:

- If SRS and PUCCH format 2/2a/2b transmissions happen to coincide in the same subframe

- Whenever SRS and ACK/NAK and/or positive SR transmissions happen to coincide in the same subframe unless the parameter *Simultaneous-AN-and-SRS* is TRUE

If the UE is equipped with two transmit antennas, then it alternates between two-antennas every time the SRS is transmitted. This allows the eNode-B to select the transmit antenna if the closed-loop antenna selection is enabled.

9.5 Buffer Status Reporting in Uplink

A Buffer Status Report (BSR) is sent from the UE to the serving eNode-B to provide information about the amount of pending data in the uplink buffer of the UE. The buffer status, along with other information, such as priorities allocated to different logical channels, is useful for the uplink scheduling process to determine which UEs or logical channels should be granted radio resources at a given time.

A BSR is triggered if any of the following events occurs:

- Uplink data for a logical channel becomes available for transmission, and either the data belongs to a logical channel with higher priority than the priorities of the logical channels for which data is already available for transmission, or there is no data available for transmission for any of the logical channels. In this case, the BSR is referred to as "regular BSR."

- Uplink resources are allocated and the number of padding bits is equal to or larger than the size of the BSR MAC control element, in which case the BSR is referred to as "padding BSR."

- A serving cell change occurs, in which case the BSR is referred to as "regular BSR."

- The retransmission BSR timer expires and the UE has data available for transmission, in which case the BSR is referred to as "regular BSR."

- The periodic BSR timer expires, in which case the BSR is referred to as "periodic BSR."

The buffer status is reported on a per radio bearer[1] (logical channel) group basis, where a radio bearer group is defined as a group of radio bearers with similar QoS requirements and belong to the same QCI (QoS Class Identifier). There are two BSR formats used in the LTE uplink: short BSR that reports only one radio bearer group, and long BSR that reports multiple radio bearer groups. For regular and periodic BSR, if more than one radio bearer group has data available for transmission in the TTI where the BSR is transmitted, long BSR is reported; otherwise, short BSR is reported. For padding BSR:

- When the number of padding bits is equal to or larger than the size of the short BSR plus its subheader but smaller than the size of the long BSR plus its subheader, truncated BSR with the highest priority logical channel is reported if more than one logical channel group has buffered data; otherwise, short BSR is reported.

- If the number of padding bits is equal to or larger than the size of the long BSR plus its subheader, long BSR is reported.

When the BSR procedure determines that at least one BSR has been triggered, and then if the UE has been allocated uplink resources, a buffer status report is transmitted; if a regular BSR has been triggered and the UE has no allocated uplink resource, a scheduling request for a BSR transmission is triggered. A MAC PDU shall contain at most one MAC BSR control element, even when multiple events trigger. In this case, the regular BSR and the periodic BSR shall have precedence over the padding BSR. All triggered BSRs shall be cancelled in the following two scenarios:

- The uplink grant can accommodate all pending data available for transmission but is not sufficient to additionally accommodate the BSR MAC control element.

- A BSR is included in a MAC PDU for transmission.

---

1 The radio bearer transfers data between a UE and the E-UTRAN with support of a set of specific QoS requirements, and it is mapped to a logical channel. This will be further discussed in Chapter 10.

9.6 Scheduling and Resource Allocation

The main purpose of scheduling and resource allocation is to efficiently allocate the available radio resources to UEs to optimize a certain performance metric with QoS requirement constraints. Scheduling algorithms for LTE can be divided into two categories:

- **Channel-dependent scheduling:** The allocation of resource blocks to a UE is based on the channel condition, e.g., proportional fairness scheduler, max CI (Carrier to Interference) scheduler, etc.

- **Channel-independent scheduling:** The allocation of resource blocks to a UE is random and not based on channel condition, e.g., round-robin scheduler.

In a multicarrier system such as LTE, channel-dependent scheduling can be further divided into two categories:

- **Frequency diverse scheduling:** The UE selection is based on wideband CQI. However, the PRB allocation in the frequency domain is random. It can exploit time selectivity and frequency diversity of the channel.

- **Frequency selective scheduling:** The UE selection is based on both wideband and subband CQI, and the PRB allocation is based on the subband CQI. This can exploit both time and frequency selectivity of the channel.

In this section, we mainly focus on the frequency selective scheduling.

Dynamic channel-dependent scheduling is one of the key features to provide high spectrum efficiency in LTE. To better exploit the channel selectivity, the packet scheduler is located in the eNode-B, which allocates physical layer resources for both the DL-SCH and UL-SCH transport channels every TTI. Resource assignment consists of PRBs and MCS. Such scheduling depends heavily on the channel information available at the eNode-B, which is provided by the uplink CQI reporting for the downlink channel and by channel sounding for the uplink channel, as discussed in Section 9.2 and Section 9.4, respectively. The scheduler should also take account of the traffic volume and the QoS requirement of each UE and associated radio bearers. Due to the implementation of OFDMA/SC-FDMA, LTE is able to exploit the channel variation in both the time and frequency domain, which is a major advantage compared to HSPA, which is able to exploit channel variation only in the time domain.

The objective of channel-dependent scheduling, as discussed in Chapter 4, is to exploit multiuser diversity to improve the spectrum efficiency. Meanwhile, it should also consider such issues as fairness and QoS requirements. In addition, scheduling is tightly integrated with link adaptation and the H-ARQ process. The scheduling algorithm is not standardized and is eNode-B vendor specific. See [10–13] for the investigation of different scheduling schemes in LTE, and refer to Chapter 4 for related discussion. In this section, we focus on the signaling for both downlink and uplink scheduling. Dynamic scheduling is mainly applied on the data traffic, which is the focus in this section. The scheduling of VoIP services will be discussed in Section 9.7.

9.6.1 Signaling for Scheduling in Downlink and Uplink

For both downlink and uplink, the eNode-B scheduler dynamically controls which time-frequency resources are allocated to a certain UE. The resource assignments, including the assigned time/frequency resources and respective transmission formats, are conveyed through downlink control signaling. The minimum size of radio resource that can be allocated to a UE corresponds to two resource blocks, which is 1 ms duration in the time domain and 180kHz in the frequency domain. Both downlink and uplink employ orthogonal transmission, so each resource block is allocated to a single UE except in the MU-MIMO mode. Both localized and distributed resource allocations are supported in the downlink, while in the uplink UEs are always assigned contiguous resources, i.e., only localized allocation is supported. In addition, there is a strict constraint on the UE transmit power in the uplink, which is subject to the uplink power control that will be discussed in Section 9.10.

Signaling for Downlink Scheduling

The channel state information at the eNode-B for the downlink scheduling is obtained through CQI reporting from UEs, as discussed in Section 9.2. To enable frequency selective scheduling, subband CQI reporting is required. The eNode-B dynamically allocates resources to UEs at each TTI. A UE always monitors the PDCCH for possible allocations. For dynamically scheduled data traffic, the UE is configured by the higher layers to decode the PDCCH with CRC scrambled by the C-RNTI.[2] The UE shall decode the PDCCH and any corresponding PDSCH according to the respective combinations defined in Table 9.16. For example, when a UE configured in transmission mode 3 or 4 (OL and CL spatial multiplexing) receives a DCI format 1A assignment, it shall assume that the PDSCH transmission is associated with transport block 1 and that transport block 2 is disabled, and transmit diversity is applied. The DCI carries the downlink scheduling assignment and other information necessary to decode and demodulate data symbols. The transport channel processing of DCI was described in Section 7.3.

As shown in Section 6.3.3, in the downlink, while the two distributed allocation types (resource allocation type 0 and type 1) provide better performance with a high overhead, the localized allocation type (resource allocation type 2) provides a low overhead alternative at the cost of limited scheduling flexibility. The UE shall interpret the resource allocation field depending on the PDCCH DCI format detected. PDCCH DCI formats 1, 2, and 2A with type 0 and with type 1 resource allocation have the same format and are distinguished via the single bit resource allocation header field, where type 0 is indicated by 0 value and type 1 is indicated otherwise. PDCCH with DCI format 1A, 1B, 1C, and 1D have a type 2 resource allocation while PDCCH with DCI format 1, 2, and 2A have type 0 or type 1 resource allocation. The details of the resource assignment can be interpreted from DCI for different formats.

To determine the modulation order and transport block size, the UE shall first read the 5-bit "modulation and coding scheme" field (I_{MCS}) in the DCI, based on which a Transport Block Size (TBS) index can also be determined. The mapping between the MCS index I_{MCS}, the modulation order, and TBS index I_{TBS} for PDSCH is shown in

---

2 This is the unique identification used for identifying RRC connection and scheduling.

Table 9.16 PDCCH and PDSCH Configured by C-RNTI

UE DL Transmission Mode	DCI Format	Transmission Scheme of PDSCH
Mode 1	DCI format 1A	Single-antenna port, port 0
	DCI format 1	Single-antenna port, port 0
Mode 2	DCI format 1A	Transmit diversity
	DCI format 1	Transmit diversity
Mode 3	DCI format 1A	Transmit diversity
	DCI format 2A	OL spatial multiplexing or transmit diversity
Mode 4	DCI format 1A	Transmit diversity
	DCI format 2	CL spatial multiplexing or transmit diversity
Mode 5	DCI format 1A	Transmit diversity
	DCI format 1D	Multiuser MIMO
Mode 6	DCI format 1A	Transmit diversity
	DCI format 1B	Closed-loop Rank = 1 precoding
Mode 7	DCI format 1A	If the number of PBCH antenna ports is one, single-antenna port (port 0); otherwise, transmit diversity
	DCI format 1	Single-antenna port, port 5

Table 9.17. The TBS can then be determined based on I_{TBS} and the total number of allocated PRBs. Note that in Table 9.17 different MCS indices may be mapped to the same TBS, e.g., $I_{MCS} = 9, 10$ are mapped to $I_{TBS} = 9$, resulting in the same data rate. Such modulation overlap is adopted to improve the performance around the modulation switching points, as different combinations of modulation and coding with the same rate may provide different performance in different scenarios. For $29 \leq I_{MCS} \leq 31$, the TBS is determined from the previous scheduling grant for the same transport block using $0 \leq I_{MCS} \leq 28$.

Signaling for Uplink Scheduling

In the uplink, the channel state information is estimated at the eNode-B with the help of sounding reference signals, as discussed in Section 9.4. A UE always monitors the PDCCH in order to find possible allocation for uplink transmission. Only contiguous resource blocks can be allocated to a UE due to the SCFDMA nature of the UL transmission'. Frequency hopping can be applied to provide additional diversity. The UE obtains the uplink resource allocation as well as frequency hopping information from the uplink scheduling grant received four subframes earlier, i.e., if the UE detects a PDCCH with DCI format 0 in subframe n intended for this UE, it will adjust the corresponding PUSCH transmission in subframe $n + 4$ accordingly.

Table 9.17 Modulation and TBS Index for PDSCH

MCS Index I_{MCS}	Modulation Order	TBS Index I_{TBS}
0	2	0
1	2	1
2	2	2
3	2	3
4	2	4
5	2	5
6	2	6
7	2	7
8	2	8
9	2	9
10	4	9
11	4	10
12	4	11
13	4	12
14	4	13
15	4	14
16	4	15
17	6	15
18	6	16
19	6	17
20	6	18
21	6	19
22	6	20
23	6	21
24	6	22
25	6	23
26	6	24
27	6	25
28	6	26
29	2	reserved
30	4	reserved
31	6	reserved

To determine the modulation order, redundancy version, and transport block size for the PUSCH, the UE shall first read the 5-bit "modulation and coding scheme and redundancy version" field (I_{MCS}) in the DCI. The mapping between I_{MCS}, modulation order, and I_{TBS} for the PUSCH is shown in Table 9.18. Note that I_{MCS} also indicates the H-ARQ redundancy version. The redundancy version 1, 2, or 3 is indicated by $I_{MCS} = 29, 30, 31$, respectively, in which case the modulation order is assumed to be

Table 9.18 Modulation, TBS Index, and Redundancy Version for PUSCH

MCS Index I_{MCS}	Modulation Order	TBS Index I_{TBS}	Redundancy Version
0	2	0	0
1	2	1	0
2	2	2	0
3	2	3	0
4	2	4	0
5	2	5	0
6	2	6	0
7	2	7	0
8	2	8	0
9	2	9	0
10	2	10	0
11	4	10	0
12	4	11	0
13	4	12	0
14	4	13	0
15	4	14	0
16	4	15	0
17	4	16	0
18	4	17	0
19	4	18	0
20	4	19	0
21	6	19	0
22	6	20	0
23	6	21	0
24	6	22	0
25	6	23	0
26	6	24	0
27	6	25	0
28	6	26	0
29	reserved	reserved	1
30	reserved	reserved	2
31	reserved	reserved	3

the one indicated in the initial grant. Similar to the downlink, there is also modulation overlap around the switching points, e.g., $I_{MCS} = 10, 11$ are both mapped to $I_{TBS} = 10$. The transport block size can be determined from I_{MCS} and I_{TBS}. For $20 \leq I_{MCS} \leq 31$, the transport block size is assumed to be as determined from DCI transport in the initial PDCCH for the same transport block using $0 \leq I_{MCS} \leq 28$.

9.6.2   Multiuser MIMO Signaling

If MU-MIMO is used in the uplink, then it is transparent to the UE with the exception that two UEs should transmit orthogonal reference signals in order for the eNode-B to separate them. The uplink resource allocation is indicated on PDCCH using DCI format 0, which contains a 3-bit field to indicate the cyclic shift in the reference signal to be used by each UE.

When MU-MIMO is used in the downlink, two rank-1 UEs are multiplexed on the same physical resource. Unlike SU-MIMO, in this case the power for each UE is reduced by 3 dB. This is indicated by the power offset field in DCI format 1D, which is used for MU-MIMO scheduling.

9.7   Semi-persistent Scheduling for VoIP

Although the revenue from data services is increasing, voice services still provide the majority of operators' revenue. In current cellular systems, including WCDMA and HSPA, there is a Circuit Switched (CS) domain to provide efficient CS voice service. On the contrary, LTE is based on all-IP packet switching, and there is no CS domain. For the commercial success of LTE, it should be able to provide voice quality comparable to that based on CS. In LTE, VoIP can be used to provide voice service. In this section, we discuss the challenge of scheduling VoIP packets, and present the semi-persistent scheduling that is included in LTE [4, 5].

9.7.1   Motivation for Semi-persistent Scheduling

VoIP is characterized by the small packet size with very stringent delay and jitter requirements, and a large number of simultaneous users. In LTE, the scheduling of the data traffic is based on the shared-channel transmission and the channel-dependent resource allocation. The eNode-B allocates radio resources in units of resource blocks to UEs, and informs the scheduling information to each UE on PDCCH. Such dynamic channel-dependent scheduling can exploit the selectivity in both time and frequency domain, and significantly improve the system throughput. However, to apply dynamic scheduling directly for VoIP packets is not desirable. This is mainly due to the small packet size and the constant inter-arrival time of VoIP packets, which results in large control overhead as control information should be transmitted per TTI. Many UEs may be scheduled simultaneously, so the limited resources available on PDCCH for control signaling become a bottleneck for the VoIP capacity.

To reduce the amount of control signaling, persistent scheduling can be applied, where a fixed allocation is valid until the next allocation is informed. With persistent scheduling, the H-ARQ operation can be implemented by sending each packet a fixed number of times, and then no H-ARQ ACK/NAK is required. However, the inflexibility of such resource allocation degrades the performance compared to the dynamic scheduling, especially due to the mismatch between the allocated resource and the actual radio channel for multiple H-ARQ processes.

Semi-persistent scheduling is proposed to exploit the benefits of both dynamic and persistent scheduling: the initial transmissions are based on persistent scheduling, while the H-ARQ retransmissions are through dynamic scheduling [8]. In this way, it efficiently reduces the control overhead and also exploits the channel selectivity.

9.7.2 Changes in the Signaling Structure

When semi-persistent scheduling is enabled, the following information is provided by the Radio Resource Control (RRC) layer:

- Semi-persistent scheduling C-RNTI, which is a unique identification used for semi-persistent scheduling

- Uplink semi-persistent scheduling interval, if semi-persistent scheduling is enabled for the uplink

- Downlink semi-persistent scheduling interval, if semi-persistent scheduling is enabled for the downlink

To check the PDCCH validation for semi-persistent scheduling, a UE shall check the following conditions for DCI formats 0, 1, 1A, 2, and 2A:

- The CRC is scrambled by the semi-persistent C-RNTI.

- In case of DCI formats 2 and 2A, the new data indicator field is set to '0'.

- All the conditions for the respective used DCI format according to Table 9.19 are met.

Table 9.19 Special Fields for Semi-persistent Scheduling PDCCH Validation

	DCI Format 0	DCI Format 1/1A	DCI Format 2/2A
TPC command for scheduled PUSCH	Set to '00'	N/A	N/A
Cyclic shift for demodulation reference signal	Set to '000'	N/A	N/A
MCS and redundancy version	MSB is set to '0'	N/A	N/A
H-ARQ process number	N/A	FDD: Set to '000'; TDD: Set to '0000'	FDD: Set to '000'; TDD: Set to '0000'
MCS	N/A	MSB is set to '0'	For the enabled transport block: MSB is set to '0'
Redundancy version	N/A	Set to '00'	For the enabled transport block: Set to '00'

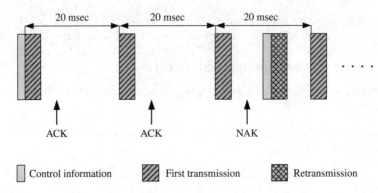

Figure 9.3 An example of semi-persistent scheduling in the downlink.

If all the conditions are met, the UE shall consider the received DCI information as a valid semi-persistent assignment/grant.

For the first H-ARQ transmissions, the eNode-B allocates semi-persistent resources to UEs. The corresponding PDCCH allocation indicates that the downlink grant is a semi-persistent one, so it can be implicitly reused in the following TTIs according to the periodicity defined by RRC. In the subframes where the UE has semi-persistent downlink resource, if the UE cannot find its C-RNTI on the PDCCH(s), a downlink transmission according to the semi-persistent allocation is assumed. Otherwise, the PDCCH allocation overrides the semi-persistent allocation for that TTI and the UE does not decode the semi-persistent resources.

For the H-ARQ process, in the downlink, retransmissions are explicitly signalled via the PDCCH. In the uplink, retransmissions are either implicitly allocated, in which case the UE uses the semi-persistent uplink allocation, or explicitly allocated via PDCCH, in which case the UE follows the new allocation. An illustrative example of semi-persistent scheduling in the downlink is shown in Figure 9.3. It shows that if an ACK is received, the next new transmission follows the persistent allocation without the scheduling control information; if an NAK is received, the new allocation is contained in PDCCH for the retransmission, which depends on the current channel state.

9.8   Cell Search

When a UE powers on, it needs to acquire time and frequency synchronization with a cell and detect the physical-layer cell ID of that cell through the cell search procedure or synchronization procedure. Such synchronization is especially important for LTE, as the performance of LTE systems relies on the orthogonal intra-cell transmission in both uplink and downlink. During cell search, different types of information need to be identified by the UE, including symbol and frame timing, frequency, cell identification, transmission bandwidth, antenna configuration, and the cyclic prefix length.

LTE uses a hierarchical cell search scheme similar to WCDMA, demonstrated in Figure 9.4. As described in Section 7.6.2, a primary synchronization signal carrying the information about the physical-layer ID within the cell-ID group ($N_{ID}^{(2)} = 0, 1, 2$) and

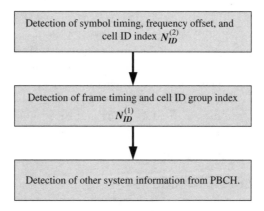

Figure 9.4 The cell search process.

a secondary synchronization signal carrying the physical-layer cell-ID group ($N_{ID}^{(1)} = 0, 1, \ldots, 167$) are defined. The cell ID is then determined as $N_{ID}^{cell} = 3N_{ID}^{(1)} + N_{ID}^{(2)}$. Different from WCDMA, the cell search in LTE needs to consider different system bandwidths and different duplexing schemes, i.e., TDD and FDD. This is achieved by defining a common synchronization signal structure for all supported bandwidths, which occupies six resource blocks (72 subcarriers) centered around the DC subcarrier, corresponding to the most narrow bandwidth supported in LTE. In the time domain, there are two pairs of primary and secondary synchronization signals in each radio frame. The arrangement of the primary and secondary synchronization is done in a manner such that it is compatible with both the TDD and FDD frame structure.

In the first step of cell search, the UE detects the symbol timing and the cell ID index $N_{ID}^{(2)}$ from the primary synchronization signal. This can be achieved, e.g., through matched filtering between the received signal and the primary synchronization sequences. As there are three orthogonal sequences defined for the primary synchronization signal, the cell ID index $N_{ID}^{(2)}$ can be detected by identifying the received sequence. Frequency and Time synchronization can be performed based on the primary synchronization signal. OFDM symbol timing can be detected, but as there are two primary synchronization signals transmitted in each frame that are indistinguishable, frame timing cannot be detected.

In the next step, the UE detects the cell ID group index $N_{ID}^{(1)}$ and frame timing from the secondary synchronization signal. The index $N_{ID}^{(1)}$ is detected by identifying the shift in the m-sequence in the received signal. For detecting the frame timing, the pair of secondary synchronization signals in a radio frame has a different structure than primary synchronization signals: If the sequence pair of secondary synchronization signals $(\mathbf{d_1}, \mathbf{d_2})$ is defined, then $(\mathbf{d_2}, \mathbf{d_1})$ is not allowed. This property is used to resolve the 5-ms timing ambiguity in the first step, based on which the frame timing can be determined.

After the cell search, the UE can detect the broadcast channel to obtain other physical layer information, e.g., system bandwidth, number of transmit antennas, and system frame number. As discussed in Section 7.4, the system information is divided into Master

Information Block (MIB) transmitted on the PBCH and System Information Blocks (SIB) transmitted on the PDSCH. At this stage, the UE detects MIB from the PBCH.

To maintain the uplink intra-cell orthogonality, uplink transmissions from different UEs should arrive at the eNode-B within a cyclic prefix. This is achieved through the timing advance procedure. The timing advance is obtained from the uplink received timing and sent by the eNode-B to the UE. The UE advances or delays its timing of transmissions to compensate for propagation delay and thus time-aligns its transmissions with other UEs. The timing advance command is on a per-need basis with a granularity in the step size of $0.52\mu s$ ($16 \times T_s$).

9.9   Random Access Procedures

In LTE, there are two random access mechanisms:

- **Non-synchronized random access:** Non-synchronized random access is used when the UE uplink has not been time synchronized, or when the UE uplink loses synchronization. Its main purpose is to obtain synchronization of the uplink, notify the eNode-B that the UE has data to transmit, or transmit a small amount of control information and data packets.

- **Synchronized random access:** Synchronized random access is used when uplink synchronization is present. Its main purpose is to request resources for uplink data transmission from the eNode-B scheduler.

In this section, we focus on non-synchronized random access. The procedure of synchronized random access is similar except that it does not need the response of uplink timing information.

After the cell search procedure, the UE has obtained downlink synchronization. However, the uplink timing is not established due to the round-trip propagation delay. The non-synchronized access allows the eNode-B to estimate the UE transmission timing to within a fraction of the cyclic prefix and inform the UE about the timing correction. With uplink synchronization, the UE may request resources for uplink transmission. The eNode-B can also schedule data transmission in the resource blocks reserved for random access channel preamble transmission.

Prior to initiation of the non-synchronized random access procedure, each UE obtains the following information broadcast from eNode-B: random access channel parameters, including PRACH configuration; frequency position and preamble format; parameters for determining the root sequences, and their cyclic shifts in the preamble sequence set for the cell.

The non-synchronized random access procedure, which consists of four steps, is depicted in Figure 9.5 and described here:

1. First, multiple UEs transmit randomly selected random access code.

2. Second, eNode-B conducts a multiuser detection process and allocates resources to the detected UEs.

3. Third, each UE transmits detailed information using allocated resources.

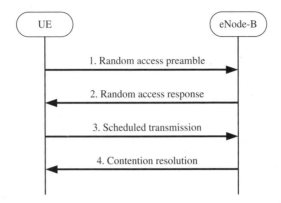

Figure 9.5 The non-synchronized random access procedure.

4. Fourth, the eNode-B transmits the contention-resolution message on the DL-SCH. When the previous steps are finished successfully, eNode-B and each UE initiate data communication.

Step 1: Random Access Preamble Transmission Based on the information obtained from eNode-B, the UE randomly selects a random access preamble, and transmits on the PRACH physical channel. The processing of random access channels and the random access preamble were discussed in Section 8.5. Open-loop power control is used to determine the initial transmit power level. Multiple UEs may transmit their random access preambles simultaneously through the same channel, and the eNode-B monitors the random access channel and conducts multiuser detection identifying each RACH transmission. The RACH signals from the different UEs are based on the Zadoff-Chu sequence with different cyclic shift resulting in a zero cross-correlation between them. This zero cross-correlation of the Zadoff-Chu sequence allows the eNode-B to simultaneously detect multiple UEs using a correlation-based detection process. The eNode-B also calculates the timing correction for the uplink transmission for each UE.

Step 2: Random Access Response If a random access attempt is detected, the eNode-B transmits the corresponding random access response on the DL-SCH, which contains the identity of the detected preamble, the timing correction for uplink transmission, a temporary identity for transmission in following steps, and an initial uplink resource grant. The random access response message can also include a backoff indicator to instruct the UE to back off for a period of time before retrying another random access attempt. The uplink scheduling grant for the following uplink transmission contains 20 bits, and the content is illustrated in Table 9.20. For the UE, once the random access preamble is transmitted, it will monitor the PDCCH for random access response identified by the Random Access Radio Network Temporary Identifier (RA-RNTI), as the time-frequency slot carrying the preamble is associated with an RA-RNTI. If the received random access response matches the transmitted preamble, the UE may stop monitoring.

Step 3: Scheduled Transmission After step 2, the UE is uplink synchronized, and can transmit additional messages on scheduled UL-SCH. This step is to assist contention resolution. If the UEs that perform random access attempts in the same time-frequency

Table 9.20 The Content of Random Access Response Grant

Information Type	Number of Bits	Purpose
Hopping flat	1	Indicates whether PUSCH frequency hopping is applied in the following step.
Fixed-size resource block assignment	10	Indicates the assigned radio resource for the following transmission.
Truncated modulation and coding scheme	4	Determines the modulation and coding scheme.
TPC command for scheduled PUSCH	3	Adjusts the transit power of PUSCH.
UL delay	1	Adjusts the uplink transmission timing.
CQI request	1	Used in non-contention-based random access procedure to determine whether an aperiodic CQI report is included in the corresponding PUSCH transmission.

resource use different preambles, different UEs can be identified by the eNode-B and there is no collision. However, it is possible that multiple UEs select the same preamble, which causes a collision. To resolve the contention for access, the UE that detects a random access preamble transmits a message containing a terminal identity. If the UE is connected to a cell, Cell Radio Network Temporary Identifier (C-RNTI) will be used, which is a unique UE ID at the cell level; otherwise, a core network identifier is used. In step 3, the H-ARQ protocol is supported to improve the transmission reliability.

Step 4: Contention Resolution Contention resolution is the key feature of the random access channel. In this step, the eNode-B transmits the contention-resolution message on the DL-SCH, which contains the identity of the winning UE. The UE that observes a match between this identity and the identity transmitted in step 3 declares a success and completes its random access procedure. If this UE has not been assigned a C-RNTI, the temporary identity is then set as its C-RNTI. The H-ARQ protocol is supported in this step, and the UE with successful access will transmit an H-ARQ acknowledgment.

9.10 Power Control in Uplink

With SC-FDMA-based transmission in the LTE uplink, orthogonality between intra-cell transmission from multiple UEs is achieved, which removes the intra-cell interference and the near-far issue typical of CDMA-based systems such as W-CDMA/HSPA. This leaves inter-cell interference as the major cause of interference and performance degradation, especially for the cell-edge UEs. In LTE, the power control in the uplink is to control the interference caused by UEs to neighboring cells while maintaining the required SINR at the serving cell. In this section, we describe the power control scheme for the PUSCH transmission in the uplink.

Conventional power control in the uplink is to achieve the same SINR for different UEs at the base station, also known as full compensation, but it suffers low spectral efficiency as the common SINR is limited by the cell-edge UEs. LTE specifies Fractional Power Control (FPC) as the open-loop power control scheme, which allows for full or partial compensation of path loss and shadowing [7, 9, 14]. FPC allows the UEs with higher path loss, i.e., cell-edge UEs, to operate with lower SINR requirements so that they generate less interference to other cells, while having a minor impact on the cell-interior UEs so that they are able to transmit at higher data rates. Besides open-loop power control, there is also a closed-loop power control component, which is to further adjust the UE transmission power to optimize the system performance.

We first describe the FPC scheme, based on which the UE adjusts the transmission power according to:

$$P = \min\{P_{max}, 10 \log M + P_0 + \alpha \cdot PL\} \text{ [dBm]}, \tag{9.11}$$

where P_{max} is the maximum UE transmission power, M is the number of assigned PRBs, P_0 is a parameter that controls the mean received SINR, α is the cell-specific path loss compensation factor, and PL is the downlink path loss estimate calculated in the UE. Note that the transmit power increases with M, which is to to ensure the same power spectral density irrespective of the number of PRBs.

If we only consider path loss and assume $10 \log M + P_0 + \alpha \cdot PL \leq P_{max}$, then the received signal power at the eNode-B is

$$P_r = P - PL = 10 \log M + P_0 + (\alpha - 1) \cdot PL \text{ [dBm]}. \tag{9.12}$$

- If $\alpha = 1$, each UE has a constant received power, which corresponds to full compensation, or channel inversion.

- If $\alpha = 0$, each UE has the same transmission power that is independent of the path loss, i.e., no power control.

- For $0 < \alpha < 1$, it is the FPC, and different UEs will have different P_r, depending on their path loss to the serving base station.

We see that reducing the value of α mainly decreases the transmission power of cell-edge UEs, which have large PLs and are likely to cause a high level of interference to neighboring cells. Therefore, by adjusting the path loss compensation factor α, we can reduce inter-cell interference and improve the spectrum efficiency.

Considering both open-loop and closed-loop components, the UE sets its total transmission power using the following formula:

$$P = \min\{P_{max}, 10 \log M + P_0(j) + \alpha(j) \cdot PL + \Delta_{MCS} + f(\Delta_i)\} \text{ [dBm]}. \tag{9.13}$$

There are three different PUSCH transmission types, corresponding to $j = 0, 1, 2$:

- For PUSCH (re)transmissions corresponding to a semi-persistent grant, $j = 0$.

- For PUSCH (re)transmissions corresponding to a dynamic scheduled grant, $j = 1$.

- For PUSCH (re)transmissions corresponding to the random access response grant, $j = 2$.

The parameters in (9.13) are described as follows:

- For $j = 0$ or 1, P_0 is composed of the sum of a cell-specific nominal component and a UE-specific component, provided by higher layers; for $j = 2$, P_0 is a cell-specific parameter signalled from higher layers.

- For $j = 0$ or 1, $\alpha(j)$ is a 3-bit cell-specific parameter, $\alpha(j) \in \{0, 0.4, 0.5, 0.6, 0.7, 0.8, 0.9, 1\}$; for $j = 2$, $\alpha(j) = 1$.

- Δ_{MCS} is a UE-specific parameter depending on the chosen modulation and coding scheme (MCS). A large value of Δ_{MCS} corresponds to higher coding rate and/or higher modulation order.

- Δ_i is a UE-specific closed-loop correction value included in the PDCCH, which is also referred to as a Transmit Power Control (TPC) command. This is to compensate the following effects including power amplifier error, path loss estimation error, and inter-cell interference level changes.

- The function $f(\cdot)$ is to perform closed-loop power control based on Δ_i. It is UE specific. There are two types of closed-loop power control defined in LTE:

    - **Accumulated:** The UE applies an offset based on Δ_i using the latest transmission power value as reference:

$$f(\Delta_i) = f(\Delta_{i-1}) + \Delta_{i-K}. \tag{9.14}$$

    The value of Δ_i is $\Delta_i \in \{-1, 0, 1, 3\}$ [dB]. For the FDD mode, $K = 4$, and for the TDD mode, the value of K depends on the UL/DL configuration [3].

    - **Absolute:** The UE adjusts the transmission power with an absolute value based on Δ_i:

$$f(\Delta_i) = \Delta_{i-K}. \tag{9.15}$$

    For this case, the value of Δ_i is $\Delta_i \in \{-4, -1, 1, 4\}$ [dB]. For the FDD mode, $K = 4$, and for the TDD mode, the value of K depends on the UL/DL configuration [3].

A similar power control scheme employing FPC is used for sounding reference signals.

9.11 Summary and Conclusions

In this chapter, we specified the physical layer procedures that provide services to upper layers.

- CQI feedback from UEs and channel sounding procedure provide the eNode-B with channel quality information for downlink and uplink channels, respectively, which are then used per UE scheduling and link adaptation. For CQI feedback, to enable frequency-selective scheduling and also to keep the overhead low, various reporting modes are supported, including period and aperiodic reporting, with both wideband and subband reporting. For MIMO modes, RI and PMI feedback are also reported from UEs.

- Both downlink and uplink scheduling are performed at the eNode-B. For uplink scheduling, buffer status reporting is required from UEs. The resource assignments, including the assigned time/frequency resources and respective transmission formats, are conveyed through downlink control signaling on PDCCH.

- Semi-persistent scheduling, which is a combination of dynamic scheduling and persistent scheduling, is proposed for the VoIP service in LTE. The initial transmission follows persistent scheduling, while retransmissions follow dynamic channel-dependent or persistent scheduling.

- The very first procedure a UE needs to do after powering on is to acquire time and frequency synchronization with a cell and obtain necessary system information. Then the UE can carry out the uplink synchronization and inform the eNode-B if it has data to transmit through the random access procedure. Cell search and random access procedures were discussed in Section 9.8 and Section 9.9, respectively.

- Intra-cell orthogonality (due to SC-FDMA) in uplink transmission makes the uplink power control less critical in LTE than in W-CDMA/HSPA. LTE uplink power control is used primarily to control inter-cell interference, which includes an open-loop component employing FPC and a closed-loop component.

Bibliography

[1] 3GPP TS 36.211: "Evolved Universal Terrestrial Radio Access (E-UTRA); Physical channels and modulation."

[2] 3GPP TS 36.212: "Evolved Universal Terrestrial Radio Access (E-UTRA); Multiplexing and channel coding."

[3] 3GPP TS 36.213: "Evolved Universal Terrestrial Radio Access (E-UTRA); Physical Layer Procedures."

[4] 3GPP TS 36.300: "Evolved Universal Terrestrial Radio Access (E-UTRA) and Evolved Universal Terrestrial Radio Access Network (E-UTRAN); Overall description; Stage 2 (Release 8)."

[5] 3GPP TS 36.321: "Evolved Universal Terrestrial Radio Access (E-UTRA) Medium Access Control (MAC) protocol specification."

[6] Brueninghaus, K., D. Astely, T. Salzer, S. Visuri, A. Alexiou, S. Karger, and G.-A. Seraji, "Link performance models for system level simulations of broadband radio access systems," in *Proc. of the IEEE Int. Symp. on Personal Indoor and Mobile Radio Comm.*, Berlin, Germany, Sept. 2005, pp. 2306–2311.

[7] Castellanos, C. U., D. L. Villa, C. Rosa, K. I. Pedersen, F. D. Calabrese, P.-H. Michaelsen, and J. Michel, "Performance of uplink fractional power control in UTRAN LTE," in *Proc. IEEE Veh. Technol. Conf.*, Singapore, May 2008, pp. 2517–2521.

[8] Jiang, D., H. Wang, E. Malkamäki, and E. Tuomaala, "Principle and performance of semi-persistent scheduling for VoIP in LTE system," in *Proc. International Conference on Wireless Communications, Networking and Mobile Computing (WiCom'07)*, Sept. 2007, pp. 2861–2864.

[9] Jindal, N., S. Weber, and J. Andrews, "Fractional power control for decentralized wireless networks," in *IEEE Trans. Wireless Communications*, vol. 7, No. 12, pp. 5482–5492, Dec. 2008.

[10] Mongha, G., K. I. Pedersen, I. Z. Kovacs, and P. E. Mogensen, "QoS oriented time and frequency domain packet schedulers for the UTRAN Long Term Evolution," in *Proc. IEEE Veh. Technology Conf.*, May 2008, pp. 2532–2536.

[11] Pokhariyal, A., T. E. Kolding, and P. E. Mogensen, "Performance of downlink frequency domain packet scheduling for the UTRAN Long Term Evolution," in *Proc. IEEE Personal Indoor and Mobile Radio Communications Conference (PIMRC)*, Helsinki, Finland, Sept. 2006, pp. 1–5.

[12] Pokhariyal, A., K. I. Pedersen, G. Monghal, I. Z. Kovacs, C. Rosa, T. E. Kolding, P. E. Mogensen, "H-ARQ aware frequency domain packet scheduling with different degree of fairness for the UTRAN Long Term Evolution," in *Proc. IEEE Veh. Technology Conf.*, Apr. 2007, pp. 2761–2765.

[13] Wengerter, C., J. Ohlhorst, and A. G. E. v. Elbwart, "Fairness and throughput analysis for generalized proportional fair frequency scheduling in OFDMA," in *Proc. IEEE Veh. Technology Conf.*, Stockholm, Sweden, May 2005, pp. 1903–1907.

[14] Xiao, W., R. Ratasuk, A. Ghosh, R. Love, Y. Sun, and R. Nory, "Uplink power control, interference coordination and resource allocation for 3GPP E-UTRA," in *Proc. IEEE Veh. Technology Conf.*, Sept. 2006, pp. 1–5.

Chapter 10

Data Flow, Radio Resource Management, and Mobility Management

Building on the physical layer procedures discussed in previous chapters, in this chapter we describe higher-layer protocols and mobility management in LTE. Radio resource management and inter-cell interference mitigation techniques will also be discussed in this chapter. However, before discussing higher-layer protocols, we first introduce the concept of bearer for Quality of Service (QoS) control and the protocol architecture of LTE.

LTE is a packet-switched network from end to end that is designed primarily for high-speed data services. To efficiently support the varying QoS requirements of different IP applications, LTE uses the concept of a *bearer* as the central element of QoS control. Each EPS (Evolved Packet System) bearer (*bearer* for short) is defined between the Packet Data Network Gateway (PDN-GW) and the UE, and maps to a specific set of QoS parameters such as data rate, latency, and packet error rate. Applications with very different QoS requirements such as e-mail and voice can be put on separate bearers that will allow the system to simultaneously meet their QoS requirements. The end-to-end connectivity through the network is made via the bearer service, and the bearer service architecture is shown in Figure 10.1. An EPS bearer has to cross multiple interfaces, and across each interface it is mapped to a transport layer bearer. An *S5/S8 bearer* transports the packets of an EPS bearer between a Serving GW (S-GW) and a PDN-GW, while an *S1 bearer* transports the packets of an EPS bearer between an eNode-B and an S-GW. Over the radio interface the bearer is referred to as the *radio bearer*, which transfers data between a UE and the E-UTRAN. Signaling Radio Bearers (SRBs) carry the Radio Resource Control (RRC) signaling messages, while the Data Radio Bearers (DRBs) carry the user plane data. Radio bearers are mapped to logical channels through Layer 2 protocols.

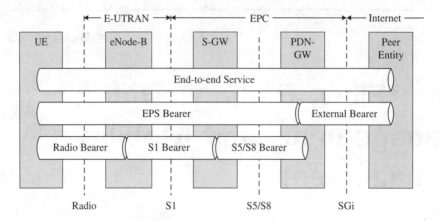

Figure 10.1 EPS bearer service architecture.

Broadly, the bearers can be divided into two classes:

- **Guaranteed Bit Rate (GBR) bearers:** These bearers define and guarantee a minimum bit rate that will be available to the UE. Bit rates higher than the minimum bit rate can be allowed if resources are available. GBR bearers are typically used for applications such as voice, streaming video, and real-time gaming.

- **Non-GBR bearers:** These bearers do not define or guarantee a minimum bit rate to the UE. The achieved bit rate depends on the system load, the number of UEs served by the eNode-B, and the scheduling algorithm. Non-GBR bearers are used for applications such as web browsing, e-mail, FTP, and P2P file sharing.

Each bearer is associated with a QoS Class Identifier (QCI), which indicates the priority, packet delay budget, acceptable packet error loss rate,[1] and the GBR/non-GBR classification [3]. The nine standardized QCI defined in the LTE are shown in Table 10.1. One EPS bearer is established when the UE connects to a Packet Data Network (PDN), and that remains established throughout the lifetime of the PDN connection to provide the UE with always-on IP connectivity to that PDN. This is referred to as the *default bearer*. Any additional EPS bearer that is established to the same PDN is referred to as a *dedicated bearer*. The core network handles the establishment and modification of the dedicated bearer.

The protocol architecture in LTE between the UE and the core network is divided into the user plane protocol stack and the control plane protocol stack, as shown in Figure 10.2 and Figure 10.3, respectively. The user plane is responsible for transporting IP packets carrying application-specific data from the PDN-GW to the UE. This is done by encapsulating the IP packets in an Evolved Packet Core (EPC)-specific protocol

---

1 The packet error loss rate defines an upper bound for the rate of IP packets that have been processed by the sender of a link layer protocol (e.g., RLC in E-UTRAN) but that are not successfully delivered by the corresponding receiver to the upper layer (e.g., PDCP in E-UTRAN). Thus, it defines an upper bound for a rate of non-congestion-related packet losses.

Table 10.1 Standardized QoS Class Identifiers (QCIs) for LTE

QCI	Resource Type	Priority	Packet Delay Budget (ms)	Packet Error Loss Rate	Example Services
1	GBR	2	100	10^{-2}	Conversational voice
2	GBR	4	150	10^{-3}	Conversational video (live streaming)
3	GBR	3	50	10^{-3}	Real-time gaming
4	GBR	5	300	10^{-6}	Non-conversational video (buffered streaming)
5	Non-GBR	1	100	10^{-6}	IMS signaling
6	Non-GBR	6	300	10^{-6}	Video (buffered streaming), TCP-based (e.g., WWW, e-mail, chat, FTP, etc.)
7	Non-GBR	7	100	10^{-3}	Voice, video (live streaming), interactive gaming
8	Non-GBR	8	300	10^{-6}	Video (buffered streaming), TCP-based (e.g., WWW, e-mail, chat, FTP, etc.)
9	Non-GBR	9	300	10^{-6}	

and tunneling them from the PDN-GW to the eNode-B using the GPRS Tunneling Protocol (GTP). From the eNode-B the packets are transported to the UE using the Packet Data Convergence Protocol (PDCP). On the other hand, the control plane is used for transporting signaling between the Mobility Management Entity (MME) and the UE. The type of signaling handled over the control plane is typically related to bearer management, QoS management, and mobility management including functions such as handover and paging.

In LTE, Layer 2 of the protocol stack is split into the following sublayers: Medium Access Control (MAC), Radio Link Control (RLC), and PDCP. The Layer 2 structure

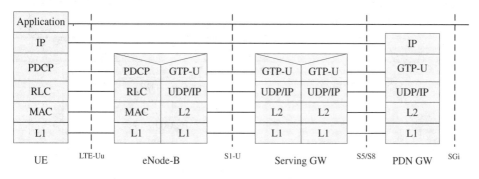

Figure 10.2 User plane protocol stack.

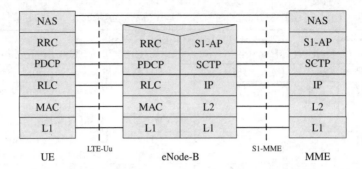

Figure 10.3 Control plane protocol stack.

for the downlink is depicted in Figure 10.4. Radio bearers are mapped to logical channels through PDCP and RLC sublayers. The Service Access Point (SAP) between the physical layer and the MAC sublayer provides the transport channels that are used by the physical layer to provide services to the MAC. Similarly, the SAP between the MAC sublayer and the RLC sublayer provides the logical channels that are used by the MAC layer to provide services to the RLC. In LTE, there is one RLC and PDCP entity per radio bearer in the UE and eNode-B. However, only one MAC entity exists in the UE and the eNode-B for all the radio bearers. The single MAC layer multiplexes the data and control information from all the radio bearers at the eNode-B and UE, i.e., it multiplexes several logical channels on the same transport channel (i.e., transport block).

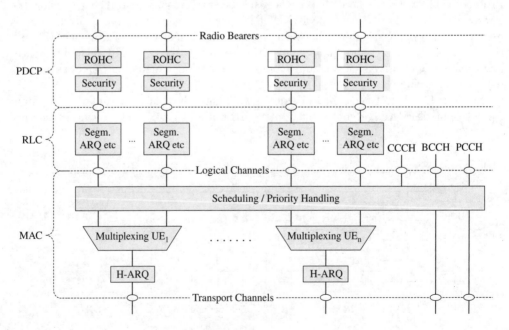

Figure 10.4 Layer 2 structure for downlink.

In W-CDMA, the RLC, PDCP, and RRC entities are in the Radio Network Controller (RNC), and the MAC entity is either in the Node-B (HSPA) or in the RNC (Release 99 W-CDMA). In LTE, all of these entities are contained in the eNode-B. At the transmit side, each protocol layer receives a service data unit (SDU) from the higher layer, and presents a protocol data unit (PDU) to the layer below. There are protocols between the core network and the UE that are transparent to the radio interface and referred to as Non-Access Stratum (NAS) signaling. In EPS, the NAS protocols consist mainly of the protocols for mobility management and session management between the UE and the MME. In this chapter we will discuss Layer 2 protocols, including the PDCP, RLC, and MAC sublayers. The RRC protocol will also be introduced, including the RRC states and different functions provided by RRC.

10.1 PDCP Overview

A PDCP entity is associated either with the control plane or with the user plane depending on which radio bearer it is carrying data for [7]. Each radio bearer is associated with one PDCP entity, and each PDCP entity is associated with one or two RLC entities depending on the radio bearer characteristic (uni-directional or bi-directional) and the RLC mode. PDCP is used only for radio bearers mapped on DCCH and DTCH types of logical channels.

The main services and functions of the PDCP sublayer for the user plane and control plane as shown in Figure 10.5 are as follows.

For the user plane:

1. Header compression and decompression of IP data flows with the RObust Header Compression (ROHC) protocol

2. Ciphering and deciphering of user plane data

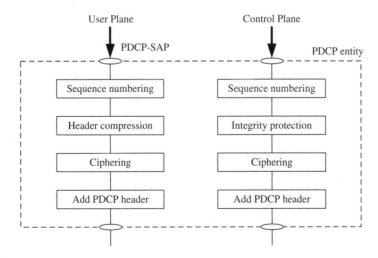

Figure 10.5 PDCP functions for the user plane and the control plane.

3. In-sequence delivery and reordering of upper-layer PDUs at handover

4. Buffering and forwarding of upper-layer PDUs from the serving eNode-B to the target eNode-B during handover

5. Timer-based discarding of SDUs in the uplink

For the control plane:

1. Ciphering and deciphering of control plane data

2. Integrity protection and integrity verification of control plane data

3. Transfer of control plane data

The PDCP PDUs can be divided into two categories:

- **The PDCP data PDU** is used in both the control and user plane to transport higher-layer packets. It is used to convey either user plane data containing a compressed/uncompressed IP packet or control plane data containing one RRC message and a Message Authentication Code for Integrity (MAC-I) field for integrity protection, which will be described in detail later in this section.

- **The PDCP control PDU** is used only within the user plane to convey a PDCP status report during handover and feedback information for header compression. Thus, unlike a PDCP data PDU, the PDCP control PDU does not carry any higher-layer SDU but rather is used for peer-to-peer signaling between the PDCP entities at two ends.

The constructions of the PDCP data PDU formats from the PDCP SDU for the user plane and the control plane are shown in Figure 10.6. The various types of PDCP PDU carried on the user and control plane are shown in Table 10.2. There are three different types of PDCP data PDUs, distinguished by the length of the Sequence Number (SN). The PDCP SN is used to provide robustness against packet loss and to guarantee sequential delivery at the receiver. The PDCP data PDU with the long SN is used for the Unacknowledge Mode (UM) and Acknowledged Mode (AM) and the PDCP data PDU with the short SN is used for the Transparent Mode (TM). Besides the SN field and the ciphered data, the PDCP data PDU for the user plane contains a 'D/C' field that is

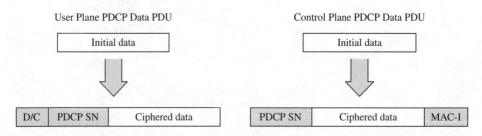

Figure 10.6 PDCP data PDU formats for the user plane and the control plane.

Table 10.2 PDCP Data Units

PDCP PDU Type	SN Length	Applicable RLC Mode
User plane PDCP data PDU (long SN)	12 bits	AM/UM
User plane PDCP data PDU (short SN)	7 bits	UM
Control plane PDCP data PDU	5 bits	AM/UM
PDCP control PDU for ROHC feedback	N/A	AM/RM
PDCP control PDU for PDCP status report	N/A	AM

to distinguish data and control PDUs. This is required since the PDCP data PDU can carry both user plane and control plane data. Also, the PDCP data PDU for the control plane comprises a MAC-I field of 32 bits for integrity protection. In the remainder of this section, we will discuss header compression, integrity, and ciphering performed by the PDCP entity.

10.1.1 Header Compression

The header compression protocol in LTE is based on the RObust Header Compression (ROHC) framework defined by the Internet Engineering Task Force (IETF) [12]. PDCP entities are configured by upper layers to use header compression, which is only performed on user plane data. The requirement for header compression comes from the fact that all the services in LTE are IP-based, and are based on the framework of IP and other related IETF protocols. Since the IP framework is native to the Internet and provides the most cost-effective mechanism for delivery of high-bandwidth data, it was determined in 3GPP that this was the optimum choice for LTE. However, these protocols bring a significant amount of header overhead at the network layer (IP), transport layer (TCP, UDP), and application layer (RTP), which contains redundant and repetitive information and unnecessarily consumes precious radio resources.[2] Therefore, an efficient header compression scheme is required, especially for VoIP services where the IP-related repetitive information in the header field is large relative to the actual speech packets. There are multiple header compression algorithms, called profiles, defined for the ROHC framework. Each profile is specific to the particular network layer, transport layer, or upper-layer protocol combination, e.g., TCP/IP and RTP/UDP/IP. The supported profiles in 3GPP Release 8 are listed in Table 10.3.

10.1.2 Integrity and Ciphering

The security-related functions in PDCP include integrity protection and ciphering. A PDCP PDU counter, denoted by the parameter COUNT, is maintained and used as an input to the security algorithm. The format of COUNT is shown in Figure 10.7, which has a length of 32 bits and consists of two parts: the Hyper Frame Number (HFN) and the PDCP SN. The SN is used for reordering and duplicate detection of RLC packets at the receive end.

---

2 TCP: Transmission Control Protocol; IP: Internet Protocol; RTP: Real-Time Transport Protocol; UDP: User Datagram Protocol.

Table 10.3 Supported Header Compression Protocols and Profiles

Profile ID	Usage	Reference
0x0000	No compression	RFC 4995
0x0001	RTP/UDP/IP	RFC 3095, RFC 4815
0x0002	UDP/IP	RFC 3095, RFC 4815
0x0003	ESP/IP	RFC 3095, RFC 4815
0x0004	IP	RFC 3843, RFC 4815
0x0006	TCP/IP	RFC 4996
0x0101	RTP/UDP/IP	RFC 5225
0x0102	UDP/IP	RFC 5225
0x0103	ESP/IP	RFC 5225
0x0104	IP	RFC 5225

The integrity protection function includes both integrity protection and integrity verification and is performed only for control plane data as indicated in Figure 10.6. The data unit that is integrity protected is the PDU header and the data part of the PDU before ciphering. Integrity protection is provided by the field MAC-I of 32-bit length. At transmission, the value of the MAC-I field is calculated based on the keys provided by RRC, the radio bearer identifier, the COUNT value, and the direction of the transmission. The receiver computes the expected message authentication code on the received message using the same parameters and algorithm used by the sender. If this does not match the MAC-I field, then the PDCP PDU does not pass the integrity check, and the PDCP PDU will be discarded.

The ciphering function includes both ciphering and deciphering. It is performed on both control plane data and user plane data. For the control plane, the data unit that is ciphered is the data part of the PDCP PDU and the MAC-I; for the user plane, the data unit that is ciphered is the data part of the PDCP PDU. Neither integrity nor ciphering is applicable to PDCP control PDUs. The ciphering function is activated by upper layers, which also configures the ciphering algorithm and the ciphering key to be used. The ciphering is done by an XOR operation of the data unit with the ciphering stream. The ciphering stream is generated by the ciphering algorithm based on ciphering keys, the radio bearer identity, the value of COUNT, the direction of the transmission, and the length of the key stream, as specified in [4].

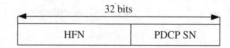

Figure 10.7 Format of COUNT.

10.2 MAC/RLC Overview

As there is close interaction between MAC and RLC sublayers [5, 6], we discuss them together in this section. The RLC layer performs segmentation and/or concatenation on PDCP PDUs based on the size indicated by the MAC. RLC also reorders the RLC PDUs once they are received out of order possibly due to H-ARQ processes in the MAC layer. The RLC layer also supports an ARQ mechanism, which resides on top of the MAC layer H-ARQ and is used only when all the H-ARQ transmissions are exhausted and the RLC PDU has not yet been received without errors. As mentioned previously, at the transmitter and the receiver there is one RLC entity per radio bearer. The MAC layer performs multiplexing and demultiplexing of the various logical channels on to the transport channels. At the eNode-B, this includes multiplexing and prioritizing various UEs that are being served by the eNode-B as well as multiplexing and prioritizing the various radio bearers within a given UE. At the UE, the MAC layer only performs the task of multiplexing and prioritizing the various radio bearers associated with the UE. The MAC layer provides services to the RLC layer through logical channels, while it accesses the data transfer services provided by the PHY layer through transport channels.

10.2.1 Data Transfer Modes

Functions of the RLC layer are performed by RLC entities. Each RLC entity can be operated in three different modes: the Transparent Mode (TM), the Unacknowledged Mode (UM), and the Acknowledged Mode (AM).

The Transparent Mode (TM)

The TM mode is the simplest one. The RLC entity does not add any RLC header to the PDU and no data segmentation or concatenation is performed. This mode is suitable for services that do not need retransmission or are not sensitive to delivery order. Only RRC messages such as broadcast system information messages and paging messages use the TM mode. The TM mode is not used for user plane data transmission. The RLC data PDU delivered by a TM RLC entity is called the TM Data (TMD) PDU.

The Unacknowledged Mode (UM)

The UM mode provides in-sequence delivery of data that may be received out of sequence due to the H-ARQ process in MAC, but no retransmission of the lost PDU is required. This mode can be used by delay-sensitive and error-tolerant real-time applications, such as VoIP. The DTCH logical channel can be operated in the UM mode, and the RLC data PDU delivered by an UM RLC entity is called the UM Data (UMD) PDU. At the transmit end, the UM RLC entity segments and/or concatenates the RLC SDUs according to the total size of RLC PDUs indicated by the MAC layer. Relevant RLC headers are also included in the UMD PDU. The receiving UM RLC entity performs duplicate detection, reordering, and reassembly of UMD PDUs.

The Acknowledged Mode (AM)

The AM mode is the most complex one, which requests retransmission of missing PDUs in addition to the UM mode functionalities. It is mainly used by error-sensitive and delay-tolerant applications. An AM RLC entity can be configured to deliver/receive RLC PDUs through DCCH and DTCH. An AM RLC entity delivers/receives the AM Data (AMD) PDU and the STATUS PDU indicating the ACK/NAK information of the RLC PDUs. When the AM RLC entity needs to retransmit a portion of an AMD PDU, which results from the ARQ process and segmentation, the transmitted PDU is called the *AMD PDU segment*. The operation of the AM RLC entity is similar to that of the UM RLC entity, except that it supports retransmission of RLC data PDUs. The receiving AM RLC entity can send a STATUS PDU to inform the transmitting RLC entity about the AMD PDUs that are received successfully and that are detected to be lost.

10.2.2   Purpose of MAC and RLC Layers

The main services and functions of the RLC sublayer include

- Transfering/receiving PDUs from upper layers, i.e., from RRC for the CCCH logical channel or from PDCP for other cases

- Error correction through ARQ (only when the RLC is operated in the AM mode)

- Concatenation,[3] segmentation, and reassembly of RLC SDUs (only for UM and AM data transfer)

- Re-segmentation of RLC data PDUs (only for AM data transfer)

- In-sequence delivery of upper-layer PDUs (only for UM and AM data transfer)

- Duplicate detection (only for UM and AM data transfer)

- Protocol error detection and recovery

- RLC SDU discard (only for UM and AM data transfer)

- RLC re-establishment

LTE defines two MAC entities: one in the UE and one in the eNode-B. The exact functions performed by the MAC entities are different in the UE from those performed in the eNode-B. The main services and functions of the MAC sublayer include

- Mapping between logical channels and transport channels, which was discussed in detail in Chapter 6

- Multiplexing/demultiplexing of MAC SDUs belonging to one or different logical channels into/from the same transport block

- Scheduling for both downlink and uplink transmission, which was discussed in Chapter 9

- Error correction through H-ARQ, which has tight interaction with ARQ in the RLC layer and will be discussed later in this section

---

3 Concatenation, which helps in reducing the total number of physical layer transmissions, can be utilized to decrease not only the protocol overhead but also the scheduling-related signaling load.

- Priority handling between logical channels of one UE or between UEs by means of dynamic scheduling

- Transport format selection, i.e., the selection of the Modulation and Coding Scheme (MCS) for link adaptation

- Padding if a MAC PDU is not fully filled with data

10.2.3 PDU Headers and Formats

RLC PDU Formats

RLC PDUs can be categorized into RLC data PDUs and RLC control PDUs. As discussed in the previous subsection, RLC data PDUs are used by TM, UM, and AM RLC entities to transfer upper-layer PDUs, called the TM Data (TMD) PDU, the UM Data (UMD) PDU, and the AM Data (AMD) PDU, respectively. On the other hand, RLC control PDUs are used for peer-to-peer signaling between the AM RLC entities at the two ends for ARQ procedures.

The formats of different RLC Data PDUs are shown in Figure 10.8. The TMD PDU only consists of a Data field, as no RLC header is added. The RLC headers are different for UMD PDU and AMD PDU, but they contain common fields including:

- **Framing Info (FI) field:** The FI field indicates whether a RLC SDU is segmented at the beginning and/or at the end of the Data field.

- **Length Indicator (LI) field:** The LI field indicates the length in bytes of the corresponding Data field element present in the UMD or AMD PDU.

- **Extension bit (E) field:** The E field indicates whether a Data field follows or a set of E field and LI field follows.

- **SN field:** The SN field indicates the sequence number of the corresponding UMD or AMD PDU. It consists of 10 bits for AMD PDU, AMD PDU segments, and STATUS PDUs, and 5 bits or 10 bits for UMD PDU. The PDU sequence number carried by the RLC header is independent of the SDU sequence number, i.e., the PDCP sequence number.

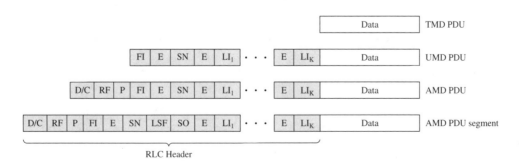

Figure 10.8 Formats of RLC Data PDUs.

For AMD PDU and AMD PDU segments, additional fields are available:

- **Data/Control (D/C) field:** The D/C field indicates whether the RLC PDU is an RLC Data PDU or an RLC Control PDU.

- **Re-segmentation Flag (RF) field:** The RF field indicates whether the RLC PDU is an AMD PDU or an AMD PDU segment.

- **Polling bit (P) field:** The P field indicates whether the transmitting side of an AM RLC entity requests a STATUS report from its peer AM RLC entity.

Additionally, the RLC header of an AMD PDU segment contains special fields including:

- **Segment Offset (SO) field:** The SO field indicates the position of the AMD PDU segment in bytes within the original AMD PDU.

- **Last Segment Flag (LSF) field:** The LSF field indicates whether the last byte of the AMD PDU segment corresponds to the last byte of an AMD PDU.

The STATUS PDU is used by the receiving AM RLC entity to indicate the missing portions of AMD PDUs. The format of the STATUS PDU is shown in Figure 10.9, which consists of the following fields:

- **Control PDU Type (CPT) field:** The CPT field indicates the type of the RLC control PDU, and in Release 8 the STATUS PDU is the only defined control PDU.

- **Acknowledgment SN (ACK_SN) field:** The ACK_SN field indicates the SN of the next not received RLC Data PDU, which is not reported as missing in the STATUS PDU.

- **Extension bit 1 (E1) field:** The E1 field indicates whether a set of NACK_SN, E1, and E2 follows.

- **Extension bit 2 (E2) field:** The E2 field indicates whether a set of SOstart and SOend follows.

- **Negative Acknowledgment SN (NACK_SN) field:** The NACK_SN field indicates the SN of the AMD PDU (or portions of it) that has been detected as lost at the receiving side of the AM RLC entity.

- **SO start (SOstart) field and SO end (SOend) field:** These two fields together indicate the portion of the AMD PDU with SN = NACK_SN that has been detected as lost at the receiving side of the AM RLC entity.

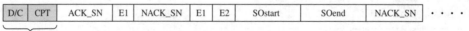

| D/C | CPT | ACK_SN | E1 | NACK_SN | E1 | E2 | SOstart | SOend | NACK_SN | ▪ ▪ ▪ ▪ |

RLC Header

Figure 10.9 The format of STATUS PDU.

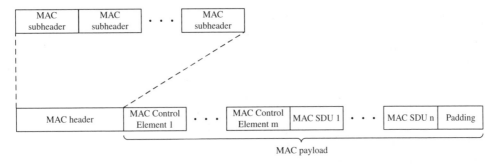

Figure 10.10 An example of MAC PDU consisting of MAC header, MAC control elements, MAC SDUs, and padding.

MAC PDU Formats

The MAC layer receives data from RLC as MAC SDUs, and passes the MAC PDUs to PHY. A MAC PDU consists of two parts: a MAC header and a MAC payload, as shown in Figure 10.10. The MAC payload consists of zero or more MAC SDUs, zero or more MAC control elements, and optional padding; the MAC PDU header consists of one or more MAC PDU subheaders, while each subheader corresponds to either a MAC SDU, a MAC control element, or padding. Therefore, both the MAC SDU and the MAC header are of variable sizes.

The format of a typical MAC subheader is shown in Figure 10.11, which contains five different fields as explained in the following:

- **"R" field:** It is currently reserved always set to "0."

- **"E" field:** It is an extension field as a flag indicating if more fields are present in the MAC header. If it is set to "1," another set of at least R/R/E/LCID fields follows; otherwise, either a MAC SDU, a MAC control element, or padding follows.

- **"LCID" field:** This Logical Channel ID (LCID) field identifies the logical channel instance of the corresponding MAC SDU or the type of the corresponding MAC control element or padding. There is one LCID field for each MAC SDU, MAC control element, or padding included in the MAC PDU.

- **"F" field:** This format indicates the size of the Length field. It is set to "0" if the size of the MAC SDU or MAC control element is less than 128 bytes; otherwise, it is "1." There is one F field per MAC PDU subheader except for the last subheader and the subheader corresponding to fixed-sized MAC control elements.

- **"L" field:** This Length field indicates the length of the corresponding MAC PDU or MAC control element in bytes. The size of the L field is indicated by the F field.

R	R	E	LCID	F	L

Figure 10.11 An example of the MAC subheader.

For the last subheader in the MAC PDU, the MAC PDU subheader corresponding to padding, and subheaders for fixed size MAC control elements, there are only four header fields: R/R/E/LCID.

The MAC control element can be used for signaling for buffer status reporting, Discontinuous Reception (DRX) command, timing advance command, UE's power headroom, and UE contention resolution. There is also a transparent MAC PDU consisting solely of a MAC SDU without any MAC header, which can be used if there is a one-to-one correspondence between a MAC SDU and a MAC PDU.

The MAC PDU for random access response has a different format, as shown in Figure 10.12. In the case of random access, there is a MAC header that consists of one or more MAC PDU subheaders, where each subheader contains information about the payload. The MAC payload consists of one or more MAC Random Access Responses (MAC RAR) and optional padding. Each MAC RAR is of fixed size and consists of four fields, described as follows:

- **Reserved Bit:** It is set to "0."

- **Timing Advance Command:** It indicates the index value used to control the amount of timing adjustment that UE has to apply. It is of 11 bits.

- **UL Grant:** It indicates the resources to be used on the uplink, and is of 20 bits.

- **Temporary C-RNTI:** This field indicates the temporary identity that is used by the UE during random access. The size is 16 bits.

The random access procedure was described in Section 9.9.

10.2.4   ARQ Procedures

To better support upper-layer services, LTE applies a dynamic and efficient two-layer retransmission scheme: A fast H-ARQ protocol with low latency and low overhead feedback in the MAC layer and a highly reliable selective repeat ARQ protocol in the RLC layer [5, 6, 15]. The H-ARQ protocol is responsible for handling transmission errors by

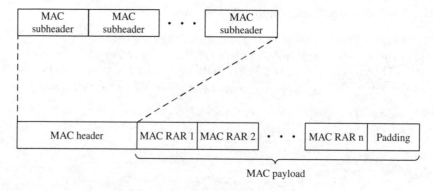

Figure 10.12 The MAC PDU for random access response.

performing retransmissions based on H-ARQ processes with incremental redundancy or chase combining, which is handled by the PHY layer. The H-ARQ protocols for downlink and uplink were discussed in Chapters 7 and 8, respectively. The ARQ protocol in the RLC layer is to correct residual H-ARQ errors, mainly due to the error in H-ARQ ACK feedback. ARQ procedures are only performed in the AM transfer mode by an AM RLC entity and unlike H-ARQ, the latency associated with the RLC layer ARQ is much larger.

The reliability of the H-ARQ protocol is determined by the error rate of the feedback. It is costly to achieve a sufficiently reliable H-ARQ-ACK feedback. The solution adopted in LTE is to use a second-layer ARQ protocol, which is to correct the error event due to H-ARQ feedback errors. This additional ARQ protocol provides a much more reliable feedback protected by a CRC. This design yields low latency and low overhead without sacrificing reliability. Most errors are captured and corrected by the low-overhead H-ARQ protocol, and the more resource-demanding ARQ retransmissions are only rarely needed.

ARQ retransmission is triggered by an ARQ NAK received at the transmit side of an AM RLC entity. The ARQ NAK is received either by the STATUS PDU from its peer AM RLC entity or by H-ARQ delivery failure notification from the transmit MAC entity, which can happen when the maximum number of H-ARQ transmissions is exhausted without a successful transmission of the transport block. The STATUS reporting is triggered by setting the Polling field of the RLC data PDU to "1," and the NAK reporting is contained in the STATUS PDU as shown in Figure 10.9. An H-ARQ delivery failure is notified by the MAC entity when the MAC PDU is not delivered successfully after the maximum number of H-ARQ retransmissions. Upon receiving an ARQ NAK, the transmit side of an AM RLC entity will deliver the AMD PDU if it fits within the total size of RLC PDU indicated by the lower layer; otherwise, it segments the AMD PDU and forms a new PDU segment that fits the PDU size. If the maximum number of ARQ retransmissions is reached, the AM RLC entity will notify the upper layers.

In HSPA, the H-ARQ protocol of the MAC layer is terminated in the Node-B, while ARQ of the RLC layer is terminated in the RNC. In LTE, both of them are terminated in the eNode-B, which enables a tighter interconnection between the H-ARQ and ARQ protocols. The benefits of this architecture include fast handling of residual H-ARQ errors and variable ARQ transmission size.

10.3 RRC Overview

The RRC layer takes care of RRC connection management, radio bearer control, mobility functions, and UE measurement reporting and control. It is also responsible for broadcasting system information and paging. In this section, we discuss the two RRC states in LTE and the functions provided by the RRC protocol.

10.3.1 RRC States

Compared to UMTS, which has four RRC states, LTE has only two states: RRC_IDLE and RRC_CONNECTED, as depicted in Figure 10.13. This simplifies the RRC state machine handling and the radio resource management, which controls the RRC state. A UE is in the RRC_CONNECTED state when an RRC connection has been established; otherwise, the UE is in the RRC_IDLE state.

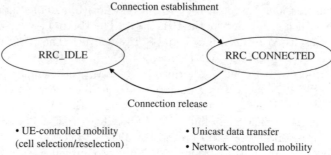

Figure 10.13 RRC states in LTE.

In the RRC_IDLE state, the UE can receive broadcasts of system information and paging information. There is no signaling radio bearer established, so there is no RRC connection. In the RRC_IDLE state, the mobility control is handled by the UE, which performs neighboring cell measurements and cell selection/reselection. The system information mainly contains parameters by which E-UTRAN controls the cell selection/reselection process, such as priorities of different frequencies. The UE shall have been allocated an ID that uniquely identifies the UE in a tracking area. The UE also monitors a paging channel to detect incoming calls, and it specifies the paging Discontinuous Reception (DRX) cycle.

In the RRC_CONNECTED state, the UE has an E-UTRAN RRC connection and a context in the E-UTRAN, so it is able to transmit and/or receive data to/from the network (eNode-B). The UE monitors control channels (PDCCH) associated with the shared data channel to determine if data is scheduled for it. The UE can also report channel quality information and feedback information to the eNode-B to assist the data transmission. In the RRC_CONNECTED state, the network controls mobility/handover of the UE, while UEs provide neighboring cell measurement information.

10.3.2   RRC Functions

Before going into different functions provided by the RRC protocol, we first introduce the concept of Signaling Radio Bearers (SRBs). SRBs are defined as radio bearers that are used only for the transmission of RRC and NAS messages. There are three different SRBs defined in LTE [8]:

- SRB0 is for RRC messages using the CCCH logical channel.

- SRB1 is for RRC messages and NAS messages prior to the establishment of SRB2, all using the DCCH logical channel.

- SRB2 is for NAS messages, using DCCH logical channel. SRB2 has a lower-priority than SRB1 and is always configured by the E-UTRAN after security activation.

Following are the main functions of the RRC protocol.

- **Broadcast of system information,** which is divided into the Master Information Block (MIB) and a number of System Information Blocks (SIBs). The MIB includes a limited number of the most essential and most frequently transmitted parameters that are needed to acquire other information from the cell, and is transmitted on the BCH logical channel. SIBs other than SIB Type 1 are carried in System Information (SI) messages. SIB Type 1 contains parameters needed to determine if a cell is suitable for cell selection as well as information about the time-domain scheduling of the other SIBs. SIB Type 1 and all SI messages are transmitted on DL-SCH.

- **RRC connection control** includes procedures related to the establishment, modification, and release of an RRC connection, including paging, initial security activation, establishment of SRBs and radio bearers carrying user data, radio configuration control and QoS control, and recovery from the radio link failure.

- **Measurement configuration and reporting** includes establishment, modification, and release of measurements, configuration, and (de-)activation of measurement gaps, and measurement reporting for intra-frequency, inter-frequency, and inter-RAT (Radio Access Technology) mobility. Details about mobility management will be provided in Section 10.4.

- **Other functions** include transfer of dedicated NAS information and non-3GPP dedicated information, transfer of UE radio access capability information, and support of self-configuration and self-optimization.

10.4 Mobility Management

LTE mobility management functions can be categorized into two groups: a) mobility within the LTE system (intra-LTE mobility) and b) mobility to other systems such as other 3GPP systems (e.g., UMTS) and non-3GPP systems (inter-RAT mobility). Intra-LTE mobility can happen either over the S1 interface or over the X2 interface. When the UE moves from one eNode-B to another eNode-B within the same Radio Access Network (RAN) attached to the same MME, the mobility takes place over the X2 interface. On the other hand, when the UE moves from one eNode-B to another that belongs to a different RAN attached to different MMEs or if the two eNode-Bs are not connected over an X2 interface, then the mobility takes place over the S1 interface. The inter-RAT mobility essentially uses the S1-mobility with the only difference being that in this case the PDCP context is not continued and the UE needs to re-establish its session once it moves to the target non-LTE system.

10.4.1 S1 Mobility

S1 mobility is very similar to the UMTS Serving Radio Network Subsystem (SRNS) relocation procedure and consists of the following steps (shown in Figure 10.14):

1. **Preparation Phase**: Once a decision has been made for a handover and a target MME and eNode-B have been identified, the network needs to allocate resources

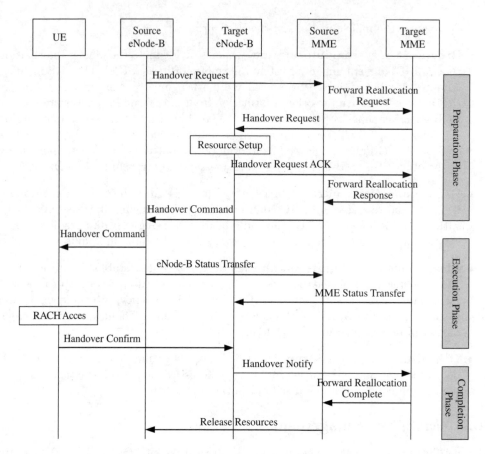

Figure 10.14 Mobility management over the S1 interface.

on the target side for the impending handover. The MME sends a handover request to the target eNode-B requesting it to set up the appropriate resources for the UE. Once the resources have been allocated at the target eNode-B, it sends a handover request ACK to the MME. Once this message is received by the MME, it sends a handover command to the UE via the source eNode-B.

2. **Execution Phase**: Once the UE receives the handover command, it responds by performing the various RAN-related procedures needed for the handover including accessing the target eNode-B using the Random Access Channel (RACH). The RAN-related procedures of a handover are discussed in detail later in this section. While the UE performs the handover, the source eNode-B initiates the status transfer where the PDCP context of the UE is transferred to the target eNode-B. The source eNode-B also forwards the data stored in the PDCP buffer to the target eNode-B. Once the status and data have been transferred to the target eNode-B and the UE is able to establish a Radio Access Bearer (RAB) on the target eNode-B, it sends the handover confirm message to the target eNode-B.

3. **Completion Phase**: When the target eNode-B receives the handover confirm message, it sends a handover notify message to the MME. The MME then informs the source eNode-B to release the resources originally used by the UE.

10.4.2   X2 Mobility

The mobility over the X2 interface is the default mode of operation in LTE unless an X2 interface is not available between the source and target eNode-Bs. When this is the case, the mobility over S1 interface is triggered as mentioned in the previous section. Mobility over the X2 interface also consists of three steps (shown in Figure 10.15):

1. **Preparation Phase**: Once the handover decision has been made by the source eNode-B, it sends a handover request message to the target eNode-B. The target eNode-B upon receipt of this message works with the MME and S-GW to set up the resources for the UE. In the case of mobility over X2 interface, it is possible to set up resources on a per-RAB basis, which implies that upon the completion of the handover the UE will have the same RABs at the target eNode-B with the

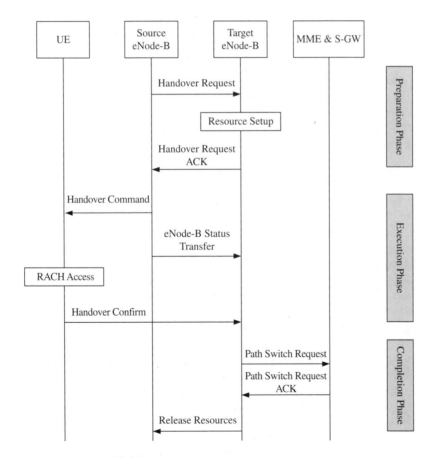

Figure 10.15 Mobility management over the X2 interface.

same set of QoS as it had on the source eNode-B. This process makes the handover quick and seamless and the UE is not required to set up the RAB with the target eNode-B once the handover is completed. The target eNode-B responds to the source eNode-B with a handover request ACK once it is ready.

2. **Execution Phase**: Upon receiving the handover request ACK, the source eNode-B sends a handover command to the UE. While the UE completes the various RAN-related handover procedures, the source eNode-B starts the status and data transfer to the target eNode-B. This is done on a per-RAB basis for the UE.

3. **Completion Phase**: Once the UE completes the handover procedure, it sends a handoff complete message to the target eNode-B. Then the target eNode-B sends a path switch request to the MME/S-GW and the S-GW switches the GTP tunnel from the source eNode-B to the target eNode-B. When the data path in the user plane is switched, the target eNode-B sends a message to the source eNode-B to release the resources originally used by the UE.

In the case of X2 mobility, the source eNode-B can select a lossless handover for one or more of the RABs. In this case, both the PDCP-processed and PDCP-unprocessed packets are sent to the target eNode-B during the status transfer. The PDCP-processed packets are the data packets that have been transmitted by the source eNode-B to the UE but the UE has not yet acknowledged the receipt of such packets. On the other hand, PDCP-unprocessed packets are the packets buffered by the PDCP layer that are yet to be transmitted by the source eNode-B. In LTE there is an additional feature called *selective retransmission*, which is enabled where the target eNode-B may not retransmit the PDCP-processed packets that were forwarded but were acknowledged by the UE after the status transfer was initiated.

10.4.3   RAN Procedures for Mobility

In the previous section we described the various mechanism and signaling procedures between the various network elements of LTE that enable the mobility management over the S1 and the X2 interfaces. However, we did not cover various aspects of the mobility management within the RAN that are used to determine when a handover (or cell reselection) should happen or how a UE accesses the target eNode-B when it executes a handover. These RAN-related mobility management procedures happen between the UE and the eNode-B or between the UE and the MME in order to enable the UE to handover from one eNode-B to another. These procedures can be classified into two distinct cases: a) mobility in the RRC_IDLE state and b) mobility in the RRC_CONNECTED state. The mobility management in these two RRC states was designed to be consistent, i.e., to prevent the ping-pong between two eNode-Bs when the UE undergoes RRC state transitions and also to be applicable in a host of different scenarios such as network sharing, country border, and home deployment (femto cells).

In LTE, like other radio access technologies, radio link quality is the primary measure that is used in intra-frequency handover, i.e., the UE selects the eNode-B with the best radio link quality. In LTE, the radio link quality is indicated by the Reference Signal Received Power (RSRP) for an LTE cell and by the Reference Signal Code Power (RSCP) for a UMTS cell. Selecting the eNode-B/Node-B with the best radio link quality is optimum from both an interference management and a battery life point of view. However, for inter-frequency handover and/or inter-RAT handover, radio link quality is not the primary measure on which the handover is based. Other factors such as UE capability, call type, QoS requirements, and other policy-related aspects are also included in the handover decision process. The *measurement report* from the UE, which contains the radio link measurement for the neighboring eNode-B, is the primary mechanism used by the network to trigger and control a handover procedure. The serving eNode-B provides the UE with the list of the neighboring cells and the frequencies that it ought to measure and report when a measurement report is requested.

For intra-LTE handover there are five events that trigger measurement reporting:

- **Event A1**: The serving cell radio link quality becomes better than an absolute threshold.

- **Event A2**: The serving cell radio link quality becomes worse than an absolute threshold.

- **Event A3**: The neighbor cell radio link quality becomes better than an offset relative to the serving cell.

- **Event A4**: The neighbor cell radio link quality becomes better than an absolute threshold.

- **Event A5**: Serving cell radio link quality becomes less than an absolute threshold and the neighbor cell radio link quality becomes better than another absolute threshold.

Similarly, for inter-RAT handover there are two events that can trigger a measurement report:

- **Event B1**: Neighbor cell radio link quality on a different RAT becomes better than an absolute threshold.

- **Event B2**: Serving cell radio link quality becomes worse than an absolute threshold and the neighbor cell radio link quality on a different RAT becomes better than another threshold.

For all these events the E-UTRAN can specify a *timeToTrigger* parameter, which is the amount of time each of these events must be satisfied before a measurement report is triggered. This *timeToTrigger* parameter is chosen to prevent the UE from ping-ponging between eNode-Bs, which can happen if no such parameter is used. The RAN mobility management in LTE had been designed to trigger a measurement report whenever there is a significant change in the radio link quality even if it is for the better. This is why the event type A1 has been defined, which would seem to be redundant at first since improving link quality is not usually a harbinger to an impending handover. But in a multicell network it is possible to envision a situation where this could be the case—for example, if the UE is moving toward an eNode-B in a direction such that it is closer to the inter-sector boundary. In this case, even though the serving cell radio link quality improves over time as the UE transitions the inter-sector boundary, the neighboring sector becomes a candidate for handover. In this scenario, the event type A1 would be needed to trigger a measurement report and start the handover procedure.

In the RRC_IDLE state, the UE decides when a handover is required and which cell/frequency the UE should target. The E-UTRAN allocates absolute priorities to the different frequencies. These priorities are conveyed by the system information message carried over the BCH. The priority of each cell is determined by the UE based on the priority of the frequency and the radio link quality of the cell.

In the RRC_CONNECTED state, the E-UTRAN determines the optimum cell and frequency for the target eNode-B in order to maintain the best radio link quality. Normally, the handover is initiated by the E-UTRAN based on one or more of the events that trigger a measurement report (A1-A5) and (B1-B2). However, the E-UTRAN may initiate a handover without any of these trigger events, also called a blind handover. In LTE all handovers are hard handovers, i.e., a UE can be connected to only one eNode-B at a time. This hard handover process is usually a "backward" handover where the source eNode-B controls the handover and requests the target eNode-B to prepare for the handover and allocate resources for the UE. When the resources are allocated and the target eNode-B is ready to send an RRC message (relayed by the source eNode-B) requesting the UE to perform the handover, the UE uses the random access procedure in the target eNode-B to establish a connection and execute the handover. Even though in the case of handover in the RRC_CONNECTED state the resources have been allocated at the target eNode-B, the UE still needs to use the RACH in order to obtain physical layer synchronization such as time and frequency synchronization, and initial open-loop power control estimates. However, unlike the network entry procedure, in this case the UE can use dedicated RACH resources, thus eliminating the possibility of a collision.

10.4.4   Paging

Paging is a connection control function of the RRC protocol. The Paging message is used to inform the UEs in the RRC_IDLE or RRC_CONNECTED state about a system information change and/or about an Earthquake and Tsunami Warning System (ETWS) notification.[4] The UE in the RRC_IDLE state also monitors a Paging channel to detect incoming calls.

Change of system information only occurs at specific radio frames, and the concept of a modification period is used. Within a modification period, system information can be transmitted a number of times with the same content. Upon receiving a change notification contained in the Paging message, the UE knows that the current system information is valid until the next modification period boundary. After this boundary, the UE will re-acquire the required system information. If the ETWS notification is indicated, the UE that is ETWS capable will re-acquire the system information block related to ETWS immediately without waiting for the next system information modification boundary.

E-UTRAN initiates the paging procedure by transmitting the Paging message at the UE's paging occasion. One Paging Frame (PF) is one radio frame in which the

---

4 Earthquake and Tsunami Warning System (ETWS) is a type of Public Warning System that broadcasts warnings of earthquakes and tsunamis to any UE that is capable of receiving them [1].

E-UTRAN can page the UE. One PF may contain one or multiple subframe(s) in which a Paging message can be transmitted. Each such subframe is called a Paging Occasion (PO), which is configured by the E-UTRAN. The paging information is carried on the PDSCH physical channel. In a certain PO, the UE is configured to decode PDCCH with CRC scrambled by the Paging-Radio Network Temporary Identifier (P-RNTI), and then decode the corresponding PDSCH for the paging information. To reduce power consumption, the UE may use Discontinuous Reception (DRX) in the idle mode, so it needs only to monitor one PO per DRX cycle. After receiving the Paging message, the UE can switch off its receiver to preserve battery power. The DRX cycle is configured by the E-UTRAN [8].

10.5 Inter-Cell Interference Coordination

In cellular networks, each UE suffers Inter-Cell Interference (ICI) due to frequency reuse in other cells. Conventional cellular networks by design are interference-limited: if they were not, it would be possible to increase the spectrum efficiency by lowering the frequency reuse or increasing the average loading per cell. To meet the spectrum efficiency target, LTE will be deployed with universal frequency reuse, i.e., the same spectrum will be reused in each cell. This will cause a high level of ICI, especially for UEs at the cell edge. Meanwhile, LTE also has a mandate to increase cell edge throughput. Therefore, ICI control techniques must be applied [10, 11, 13, 14, 17]. In this section, we discuss ICI mitigation techniques for both downlink and uplink transmissions. ICI suppression through base station coordination, or networked MIMO, has been discussed in Section 5.9.2, where the associated opportunities and challenges were highlighted.

10.5.1 Downlink

In the downlink, there are three basic approaches to mitigate ICI:

- **ICI randomization** This is achieved by scrambling the codeword after channel coding with a pseudo-random sequence, as discussed in Section 7.1.2. With cell-specific scrambling, ICI from neighboring cells is randomized, and then interference suppression is achieved thanks to the processing gain provided by the channel code. Without scrambling, the channel decoder might be equally matched to interfering signals as to the desired signals on the same radio resource. ICI randomization has been applied in systems such as UMTS.

- **ICI cancellation** If a UE is able to decode the interfering signals, it can regenerate and then subtract them from the desired signal. This can be achieved with a multiuser detector [16] at the UE. However, to decode the interfering signal from neighboring cells, the UE needs to know its transmission format, which is not available as the UE cannot decode the PDCCH from neighboring cells. Alternatively, ICI cancellation can also be performed in the spatial domain, as discussed in Section 5.4. As shown in Section 5.4.3, linear spatial interference cancellation with statistical knowledge of interference channels is a practical option for ICI cancellation, but application in the downlink is limited by the capability and the number of antennas at UEs.

- **ICI coordination/avoidance** This is achieved by applying restrictions to the downlink resource management in a coordinated way between neighboring cells. The restrictions can be on time/frequency resources or transmit power used at each eNode-B. It requires additional inter-eNode-B communication and UE measurements and reporting.

In this subsection, we will focus on ICI coordination/avoidance, which is a more advanced technique and requires additional signaling. ICI coordination/avoidance can be either static or semi-static, with different inter-eNode-B communication requirements and different performance.

- **Static ICI coordination/avoidance** This is mainly done during the cell planning process and does not require frequent reconfiguration. An example is static Fractional Frequency Reuse (FFR), as discussed in Section 4.6.2. Static coordination strategy requires no or little inter-eNode-B signaling, but there is performance limitation as dynamic characteristics such as cell loading or user distributions are not taken into consideration.

- **Semi-static ICI coordination/avoidance** Semi-static coordination typically requires reconfigurations on a time-scale of the order of seconds or longer, and inter-eNode-B communication over the X2 interface is needed. The information exchanged between neighboring eNode-Bs can be transmission power and/or traffic load on different resource blocks. By considering such information at neighboring eNode-Bs, ICI suppression is more efficient.

From the above discussion, we see that ICI coordination/avoidance is mainly a scheduler implementation issue at eNode-Bs. To assist such coordination, the LTE system defines eNode-B power restriction signaling in the downlink, which is a bitmap termed the Relative Narrowband Transmit Power (RNTP) indicator that can be exchanged between eNode-Bs over the X2 interface. Each bit of the RNTP indicator corresponds to one Physical Resource Block (PRB) and is to indicate the maximum anticipated transmit power on that PRB. Based on the RNTP indicators from neighboring cells, each eNode-B is able to improve the performance of UEs in its own cell by scheduling and power allocation. Figure 10.16 shows a simple example of power patterns in three neighboring cells.

Coordinated Multi-Point Transmission

In LTE-Advanced, to further improve cell-edge performance, advanced techniques with more sophisticated coordination will be developed for ICI mitigation. One such technique is called Coordinated Multi-Point (CoMP) transmission/reception [2]. Downlink CoMP transmission implies dynamic coordination among multiple geographically separated transmission points. It can be deployed in the form of coordinated scheduling and/or beamforming, or multicell joint transmission, which is essentially the same as the networked MIMO discussed in Section 5.9.2. As shown in Section 5.9.2, CoMP with joint transmission theoretically can eliminate all the ICI and transfer the cellular network from an interference-limited system to a noise-limited system. However, there are many practical issues associated with CoMP transmission. It is a type of dynamic ICI

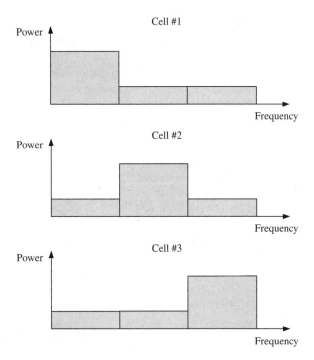

Figure 10.16 Possible downlink power levels of three neighboring cells. Edge users in each cell would be allocated to the higher power levels.

coordination. Deploying it will have great impacts on radio-interface specifications, such as feedback and measurement mechanisms from the UE, inter-eNode-B signaling, and downlink control and reference signal design.

10.5.2 Uplink

The basic approaches for uplink ICI mitigation are as follows:

- **ICI randomization** Similar to the downlink, ICI randomization in the uplink is achieved by scrambling the encoded symbols prior to modulation. Instead of cell-specific scrambling as used in the downlink, UE-specific scrambling is used in the uplink as ICI comes from multiple UEs in neighboring cells.

- **ICI cancellation** ICI cancellation is more applicable in the uplink than in the downlink, as the eNode-B has higher computational capability and usually more antenna elements.

- **Uplink power control** Power control is an efficient way to suppress ICI in the uplink. Fractional Power Control (FPC) is used in LTE, as discussed in Section 9.10.

- **ICI coordination/avoidance** Similar coordination techniques discussed for downlink can be applied in the uplink, such as FFR.

To assist uplink ICI coordination, two messages are defined in LTE that can be exchanged over the X2 interface between eNode-Bs for power allocation and user scheduling: interference Overload Indicator (OI) and High Interference Indicator (HII) [9]. OI indicates physical layer measurements of the average uplink interference plus noise for each PRB, based on which eNode-Bs can adjust uplink power to suppress ICI. HII indicates which PRBs will be used for cell-edge UEs in a certain cell. Neighboring cells may then take this information into consideration when scheduling their own users to avoid high interference.

Coordinated Multi-Point Reception

Similar to the downlink, CoMP reception will be developed for uplink in LTE-Advanced. This means coordinated reception at multiple eNode-Bs of transmitted signals from multiple geographically separated UEs in different cells. In contrast to downlink, uplink CoMP reception is expected to have very limited impact on the radio-interface specifications. As uplink scheduling is performed at the eNode-B, coordinated inter-cell scheduling can be applied to control ICI, which, however, will have impact on radio-interface specifications.

10.6   Summary and Conclusions

This chapter described higher-layer protocols, and the mobility management and inter-cell interference coordination in LTE.

- The EPS bearer is used as the central element for the QoS control in LTE. Each bearer is associated with a QCI, which indicates its priority, packet delay budget, acceptable packet error loss rate, and the GBR/non-GBR classification.

- Layer 2 of the LTE protocol stack is split into PDCP, RLC, and MAC sublayers.

  - The main functions of the PDCP sublayer include header compression for user plane data, integrity protection of control plane data, ciphering, and in-sequence delivery and duplicated elimination.

  - The RLC sublayer performs segmentation and/or concatenation on PDCP PDUs, and reorders the RLC PDUs that are received out of order.

  - The MAC sublayer performs multiplexing and demultiplexing between logical channels and transport channels.

  - LTE applies a two-layer retransmission scheme: A fast H-ARQ protocol with low overhead feedback in the MAC layer and a highly reliable selective repeat ARQ protocol in the RLC layer.

- In LTE, there are two RRC states: RRC_IDLE and RRC_CONNECTED, compared to four RRC states in UMTS. The RRC protocol mainly includes functions such as broadcast of system information, RRC connection control, and measurement configuration and reporting.

- In LTE, there are two categories of mobility management: intra-LTE mobility and inter-RAT mobility. Intra-LTE mobility can happen either over the S1 interface or over the X2 interface, while inter-RAT mobility happens over the S1 interface. In the RRC_IDLE state the mobility control is handled by the UE, while in the RRC_CONNECTED state the eNode-B controls mobility/handover of the UE.

- Inter-cell interference control is important for cell-edge throughput. Different interference mitigation techniques are available, including interference randomization, interference cancellation, and interference coordination/avoidance. LTE defines specific messages to assist interference coordination: RNTP indicator for downlink coordination, and OI and HII for uplink coordination.

Bibliography

[1] 3GPP TR 23.828: "Earthquake and Tsunami Warning System (ETWS) Requirements and Solutions; Solution Placeholder."

[2] 3GPP TR 36.814: "Further Advancements for E-UTRA Physical Layer Aspects (Release 9)."

[3] 3GPP TS 23.203: "Technical Specification Group Services and System Aspects; Policy and charging control architecture."

[4] 3GPP TS 33.401: "3GPP System Architecture Evolution: Security Architecture."

[5] 3GPP TS 36.321: "Evolved Universal Terrestrial Radio Access (E-UTRA) Medium Access Control (MAC) protocol specification."

[6] 3GPP TS 36.322: "Evolved Universal Terrestrial Radio Access (E-UTRA) Radio Link Control (RLC) protocol specification."

[7] 3GPP TS 36.323: "Evolved Universal Terrestrial Radio Access (E-UTRA); Packet Data Convergence Protocol (PDCP) specification."

[8] 3GPP TS 36.331: "Evolved Universal Terrestrial Radio Access (E-UTRA) Radio Resource Control (RRC); Protocol specification."

[9] 3GPP TS 36.423: "Evolved Universal Terrestrial Radio Access Network (E-UTRAN); X2 application protocol (X2AP)."

[10] 3GPP TSG RAN WG1 R1-050507: "Soft frequency reuse scheme for UTRAN LTE," Huawei, Tech. Rep., Athens, Greece, May 2005.

[11] 3GPP TSG RAN WG1 R1-050764: "Inter-cell interference handling for E-UTRA," Ericsson, Tech. Rep., 2005.

[12] IETF RFC 4995: "The RObust Header Compression (ROHC) Framework."

[13] Andrews, J. G., W. Choi, and R. W. Heath Jr., "Overcoming interference in spatial multiplexing MIMO cellular networks," *IEEE Wireless Commun.*, vol. 14, no. 6, Dec. 2007, pp. 95–104.

[14] Boudreau, G., J. Panicker, N. Guo, R. Chang, N. Wang, and S. Vrzic, "Interference coordination and cancellation for 4G networks," *IEEE Commun. Mag.*, Apr. 2009, pp. 74–81.

[15] Meyer, M., H. Wiemann, M. Sagfors, J. Torsner, and J.-F. Cheng, "ARQ concept for the UMTS long-term evolution," in *Proc. IEEE Veh. Technol. Conf.*, Montreal, Canada, Sept. 2006, pp. 1–5.

[16] Verdú, S. *Multiuser Detection.* Cambridge University Press, 1998.

[17] Weber, T., I. Maniatis, A. Sklavos, Y. Liu, E. Costa, H. Haas, and E. Schulz, "Joint transmission and detection integrated network (JOINT), a generic proposal for beyond 3G systems," in *Proc. of 9th International Conf. on Telecommunications*, Beijing, China, 2002, pp. 479–483.

Index

Credits and Permissions

| 3GPP TS 23.203   v8.9.0 | Table 6.1.1 |

©2010. 3GPP^{TM} TSs and TRs are the property of ARIB, ATIS, CCSA, ETSI, TTA and TTC who jointly own the copyright in them. They are subject to further modifications and are therefore provided to you "as is" for information purposes only. Further use is strictly prohibited.

| 3GPP TS 36.323   v8.6.0 | Table 5.5.1.1 |

©2009. 3GPP^{TM} TSs and TRs are the property of ARIB, ATIS, CCSA, ETSI, TTA and TTC who jointly own the copyright in them. They are subject to further modifications and are therefore provided to you "as is" for information purposes only. Further use is strictly prohibited.

3GPP TS 36.211 v8.5.0	Figures 4.1.1, 4.2.1, 5.2.1-1, 5.4.3-1, 5.7.1-1, 6.10.1.2-1, 6.10.2.2-1, 6.10.3.2-1, 6.2.2-1, 6.3-1. Tables 5.4.1-1, 5.4.2-1, 5.4-1, 5.7.1-1, 6.12-1, 6.3.4.2.2-1, 6.3.4.2.3-1, 6.3.4.2.3-2, 6.7-1, 6.8.1-1
3GPP TS 36.212 v8.5.0	Figures 5.1.3-1, 5.1.3-2 Tables 5.2.2.6-5, 5.2.2.6-6, 5.2.3.3-1, 5.3.1.1-1, 5.3.3.2-1, 5.3.4-1
3GPP TS 36.213 v8.5.0	Tables 10.1-1, 7.1.7.1-1, 7.2.1-1, 7.2.2-1, 7.2.2-2, 7.2.2-3, 7-1, 8.3-1, 8-1, 8-2, 8-2a, 9.2-1
3GPP TS 36.303 v8.7.0	Figures 5.3.1-1, 5.3.1-2, 6.1.3.1-1, 6.1.3.2-1

©2008. 3GPP^{TM} TSs and TRs are the property of ARIB, ATIS, CCSA, ETSI, TTA and TTC who jointly own the copyright in them. They are subject to further modifications and are therefore provided to you "as is" for information purposes only. Further use is strictly prohibited.

Chapter #	Table/Figure #	3GPP Reference Document	Detailed reference (in the specified document)
Chapter 6	Figure 6.6 & 6.7	TS 36.300-870	Figure 5.3.1-1, 5.3.1-2, 6.1.3.1-1, and 6.1.3.2-1
Figure 6.8 -& 6.9	TS 36.211-850	Figure 4.1-1 and 4.2-1	
Figure 6.10	TS 36.211-850	Figure 6.2.2-1	
Figure 6.12	TS 36.211-850	Figure 5.2.1-1	
Chapter 7	Figure 7.1	TS 36.211-850	Figure 6.3-1
	Figure 7.3	TS 36.212-850	Figure 5.1.3-1
	Figure 7.4	TS 36.212-850	Figure 5.1.3-2
	Table 7.6	TS 36.211-850	Table 6.12-1
	Table 7.7	TS 36.211-850	Table 6.3.4.2.2-1
	Table 7.8	TS 36.211-850	Table 6.3.4.2.3-1
	Table 7.9	TS 36.211-850	Table 6.3.4.2.3-2
	Table 7.12	TS 36.212-850	Table 5.3.3.2-1
	Table 7.13	TS 36.211-850	Table 6.7-1
	Table 7.14	TS 36.211-850	Table 6.8.1-1
	Table 7.15	TS 36.212-850	Table 5.3.4-1
	Table 7.16	TS 36.212-850	Table 5.3.1.1-1
	Figure 7.10	TS 36.211-850	Figure 6.10.1.2-1
	Figure 7.11	TS 36.211-850	Figure 6.10.2.2-1
	Figure 7.12	TS 36.211-850	Figure 6.10.3.2-1
	Table 7.17	TS 36.213-850	Table 7-1
Chapter 8	Table 8.3	TS 36.212-850	Table 5.2.3.3-1
	Table 8.4 & table 8.6	TS 36.211-850	Table 5.4-1
	Table 8.5	TS 36.212-850	Table 5.2.2.6-5 & 5.2.2.6-6
	Table 8.7	TS 36.211-850	Table 5.4.1-1
	Table 8.8	TS 36.211-850	Table 5.4.2-1
	Figure 8.7	TS 36.211-850	Figure 5.4.3-1
	Table 8.10	TS 36.211-850	Table 5.7.1-1
	Figure 8.11	TS 36.211-850	Figure 5.7.1-1
	Table 8.12	TS 36.213-850	Table 8-1
	Table 8.13 & 8.14	TS 36.213-850	Table 8-2 & 8-2a
Chapter 9	Table 9.1	TS 36.213-850	Table 10.1-1
	Table 9.2	TS 36.213-850	Table 8.3-1
	Table 9.3	TS 36.213-850	Table 7.2.3-1
	Table 9.5	TS 36.213-850	Table 7.2.1-1
	Table 9.4	TS 36.213-850	Table 7.2.2-1
	Table 9.7	TS 36.213-850	Table 7.2.2-3
	Table 9.8	TS 36.213-850	Table 7.2.2-2
	Table 9.13	TS 36.212-850	Table 5.2.2.6-5 & 5.2.2.6-6
	Table 9.17	TS 36.213-850	Table 7.1.7.1-1
	Table 9.19	TS 36.213-850	Table 9.2-1
Chapter 10	Table 10.1	TS 23.303-890	Table 6.1.7
	Table 10.3	TS 23.323-860	Table 5.5.1.1

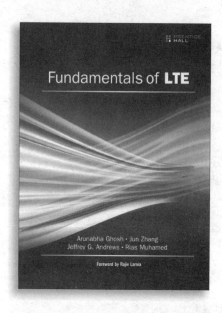

FREE Online Edition

Your purchase of **Fundamentals of LTE** includes access to a free online edition for 45 days through the Safari Books Online subscription service. Nearly every Prentice Hall book is available online through Safari Books Online, along with more than 5,000 other technical books and videos from publishers such as Addison-Wesley Professional, Cisco Press, Exam Cram, IBM Press, O'Reilly, Que, and Sams.

SAFARI BOOKS ONLINE allows you to search for a specific answer, cut and paste code, download chapters, and stay current with emerging technologies.

Activate your FREE Online Edition at www.informit.com/safarifree

> **STEP 1:** Enter the coupon code: ZMMAHAA.

> **STEP 2:** New Safari users, complete the brief registration form.
> Safari subscribers, just log in.

If you have difficulty registering on Safari or accessing the online edition, please e-mail customer-service@safaribooksonline.com